Phantom Risk

Phantom Risk

Scientific Inference and the Law

edited by Kenneth R. Foster, David E. Bernstein, Peter W. Huber

The MIT Press
Cambridge, Massachusetts
London, England

First MIT Press paperback edition, 1999

© 1993 Massachusetts Institute of Technology

Published for the Manhattan Institute by The MIT Press.

This book was set in Bembo by Compset Inc and printed and bound in the United States of America.

Library of Congress Cataloging-in-Publication Data
Phantom risk : scientific inference and the law / edited by Kenneth R. Foster,
  David E. Bernstein, Peter W. Huber.
    p. cm.
  Includes bibliographical references and index.
  ISBN 0-262-06156-2 (hc), 0-262-56119-0 (pb)
  1. Science and law. 2. Torts. 3. Causation. 4. Risk. I. Foster, Kenneth R.
II. Bernstein, David E. III. Huber, Peter W. (Peter William), 1952–
K487.S3P43   1993
346.03—dc20
[342.63]   92-36137
                                                                      CIP

Contents

Preface   vii

Contributors   ix

1   **A Scientific Perspective**   1

2   **A Legal Perspective**   27

I   **Phantom (Or Not So Phantom) Risks**   45

3   **Weak Magnetic Fields: A Cancer Connection?**   47
Kenneth R. Foster

4   **Spermicides and Birth Defects**   87
James L. Mills

5   **Bendectin and the Language of Causation**   101
Louis Lasagna and Sheila R. Shulman

6   **Miscarriage and Video Display Terminals: An Update**   123
Kenneth R. Foster

The Legal Context   137

II   **Just a Little Bit of Poison**   151

7   **Environmental Pollution and Cancer:
Some Misconceptions**   153
Bruce N. Ames and Lois Swirsky Gold

8   **Asbestos: The Hazard, the Risk, and Public Policy**   183
Ralph D'Agostino, Jr., and Richard Wilson

9   **The Human Health Effects of Polychlorinated Biphenyls**   211
Renate D. Kimbrough

10   Trichloroethylene: Toxicology and Epidemiology:
      A Critical Review of the Literature   229
      Rudolph J. Jaeger and Arlene L. Weiss

11   Dioxin: Perceptions, Estimates, and Measures   249
      Michael Gough

12   The Three Mile Island Nuclear Accident and
      Public Health Consequences   279
      George K. Tokuhata

13   The Fallout Controversy   299
      Ralph E. Lapp

14   The Saga of Fernald   319
      Bernard L. Cohen

      The Legal Context   337

III   Medical Controversy   357

15   Trauma and Cancer   359
      Marvin M. Romsdahl

16   Chemical Pollutants and "Multiple Chemical
      Sensitivities"   379
      Michael I. Luster, Gary J. Rosenthal, and Dori R. Germolec

17   Immunologic Laboratory Tests: A Critique of the
      Alcolac Decision   401
      Richard S. Cornfeld and Stuart F. Schlossman

      The Legal Context   425

IV   Conclusion: Phantom Risk—A Problem at the Interface of
      Science and the Law   431

      Abbreviations and Acronyms   445
      Index   449

Preface

This book examines two intersecting themes: the problems of assessing subtle environmental or occupational risks, and the havoc this creates in the courtroom. In each chapter, a scientist addresses an occupational or environmental health issue that has figured prominently in tort litigation. Each section concludes with a brief summary of the litigation. The final chapter offers guidelines to help the legal system deal with the very real problem of phantom risk.

The editors and authors strive to discuss the scientific and legal issues in a way that will be accessible to the "intelligent lay reader," who—despite occasional claims to the contrary—is not an endangered species.

We gratefully acknowledge the generous support of the Sloan Foundation and the Manhattan Institute for Policy Research. We thank the authors of these chapters and many colleagues for suggestions and helpful discussions, with special thanks to Michael Gough and Isadore Rosenthal. We have also benefited from the excellent secretarial assistance of Marilyn Leeland and our paralegal assistant, Karin Albani.

Contributors

Bruce N. Ames and
Lois Swirsky Gold
Division of Biochemistry and
Molecular Biology
401 Barker Hall
University of California
Berkeley, CA 94720

David E. Bernstein
Crowell and Moring
1001 Pennsylvania Avenue, N.W.
Washington, DC 20004

Bernard L. Cohen
Department of Physics
and Astronomy
University of Pittsburgh
100 Allen Hall
3941 O'Hara Street
Pittsburgh, PA 15260

Richard S. Cornfeld
Coburn, Croft & Putzell
One Mercantile Center
Suite 2900
St. Louis, MO 63101

Kenneth R. Foster
Department of Bioengineering
University of Pennsylvania
220 South 33rd Street
Philadelphia, PA 19104-6392

Michael Gough
Office of Technology Assessment
U.S. Congress
Washington, DC 20510-8025

Peter W. Huber
5029 Edgemoor Lane
Bethesda, MD 20814

Rudolph J. Jaeger and
Arlene L. Weiss
Environmental Medicine, Inc.
263 Center Avenue
Westwood, NJ 07675

Renate D. Kimbrough
Institute for Evaluating Health Risks
Suite 608
1101 Vermont Ave., N.W.
Washington, DC 20090-1195

Ralph E. Lapp
7215 Park Terrace Road
Alexandria, VA 22307

Louis Lasagna and
Sheila R. Shulman
Center for the Study of
Drug Development
Tufts University
192 South Street
Boston, MA 02111

Michael I. Luster,
Gary J. Rosenthal, and
Dori R. Germolec
Systems Toxicity Branch
National Toxicology Program
National Institute of Environmental
Health Sciences
Research Triangle Park, NC 27709

James L. Mills
Epidemiology Branch
Prevention Research Program
National Institute of Child Health and
Human Development
National Institutes of Health
6100 Building
Room 7B03
Bethesda, MD 20892

Marvin M. Romsdahl
University of Texas
M.D. Anderson Cancer Center
1515 Holcombe Boulevard
Houston, TX 77030

Stuart F. Schlossman
Dana-Farber Cancer Institute
Harvard Medical School
44 Binney Street
Boston, MA 02115

George K. Tokuhata
410 Rupley Road
Camp Hill, PA 17011

Ralph D'Agostino, Jr.
and **Richard Wilson**
Lyman Laboratory of Physics
Harvard University
Cambridge, MA 02138

Cognitive dissonance is all but unavoidable when the data are ambiguous and the stakes are high.

Weinberg 1985, p. 67

We would know nothing at all about chronic risk attributable to most toxic substances if scientists had not detected and evaluated them. Our response to such risks, therefore, must be based on a set of scientific findings. Science, however, is hardly ever unambiguous or unanimous, especially when the data on which definitive science must be founded scarcely exist.

Ruckelshaus 1985, p. 26

1

A Scientific Perspective

Phantom risk is not lung cancer from smoking, or pelvic inflammatory disease (PID) from one intrauterine contraceptive device, the Dalkon Shield. It is not mesothelioma from asbestos; it is surely not AIDS from unprotected sex.

Phantom risk is, arguably: miscarriage resulting from work at video display terminals, birth defects in children caused by the mother's use of the drug Bendectin, cancer from low-intensity magnetic fields, lung cancer produced by the very slight levels of airborne asbestos in buildings with intact asbestos insulation, or cancer resulting from a slip and fall in a grocery store. By *phantom risk* we mean cause-and-effect relationships whose very existence is unproven and perhaps unprovable.

In using the term *phantom risk* we do not question the existence of human tragedies or imply lack of sympathy for the affected individuals. A family that has a child with a major birth defect has suffered real tragedy, whatever caused it. The problem we address is whether its cause can be identified and (inevitably in our litigious society) how to resolve the resulting legal claims. Phantom risk is a problem at the interface of science and the law.

We are interested, for present purposes, in the problems that arise in tort litigation in proving that an injury did (or did not) arise from low-level exposure to a potentially hazardous substance. Phantom risk also causes problems in the regulatory process, but that is not of principal concern in this book. The issues we discuss aroused much public anxiety and litigation, yet the hazards were never proven, or at least not proven to be serious at the levels of exposure that litigants experienced.

This book explores two intersecting problems. The first is the great disparity between the ease with which a controversy about a suspected hazard can begin and the difficulty in resolving the nature of the connection, if any, between the suspected hazard and a health effect. The second is the havoc the resulting confusion wreaks in the courts. The two problems cannot be separated: litigation may reflect scientific controversy, but it may also help to create it.

Phantom risk can arise from chance observations in everyday life. Breast cancer developing after serious trauma to the chest (chapter 15), the birth of a child with a major defect following use of the drug Bendectin by the mother (chapter 5), miscarriage in a user of a video display terminal (chapter 6), the illness of a child after a vaccination, or the appearance of essentially any cancer in a person exposed to a pesticide might understandably appear as causal sequences to the people concerned. Such incidents, which in retrospect (and in the light of accepted scientific theory and clinical practice) might be regarded as chance occurrences, helped to fuel the scientific and legal controversies discussed in this book.

Phantom risk may also arise from errors and ambiguity in science itself. Often in science, the first studies in a new line of investigation are preliminary in design, crude in execution, or flawed in concept. Follow-up studies are often better designed, more focused, better executed, and less ambiguous in interpretation. Phantom risk is a manifestation of the confusion and uncertainty that invariably accompany risk research, a science that in all respects is in its early stages of development. This confusion is particularly troublesome in epidemiology, which is an observational (rather than experimental) science and therefore more subject to ambiguity in interpretation than an "exact" science such as physics.

Setting the Stage

Risk in technical usage is the probability that a person will experience an adverse effect from some activity or exposure. *Risk assessment* is the process of quantifying and evaluating risk. Risk assessment occupies the time of many scientists and physicians in academia, industry, and government, and a vast literature exists on the subject. [Good introductions are the collection of readings by Glickman and Gough (1990) and the book by Rodricks (1992)].

A broad perspective of the process of risk assessment is given in an influential 1983 report by the National Research Council. According to this report, risk assessment can be broken down into four stages:

Hazard identification is the process of determining whether exposure to an agent can cause an adverse health effect, such as an increase in incidence of cancer or miscarriage. The question "Can ionizing radiation cause cancer?" is one of hazard identification. (The answer is an unqualified yes.)

Dose-response assessment is the process of quantifying the relation between the dose of an agent and the increase in incidence of the health effect. The question "How much exposure to ionizing radiation is needed to produce a 50 percent increase in the incidence of leukemia?" is one of dose-response assessment. (A great deal of exposure is needed, roughly comparable with what many people experienced at Hiroshima when the atomic bomb exploded.) Many of the controversies described in this book involve claims of injury from far smaller exposures.

Exposure assessment is the process of measuring how much exposure people actually receive from a potentially hazardous agent. The question "How much exposure did people receive from radioactive fallout from atmospheric weapons testing?" is one of exposure assessment. (The answer, for most people, is very little, compared with other sources of exposure; see chapter 13).

Finally, *risk characterization* involves the estimate of the magnitude of the public health problem involved with exposure to a potentially hazardous agent and other study of the problem.

Thus, at least three factors must be considered when assessing the likelihood that a person was harmed by exposure to an agent (which is, after all, the central question in personal injury suits). The first is the existence of a hazard, that is, the potential health effect. The second is the exposure the person received, and the third is the level of risk associated with that exposure. Public discourse (and media coverage) about subtle environmental hazards usually focuses on the first of these factors (e.g., whether radiation causes cancer); the other two need to be considered as well.

Association and Causation

The most direct way to identify a hazard is to observe human populations. Epidemiology, as defined by one authority, is "the branch of applied statistics that studies the determinates and correlates of human disease" (Bailar 1989). Epidemiology has a strong medical component also; perhaps the most famous collaboration in epidemiology in recent decades has been between Richard Peto (a biostatistician) and Richard Doll (a physician/epidemiologist).

By observing human populations, epidemiologists try to identify statistical associations between exposure (use of a drug or exposure to an environmental chemical, for example) and incidence of a disease.

For example, consider the birth of a child with a major defect to a woman who had used the drug Bendectin during pregnancy. This event, certainly tragic to the family, is not necessarily an adverse effect of the drug. Major birth defects occur in roughly 3 percent of all pregnancies, including users of Bendectin even if the drug had no effect on the outcome of the pregnancy. As Lasagna and Shulman point out (chapter 5), the interpretation of such an event depends on whether exposure to the drug is associated with an increase over the usual incidence of such outcomes. This problem is best approached by means of controlled observations on populations of users and nonusers of the drug.

For such purposes, a useful concept is *relative risk,* in this case the incidence of serious birth defects in a population of Bendectin users, divided by that in a population of nonusers. A relative risk of 1 indicates lack of association between use of Bendectin and birth defects in the child; progressively higher values indicate progressively stronger associations. As Lasagna and Shulman point out, epidemiologic studies failed to make a strong case linking birth defects and the mother's use of Bendectin, despite heart-rending cases that were well publicized in the media.

Consider, by contrast, smoking and lung cancer. Epidemiologic studies by Doll and Hill (1952) conducted in the early 1950s strongly indicated that a pack-a-day smoker has a tenfold higher chance of developing lung cancer than a nonuser. These studies (which have been repeatedly confirmed by other investigators) stand as classics in their field; some of their results are shown in chapter 3. Moreover, lung cancer is a major public health problem, and one that is largely avoidable. The disease, primarily a result of smoking, now accounts for the largest number of new cancer cases in the United States, about 157,000 cases in 1990 (Henderson et al. 1991).

Epidemiology provides information that is directly relevant to health and disease in humans. This must be weighted against the frequent difficulty in interpreting the evidence, and the frequent inconsistency of epidemiologic findings. Our authors emphasize the need to examine the whole body of evidence about a suspected hazard, and judge what can be concluded reliably in spite of inconsistency and confusion.

Interpreting the Evidence

The authors in this book are clearly optimistic about the use of science to detect and evaluate risks. But they point to the need to weigh conflicting scientific evidence and to debate interpretations of data. In so doing, they often return to two major themes. The first is the difficulty of inferring cause-and-effect relationships from epidemiologic evidence. The second is the difficulty of inferring risks to humans from high-dose animal experiments.

In sorting through the evidence, our authors repeatedly evaluate epidemiologic studies along several dimensions. The first is the strength of association between exposure and a disease, that is, the relative risk. Many arguments about phantom risk revolve about small relative risks, that is, about weak statistical associations. A relative risk close to 1 implies that the exposure is, at best, only one of perhaps many factors that contribute to the development of a disease.

The second dimension is *significance of association*. Because of statistical uncertainties (such as sampling error), the results of an epidemiologic study are surrounded by a penumbra of uncertainty. The size of a study is an important factor; sampling error declines as study size increases. A study might report a relative risk greater than 1 (indicating an increase in risk), but with a margin of sampling error that includes a relative risk of 1. Thus, the increase is not statistically significant, which means that it has an uncomfortably high probability of arising from sampling error. This creates obvious problems for laymen on juries who must interpret such evidence, as happened in the Bendectin litigation.

A related problem, mentioned by several authors, is that some risks are reported on the basis of very limited data. Foster notes (chapter 3) that the claim, often repeated in the lay media, that 10–15 percent of all childhood cancers result from exposure to magnetic fields, derives from data from a group of 27 households in Denver. In statistical jargon, such results are unstable, that is, highly uncertain because of the small numbers of subjects.

The final dimension is *validity of a study*. Epidemiologic studies are susceptible to many potential errors, which are particularly difficult to control in early stages of research on a problem whose dimensions and nature are unknown. For example, Mills suggests (chapter 4) that early studies linking spermicides and birth defects were flawed and seriously misleading. Kimbrough describes major flaws in early studies that reported adverse health effects of polychlorinated biphenyls (PCBs) (chapter 9). Gough (chapter 11) describes studies that are inconsistent with (and probably invalidate) the earliest studies that linked low-level exposure to dioxin and cancer. In all of these cases, the early positive findings were not confirmed by later investigation and are presumably wrong.

Recall bias is one potential difficulty that several of our authors mention. This problem arises if some individuals in a study are more likely than others to report using a drug or remember an exposure. Epidemiologists have learned, through hard experience, that external factors such as bad publicity about a drug will affect the likelihood that a person will report having used it. Recall bias may have been a factor in studies of miscarriage and video display terminals (chapter 6) or birth defects and spermicides (chapter 4) or Bendectin (chapter 5). Again, these early studies were not confirmed by later investigations and are presumably in error.

Another problem that our authors frequently mention is the multiple comparison effect. An investigator who makes enough comparisons in a study will surely find many "statistically significant" associations in the data, merely because of chance. For example, there are many different kinds of birth defects, and an investigator fishing for some connection between use of a drug and birth defects can make many comparisons, each of which (under the statistical rules most investigators adopt for interpreting such studies) has 1 chance in 20 of yielding a "statistically significant" difference, even though there may be no real effect of the drug. There are many occupations and many forms of cancer, and an investigator who performs enough comparisons will surely find associations between the two.

This problem is obvious enough, but it is a recurrent and hard-to-prove source of error. According to our authors, initial reports of associations between Bendectin and birth defects (chapter 5), or dioxin and cancer (chapter 11), or "electrical" occupation and cancer (chapter 3), or PCBs and diverse health effects (chapter 9) may have been false-positive errors that arose from the many comparisons the investigators performed. The initially reported "associations" were not confirmed by later studies, which were more focused and less susceptible to the multiple comparison problem.

Some errors might lead an investigator to *underestimate* a risk. One common problem is the misclassification of subjects according to their exposure. A study that randomly grouped its subjects as "exposed" or "unexposed" to a suspected hazardous agent would detect no effect, even if one existed. Smaller misclassification errors will tend to diminish the size of any detected effect.

For this and other reasons, a scientist might view the borderline results of a study as suggesting a large effect. If so, additional studies with better exposure assessment will show the effect more clearly. For the scientific issues discussed in these pages, the trend has been in the opposite direction.

Much of the legal controversy in these pages turns on different interpretations of epidemiologic evidence. In epidemiology, as in any science, the search for small effects is uncertain and confusing; and epidemiology is hardly an exact science in any event. Unfortunately, the irreducible uncertainties in epidemiology are frequently large enough to be legally significant. The usual test in civil litigation is whether the suspected agent "more likely than not" caused a claimant's disease. This might be interpreted as whether the exposure doubled the risk. Many epidemiologists, if pressed, would admit that twofold increases in risk are difficult to measure reliably, except under special circumstances.

Assessing Causation

Epidemiology relies on statistics, and it is a cardinal rule of science that statistics cannot prove causation. For this reason scientists are usually reluctant to speak of exposure "causing" a disease on the basis of epidemiologic data alone. We consider different criteria for medicine and epidemiology that scientists have developed to weigh inferences about causation.

Henle-Koch-Evans (HKE) postulates. HKE postulates were first proposed by the famous bacteriologist and Nobel Prize (1905) winner Robert Koch (1843–1910) during the nineteenth century, when medicine was struggling with cholera, typhus, typhoid fever, and tuberculosis. Some of these postulates were enunciated as early as 1840 by Koch's teacher Henle. They were restated in 1976 by Evans, and are best referred to now as the Henle-Koch-Evans (HKE) postulates (Evans 1976, 1977). They are listed below.

1. The disease is significantly more prevalent in those exposed to the hypothesized cause than in unexposed controls.
2. Exposure is more frequent among those with the disease than in controls without the disease.
3. Prospective studies (which begin with an entirely healthy population) show a significantly higher incidence of disease in those exposed than in those not exposed.
4. Disease should follow exposure after an incubation period that tracks a lognormal curve.
5. Responses follow exposure along a logical biologic gradient from mild to severe.
6. Exposure triggers a measurable response (e.g., antibodies, cancer cells), with a high probability after exposure, or increases the number of responses if already present before exposure. This response pattern occurs infrequently or never in persons not exposed.
7. Experimental reproduction of the disease, in volunteers or laboratory experiments, or by controlled regulation of natural exposure, occurs more frequently in exposed animals or humans than in those not exposed.

8. Elimination of the suspected agent (e.g., control of polluted water, removal of tar from cigarettes) decreases the incidence of the disease.
9. Modification of the host's response on exposure (e.g., by immunization, or drugs to lower cholesterol) should decrease or eliminate the disease.
10. All of the relationships and findings should make scientific sense.

Most scientists would agree that evidence that satisfies the HKE postulates would make a compelling case for causation. They are most easily satisfied for infectious diseases, when the investigator believes that he or she has isolated the infectious agent. The postulates played a role in the scientific debates about the cause of AIDS. Virtually all scientists now agree that the HIV virus causes AIDS; what appears to be the last remaining holdout of high stature based his argument on the denial that the evidence satisfies these postulates (Duesberg 1989). Duesberg's views have been hotly contested by other scientists, and remain very much a minority position.

Hill's Criteria for Assessing Causation From Epidemiologic Studies. Most chronic diseases have an unknown cause, and some perhaps have multiple causes. For them, the scientific evidence does not—and may never—satisfy the HKE postulates. Nevertheless, epidemiologic studies can identify factors that increase a person's risk for a disease and allow effective public health measures to be developed to reduce the problem.

Some diseases rarely occur except in association with exposure to some hazardous substance. Mesothelioma rarely occurs except following exposure to asbestos (although other fibers may also produce it; see chapter 8); vaginal adenocarcinoma is unequivocally associated with in utero exposure to the drug DES; fetal alcohol syndrome arises from alcohol consumption by the mother. These "signature diseases" are characterized by very high values of relative risk, and for most purposes the question of causation is moot.

Other diseases are strongly but not uniquely associated with some risky behavior: smoking and lung cancer. Some associations may be weak (passive smoking and lung cancer). Most reported associations between passive smoking and cancer, in fact, are not statistically significant, but are accepted as real by many scientists because of the much stronger data from smokers.

In his celebrated lecture of 1965, Sir Austin Bradford Hill proposed nine criteria to help decide whether a reported association is causal or spurious. The criteria are summarized below, with Hill's comments (Hill 1965, 295–300).

1. *Strength of association.* "First upon my list I would put the strength of association. To take a very old example, by comparing the occupations of patients with scrotal cancer with the occupations of patients presenting with other diseases, Percival Pott could reach the correct conclusion because of the *enormous* increase of scrotal cancer in the chimney sweeps."
2. *Consistency.* "Next on my list of features to be specifically considered I would place the *consistency* of association. Has it been repeatedly observed by different persons, in different places, circumstances and times?"
3. *Specificity.* "If . . . the association is limited to specific workers and to particular sites and types of disease and there is no association between the work and other modes of dying, then clearly that is a strong argument in favor of causation."
4. *Temporality.* ". . . [W]hich is the cart and which the horse?"
5. *Biological gradient.* "Fifthly, if the association is one which can reveal a biological gradient, or dose-response curve, then we should look most carefully for such evidence. . . . The clear dose-response curve admits of a simple explanation and obviously puts the case in a clearer light."
6. *Plausibility.* "It would be helpful if the causation we suspect is biologically plausible. But this is a feature I am convinced we cannot demand. What is biologically plausible depends on the biological knowledge of the day."
7. *Coherence.* ". . . [T]he cause-and-effect interpretation of our data should not seriously conflict with the generally known facts of the natural history and biology of the disease. . . ."
8. *Experiment.* "Occasionally it is possible to appeal to experimental . . . evidence. . . . Here the strongest support for the causation hypothesis may be revealed."
9. *Analogy.* "In some circumstances it would be fair to judge by analogy. With the effects of thalidomide and rubella before us we would surely be ready to accept slighter but similar evidence with another drug or another viral disease in pregnancy."

According to Hill, the case for causation becomes stronger when the association is strong, independently confirmed, biologically plausible—*makes sense*. He cautioned that

[n]one of my nine viewpoints can bring indisputable evidence for or against the cause-and-effect hypothesis and none can be required as a *sine qua non*. What they can do . . . is to help us make up our minds on the fundamental question—is there any other way of explaining the set of facts before us, is there any other answer equally, or more, likely than cause and effect? (Hill 1965)

Several authors in this volume apply Hill's criteria: Lasagna and Shulman (chapter 5) to epidemiologic evidence linking Bendectin and birth defects, Mills (chapter 4) to spermicides and birth defects, Foster (chapter 3) to electromagnetic fields and cancer, Kimbrough (chapter 9) to human health effects of PCBs, Jaeger and Weiss (chapter 10) to trichlo-

contaminated water and leukemia, and Gough (chapter 11) to dioxin and cancer. In each case, they find the evidence unpersuasive.

Philosophers of science and epidemiologists have debated Hill's criteria (Rothman 1988), and other scientists have proposed criteria of their own (e.g., Susser 1973, 1991). Most scientists would agree that they are not standards of scientific proof, or at least are not the high standards that the HKE postulates are generally assumed to be. Nevertheless, Hill's criteria have been widely influential in epidemiology. The fact that epidemiologists feel it necessary to debate them at all underscores the frequent difficulty of interpreting epidemiologic evidence. At the least, it points to the need for a holistic assessment of the data, and the recognition that the evidence will never be completely consistent.

These issues are complex and contentious. A rancorous debate has raged for two decades between Alvan Feinstein, the eminent Yale epidemiologist, and other epidemiologists. Feinstein has published blunt commentaries that point out methodologic and conceptual problems in many epidemiologic studies (e.g., Feinstein 1973, 1979, 1982, 1985, 1988) which, in his view, negate their validity. His opponents (e.g., Savitz et al. 1990) reply in effect that Feinstein's standards of inference are too high. The very existence of this controversy speaks volumes about the "rigors" of science.

Animal Studies

Animal studies can give information about risks from toxic substances without exposing human subjects. They are far more easily controlled than epidemiologic studies, and they allow the experimenter to vary conditions of exposure in a way that is not possible with humans. Notwithstanding the complaints of animal rights activists, animal studies provide important and necessary information that can help scientists understand the risks of toxic substances to humans, and compare the relative toxicity of different substances. A chemical that readily kills a rat would no doubt do the same to a human being, but not necessarily at comparable doses.

The most direct approach in animal studies is to expose animals to a chemical, then wait and see what happens. This, in a highly controlled form, is the basis of standardized cancer screening tests and other toxicologic assays.

For several reasons, scientists have great difficulty in studying the effects of small chemical exposures in animals. Small effects are undetectable by animal studies of any reasonable size; an exposure that causes one excess cancer death in a million rats (which for humans is the level of safety that American regulators typically strive for) would produce no detectable effects in a test using 100 animals (the typical size of such a test). Animals, like humans, frequently develop chronic disease in old age, and an investigator seeking an effect of some exposure must contend with a high background rate of naturally occurring disease.

To increase the sensitivity of a study, investigators commonly expose animals to high doses of a test substance, often the maximum tolerated dose (MTD). But then the relevance of the study to low-level human exposure becomes unclear. Some way is needed to extrapolate to exposure levels that are more typical of human exposure.

As several authors in this volume point out, animal studies are particularly difficult to interpret when the substances are relatively nontoxic and massive doses are required to produce observable effects. Birth defects, cancer, and other adverse effects observed at high exposure levels might imply no increase in risk at lower levels of exposure. As Ames and Gold note (chapter 7), the chronic irritation that many chemicals produce at high exposure levels is itself a cause of cancer. This issue came vividly to public attention a few years ago during the debates about the supposed carcinogenicity of saccharine, when editorial-page cartoonists made great fun of the matter, showing bloated rats surrounded by huge bags of the stuff.

A second problem is the relevance of *animal tests* to *human health risks*. It depends on how similar the exposure is to actual human exposures, biological similarities and differences between the animals and humans, and the nature of the effects produced by high doses in the animals. A human is not a 70-kilogram rat.

The question of relevance of high-dose animal tests to human health is one of the most interesting controversies in science today (Ames et al. 1987; Epstein and Schwarz 1988; Ames and Gold 1988; Abelson 1990). One side—most prominently represented by the eminent epidemiologist Peto (1985) and eminent biochemist Ames (in many publications)—argues that such tests provide little useful information for calculating risks to humans from low-level exposure. The other side (much of the toxicology establishment and all regulatory laws) concedes the point but argues that no better alternative exists. A few scientists and physicians (most prominently Epstein) are far more ready to infer distressing implications from positive results of high-dose animal studies (Epstein 1978; Epstein and Schwarz 1988).

For risk assessment, such questions are both crucially important and difficult (or, one may argue, impossible) to resolve. Current U.S. regulatory policy and most scientists agree that, at least for practical purposes, a "threshold" dose must be exceeded before exposures cause an increased risk for most adverse health effects other than cancer. This is true for, say, organ damage, neurological, and pulmonary effects. While a few scientists argue that no threshold exists for such effects, the majority of scientists and regulators accept one.

The situation is quite different for cancer. U.S. regulatory policy and many scientists assume that there is no threshold dose that must be exceeded to cause an increase in cancer risk. This idea gained currency from the years-ago observation that many carcinogens (agents that cause cancer) including radiation can mutate (alter) DNA, the genetic material. A single particle of ionizing radiation, or a single chemical molecule, might alter a single DNA molecule and eventually lead to the development of cancer. As Ames and Gold point out (chapter 7), this occurs against a very high background rate of exactly similar damage to DNA from natural causes, and the body has effective methods to repair the damage and suppress any tumors that develop in early stages.

The situation has become still more complex with recent advances in understanding of cancer. Almost all scientists accept that no threshold dose is necessary for carcinogens that are capable of mutating DNA. However, the testing of many chemicals within the past 15 years has revealed that only about one-half of all carcinogens are capable of causing mutations. Scientists now debate whether or not a threshold dose must be exceeded for a non-mutagenic carcinogen to increase the risk of cancer. It is difficult (so far, impossible) to directly answer the threshold/no-threshold question for most substances because of the difficulty of testing very large populations of animals for rare occurrences of adverse effects.

Recently (March 1992), National Public Radio offered a nice analogy, in a balanced program on the role of animal studies in risk assessment. If a glass bottle is dropped from a height of ten feet onto a concrete floor, it will probably break. But what about dropping ten bottles from a height of one foot? Or a thousand bottles from 1/100 feet? Or a million bottles from 1/100,000 feet? By linear extrapolation, which underlies much risk assessment in the United States, we would expect one bottle to break in each case. Whether such extrapolations are warranted depends on how the system fails. For the glass bottles a "linear dose-response model" is clearly absurd. In toxicology the situation is much less clear.

Clearly, high-dose animal studies are only one part of the toxicologic puzzle and their relevance to low environmental exposures is indirect at best and possibly nil. As Luster and colleagues point out (chapter 16), the use of high-dose animal studies as evidence in court, outside the context of a careful risk assessment, is a gross misuse of scientific data.

Putting It All Together

The authors discuss two kinds of evidence: epidemiologic studies, often on groups of workers who have been exposed to the toxic substance in question, but sometimes on environmentally exposed populations where the exposure is in doubt, and animal studies. The epidemiologic studies are frequently inconsistent; the animal studies often show clear toxic effects, but at levels that vastly exceed any reasonable human exposure. Although the issues vary, similar themes constantly reappear.

Compared with other organic solvents, for example, trichloro-ethylene (TCE) is rather benign, with obvious toxic effects only at high levels of exposure. But, in massive doses, it produces cancer in animals. Can one infer that TCE causes cancer in humans at very low levels of exposure? Probably not, as Jaeger and Weiss (chapter 10) argue; the great disparity in doses and biological differences between the test animals and humans makes the relevance of the animal data very uncertain. The epidemiologic studies on TCE and cancer risk are inconsistent but, considered as a whole, negative. The outcome of litigation (for example, that related to TCE-tainted drinking water in Woburn, Massachusetts) has turned upon the interpretation of such inconclusive evidence by juries.

The evidence regarding PCBs raises other kinds of problems. As Kimbrough points out (chapter 9), commercially-used PCBs were mixtures of chemicals of varying (but generally moderate) toxicity. In massive doses (compared with typical environmental exposures) some PCB mixtures produce cancer in laboratory animals. However, there is no convincing evidence that PCBs caused any human illness. Some well-publicized incidents, for example the tragic poisoning of people in Japan and Taiwan who had ingested rice oil contaminated with PCBs and other chemicals, were later traced to contaminants other than PCBs. In the plenitude of toxic substances, PCBs have received excessive notoriety.

A difficulty of another sort is presented by the dioxins, a class of chemicals of which one (TCDD) is an extremely potent carcinogen in rodents. TCDD is present at trace levels as a contaminant of herbicides (including Agent Orange) and other industrial chemicals. But the epidemiologic evidence linking TCDD and human cancers (chapter 11) is equivocal and appears to be growing weaker as more studies are reported.

As Gough points out (chapter 11), the evidence regarding dioxin has a simple interpretation: the risks if any were just too small to measure. TCDD may well be a human carcinogen at near toxic doses, as it is in rodents. But people were not exposed at levels that caused cancer in rats, and it seems that TCDD is less toxic to humans than to rodents in any event. The studies on individuals with relatively high exposures were small and comparatively insensitive. The larger studies involved individuals with much smaller exposures (and presumably much smaller risks). While some did report increases in cancers, it is unclear whether dioxin (as opposed to other chemicals or smoking) was responsible. Taken together, the weak and inconsistent epidemiologic evidence makes no strong case that dioxin at any past level of exposure caused cancers in humans.

These issues have important implications both for public policy and for the law. The scientific evidence regarding subtle hazards is bound to be confusing and inconsistent, particularly when the risks are small. Surely asbestos, ionizing radiation, and dioxin are nasty things at high levels of exposure, and they unquestionably have harmed people exposed to them under uncontrolled conditions in the bad old days before strict regulatory controls were established. Even recently, as Ames and Gold point out in chapter 7, some workers have been exposed to specific chemicals at levels that are comparable with those producing cancer in test animals. In such cases, strict controls are prudent, with safety factors that take into account the uncertainty of scientific knowledge.

By contrast, the exposure of most people to PCBs, asbestos (in buildings with intact asbestos insulation), and most other toxic substances in the environment is very much below levels that are obviously dangerous. Small risks, if assumed by many people, could add up to a significant health problem. However—despite hysterical claims that were widely publicized during the 1970s—typical environmental exposures to most chemicals are too low to be a major (or even detectable) source of illness. Gough (1989) reviewed the Environmental Protection Agency's estimates of cancer risk from environmental pollution, and identified a total of 6,000 to 11,000 cancer deaths per year that might be associated with environmental exposure to manmade carcinogens—or 1.5–3 percent of all cancer deaths. By the EPA's own estimates, the expenditure of large resources to further reduce public exposure to these chemicals is unlikely to have a measurable effect on public health.

The perspective of someone who has fallen victim to disease is vastly different. That the disease might be rare (or the risk of developing it low) no longer matters—the victim has already lost that particular gamble. The victim will ask whether exposure to some toxic substance might have caused it. Perhaps a strong case can be made, perhaps not. As the following chapters show, anyone who searches through the scientific literature will find many bits of inconsistent and often disquieting pieces of evidence. A person who insists on unambiguous proof of safety will never receive a satisfactory answer from science.

Risk and Non-Risk

The law frequently demands positive statements by scientists that a risk does, or does not, exist. There is, however, a great asymmetry between such claims that leads to unnecessary confusion and controversy.

For example, consider the statement "Smoking causes lung cancer." We know this to be true, with a high (but not absolute) level of certainty. This claim is supported by decades of epidemiologic and laboratory studies. The former show that smoking dramatically increases the risk of lung cancer; the latter have begun to trace the causal chain in the process.

This claim rests on the fact that pack-a-day smokers have roughly a tenfold increase in risk of lung cancer. Yet some residual uncertainty exists. For example, some epidemiologic studies report a fivefold, and some a fifteenfold, increase in cancer risk for a pack-a-day smoker. But this does not negate the fact that smoking is linked with greater risk of lung cancer (and many other diseases as well).

But the claim that smoking *causes* lung cancer is more difficult to prove. The tobacco industry for many years has cynically argued that smoking is an unproven cause of lung cancer. Nevertheless, the epidemiologic evidence and laboratory evidence, taken together, make a case of overwhelming strength. Ironically, personal injury suits by lung cancer victims against tobacco companies have been uniformly unsuccessful.

Consider, by contrast, the statement "Sudden trauma does not cause cancer." Such a negative proposition is unprovable and, in some philosophical sense, meaningless. No study could prove the absence of any association between trauma and cancer; at best one might place an upper limit on the risk. A more defensible statement is that, despite much research, no strong case has emerged that simple trauma is a sufficient cause of cancer. How much evidence is needed to make a "strong case," and what to make of the bits and pieces of evidence that don't fit together, is obviously a contentious problem.

In fact, as Romsdahl notes in chapter 15, most authorities at the beginning of the twentieth century *did* believe that simple trauma might cause cancer, although with sufficient reservations to keep the question alive. The theory is credited to the eminent English surgeon Richard Wiseman, who in 1676 reported two interesting cases of cancer (*see* Stoll 1962). Both patients, he observed, "thought [the cancer] came from an accidental bruise" (quoted in Behan 1939). The theory had its ups and downs but eventually came to be widely accepted. It was supported neither by controlled studies nor by convincing laboratory evidence.

The difficulty with the theory is that many people break their bones, are traumatized by surgery, are injured at work, or are wounded in war—without developing the kinds of cancer (sarcomas) supposedly caused by trauma. Many sarcomas develop without obvious association with trauma. After physicians developed objective criteria to identify trauma-induced cancer, the number of such cases declined. The theory is now dead—or rather, most of its advocates are dead, neatly illustrating Kuhn's concept of a paradigm shift in science. But for many years it figured prominently in claims for compensation (e.g., *Menarde* v. *Philadelphia Transportation,* 376 Pa. 497; 103 A.2d 681 (1954)), and to this day is still resurrected occasionally in lawsuits.

Certainly, the laws of nature do not exclude trauma as a cause of cancer. As Ames and Gold argue in another context (chapter 7), rapidly proliferating cells (such as found in healing wounds) are at greater risk of becoming transformed into cancer cells. Chronic irritation is well known to be associated with cancer, for example, in the strong association between presence of gallstones (which abrade the gallbladder wall) and gallbladder cancer (Henderson et al. 1991). Evidently, the probability of such a transformation occurring during the healing of a simple wound is too small to detect. Surgical trauma to animals increases the chance that an implanted tumor will grow in their bodies. In retrospect, links do exist between trauma and cancer, but they are more subtle and complex than physicians and judges and juries originally believed.

Scientific Speculation

From the above discussion, it is clear that risk research often yields ambiguous answers, and that there is room for informed debate about the interpretation of the evidence. There is a spectrum of opinion held by mainstream scientists on issues such as whether dioxin is a human carcinogen, or the risks of PCBs, or what to make of the many studies suggesting links between exposure to electromagnetic fields and cancer.

The breadth of this spectrum, and the points about which scientists disagree, are often hard to judge from media accounts of the controversies. A different problem, in court, is what to make of the questionable observations and bizarre theories that expert witnesses sometimes present, which are well outside the spectrum of opinion held by most scientists.

Some spectacularly original scientific theories have led to fundamental changes in the way that scientists view the world. For example, many geologists initially dismissed Alfred Wegener's theory of continental drift (Takeuchi et al. 1967), but it eventually prevailed and now is a central organizing concept of modern geology. As Kuhn points out in *The Structure of Scientific Revolutions,* however, most revolutionary theories just sputter out, gaining little acceptance except by a small group of scientists who vociferously defend them.

Several of the chapters discuss questionable medical theories. For example, Romsdahl (chapter 15) reviews the complex and ambiguous relations between trauma and cancer. Expert witnesses have argued in court for a much simpler theory—that simple trauma *causes* cancer—and have claimed to be able to identify traumatic origins of a plaintiff's disease.

Another questionable theory addresses the issue of "multiple chemical sensitivities" (MCS). As Luster and colleagues point out in chapter 16, many people believe that they are highly sensitive to low levels of chemicals in the environment, and are sometimes affected to the point of inability to function in society. Medical scientists have been unable to identify any specific physiological condition associated with MCS. *Something* is clearly the matter with these individuals, but mainstream scientists and physicians cannot identify just what the problem might be, and are generally unsuccessful in treating it. Physicians describe MCS as a complex psychosocial problem, which is to say they don't really know what it is.

Members of a controversial medical discipline, clinical ecology, have a different view: MCS arises from toxic effects of environmental pollutants on the immune system. They justify this theory by using methods that have been widely criticized by mainstream scientists and physicians. Some clinical ecologists have been prominent as expert witnesses in personal injury suits, offering alarming (and grossly inappropriate) diagnoses such as "chemically induced AIDS" in support of claimants' cases.

The problem is compounded by the fact that many immune-system tests are difficult to interpret and yield variable results in normal individuals. Often small deviations from "normal" have no clear relation to clinical disease. The problem of interpreting immunological tests is touched upon by Luster et al. (chapter 16), Cornfield and Schlossman (chapter 17), and other authors.

Phantom Risk and Pathological Science

Science has a long history of phenomena that are reported, create much excitement, and then vanish upon further investigation—cold fusion, for example. Nobel Chemist Irving Langmuir described, in a cynical but

amusing lecture (reprinted in 1989), the science "of things that aren't so."
He proposed criteria to help scientists recognize such nonphenomena:

1. The maximum effect that is observed is produced by a causative agent of
barely detectable intensity, and the magnitude of the effect is substantially independent of the intensity of the cause.
2. The effect is of a magnitude that remains close to the limit of detectability, or
many measurements are necessary because of the very low statistical significance
of the results.
3. There are claims of great accuracy.
4. Fantastic theories contrary to experience are suggested.
5. Criticisms are met by *ad hoc* excuses thought up on the spur of the moment.
6. The ratio of supporters to critics rises to somewhere near 50 percent and then
falls gradually to oblivion.

Langmuir, a chemist, came from an intellectual tradition quite different from Hill's. However, his criteria bear a striking resemblance to
Hill's. His caution against "fantastic theories, contrary to evidence"
echoes Hill's insistence that a supposed cause-effect relation be plausible.
Both scientists urge caution in accepting claims about effects that are at
the very edge of detectability.

One of Langmuir's criteria has important implications for the courtroom. In initial stages of a controversy, the numbers of supporters and
skeptics of a new discovery are similar. As time goes on, the balance of
scientific opinion shifts, as some (but not all) of the original advocates
change their minds and many other scientists come to reject the claims.
However, any scientific cause, no matter how hopeless it might be, will
find at least some scientists to support it. Such people, taking positions
on issues of health and safety, are useful as expert witnesses in personal
injury suits. These "experts" might have negligible impact on science,
but exert a considerable influence in the courtroom. Indeed, since many
plaintiffs' cases might be based on the views of these few scientists, were
it not for their availability as expert witnesses many suits would not have
been filed at all.

The issues that Langmuir raised lie just beneath the surface in many
debates about subtle hazards. One authority observed that many reported biological effects of power line fields satisfy many of the criteria
of pathological science (Carstensen 1987).

Much of the evidence discussed in this book concerns barely detectable increases in risk and claims of health effects of questionable plausibility. For example, the debates among scientists about possible health
effects of low-level ionizing radiation involve different interpretations of
epidemiologic studies of workers exposed to radiation that identified

only a few cases of disease, or questionable interpretations of the much larger body of evidence from the Hiroshima bomb survivors [see, for example, the exchange of letters between Morgan and Cameron (1992) and the studies cited therein]. Disputes about radiation effects from the accident at Three Mile Island, above-ground weapons testing, and a uranium processing plant are discussed in chapters 12 through 14.

Langmuir's criteria are useful mostly in hindsight. They do not relieve scientists of the responsibility of following up reported discoveries that might be significant, up to a point. But they warn scientists of the likely presence of the Cheshire cat.

Science is more than tests and observations; it is also the construction of theories and the testing of theories by experiments. Science advances by a winnowing and sifting process (in the words of Yale physicist Robert K. Adair) through which sound hypotheses become accepted and incorrect data and ideas are forgotten. Science *converges*. This convergence occurs in risk research as accumulating epidemiologic evidence becomes stronger and other scientists begin to work out the underlying biological mechanisms for the effects. It occurred, for example, with Wegener's theory of continental drift, and not (so far) with cold fusion. Whether it *will* occur with cold fusion cannot be predicted, strictly speaking, but the trend is clearly in the opposite direction.

Ultimately, truth in science is established by its ability to make successful predictions. Thus, a good theory about the toxic effects of an agent should encompass the results of animal and epidemiologic studies without having to make exceptions for all sorts of special cases. A theory constructed by means of special pleading and on the basis of a few observations selected from a multitude is not satisfactory. Repeatedly in the chapters that follow, the authors reveal the weakness of purported associations between exposures and disease. If the initial studies, which often associated large risks with tiny exposures, are correct, then much larger risks should be identified by later studies in which the subjects' exposure was greater or more accurately measured. If they are not, then the initial theory of the association was suspect, and probably wrong.

Given time and resources, science will sort out such muddles. However, this process is slow, and it constantly generates still other questions. The controversy about miscarriage and use of video display terminals took ten years to resolve. The clusters of miscarriages were never adequately explained and may have had no connection with the terminals. But once the question was opened, a dozen studies were required to put the matter to rest; some critics may still argue that the matter remains unresolved. Centuries were required for the theory that simple trauma is a sufficient cause of cancer to disappear. Some controversies described in this volume took years to resolve; others continue after years of investigation with no certain prospects of resolution. Scientists view ambiguity simply as an invitation to further study.

The problem is with the use of science in human affairs and the law. Juries and policymakers must decide on the basis of ambiguous scientific (or pseudoscientific) data, often in the face of great public concern. Most scientists would agree that, depending on the circumstances, policy makers might properly take action even though the scientific evidence about a risk is incomplete. In the words of Savitz et al. (1990, p. 82), "Physicians and policy makers should consider both the costs and benefits of actions, bearing in mind the uncertainties in causal inference and the impossibility of perfect decision rules." Just where the guidelines for scientific inference (such as the HKE postulates or Hill's criteria) stand in relation to the "preponderance of evidence" standard of legal proof or the standards of evidence required for regulatory action remains unclear.

The considerations that scientists bring to bear when evaluating scientific evidence about risk seldom appear in coverage of health issues by the lay media; it is as if scientists and the lay public inhabit different worlds entirely. One needs only to compare the chapters in this book with articles on similar topics in magazines in the local supermarket to get the point. In the words of the eminent epidemiologist Richard Doll,

> . . . hardly a day passes without some reference being made [in the media] to the hazards associated with radioactivity, chemical waste, food additives, contraceptives, medicines, the so-called drugs of solace, or new sources of infection. Unfortunately, claims about the existence of hazards are often based on half-baked and preliminary findings without adequate allowance for the vagaries of chance, bias in reporting, and the complexity caused by the way different social and environmental factors are interrelated. They may consequently cause much unnecessary . . . anxiety for the public. (Hennekens et al. 1987, pp. xi–xii)

Scientists need to do a better job in communicating their concerns to the public, and lay people who engage in debates about risk (and they should) need to try to understand what the scientists are talking about.

Phantom Risk and Phantom Cure

Phantom risk is the mirror image of phantom cure. Both arise from the layman's faith in science to improve (or diminish) life. The advent of electricity brought electric belts from the McIntosh Galvanic and Faradic Battery Company of Chicago, because "Disease Yields Under Electrical

Treatment" (Resneck 1988). Electricity also shattered the peace of mind of James Thurber's grandmother (among many others), who (as Thurber described in a delightful 1933 essay) "lived the latter years of her life in the horrible suspicion that electricity was dripping invisibly all over the house." The lay media have variously reported insidious dangers and remarkable healing powers of magnetic fields, X rays, microwaves, ultradilute solutions of various toxins, and oil from venomous snakes. Even now, health food stores are parodies of pharmacies, their shelves filled with unproved nostrums. Both phantom risk and phantom cure trade upon the power of myths inspired by science and accepted by the public.

Phantom risks and phantom cures are justified by remarkably similar arguments. Magazine writers, in an attempt to put a human face on otherwise abstract discussions of risk, describe horrible things that have happened to people living near electrical substations or downwind of nuclear test sites. In testimonials, satisfied consumers describe the good things they experienced after taking a nostrum. The famous shrine at Ste. Anne de Beaupré in Quebec has a large display of crutches and other appliances, cast off by the faithful after being cured with the help of prayer.

Nevertheless, the proper interpretation of such events depends on the frequency of similar outcomes in all people, and testimonials based on individual cases can be misleading. For that reason, the U.S. Food and Drug Administration requires extensive and statistically meaningful clinical tests of drugs, and for that reason distributors of nostrums sold in health food stores carefully avoid making health claims for their products. (They leave that task to magazine writers, who are not constrained by the Food and Drug Administration.)

Phantom cure is, of course, a source of *real* risk. The Curies' discovery of radium, for example, kicked off the Milk Radium Therapy movement among American socialites, and precipitated a lucrative trade in radium-based belts, hearing aids, toothpaste, face cream, and hair tonic. Most lucrative of all was Radiothor, a glow-in-the-dark mineral water that promised a cure for more than 150 maladies. The Federal Trade Commission, ever vigilant, cracked down on competing potions that *lacked* advertised levels of radioactivity. The steel mogul, socialite, and amateur golf champion Eben MacBurney Byers faithfully drank Radiothor every day from 1926 to 1931. By the latter year he had developed cancer of the jaw, a presumed but unproved consequence of the radiation. He died miserably in 1932 (Brenner 1989). (This well publicized incident alerted the public to the dangers of ionizing radiation, and helped spur much-needed government action.) Even today, radon (a radioactive gas that is a real environmental hazard) is the chief selling point in abandoned mines in Montana that are open to the public, and "radon baths" are widely prescribed throughout the former Soviet Union (Brenner 1989).

Views from the Mainstream

Chapter 2 discusses phantom risk from a legal perspective, and the legal rules of evidence that apply in toxic tort suits. How do judges decide who will be allowed to testify? How have juries treated animal or epidemiologic data on Bendectin or electromagnetic fields? What procedures have they used, with what effectiveness, to separate science from emotion in cases involving children whose birth defects are alleged to be caused by Bendectin? How do judges view peer review, refereed publication, and the other quality-control mechanisms of science? Indeed, how do judges view science itself?

The first step in resolving the issues is to carefully delineate what can be inferred reliably from the scientific evidence. In addressing questions of this kind, European judges routinely summon their own expert witnesses, in the hope of receiving nonpartisan advice on the kinds of scientific questions addressed in this book. American judges have similar powers but seldom exercise them.[1] If they did, the memoranda they would receive might resemble the chapters in this book.

Each chapter provides a scientist's perspective on a drug, product, chemical, or form of radiation whose supposed hazards have attracted the interest of lawyers and scientists. Without reviewing trials blow by blow, we conclude each section with a brief summary of the legal context in which these scientific issues have arisen.

Perhaps the litigators who have pursued traumatic cancer, teratogenic spermicides, Bendectin, and other such issues will someday be vindicated. Perhaps the generally optimistic views of our authors will be proved wrong. Some serious and reputable scientists may disagree, in part or in whole, with our authors' description of the issues. Nevertheless, the scientific consensus emerging on the issues discussed here is reasonably strong. The final judgment on these phantom (or possibly not so phantom) risks will be the test of time.

The final chapter addresses a single question that has proved exceptionally difficult for both scientists and lawyers: How can the effects of phantom risks on society be reduced? It is not enough to diagnose an illness; preventive or curative measures must be found. We offer only tentative suggestions and welcome further contributions on this important question from our readers.

Notes

1. Lee, *Court-appointed experts and judicial reluctance: A proposal to amend Rule 706 of the Federal Rules of Evidence,* 6 Yale Law & Policy Rev. 480 (1988). *In re Swine Flu Immunization Products Liability Litigation,* 495 F. Supp. 1185 (1980), *aff'd* 707 F.2d 1141. Harris, Louis and Assoc. 1987. Judges' opinions on procedural issues 45, Table 6.1. Study no. 874017. Cited in Elliot, Issues of science and technology facing the federal courts 11 (draft of Apr. 4, 1988).

References

Abelson, P. H. 1990. Testing for carcinogens with rodents. 249 *Science* 1357.

Ames, B. N., and L. S. Gold. 1988. Carcinogenic risk estimation—response. 240 *Science* 1045–1047.

Ames, B. N., R. Magaw, and L. S. Gold. 1987. Ranking possible carcinogenic hazards. 236 *Science* 271–280.

Bailar, J. C. 1989. Research on the health effects of electromagnetic fields: Science, uncertainty, and stopping rules. *Paper presented at* VIII ASA Conference on Radiation and Health, Alexandria, VA, July 9–13.

Behan, R. F. 1939. *Relation of trauma to new growths: Medico-legal aspects.* Baltimore: Williams and Wilkins.

Brenner, D. J. 1989. *Radon: risk and remedy.* New York: W. H. Freeman and Sons.

Cameron, J. 1992. *Physics Today,* August, p. 9. Letter.

Carstensen, E. L. 1987. *Biological effects of transmission line fields.* New York: Elsevier.

Doll, R., and A. B. Hill. 1952. A study of aetiology of carcinoma of the lung. 2 *Br. Med. J.* 1271–1286.

Duesberg, P. H. 1989. Human immunodeficiency virus and acquired immunodeficiency syndrome—correlation but not causation. 86 *Proc. Nat. Acad. Sci.* 755–764.

Epstein, S. S. 1978. *The politics of cancer.* San Francisco: Sierra Club Books.

Epstein, S. S., and J. B. Schwarz. 1988. Technical comment: Carcinogenic risk estimation. 240 *Science* 1043–1045.

Evans, A. S. 1976. Causation and disease: The Henle-Koch postulates revisited. 49 *Yale J. Bio. & Med.* 175–195.

Evans, A. S. 1977. Limitations of Koch's postulates. 2 (8051) *The Lancet* 1277.

Feinstein, A. R. 1973. Clinical biostatistics. XX. The Epidemiologic Trohoc, the Ablative Risk Ratio, and 'Retrospective' Research. 14 *Clin. Pharmacol. Ther.* 291–307.

Feinstein, A. R. 1979. Methodologic problems and the standards in case-control research. 32 *J. Chronic Dis.* 35–41.

Feinstein, A. R. 1982. Double standards, scientific methods, and epidemiologic research. 307 *N. Engl. J. Med.* 1611–1617.

Feinstein, A. R. 1985. *Clinical epidemiology.* Philadelphia: W. B. Saunders.

Feinstein, A. R. 1988. Scientific standards in epidemiologic studies of the menace of everyday life. 242 *Science* 257–1263.

Glickman, T. S., and M. Gough. 1990. *Readings in risk.* Washington DC: Resources for the Future.

Gough, M. 1989. Estimating cancer mortality. 23 *Environ. Sci. & Tech.* 925–930.

Henderson, B. E., R. K. Moss, and M. C. Pike. 1991. Toward the primary prevention of cancer. 254 *Science* 1131–1138.

Hennekens, C. H., J. E. Buring. 1987. *Epidemiology in medicine.* Boston: Little, Brown and Co.

Hill, A. B. 1965. The environment and disease: association or causation? 58 *Proc. R. Soc. Med.* 295–300.

Holden, C. 1989. Science in court. 243 *Science* 1658–59.

Langmuir, I. 1989. Pathological science. 42 *Physics Today* 36–48.

Morgan, K. Z. 1992. *Physics Today* 9, August. Letter.

National Research Council. 1983. *Risk assessment in the federal government: Managing the process.* Washington, DC: National Academy Press.

Peto, R. 1985. Epidemiologic reservations about risk assessment. In Woodhead, A. D., C. J. Shellabarger, V. Pond, and A. Hollaender (eds). *Assessment of risk from low-level exposure to radiation and chemicals.* New York: Plenum Press.

Resneck 1988. *Insight.* Letter to the editor. August 1.

Rodricks, J. 1992. *Calculated risks.* Cambridge UK: Cambridge Univ. Press.

Rothman, K. J. 1988. *Causal inference.* Chestnut Hill, MA: Epidemiology Resources.

Ruckelshaus, W. D. 1985. Risk, science, and democracy. 1 *Iss. in Sci. & Tech.* 19–38.

Savitz, D. A., S. Greenland, P. D. Stolley, and J. L. Kelsey. Scientific standards of criticism: A reaction to "scientific standards in epidemiologic studies of the menace of daily life" by A. R. Feinstein. 1 *Epidemiology* 78–83.

Stoll, H. L. and J. T. Crissey. 1962. Epithelioma from single trauma. 62 *N. Y. J. Med.,* 496–500.

Susser, M. 1973. *Causal thinking in the health sciences: Concepts and strategies in epidemiology.* Oxford University Press.

Susser, M. 1991. What is a cause and how do we know one? A grammar for pragmatic epidemiology. 133 *Am. J. Epidem.* 635–648.

Takeuchi, H., S. Uyeda, and H. Kanamori. 1967. *Debate about the earth*. Freeman, Cooper and Co.

Thurber, J. 1933, 1971. The car we had to push. In *My life and hard times*. New York: Harper & Row 1933, *repr.*: Bantam Press.

Weinberg, A. M. 1985. Science and its limits: The regulator's dilemma. 2 *Iss. Sci. & Tech*. 59–72.

2

A Legal Perspective

Tort law approaches the question of risk quite differently than does science. A store owner defending himself against a claim that a slip and fall caused breast cancer need not prove generally that trauma does not cause breast cancer; he need only show that *this* trauma probably did not cause *that* cancer, whether or not other traumas cause other cancers elsewhere. Conversely, the plaintiff needs only to sell a diagnosis: *this* breast cancer was caused by *that* fall. The jury is supposed to decide in favor of the side that has established its claim by the "preponderance of the evidence."

Thus, at one level, the legal system is more symmetric than science in its approach to risk. In an individual trial, one side affirms, the other denies, and the matter is resolved in favor of one side or the other by the jury. Each side can hire its own expert witnesses, and in theory (and quite often in practice) the jury's decision will reflect the strengths of the scientific arguments that are presented.

But in a larger sense the legal system is highly asymmetric in its handling of technological risk. The problem is associated with the avalanche of litigation that may be filed because of a real or presumed risk. So much litigation arose because the Dalkon Shield led to pelvic infection in some of its users, and asbestos led to lung disease in some workers, that A. H. Robins and the Johns-Manville Company were both driven into bankruptcy. These were real problems, although one might question whether more effective means of compensating the victims might have been devised.

Ending baseless claims—that trauma caused a cancer, or Bendectin caused a birth defect—is far more difficult. The individual claimant may lose, and the case will then be closed. But for legal purposes the issue remains open, to be raised again any number of times by others elsewhere. Everyone is entitled to at least one day in court, and the same question can be litigated indefinitely.

In a mass market, a manufacturer is potentially exposed to many lawsuits if something goes wrong, and even questionable claims may result in endless litigation. If 30 million women used Bendectin, and 900,000 of them bore children with birth defects (as expected from the 3 percent incidence of major birth defects in the population at large), then 900,000 different juries could (in principle) be asked to determine whether Bendectin causes birth defects. The legal rule of collateral estoppel, which sometimes bars a defendant from litigating an issue he or she has already lost, does not stop a new plaintiff from relitigating an issue that other plaintiffs have lost elsewhere. Class actions—the main procedural device courts use to resolve common questions of law or fact— have not been invoked with any consistent success in personal injury litigation. In court, scientific facts can remain perpetually in play.

Tort lawyers might suggest that this makes the legal system more faithful to the scientific ideal. Science issues no final judgments; since the time of Galileo, the scientist's most cherished freedom has been the freedom to doubt, to disagree, to question anew, and to reconsider. But this analogy between an open-ended legal process and open-ended science is incomplete. While science respects the individual's freedom to keep an open mind, it also depends on the sifting and winnowing process. Science converges. Tort law does not, at least not over a time scale that is sufficiently short to prevent catastrophic losses to its victims.

Legal Risk and Litogens

Most of the chapters in this book concern substances that have attracted the attention of many plaintiffs and their lawyers, in most cases for exposures that were far too low to be obviously harmful. Some substances are carcinogens (cause cancer) or teratogens (cause birth defects). A litogen, by contrast, attracts litigation (Mills and Alexander 1986). Before discussing the legal issues, let us briefly consider some of the factors that help make something a lightning rod for litigation.

Often litigation is triggered by tentative scientific results that are seized upon by lawyers, even as later developments failed to support the concern. For example, several Boston investigators published a paper entitled "Vaginal Spermicides and Congenital Disorders" in the April 1981 issue of the *Journal of the American Medical Association* (Jick et al. 1981). The paper suggested that spermicides might be associated with certain types of birth defects. But the authors added a caution: "Since a well-defined syndrome among babies with congenital disorders whose mothers used spermicides was not present, these results should be considered tentative until confirmed by other data" (Jick et al. 1981, p. 1329).

In 1985, however, in large part justified by this study, a federal judge awarded a $5.1 million judgment against the Ortho Pharmaceutical Corporation for congenital injuries to Katie Wells said to have been caused by a spermicide. In affirming the verdict, a court of appeals stated: "[I]t does not matter in terms of deciding the case that the medical community might require more research and evidence before conclusively resolving the question."[1] A year after the verdict the authors of the original study spoke out again. One acknowledged (Watkins 1986) that their work "was not corroborated by subsequent studies." Another conceded: "I believe our article should never have been published. In our present litigious environment, the reservations and qualifications written into a published report are often ignored, and the article is used as 'proof' of a causal relationship." Two physicians from the National Institute of Child Health and Human Development noted that "the overwhelming body of evidence indicates that spermicides are not teratogenic" (Mills and Alexander 1986).

Litigation over the pertussis (whooping cough) vaccine developed along similar lines. Undisputably, the vaccine has virtually ended the disease, of which 265,000 cases and 7,500 pertussis-related deaths were recorded in the years before 1949, when the vaccine was first licensed (Hinman and Koplan 1984). But a 1984 English study, serious and cautiously phrased, suggested that the vaccine might cause 25 cases a year of serious brain damage in the United States. An avalanche of litigation followed, blaming the vaccine for brain damage, unexplained coma, Reyes' syndrome, epilepsy, sudden infant death, and other afflictions. Concerned about liability, several pharmaceutical companies abandoned the market, and at one time it seemed that the last U.S. manufacturer of the product would be leaving, too. Later, more reassuring evidence on the vaccine's safety began to accumulate. In March 1990, a report of a study of 230,000 children and 713,000 immunizations concluded that the vaccine had caused *no* serious neurological complications of any kind, and no deaths (Griffin et al. 1990). "It is time for the myth of pertussis vaccine encephalopathy to end," declared an editorial in the *Journal of the American Medical Association*. "Unfortunately, because of the sensationalistic media, the organization of a group of parents who attribute their children's illnesses and deaths to the pertussis vaccine, and the unique destructive force of personal injury lawyers, we now have a national problem that shouldn't be. . . . We need to end this national nonsense" (Cherry 1990).

Litigation also has resulted from expectations raised by new technology. Physicians, for example, were long mystified by cerebral palsy but usually attributed its cause either to trauma or to oxygen deprivation during labor. Doctors needed, some believed, a better way to detect signs of trouble during delivery, before trouble became disaster. In 1972, the electronic fetal monitor (EFM) arrived on the scene. A sensor attached to the baby's scalp in the early stages of labor was used to record the infant's heartbeat and the mother's contractions.

Many doctors enthusiastically welcomed EFM as "a medical breakthrough that could reduce the incidence of cerebral palsy, stillbirth and infant death" (Lewin 1988). EFM would flag fetal distress, allowing doctors to prevent trauma or hypoxia by performing cesarean sections. Then, starting in the 1970s, obstetricians who delivered babies with cerebral palsy began to be sued in record numbers. EFM and aggressive surgical intervention quickly became the legally established standards for prudent care. Then the medical consensus began to move in the opposite direction. A major report of the Institute of Medicine concluded that "overwhelming evidence" shows that EFM "does not improve neonatal mortality and morbidity rates" (Committee to Study Medical Professional Liability 1989).

Still other litigation develops at the periphery of real hazards, for example, in the emotional issues of intrauterine contraceptive devices (IUDs) and asbestos.

The first half of the IUD story is very familiar. Soon after Robins placed the Dalkon Shield on the market in 1971, doctors began observing pelvic inflammatory disease (PID) among its users. The U.S. Food and Drug Administration then lacked strong enforcement powers over medical devices, but it nevertheless asked Robins to halt sales. Robins complied in June 1974. Several years of intensive scientific study (Lee et al. 1983) confirmed that the Shield increased risks of PID in sexually active women by six to ten times. An outpouring of IUD litigation followed that quickly enfolded other IUDs as well, including the Lippes Loop, the Saf T Coil, and the Copper 7. The IUD market folded.

Scientists eventually traced the problems with the Dalkon Shield to its nylon multifilament tail, which served as a wick for bacteria, especially after prolonged exposure to body fluids. Other IUDs lacked this flaw. An initial epidemiologic study by Lee et al. (1983) of the Centers for Disease Control confirmed the high PID rates for Dalkon Shield users. Two large studies in Boston and Seattle (Dahling et al. 1985; Cramer et al. 1985), confirmed that the Dalkon Shield posed a sharply higher risk than other IUDs.

Epidemiologic studies have failed to implicate other IUDs. In 1988, Lee reported a study (Lee et al. 1988) that took careful account of the sexual habits of its subjects. The investigators concluded that stably monogamous users of any IUD other than the Dalkon Shield faced no significantly increased risk of PID, except for a very modest increase in risk in the month or two following the insertion of the device. Other studies showed that oral contraceptives also increase risks of PID two-fold to three-fold, apparently because sexually transmitted pathogens grow in a region of the cervix that is enlarged by sex hormones. Lee concluded: "The IUD is a good contraceptive choice for women who are in mutually monogamous relationships and, therefore, at low risk of acquiring sexually transmitted infections" (Lee et al. 1988). A major 1987 review of the literature (Grimes 1987) reached a similar conclusion that most IUDs have been "guilty by association." A year earlier, however, the legal system had delivered its verdict to the contrary. A headline in the *New York Times* summarized it (February 2, 1986): "No more IUD's in U.S."

The asbestos story unfolded similarly, and again the legal system had trouble keeping pace with the science. From the start of World War II through the 1970s, some 10 million people were exposed to high levels of asbestos in shipyards and other industries. Epidemiologic studies clearly showed that such exposure multiplies the risk of lung cancer by five to seven times in nonsmokers, and by a far greater amount in smokers (chapter 8).

An avalanche of litigation followed. The notion developed that asbestos is a uniquely potent poison that produces lung disease whenever it is on the scene. Lawyers then unleashed a wave of lawsuits against suppliers of asbestos in building materials, car brakes, and home hair dryers.

Present scientific knowledge suggests that many concerns about asbestos are exaggerated. The risks from occupational exposure to high levels of asbestos are grave. But risks from low-level exposure (for example, in buildings with intact asbestos insulation) are much smaller and apparently insignificant (Mossman et al. 1990). Typical asbestos levels in U.S. schools and buildings are 10,000 to 100,000 times lower than occupational levels known to cause disease (Mossman et al. 1990).

Moreover, there are two major forms of asbestos with greatly different hazards. The form usually found in buildings is probably much less hazardous than that used in World War II shipyards. D'Agostino and Wilson discuss this further in chapter 8.

Phantom Risk and the Media

Public reaction to a risk is strongly shaped by the media, particularly by the sensationalism that often afflicts reporting of technological risk. The first shot in the Bendectin litigation, for example, was fired by a story in the *National Enquirer* published in October 1979. In the next five years, leading up to Merrell Dow's $120 million offer to settle all outstanding claims, the media played a critical role in mobilizing Bendectin lawyers and their clients. Media attention to asbestos, Agent Orange, and the accident at Three Mile Island likewise fueled public concern, mobilized claimants, and triggered lawsuits seeking compensation for fear of cancer, anxiety, declining property values, and so on. Indeed, media coverage of a toxic exposure may lead people to report symptoms, even though their actual exposure was very slight (Lees-Haley and Brown 1992).

. . . and Politics

Political pressures are often important as well. In 1970, Senator Gaylord Nelson held widely publicized hearings on the supposed risks of oral contraceptives. The dramatic testimony, based on preliminary scientific evidence and studies that have since been largely repudiated, was extensively covered by the press. Millions of young women began searching for a safer contraceptive option. At Nelson's hearings, a persuasive critic of the pill's risks and advocate of safer alternatives was Dr. Hugh J. Davis of Johns Hopkins University. Four years earlier he had developed one such alternative, the Dalkon Shield.

Our authors frequently turn to the interplay between politics and science. Lasagna and Shulman (chapter 5) note that the Bendectin controversy was sharpened by publicity and demands for FDA action by the Public Citizen's Health Research Group. Gough points out (chapter 11) that "the political stakes are higher for dioxin than for other toxic substances. Any change in popular perceptions of dioxin would be a sharp challenge to the idea that cleaning up tiny amounts of chemicals in the environment will significantly improve human health." The same could be said for PCBs, or asbestos, or other high-profile substances whose presence in the environment was the justification for major legislation.

Political pressures can affect the way that government agencies consider risks. D'Agostino and Wilson (chapter 8) note that EPA documents on asbestos often "fail[] to differentiate between smokers and nonsmokers"; the omission is "widely believed to be due to political pressure on EPA management by senators from tobacco growing states."

Scientists themselves might overstate a problem as they lobby to elevate their research areas on the public agenda. An amusing example is the threat of sudden annihilation by a "killer asteroid" that is presently receiving media coverage. That unlikely hazard is being promoted by weapons scientists as a real threat (nuclear war with the former Soviet Union) and the accompanying funds for weapons development recede from view. There is not much in killer asteroids to interest tort lawyers; there is nobody to sue, and the accident is unlikely to occur anytime soon in any event. The remedy the scientists propose (a nuclear weapons program to shoot down a threatening asteroid) has its own obvious risks, by the way.

. . . and Fear

Litigation often turns on fear. A legal theory now held by some academics and jurists links legal rights not just to the actuality of risk but also to the public's widely shared fears. Some courts permit recovery only if a claimant's anxiety about rabies or cancer (say) is scientifically reasonable, and would be shared by a knowledgeable doctor or scientist in the same position. But others ask only whether the public at large shares the fear; the factual basis for the fear is irrelevant. Real fear is easier to prove than real hazard.

Some fears are perfectly rational; people *should* fear real risks. However, people often underestimate familiar risks and excessively fear new or unfamiliar ones.

Consider the Three Mile Island (TMI) nuclear plant and a large coal-burning power plant. Statisticians have estimated that the radiation released from the TMI accident will result in less than one excess death over the remaining lifetimes of the nearby population. In contrast, a large coal-burning power plant might cause dozens of excess deaths every year from air pollution (chapter 12). TMI became a lightning rod for litigation, but there has been no wave of personal injury suits against coal-burning power plants. The federal or state government might crack down on a power plant because of regulatory issues, but that is a different matter entirely.

The Outrage Factor

As Sandman has argued (1985, 1987), the severity of a "risk problem" is defined by a combination of risk and the "outrage factor." The latter depends on whether the risk is voluntary or involuntary, familiar or unfamiliar, detectable or undetectable, under an individual's control or not, and other variables.

For example, people typically react more strongly to risks that are imposed on them involuntary than to those assumed by choice. Smoking and alcohol consumption are truly hazardous, and are leading causes of otherwise preventable disease. But they have not engendered much tort litigation on account of their health risks. In contrast, people "know" that dioxin or PCBs are hazardous, and may be more likely to attribute their problems to slight exposure to these chemicals—particularly if their exposure was a result of a corporation's negligence. PCBs and dioxin are litogens; beer and wine are not (notwithstanding an occasional lawsuit over fetal alcohol syndrome).

Corporate negligence, even if it did not create a significant health hazard, can easily ignite the "outrage factor." A company that responds to concerns about the safety of its products by denying the problem, holding back information, stonewalling, putting on a happy face—all common bureaucratic responses to external challenge—will outrage the public, however firm or weak may be the legal grounds for its actions. The company will send a message that it doesn't *care,* that it is more interested in protecting itself from litigation than in the health of its customers. The result is likely to be an avalanche of litigation.

Most people care deeply about the environment, and environmental issues can engender a sense of outrage. Many people view with distaste a high-voltage power line running through pristine wilderness. Chemical pollution is disagreeable whether or not it poses any real risk of disease. In public discourse, environmental issues are often conflated with health issues, and a company that visibly (or invisibly) pollutes the environment—and most industrial activities do, at some level—can become a lightning rod for personal injury suits. Environmental issues have attained a certain political correctness, which complicates any fair assessment of environmental health issues.

The "outrage factor" also helps to determine the outcome of litigation. If jurors perceive a defendant to be an aesthetic or environmental polluter, they are inclined to find that defendant liable in a personal injury action to punish it, whether or not the defendant caused the injury in question or whether or not the injury even exists. This is particularly true if the plaintiffs were involuntarily exposed to a risk, however small (Elliott 1985).

For example, with unusual candor, one jury in a dioxin case returned a verdict of $1 for compensation, and $16 million in punishment (chapter 11). The jury called the science correctly—it found no credible evidence of physical harm to the plaintiffs. But a spill had occurred, and the jury concluded that the responsible company should pay heavily for exposing the plaintiffs to an involuntary risk, notwithstanding the absence of injury. That decision was reversed on appeal, but in many other cases, where jury misconduct is not nearly so blatant, the verdict stands and the defendant pays.

Financial Incentives

For a tort lawyer, speculative litigation can be a rewarding business. Even if most of the cases are lost, the rewards from the occasional successful case may be enough to justify the whole enterprise.

Sometimes a lawyer can win just by getting the game in play. Deterred by the possibility of large awards from unpredictable juries, high legal costs, and the notoriety of a trial, many defendants can be induced to offer huge settlements to buy their way out of the litigation. This happened in some cases related to Bendectin, dioxin, Fernald, trichloroethylene, and PCBs, as described in Part II. The merits (or lack thereof) of the cases were never decided by a jury.

Consider, for example, the Bendectin litigation. The first thousand claims in the giant class action suit were resolved in line with mainstream science, though not before Merrell was impelled to offer $120 million to escape from the legal quagmire. (See chapter 5). The plaintiffs' lawyers declined the offer, and the cases went to trial. Merrell ultimately won most of the individual trials. Most juries made no award, but some returned verdicts ranging from $20,000 to $95 million. Most of these verdicts were overturned on appeal, but some survived that additional test. The average award (the total awarded in all the trials, divided by the number of trials) was close to $100,000.

To the individual claimant, the results of this process are very uncertain. But to a tort lawyer who operates on a contingency basis it can be profitable: a single million-dollar verdict that survives all appeals can more than offset a long string of losses. To the company that has to defend itself against these many claims, the result is a disaster, even if it "wins" most of the cases.

Legal risk is increased by the ruling, in a growing number of courts, that a plaintiff need not prove actual injury to collect in some toxic tort suits. If the plaintiff claims that a defendant's product or technology causes negative health effects, the plaintiff (in these courts) need not present any evidence that the product actually hurt him or her, but only that the product caused a fear of potential negative health effects.

In some jurisdictions, this liberal standard of recovery is mitigated somewhat by a rule that the plaintiff must prove through competent scientific evidence that the fear is reasonable. But in other jurisdictions the plaintiff need only show that he or she suffers from fear and that the fear is widespread in the community. The latter rule has been widely adopted in power line cases (see chapter 3). In cases in which that rule is applied, legal risk has nothing to do with scientific risk. Rather, the results of litigation turn on the success of those who oppose the product or technology—for legal, political, aesthetic, or other reasons—in persuading the public that the product or technology should be feared.

Finally, there are the obvious financial incentives to the plaintiff. The plaintiff in most cases has suffered some illness or injury, and often has crushing financial burdens that are not adequately covered by insurance. Why suffer from an act of God when a potential defendant with deep pockets can be found?

Financial incentives for potential plaintiffs can create and sustain a scientific controversy that would otherwise fade away. Consider, for example, the theory of traumatic cancer (chapter 15). The theory originated in the seventeenth century, but was in decline by the nineteenth. Then, quite abruptly, many doctors began to become interested in the theory once again. The rapid shift in medical attitudes began in Germany in the 1880s, and swept across the American continent in the first decades of the twentieth century.

The change was motivated by social and legal developments, not by scientific progress. Germany introduced the world's first worker's compensation program in 1884, and by the early 1920s all but eight American states had enacted similar programs. Sympathetic doctors, acting to ensure that cancer patients and their families were not financially ruined, frequently attributed cancers to traumas suffered on the job. With so many anecdotal reports of traumatic cancer, and the medical establishment at a loss for any other explanation, the connection between trauma and cancer became accepted by many physicians.

As one observer noted in 1959, the carcinogenic properties of trauma "increase[d] in potency each year and in direct proportion to the broadening of insurance coverage" (Crane 1959). "The cancerigenic potentialities of mechanical trauma would probably have long since ceased to stimulate any significant amount of scientific interest," wrote one commentator in 1954, "were it not for the fact that so many claims for compensation are filed each year" (Moritz 1954; see also Curphey 1956). Traumatic cancer would have been "relegated to limbo" far sooner, declared a Mayo Clinic review 20 years later, but for "lawyers constantly keeping the question alive" (Monkman et al. 1974).

The Expert Witness and Rules of Evidence

In a personal injury suit, factual issues are decided by juries composed of ordinary citizens. Often baffled by weeks or months of complex scientific testimony, jurors may be left to rely on their instincts, "common sense," sense of justice—and impressions made by the expert witnesses who appeared at the trial.

Many of the lawsuits mentioned in this book turned on the testimony of expert witnesses that was sharply at odds with conventional scientific understanding of the issues. Some of these witnesses reappear in many lawsuits; Lapp (chapter 13) mentions a few expert witnesses who appeared in numerous cases, describing fearsome risks of exposure to radioactive fallout and other sources of low-level radiation. Some clinical ecologists have turned up repeatedly in cases involving TCE, dioxin, PCBs, and even traumatic cancer.

Clearly, risk research is a confusing business, and there is considerable room for differences of opinion by scientists themselves. In many lawsuits, both sides present distinguished mainstream scientists and physicians to argue in support of different interpretations of the evidence. In theory (and usually in practice) a case is decided in a way that is consistent with a broad spectrum of mainstream scientific opinion.

The problem is what to make of witnesses who present radically different views. Such witnesses typically have scientific or medical degrees or other credentials to qualify as experts in their areas under legal rules of evidence. Some, like Karl Z. Morgan (who frequently testified in support of claims for injury from low-level ionizing radiation) even have attained high professional distinction. Their unambiguous diagnoses and passionately argued theories are often crucial to a plaintiff's case. But their theories are not generally accepted by the scientific community at large. Sometimes their interpretations represent those of an extreme minority of scientists.

Consumer activists and tort lawyers often claim that such experts are not on the fringe of science but, rather, are closer to the truth than "mainstream" scientists and physicians who, for reasons of self-interest, want to cover up hazards. Such theories—and conspiracy theories in general—are easy to propose, and evidently appeal to many people.

For at least two reasons such arguments make little sense for the issues discussed in this book. The first is that *too many people* were involved with these issues for any real evidence of hazard to be covered up. Many scientists have reviewed the evidence, outside of the context of litigation, and many expert assessments have been published by a variety of scientific groups of diverse composition. A scientist whose views are outside of the spectrum of mainstream scientific opinion is, most likely, simply wrong.

The second is that the validity of a scientific opinion is decided, not by the personal interests of the scientists, but by its *verifiability*. *Ad hominem* judgments have a certain appeal to laypeople (judging from the frequency with which they appear in the lay media) but have little bearing on the truth or falsity of a scientific argument.

Should witnesses be allowed to present scientific testimony to a jury that is not consistent with mainstream science? Some jurists have argued that such testimony may add information that will help a jury decide, and that the witnesses' theories can be tested on cross examination. But ordinary citizens are not equipped to sort out the complex scientific issues that arise in hazardous exposure cases (which, of course, is why expert testimony is needed in the first place). The fairest approach in toxic tort litigation (we argue) is to ensure that scientific testimony that is presented to the jury is *verifiable* and, as far as possible, reflects consensus scientific judgments about the matter at hand. Verifiability and scientific consensus do not guarantee the absence of error, but they are the best we have.

American courts have employed diverse and shifting rules that govern the qualification of witnesses and admissibility of scientific evidence. Until the mid-1970s, most courts employed the *Frye* rule, named after a 1923 federal court decision.[2] According to this rule, expert testimony was to be admitted only when it had received "general acceptance" in the relevant scientific community. Thus, a witness's educational qualifications were not sufficient for his or her testimony to be admitted; his or her testimony had also to be consistent with mainstream scientific understanding of an issue.

For half a century, the *Frye* rule served reasonably well to exclude unreliable or eccentric scientific evidence from the courtroom. The rule came under attack, however, in the 1960s and 1970s. Many lawyers viewed the rule as elitist and unhelpful, particularly in cases involving new pollutants and unfamiliar hazards. New theories of liability evolved to give plaintiffs a greater advantage at trial (Olson 1991). Critics of the *Frye* rule argued that an alleged victim of chemical poisoning or some other "toxic tort" should not be denied compensation just because the plaintiff's offer of proof could not meet the standards of acceptance by a broader scientific community.

In 1975, Rule 702 of the Federal Rules of Evidence (which significantly influenced state rules of evidence) was promulgated. It stated that any qualified scientific expert may testify at a trial if he or she possesses "scientific, technical, or other specialized knowledge [which] will assist the trier of fact to understand the evidence or to determine a fact." Many courts and commentators believed that Rule 702 replaced the *Frye* rule with a relevancy test, that is, whether the scientific testimony was relevant to the issue at hand.

Many courts defined the concept of relevancy loosely. Thus "relevant" scientific evidence would not persuade scientists that the product or technology in question actually harmed, or even could have harmed, the plaintiffs. Rather, courts defined relevancy in layman's terms: any study reporting a correlation between a product or technology and injury, no matter how weak the study or inconclusive its results, was deemed relevant.

The "relevance" of particular kinds of scientific evidence to human health is a matter on which scientists and the law clearly diverge. For example, Kimbrough (chapter 9), Luster et al. (chapter 16), and Cornfeld and Schlossman (chapter 17) comment on the remote connection between many tests of immune function and clinical illness. Yet results of such tests have frequently been admitted as "relevant" evidence in cases alleging injury in the form of suppression of the immune system.

Federal Rule of Evidence 703, also promulgated in 1975, continued the liberal trend regarding the admission of scientific evidence. This rule holds that an expert may base his or her testimony on facts or data that are not admissible into evidence, if they are of a type reasonably relied upon by experts in the particular field in forming opinions or inferences upon the subject. Many judges and legal scholars argue that Rule 703 also implicitly demands that an expert witness whose facts or data are admissible into evidence may base his or her testimony on them, even if experts in the field would not rely on them for the proposition asserted. In other words, the rule would allow an expert to interpret the data in a way that few scientists or physicians would accept.

This liberalization of standards for scientific evidence led to an avalanche of questionable testimony on scientific issues in the courtroom. Brokers of expert witnesses flourished, matching malleable witnesses to eager attorneys. Eventually, however, the need for reform became recognized within and without the legal world, following a series of embarrassing federal court decisions (some of which are described later in this book).

Judge Patrick Higginbotham of the Fifth Circuit Court of Appeals fired the first major shot when he declared that henceforth his court would keep a "sharp eye" on instances where "the decision to receive expert testimony was simply tossed off to the jury under a 'let it all in' philosophy. . . . Our message to our able trial colleagues: it is time to take hold of expert testimony in federal trials."[3]

Soon thereafter, some courts began to interpret the Federal Rules of Evidence more strictly, so that legal standards would be more in line with scientific standards (Bernstein 1990). Some courts held that for scientific testimony to be relevant under Rule 702, it had to conform to a generally accepted explanatory theory, thereby implicitly or explicitly reincorporating the *Frye* rule into the rules of evidence.[4]

Other courts have reinterpreted Rule 703 as holding that courts must examine the bases of an expert's opinion. If scientists would not reasonably rely on those bases for the conclusions urged by the expert, the expert's testimony must be excluded. Judge Jack Weinstein, for example, relied on Rule 703 in excluding various expert testimony, including testimony about studies of animals and people exposed to extremely high doses of dioxin, from the Agent Orange litigation (see chapter 11).

Another recent trend in the courts has been to strictly apply more general rules of evidence to scientific cases. Of particular importance is Federal Rule of Evidence 403, which requires that judges must exclude testimony that is more prejudicial than probative. Court are slowly approaching the consensus that scientific studies that have not been subjected to peer review have little if any probative value.[5] They recognize that peer review—which typically consists of review of a scientific paper by several anonymous scientists before its acceptance by a journal—is an important means of quality control in science. (As we discuss in the concluding chapter, peer review is a qualifying step for publication, and not a guarantee of accuracy.)

The insistence on stricter standards for the admission of scientific evidence is by no means universal. Some jurisdictions still adhere to a liberal relevancy standard under Rule 702,[6] refuse to exclude evidence under Rule 703,[7] and do not require scientific studies to be peer-reviewed before they are admissible at trial.[8]

Some judges have also based their opinions on odd sources of scientific knowledge. In one case, the New Jersey Supreme Court relied on an article written by a law student for a crucial (but dubious) scientific proposition.[9] The law student had relied on two other law review articles.[10] Science itself was somehow lost in the process.

Proposals to create stricter standards for admissible scientific evidence continue to be debated, and may be promulgated. Even if the rules remain unchanged, courts—as they become more aware of the ambiguities inherent in risk research and the resulting problems in the courtroom—may scrutinize expert testimony more carefully. Judges have the authority to do so: Rule 102 of the Federal Rules of Evidence commands that the rules "shall be construed to secure . . . promotion of growth and development of the law of evidence to the end that the truth may be ascertained and proceedings justly determined." As this book goes to press, the United States Supreme Court has agreed to review the standards for scientific evidence in federal cases. The issues to be determined are right on point—the survival of the *Frye* rule in the face of Rule 702 (see note 5).

Notes

1. 788 F.2d at 745.

2. *Frye* v. *United States,* 293 F. 1013 (D. C. Cir. 1923).

3. *In re Air Crash Disaster at New Orleans (Eymard* v. *Pan American Airways),* 795 F.2d 1230, 1234 (5th Cir. 1986).

4. *Sterling* v. *Velsicol,* 855 F.2d 1188, 1208 (6th Cir. 1988); *Daubert* v. *Merrell Dow Pharmaceuticals, Inc.,* 951 F.2d 1128, 1130 (9th Cir. 1991); *Christophersen* v. *Allied-Signal Corp.,* 939 F.2d 1106 (5th Cir. 1991) (en banc).

5. E.g., *Daubert* v. *Merrell Dow Pharmaceuticals, Inc.,* 951 F.2d 1128, 1130 (9th Cir. 1991, cert. granted.); *Lynch* v. *Merrell-National Laboratories,* 830 F.2d 1190, 1195 (1st Cir. 1987). *Daubert* was accepted in early 1993 for review by the U.S. Supreme Court—see 61 U.S.L.W. 3284).

6. E.g., *In re Paoli Railroad Yard PCB Litigation,* 916 F.2d 829 (3d Cir. 1990).

7. E.g., *DeLuca* v. *Merrell Dow Pharmaceuticals Inc.,* 911 F.2d 941 (3d Cir. 1990).

8. *Rubanick* v. *Witco,* 125 N.J. 421, 593 A.2d 733 (1991).

9. *Id.* 593 A.2d at 747.

10. *Tort actions for cancer: Deterrence, compensation, and environmental carcinogenesis,* 90 Yale Law J. 840, n.1 (1981).

References

Anonymous 1979. Experts reveal . . . common drug causing deformed babies. National Enquirer 20. October 9.

Bernstein, D. 1990. Out of the Fryeing pan and into the fire: The expert witness problem in toxic tort litigation. 10 *Rev. Litig.* 117–159.

Cherry, J. D. 1990. Pertussis-vaccine encephalopathy—it is time to recognize it as the myth that it is. 263 *J. Am. Med. Assn.* 1679–1680.

Committee to study medical professional liability and the delivery of obstetrical care. 1989. Division of Health Promotion and Disease Prevention. 1 Medical Professional Liability and the Delivery of Obstetrical Care 78. Institute of Medicine.

Crane, R. 1959. The relationship of a single of trauma to subsequent malignancy. In Moritz and Helberg, ed., *Trauma and disease* 147 n. 148. *Quoted* in Comment, *Sufficiency of proof in traumatic cancer: A medico-legal quandary,* 16 *Ark Law Rev.* 243.

Cramer D. W., M. J. Berger, S. Belisle, B. Albrecht, M. Gibson, B. V. Stadel, R. J. Stillman, S. C. Schoenbaum, M. Seibel, E. Wilson, and I. Schiff. 1985. *Tubal infertility and the intrauterine shield.* 312 *N. Eng. J. Med.* 941–947.

Curphey 1985. Trauma and tumors. 1 *J. For. Sci.* 27.

Daling, J. R., W. H. Chow, N. S. Weiss, R. M. Sonderstrom, L. R. Spadoni, B. V. Stadel, and D. E. Metch. 1985. Primary tubal infertility in relation to the use of an intrauterine device. 312 *New Eng. J. Med.* 937–941.

Elliott, D. 1985. Why courts? Comment on Robinson. 14 *J. Leg. Stud.* 799, 801–802.

Griffin, M. R., W. A. Ray, E. A. Mortimer, G. M. Fenichel, and W. Schaffner. 1990. Risk of seizures and encephalopathy after immunization with diptheria-tetanus-pertussis vaccine. 263 *J. Am. Med. Assn.* 1641–1645.

Grimes, D. A. 1987. Intrauterine-devices and pelvic inflammatory disease—recent developments. 36 *Contraception* 97–109.

Hinman, A. R., and J. P. Koplan. 1984. Pertussis and pertussis vaccine—reanalysis of benefits, risks, and costs. 251 *J. Am. Med. Assn.* 3109–3113.

Holmes 1986. Vaginal spermicides and congenital disorders: the validity of a study. 256 *J. Am. Med. Assn.* 3095. Letter.

Jick, H., A. M. Walker, K. J. Rothman, J. R. Hunter, L. B. Holmes, R. N. Watkins, D. C. D'Ewart, A. Danford, and S. Madsen. 1981. *Vaginal spermicides and congenital disorders,* 245 J. of the Am. Med. Ass'n 1329–1332.

Lee, N. C., G. L. Rubin, H. W. Ory and R. L. Burkman. 1983. Type of intrauterine device and the risk of pelvic inflammatory disease. 62 *Obstet. & Gynecol.* 1–6.

Lee, N. C., G. L. Rubin, and R. Borucki. 1988. The intrauterine-device and pelvic inflammatory disease revisited—new results from the women's health study. 72 *Obstet. & Gynecol.* 1–6.

Lees-Haley, P. and R. S. Brown. 1992. Biases in perception and reporting following a perceived toxic exposure. 75 Percept. Motor Skills 531–544.

Lewin 1988. Despite criticism, fetal monitors are likely to remain in wide use. New York Times, § 1, 24.

Mills, J. L., and D. Alexander. 1986. Teratogens and "litogens." 315 *N. Eng. J. Med.* 1234–1236.

Monkman, G., G. Orwoll, and J. C. Ivins. 1974. Trauma and oncogenesis. 49 *Mayo Clinic Proc.* 157–163.

Moritz, 1954. *Pathology of trauma* 116. 2d ed.

Mossman, B. T., J. Bignon, M. Corn, A. Seaton, J. B. L. Gee. 1990. Asbestos-scientific developments and implications for public policy. 247 *Science* 294–301.

Olson, W. K. 1991. *The Litigation Explosion*. New York: Dutton.

Sandman, P. M. 1985. Getting to maybe: Some communications aspects of siting hazardous waste facilities. 9 *Seton Hall Leg. J.* 442–465.

Sandman, P. M. 1987. *Risk communications: Facing public outrage*. Washington, DC: EPA Journal, 21–22.

Watkins 1986. Vaginal spermicides and congenital disorders: the validity of a study. 256 *J. Am. Med. Assn.* 3096. Reply.

I

Phantom (Or Not So Phantom) Risks

. . . the connection between low-level insult and bodily harm is probably as difficult to prove as the connection between witches and failed crops.

Weinberg

In this first section, we consider hazards whose very existence is somehow in doubt. Each issue arose from preliminary scientific evidence or from anecdotal reports that seemed to indicate a hazard. In later studies, however, the evidence became weaker and in retrospect it is questionable whether any hazard existed at all.

For example, Mills (chapter 4) describes the issue of spermicides and birth defects. This issue arose with the publication of three epidemiologic studies in 1981–1982 reporting a link between the use of spermicides prior to or soon after conception, and the birth of a child with major congenital defects. Half a dozen subsequent studies showed no such connection.

According to Mills, the early studies were deficient in several respects, the most important of which was lack of information about the women's use of the spermicides during or just before pregnancy. Another potential difficulty was the possibility of spurious associations, because of the many comparisons the investigators could have been made between use of spermicides and the many different kinds of birth defects. The initial positive results were not confirmed by later, more focused investigations.

A different issue, Bendectin and birth defects, began with the publication in 1969 of a letter in a medical journal reporting cases of deformed children born to women who had used the drug during pregnancy. As Lasagna and Shulman point out in chapter 5, such reports are difficult to evaluate, since major birth defects are regrettably common, occurring in 1 percent to 7 percent of newborns, and will occur in any group of children regardless of any connection with their mothers' use of a drug.

As Lasagna and Schulman observe, "The degree to which such data are compelling rests not on individual cases but on collective evidence showing that the drug's use has been associated with an increase over the usual incidence of fetal abnormalities." Two early studies reported weak associations between Bendectin and birth defects. However, later epidemiologic studies failed to observe any associations between Bendectin and congenital malformations. In 1986 the drug was removed from the market, ending the scientific controversy.

Foster (chapters 3 and 6) reviews two issues related to possible hazards from low-level electromagnetic fields. The first issue is electromagnetic fields and cancer, a source of unresolved controversy since the late 1970s. Over four dozen epidemiologic studies have been reported, many claiming increased cancer risk to workers in "electrical" occupations or from residential exposure to electromagnetic fields. But the data are inconsistent and the case for real hazard remains weak.

The second issue is video display terminals (VDTs) and miscarriage. This controversy originated with reports in 1980 in the lay media of clusters of miscarriages among women users of VDTs. A dozen epidemiologic studies during the following ten years produced results that were overwhelmingly (but not totally) negative.

Reference

Weinberg, A. M. 1985. Science and its limits, 2 *Issues in Science and Technology* 59–72.

3

Weak Magnetic Fields: A Cancer Connection?

Kenneth R. Foster

Some hazards of electricity are painfully obvious. For example, the *New York Times* once described a hang glider that had fallen into power lines, its dead pilot a modern Icarus. In less spectacular ways, hundreds of other Americans die each year from accidental electrocution. These tragedies seem to have raised little controversy in the scientific or legal arena.

A more interesting controversy surrounds the possibility of hazard from electric or magnetic *fields* associated with power lines or household appliances. For many years there has been some level of public concern about electric fields; James Thurber once satirized his grandmother's fears of electricity leaking from household wiring (Thurber 1933). More recently, a larger public issue has developed, fueled in part by sensationalized lay accounts of scientific research (e.g., Brodeur 1989), with substantial impact in legal and government arenas.

In this chapter I address one issue: whether a link might exist between power-frequency magnetic fields and cancer. Its scientific basis consists of roughly four dozen epidemiologic studies, mostly undertaken during the 1980s, and many other laboratory studies. For reasons discussed below, the case for any real hazard is very weak, and I doubt whether any exists at all. But the controversy raises important questions about scientific ambiguity in the search for subtle hazards.

The Fields

Magnetic fields are ubiquitous in our environment. The earth's magnetic field has a strength, more correctly called flux density, of around 500 milligauss.[1] The use and distribution of electric power gives rise to other magnetic fields at the power-line frequency, 60 hertz (Hz).

Figure 3.1 compares the 60 Hz magnetic fields from several common sources. The strongest fields most people are likely to encounter are

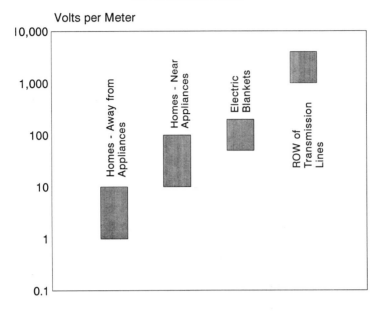

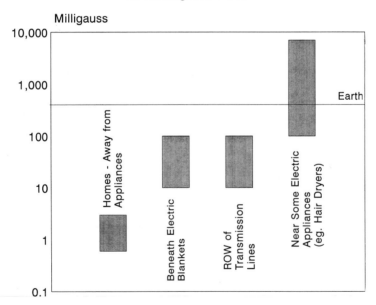

Figure 3.1
Electric and magnetic fields found under typical environmental conditions
Source: Nair et al. 1989.

in the home, associated with appliances. Within a foot or so of common household appliances, the flux density of 60 Hz magnetic fields might be in the range of 100–1,000 milligauss (mG); away from appliances ambient levels are about 1 mG. Beneath high-voltage transmission lines, flux densities are typically in the range of 30–100 mG.

A few medical devices create far higher fields. Magnetic resonance imaging (MRI) scanners can generate detailed images of the interior of the body, and employ constant magnetic fields of several thousand gauss. Thousands of patients have been briefly exposed to such fields with no apparent ill effect. Experimental devices can stimulate neurons in the brain by application of short pulses of magnetic fields of tens of thousands of gauss (Barker et al. 1985). The stimulation arises from electric currents induced in the brain and no other effects are apparent.

Hundreds of studies have been conducted on biological effects of 50–60 Hz electric or magnetic fields; the appendix lists some reviews of this field. The few proven hazards of electric fields are obvious and easily avoided—for example, a person might be shocked by touching a large conductive object located in a strong field. Alternating magnetic fields will induce electric currents in the body, which might conceivably lead to shock. However, that would require magnetic fields far stronger than any likely to be encountered in the environment. Such hazards require exposure to strong fields, and there is clearly a threshold below which these hazards do not exist.

The Epidemiologic Evidence

More controversial is the possibility of subtle hazard from long-term exposure to weak fields. The evidence consists of roughly four dozen epidemiologic studies published over a decade or more. A detailed review of this literature would exceed the space available here, and would tax the patience of most readers. Instead, I will summarize the chief results and the problems with their interpretation. My summary of the occupational studies largely follows an unpublished review by Cole (1987) with more recent results included as needed. The discussion is based in part on Hill's criteria for assessing causation in epidemiologic studies (Hill 1965; see chapter 1).

An interesting starting point for this discussion is the evidence for a *real* hazard—lung cancer (carcinoma of the lung) from smoking, from the study by Doll and Hill (1952). These investigators identified 1,465 patients of both sexes with lung cancer, and an equal number of controls who had other diseases. Considering only men, the study included 1,357 cases and an equal number of controls. Of these, only 7 cases and 61 controls were nonsmokers; 475 cases and 431 controls smoked a pack of cigarettes a day. These figures indicate (Figure 3.2) that a pack-a-day smoker is 14 times more likely to develop lung cancer than a nonsmoker. The association is very strong, and increases with increasing dose—two factors that suggest a cause-effect relation between smoking and lung cancer. Smoking is, in fact, a serious health problem and the cause of much preventable disease.

By contrast, much of the controversy about health effects of magnetic fields pertains to rare diseases—various childhood cancers, for example—and to barely detectable increases in risk. For reasons that are discussed in chapter 1 and elsewhere in this book, such risks are frequently very difficult to measure reliably. After summarizing the epidemiologic evidence, I consider some of the difficulties in its interpretation.

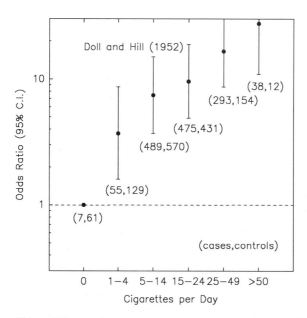

Figure 3.2
Relative risk for lung cancer in men, in relation to average number of cigarettes smoked per day during ten years before onset of the disease
The error bars indicate the 95 percent confidence limits, calculated using the method of Miettinen (see Feinstein 1985, 432). Note the clear biological gradient in response: the risk increases progressively with smoking. The cases were a group of 1,357 men with lung cancer; the controls were an equal number of men with other diseases.
Source: Doll and Hill 1952.

Occupational Studies

The epidemiologic studies fall into two broad classes: occupational and residential studies. Following Cole (1987), I group the occupational studies into three major classes, depending on their study design and the method they used to estimate relative risk.

Proportionate Mortality or Morbidity Ratios. These studies compare the proportions of total deaths in different groups of people. Proportionate mortality studies typically are based on an evaluation of death certificates, which are readily available and indicate (often unreliably) the cause of death and the occupation of the decedent. The proportionate mortality ratio, or PMR, is the fraction of individuals in the exposed groups who have died of a disease, divided by the fraction of nonexposed individuals. Thus, the PMR is the ratio of two death rates, for "exposed" and "control" individuals; a PMR of 1 corresponds to no difference in risk in the two groups being compared. An analogous quantity, the proportionate morbidity ratio (also PMR), compares the incidence of a disease and is obtained from other health records.

Figure 3.3 summarizes the results of six PMR studies that compared workers in "electrical" occupations with other groups of workers (Milham 1982; Wright et al. 1982; Coleman et al. 1983; McDowall 1983; Calle and Savitz 1985; Milham 1985) or radio amateurs with control populations (Milham 1982, 1985). The figure shows only the PMR for all forms of leukemia; most of the studies also presented similar PMRs for different subclassifications of the disease.

Two of these six studies (both by Milham) reported PMRs for leukemia that are significantly higher than 1; two other studies reported PMRs that exceeded 1 but for which the increases were not statistically significant. Two of the studies reported no appreciable increase at all. Milham has argued that his results support the hypothesis that electromagnetic fields are carcinogenic.

Proportionate mortality studies are comparatively easy to do but have potentially serious weaknesses. As several authors emphasize (e.g., chapters 9 and 11), death certificates are unreliable sources of information about the cause of death and the occupation of the decedent.

Also, the PMR can be misleading when comparing groups of people with different overall death rates. To give an extreme example, college students may have a far higher PMR for leukemia than soldiers in wartime even though their risk of developing the disease might be the same; while their overall death rate is lower, a greater proportion of the students that do die are carried away by the disease.

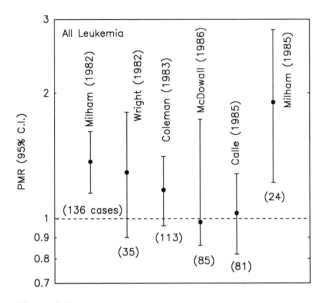

Figure 3.3
Results of proportionate mortality or morbidity studies
Sources: Milham 1982 (deceased men occupationally exposed to electromagnetic fields); Wright 1983 (Los Angeles men occupationally exposed to fields); Coleman et al. 1983 (British men in electrical occupations); McDowall 1983 (deceased electrical workers in England and Wales); Calle and Savitz 1985 (deceased Wisconsin men in electrical occupations); Milham 1985 (deceased male amateur radio operators).

A less extreme form of this problem appears in many occupational studies. Workers as a group are often healthier than nonworkers of similar age, and thus have a higher PMR for a disease (a greater fraction of them die from it) even though the incidence of the disease might be the same in both groups. For these and other reasons, Feinstein (1985) described the PMR as "too unstable to warrant serious scientific attention."

Case-Control Studies and Odds Ratio.   A "case-control" study compares cases (people with the disease) and controls (people without the disease) with respect to exposure. The odds ratio is the ratio of exposed to unexposed individuals among the cases, divided by the similar ratio of controls, and is a good estimate of the relative risk. The study by Doll and Hill (1952) that I described above was of this type.

   Case-control studies are well suited for the study of rare diseases such as childhood cancers, since the investigator can easily locate cases by searching through medical records. However, their validity depends critically on how well the controls are chosen. Any inadvertent tendency to exclude exposed individuals from the controls will introduce bias into the study. For example, had Doll and Hill chosen their controls from a group of Mormons (who do not smoke), their study would have been dramatically in error. Such an error would have been very obvious; but in other studies bias can be subtle and difficult to identify. Rothman (1986) offered the opinion that case-control studies "present more opportunities for bias and mistaken inference than other types of research." (Rothman figured prominently in the controversy about a possible association between spermicides use and birth defects, as described in chapter 4).

Figure 3.4 summarizes the results from 12 case-control studies (McDowall 1983; Pearce et al. 1985 (corrected in 1988); Swerdlow 1983; Lin et al. 1985; Spitz and Johnson 1985; Flodin et al. 1986; Stern et al. 1986; Speers et al. 1988; Nasca et al. 1988; Thomas et al. 1987; Wilkins and Hundley 1990; Bunin et al. 1990). These studies considered many

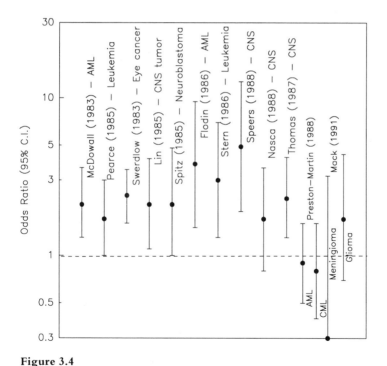

Figure 3.4
Results from case-control studies
Note: The studies by Spitz (1985) and Nasca (1988) related to parents' occupations to cancer risk in children.

different diseases: a variety of central nervous system tumors, various subcategories of leukemia, and other diseases such as melanoma of the eye. Their subjects were workers in "electrical" occupations, or (in a few studies) children of "electrical" workers.

These studies ranged widely in size, approach, and quality. Nevertheless, most of them reported odds ratios that were slightly but significantly higher than 1, albeit close to the margins of sampling error.

Retrospective Follow-up Studies.   A third approach is to calculate the rates of disease or death for groups of people, and compare them with rates in the population at large. Such studies can be done by using the extensive data in national disease registries; Sweden, for example, maintains an exhaustive tumor registry together with extensive records of other vital statistics of its population. An investigator with access to such data can design very large studies that cover virtually the entire country's population for periods of a decade or more.

The incidence of diseases usually depends strongly on age, sex, and other variables. Investigators typically correct (standardize) data to account for such variables. The standardized mortality (or morbidity) ratio, SMR, is the ratio of the standardized death rate (or disease incidence) for the group being studied, divided by the corresponding figure for the comparison group.

Figure 3.5 summarizes the results of eight SMR studies (Vågerö and Olin 1983; Vågerö et al. 1985; Olin et al. 1985; Barregård et al. 1985; Törnqvist et al. 1986; McLaughlin et al. 1987; Juutilainen et al. 1988; Milham 1988). The subjects ranged from workers in "electrical" occupations, to workers employed at a chlorine plant that used large amounts of electrical power in an electrolysis process, to amateur radio operators.[2] The studies by Vågerö (1983, 1985) and Linet et al. (1988), in particular, were based on the Swedish cancer registry and included many subjects.

None of the data shown in this figure indicate an increase in cancer risk. However, many of these studies did report increased SMRs for specific cancers (not shown in this figure) for subgroups of the populations studied. For example, in 1983 Vågerö and Olin reported an excess of lung cancers in workers in the electronics industry; in 1985 Vågerö reported an increase in melanoma in telecommunications workers. In fact, *most* of these studies reported some increase in risk, for some kind of cancer, for some subgroups of workers with an "electrical" occupation.

On looking over these figures, one gets the impression of a slight but consistent increase in cancer risk among "electrical" workers. The diseases that are most frequently mentioned are leukemia in its various

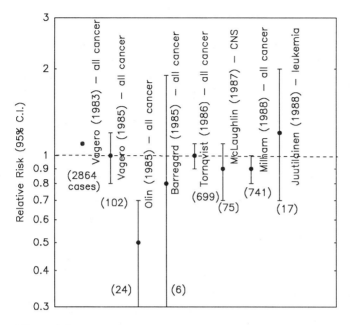

Figure 3.5
Results from retrospective follow-up studies

forms and brain tumors. The studies, however, include many different occupational groups and diverse diseases. Savitz and Calle (1987) combined the data from many of these studies to estimate the risk of leukemia among workers in 12 "electrical" occupations (Table 3.1). Their analysis suggests that the leukemia risk for these "electrical" workers is 10–30 percent higher than for the diverse groups of people used as controls; Savitz and Calle found similar increases for various subclassifications of the disease.

More Recent Occupational Studies
Many other studies are under way, and the epidemiologic literature relating to occupational exposure to electromagnetic fields and cancer is growing rapidly. One extensive case-control study was reported by Loomis and Savitz (1990). The cases consisted of 2,173 men who had died of brain cancer, and 3,400 men who had died of leukemia, in 16 states during 1985–1986. The controls were men who had died of other causes during that period. The diagnosis of disease was obtained from death certificates, as encoded in computer data bases.

The results (Table 3.2) suggest a slight increase in risk of brain cancer to workers in some "electrical" occupations. However, the increases are

Table 3.1
Leukemia risk for workers in "electrical" occupations

Occupation	Relative risk (95% confidence interval)
Electrical equipment assemblers	2.4 (1.0 − 4.8)
Aluminum workers	1.9 (1.2 − 2.9)
Telegraph, radio, and radar operators	1.8 (1.4 − 2.6)
Streetcar, subway, and elevated railway motormen	1.7 (0.7 − 3.3)
Power station operators	1.6 (0.8 − 3.0)
Electronics technicians	1.3 (0.9 − 1.8)
Power and telephone linemen	1.3 (1.0 − 1.6)
Electrical and electronic engineers	1.2 (1.0 − 1.5)
Electricians	1.1 (0.9 − 1.2)
Motion picture projectionists	1.1 (0.5 − 2.2)
Telephone repairers and installers	0.9 (0.7 − 1.3)
Welders and flame cutters	0.9 (0.7 − 1.2)
TOTAL	1.2 (1.1 − 1.3)

Note: Calculated from many of the studies in Figures 3.3–3.5. The relative risk pertains to all forms of leukemia; similar results were found for different subclassifications of the disease.
Source: Adapted from Savitz and Calle 1987.

Table 3.2
Odds ratios for association of death from brain cancer and leukemia with occupation

Occupational group	Leukemia odds ratio (95% confidence interval) [number of cases]	Brain tumor odds ratio (95% confidence interval) [number of cases]
Electrical and electronic engineers and technicians	1.3 (1.0–1.7) [19]	2.7 (2.1–3.4) [29]
Electrical and electronic equipment repairers	1.0 (0.7–1.4) [11]	1.0 (0.6–1.6) [6]
Telephone and telephone line installers and repairers	1.1 (0.7–1.7) [6]	1.6 (1.1–2.4) [9]
Electricians and apprentices	0.8 (0.7–1.0) [29]	1.0 (0.8–1.3) [24]
Electric power installers and repairers	1.2 (0.8–1.9) [6]	1.7 (1.0–2.7) [5]
Other electrical occupations	0.8 (0.3–1.3) [5]	0.4 (0.2–0.8) [2]

Source: Loomis and Savitz 1990.

small—only two of these increases are statistically significant; two others are at the very edge of significance. Curiously, the results for leukemia were essentially negative.

Residential Studies
Other studies examined a possible link between cancer and *domestic* exposure to electric or magnetic fields (Wertheimer and Leeper 1979; Fulton et al. 1980; Wertheimer and Leeper 1982; Myers et al. 1985; McDowall 1986; Tomenius 1986; Savitz et al. 1988; Preston-Martin et al. 1988; Severson et al. 1988; Lin 1989; Coleman et al. 1989; London et al. 1991). All except one were case-control studies that individually estimated their subjects' exposure, in most cases by the proximity of residence to power lines or electrical substation. The more recent studies attempted direct field measurements as well.

Collectively, these studies examined many diseases; most focused on childhood cancers, of which leukemia is the most common. Figure 3.6 summarizes the data on this neoplasm.

The Wertheimer–Leeper Studies.   The earliest (and in public discussion the most widely cited) of the group was a case-control study by Wertheimer and Leeper (1979) on childhood cancer. The cases included 344 children in the Denver area who had died of any form of cancer during the years 1950–1973; the controls were an equal number of children, without cancer, who had been randomly chosen from county birth records.

Wertheimer and Leeper classified a home according to a four level "wiring configuration code" depending on its proximity to an electrical substation or a primary or secondary distribution line. The investigators

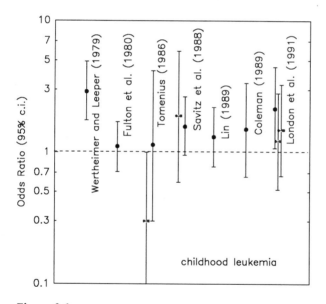

Figure 3.6
Summary of results of epidemiologic studies on childhood leukemia risk associated with domestic exposure to fields
Exposure was judged by the proximity of the home to neighborhood distribution facilities or wiring configuration code (closed circles), spot measurements of magnetic fields in or near the homes (open circles), or measurements of the 24-hour arithmetic mean magnetic fields in the child's bedroom (open triangle).
Source: Foster (1992). Reprinted from the journal *Health Physics* with permission from the Health Physics Society.

suggested that the wiring configuration code is a measure of a child's exposure to 60 Hz magnetic fields, in particular to fields produced by power distribution lines near the home.

The investigators found that a disproportionate fraction of children who had died of cancer lived in "high current configuration" homes (Figure 3.7). The odds ratios for all childhood cancers combined (most frequently leukemia but also other diseases including lymphoma and brain tumors) increased progressively with the wiring code. The most striking increase occurred in homes near electric substations; but the number of subjects in this exposure class was very small. In their paper, Wertheimer and Leeper suggested that 60 Hz magnetic fields might have been a causative factor, apparently for lack of any other obvious risk factor that might be plausibly connected with the wiring configuration code.

In 1982, the same investigators published results of a similar study on adult cancer, including 1,200 adult cancer cases and the same number of controls. They reported an odds ratio of approximately 2 for all can-

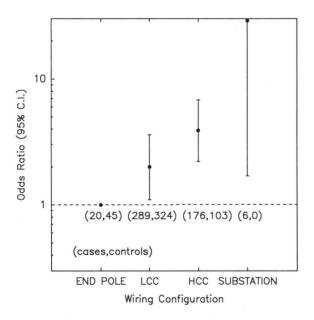

Figure 3.7
Results of the Wertheimer–Leeper Study (1979) on childhood cancer and wiring configuration code
Note: The wiring configuration code is calculated from the proximity of the home to power distribution lines.
Source: Wertheimer and Leeper 1979.

cers, for people living in homes with the highest wiring configuration code.

The Wertheimer–Leeper studies attracted wide public attention, and other investigators soon followed up their findings:

Fulton's Study.   Fulton et al. (1980) reported a case-control study on childhood leukemia patients in Rhode Island. They found no statistically significant association between the wiring configuration code and risk of childhood leukemia; Wertheimer and Leeper (1980) argued that the control children in this study had been chosen in a way that might have caused the investigators to overlook a real effect.

Myers's Study.   Myers et al. (1985) reported a case-control study on children in the United Kingdom who had suffered from various childhood cancers. They reported weak associations between childhood cancers (including leukemia and solid tumors) and the distance from the child's home to an overhead power line; however, the differences were small and not statistically significant.

Tomenius's Study.   Tomenius (1986) reported a case-control study on children in Stockholm County, Sweden. He reported that children with cancer were slightly more likely than control children to live within 150 meters of an "electrical construction" (with an odds ratio of 1.3), or to live in homes with 3 mG field strength (odds ratio of 2.1). The study reported an increase in brain tumors, not in childhood leukemia, as reported by Wertheimer and Leeper. Curiously, the study found an *inverse* relation between cancer risk and distance from the child's house to transmission lines—the closer the child lived to the line, the lower the risk of cancer.

These studies can be criticized on several grounds, the most important of which is inadequate exposure assessment. Most lacked any direct measurement of exposure and relied on indirect measures such as a "wiring configuration code" (Wertheimer and Leeper, Myers), the proximity of the child's home to a power line (Myers), or the proximity of a house to "electrical construction" (Tomenius).[3]

The Savitz and Severson Studies.   To address the concerns that these studies raised, the New York State Power Lines Project[4] commissioned two case-control studies of cancer and domestic exposure to electric and magnetic fields. One, by Severson et al. (1988), examined 114 adults with nonlymphocytic leukemia in Seattle. The other, by Savitz et al.

(1988), included 356 cases—every child who had been diagnosed with cancer in the Denver metropolitan area during the years 1976–1983. Savitz' study was comparable in design and examined the same metropolitan area as the earlier study by Wertheimer and Leeper, but considered a different period of time and hence different children.

In important respects, these two studies were significant improvements over earlier ones. Both measured the exposure of individuals in multiple ways: using a wiring configuration code similar to that employed by Wertheimer and Leeper, and by direct measurements of electric and magnetic fields in the home. Where possible, Savitz found the wiring configuration codes of homes in which the children had previously lived. Severson and colleagues questioned the subjects about their use of electric blankets.

Neither study found any striking increase in risk. Severson reported no statistically significant association between cancer risk and the wiring code, the strength of magnetic fields measured in the home, or the use of electric blankets.

Savitz's results are summarized in Figure 3.8. While the investigators reported many odds ratios above 1, few of these increases were statistically significant; the only striking result in Figure 3.8 involved a comparison between two very small groups.[5] The lay press has often described Savitz's study as "conforming" the Wertheimer–Leeper study. In fact, its results were far weaker (compare Figures 3.7 and 3.8) and in most respects negative.

Curiously, the odds ratios calculated from the magnetic fields that were measured in the home were smaller (in fact, not significantly different from 1) than for the wiring configuration code. This raises a paradox that casts doubt on the role of "fields": if the children's cancers were related to exposure to magnetic fields, a stronger association should be found when the exposure was measured directly than estimated with a crude surrogate (the wiring configuration code).

McDowall's Study. McDowall (1986) surveyed the mortality of nearly 8,000 people in East Anglia (England) over the period 1971–1983. All of these people lived in the vicinity of electrical transmission facilities, either within 50 meters of an electrical substation or within 30 meters of an overhead power line. McDowall concluded "overall mortality was lower than expected and no evidence of major health hazards emerged." This result contrasts sharply with sensationalized reports in the lay media of hazards from living near electrical substations (Brodeur 1990).

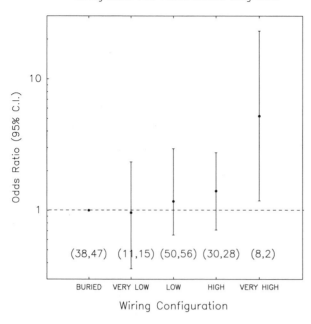

Wiring Code Two Years Before Diagnosis

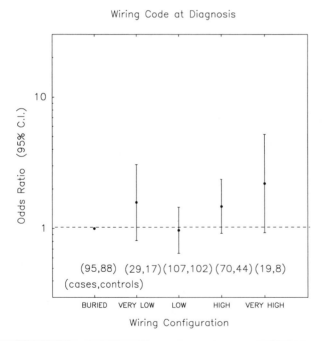

Wiring Code at Diagnosis

Figure 3.8
Results of the Savitz study on childhood cancer and residential exposure to magnetic fields
Note: The number of cases in each group is indicated in parentheses. The study was conducted in the same metropolitan area as the Wertheimer-Leeper study

Measured Magnetic Field — Low Power Use

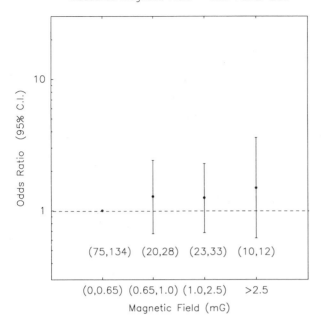

Measured Electric Field

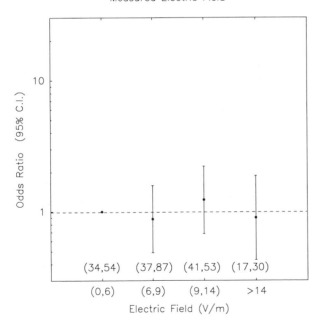

Figure 3.8 (continued)
(Denver) with a different set of subjects. The wiring configuration code was similar
to that used by the Wertheimer–Leeper study.
Source: Savitz et al. 1988.

The Coleman Study. This case-control study (1989) identified 771 leukemia cases in southeast England; the controls were 1,432 people diagnosed with another kind of cancer and 231 other people from the general population. The study failed to observe a clear association between leukemia risk and living near electrical transmission or distribution equipment; while some of the odds ratios were slightly above 1, none of the increases were statistically significant and there was no trend toward increased risk at closer distances to the equipment.

The Peters' Study. A case-control study, conducted under the direction of Peters (London et al. 1991), was comparable in design to the Wertheimer-Leeper and Savitz studies. The cases were 232 children who had been diagnosed with leukemia in Los Angeles County; the controls were an equal number of healthy children. The investigators measured exposure in three different ways: by using a wiring configuration code, by spot measurements of the magnetic and electric fields in the homes, and by means of 24-hour recordings of the magnetic field exposure of the children. The investigators also determined the parents' and children's use of various appliances.

The investigators reported a small association between the wiring configuration code and cancer risk, but none with measured electric or magnetic fields. The investigators also reported slight (but statistically significant) associations between the children's use of hair dryers and black-and-white television sets, but not color television sets or other appliances.

Cancer and Electric Blankets

One group of people has unequivocally high exposure to magnetic fields: users of electric blankets. The magnetic fields associated with electric blankets are typically 10–100 times stronger than found elsewhere in the home; users will typically bask in their warmth for eight hours a day, on a daily basis for much of the year. Such users are an excellent group to study potential adverse health effects of magnetic fields. Four case-control studies have examined the use of electric blankets as related to cancer risk:

Preston-Martin Study. Preston-Martin et al. (1988) studied acute and chronic myelogenous leukemia as related to use of electric blankets in a case-control study with 224 cases (cancer patients) and an equal number of controls chosen at random from the cases' neighborhoods. They reported no increase in the risk of leukemia associated with use of electric blankets.

Savitz Study.   Savitz et al. (1990) reexamined the data from their earlier study on childhood cancer, searching for any connection between childhood cancer risk and use of electric blankets. They reported a slight association between childhood cancer and either prenatal or postnatal exposure to the blankets. However, the odds ratios were small, and the increases were not statistically significant.

Verreault Study.   Verreault et al. (1990) reported a study on testicular cancer related to use of electric blankets. They concluded that use of electric blankets added little if any to the risk of this cancer.

Vena Study.   Vena et al. (1991) reported a study on 821 postmenopausal women, including 382 breast cancer patients and 439 randomly selected controls. Their findings did "not support the hypothesis that electric blanket use is associated with an increased risk for breast cancer."

London Study.   London et al. (1991) searched for an association between the use of an electric blanket by the mother during pregnancy, and childhood leukemia. The odds ratios were slightly above 1 but the increase was not statistically significant.

The results of these studies are summarized in Figure 3.9. Nothing in these studies indicates any significant cancer risk from use of electric blankets, despite the unequivocally high exposure involved.

Barriers to Inference

What is one to make of these results? A careful analysis would have to consider each study individually. Collectively, the studies considered many diseases (several forms of leukemia, brain tumors, melanoma of the eye, breast cancer in men, and diverse childhood cancers) and the diverse exposures (occupational, residential, or from use of appliances). This is beyond the scope of this chapter; several major reviews are cited in the appendix-bibliography.

Nevertheless, the ambiguities in interpretation are so great that one can draw no conclusions about possible carcinogenic effects of electromagnetic fields. This applies to individual studies, or collected evidence on particular diseases.

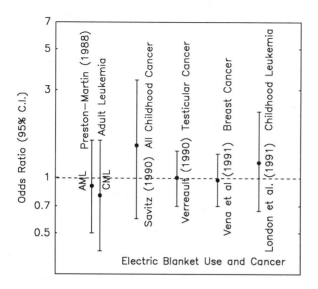

Figure 3.9
Cancer risk as related to use of electric blankets
Note: The studies by Savitz et al. and London et al. examined children's cancer
risk associated with their mothers' use of electric blankets.

Occupational Studies

The occupational studies are the most difficult to interpret. Many are
preliminary or too briefly reported to assess (indeed, many are just letters
to the editors of medical journals). Most can be criticized on technical
grounds as well.

One important limitation is *inadequate exposure assessment.* Most of
these studies classified their subjects on the basis of occupational title
alone, without measurements of the actual exposures of their subjects.
Are "electrical" workers really exposed to stronger fields than other
workers? And what is the nature of their exposure?

Another problem is *neglect of potential confounding variables.* Such
workers, such as welders or electrical equipment assemblers, might be
exposed to various toxic fumes or solvents, which were potential confounding factors that were often mentioned by the authors but not adequately addressed by the study design.

Collectively, the occupational studies have many inconsistencies and
contradictions. For example, Linet et al. (1988) searched through the
Swedish national cancer registry for associations between occupation and
leukemia. They found no association between any "electrical" occupation and any form of leukemia—with one exception. They identified 13

cases of chronic lymphocytic leukemia among power linemen, twice the expected number. Loomis and Savitz (1990), in their more focused study, reported no such increase (Table 3.2). Perhaps Linet's finding was a false positive result due to the many comparisons the investigators performed. Or perhaps Loomis' study was too small to detect a doubling of incidence of a rare disease in a small occupational group. It is premature to conclude that power linemen have increased risk for chronic lymphocytic leukemia.

Residential Studies
The residential studies had far greater impact on public opinion. These studies were broadly similar in design (all are case-control studies) and are easier to compare. They, too, suffer from important limitations.

Technical Limitations.   The Wertheimer–Leeper studies are particularly weak. Their 1979 study was not blinded (the investigators knew whether a house belonged to a case or control child as they determined its wiring configuration code) and therefore might be subject to bias.

Moreover, the Wertheimer–Leeper papers are often unclearly written, and the data are often analyzed or presented in unconventional ways. Cole (1987) has pointed to an "inordinate consistency" of the results of their 1979 paper on childhood cancer: of the approximately 30 comparisons the investigators reported, all but one yielded odds ratios within the range of 2–3—which, in Cole's words, "stretch[es] credulity." Later studies (particularly the childhood cancer studies by Savitz and Peters) were superior in design and more carefully analyzed—and reported far smaller increases in odds ratios.

Even the Savitz and Peters studies had serious limitations, which the investigators themselves acknowledged. One troubling problem was the method that both studies employed to choose controls, randomly calling telephone numbers. In both studies, the investigators called far more people than they recruited as controls. (In Peters' study, for example, the investigators had to call 4,424 numbers to recruit 102 controls.) In contrast, case children were chosen from health records.

This method of choosing controls clearly opens the door to subtle bias: an increase in odds ratio might arise from proportionately *more* case children in the "high-wiring code" group, or proportionately *fewer* control children in this same category. Any tendency to exclude families in high wiring code homes from the control group would bias the studies in the direction of the reported results. Given the large number of calls the investigators made, and the small odds ratios they reported, any small error would be sufficient.

The wiring code is determined by the distance of a house from electrical distribution lines and distribution transformers. But it indirectly reflects the setback of the house from the street, the building density along a street, which in turn reflect cost of housing and other sociodemographic variables. High-code homes are often inexpensive rental units on busy streets. Perhaps the families who occupy them are harder to reach than those in suburban (low-code) homes. Or perhaps the wiring configuration code is an indication of some (as yet unknown) sociodemographic variable that influences cancer risk. No such error has been demonstrated, however, despite careful analysis of the data by the investigators.

Inadequate Exposure Assessment.   Everybody in modern society is exposed to magnetic fields, at highly variable levels, which makes it difficult to separate people reliably into high-exposure and low-exposure categories.

Most of the residential studies relied on indirect indices of exposure (such as the wiring configuration code) or limited field measurements in the subjects' homes (the studies by Savitz and Severson) or at their doorsteps (Tomenius's study). Peters's study, by contrast, included 24-hour measurements of the magnetic field exposure of the subjects.

Several engineering studies have shown that the wiring configuration code of a home is a poor indication of a person's actual exposure to magnetic fields. For example, the Savitz and Severson studies both recorded the wiring configuration code for each house, and performed spot measurements of fields within the homes. The wiring configuration code accounted for only 16 to 19 percent of the variability in the fields directly measured in the homes away from appliances (Kaune et al. 1987; Barnes et al. 1989). (See Figure 3.10.)

At best, the wiring configuration code can indicate exposure from sources outside the home, in particular neighborhood distribution lines. There are many other sources of exposure to magnetic fields in the home. For example, ground return currents in water pipes contribute as much or more to the magnetic fields in a room as outside distribution lines (Mader et al. 1990). Appliances generate high localized fields. The wiring configuration code cannot account for such exposure.

Surveys using electromagnetic dosimeters worn on the body show how bad the problem really is. Figure 3.11 shows a recording of the 60 Hz magnetic fields to which an 8-year-old girl was exposed in the course of one day (Silva private communication). The high exposure at night is

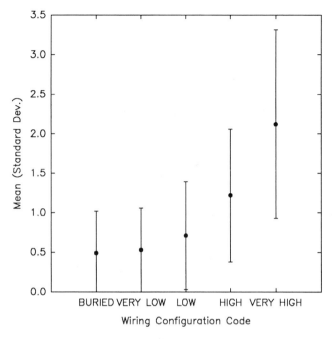

Figure 3.10
Mean and standard deviation of magnetic flux density in the home (in milligauss)
Source: Barnes et al. 1989. Reprinted from Foster 1992 from the journal *Health Physics* with permission from the Health Physics Society.

from use of an electric blanket; the peaks during the day result from localized sources such as appliances. The figure also shows the average magnetic flux densities corresponding to the different wiring configuration codes in the Savitz study. Clearly, a person's actual exposure might vary over greater ranges than the differences between the wiring configuration codes.

Then what does the wiring configuration code really measure? Some scientists have argued that the code is a more useful measure of long-term exposure to fields than spot measurements, or even 24-hour recordings with a dosimeter. This speculation, however, is impossible to prove one way or the other.

Some critics have argued that the increases in odds ratio obtained using the wiring configuration code might reflect a *very large* risk, that is obscured by the imprecision of the code. This will cause investigators to misclassify subjects as "exposed" or "unexposed." While exceptions can be contrived (Dosemeci et al. 1990), this will usually diminish the size of a real effect.

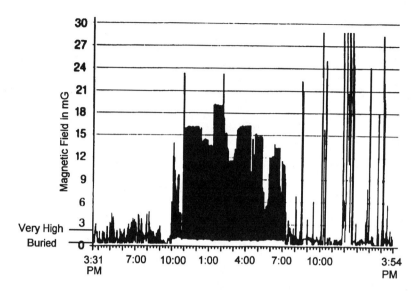

Figure 3.11
Exposure of an eight-year-old schoolgirl to 60 Hz magnetic fields
Note: The period of high exposure from 10 PM to 7 AM arises from use of an electric blanket; other brief periods of high exposure result from appliances. Also shown on the axis on the left are the mean magnetic flux densities corresponding to the lowest and highest wiring configuration code used in the Savitz childhood cancer study.
Source: (adapted from J. Michael Silva by permission.)

If so, a study that employed better dosimetry would show a stronger effect. In fact, the opposite is found. As shown in Figure 3.6, the strongest associations are generally found using the wiring configuration code, rather than direct measurements of fields. There is little to suggest that "fields" are the problem. But no positive explanation has been demonstrated, and perhaps none may appear.

Assessing Causation
It is useful to consider the evidence in light of Hill's criteria that are listed in chapter 1. To summarize:

Strength of Association.   All of the reported associations described above were weak—close to, if not below, the margins of sampling error.

Consistency of Association.   Many inconsistencies emerge, particularly in the occupational studies. For example, several investigators reported associations between work in specific "electrical" occupations and leukemia. These were contradicted by other studies, some of which were based on very large tumor registries (Vågerö and Olin 1983; Vågerö et al. 1985; Törnqvist et al. 1986; Linet et al. 1988) and the study by Loomis and Savitz (1990).

The domestic studies show other kinds of inconsistency. Wertheimer and Leeper (1982) reported a strong association between childhood cancer and residence near electrical substations; the large study by McDowall (1986) found none. Wertheimer and Leeper reported an increase in childhood leukemia in children whose homes were near electrical distribution equipment; Tomenius (1986) reported an increase in childhood brain tumors but a *decrease* in leukemia.

Specificity of Association. The occupational studies point in many different directions. The diseases that are most often mentioned include several forms of leukemia and brain tumors. But other diseases have been mentioned as well, including melanoma of the eye and (in two reports) breast cancer in male electrical workers (Matanoski et al. 1991; Demers et al. 1991). If there had been some "signature" disease (such as the mesothelioma associated with asbestos exposure), the evidence would have been far easier to deal with.

The evidence from the residential studies by Wertheimer and Leeper and by Savitz et al. (1990) suffer from a lack of specificity of another sort. Their principal results were increased odds ratios for all childhood cancers combined (of which the most common form is leukemia). Although the odds ratios for individual neoplasms have much larger statistical uncertainties (because of the smaller numbers of cases), they seem to be increased slightly for a range of childhood cancers, including leukemia, brain tumors, and lymphomas. The idea that magnetic fields might increase the incidence of such a wide range of diseases (in Cole's words) "strains credulity."

Temporality of Association. A stronger case could be made had any study shown that its subjects were exposed to fields before developing cancer. All of the studies reviewed above were *retrospective,* that is, they examined their subjects after their disease had been diagnosed. No information is available about the subjects' exposure when the cancer developed, which might have occurred years before the study was done.

A *prospective study* could avoid this problem. For the rare diseases considered here, in particular the childhood cancers, it is difficult to imagine how such a study could be mounted. Leukemia, the most common childhood cancer, strikes approximately 5 children per 100,000 each year. A study would have to follow a million children for ten years to obtain 500 cases, preferably measuring the exposure of each child individually. This is clearly an impossible task.

Biologic Gradient. A clear dose-response function provides a much stronger case for causation. None of the occupational studies found a dose-response relationship; none measured "dose." The Wertheimer and Leeper study on childhood cancer suggested a dose-response relationship; no such relation is apparent in the studies by Savitz et al. (1988) and London (1991). (These studies did, however, report the highest odds ratios for children in the group of homes with the highest wiring code.)

Biologic Plausibility and Supporting Experimental Evidence. This is a difficult issue because of the great diversity of the biological research. Many investigators have reported biological effects of 50–60 Hz electric or magnetic fields. Most of these effects appear at field strengths that far exceed those commonly found in the environment, and have no apparent relevance to human health. Many reported effects cannot be independently confirmed and their very existence is in doubt (Carstensen 1987). The bioeffects literature is awash with speculation about possible mechanisms by which weak fields might influence biological function (Foster 1992).

For risk assessment, the more relevant question is whether standard assays, either in vitro or in vivo, disclose carcinogenic or tumor promoting effects of electromagnetic fields. Many such tests have already been done, and many others are in progress. So far, the results are overwhelmingly negative.

Most of these tests have been in vitro, i.e. using cell cultures. Few standardized animal screening studies have been reported; a National Toxicology Program study with 60 Hz magnetic fields is now being planned.

There is insufficient space for a comprehensive review of all of this work; instead, I mention two well-done animal studies that might have uncovered a cancer-producing or -promoting effect, but did not. Both involved magnetic field exposures thousands of times stronger than those implicated by the residential studies.

The first is the study by Benz and Carsten (1987), who exposed large numbers of mice to strong 60 Hz fields (up to 10,000 mG magnetic field and 50 kV/m electric fields) for 3 generations. The investigators reported no reduction in lifespan or increase in cancer mortality in the exposed animals. This study was not a standard carcinogen assay (but rather was a screening study for toxic or mutagenic effects); nevertheless its design was adequate to detect a pronounced increase in cancer incidence from these (comparatively very strong) electric and magnetic fields.

The second is a study by Thomson et al. (1988) to test for possible effects of magnetic fields on tumor promotion or progression. In this study, mice were implanted with leukemia cells and exposed to 60 Hz magnetic fields up to 5000 mG. The investigators detected "no effect on the incidence or progression" of the disease.

Many in vitro studies have been conducted on cultured cells, employing carcinogen screening tests. None have provided evidence that 60 Hz fields can induce or promote tumors. Alice Martin, a senior cytogeneticist who was a member of the Scientific Advisory Panel of the New York State Power Lines Project, surveyed 23 studies on animals or cultured cells. She concluded:

Neither electric nor magnetic, nor combined exposures have produced evidence from standard laboratory assays that EMF [electromagnetic fields] are cancer initiators or promoters. However, many studies are now currently underway that will be completed in 3 to 4 years. The design of these studies included magnetic field exposures. Final determination awaits completion of these studies. However, strong and/or standard carcinogenic properties of EMF would have been detected by previous studies. (Martin 1989)

Coherence. This criterion is hard to apply because of the complexity and diversity of the epidemiologic evidence.

One related issue is the strength of the fields implicated by the epidemiologic evidence, compared to those naturally present within the body (Table 3.3). The residential studies implicate magnetic fields of 1–2 milliGauss. By contrast, the earth's magnetic field has a flux density of about 500 mG. A person who moves about in the earth's field will experience time-varying magnetic fields within his or her body that are far greater than those resulting from ordinary domestic exposure.

One might argue that the causal factor is the electric field induced by an alternating magnetic field within the body. But such fields are, for any reasonable level of exposure, a million times or more smaller than electric fields already present within the body due to electrical activity in the brain, heart, or other sources (Carstensen 1987).

Analogy. In lay discussions of the issue, a false analogy sometimes arises with ionizing radiation, a known cause of cancer. The profound biological activity of ionizing radiation arises from its ability to break chemical bonds and ionize molecules. By contrast, the energy carried by a photon of 60 Hz electromagnetic energy is many orders of magnitude too small to produce these effects.

Is There Evidence for a Causal Connection?

Critics have cited some reported effects of 60 Hz electric or magnetic fields as suggesting a health hazard from low-level fields. I summarize some of this evidence.

Many Reported Biological Effects of 60 Hz Fields

The literature on biological effects of 60 Hz electric and magnetic fields is vast, speculative, and inconsistent. In his review, Carstensen (1987) lists over 100 reported biological effects of low-frequency magnetic fields, at flux densities ranging from 20,000 gauss down to 0.01 mG. Only a few of these effects have been independently confirmed—one is the excitation of nerves by time-varying fields at 2,000 gauss. Many others could not be confirmed by independent studies and presumably are artifacts. Most reported effects have never been independently followed up, and their very existence is uncertain. Most of these effects have only speculative relevance to human health in any event.

Expert panels have repeatedly surveyed this vast literature, and found no convincing evidence for a hazard from 50–60 Hz fields of even

Table 3.3
Comparison of induced electric fields with naturally occurring electric fields in the body

Field	Head	Trunk
Naturally occurring electric fields	1 mV/m (scalp)	10–50 mV/m (surface of the chest)
	1 V/m (brain)	1–10 V/m (surface of the heart)
Electrically induced 60 Hz fields	0.5 mV/m	1 mV/m
Magnetically induced 60 Hz fields	0.1 mV/m	0.4 mV/m

Note: The calculations assume an erect human located in a 1 kv/m electric field or 100 mG magnetic field.
Source: Adapted from Carstensen 1987.

high intensity. The Appendix-bibliography at the end of this chapter lists several of their reports.

However, some critics point to these many reported effects, and argue that these effects demonstrate a biological activity of weak fields that might lead to some as yet unproven unrecognized hazard. This argument has strong emotional appeal but is very slippery. Advocates frequently advance similar arguments—the collective impression of individually inconclusive observations—to "prove" the existence of extrasensory perception or unidentified flying objects.

Some critics have cited—in court—a few laboratory studies to support the argument that weak electric or magnetic fields might increase cancer risk in humans.

Cell Growth (Clonogenicity)

Phillips et al. (1986) investigated the growth properties of tumor cells on soft agar when exposed to 60 Hz magnetic fields. They reported that exposure to alternating magnetic fields of 1 gauss amplitude increases the growth rate of the cells. The sponsor of the study (the New York Power Lines Project) in its final report criticized this study on technical grounds and disputed its relevance to any health effect of the fields. The Project's final report describes the unsuccessful attempts of one investigator to confirm these results.

Ornithine Decarboxylase (ODC)

Byus and colleagues (1987) reported that 60 Hz electric fields increased the content of ODC in tumor cells in culture. This substance, associated with growth of cells, increases dramatically when tissues are exposed to tumor-promoting agents. Byus's finding has prompted the speculation that 60 Hz *electric* fields might be tumor promoters. Since 60 Hz *magnetic* fields induce electric fields in the body, this conclusion presumably would apply to magnetic fields as well. The hypothesis that the magnetic fields might be tumor promoters (rather than direct carcinogens) apparently was first suggested by Wertheimer and Leeper in their 1979 study on childhood cancer.

However, the implication of Byus's finding to possible tumor promotion by 60 Hz fields is unclear. Ornithine decarboxylase is associated with cell *growth,* not necessarily tumor development (Jänne et al. 1978). Byus' experiments were conducted on cancer cells, which had already undergone the stage of promotion. Furthermore, the increase of ODC they reported was small compared with increases produced in other cells by known tumor promoters.

Melatonin

Wilson et al. (1986) reported that rats when exposed to strong 60 Hz electric fields (39 kV/m) show reduced concentrations of melatonin (a substance that is produced naturally in the body by metabolic processes) in their blood. The significance of this finding is unclear; some investigators believe that melatonin is connected with tumor growth. Grota et al. (1991) could not confirm the finding. More recently, Reiter et al. reported effects of weak *magnetic* fields on melatonin synthesis or related processes in intact animals or excised pineal glands (Lerchl et al 1990, 1991). These effects were observed after an abrupt change in the ambient magnetic field corresponding to sudden inversion of the earth's field. So far, these results have not been independently confirmed.

For several reasons, the health implications of these studies is unclear. Most employed fields far above typical environmental levels. For example, the experiments of Byus et al. involved *electric* fields of 0.1 to 10 mV/cm within the medium surrounding the cells. To produce the same field within the human body would require unrealistically strong 60 Hz electric fields above 10 kV/m; those of Phillips et al. involved magnetic flux densities of 1 gauss. Also, the biological significance of the findings is unclear, assuming that the effects themselves are real. For example, the physiological significance of the changes in melatonin to the exposed animals—let alone to humans—is not yet established.

In short, the health significance of these effects is unclear, and in several cases there is reason to question their existence. Given the dismal record for reproducibility of bioeffects studies, an important next step should be the independent confirmation and study of these effects.

Resolution of the Issue

The epidemiologic evidence gives the impression of a slight increase in cancer risk that is somehow associated with electromagnetic fields, and this impression has clearly aroused great public concern. The impression that "something is there" might be just the accumulated effect of scientific noise.

How can this issue be resolved? A dozen major epidemiologic studies are underway (Coleman 1990). In view of the past history of this field, we can expect that their results will be inconsistent whatever their overall trend. The only way to unambiguously resolve the issue would be to identify some real hazard. If the weak magnetic fields in a home caused a detectable increase in disease, a population might exist that has unambiguously high exposure—and a very high incidence of disease. Four dozen epidemiologic studies have failed to identify reliably any such group, notwithstanding occasional reports of rare tumors in some occupational groups (such as a few cases of breast cancer in a cohort of male telephone workers reported by Matanoski et al. 1991).

Unless some breakthrough occurs in the epidemiology, the issue will probably turn on the outcome of animal studies. As of this writing, dozens of animal studies are being planned or are in progress, including a 56-month, $8.3 million animal screening study at the Illinois Institute of Technology, announced in August 1992.

Some of these studies involve exposing the animals to known carcinogens in addition to magnetic fields, to see whether the exposure has any effect on the development of disease. If positive, these studies might provide hypotheses by which to design further epidemiologic studies. However, most are not standardized carcinogen assays. If the relevance of standardized carcinogen assays for risk assessment is questionable, that of these studies with magnetic fields is even more so. At least standard carcinogen assays have been in use for a long time, and the issues surrounding their interpretation have been well explored (if not settled). For risk assessment, the planned studies with magnetic fields break new ground, and their role will not be easily defined. One may question how much effort should be spent on these studies, given the negative results of standard carcinogen assays.

The model of risk assessment of the National Academy of Sciences (chapter 1) offers a broader perspective. So far, scientists have not completed the first step in the process of risk assessment: hazard identification. Granted, engineers are working on a later stage of the process, exposure assessment, as they develop instruments for recording magnetic field exposure of individuals and conduct surveys. (They don't know what to measure, however, in the absence of any scientific understanding of what parameters of exposure may be important.) The goal is to *reduce risk,* and this requires some clear understanding of the nature of a problem and the conditions of exposure under which it occurs. With magnetic fields, no such understanding exists, and none may develop in the future.

Another issue is the public's interest. Many health claims regarding electromagnetic fields have been presented in the scientific literature. Other questionable claims involve miscarriage and use of video display terminals (chapter 6); miscarriage and use of electric blankets (Wertheimer and Leeper 1986) or electric ceiling heat (Wertheimer and Leeper

1989); suicide and residence near power lines (Reichmanis et al. 1979); cataracts in radio linemen (Hollows and Douglas 1984); and a "neurasthenic" syndrome among workers in radio equipment factories in the former Soviet Union (Roberts and Michaelson 1985). These claims have engendered endless controversy and an increasing amount of litigation but have resulted in little, if any, demonstrable benefit to public health. If some real hazard exists, we need to identify it and remedy the problem; if it does not, we need to redirect our attention to more pressing issues.

How should laymen respond to the findings summarized in this chapter? John Bailar, an epidemiologist from McGill University (and 1990 MacArthur Fellow), offered this reasonable perspective for the layman:

Pregnant women may well want to stow their electric blankets, but until scientists sort out the risks, people should concern themselves with other, larger issues. There is a clear causal link between excessive exposure to sunlight or X-rays and health hazards. But with lower frequency electromagnetic fields, hazards are more difficult to detect. It's ludicrous to find people worried about this kind of exposure while they continue to smoke, continue to eat a rotten diet, or drive around without seat belts. (1990)

Finally, this controversy demonstrates once again the great asymmetry in risk research: a hazard can be proven, the absence of hazard cannot. In science one can draw no conclusions from unexplained phenomena or inconclusive studies. But in the courtroom it is sometimes enough just to raise questions. And these studies have done that very well.[6]

Notes

1. The conventional measure of magnetic field exposure is the gauss or tesla (10,000 gauss); 1 mG $= 10^{-3}$ gauss. The gauss is, strictly speaking, a measure of flux density; for historical reasons the term "field strength" applies to a different quantity. For nonmagnetic materials this distinction has little practical consequence.

2. Most of the studies calculated SMRs for different diseases. To reduce the amount of detail in Figure 3.5, only the SMR for the cancer involving the largest number of individuals in each study is shown.

3. Tomenius's study also measured the 50 Hz magnetic fields at the front door of the children's homes; however, the relation between this measurement and the exposure of a child moving about the home is highly uncertain.

4. This was set up as part of a settlement of a lawsuit in New York concerning possible health hazards from a proposed 765 kV power line (see the legal summary at the end of Part 1).

5. The media have frequently quoted an estimate (from the final report of the New York Power Lines Project) that 10–15 percent of childhood leukemia in America is associated with domesteic exposure to magnetic fields. This estimate was based on the odds ratio for the highest exposure group in Figure 3.8b—involving 27 houses!

6. In November 1992, two case-control Swedish epidemiologic studies were reported at a conference (but so far not published in detail), linking leukemia and residence near power lines or "electrical" occupation. Both studies were small, and their results were near the limits of statistical significance; the residential study did, however, feature somewhat improved dosimetry. The Swedish Board for Industrial and Technical Development announced that it will act on the assumption that there is a causal link between power-frequency magnetic fields and leukemia. At about the same time, the (U.S.) Office of Science and Technology Policy released a report that concluded that there is no convincing evidence for a causal link and recommended that EMF research be given low priority. The National Institute of Environmental Health Sciences is about to embark on a $65 million, 5-year research program, however. See R. Stone, "Polarized debate: EMFs and cancer," 258 *Science,* 1724–1725 (1992).

Appendix: Bibliography

This chapter provided only a brief introduction to a vast and confusing subject. For a more extensive review, I particularly recommend Carstensen's monograph and the reviews by Tenforde and Kaune and by Aldrich and Easterly. ·

Review Articles
Ahlbom, A. 1988. A review of the epidemiologic literature on magnetic fields and cancer, 14 *Scand. J. Work Environ. Health* 337–343.

Aldrich, T. E., and C. E. Easterly. 1987. Electromagnetic fields and public health, 75 *Envir. Health Persp.* 159–171.

Coleman, M., and V. Beral, A review of epidemiological studies of the health effects of living near or working with electricity generation and transmission equipment, 17 *Int. J. Epidemiol.* 1–13.

Savitz, D. A., and E. E. Calle. 1987. Leukemia and occupational exposure to electromagnetic fields: review of epidemiologic surveys, 29 *J. Occup. Med.* 47–51.

Sheikh, K. 1986. Exposure to electromagnetic fields and risk of leukemia, 41 *Arch. Environ. Health* 56–63.

Tenforde, T. S., and W. T. Kaune. 1987. Interaction of extremely low frequency electric and magnetic fields with humans, 53 *Health Physics* 585–606.

Other
Carstensen, E. L. 1987. *Biological effects of transmission line fields.* Amsterdam: Elsevier. A comprehensive monograph with extensive introductory material.

Florig, H. K. 1992. *Containing the costs of EMF litigation,* 257 *Science* 468–490.

Morgan, M. G. 1989. *Electric and magnetic fields from 60 Hertz electric power: What do we know about possible health risks?* Pittsburgh: Carnegie-Mellon University.

Nair, I., M. G. Morgan, and H. L. Florig. 1989. *Power-frequency electric and magnetic fields exposure, effects, research, and regulation.* Washington, DC: U.S. Government Printing Office.

Consensus/Group Reports

American Institute of Biological Sciences. 1985. *Biological and human health effects of extremely low frequency electromagnetic fields.* NTIS no. AD-A152 731.

Florida Electric and Magnetic Fields Science Advisory Commission. 1985. *Biological effects of 60-Hz power transmission lines.* NTIS no. PB-85200871.

International Non-Ionizing Radiation Commission of the International Radiation Protection Association. 1990. Interim guidelines on limits of exposure to 50/60 Hz electric and magnetic field. 58 *Health Physics* 113–122.

New York State Power Lines Scientific Advisory Panel. 1987. *Biological effects of power line fields.* Albany: The Panel.

West Associates. 1986. *A critical review of the scientific literature on low frequency electric and magnetic fields: Assessment of possible effects on human health and recommendations for research.* Prepared for Southern California Edison, Co.

World Health Organization. 1984. *Extremely low frequency (ELF) fields.* Environmental Health Criteria 35.

World Health Organization. 1987. Magnetic fields. Environmental Health Criteria 69.

References

Ahlbom, A., et al. 1987. *Biological effects of power line fields.* Albany: New York State Power Lines Scientific Advisory Panel.

Bailar, J., Quoted in P. Raeburn. 1990. The switched-on house. *Am. Health.* (Quotation verified by personal communication with Bailar.)

Barker, A. T., R. Jalinous, and I. L. Freeston. 1985. Non-invasive magnetic stimulation of the human motor cortex. 1 *The Lancet* 1106–1107.

Barnes, F., H. Wachtel, D. A. Savitz, and J. Fuller. 1989. Use of wiring configuration codes for estimating externally generated electric and magnetic fields. 10 *Bioelectromagnetics* 13–21.

Barregård, L., B. Järvholm, and E. Ungethüm. 1985. Cancer among workers exposed to strong static magnetic fields. 2 *The Lancet* 892.

Benz, R. D., A. L. Carsten, J. W. Baum, and A. V. Kuehner. 1987. *Mutagenicity and toxicity of 60 Hz magnetic and electric fields.* Albany: New York State Power Lines Project, Wadsworth Center for Laboratories and Research.

Brodeur, P. 1989. *Currents of death.* New York: Simon and Schuster.

Brodeur, P. 1990. Calamity on Meadow Street. *New Yorker,* July 9, 38–72.

Bunin, G. R., E. Ward, S. Kramer, C. A. Rhee, and A. T. Meadows. 1990. Neuroblastoma and parental occupation. 131 *Am. J. Epidemiol.* 776–780.

Byus, C. V., S. E. Pieper, and W. R. Adey. 1987. The effects of low-energy 60 Hz environmental electromagnetic fields upon the growth-related enzyme ornithine decarboxylase. 8 *Carcinogenesis* 1385–1389.

Calle, E. E., and D. A. Savitz. 1985. Leukemia in occupational groups with presumed exposure to electrical and magnetic fields. 313 *N. Eng. J. Med. 1476–1477.* Letter.

Carstensen, E. L. 1987. *Biological effects of transmission line fields.* Amsterdam: Elsevier.

Cole, P. 1987. An epidemiologic perspective on electromagnetic fields and cancer. Manuscript on file with Department of Epidemiology, University of Alabama at Birmingham.

Coleman, M. P. 1990. Extremely low-frequency electric and magnetic fields and risk of human cancer. 11 *Bioelectromagnetics* 91–99.

Coleman, M. P., C. M. J. Bell, H.-L. Taylor, and M. Primic-Zakelj. 1989. Leukaemia and residence near electricity transmission equipment: A case-control study. 60 *Br. J. Cancer* 793–798.

Coleman, M. P., J. Bell, and R. Skeet. 1983. Leukaemia incidence in electrical workers. 1 *The Lancet* 982–983. Letter.

Demers, P. A., D. B. Thomas, K. A. Rosenblatt, L. M. Jimenez, A. McTiernan, H. Stalsberg, A. Stemhagen, W. D. Thompson, M. G. M. Curnen, W. Satariano, D. F. Austin, P. Isacson, R. S. Greenberg, C. Key, L. N. Kolonel, and D. W. West. 1991. Occupational exposure to electromagnetic fields and breast cancer in men. 134 *Am. J. Epidemiol.* 340–347.

Doll, R. and A. B. Hill. 1952. A study of the aetiology of carcinoma of the lung. 2 *Br. Med. J.* 1271–1286.

Dosemeci, M., S. Wacholder, and J. H. Lubin. 1990. Does nondifferential misclassification of exposure always bias a true effect toward the null value? 132 *Am. J. Epidemiol.* 746–748.

Feinstein, A. R. 1985. *Clinical epidemiology.* Philadelphia: W. B. Saunders.

Flodin, U. L. R., M. Fredriksson, O. Axelson, B. Persson, L. Hardell. 1986. Background radiation, electrical work, and some other exposures associated with acute myeloid leukemia in a case-referent study. 41 *Arch. Environ. Health* 77–84.

Foster, K. R., and W. F. Pickard. 1987. Microwaves: The risks of risk research. 330 *Nature* 531–532.

Foster, K. R. 1992. Health effects of low-level electromagnetic fields: Phantom or not-so-phantom risk? 62 *Health Physics* 429–435.

Fulton, J. P., S. Cobb, L. Preble, L. Leone, and E. J. Forman. 1980. Electrical wiring configurations and childhood leukemia in Rhode Island. 111 *Am. J. Epidemiol.* 292–296.

Grota, L. J., S-T Lu, R. Reiter, S. Pettit, C. Borkhuis, P. Keng, and S. Michaelson. 1991. Melatonin secretion by rats exposed to electric fields. Abstract presented at Annual Meeting of the Bioelectromagnetics Society, June 23–27.

Hill, A. B. 1965. The environment and disease: Association or causation? 58 *Proc. R. Soc. Med.* 295–300.

Hollows, F. C., and J. B. Douglas. 1984. Microwave cataract in radiolinemen and controls. 2 *The Lancet* 406–407.

Jänne, J., H. Pösö, and A. Raina. 1978. Polyamines in rapid growth and cancer. 473 *Biochim. Biophys. Acta* 241–293.

Juutilainen, J., E. Pukkala, and E. Laara. 1988. Results of epidemiological cancer study among electrical workers in Finland. 7 *J. Bioelect.* 119–121.

Kaune, W. T., R. G. Stevens, N. J. Callahan, R. K. Severson, and D. B. Thomas. 1987. Residential magnetic and electric fields. 8 *Bioelectromagnetics* 315–335.

Lerchl, A., K. O. Nonaka, K. A. Stokkan, and R. J. Reiter. 1990. Marked rapid alterations in nocturnal pineal serotonin metabolism in mice and rats exposed to weak intermittent magnetic fields. 169 *Biochem. Biophys. Res. Commun.* 102–108.

Lerchl, A., R. J. Reiter, K. A. Howes, K. O. Nonaka, and K. A. Stokkan. 1991. Evidence that extremely low frequency Ca^{2+}-cyclotron resonance depresses pineal melatonin synthesis in vitro. 124 *Neuroscience Lett.* 213–215.

Lin, R. S., P. C. Dischinger, J. Conde, and K. P. Farrell. 1985. Occupational exposure to electromagnetic fields and the occurrence of brain tumors. 27 *J. Occup. Med.* 413–419.

Lin, R. S., and P. Y. Lu. 1989. An epidemiologic study of childhood cancer in relation to residential exposure to electromagnetic fields. In Ann. rev. of res. on biol. effects of 50 and 60 Hz electric and magnetic fields. Conference sponsored by Electric Power Research Institute and Department of Energy, Portland OR, Nov. 13–16.

Linet, M. S., H. S. R. Malker, J. K. McLaughlin, J. A. Weiner, B. J. Stone, W. J. Blot, J. L. E. Ericsson, and J. F. Fraumeni, Jr. 1988. Leukemias and occupation in Sweden: A registry-based analysis. 14 *Am. J. Indus. Med.* 319–330.

London, S. J., D. C. Thomas, J. D. Bowman, E. Sobel, T.-C. Cheng, and J. M. Peters. 1991. Exposure to residential electric and magnetic fields and risk of childhood leukemia. 134 *Am. J. Epidemiol.* 923–937.

Loomis, D. P., and D. A. Savitz. 1990. Mortality from brain cancer and leukaemia among electrical workers. 47 *Brit. J. Indus. Med.* 633–638.

Mack, W., S. Preston-Martin, and J. M. Peters. 1991. Astrocytoma risk related to job exposure to electric and magnetic fields. 12 *Bioelectromagnetics* 55–66.

Mader, D. L., D. A. Barrow, K. E. Donnelly, R. R. Scheer, and M. D. Sherar. 1990. A simple model for calculating residential 60-Hz magnetic fields. 11 *Bioelectromagnetics* 283–296.

Martin, A. O. 1989. EMF and Cancer. Paper presented at the 1989 EPRI Utility Seminar, Sept.

Matanoski, G. M., P. N. Breysse, and E. A. Elliott. 1991. Electromagnetic field exposure and male breast cancer. 1 *The Lancet* 737. (Letter).

McDowall, M. E. 1983. Leukaemia mortality in electrical workers in England and Wales. 1 *The Lancet* 246.

McDowall, M. E. 1986. Mortality of persons resident in the vicinity of electricity transmission facilities. 53 *Br. J. Cancer* 271–279.

McLaughlin, J. K., H. S. R. Malker, W. J. Blot, B. K. Malker, B. J. Stone, J. A. Weiner, J. L. E. Ericsson, and J. F. Fraumeni, Jr. 1987. Occupational risks for intracranial gliomas in Sweden. 78 *J. Natl. Cancer Inst.* 253–257.

Milham, S., Jr. 1982. Mortality from leukemia in workers exposed to electrical and magnetic fields. 307 *N. Engl. J. Med. 249* Letter.

Milham, S., Jr. 1985. Silent keys: Leukaemia mortality in amateur radio operators. 1 *The Lancet* 812. Letter.

Milham, S., Jr. 1988. Mortality by license class in amateur radio operators. 128 *Am. J. Epidemiol.* 1175–1176. Letter.

Myers, A., R. A. Cartwright, J. A. Bonnell, J. C. Male, and S. C. Cartwright. 1985. Overhead power lines and childhood cancer presented at the IEE International Conference on Electric and Magnetic Fields in Medicine and Biology, London, December 4–5, pp 126–130.

Nasca, P. C., M. S. Baptiste, P. A. MacCubbin, B. B. Metzger, K. Carlton, P. Greenwald, V. M. Armbrustmacher, K. M. Earle, and J. Waldman. 1988. Epidemiologic case-control study of central nervous system tumors in children and parental occupational exposures. 128 *Am. J. Epidemiol.* 1256–1265.

National Research Council. 1983. *Risk assessment in the federal government: Managing the process.* Washington, DC: National Academy Press.

Olin, M, D. Vågerö, and A. Ahlbom. 1985. Mortality experience of electrical engineers. 42 *Br. J. Indus. Med.* 211–212.

Pearce, N. E., R. A. Sheppard, J. K. Howard, J. Fraser, and B. M. Lilley. 1985 Leukaemia in electrical workers in New Zealand. 1 *The Lancet* 811–812. Letter.

Pearce, N. E. 1988. Leukemia in electrical workers in New Zealand: A correction, 2 *The Lancet* 48.

Phillips, J. L., W. D. Winters, and L. Rutledge. 1986. In vitro exposure to electromagnetic fields: Changes in tumour cell properties. 49 *Int. J. Rad. Biol.* 463–469.

Preston-Martin, S., J. M. Peters, M. C. Yu, D. H. Garabrant, and J. D. Bowman. 1988. Myelogenous leukemia and electric blanket use. 9 *Bioelectromagnetics* 207–213.

Reichmanis, M., F. S. Perry, A. A. Marino, and R. O. Becker. 1979. Relation between suicide and the electromagnetic field of overhead power lines. 11 *Physiol. Chem. Phys.* 395–403.

Roberts, N. J., and S. M. Michaelson. 1985. Epidemiological studies of human exposures to radiofrequency radiation. A critical review. 56 *Int. Arch. Occup. Environ. Health* 169–178.

Rothman, K. K. 1986. *Modern epidemiology*. Boston: Little, Brown.

Savitz, D. A., E. M. John, R. C. Kleckner. 1990. Magnetic field exposure from electric appliances and childhood cancer. 131 *Am. J. Epidemiol.* 763–773.

Savitz, D. A., and E. E. Calle. 1987. Leukemia and occupational exposure to electromagnetic fields: Review of epidemiologic surveys. 29 *J. Occup. Med.* 47–51.

Savitz, D. A., H. Wachtel, F. A. Barnes, E. M. John, and J. G. Tvrdik. 1988. Case-control study of childhood cancer and exposure to 60-Hz magnetic fields. 128 *Am. J. Epidemiol.* 21–38.

Severson, R. K., R. G. Stevens, W. T. Kaune, D. B. Thomas, L. Heuser, S. Davis, and L. E. Sever. 1988. Acute nonlymphocytic leukemia and residential exposure to power-frequency magnetic fields. 128 *Am. J. Epidemiol.* 10–20.

Speers, M. A., J. G. Dobbins, and V. S. Miller. 1988. Occupational exposures and brain cancer mortality: A preliminary study of East Texas residents. 13 *Am. J. Indus. Med.* 629–638.

Spitz, M. R., and C. C. Johnson. 1985. Neuroblastoma and paternal occupation. A case-control analysis. 121 *Am. J. Epidemiol.* 924–929.

Stern, F. B., R. A. Waxweiler, J. J. Beaumont, T. L. Shiu, R. A. Rinsky, R. D. Zumwalde, W. E. Halperin, P. J. Bierbaum, P. J. Landrigan, and W. E. Murray, Jr. 1986. A case-control study of leukemia at a naval nuclear shipyard. 123 *Am. J. Epidemiol.* 980–992.

Swerdlow, A. J. 1983. Epidemiology of eye cancer in adults in England and Wales, 1962–1977. 118 *Am. J. Epidemiol.* 294–300.

Thomas, T. L., P. D. Stolley, A. Stemhagen, E. T. H. Fontham, M. L. Bleecker, P. A. Stewart, and R. N. Hoover. 1987. Brain tumor mortality risk among men with electrical and electronics jobs: A case-control study. 79 *J. Natl. Cancer Inst.* 233–238.

Thomson, R. A. E., S. M. Michaelson, and Q. A. Nguyen. 1988. Influence of 60-Hertz magnetic fields on leukemia. 9 *Bioelectromagnetics* 149–158.

Thurber, J. 1933, 1973. The car we had to push. In his *My life and hard times*. New York: Harper and Row; rep. New York: Bantam.

Tomenius, L. 1986. 50-Hz electromagnetic environment and the incidence of childhood tumors in Stockholm County. 7 *Bioelectromagnetics* 191–207.

Tornqvist, S., S. Norell, A. Ahlbom, and B. Knave. 1986. Cancer in the electric power industry. 43 *Br. J. Indus. Med.* 212–213.

Vågerö, D., and R. Olin. 1983. Incidence of cancer in the electronics industry: Using the new Swedish cancer environment registry as a screening instrument. 40 *Br. J. Indus. Med.* 188–192.

Vagero, D., A. Ahlbom, R. Olin, and S. Sahlsten. 1985 Cancer morbidity among workers in the telecommunications industry. 42 *Br. J. Indus. Med.* 191–195.

Vena, J. E., S. Graham, R. Hellmann, M. Swanson, and J. Brasure. 1991. Use of electric blankets and risk of postmenopausal breast cancer. 134 *Am. J. Epidemiol.* 180–185.

Verreault, R., N. S. Weiss, K. A. Hollenbach, C. H. Strader, and J. R. Daling. 1990. Use of electric blankets and risk of testicular cancer. 131 *Am. J. Epidemiol.* 759–762.

Wertheimer, N., and E. Leeper. 1979. Electrical wiring configurations and childhood cancer. 109 *Am. J. Epidemiol.* 273–284.

Wertheimer, N., and E. Leeper. 1982. Adult cancer related to electrical wires near the home. 11 *Int. J. Epidemiol.* 345–355.

Wertheimer, N., and E. Leeper. 1980. Electrical wiring configurations and childhood leukemia in Rhode Island. 111 *Am. J. Epidemiol.* 461–462. Letter.

Wertheimer, N. and E. Leeper. 1989. Fetal loss associated with two seasonal sources of electromagnetic field exposure. 129 *Am. J. Epidemiol.* 220–224.

Wertheimer, N. and E. Leeper. 1986. Possible effects of electric blankets and heated waterbeds on fetal development. 7 *Bioelectromagnetics* 13–22.

Wilkins III, J. R., and V. D. Hundley. 1990. Paternal occupational exposure to electromagnetic fields and neuroblastoma in offspring. 131 *Am. J. Epidemiol.* 995–1008.

Wilson, B. W., E. K. Chess, and L. E. Anderson. 1986. 60-Hz electric field effects on pineal melatonin rhythms: time course for onset and recovery. 7 *Bioelectromagnetics* 239–242.

Wright, W. E., J. M. Peters, and T. M. Mack. 1982. Leukaemia in workers exposed to electrical and magnetic fields. 2 *The Lancet* 1160–1161. Letter.

Biographical Sketch

Kenneth R. Foster is Associate Professor in the Department of Bioengineering at the University of Pennsylvania. After earning his Ph.D. in Physics (Indiana University, 1971) he served for 4 ½ years as a Lieutenant in the US Navy, assigned to the Naval Medical Research Institute in Bethesda MD where he studied the interactions of microwave energy with biological systems. Since 1977 he has been a member of the faculty of the Department of Bioengineering.

His research interests are the interactions between electromagnetic fields and biological systems, particularly the mechanisms of interactions. He has published 70 papers in peer reviewed scientific journals, over a range of subjects including electrical properties of tissues, interactions between electromagnetic fields and tissues, and public health issues involving electromagnetic fields. He has also written on these issues in more popular journals including Scientific American and American Scientist, and the Magazine of the IEEE Engineering in Medicine and Biology Society.

Dr. Foster is a Fellow of the Institute of Electrical and Electronics Engineers, a member of the Electromagnetics Academy, and Fellow of the American Institute of Medical and Biological Engineering.

4

Spermicides and Birth Defects

James L. Mills

Introduction

Spermicides are a very old method of contraception. One of the earliest known medical texts, the Petri Papyrus (ca. 1850 B.C.), provides instructions for compounding spermicides (Seregely 1981). The most remarkable ingredient was crocodile dung. Unfortunately for our purposes, the papyrus does not discuss the adverse effects, if any, of these compounds.

In fact, spermicides were used for many centuries without much attention to complications resulting from their use. Both the general public and the medical profession grew to regard them as safe. The problems noted were minor, relating to local sensitivity and allergic reactions. The *1980 Physician's Desk Reference for Nonprescription Drugs* warned of only "burning and/or irritation of the vagina or penis" as potential complications of one popular spermicide.

Medical researchers began to look seriously at the drugs and contraceptive methods women were using around the time of conception only after they became generally aware that maternal exposures during pregnancy could damage the developing embryo. Some early studies suggested that oral contraceptives might be teratogenic (cause birth defects), particularly when used accidentally after conception. Spermicides, however, received little attention.

Other studies mentioned spermicides in relation to birth defects almost in passing. A 1980 study of oral contraceptives by Janerich et al. (1980) noted that women who used chemical contraceptives after their last menstrual period had no more malformed infants than did control subjects. The Collaborative Perinatal Project, a massive study of over 50,000 pregnancies, reported its findings on birth defects in a book entitled *Birth Defects and Drugs in Pregnancy* (Heinonen et al. 1977). One table in this book is devoted to hormones, hormone antagonists, and contraceptives. The last section of this table contains data on birth defects in offspring of women exposed to local contraceptives (including spermicides) in the first four lunar months of pregnancy. The relative risk of birth defects in these children compared with other, nonexposed children was very close to 1; there was, in other words, no increase in birth defects related to spermicides.

Throughout the 1970s the possibility that oral contraceptives could cause birth defects was examined thoroughly. Yet virtually no studies focusing on spermicides were performed, perhaps because of the widely held belief that they posed no such risk.

Spermicides Linked to Birth Defects

The situation changed dramatically in April 1981 when Dr. Hershel Jick and other investigators in Boston published a paper entitled "Vaginal Spermicides and Congenital Disorders" in the *Journal of the American Medical Association*. These investigators had studied women who became pregnant and gave birth while members of a Seattle health maintenance organization, The Group Health Cooperative. Medical records were used to identify infants with a wide range of birth defects. Because the cooperative dispensed spermicides through its pharmacy, pharmacy records were abstracted to determine who had had a prescription for spermicide filled; a woman was considered to be a user "if a prescription for spermicide was filled 600 days or less before delivery or abortion."

On the 4,772 women studied, 17 percent (790) fit the authors' definition of a spermicide user. A comparison of malformation rates in the offspring of users and nonusers of spermicides revealed a significantly higher rate of four types of anomalies in the offspring of users. The authors did not state how many different individual malformations were studied; they did indicate that 23 categories of malformations were examined. The four types of anomalies associated with spermicide use were heterogeneous. The first, limb reduction defects, consisted of underdevelopment or absence of a finger, toe, hand, foot, leg, arm, or thigh. The second, neoplasms, included a malignant brain tumor and a failure of the beta (insulin-secreting) cells of the pancreas to mature. The third, chromosomal anomalies, consisted of three cases of Down's syndrome. The fourth, hypospadias, was an abnormality in which the urethral opening is not located at the tip of the penis.

The investigators suggested that use of spermicides by the children's mothers caused these particular malformations. In their original report they cautioned: "Since a well-defined syndrome among babies with congenital disorders whose mothers used spermicides was not present, these results should be considered tentative until confirmed by other data." Unfortunately, this message was lost in the process of communicating the results of the study to the general public.

For several reasons, the findings of the Jick study were correctly described as tentative. I will briefly review the study's design and methods of analysis, and the biological implications of its findings. This review demonstrates some of the study's weaknesses, and helps to explain why it was subsequently found to be incorrect.

Jick et al. obtained data on spermicide use before the outcome of the subjects' pregnancies was known. This design, called a prospective design, is attractive because data on the exposure of interest (spermicides) are not biased by knowledge of the outcome (birth defects). That is to say, women who have had a bad outcome may be more likely to recall spermicide use than women who have had a normal outcome. I will return to this concept in more detail shortly.

But the study did not adequately establish the exposure of the women to spermicides. Women who did not fill prescriptions at the dispensary were considered unexposed—but they might have purchased spermicides over the counter at virtually any pharmacy. Conversely, women who did fill a prescription at the dispensary may not have used it.

Moreover, the investigators considered a woman "exposed" to spermicides if she had filled a prescription within 600 days of the outcome of her pregnancy. Since a term pregnancy lasts about 280 days, she might have stopped using the spermicides long before conception. There is no obvious reason why the investigators chose 600 days prior to a pregnancy outcome as the exposure interval. Unless the investigators had some (unstated) reason to assume a persistent toxic effect of spermicide use, a more logical to choice would be an interval closer to the duration of a normal term pregnancy.

There are also unanswered questions about the method the investigators used to analyze their data. The categories of malformations chosen for analysis are somewhat unusual. Cancers and developmental anomalies such as pancreatic defects are not often included in malformation studies. More important, Jick et al. did not report how many comparisons they had made before identifying the four categories of excess malformations. Because of the multiple comparison problem (chapter 1), it is impossible to say whether the positive findings might have resulted by chance.

The final questions about the results of the Jick study relate to the biological plausibility of its findings. I will discuss this topic in more detail later. For now I will simply note that the reported malformations occurred at different times during development. Down's syndrome results from a failure of chromosome 21 to divide before the egg and sperm meet. Hypospadias and limb reduction defects occur during the first trimester of pregnancy. The pancreatic defect probably represents a persistence of embryonic cells or a failure of the pancreatic cells to mature during pregnancy. To cause all of these reported defects, spermicides would have had to act in at least three different ways at different times during pregnancy. How spermicides would have caused chromosomes to fail to divide is not obvious.

A second study linking spermicides and birth defects was reported by Rothman in 1982. This study used an unusual population: children with congenital heart disease, some of whom also had Down's syndrome, and normal children. Rothman compared the use of spermicides before pregnancy in three groups of women: mothers of children with Down's syndrome (and heart disease), mothers of children with heart disease (but not Down's syndrome), and mothers of normal children used as controls.

Rothman found that mothers with Down's syndrome children were significantly more likely to have used spermicides than mothers of control children. Mothers of Down's syndrome children were also somewhat more likely to have used spermicides than mothers of children with congenital heart disease but not Down's syndrome. The analysis excluded women who reported using diaphragms, which is surprising because women who use diaphragms use spermicides as well. When the analysis was repeated with diaphragm users included in the spermicide user group, the significant relationship between spermicide use and Down's syndrome disappeared. Although a higher rate of spermicide use was still present in the mothers of the Down's syndrome subjects, the rate was based on only 16 subjects and, therefore, unstable (unreliable because of small numbers).

Rothman concluded that his study tentatively confirmed the hypothesis that spermicides cause Down's syndrome. There are, however, several reasons to question this conclusion. The only statistically significant association between spermicide use and Down's syndrome occurred when the Down's syndrome group was compared with the normal control group. This comparison is the most susceptible to recall bias: women with bad pregnancy outcomes (Down's syndrome) might try harder to remember what they did that could have caused the outcome than normal controls, and be more likely to recall spermicide exposure. This differential recall would produce a false association between spermicide use and Down's syndrome. Epidemiologists deal with this problem by including a control group with another kind of bad outcome, whose members presumably are also highly motivated to recall exposure. If this group also reports a significantly lower rate of exposure (spermicide use), then one can assume that the difference is not due to recall bias.

In this instance, comparing women whose children had other bad outcomes (heart disease) with women whose children had Down's syndrome did not reveal a significant association between spermicide use and Down's syndrome. Several other limitations of this study should be noted. Diaphragm users should have been included in the main analysis as spermicides users; including them weakened the reported association between spermicide use and Down's syndrome because it increased the number of spermicide users in the control groups. Also, the Down's syndrome group in this study was probably not representative of all cases of Down's syndrome because the children had to have heart disease as well as Down's syndrome to be included in the original study from which this study derived.

Rothman's study could be considered to show a relationship between spermicides and Down's syndrome. The lack of consistency of the association when using different control groups and different definitions of spermicide exposure cast its results into doubt. These limitations were sufficiently serious to make the author's conclusion prudent, *i.e.* the study provided "tentative" confirmation of the previous study.

One other study supporting a connection between spermicides and adverse pregnancy outcome appeared in 1982 (Jick et al. 1982). This study reported that women who had experienced a spontaneous abortion were more likely to have used spermicides than women who used either oral contraceptives or neither method of contraception. This study did not examine the question of congenital malformations and will not be reviewed in detail here. But it further increased concerns about the safety of spermicides.

Thus, by April 1982 three articles had suggested that spermicides caused bad outcomes in pregnancy. One reported that spermicide use increased the risk of miscarriage. The other two found an association between maternal spermicide exposure and birth defects: Down's syndrome, limb defects, neoplasms, and defects of the penis. Unfortunately, there was little evidence available to demonstrate the safety of spermicides. The result was great public concern.

How Do Scientists Establish Cause and Effect?

Much has been written on how one "proves" cause and effect in science. The more one looks at the criteria for proof, the more obvious it becomes that proof in any rigorous sense is elusive if not illusory. But there is wide agreement about methods for weighing evidence to determine whether the relationship between an exposure and a disease is one of cause and effect. I will discuss the strength of the evidence in terms of Hill's criteria (listed in chapter 1).

Biological plausibility is the most important criterion. "Bad air," for example, was once thought to cause malaria (hence the name, *mal-aria*). Once the microbial nature of infectious disease was understood, the "bad air" hypothesis was abandoned as biologically implausible. We now know that the "bad air" theory was a relevant association, though not properly termed one of cause and effect, because mosquitoes that transmit malaria breed in swamps.

Are the claimed links between spermicides and birth defects biologically plausible? A sperm that comes into contact with spermicide would probably have its outer capsule removed, and be unlikely to penetrate and fertilize the ovum. If, however, spermicides are absorbed by the mother through the vaginal wall, which in itself is unclear, they might conceivably reach a developing embryo and cause defects. Therefore, spermicide exposure might plausibly cause birth defects, but it is by no means clear how.

Medical evidence or animal studies demonstrating that the proposed cause can produce the proposed effect is often very helpful. No animal experiments demonstrated that spermicides cause birth defects. Using data from animal studies can be tricky, however. Some known human teratogens did not cause birth defects in the animals in which they were initially tested. Conversely, of the hundreds of known animal teratogens; only 20 or so are known to cause birth defects in humans.

Temporality is another critical criterion for establishing causal relationships, and the simplest. A cause must always precede its effect. The cell division that imparts 23 chromosomes to an egg or sperm takes place *before* exposure to spermicides is likely to occur; Down's syndrome is due to an unequal division of chromosomal material and is therefore unlikely to be influenced by spermicide exposure. The other birth defects postulated to be caused by spermicide exposure occur after conception and presumably after spermicide exposure. For these defects the temporal sequence is correct.

Strength of association is a criterion frequently relied upon by epidemiologists to determine causality. The larger the relative risk, the more likely it is that the association is real and not due to chance.

However, the strength of the association must considered along with its stability. The relative risks of spermicides did appear to be high, but they were based on very small numbers of cases and hence the results were unstable. In practical terms, therefore, the strength-of-association criterion is not helpful in assessing the causal link between spermicides and birth defects.

Specificity is another criterion sometimes applied to determine causality. Specificity means that a given exposure is linked to a specific type of disease or site for the disease. This is a controversial criterion because some agents, such as cigarettes, can cause more than one disease (cancer, emphysema) and can cause one disease (cancer) at more than one site (lung, larynx). Nevertheless, birth-defects research has relied on this concept. A drug or other exposure is considered more likely to be a cause of birth defects if it produces a syndrome or specific group of defects. Spermicides did not do this.

Dose response is yet another important consideration in assessing cause and effect. For cigarette smoking, the higher the dose, the greater the risk of lung cancer. (Figure 2, chapter 3).

Applying the dose-response criterion to the spermicide-birth defects issue is difficult. First, it is not clear whether exposure prior to pregnancy should be included in estimating "dose." Second, it is difficult to measure a woman's total exposure to spermicides accurately because the drugs are used episodically. The problem is magnified when an investigator attempts to obtain the information long after the event. For these reasons, the dose-response criterion was not applied to the spermicide question.

The last, but by no means least important, criterion for determining causality is *consistency*. The same association should be found in different studies using different designs and different populations, preferably in both prospective and retrospective studies, and in both clinical trials and observational studies. Scientists are seldom fortunate enough to have all these different types of evidence available. But many scientists, particularly epidemiologists, do expect to see results replicated before accepting them as true. The question of consistency in the spermicide investigations is the one to which I now turn.

Do Spermicides Cause Birth Defects?

The need for additional research to confirm or refute the association between birth defects and spermicides was widely recognized by 1982. The clinical trial is generally considered the best way to test an exposure. In a clinical trial, one group receives the substance of interest (usually a drug) and the other group does not. One hardly needs to be an epidemiologist to see how impractical it would be to assign one group of women to use spermicides and one group to abstain from spermicide use, then wait for them to decide to get pregnant, stop spermicide use, get pregnant, and, finally, examine their offspring for malformations. Unsurprisingly, no one has suggested a clinical trial to examine the safety of spermicides.

Prospective studies are a second, highly regarded type of epidemiologic study, in which the investigator identifies the exposure and waits for the disease to occur. With spermicides, for example, exposure might have been ascertained in a population *before* or *during* pregnancy. The investigator would then record the number of birth defects in the children. It is easier to identify exposures in such studies, and that information is less likely to be biased by knowledge about the final outcome. Prospective studies can also provide information on multiple outcomes. Once a group of pregnant women has been identified and asked about spermicide use, for example, users and nonusers can be compared on stillbirth rates, infant birth weights, or any of a number of other outcomes.

Unfortunately, prospective studies have several disadvantages. They are logistically difficult and costly because subjects must be followed until the outcomes occur. They also require large numbers of subjects to answer most questions. For example, 100 pregnancies would ordinarily result in 2 children with major birth defects and 98 normal children. Identifying teratogenic effects of a chemical or drug would require monitoring thousands of pregnancies, even if the exposure was relatively common. Determining whether an agent increased a specific type of birth defect might require study of tens or even hundreds of thousands of pregnancies, depending on the rate of occurrence of the defect and how common the exposure was. For these reasons prospective studies may be impractical to address general questions about birth defects and frequently cannot answer questions about specific types of birth defects.

Because of these limitations, scientists frequently resort to a third type of study, the retrospective case-control study. In this type of study, the outcome is known and potential explanations (exposures) are looked for after the fact (retrospectively). Subjects with the disease to be studied (cases) and a suitable comparison group of control subjects without the disease of interest are gathered, and their exposures are compared. This kind of study has several practical advantages. It is faster, cheaper, and easier to assemble a group of known cases and suitable control subjects than to wait for enough cases to occur in a prospective study. For rare conditions such as limb reduction defects, only retrospective studies will be able to assemble enough cases to test some possible links.

But the retrospective case-control approach has substantial disadvantages. Recall bias may be a problem. Moreover, if the investigator chooses cases that for some reason are unrepresentative of all cases of the disease, the conclusions of the study may be in error. Finally, the choice of control subjects is critical and often difficult. For example, one early study of lung cancer and smoking used patients with emphysema as control subjects. Smoking causes both lung cancer and emphysema, but the investigators did not know that. Both cases (subjects with lung cancer) and controls (emphysema patients) reported high rates of cigarette smoking. These researchers might have mistakenly concluded that cigarettes were not related to lung cancer, because both groups could have had equal rates of smoking. However, smoking is such a potent cause of lung cancer that even when patients with another disease caused by smoking were used as the control group, the association between smoking and cancer was still detected. These investigators were lucky; but the problem of poorly chosen control groups is nonetheless very real. For these reasons, most epidemiologists consider retrospective case-control studies to be somewhat less reliable than clinical trials and prospective epidemiologic studies.

In summary, there are strengths and weaknesses to both prospective and retrospective studies. Frequently, a combination of the two approaches is required to resolve a difficult question. The birth defects-spermicides issue was, in fact, resolved using both prospective and retrospective studies.

Articles questioning the reported link between spermicides and birth defects began appearing in May 1982. The first of these studies was by Shapiro and colleagues (1982), who used data from a large, prospective, multicenter study conducted between 1959 and 1965, with data on 50,282 pregnancies. In the time period of the study, many subjects had used spermicides that contained mercury. Because of the toxicity of mercury, these spermicides had been removed from the market and were no longer considered relevant to the spermicides-birth defects question. Nonetheless, the study included data from 462 women who had used non-mercurial spermicides.

The investigators found that the overall rates of birth defects in children of spermicide users was slightly *lower* than for children of nonusers, with no excess in the specific kinds of defects that had been previously linked to spermicides. This study had the typical strengths of prospective studies: the mothers' use of spermicides was ascertained shortly after the event and not biased by knowledge of the outcomes of their pregnancy. The study also had the problems inherent in prospective studies. In particular, the number of spermicide users was modest, so the investigators could rule out only a very large increase for some of the defects previously linked to spermicide use.

Shortly after this study was published, I reported a large prospective study on 34,460 pregnant women who belonged to a health maintenance organization. (Mills et al. 1982). Information gathered at their first prenatal visit showed that 3,146 women had used spermicides before their last menstrual period but not after. An additional 2,282 women had used spermicides after their last menstrual period. We compared the rates of birth defects in their children with those of children of 13,148 women who used other contraceptive methods before their last menstrual period but not after, and with 2,831 women who used other contraceptive methods after their last menstrual period, respectively.

Mills et al (1982) also found no evidence linking spermicides and birth defects. The study was relatively large and would have been virtually certain to detect a 50 percent increase in the rate of all birth defects. We found no association between spermicide use and total rate of defects, or rate of specific defects including chromosomal defects, limb defects, or defects of the genital system (a category that would include hypospadias). As often occurs in prospective studies, the study could rule out a large increase in these specific defects but not weaker links. A companion study using the same subjects later demonstrated that there was no spermicide syndrome or pattern of defects found in the offspring of spermicide users (Mills et al. 1985). That study also found no association between spermicides and spontaneous abortion, preterm delivery, or low birth weight.

Taken together, these two large prospective studies provided considerable reassurance that spermicide use is not associated with higher rates of birth defects in general and provided some indication that spermicides are not associated with the individual defects that had initially been linked to their use.

Soon after these studies appeared, several more modest studies were published. These, too, showed no evidence of a relationship between spermicide use around the time of conception and an increased rate of birth defects. These studies, however, were too small to provide any assurance regarding the risk of individual defects.

In early 1983, a case-control study by the Metropolitan Atlanta Congenital Defects Program (Cordero and Layde 1983) tackled the remaining question of whether spermicides really cause chromosomal anomalies or limb reduction defects. The investigators asked mothers of children with chromosomal anomalies, limb reduction defects, or a variety of other birth defects about their use of spermicides prior to conception and in the first trimester of pregnancy. The mothers of children with other birth defects were used as a control group, on the assumption that spermicides were not related to these defects. The rate of spermicide exposure was found to be 4.5 percent in the chromosomal-anomalies group, 3.8 percent in the limb reduction group, and 3.8 percent in the control group. These differences were not statistically significant, and the investigators concluded that spermicide use did not increase the risk of either chromosomal anomalies or limb reduction defects. This study provided important support for the claim that spermicides did not cause birth defects.

The issue seemed resolved: the vast majority of evidence found no association between spermicide use and birth defects. The Fertility and Maternal Health Drugs Advisory Committee of the Food and Drug Administration met in December 1983 to review the safety of vaginal spermicides. The committee concluded that "the information presented was insufficient to warrant a special warning on vaginal contraceptive product labeling regarding the risk of fetal anomalies and chromosomal anomalies with spermicide use during pregnancy" (FDA 1983).

This report was followed in November 1986 by a notice in the *FDA Drug Bulletin* entitled *"Data Do Not Support Association Between Spermicides, Birth Defects"* (FDA 1986). The notice stated: "After reviewing all available scientific data, the FDA has concluded that the weight of the present evidence does not support an association between the use of spermicides and birth defects or miscarriage." The FDA reaffirmed its decision not to add a warning to products containing spermicides and announced that it would continue to monitor the situation. Since that announcement, no new data have appeared suggesting that spermicides cause birth defects.

What may well be the final chapter of the saga concerning spermicides and birth defects appeared in the form of two reports in the *New England Journal of Medicine* on August 20, 1987. These studies had been performed under contracts from the National Institute of Child Health and Human Development. The contracts were let to provide additional information regarding the four types of birth defects initially linked to spermicide use: chromosomal anomalies, hypospadias, limb reduction defects, and neoplasms.

In the first of these studies, investigators interviewed women undergoing prenatal diagnosis before they knew the results of their diagnostic procedures (Warburton et al. 1987). Among the 13,729 women interviewed, 154 had fetuses with trisomies, 98 of which were Down's syndrome. For each of these case women, the investigators chose four matched control women who had chromosomally normal fetuses. The investigators found no association between spermicide use and trisomy (all types) or the particular type of trisomy known as Down's syndrome.

In the second study, investigators identified infants with birth defects in the first six months of life by reviewing medical records from 188 institutions (Louik et al. 1987). The case group included mothers of 265 children with Down's syndrome, of 396 children with hypospadias, of 146 children with limb reduction defects, and of 116 children with neoplasms. A control group consisted of mothers of 3,442 infants with a variety of other defects. All mothers were asked about spermicide use both before and after conception (because of the different times at which these defects occur). The investigators found no significant differences in the rates of spermicide exposure in the case versus control groups. They concluded that the risks for the birth defects they examined were not increased by exposure to spermicides.

Ironically, one of the authors of the original study linking spermicides and birth defects published a reappraisal of the study in 1986. He reexamined the medical records to determine whether the "exposed" women who bore children with birth defects had used spermicides around the time they conceived. He discovered that many of these women had *planned* their pregnancies; that is, they were not using spermicides around the time of conception. "[O]ur study's definition of exposure to spermicide near the time of conception was grossly inaccurate," he concluded (Watkins 1986). He stated that the article's "conclusion is unsupported by more complete evidence from its subjects. Our article did not suggest that exposure other than near the time of conception might cause birth defects, and neither have subsequent investigators made this suggestion." Another of the study's authors replied: "In retrospect, I believe our article should never have been published. In our present litigious environment, the reservations and qualifications written into a published report are often ignored, and the article is used as 'proof' of a causal relationship" (Holmes 1986).

References

Cordero, J. F., and P. M. Layde. 1983. Vaginal spermicides, chromosomal abnormalities and limb reduction defects. 15 *Fam. Plan. Perspec.* 16–18.

Food and Drug Administration. 1983. Memorandum from executive secretary, Fertility and Maternal Health Drugs Advisory Committee. December 21.

Food and Drug Administration. 1986. *FDA Drug Bulletin*. November 16.

Heinonen, O. P., D. Slone, and S. Shapiro. 1977. *Birth defects and drugs in pregnancy*. 391–392. Littleton, MA: Publishing Sciences Group.

Holmes, L. B. 1986. Vaginal spermicides and congenital disorders: the validity of a study [in reply]. 256 *J. Am. Med. Assn.* 3096.

Janerich, D. T., J. M. Piper, and D. M. Glebatis. 1980. Oral contraceptives and birth defects. 112 *Am. J. Epidemiology* 73–79.

Jick, H., A. M. Walker, K. J. Rothman, J. R. Hunter, L. B. Holmes, R. N. Watkins, D. C. D'Ewart, A. Danford, S. Madsen. 1981. *Vaginal spermicides and congenital disorders,* 245 J. of the Am. Med. Assn. 1329–1332.

Jick, H., K. Shiota, T. H. Shepard, J. R. Hunter, A. Stergachis, S. Madsen, and J. B. Porter. 1982. Vaginal spermicides and miscarriage seen primarily in the emergency room. 2 *Teratogenesis, Carcinogenesis, & Mutagenesis* 205–210.

Louik, C., A. A. Mitchell, M. M. Werler, J. W. Hanson, and S. Shapiro. 1987. Maternal exposure to spermicide in relation to certain birth defects. 317 *N. Eng. J. Med.* 474–478.

Mills, J. L., E. E. Harley, G. F. Reed, H. W. Berendes. 1982. Are spermicides teratogenic? 248 *J. Am. Med. Assn.* 2148–2151.

Mills, J. L., G. F. Reed, R. P. Nugent, E. E. Harley, and H. W. Berendes. 1985. Are there adverse effects of periconceptual spermicide use? 43 *Fertility & Sterility* 442–446.

Physician's desk reference for nonprescription drugs. 1980. Oradell, NJ: Medical Economics.

Rothman, K. J. 1982. Spermicide use and Down's syndrome. 72 *Am. J. Pub. Health* 399–401.

Seregely, G. 1981. *Contraception*. 4th ed. Budapest: Medicina.

Shapiro, S., D. Slone, O. P. Heinonen, D. W. Kaufman, L. Rosenberg, A. A. Mitchell, and S. P. Helmrich. 1982. Birth defects and vaginal spermicides. 247 *J. Am. Med. Assn.* 2381–2384.

Warburton, D., R. H. Neugut, A. Lustenberger, A. G. Nicholas, and J. Kline. 1987. Lack of association between spermicide use and trisomy, 317 *N. Eng. J. Med.* 478–482.

Watkins, R. N. 1986. Vaginal spermicides and congenital disorders: The validity of a study. 256 *J. Am. Med. Assn.* 3095–96.

Biographical Sketch

James L. Mills is chief of the Pediatric Epidemiology Section of the Prevention Research Program at the National Institute of Child Health and Human Development. He received his medical training at New York Medical College, his pediatric specialty training at Cornell Medical College and his subspecialty training in pediatric endocrinology at the University of Pennsylvania (Children's Hospital of Philadelphia). He has a master's degree in epidemiology from the University of Pennsylvania.

Dr. Mills is particularly interested in birth defects and has led several major studies examining adverse effects of spermicides.

Dr. Mills is Fellow of the American College of Epidemiology; a member of the American Epidemiological Society, American Pediatric Society, and Society for Pediatric Research; and an associate in the Department of Epidemiology at Johns Hopkins University.

5

Bendectin and the Language of Causation

Louis Lasagna and Sheila R. Shulman[1]

Bendectin was the only medication ever approved in the United States for treatment of the nausea and vomiting associated with pregnancy. It entered the U.S. market in 1956, and was sold in 22 countries before the manufacturer withdrew it in 1983. The drug was sold by the William S. Merrell Company of Cincinnati, the same company that had been preparing to market thalidomide in the United States when that drug's potent teratogenic effects were uncovered by European scientists.

Bendectin enjoyed considerable popularity among prescribing physicians but encountered a challenge in 1972 in the wake of the Drug Efficacy Study Implementation (DESI)[2] review. At that time, the manufacturer was asked to demonstrate that each of Bendectin's three ingredients contributed to the suppression of nausea. Merrell conducted clinical trials, and one of the ingredients, the antispasmodic dicyclomine, showed no evident benefit. In 1976, Bendectin was reconstituted as a two-ingredient medication, containing doxylamine (a sedative antihistamine) and the vitamin pyridoxine (B_6).

The first suggestions that Bendectin might cause birth defects came in case reports in the medical literature. These anomalies included limb deformities (limb reductions), omphalocele-gastroschisis (abnormality of the umbilicus and intestines), and neural tube defects. The first report came from Canada in 1969 (Paterson 1969); the same author described a similar case eight years later (Paterson 1977). An English report the following year (Donnai and Harris 1978) and subsequent letters to the editor (Menzies 1978; Frith 1978; Mellor 1978) suggested teratogenicity for the 3-ingredient product (called Debendox) on sale in the United Kingdom. Other case reports associated Bendectin use with a variety of congenital anomalies (Fisher et al. 1982; Grodofsky and Wilmott 1984). In some cases, however, the mother had used other drugs during the first trimester of pregnancy.

All of these reports relied on *post hoc, ergo propter hoc* deduction, as do all case reports. Similar reports had originally alerted McBride (1981, 1984) in Australia and Lenz in Germany to the possibility that thalidomide was a teratogen. The degree to which such data are compelling rests not on individual cases but on collective evidence showing that the drug's use has been associated with an increase over the usual incidence of fetal abnormalities.

Congenital anomalies are quite common. The exact rate is difficult to quantify, since it depends in part on the definition of anomaly, the skill of the observing medical staff, and the time after birth at which the child is examined. Estimates thus range from 1 to 7 percent; a 3 percent figure is often quoted. In 1983, Brent estimated that some 30 million infants had been exposed to Bendectin early in pregnancy; chance alone could have accounted for 900,000 malformed infants in a population of this size. The rate of spontaneous occurrence of limb reduction defects is considered to be 1 in 3,000; hence 10,000 such defects would have occurred by chance alone in Bendectin-exposed infants.

Nonetheless, the alleged association between Bendectin and congenital defects provoked over 1,000 legal claims between 1977 and 1986; it was this deluge of litigation, combined with high insurance rates, that forced the product from the market.

This chapter examines the complex issue of causation in light of the Bendectin experience. We present the conclusions of a range of Bendectin studies and survey the scientific evidence used by parties in the Bendectin litigation. We review how four different courts interpreted and analyzed the scientific data, and examine how well legal findings of causation meet the criteria that permit an inference of causation in epidemiology. We conclude by discussing whether existing legal procedures are appropriate for determining the question of causation in cases of this type.

The Science of Bendectin

Epidemiologic Studies

Epidemiology supplies the best available evidence of the causal link, if any, between Bendectin and congenital anomalies. Epidemiologic studies, however, have their own pitfalls. Recall bias is a significant problem: mothers of deformed babies are more likely to remember correctly use of drugs during pregnancy (Werler et al. 1989). Modest increases in rates of congenital anomalies can be easily missed unless very large numbers of subjects are studied. On the other hand, repeated dredging of epidemiologic data will predictably turn up spurious correlations by chance.[3]

Rothman and his colleagues (1979), for example, conducted an epidemiologic study that found an association between Bendectin and some congenital heart defects. The association was weak, and the study revealed that aspirin, ampicillin, and codeine—all drugs not thought to be teratogens—were taken more frequently by the mothers of the affected children. A retrospective case control study conducted by a team in Oxford found an excess of infants with cleft lips among mothers who had used Bendectin, but the report cautioned that "this result was not thought to be conclusive evidence of a teratogenic effect" (Golding et al. 1983).

Standing against the few studies that have found a positive association between Bendectin and congenital malformations are numerous prospective and retrospective studies that failed to find any such correlation. Two years after the Oxford study, for example, another British group using data from Cardiff and Aberdeen was unable to confirm any teratogenic property of Bendectin (Elbourne et al. 1985). An earlier study correlating Bendectin prescription and congenital anomalies in Northern Ireland similarly found no association (Harron et al. 1980). Several cohort studies, some prospective and some retrospective, were published between 1976 and 1981 (Gibson et al. 1981; Jick et al. 1981; Smithells and Sheppard 1978; Fleming et al. 1981; Newman et al. 1977; Milkovich and van den Berg 1976).

Despite differences in design and sensitivity, all of these studies failed to find any significant elevation of malformations in infants exposed to Bendectin. MacMahon (1981) analyzed the more recent of these studies and concluded that they show that Bendectin presents a relative risk of 0.89, which is to say that the studies overall revealed Bendectin babies had no more anomalies than expected by pure chance. The reliability of this 0.89 estimate is indicated by the 90 percent confidence limits that MacMahon placed on it, which ranged from 0.76 to 1.04. That is, they span the range from a modest protection against congenital anomalies to a tiny increase in risk.

Other published reports from the United States, Great Britain, West Germany, and Australia also failed to show a teratogenic potential in Bendectin (McCredie et al. 1984; Aselton et al. 1985; Nelson and Forfar 1971; Zierler and Rothman 1985; Clarke and Clayton 1981; Michaelis et al. 1983). In one large prospective study, Milkovich and van den Berg (1976) failed to find any difference in the rates of severe congenital anomalies or of perinatal death between children born to mothers who had used antinauseant drugs during pregnancy and those who had not. Thirteen years earlier, a retrospective survey of physician records by Bunde and Bowles (1963) had come to similar conclusions about the safety of Bendectin. This study of 4,436 women attempted to account for possible differences in temporal effects, hospital facilities, physician clientele, obstetrical skill, and ability to diagnose malformations, by comparing the incidence of anomalies in Bendectin babies with the incidence in other babies delivered at roughly the same time in the same hospital by the same physician. The two groups exhibited no statistically significant difference in either incidence or type of malformations. In fact, there were more anomalies in the controls than among the Bendectin babies. Although not a controlled trial (which would have been difficult or impossible to carry out), this early study represented an imaginative approach to the acquisition of meaningful (and reassuring) data.

In another prospective cohort study, Shapiro et al. (1977) found no indication that doxylamine or dicyclomine was harmful to the fetus in over 1,000 women exposed to these drugs during the first four lunar months of pregnancy. (The third ingredient of Bendectin, pyridoxine, was not evaluated because most pregnant women take supplemental vitamins.)

Morelock et al. (1982) conducted a prospective study of maternal habits and characteristics during pregnancy and their impact on fetal development. Of the 1690 mother/infant pairs, 375 involved the use of Bendectin during pregnancy. Again, Bendectin exposure was not found to be associated with adverse fetal outcome. The authors calculated that the study had a power of 82 percent, that is, there was "only an 18 percent chance of missing a two-fold increased risk to Bendectin-users."

Two case-control studies attempted to control for recall bias by comparing Bendectin exposure among infants having one type of malformation with exposure for infants having other malformations. Mitchell et al. found no evidence that early exposure to Bendectin in utero increased the risk of oral clefts or heart defects (1981), or that Bendectin was associated with pyloric stenosis (narrowing of the outlet to the stomach) in newborns (1983). This latter result contradicted an epidemiologic study by Eskenazi and Bracken (1982). Cordero and associates (1981) found no significant differences in exposure to Bendectin for any of 12 different defect categories. For six subgroups of infants with limb reduction defects, only the group with amniotic bands[4] had a significantly increased exposure to Bendectin. Weak associations were found for esophageal atresia,[5] encephalocele,[6] and amniotic bands, but the authors concluded that the study did not establish a causal relation between Bendectin exposure and the birth defects studied.

Brent (1985a) looked specifically at ventricular septal defects, which are openings in the dividing wall between the lower chambers of the heart. He plotted Bendectin sales in the United States against the incidence of such defects as reported to the Centers for Disease Control. Reported defects rose steadily from 1970 to 1983; Bendectin sales, however, plateaued in the first years of this period, then declined rapidly (to zero) in the last five.

Animal Testing

Do animal studies shed any light on possible teratogenic effects of Bendectin? Gibson et al. (1968) performed teratology studies in rabbits and reproduction studies in rats with Bendectin and with its two nonvitamin components. Rabbits were artificially inseminated and then given various doses of the drug orally on days 9 through 16 of the gestation period. Any rabbits that died were autopsied, and surviving rabbits were sacrificed on day 26 or 28. All live fetuses were weighed; and the number of live, dead, and resorbed fetuses was recorded; and the fetuses were examined.

The only effects the investigators observed were at the highest doses of doxylamine and dicyclomine. High dosages of doxylamine were associated with an increase in the mean number of fetuses resorbed and with three fetuses whose skeletons were malformed. High dosages of dicyclomine were associated with a similar increase in fetal resorption but no malformations. Rabbits given the highest dose of Bendectin produced four fetuses with minor skeletal malformations, compared with two in the control group and none and two in the groups given lower doses of Bendectin. The effects seen with the highest doses of dicyclomine and doxylamine were attributed to toxic effects of the drugs to the mothers, since there were more deaths of the does in these groups.

In the rat experiments, both male and female rats were dosed with doxylamine, dicyclomine, or Bendectin for at least 80 days prior to breeding and during the raising of 1 or 2 successive litters. To identify any latent effects on reproduction or fetal development, male and female progeny from control and drug groups were bred and the females allowed to deliver and nurse their young for a week. No drugs were administered during this portion of the study. No malformations were noted in the fetuses of any of the doxylamine-treated rats. With dicyclomine, one fetus in the high-dose group had exencephaly.[7] Bendectin produced no anomalies, and the reproductive testing of Bendectin-treated progeny showed no abnormalities. The authors of this study were not impressed with the malformations they observed in these animals, because they were of a nature and frequency seen in control animal populations.

In 1984, McBride published some data on the effects of doxylamine on rabbits. He found 32 percent of fetuses to be malformed, as opposed to none in the controls, but he used high doses—up to 330 mg/kg by mouth daily. Oral doses of 250 mg/kg are typically enough to kill half of the animals receiving them; indeed, 19 of 48 tested animals died of drug toxicity. McBride had earlier (1981) placed large doses of dicyclomine directly in chick eggs and produced dose-related gastroschisis and other defects at the highest dosage.

In 1988 Tyl et al. evaluated the maternal and developmental effects of doxylamine and pyridoxine in rats, using doses that at the highest end of the range killed a significant fraction of the animals (17.1 percent). The proportion of litters with malformed fetuses was higher than controls only at doses of 800 mg/kg/day, with the dominant anomaly being a short thirteenth rib (an anomaly to which the rat is predisposed). By contrast, a positive control (nitrofen) produced 85 percent malformed fetuses, the predominant malformation being diaphragmatic hernia.

In the cynomolgus monkey, Hendrickx et al. (1985a) used doses approximately 2, 5, and 20 times the human dose equivalent from days 20 to 50 of gestation. The investigators observed no evidence at the end of pregnancy of either teratogenicity or toxicity to mother, embryo, or fetus. These same authors also studied the effects of Bendectin administered to rhesus monkeys and baboons at doses 10 to 40 times the human dose equivalent (Hendrickx et al. 1985b). Ventricular septal defects were found in 18–40 percent of the primates examined prenatally. These lesions were not, however, seen at term, suggesting a drug-related delay in spontaneous closure of the defect with minimal clinical implications.

We have already noted some of the deficiencies of the epidemiologic studies. Animal studies also have their failings. As one of us has pointed out (Lasagna 1987), such tests can have both false positive results (suggesting the presence of an effect when none exists) and false negatives (missing a real effect). Thalidomide, for example, was finally shown to be a teratogen in several animal species, but only after many negative animal tests.

One peculiar problem arises when testing relatively nontoxic drugs that can be given to animals in doses far higher than those used in humans (as is the case with Bendectin). It is then difficult to interpret the results and judge their implications for human health. As Brent (1985b) has pointed out, drugs with small margins of safety, such as morphine and digitalis, "are not of reproductive concern because they kill the pregnant animal." One may also question the relevance to human health of studies (as was the case with Bendectin) where drugs are given to animals of both sexes for months prior to mating as well as during all of pregnancy.

The Food and Drug Administration

In September 1980, responding to anecdotal reports and a request from the American College of Obstetrics and Gynecology, the FDA's Fertility and Maternal Health Drugs Advisory Committee reviewed the available scientific information about Bendectin's association with birth defects. The FDA invited experts to share their views on whether Bendectin was associated with increased risk for human birth defects and, if so, whether the benefits of therapy outweighed the risks.

The committee concluded that existing data did not show an association between Bendectin and human birth defects. Two of 13 studies suggested a possible association, but these studies had been exploratory only, and could not be taken to contradict the more formal, large-scale epidemiologic studies. The committee decided that the available studies were sufficiently large to have detected a doubling of the overall malformation rate, but not large enough to rule out a doubling of any single malformation. It recommended that the FDA should monitor three ongoing epidemiologic studies and limit Bendectin use to patients for whom nondrug therapies had failed (Public Health Service 1980).

In December 1980, the FDA proposed a patient package insert for Bendectin, that read in part:

It is not possible to prove that any drug . . . [is] totally free of risk, or absolutely safe, if taken during pregnancy. In 11 of 13 studies of women who took this drug during pregnancy, there has been no evidence that it increased the risk of birth defects. . . . [T]his drug has been the most carefully studied of all drugs which could be used to treat the nausea and vomiting of pregnancy. There is no evidence that any other drug is safer in treating the nausea and vomiting of pregnancy. (Federal Register 1980, 80740-80743)

In June 1981, the Public Citizen's Health Research Group (HRG), a consumer advocate organization, petitioned Health and Human Services Secretary Richard Schweiker to remove Bendectin from the market immediately, pursuant to section 355(e) of the Federal Food, Drug, and Cosmetic Act. The HRG argued that there was an absence of substantial evidence of Bendectin's effectiveness in patients with severe nausea and vomiting or those who could not be helped with nondrug measures, although the HRG did not deny that the drug effectively relieved morning sickness. The petition contended further that pyridoxine inhibited doxylamine's antiemetic action and that no evidence showed that Bendectin was a rational mixture. The petition based its claims on Merrell's 1975 clinical efficacy study. In February 1982, FDA Commissioner Dr. Arthur Hayes denied the petition.

In June 1982, the HRG again petitioned the Health and Human Services to remove the drug, arguing that neither the drug's safety nor a consumer need for it had been demonstrated. This petition stated: "Based on substantial dose-dependent increase in diaphragmatic hernias following the administration to animals, and a statistical association between Bendectin use and birth defects in humans, Bendectin is unsafe for human use." The petition further claimed that "Bendectin is rarely if ever necessary," and that the drug should not be indicated for use during pregnancy, since one of its components, doxylamine, was sold over the counter with a warning that it should not be taken during pregnancy.

This petition cited an unpublished West German study conducted on rats in 1981, that demonstrated a significant correlation between Bendectin and diaphragmatic hernias and wavy ribs (but these results were not replicated in subsequent studies), and epidemiologic data from four major U.S. cohort studies showing weak associations between Bendectin and various malformations. The HRG used data from the latter studies to conclude that there was an increase in the rate of diaphragmatic defects among offspring of Bendectin users.

The FDA first responded informally to this petition in July 1982 by reiterating its support for Bendectin when used as indicated (FDC Reports 1982). An exchange of letters between the FDA's Center for Drugs and Biologics and the HRG followed. In the last exchange, in January 1983, the FDA wrote that it considered Bendectin a priority item, although additional time was required to provide a thorough reply (Morrison 1983). The manufacturer of Bendectin discontinued production, however, before the FDA responded formally to this petition. In March 1983, the HRG wrote to Commissioner Hayes, complaining that Merrell-Dow was negligently lax in conducting studies and that the FDA had acted negligently in permitting Merrell-Dow to delay. Commissioner Hayes responded (Hayes 1983) that the FDA's support of Bendectin was unchanged.

In May 1983, HRG wrote to FDA Commissioner Hayes urging the FDA to require a box warning directly informing women of a serious risk of birth defects. The letter argued that the current package insert was inaccurate because it failed to refer specifically to the 1981 West German study or to animal studies suggesting that the drug might cause birth defects.

Meanwhile, in June 1981, the House Committee on Science and Technology, Subcommittee on Investigations and Oversight, had held a hearing on the effects of prescription drugs during pregnancy. Although the hearings were not intended to address Bendectin's safety or the FDA's regulation of the drug specifically, consumer fears regarding Bendectin were apparently involved in the decision to conduct them.

The subcommittee questioned FDA Commissioner Hayes and other FDA officials about the agency's procedure for evaluating safety issues, monitoring adverse drug reactions, and making recommendations (U.S. House Committee on Science and Technology 1981). Commissioner Hayes described the FDA's use of numerous sources to obtain information on birth defects: the National Institutes of Health collaborative perinatal study of 50,000 women and their pregnancies, the Kaiser-Oakland study of 20,000 pregnant women, an ongoing Centers for Disease Control study of yearly trends in birth defects, case-control studies of birth defects by the Centers for Disease Control and the Boston Drug Epidemiology Unit, the Columbia University study of spontaneous abortions, and the ongoing analysis of the Group Health Cooperative of Puget Sound data base of 7000 pregnancies. Dr. Hayes further defended the agency's attention to safety by pointing to the FDA's formation of the Maternal-Child Task Force, its review of all birth defects and perinatal adverse effects (including spontaneous abortions), coordination of data sources on birth defects, financial support of epidemiologic studies, and communication to the medical community. Dr. Hayes reiterated the FDA's determination that Bendectin did not cause birth defects.

In summary, the scientific evidence seems sufficient to rule out the possibility that Bendectin is a powerful cause of birth defects. The possibility that it might cause undetectably small increases in the rate of birth defects cannot be ruled out by scientific data. Proving that Bendectin does not cause birth defects is logically impossible.

The demise of Bendectin might be attributed to a number of factors: the thalidomide experience, the significant incidence of congenital anomalies even in the absence of identifiable causal agents, the way our social system deals with putative drug-induced damage, the popularity of litigation, and the difficulties experienced by both judges and juries in dealing with statistical concepts.

It is difficult to see how a new drug for the treatment of morning sickness will ever be marketed in the United States. Canada, however, has approved the marketing of 2-ingredient Bendectin. Doxylamine is available in the United States in various over-the-counter preparations, and dicyclomine is still marketed as an antispasmodic for gastrointestinal disorders.

Bendectin Litigation: The Merger of Law and Science

Prior to jury selection in the 1985 litigation consolidating 818 Bendectin cases, Chief Judge Carl B. Rubin offered the parties to the litigation an interesting option.[8] Assuming a consensus among all those involved in the proceeding, the court authorized the impanelment of a jury with "special qualifications." The judge suggested that the parties might select either a "blue, blue ribbon jury" or a "blue ribbon jury." The "blue, blue ribbon jury" would be composed of persons knowledgeable in the fields represented by the expert witnesses in the case; a "blue ribbon jury" would be selected from those persons having the most formal education among the jury panel. As the court acknowledged, neither concept is recognized in the Federal Rules of Civil Procedure. However, the antic-ipation of highly technical and complex testimony by expert witnesses on the key issue of causation motivated the court to consider a departure from traditional practice.

The plaintiffs rejected the offer. The jury that was eventually im-paneled had six members, ranging in education from nonattendance at high school to possession of a graduate degree. The tendering of the offer, however, was significant. It acknowledged the challenge confront-ing the courts as they attempt to deal with the difficult and controversial evidentiary issues raised in toxic tort litigation. Courts have admitted that judges lack special competence to resolve the complex questions of causality.[9] The task for a lay jury in such cases can be formidable.

With the growth in hazardous substance litigation since the early 1980s, an increased reliance on detailed scientific data has emerged not only in the Bendectin cases but also in toxic tort cases involving radiation fallout,[10] the defoliant Agent Orange,[11] swine flu vaccine,[12] and chemical contamination of community water supplies.[13] An expanding body of law recognizes the importance of epidemiologic evidence in particular as a foundation for expert opinion where no direct evidence is available on the issue of causation (Dangell 1989).

The Bendectin decisions affirm this trend. In *Brock v. Merrell Dow Pharmaceuticals, Inc.,*[14] the Fifth Circuit concluded that epidemiologic studies constitute "the most useful and conclusive type of evidence" and, in cases of this type, "speculation unconfirmed by epidemiologic proof cannot form the basis for causation in a court of law." The First Circuit affirmed summary judgment for the defendant in a Bendectin case in Massachusetts[15] where the plaintiffs failed to present acceptable confirmatory epidemiologic data to support their experts' opinions on the issue of causation.

Some authors have questioned the way in which epidemiologic data have been integrated into the legal framework with its clearly defined rules of evidence (Hoffman 1984; Harter 1986). While causation is an important element in an inquiry conducted by either discipline, the methods of determining causation are different in law and epidemiology. In *Ferebee* v. *Chevron Chemical Co.*,[16] a case involving the herbicide paraquat, the court drew a distinction between the demands of the two disciplines: "In a courtroom, the test for allowing a plaintiff to recover in a tort suit of this type is not scientific certainly but legal sufficiency."

It seems reasonable, therefore, to ask what quality, quantity, or standard of scientific evidence is required to justify a determination of legal causation.

Legal v. Epidemiologic Causation

The following question was put to the jury by the U.S. District Court in Ohio in the consolidated Bendectin litigation:

Have the plaintiffs established by a preponderance of the evidence that ingestion of Bendectin at therapeutic doses during the period of fetal organogenesis is a proximate cause of human birth defects?[17]

The jury unanimously answered in the negative. The plaintiffs had failed, in the jury's opinion, to meet the burden of proof required to establish legal causation.

What, exactly, is that burden? The plaintiff must establish the fact of causation by a preponderance of the evidence. This burden is generally defined as evidence that would render a fact more likely than not. To prevail in a toxic tort case, the plaintiff must introduce evidence which affords a reasonable basis for the conclusion that it is more likely or probable than not that exposure to the substance in question was a substantial contributing factor to the plaintiff's injury (Prosser and Keeton 1984).

This process requires a two-step analysis (Whitehead and Espel 1988). The first focuses on generic causation, that is, whether exposure to the substance in question causes harm of the kind reported by the plaintiff. The second step, which must be addressed only if the first is answered affirmatively, is whether the exposure in fact caused harm to this particular plaintiff. As both steps in the analysis, a mere possibility of causation is insufficient (Whitehead and Espel 1988); however, the requirement is far from one of certainty. This burden of proof is significantly lower than the "beyond a reasonable doubt" standard required in criminal proceedings or the "clear and convincing evidence" standard imposed in certain civil and administrative hearings.

The evidence in such cases is qualitative, and resists precise measurement. However, the rough estimate of "over 50 percent" of the evidence is generally equated with this civil burden of proof (Rosenberg 1984). The precise extent of the causal connection is not specified when legal responsibility is imposed. Therefore, while the determination of a court proceeding imposes finality in the legal sense, there may in fact be no corresponding certainty with respect to actual causality outside of the legal forum.

Most epidemiologists approach conclusions about causality with caution. The discipline is said to be characterized by uncertainty and "is by its nature inexact" (Hennekens and Buring 1987). While a long-term goal of an epidemiologic study may be to determine a cause-effect relationship, this conclusion is elusive and never unequivocal.

An epidemiologic investigation may report an association between an injury or disease and a specific exposure. The association, however, is not necessarily one of cause and effect. A more important consideration is the validity of a study. In epidemiology, a study may be considered valid if the investigator has adequately eliminated the roles of chance, bias, and confounding variables through rigor in both the study methodology and data analysis.

Scientists often employ Hill's criteria to judge whether an association as reported by an epidemiologic study reflects an underlying cause-effect relation; these criteria are listed in chapter 1. In the Bendectin decisions, courts focused on three specific measurements used in epidemiology: relative risk or risk ratio, statistical significance, and confidence intervals.

Given the difficulties in inferring cause-effect relations in epidemiology, judges and juries might be misled if they lacked a clear understanding of the requirements for proving causation in epidemiology and in law. When expert witnesses state their opinion, on the basis of epidemiologic studies, that no causal relationship exists, their responses are based on the rules of epidemiology. The jury, however, must determine causality on the basis of legal rules that impose a less rigorous standard of evidence. The point at which the "preponderance of evidence" standard and the epidemiology intersect is unclear.

Review of Four Bendectin Court Decisions

In each of the four court cases reviewed here, a limb reduction defect was alleged to have been caused by Bendectin. In each, the plaintiffs presented evidence of substantially the same type; the cases, however, followed quite different paths.

In *Lynch v. Merrell-National Laboratories,*[18] the U.S. District Court for Massachusetts granted the defendant's pretrial motion for summary judgment, and dismissed the complaint against the defendant.

In the other three cases—*Richardson v. Richardson-Merrell, Inc.,*[19] *Brock v. Merrell Dow Pharmaceuticals, Inc.,*[20] and *Oxendine v. Merrell Dow Pharmaceuticals*[21]—jury trials were conducted. In each case, the jury returned a verdict for the plaintiff. The defendants then moved for "judgment notwithstanding the verdict" which, if granted, serves to reverse the jury's verdict and to effectively dismiss the case against the defendant. The motion for was granted by the trial judge in *Richardson* and *Oxendine,* but not in *Brock.* An appeal was filed in all four cases.

In each of these four cases, the plaintiffs presented four kinds of evidence to support the opinions of their expert witnesses: reanalyses of major Bendectin studies; structure-activity data or studies of analogous chemical structures; in vivo animal studies; and in vitro studies on animal tissues. Three different views of the epidemiological and other scientific evidence emerged.

Lynch. In *Lynch,* the evidence failed to survive an initial challenge. The court found the plaintiff's evidence to be inadmissible on the issue of causation and granted summary judgment for the defendant, thus preempting the trial process.

In the opinion of the court, the plaintiff's evidence did not comport with the requirements of Rule 703 of the Federal Rules of Evidence, which permits an expert witness to base an opinion or inference on facts or data outside of personal knowledge if the facts or data are "of a type reasonably relied upon by experts in the particular field."

The court also condemned the use of animal study data and data from studies of analogous chemical structures in a determination of causation, finding the evidence to be of so little probative value as to be inadmissible. It viewed the reanalysis of a major epidemiologic study as "result-oriented" and found it, too, to be inadmissible. The court focused on the fact rather than the substance of the reanalysis: "The plaintiffs cannot merely rely on criticisms of the defendant's studies to establish causation."

The court also affirmed that plaintiffs are precluded from presenting reanalyses alleging methodological or other flaws in epidemiologic studies unless, absent the flaws, the studies "would affirmatively demonstrate that Bendectin is a teratogen at the appropriate level of statistical significance."

The summary judgment was affirmed on appeal.[22] In the course of its decision, the appeals courts noted that the reanalysis relied upon by the plaintiff had not been subjected to peer review or published in a scientific journal.

Richardson and Brock. In the *Richardson* and *Brock* cases, the evidence was not only admissible but, in the opinion of the two juries, it was sufficient to meet the burden of proof on the issue of causation. However, in affirming "judgment notwithstanding the verdict" in *Richardson* and in reversing the trial court's denial of the same in *Brock,* the appeals courts agreed that the opinions of the plaintiffs' expert witnesses were insufficient to demonstrate causation by a preponderance of the evidence. "Judgment notwithstanding the verdict" is proper when there can be only one reasonable conclusion drawn from the evidence.

In both *Richardson* and *Brock,* the courts concluded that no reasonable jury could find on the basis of the evidence presented that Bendectin more likely than not caused the birth defects. These decisions, *Brock* in particular, reveal a closer scrutiny of the data and a willingness by the courts to look behind the experts' conclusions to analyze the adequacy of their foundations. In both cases, the courts concluded that neither in vivo nor in vitro animal studies nor chemical structure analysis data, standing alone or in combination, are capable of proving causation in human beings. Reanalyses of epidemiologic studies that resulted in statistically significant results were found insufficient to support a reasonable inference of causation.

In *Brock,* the court tackled the concepts of relative risk and confidence intervals when determining the sufficiency of the epidemiologic evidence. The court acknowledged the problems created by chance, bias, and confounding variables, but proceeded on the assumption that the use of confidence intervals precluded the need to be concerned about these factors. It placed considerable emphasis on the implications of a confidence interval that included the number 1.0. The court accepted that when this occurred, the results of the study were rendered statistically insignificant.

Using this reasoning, the court discounted the data presented by the plaintiff's expert witness. This included a reanalysis of epidemiologic data that yielded a relative risk of 1.49 but had a confidence interval of 0.17 to 2.0. The court concluded that the lack of "conclusive epidemiological proof" was fatal to the Brock case.

Oxendine. The *Oxendine* case offered a third approach to the plaintiff's evidence on causation.[23] The appeals court reviewed the four types of evidence relied upon by the plaintiff's experts. It granted that each type of evidence, considered separately, established little or nothing. However, the court stated that the trial judge had erred in segregating the evidence in this way. When the results of the individual studies were combined, they formed what the court termed an "evidentiary mosaic" providing a foundation for the opinion of the plaintiff's expert that Bendectin was causally linked to birth defects.[24] The evidence of chemical structure activity provided a "clue" and the in vivo studies raised a "suspicion" of possible teratogenicity. The in vitro studies indicated that the "potential for teratogenicity" existed. Viewing these pieces together with the reanalysis of an epidemiologic study that cited faulty methodology and yielded a relative risk of 1.3–1.8, the court concluded that a reasonable jury could reach a verdict in the plaintiff's favor. Thus, in this case, the court viewed the evidence of causation as sufficient for a jury to conclude that the "preponderance of the evidence" standard has been satisfied.

The Oxendine court also revealed a more flexible approach to several epidemiologic concepts. An expert witness for the plaintiff testified that the mere fact that the number 1 appears in the confidence interval does not invalidate the study; confidence intervals are used to predict the range in which the relative risk would fall if the study were repeated several times, and "the relative risk calculation is the best estimate of the true situation" based on the study data. The court acknowledged the conflict between the parties on this point, and concluded that the contradiction was properly left for resolution by the jury. The court remarked that "the relative risk calculated for a particular study was not carved in stone" and referred to a Merrell Dow witness who calculated the relative risk for his study as 0.95 but admitted that it could also be calculated as 1.37.

Urging the courts to be cautious about setting aside jury verdicts in product liability cases involving difficult issues of causation with expert testimony going both ways, the District of Columbia Court of Appeals reinstated the jury verdict for the plaintiff and remanded the case to the trial court for further proceedings on the issue of punitive damages.

Conclusion

Our goal is not to determine which court took the correct approach or which study or type of scientific evidence has validity but, rather, to question the appropriateness of the process. This process, after all, played a crucial role in the fate of Bendectin.

In toxic tort cases, the courts have indicated that causation cannot be determined in the absence of epidemiologic evidence. Black (1988) acknowledged the developing merger of law and science and urged more thorough judicial review of scientific evidence, both to ensure that expert witnesses are held to the standards of their own disciplines and to ensure the scientific validity of their evidence. In this way, Black argued, irrational and inconsistent decisions may be avoided.

More may be required, however, if judicial scrutiny of scientific evidence is to be meaningful. In both the *Brock* and the *Oxendine* cases, the courts agreed to subject the evidence to the "standards and criteria" of epidemiology. Working with substantially the same types of evidence on precisely the same issue of causation, the two courts interpreted basic rules and principles differently, and ultimately arrived at opposite conclusions about the value of the data.

More help may be required. Perhaps the idea of a "blue, blue ribbon" panel of experts proposed by the court in an early Bendectin case might help resolve issues of causation. The validity of the scientific evidence presented by both plaintiff and defendant could then be exposed to a standardized, systematic critique with an emphasis on study design. This seems preferable to asking a lay jury to resolve conflicts in the evidence, such as that related to the significance of the number 1 in a confidence interval.

It may also be that the "all-or-nothing" result of the "preponderance of the evidence" rule is inappropriate to cases dependent on scientific evidence, as the Bendectin litigation was. A more discrete evidentiary standard could be considered. A toxic agent is rarely the exclusive cause of a given disease. This reality, together with the inherent injustice that may result in some cases where all compensation is denied, has led at least one author to argue for a shift from the traditional evidentiary rule to a standard of proportional liability (Rosenberg 1984). Under this standard, courts would impose liability in proportion to the probability of causation assigned to the substance in question, whether above or below the 50 percent. The uncertainties and imperfections of epidemiologic evidence may find a more honest fit in a system that reflects the subtleties of causation.

Notes

1. Center for the Study of Drug Development, Tufts University, Boston, Massachusetts 02111.

2. The DESI review was instituted by the FDA commissioner to assess the claims and labeling for prescription drugs approved prior to 1962.

3. This is well illustrated in a 1989 publication (40 *Teratology* 151–155) by P. H. Shiono and M. A. Klebanoff reporting on a study of 31,564 newborns. In it, of 58 categories of congenital malformations, three were statistically associated with Bendectin exposure—exactly the number of associations that would be expected by chance [i.e., a manifestation of the multiple comparison effect; cf. chapter 1.—Ed.]. Two of the three, incidentally, were strongly associated with vomiting in the *absence* of Bendectin.

4. Amniotic bands are constricting strips of tissue in the inner of the two fetal membranes.

5. Esophageal atresia refers to a lack of continuity of the esophagus due to failure in development.

6. An encephalocele is extracranial cerebral tissue with a connection to the brain.

7. Exencephaly is a developmental anomaly characterized by an imperfect cranium with the brain lying more or less outside of the skull.

8. In *re Richardson-Merrell, Inc. "Bendectin" Products Liability Litigation,* 624 F. Supp. 1212 (S.D. Ohio 1985).

9. *Ferebee* v. *Chevron Chemical Co.,* 736 F.2d 1529 (D.C. Cir.), *cert. denied,* 469 U.S. 1062 (1984).

10. *Allen* v. *United States,* 588 F. Supp. 247 (D. Utah 1984).

11. In *re "Agent Orange" Products Liability Litigation,* 597 F. Supp. 740 (E.D.N.Y. 1984).

12. *Thompson* v. *United States,* 533 F. Supp. 581 (1981); *Alvarez* v. *United States,* 495 F. Supp. 1188 (1980); *Heyman* v. *United States,* 506 F. Supp. 1145 (S.D. Fl. 1981).

13. *Sterling* v. *Velsicol Chemical Corp.,* 855 F.2d 1188 (6th Cir. 1988).

14. *Brock* v. *Merrell Dow Pharmaceuticals Inc.,* 874 F.2d 307 (5th Cir. 1989).

15. 830 F.2d 1190 (1st Cir. 1987).

16. *Ferebee* v. *Chevron Chemical Co.,* 736 F.2d 1529 (D.C. Cir.), *cert. denied,* 469 U.S. 1062 (1984).

17. *In re Richardson-Merrell Inc.,* 624 F. Supp. at 1228.

18. *Lynch* v. *Merrell-National Laboratories,* 646 F. Supp. 856 (D. Mass. 1986).

19. *In re Richardson-Merrell,* 624 F. Supp. 1212 (S.D. Ohio 1985).

20. *Brock* v. *Merrell Dow Pharmaceuticals Inc.,* 874 F.2d 307 (5th Cir. 1989).

21. *Oxendine* v. *Merrell Dow Pharmaceuticals, Inc.,* 563 A.2d 330 (D.C. App. 1989).

22. 830 F.2d 1190 (1st Cir. 1987).

23. 506 A.2d 1100 (D.C. App. 1986). Further proceedings in this case include a successful motion brought in February 1988 to vacate the judgment in the plaintiff's favor on the basis of misrepresentations by the plaintiff's sole causation witness. On appeal of this decision, the judgment was again reversed and the case remanded to reinstate the jury verdict. *Oxendine* v. *Merrell Dow Pharmaceuticals, Inc.,* 563 A.2d 330 (D.C. App. 1989).

24. *Oxendine,* 506 A.2d at 1110 & 1113 n.9 (D.C. App. 1986).

References

Aselton, P., H. Jick, A. Milunsky, J. R. Hunter, and A. Stergachis. 1985. First-trimester drug use and congenital disorders. 65 *Obstet. & Gynecol.* 451–455.

Black, B. 1988. Evolving legal standards for the admissibility of scientific evidence. 239 *Science* 1508–1512.

Brent, R. R. 1983. The Bendectin saga: Another American tragedy. 27 *Teratology* 283–286.

Brent, R. R. 1985a. Bendectin and interventricular septal defects. 32 *Teratology* 317–318.

Brent, R. R. 1985b. Editorial comment on comments on "Teratogen update: Bendectin." 31 *Teratology* 431–432.

Bunde, C. A., and D. M. Bowles. 1963. A technique for controlled survey of case records. 5 *Cur. Therapeut. Res.* 245–248.

Clarke, M., and D. G. Clayton. 1981. Safety of Debendox. 1 *The Lancet* 659–660. Letter.

Cordero, J. F., G. P. Oakley, F. Greenberg, et al. 1981. Is Bendectin a teratogen? 245 *J. Am. Med. Assn.* 2307–2310.

Dangell, E. T. 1989. Proof of causation in toxic tort cases. 74 *Massachusetts Law Review* 169–178.

Donnai, D., and R. Harris. 1978. Unusual fetal malformations after antiemetics in early pregnancy. 1 *Br. Med. J.* 691–692.

Elbourne, D., L. Mutch, M. Dauncey, H. Campbell, and M. Samphier. 1985. Debendox revisited. 92 *Br. J. Obstet. & Gynecol.* 780–786.

Eskenazi, B., and M. B. Bracken. 1982. Bendectin (Debendox) as a risk factor for pyloric stenosis. 144 *Am. J. Obstet. & Gynecol.* 919–924.

FDC Reports—"The Pink Sheet" T&G-2. 1985. Merrell-Dow's Bendectin unit-of-use package will ensure information. July 5.

Federal Register. 1980. Draft guideline patient package insert; Bendectin and other combination drugs containing doxylamine and vitamin B_6. 45(236) December 5: 80740-80743.

Fisher, J. E., S. J. Nelson, J. E. Allen, and R. S. Holzman. 1982. Congenital cystic adenomatoid malformation of the lung, A unique variant. 136 *Am. J. Dis. Children* 1071–1074.

Fleming, D. M., J. D. E. Knox, and D. L. Crombie. 1981. Debendox in early pregnancy and fetal malformation. 283 *Br. Med. J.* 99–101.

Frith, K. 1978. Fetal malformation after Debendox treatment in early pregnancy. 1 *Br. Med. J.* 925. Letter.

Gibson, G. T., D. P. Colley, A. J. McMichael, and J. M. Hartshorne. 1981. Congenital anomalies in relation to the use of doxylamine/dicyclomine and other antenatal factors, an ongoing prospective study. 1 *Med. J. Australia* 410–413.

Gibson, J. P., R. F. Staples, E. F. Larson, W. L. Kuhn, D. E. Holtkamp, and J. W. Newberne. 1968. Teratology and reproduction studies with an antinauseant. 13 *Tox. & Appl. Pharm.* 439–447.

Golding, J., S. Vivian, and J. A. Baldwin. 1983. Maternal Anti-nauseants and clefts of lip and palate. 2 *Hum. Toxicol.* 63–73.

Grodofsky, M. P., and R. W. Wilmott. 1984. Possible association of use of Bendectin during early pregnancy and congenital lung hypoplasia. 311 *N. Eng. J. Med.* 732. Letter.

Harron, D. W. G., K. Griffiths, and R. G. Shanks. 1980. Debendox and congenital malformations in Northern Ireland. 281 *Br. Med. J.* 1379–1381.

Hayes, Arthur, FDA Commissioner. 1982. Letter to Dr. Sidney Wolfe, Public Citizen's Health Research Group. February 4.

Hayes, Arthur, FDA Commissioner. 1983. Letter to Dr. Sidney Wolfe, Public Citizen's Health Research Group. May 27.

Hendrickx, A. G., M. Cukierski, S. Prahalada, G. Janos, S. Booher, and T. Nyland. 1985. Evaluation of Bendectin embryotoxicity in nonhuman primates. II. Double blind study in term cynomolgus monkeys. 32 *Teratology* 191–194.

Hendrickx, A. G., M. Cukierski, S. Prahalada, G. Janos, and J. Rowland. 1985. Evaluation of Bendectin embryotoxicity in nonhuman primates: I. Ventricular septal defects in prenatal macaques and baboon. 32 *Teratology* 179–189.

Hennekens, C. H., and J. E. Buring. 1987. 3 *Epidemiology in medicine.* 1st ed. Boston: Little, Brown.

Hoffman, R. E. 1984. The use of epidemiologic data in the courts. 120 *Am. J. Epidemiol.* 191–202.

Harter, P. J. 1986. The dilemma of causation in toxic torts. 6 *Regul. Toxicol. & Pharmacol.* 103–107.

Jick, H., L. B. Holmes, J. R. Hunter, S. Madsen, and A. Stergachis. 1981. First-trimester drug use and congenital disorders. 246 *J. Am. Med. Assn.* 343–346 (1981).

Lasagna, L. 1987. Predicting human drug safety from animal studies: current issues. 12 *J. Toxicol. Sci.* 439–450.

Lenz, W. 1988. A short history of thalidomide embryogenesis. 38 *Teratology* 203–215.

MacMahon, B. 1981. More on Bendectin. 246 *J. Am. Med. Assn.* 371–372.

McBride, W. G. 1981. The effects of dicyclomine hydrochloride on the development of the chick embryo. 19 *IRCS J. Med. Sci.* 471.

McBride, W. G. 1984. Teratogenic effect of doxylamine succinate in New Zealand white rabbits. 12 *IRCS J. Med. Sci. & Biochem.* 536–537.

McCredie, J., A. Kricker, J. Elliott, and J. Forrest. 1984. The innocent bystander, doxylamine/dicyclomine/pyridoxine and congenital limb defects, 140 *Med. J. Australia* 525–527.

Mellor, S. 1978. Fetal malformation after debendox treatment in early pregnancy. 1 *Br. Med. J.* 1055–1056. Letter to the editor.

Menzies, C. J. G. 1978. Fetal malformation after debendox treatment in early pregnancy. 1 *Br. Med. J.* 925.

Michaelis, J., H. Michaelis, E. Glück, and S. Koller. 1983. Prospective study of suspected associations between certain drugs administered during early pregnancy and congenital malformations, 27 *Teratology* 57–64.

Milkovich, L., and B. J. van den Berg. 1976. An evaluation of the teratogenicity of certain antinauseant drugs. 125 *Am. J. Obstet. & Gynecol.* 244–248.

Mitchell, A. A., P. J. Schwingl, L. Roesnberg, C. Louik, and S. Shapiro. 1983. Birth defects in relation to Bendectin use in pregnancy, II. Pyloric Stenosis. 147 *Am. J. Obstet. & Gynecol.* 737–742.

Mitchell, A. A., L. Rosenberg, S. Shapiro, and D. Slone. 1981. Birth defects related to Bendectin use in pregnancy, I. Oral clefts and cardiac defects. 245 *J. Am. Med. Assn.* 2311–2314.

Morelock, S., R. Hingson, H. Kayne, E. Dooling, B. Zuckerman, N. Day, J. J. Alpert, and G. Flowerdew. 1982. Bendectin and fetal development, a study at Boston City Hospital. 142 *Am. J. Obstet. & Gynecol.* 209–213.

Morrison, James C. Asst. Director of Regulatory Affairs, National Center for Drugs and Biologics. 1983. Letter to Dr. Sidney Wolfe, Public Citizen's Health Research Group. January 14.

Nelson, M. M., and J. O. Forfar. 1971. Associations between drugs administered during pregnancy and congenital abnormalities of the fetus. 1 *Br. Med. J.* 523–527.

Newman, N. M., J. F. Correy, and G. I. Dudgeon. 1977. A survey of congenital abnormalities and drugs in a private practice. 17 *Aust. N.Z. J. Obstet. & Gynecol.* 156–159.

Paterson, D. C. 1977. Congenital deformities associated with Bendectin. 116 *Can. Med. Assn. J.* 1348. Letter to the editor.

Paterson, D. C. 1969. Congenital deformities. 101 *Can. Med. Assn. J.* 175–176.

Public Citizen's Health Research Group. 1982. Petition to HHS Secretary Richard Schweiker. June 25.

Public Citizen's Health Research Group. 1983. Letter to FDA Commissioner Aruther Hayes. March 17.

Public Health Service. 1990. *Hearing before the Fertility and Maternal Health Drugs Advisory Committee, Department of Health and Human Services, Public Health Service, Food and Drug Administration.* 2 vols. Washington, DC: Government Printing Office.

Restatement (Second) of Torts § 432 (1974). *In* Prosser and Keeton on the Law of Torts 269. 5th ed. Minneapolis: West Publishing, 1984.

Rosenberg, D. 1984. The causal connection in mass exposure cases: A "public law" vision of the tort system. 97 *Harv. L. Rev.* 851–929.

Rothman, K. J., D. C. Fyler, A. Goldblatt, and M. B. Kreidberg. 1979. Exogenous hormones and other drug exposures of children with congenital heart disease. 109 *Am. J. Epidem.* 433–439.

Shapiro, S., O. P. Heinonen, V. Siskind, D. W. Kaufman, R. R. Monson, and D. Slone. 1977. Antenatal exposure to doxylamine succinate and dicyclomine hydro-chloride (Bendectin) in relation to congenital malformations, perinatal mortality rate, birth weight, and intelligence quotient score. 128 *Am. J. Obstet. & Gynecol.* 480–485.

Smithells, R., and S. Sheppard. 1978. Teratogenicity testing in humans: A method demonstrating safety of Bendectin (abstr.). 33 *Obstet. & Gynecol. Survey* 582–584.

Susser, M. 1986. Rules of inference in epidemiology. 6 *Regul. Toxicol. & Pharmacol.* 116–128.

Tyl, R. W., C. J. Price, M. C. Marr, and C. A. Kimmel. 1988. Developmental toxicity evaluation of Bendectin in CD rats. 37 *Teratology* 539–552.

U.S. House Committee on Science and Technology, Subcommittee on Investigations and Oversight. 198. *Effects of prescription drugs during pregnancy.* July 30.

Werler, M. M., B. R. Pober, K. Nelson, and L. B. Holmes. 1989. Reporting accuracy among mothers of malformed and nonmalformed infants. 129 *Am. J. Epidemiol.* 415–421.

Whitehead, G. M., and L. D. Espel. 1988. Proof of causation and damages in toxic tort cases, in American Law Institute—American Bar Association Study Materials 4.

Zierler, S., and K. J. Rothman. 1985. Congenital heart disease in relation to maternal use of Bendectin and other drugs in early pregnancy. 313 *N. Eng. J. Med.* 347–352.

Court Cases

Allen v. *United States,* 588 F. Supp. 247 (D. Utah 1984).

Alvarez v. *United States,* 495 F. Supp. 1188 (D. Col. 1980).

Brock v. *Merrell Dow Pharmaceuticals Inc.,* 874 F.2d 307 (5th Cir. 1989).

Ferebee v. *Chevron Chemical Co.,* 736 F.2d 1529 (D.C. Cir.), *cert. denied,* 469 U.S. 1062 (1984).

Heyman v. *United States*, 506 F. Supp. 1145 (S.D. Fl. 1981).

In re Richardson-Merrell, Inc. "Bendectin" Products Liability Litigation, 624 F. Supp. 1212 (S.D. Ohio 1985).

In re "Agent Orange" Products Liability Litigation, 597 F. Supp. 740 (E.D.N.Y. 1984).

Lynch v. *Merrell-National Laboratories*, 646 F. Supp. 856 (D. Mass. 1986).

Oxendine v. *Merrell Dow Pharmaceuticals*, 506 A.2d 1100 (D.C. App. 1986); 563 A.2d 330 (D.C. App. 1989).

Sterling v. *Velsicol Chemical Corp.*, 855 F.2d 1188 (6th Cir. 1988).

Thompson v. *United States*, 533 F. Supp. 581 (N.D. Okla. 1981).

Biographical Sketch

Louis Lasagna was appointed academic dean of the medical school and dean of the Sackler School of Graduate Biomedical Sciences at Tufts University in July 1984. Prior to that, he was chairman of the Department of Pharmacology and Toxicology (1970–1980) and professor of pharmacology and toxicology of medicine at the University of Rochester School of Medicine and Dentistry. Before moving to Rochester he spent 16 years at the Johns Hopkins University School of Medicine, where he started the first academic group devoted solely to clinical pharmacology. Dr. Lasagna received his M.D. from Columbia University in 1947.

Dr. Lasagna has worked and written extensively in the areas of clinical trial methodology, analgesics, hypnotics, medical ethics, and the placebo effect. He was a member of the Commission on the Federal Drug Approval Process that examined the drug development and approval process and reported its findings to Congress in April 1982. In 1990, Dr. Lasagna was appointed to Secretary Louis Sullivan's "blue ribbon panel" commissioned to examine the Food and Drug Administration.

Sheila Shulman, an attorney, has been a research associate at the Center for the Study of Drug Development at Tufts University since September 1987. From 1981 to 1985, she practiced law in Vancouver, British Columbia. Ms. Shulman received her law degree from the University of British Columbia, and a master's degree in public health from Boston University, and is a graduate of the Toronto Western Hospital and Montreal Neurological Institute nursing programs. At the Center, Ms. Shulman has focused on legal issues related to drug development and the delivery of health care.

6

Miscarriage and Video Display Terminals: An Update

Kenneth R. Foster

The link between miscarriages and use of video display terminals (VDTs) became a public issue around 1980 with the reports of clusters of reproductive mishaps in women users of VDTs. In 1986 I traced the development of the VDT debate (Foster 1986). Now, six years later (and a decade after the controversy began), I describe the current state of the issue.

All together, about a dozen clusters were reported. These included 7 adverse outcomes of 8 pregnancies at the offices of the solicitor general in Ottawa; 10 out of 19 at the offices of the attorney general in Toronto; 7 of 13 at the Air Canada offices at Dorval Airport, Montreal; 8 of 12 at Sears, Roebuck in Dallas, Texas; 10 of 15 at the Defense Logistics Agency in Atlanta; 3 of 5 at Pacific Northwest Bell in Renton, Washington; and 5 of 5 at Surrey Memorial Hospital in Vancouver. The problems included birth defects, spontaneous abortions, respiratory problems in the newborns, Down's syndrome, spina bifida, and premature birth.

Despite attempts by health authorities to investigate the matter, the clusters were never adequately explained. I have been able to locate reports of a follow-up investigation by the U.S. Army Environmental Hygiene Agency of the cluster at the Defense Logistics Agency (Tezak 1981), and by the Centers for Disease Control (1981) of the cluster at Sears, Roebuck. Both verified the existence of a cluster; neither established any apparent link to the women's use of VDTs.

The interpretation of a cluster is problematic. Any unexpected grouping of problems (a cluster) may indicate some problem of public health significance. More commonly, investigation by health authorities of a reported cluster fails to identify a problem that can be remedied by public health measures. However tragic the outcomes may be to the people involved, the grouping of cases may have been a statistical event with no epidemiologic significance. Roughly one pregnancy in five ends in spontaneous abortion (the reported rates vary widely, depending on how early pregnancy is diagnosed); roughly 3 children in a hundred are born with a major birth defect. Simple calculations will show that many clusters will occur every year among the 10 million North American women who use VDTs. The issue, so easily raised, took a decade to resolve.

In the remainder of this chapter, I will summarize two lines of evidence related to the possible reproductive risks from use of VDTs. The first is the many studies on possible teratological effects of electromagnetic fields; the second is the series of progressively more sophisticated epidemiologic studies searching for a possible link between adverse pregnancy outcomes and use of VDTs.

Electromagnetic Fields

Public concern about VDTs has focused on several factors. As judged by contemporary newspaper articles, initial fears concerned possible X-ray emissions from the terminals, no doubt reflecting the scare in the late 1960s about X-ray emission from color television sets (Foster 1986). However, measurements by several government agencies on thousands of terminals showed that X-ray emissions are extremely low and in the overwhelming majority of cases are unmeasurable (Zuk et al. 1983). Emissions of ultraviolet, visible, and infrared radiation are also small, and far below recommended exposure limits. VDTs produce no measurable microwave radiation, notwithstanding one early (incorrect) report by an investigator to the contrary.

In their coverage of the issue, the lay media has frequently mentioned possible effects of low-frequency magnetic fields that are present near the terminals. These fields include components at power-line frequency (50–60 Hz) associated with the power supply, and fields with a more complex time dependence from the coils that move the electron beam around the screen.

The power-frequency fields from VDTs are comparable with those from other appliances; at a distance of 30 cm from the terminal, typical field strengths are a few V/m (electric field) and 4–7 mG (magnetic flux density) (Jokela et al. 1989).

The fields from the beam deflection coils are more complex. If displayed on an oscilloscope, they would resemble a sawtooth wave with a repetition frequency of approximately 20 kHz (for the coils responsible for horizontal beam movement) and 60 Hz (vertical motion). The field from the vertical deflection coil has a peak amplitude of about 10–15 mG at a distance of 30 cm from the screen (Jokela et al. 1989); that from the horizontal deflection coil is smaller but at a higher frequency. The corresponding electric field strength is typically a few volts per meter at a distance of 30 cm from the terminals. These field strengths are far below the levels associated with known hazards of electromagnetic fields (excessive heating of tissues or nerve excitation and shock) and far below recommended exposure limits.

In Vitro and In Vivo Studies

Two lines of evidence are related to the question of possible reproductive risk from VDTs: animal studies and epidemiologic observations on human populations. I consider the first and most confusing of these: animal tests for possible teratogenic effects of low-frequency magnetic fields.

In 1982 Delgado and colleagues reported that chicken eggs exposed to pulsed magnetic fields showed a striking number of malformations in the embryos inside (Delgado et al. 1982; Ubeda et al. 1983). The fields were comparable in strength with those from VDTs but weaker than the earth's magnetic field. Further, the investigators claimed, small changes in the waveshape of the field made a large difference in the rate of the malformations that were induced. Four independent attempts to confirm the findings were unsuccessful (Maffeo et al. 1984; Stuchly et al. 1988; Sandstrom et al. 1986; Sisken et al. 1986).

Delgado's findings were widely reported in the lay media, often with speculation about their possible significance to hazards from fields from VDTs and other appliances. The unsuccessful attempts at replication received little media attention.

Project HenHouse

To address the questions that the Delgado studies raised, the US Office of Naval Research commissioned at great expense a multi-laboratory replication of the original study, under the name Project HenHouse. Six laboratories in the United States, Canada, and Europe conducted replicate experiments, using the same techniques, identical exposure apparatus, and precisely measured fields (Berman et al. 1990). Each experiment involved the exposure of fertilized chicken eggs to pulsed magnetic fields, and subsequent examination of the embryos.

The outcome of Project HenHouse was very puzzling. Four of the laboratories—including that of (now retired) Delgado—found no statistically significant differences in the rate of malformations in the exposed versus control eggs. A fifth laboratory reported a borderline-significant increase. The sixth reported a statistically significant increase (but a smaller one than originally reported by Delgado et al.). If the results of all six studies are combined, they indicate a borderline significant increase in rate of malformations in the exposed eggs—in contrast with the very striking effect originally reported by Delgado et al. (Berman et al. 1990).

Thus, the results of Project HenHouse were neither clearly positive nor clearly negative. The simplest interpretation is that five of the six studies were negative, and that the one positive study was different in some important respect from the other five. Whether the sixth was in error or whether there is something important in its results is a question that cannot at present be answered.

The latest development in this episode is the preliminary report by Litovitz et al. (1992) of a teratogenic effect of weak magnetic fields on chicken eggs. Litovitz claimed that the critical variable of exposure is the "coherence" of the field. As of this writing these results have not been published; whether they will be confirmed and accepted by other scientists remains to be seen.

In retrospect, Delgado's study probably did not merit the widespread attention it received. The biological system (fertilized chicken eggs) differs too much from human embryos for the test to have much value for risk assessment; on the other hand it is too complex to be of much use for basic scientific research on mechanisms of interaction of fields with biological systems. Chickens are genetically very diverse, and are notoriously variable in the frequency of chick malformations and fertility of eggs. Finally, a project officer from the Office of Naval Research who visited Delgado's lab (Thomas C. Rozzell, private communication) told me that the initial study used poorly characterized fields and was (I judge) of poor quality.

After ten years of research on the "Delgado effect" with so little to show for it, funding agencies and most scientists have lost interest in the matter. As well they should.

Other Animal Studies

Since the early 1980s, at least 17 animal studies have been searched for effects of pulsed magnetic fields on animal embryos. Berman (1990) provide a comprehensive review. The literature is very inconsistent, with some studies reporting effects and others (including attempts to replicate earlier positive findings) finding none. Berman concludes

. . . we cannot clearly relate an increase in the incidence of abnormal embryos resulting from exposure to pulsed magnetic fields to any patterns of pulse frequency, field intensity, pulse shape, or rate of change in the intensity. . . . Until the important variables in pulsed magnetic fields are determined and the mechanism of effects is identified, it may not be possible to extrapolate such effects to humans. (1990, p. 47)

This conflates two issues. The first is the absence of any clearly reproducible phenomena. Until some reproducible phenomenon appears, with some defined relation between dose and response, that can be consistently observed by independent investigators, it will be difficult to draw any conclusions from the data. The second is the relevance of these results to human health, assuming that the effects themselves are real. That depends on the biological similarity between the animal subjects and humans, the exposure conditions, and other factors. Whether these studies will point to a mechanism for human injury is, at present, a matter of speculation.

Epidemiologic Evidence

A much clearer picture has emerged from the epidemiologic studies. By now, a dozen epidemiologic studies have been conducted in the United States, Canada, Finland, Sweden, and elsewhere on reproductive problems associated with use of VDTs. (A good, but dated, review is Blackwell and Chang 1988.) They have been overwhelmingly—but not totally—negative, finding no links between use of VDTs and spontaneous abortion or birth defects.

The studies vary widely in their methods, and I will not review them in detail here. Table 6.1 summarizes their results in terms of the *relative risk,* which is the incidence of an undesired consequence in VDT users divided by that in otherwise similar nonusers (see chapter 1). The table also shows the 95 percent confidence intervals, *i.e.,* margins of sampling error in the studies. Virtually all of the results indicate no increase in risk associated with use of VDTs. But some of these studies did report positive or equivocal findings, which has helped to keep the issue alive. The most widely publicized of these studies was that of Goldhaber et al. (1988), who reported a 1.8-fold increase in risk of miscarriage among women who worked with VDTs for more than 20 hours a week during their first trimester of pregnancy. This increase was at the edge of statistical significance.

Goldhaber's study was generally well done, but it had one major weakness that resulted from its retrospective design. To determine the subjects' use of VDTs during pregnancy, the investigators sent them a questionnaire, as much as three years after their pregnancies. The investigators did not independently verify the subjects' actual use of the terminals. At the time the study was conducted, the possible reproductive hazards of VDTs were well publicized; it is likely, as the investigators themselves suggested, that women with adverse pregnancy outcomes

Table 6.1
Epidemiologic studies on reproductive outcomes and VDT use

Study (date)	Number of pregnancies studied	Odds ratio (95% confidence interval)	
		Spontaneous abortion (group with highest VDT use)	Birth defects (group with highest VDT use)
Kurppa (1984,1985) (case-control)	2950	(n/a)	0.9 (0.6–1.2)
Ericson (1986) (case-control)	1447	1.2 (0.9–1.7) (>10 hrs/wk exposure)	2.0 (1.2–3.2)
Westerholm (1987) (cohort)	4117	no difference	no difference
McDonald (1986) (case-control)	56012	1.12 (0.92–1.35)	0.94 (0.72–1.22)
McDonald (1988) (ecologic survey)	6876	1.06 (0.8–1.4) (current pregnancy) 1.01 (0.7–1.3) (previous pregnancy)	0.94 (0.8–1.1) (current pregnancy) 1.12 (0.89–1.43) (previous pregnancy)
Butler (1986) (cross-sectional)	728	1.13 (0.55–2.24) (>20 hrs/wk exposure)	(n/a)

Study	Sample size		
Nurminen (1988) (case-control)	613	0.8 (0.5–1.4) ("threatened abortion")	(n/a)
Goldhaber (1988) (case-control)	1575	1.8 (1.2–2.8) (>20 hrs/wk exposure)	1.4 (0.7–2.9)
Bryant (1989) (case-control)	1002	1.07 (0.54–2.11)	(n/a)
Brandt (1990) (population-based)	6541	0.75 (1.4–0.5) (>30 hrs/wk exposure)	0.9 (1.9–0.4) (>30 hrs/wk exposure)
Windham (1990) (case-control)	1361	1.2 (0.87–1.6) (>20 hrs/wk exposure)	(n/a)
Schnorr (1991) (cohort)	882	0.90 (0.55–1.47) (>25 hrs/wk exposure)	(n/a)

Note: (n/a) – not measured.

might have been more likely than other women to report using VDTs. Goldhaber's study was widely reported in the lay media, without the careful reservations of the investigators, and usually without mention of the negative findings of the other studies.

The most recent, and undoubtably the best, study on reproductive risk of VDTs was published early in 1991 in the *New England Journal of Medicine* by Schnorr and colleagues. The investigators, working for the National Institute for Occupational Safety and Health (NIOSH), conducted a retrospective cohort study that compared groups of telephone operators who used VDTs with telephone operators in otherwise similar jobs who did not. The investigators found no link between spontaneous abortion and use of VDTs during the first trimester of pregnancy. Whether this study will end the VDT debate remains to be seen.

The epidemiologic literature on the VDT-miscarriage question frequently mentions the great difficulty of measuring reproductive risk. These problems are not reflected in the 95 percent confidence intervals in the table, which show only the statistical uncertainties due to sampling error.

For example, several of the papers listed in the table discuss at length the problem of reporting bias, which might be introduced if not all of the subjects in a study were equally likely to report use of VDTs during their pregnancies. Two studies (Goldhaber et al. 1988; McDonald et al. 1988) mentioned this as a possible explanation for a small apparent excess of miscarriages among VDT users.

Another problem is the difficulty of reliably detecting miscarriages that occur early in pregnancy. Because of this difficulty, an investigator has a choice of including only miscarriages that occur after a month or more of pregnancy (and thus missing a large fraction of all miscarriages), or of including earlier miscarriages and finding some way to determine precisely when the subjects became pregnant. Most studies choose the former approach.

Still another difficulty arises from the many different birth defects that can occur. A study that retrospectively examines medical records for any association between birth defects and use of VDTs can, therefore, make many different comparisons. However, by the statistical tests that most scientists adopt, 1 comparison out of 20 will show a difference that is statistically significant—even if there is no real difference in the groups being compared. (This problem is discussed in chapter 1, and again in chapter 4.)

Because of these and other problems, one can never achieve complete consistency in epidemiologic studies—but the dozen studies summarized in the table come pretty close. They certainly rule out the large increases in risk that some people inferred from the clusters.

Recently, public concern has shifted to the much more difficult question of possible risks from the *fields* associated with the terminals, which these studies do not directly address. In the NIOSH study, for example, both the VDT and non-VDT operators were exposed to similar levels of 60 Hz electromagnetic fields from the equipment they used. Consequently, the study is inconclusive on the question of hazard from fields. This point was raised in a letter to the editor of *Science News* from the president of a company that makes radiation shields for VDTs (Doilney 1991).

An adequate epidemiologic study on reproductive risk from 60 Hz fields from VDTs would be very hard to mount. The NIOSH investigators measured the fields from the terminals, and found them to be comparable to those from many other sources in the environment.

The latest development in this issue is a preliminary report of a Finnish epidemiologic study (Hietanen et al. 1992) of a 3.5-fold increase in risk of miscarriage in VDT operators who were exposed to extremely low frequency magnetic fields greater than 9 mG from the terminals. The study has not been published as of this writing and there is no way to judge its quality. Sweden has recently adopted strict emission standards for VDTs, which will result in lower public exposure (whatever the risks).

Other Problems Associated with Use of VDTs

Of greater concern to many scientists and health authorities have been diverse ergonomic and psychosocial problems associated with the use of computers in the workplace (World Health Organization 1989).

Ergonomic problems are associated with workstation design, glare, legibility of display, seating, and keyboard height. A panel assembled by the U.S. National Research Council judged radiation hazards to be highly unlikely, and focused in its report on issues such as glare, legibility of video displays, and background lighting (National Academy of Sciences 1983).

Perhaps more important still are psychosocial problems. To my mind the fundamental problem is that many clerical workers using VDTs simply have lousy jobs. A data entry operator who spends the day keying numbers into a computer, with every keystroke counted, little opportunity for personal interaction, and rigid performance standards to meet might well experience emotional and perhaps physical problems. If only radiation shielding could fix such problems!

Carpal tunnel syndrome (CTS) is a painful condition associated with repetitive motions of the hand, that afflicts workers in many occupations, including VDT operators. CTS arises from compression of the median nerve as it passes through a small opening (the carpal tunnel) in the wrist (Spinner et al. 1989); and can be relieved by a simple operation. The problem has been reported among workers in diverse occupations, including meat cutting and clerical workers, but there are few reliable data on its incidence and the medical literature on CTS is sketchy and anecdotal. The syndrome is clearly a matter of concern to VDT operators and their employers, and might be prevented by better keyboard design or other ergonomic considerations. Clearly, more study on CTS is needed.

Other, less well defined, health problems have been reported from use of VDTs (Bergqvist 1989; Council on Scientific Affairs 1987). Since the mid-1980s, there have been scattered reports of rashes and other skin problems among VDT users; follow-up studies have been unable to find the cause of the problem or associate it with the terminals or other factors in the office environment. This has, however, led to at least one lawsuit (see "The Legal Context" at the end of Part I).

On reviewing the history of the VDT debate, I am struck by the great disparity between the ease with which concerns about reproductive hazards from the terminals were raised, and the great difficulty in adequately addressing them. The clusters, in retrospect, were probably chance events of no epidemiologic significance. But the question of whether use of VDTs increases reproductive risk took ten years and a dozen studies to address, and (from a recent preliminary report) it has still not been settled. It is time to focus instead on the more serious ergonomic and psychosocial problems associated with use of computers in the workplace.

References

Berg, M. 1988. Skin problems in workers using visual display terminals—a study of 201 patients. 19 *Contact Dermatitis* 335–341.

Bergqvist, U. 1989. Possible health effects of working with VDUs. 46 *Br. J. Indus. Med.* 217–221.

Berman, E., L. Chacon, D. House, B. A. Koch, W. E. Koch, J. Leal, S. Lovtrup, E. Mantiply, A. H. Martin, G. I. Martucci, K. H. Mild, J. C. Monahan, M. Sandstrom, K. Shamsaifer, R. Tell, M. A. Trillo, A. Ubeda, and P. Wagner. 1990. Development of chicken embryos in a pulsed magnetic field. 11 *Bioelectromagnetics* 169–187.

Berman, E. 1990. The developmental effects of pulsed magnetic fields on animal embryos. 4 *Repro. Toxicol.* 45–49.

Blackwell, R., and A. Chang. 1988. Video display terminals and pregnancy. A review. 95 *Br. J. Obstet. & Gynaecol.* 446–453.

Brandt, L. P. A., and C. V. Nielsen. 1990. Congenital malformations among children of women working with video display terminals. 16 *Scand. J. Work Environ. & Health* 329–33.

Bryant, H. E., E. J. Love. 1989. Video display terminal use and spontaneous abortion risk. 18 *Int. J. Epidemiol.* 132–8.

Butler, W. J., and K. A. Brix. 1986. Video display terminal work and pregnancy outcome in Michigan clerical workers. In *Allegations of reproductive hazards from VDUs*. Nottingham UK: *Humane Technology* 67–91.

Centers for Disease Control, Family Planning Evaluation Division. 1981. Cluster of spontaneous abortions. Report EPI-80-113-2.

Council on Scientific Affairs. 1987. Health effects of video display terminals. 257 *J. Am. Med. Assn.* 1508–1512.

Delgado, J. M. R., J. Leal. J. L. Monteagudo and M. G. Gracia. 1982. Embryological changes induced by weak extremely low frequency electromagnetic fields. 134 *J. Anat.* 533–551.

Doilney, J. A. 1991. *Science News* 387. June 22. Letter to the editor.

Ericson, A., and B. Källén. 1986. An epidemiological study of work with video screens and pregnancy outcome: II. A case-control study. 9 *Am. J. Indus. Med.* 459–475.

Foster, K. R. 1986. The VDT debate. 74 *Am. Scientist* 163–168.

Goldhaber, M. K., M. R. Polen, and R. A. Hiatt. 1988. The risk of miscarriage and birth defects among women who use visual display units during pregnancy. 13 *Am. J. Indus. Med.* 695–706.

Hietanen, M., M. L. Lindbohm, P. von Nandelstadh, P. Kyyrönen, and M. Sallmén. 1992. Effects of exposure to magnetic fields of VDTs on miscarriages (abstr), 1st Congress of the European Bioelectromagnetics Association, Brussels, Belgium. January.

Jokela, K., J. Aaltonen, and A. Lukkarinen. 1989. Measurements of electromagnetic emissions from video display terminals at the frequency range from 30 Hz to 1 MHz. 57 *Health Physics* 79–88.

Edström, R., and B. Källén. 1985. Dataskarmsarbete och graviditet. 82 *Lakartidningen* 687–688.

Kurppa, K., P. C. Holmberg, K. Rantala, and T. Nurminen. 1984. Birth defects and video display terminals, 2 *The Lancet* 1339.

Kurppa, K., P. C. Holmberg, K. Rantala, T. Nurminen, and L. Saxen. 1985. Birth defects and exposure to video display terminals during pregnancy. 11 *Scand. J. Work Environ. Health* 353–356.

Maffeo, S., M. W. Miller and E. L. Carstensen. 1984. Lack of effect of weak low frequency electromagnetic fields on chick embryogenesis. 139 *J. Anat.* 613–618.

Mackay, C. J. 1989. Work with visual display terminals: psychosocial aspects and health. 31 *J. Occup. Med.* 957–968.

McDonald, A. D., N. M. Cherry, C. Delorme, and J. C. McDonald. 1986. Visual display units and pregnancy: evidence from the Montreal Study. 28 *J. Occup. Med.* 1226–1231.

McDonald, A. D., J. C. McDonald, B. Armstrong, N. Cherry, A. D. Nolin, and D. Robert. 1988. Work with visual display units in pregnancy. 45 *Br. J. Indus. Med.* 509–515.

Miller, D. A. 1974. Electric and magnetic fields produced by commercial power systems. In J. G. Llaurado, A. Sances, and J. H. Battocletti, eds., *Biologic and clinical effects of low-frequency magnetic and electric fields* 62–70. C. Thomas.

National Academy of Sciences. 1983. *Video displays, work, and vision*. Washington DC: National Academy Press.

Nurminen, T., and K. Kurppa. 1988. Office employment, work with video display terminals, and course of pregnancy. Reference mothers' experience from a Finnish case-referent study of birth defects. 14 *Scand. J. Work Environ. Health* 293–298.

Sandstrom, M., K. H. Mild, and S. Lovtrup. 1986. Effects of weak pulsed magnetic fields on chick embryogenesis. In *Proceedings of the International Scientific Conference: Work with video display units* 60–63. Stockholm: Swedish National Board of Occupational Safety.

Schnorr, T. M., B. A. Grajewski, R. W. Hornung, M. J. Thun, G. M. Egeland, W. E. Murray, D. L. Conover, and W. E. Halperin. 1991. Video display terminals and the risk of spontaneous abortion. 324 *N. Eng. J. Med.* 727–733.

Sisken, B. F., C. Fowler, J. P. Mayaud, J. P. Ryaby, J. Ryaby, and A. Pilla. 1986. Pulsed electromagnetic fields and normal chick development. 5 *J. Bioelec.* 25–34 (1986).

Slesin, L., and M. Zybko. 1983. *Video display terminals: Health and safety*. New York: *Microwave News* 41–46.

Spinner, R. J., J. W. Bachman, and P. C. Amadio. 1989. The many faces of carpal tunnel syndrome. 64 *Mayo Clinic Proc.* 829–836.

Stuchly, M. A., et al. 1988. Teratological assessment of exposure to time-varying magnetic field. 38 *Teratology* 461–466.

Ubeda, A., J. Leal, M. A. Trillo, A. Jimenez, and J. M. R. Delgado. 1983. Pulse shape of magnetic fields influences chick embryogenesis. 137 *J. Anat.* 513–536.

Tezak, R. W. 1981. Investigations of adverse pregnancy outcomes. Service Report 66-32-1359-81. Aberdeen Proving Ground MD: U.S. Army Environmental Hygiene Agency, Defense Contract Administration.

Wahlberg, J. E., and C. Lidén. 1988. Is the skin affected by work with visual display terminals? 6 *Occup. Dermatoses* 81–85.

Westerholm, P., and A. Ericson. 1987. Pregnancy outcome and VDU-work in a cohort of insurance clerks. In B. Knave, P. G. Widebäck, eds., *Work with display units* 86, at 87–93. Amsterdam: Elsevier.

Windham, G. C., L. Fenster, S. H. Swan, and R. R. Neutra. 1990. Use of video display terminals during pregnancy and risk of spontaneous abortion, low birthweight, or intrauterine growth retardation. 18 *Am. J. Indus. Med.* 675–688.

Zuk, W. M., M. A. Stuchly, P. Dvorak, and Y. Deslauriers. 1983. Investigations of radiation emissions from video display terminals. Public Affairs Directorate, Dept. of Health and Welfare Canada, Report 83-EHD-91.

The Legal Context

Spermicides

Katie Wells was born on July 1, 1981, with tragic birth defects. Her mother successfully sued Ortho Pharmaceutical, blaming that company's spermicidal jelly, Ortho-Gynol (Bernstein 1990). The active ingredient in the gel is nonoxynol-9, also used in most other contraceptive foams, gels, and sponges, and on many condoms.

The case was tried in federal court without a jury.[1] The trial judge, Marvin Shoob, decided that the statistical studies offered by experts were inconclusive as to whether nonoxynol caused Katie Wells's birth defects. He cited several studies in his decision, but only one of them directly investigated a relationship between spermicide use and birth defects of the sort that afflicted Katie. That study had been reviewed by the Food and Drug Administration, which found it inconclusive. One of the authors of the study appeared as a witness at the trial, and warned the court not to construe the study as proving a link between spermicides and birth defects. Judge Shoob, he later remarked, had either ignored or failed to understand his testimony.[2]

In the end, Judge Shoob based his opinion on his evaluation of the "demeanor and tone" of each expert. He ultimately declared that defects in Katie's left arm and shoulder and her right hand were caused by the spermicide, while her cleft lip, nostril deformity, and right optic nerve defect were not. He awarded the plaintiffs $5.1 million.

Ortho appealed; the appelate court upheld the decision but reduced the award to $4.7 million. The court declared that the plaintiffs were not required to produce scientific studies showing a statistically significant association between spermicides and birth defects or to defer to two Food and Drug Administration studies that had found no link between spermicides and birth defects. Judge Shoob's finding was not "clearly erroneous," the court reasoned, so the appellate judges would not displace his decision. The U.S. Supreme Court refused to review the case.

The opinion was immediately and widely criticized in the medical community. The *Wells* decision, declared two doctors in the *New England Journal of Medicine,* "indicate[s] that courts will not be bound by reasonable standards of scientific proof. . . . The plaintiff won despite testimony citing the considerable medical evidence that spermicides do not cause birth defects . . . legal cases can now be decided on the type of evidence that the scientific community rejected decades ago."[3]

At that time, Ortho had "less than a handful" of similar suits pending. According to an Ortho lawyer, those suits "never got anywhere."[4] One suit had been filed in the same federal district as *Wells* at about the same time. Because of procedural delays the case was not decided until 1991. The court found for Ortho, noting that "the scientific community has arrived at a consensus that spermicide does not cause birth defects. . . ."[5]

Bendectin

Bendectin, a drug used to alleviate morning sickness, was introduced by what would later become Merrell Dow Pharmaceuticals in 1957.[6] In subsequent years, over 33 million women used the drug worldwide. In the 1960s, Dow Chemical, Merrell's parent company, had sought permission to market thalidomide in the United States. Thalidomide was never approved for use here, though it was widely distributed in Europe before its tragic link to birth defects was discovered.

Reports of a link between Bendectin and birth defects (especially limb defects) began to surface in the 1960s. The first major U.S. suit, *Mekdeci v. Merrell Nat'l Laboratories,*[7] was not filed, however, until 1977.

Elizabeth Mekdeci had taken Bendectin for morning sickness during her second pregnancy. Her son David was later born with a malformed arm and a caved-in chest. After exhaustive research and communication with the FDA, she decided that the evidence pointed to Bendectin as the source of her son's defects. She sued Bendectin's manufacturers, and in 1980 a Federal District Court jury awarded her and her husband $20,000 for medical expenses. They did not award anything to young David, however. Merrell asked the trial court for a new trial, pointing to the inconsistency of a jury's awarding medical expenses to the parents but nothing to the child allegedly injured by the product: the bizarre verdict could only mean that the jury had found no link between Bendectin and the child's injuries but had decided to award the parents something anyway. The trial judge granted a new trial, which ended in a verdict for the defense. The verdict was upheld by the Eleventh Circuit Court of Appeals in 1983.

In the interim, however, the Mekdeci litigation and associated publicity (including a melodramatic account in the *National Enquirer*[8]) had triggered a rush of litigation that, as of this writing in mid-1992, is still in progress.

In the next major Bendectin case, a Washington, D.C., jury awarded young Mary Oxendine $750,000, but District of Columbia Superior Court Judge Joseph M. Hannon overturned the award, declaring that no jury could reasonably have found Merrell responsible for Oxendine's birth defects.[9] The plaintiffs appealed, and the D.C. Court of Appeals reversed the trial judge and restored the jury's verdict for the plaintiff. The case, the court reasoned, presented a "classic battle of the experts"; it was therefore up to the jury to decide whom to believe. On remand in 1988, Superior Court Judge Peter H. Wolf granted Merrell's subsequent motion for a new trial after Merrell accused Dr. Alan K. Done, the plaintiff's only expert witness, of lying in court. Judge Wolf stated that Dr. Done's statements about his credentials had been "so deliberately false that *all* his testimony on behalf of plaintiff is suspect." The plaintiffs, however, successfully appealed Judge Wolf's decision. As of this writing, the *Oxendine* verdict still stands.

Soon after the first-round *Oxendine* verdict, U.S. District Chief Judge Carl B. Rubin of Cincinnati aggregated all 750 of the pending Bendectin cases and certified a class action. Without admitting any liability, Merrell offered $120 million in settlement of all pending and future Bendectin claims. Most of the plaintiffs' lawyers agreed, but a small group of dissenters managed to torpedo the deal on appeal to the Sixth Circuit. The appellate court ruled that Judge Rubin had exceeded his authority by forbidding plaintiffs who disliked the settlement offer to opt out of the class. Merrell then withdrew its settlement offer and went to trial. By this time more than 1,100 claims had been consolidated in Judge Rubin's courtroom.[10]

To prevent any emotional appeal to jury fears and sympathy, Judge Rubin banned the word "thalidomide"—as well as all visibly deformed children—from his courtroom. He "trifurcated" the trial; in the first round the jury would decide only whether Bendectin does cause birth defects. (Subsequent rounds, if needed, would determine negligence or strict liability, and then the measure of damages.) After hearing the testimony of 19 experts, the jury found that Bendectin did not cause the birth defects. The Court of Appeals upheld that verdict; the U.S. Supreme Court denied further review.

In subsequent suits, Merrell sought unsuccessfully to avoid retrying the issue of causation again and again by invoking the doctrine of collateral estoppel. In the opening round of *Lynch v. Merrell-National Laboratories,*[11] for example, the trial court granted summary judgment for Merrell on both causation and collateral estoppel grounds. The First Circuit Court of Appeals upheld the ruling, but only on the issue of causation.

Since that time Bendectin cases have been litigated painstakingly, one by one. Carita Richardson's mother, for example, took three Bendectin tablets a day in the early stages of her pregnancy; Carita was born with grave limb deformities. The Richardsons had originally been part of the class action in Cincinnati but had opted out and filed suit individually in federal court, in Washington, D.C.[12] The case was submitted to the jury in stages: first on causation, then on liability and damages. This time the jury found for the plaintiff, and awarded $1.16 million. Trial Judge Thomas Penfield Jackson overturned the verdict. "Though [plaintiff's expert] might disagree," he wrote, "there is now nearly a universal scientific consensus that Bendectin has not been shown to be a teratogen, and, the issue being a scientific one, reasonable jurors could not reject that consensus without indulging in precisely the same speculation and conjecture which the multiple investigations undertook, but failed, to confirm." The District of Columbia Circuit Court of Appeals affirmed.

In the wake of *Richardson,* the District of Columbia Circuit disposed of two other plaintiffs' verdicts in Bendectin cases—one involving a $95 million verdict, including $75 million dollars in punitive damages.[13] The Fifth Circuit overturned yet another jury award, declaring that "unproven medical speculation lacking any sort of consensus" had no probative value.[14] In denying a petition for rehearing, the court warned that judges should "be especially vigilant in scrutinizing the basis, reasoning and statistical significance" of epidemiologic studies.

So far, Merrell has been extremely successful in its litigation. Dozens of cases have been decided on the merits in Merrell's favor,[15] including at least 15 cases that were disposed of summarily.[16] Other than *Oxendine,* the only case that Merrell lost was *Raynor v. Merrell Dow Pharmaceuticals,*[17] but in the wake of *Richardson* and *Ealy,* that verdict will most likely be overturned; as of this writing, a motion for a judgment withstanding the verdict is pending. In early October, 1991, however, a Texas jury handed down a more than $30 million verdict against Merrell, which was later reduced by the trial court to approximately $20 million;[18] how this verdict will fare on appeal in the Texas court system is far from clear. Other cases continue to be litigated across the country.[19] One case (*Daubert v. Merrell-Dow*) was recently accepted for review by the U.S. Supreme Court. The issue is the *Frye* rule and scientific testimony (*N.Y. Times* Jan. 2, 1993).

Bendectin was withdrawn from the market on June 9, 1983. According to the American College of Obstetrics and Gynecology, Merrell Dow's decision to discontinue the production of Bendectin "create[d] a significant therapeutic gap."[20] "We wouldn't bring Bendectin back," a Merrell spokesman declared, even "if we won every lawsuit."[21]

Electromagnetic Fields

Do low-frequency electromagnetic fields cause cancer and other diseases? Recent litigation has blamed the extremely-low-frequency (ELF) fields from electric power lines and other sources for promoting cancer, leukemia, changes in behavior and mood, sleep disruption, chronic diarrhea, Crohn's disease (a chronic digestive ailment), and hormonal changes that might entail reproductive disorders. (Foster reviews the cancer issue in chapter 3.)

Initially, most of the litigation concerning electromagnetic fields concerned the siting of high-voltage transmission lines or other facilities, or land condemnation issues, and involved health concerns and other issues. There have been an increasing number of tort cases, seeking compensation for actual or feared injuries from exposure to fields.

The first important modern lawsuit began in the 1970s in New York, when the Public Utility Commission (an environmental group) sued the Power Authority of the State of New York to prevent the construction of a proposed 765 kV transmission line, citing health concerns. The case was settled, with an agreement that the line would be constructed with a wider right-of-way than originally planned, and that the utilities constructing it would establish a $5 million fund to study the possible health hazards of power lines. (This fund was administered by the State of New York, in what became the New York Power Lines Project that is mentioned in chapter 3.)

In this trial, the health concerns raised by the plaintiffs mostly concerned the strong electric fields that exist beneath the lines. Gradually, in other cases, health concerns began to shift to the magnetic fields associated with high-voltage transmission lines, and then, to magnetic fields associated with other distribution facilities and appliances.

In 1981, Houston Lighting and Power Company (HL&P) sought government condemnation of a 100-foot-wide strip of land across which it proposed to run part of a 79.2-mile, 345 kV transmission line. The strip ran next to the campuses of two schools owned by the Klein Independent School District. The district was awarded $78,000 for giving up the property.[22] HL&P took possession of the property and constructed the transmission line, which was energized in 1984.

The district objected all along, and in November 1985 added to its other complaints a claim that locating the power line on its property reflected "a callous disregard for the safety, health, and well-being of the 3,000 plus children" attending school nearby.

When the issue came to court, each side presented expert testimony on the health effects of high-voltage transmission lines. For the school district, Dr. Marvin Chadkoff testified that he had measured magnetic flux densities of 6 to 10 milligauss from the line at the school complex, some 300 feet from the line. Dr. Nancy Wertheimer testified about the studies she and others had conducted that suggested a correlation between magnetic fields and cancer (her study is reviewed in chapter 3). She concluded that children at each of the schools would probably experience an increased risk of cancer. Another expert, Dr. Jerry Phillips, testified that his laboratory studies indicated that exposure to electromagnetic fields accelerates growth of cancer cells. (As described in chapter 3, these studies have been contested by other scientists, who could not confirm their results.) He concluded that the children attending the schools faced a significantly increased risk of cancer. A final witness for the school district did not claim to know whether the lines actually posed a threat to the schoolchildren's health, but objected to what he characterized as an "inadvertent prospective experiment" on the children.

The power company responded that the fields were much weaker than the plaintiffs claimed, and that the scientific evidence of risk was far too speculative. Dr. Edwin Carstensen, an expert witness for the defense, said his measurements showed the maximum magnetic flux density at the school to be 1.5 to 2 milligauss, which is typical of magnetic fields found in normal home environments. Employees of the company, some of whose children attended the schools in question, testified that the lines would cause no adverse health effects. Among other HL&P experts, Dr. Carstensen criticized Wertheimer's and Phillips' use of unreliable epidemiologic studies. He testified that the mainstream scientific community has found no reliable evidence of adverse health effects.

As the case was presented, the jury did not actually have to resolve the competing safety claims; it had only to determine whether HL&P's actions constituted an "abuse of discretion," and whether the decision to run the line near the schools had been made "according to reason or judgment." The jury awarded the school district $104,275 in actual damages, and added a $25 million punitive verdict.

HL&P appealed. The punitive damages award was struck down on a technicality; the award for actual damages was upheld. The Supreme Court of Texas refused further review. HL&P then relocated the power line and paid the award. It still faced a separate suit over the same power line by a Houston couple who alleged that electromagnetic fields "caused at least an aggravation" of their cancer, which was later dismissed.

Faced with the difficulty of proving actual harm from electromagnetic fields, other plaintiffs have based their claims on fear of harm rather than on harm itself. In 1982, the San Diego Gas & Electric Company sought to run a power line over property belonging to the Daley family known as Rancho Jamul. The company offered $110,000 for the easement; the Daleys refused the offer. They demanded, instead, compensation for the loss of resale value of their entire property, a loss they maintained was inevitable given the public's fear and uncertainty about power line hazards. The trial judge barred the electric company from trying to prove that power lines do not, in reality, cause any health problems. As the judge saw it, the issue is not whether there really is a hazard but whether "there is a controversy as to the existence or no[n] existence of a magnetic field under high power lines, and that conflicting opinion or controversy is known by people who develop property . . . and that it plays some part in the development of property and has a negative impact so far as developers are concerned." The court would not look deeper into the basis of the scientific controversy, nor would it attempt to resolve whether fear of ELF fields is scientifically reasonable. By a 9-3 vote, the jury awarded the plaintiffs $1,035,000. (The jury also awarded interest and court costs for a grand total of more than $2 million dollars.) A California appellate court upheld the award.[23]

A similar approach was taken by a New York State landowner, who sued the New York Power Authority when it sought an easement to run a 345 kV power line across his land.[24] Initially, the plaintiff claimed that "dangerous levels of electromagnetic fields and other pollutants will emanate from the transmission line, causing biological effects resulting in health hazards and a carcinogenic atmosphere, rendering said area unsafe to reside thereon, cancer phobia, and being otherwise dangerous to the health of humans, flora and fauna." He later amended his complaint to drop the health claims, instead basing his suit on the claim that "the present state of science and the attendant publicity emanating throughout the nation that buyers have 'fear' of health risks associated with these lines." The trial judge, however, refused to follow in the tracks of the *Daley* litigation; under New York law, the judge ruled, there would have to be "proof of the existence of reasonable grounds for the fear."

New York precedent held that "some vague and ungrounded fear cannot form a basis for the recovery of consequential damage, as any such damage would be speculative and capricious in nature. Only a reluctance to purchase based on the reasonable apprehension of a potential purchaser should be considered." The most the plaintiff was able to establish, the trial judge ultimately concluded, was there is a need "for further scientific examination." This was not sufficient basis for "a reasonable fear that power lines cause health hazards." Most courts that have dealt with the power-line issue have, however, followed the California case and allowed plaintiffs to recover for fear without having to show that the fear was reasonable (McCune 1991).

Other kinds of electromagnetic field exposure cases have been filed as well. In August 1990, Boeing settled a class action suit in which a lead plaintiff alleged he had contracted leukemia after being exposed to pulses of electromagnetic fields (whose electrical characteristics are quite different from power line fields) while working as an electrical technician. The case was filed on behalf of more than 700 past and present Boeing workers. The settlement involved $500,000 in cash and purchase of an annuity for the lead plaintiff, Robert Strom, and ten years of medical monitoring of other class members. All members "also retain the right to seek compensation in the future."[25] Strom used some of his award to establish the Robert Carl Strom Foundation, to help others pursue EMF cases.[26]

Also arising out of the Strom case was a lawyers' organization known as the Electromagnetic Radiation Case Evaluation Team (EMRCET). EMRCET, formed in early 1991, is funded by ten law firms across the country with a goal of pooling data and finding clients for potential EMF personal injury suits.[27] In late 1991 and early 1992, EMRCET filed its first two lawsuits against the Connecticut Light & Power Company on behalf of plaintiffs with brain cancer and meningioma, an intracranial tumor.[28] (The plaintiffs were the subjects of a lurid article in *The New Yorker* (Brodeur 1990) about the alleged risks of electrical substations.)

One highly publicized suit was filed in May 1991 in San Diego by Ted and Michelle Zuidema. They allege that unusually high levels of magnetic fields (3.5 to 17 milligauss flux density) in their home from nearby San Diego Gas and Electric power lines led to Wilm's tumor, a kidney cancer that now affects their four-year-old daughter, Mallory.[29] As H. Dixon Montague, the attorney who represented the school district in the Klein litigation was quoted, "Personal injury cases are coming. No doubt about it."[30]

Other cases are now working their way through the courts. These include, for example, a suit by Johnny Neal and Sharon Allen seeking $5.25 billion from the Alabama Power Company for EMR exposure on behalf of their two-year-old son, Austin, who is perfectly healthy.

So far, the number of tort actions remains small; one review lists 14 personal injury suits filed in 1991 (Banks 1992). Their outcomes will probably determine how many tort actions will eventually be filed. If they are successful, the potential liability exposure of utilities and other companies could be very high.

Utilities face legal challenge on other fronts as well. Electric utilities and cellular phone companies (among other companies) must go before many local planning boards for permission to install new facilities. They are facing increased public opposition for health reasons. Power companies can appeal to state public utility commissions, and other companies can fight their way through appeals processes, but the legal costs and delays are substantial. Some proposed high voltage power lines have been in litigation for a decade or more, partly because of health concerns. The uncertainty of the process (rather than the costs, which are passed on to the consumer in any event) is probably of greatest concern to the utilities.

Video Display Terminals (VDTs) and Other Appliances

So far, few lawsuits have presented claims for serious illness arising from use of VDTs. In 1980, two Chicago women who worked together at computer terminals developed cervical cancer. Within a year, one died. The other underwent several operations and sued Raytheon, the Lexington, Massachusetts, company that manufactured the VDT in question.[31] An unsuccessful worker's compensation claim was filed in 1987 against American Telephone and Telegraph Company by a woman who attributed a skin rash to use of VDTs (VDT News 1987).

A storm of litigation is brewing, however. The same factors that have led to other questionable claims of injury from electromagnetic fields exist as well with VDTs. Several well-publicized studies have reported possible links between VDTs and adverse health effects including miscarriages and cataracts. (The evidence regarding miscarriages is described in chapter 6). But public concern is apparently shifting to another

issue, the possibility that the magnetic fields associated with the terminals (and other appliances) may increase the risk for cancer. That issue
will be very hard to resolve by scientific studies.

An article in *Best's Review,* an insurance-related publication, advises
its readers to expect a wave of litigation involving VDTs to arise soon.[32]
Many claims have already been filed concerning repetitive stress injuries
(*e.g.,* carpal tunnel syndrome) associated with use of computer key-
boards. For example, an article in the New York Times (June 3, 1992)
described a consolidated case involving 44 suits filed against several companies, and noted that an additional 100 suits were pending in New York.
One lawyer, quoted in the article, said he had more than a hundred other
such cases pending. Most of these claims are against the manufacturers
of the equipment; the injuries themselves are usually covered by workers'
compensation insurance and the employer is shielded to some extent
from litigation.

So far, few actions seek compensation for injury from exposure to
fields from such equipment. However, depending on the outcome of
several pending tort suits, many more could follow. The author of the
Best's Review article predicts that the plaintiff's bar will rely on precedents
involving hazardous substances in the workplce to argue that employers
and manufacturers should be held liable for failing to protect employees
and purchasers against the hazardous effects of VDTs.

The *Best's Review* article suggests that employers take preemptive
measures, such as purchasing radiation shields or "low emission" VDTs.
Sweden has recently adopted strict emissions standards for VDTs, with
which most VDT manufacturers around the world are now complying.
Should an employer who buys "low emission" VDTs allow employees
to use older, unshielded, VDTs? One legal standard to determine negligence is to look at the custom of the industry. If (as has already happened)
most of the computer industry begins to treat VDTs as a real threat and
adopts "low emission" VDTs, plaintiffs will use that as evidence that it
was unreasonable for other companies to ignore the "danger" from
VDTs. Most manufacturers of electric blankets have already redesigned
their products to reduce magnetic field exposure to users. What should
they tell their customers who use the old (high-exposure) blankets?

Notes

1. *Wells v. Ortho Pharmaceutical Corp.,* 615 F. Supp. 262 (N.D. Ga. 1985), *aff'd in
part, modif'd in part,* 788 F.2d 741, *reh'g denied en banc,* 795 F.2d 89 (11th Cir.), *cert.
denied,* 479 U.S. 950 (1986).

2. *Contraceptive jelly-birth defect study repudiated by its authors.* United Press International. December 11, 1986.

3. *Courts not bound by "scientific proof."* United Press International. November 6, 1986.

4. Telephone interview with corporate counsel for Johnson & Johnson, July 6, 1989.

5. *Smith v. Ortho Pharmaceutical Corp.*, 770 F. Supp. 1561 (N.D. Ga. 1991).

6. Richardson Merrell, the original manufacturer, was later acquired by Dow. For simplicity we refer to the Bendectin defendant as Merrell.

7. 711 F.2d 1510 (11th Cir. 1983).

8. *Experts reveal . . . common drug causing deformed babies.* National Enquirer. October 9, 1979, 20.

9. *Oxendine v. Richardson-Merrell*, no. 1245-82 (D.C. Super. Ct. 1983), *rev'd, Oxendine* v. *Merrell Dow Pharmaceuticals, Inc.*, 506 A.2d 1100 (D.C. App. 1986) (mem. and order), *vacated*, no. 1245-82 (D.C. Super. Ct. Feb. 11, 1988), *rev'd*, 563 A.2d 330 (D.C. App.), *cert. denied*, 110 S. Ct. 1121 (1990), *appeal after remand*, 593 A.2d 1023 (1991).

10. *In re Richardson-Merrell, Inc. "Bendectin" Products Liability Litigation.*, 624 F. Supp. 1212 (S.D. Ohio 1985), *aff'd*, 857 F. 2d 290 (6th Cir. 1988), *cert. denied sub nom., Hoffman* v. *Merrell Dow Pharmaceuticals*, 488 U.S. 1006 (1989).

11. 646 F. Supp. 856 (D. Mass. 1986), *aff'd*, 830 F.2d 1190 (1st Cir. 1987).

12. *Richardson v. Richardson Merrell, Inc.*, 649 F. Supp. 799 (D.D.C. 1986), *aff'd*, 857 F.2d 823 (D.C. Cir. 1988), *cert. denied*, 110 S. Ct. 218 (1989).

13. *Ealy v. Richardson-Merrell, Inc.*, no. 83-3504. (D.D.C. Oct. 1, 1987) (mem. and order), *rev'd*, 897 F.2d 1159, *cert. denied*, 111 S. Ct. 370 (1990).

14. *Brock v. Merrell Dow Pharmaceuticals, Inc.*, 874 F.2d 307, 315, *petition for reh'g denied*, 884 F.2d 166, *reh'g en banc denied*, 884 F.2d 167 (5th Cir. 1989) (per curiam), *cert. denied*, 110 S. Ct. 1511 (1990).

15. *Brock v. Merrell Dow Pharmaceuticals, Inc.*, 874 F.2d 307, *reh'g denied*, 884 F.2d 167 (5th Cir. 1989) (en banc), *cert. denied*, 110 S. Ct. 1511 (1990); *Richardson v. Richardson-Merrell, Inc.*, 857 F.2d 823 (D.C. Cir. 1988), *cert. denied*, 110 S. Ct. 218 (1989); *Hoffman v. Merrell Dow Pharmaceuticals, Inc.*, 857 F.2d 290 (6th Cir. 1988), *cert. denied*, 488 U.S. 1006 (1989); *Wilson v. Merrell Dow Pharmaceuticals, Inc.*, 893 F.2d 1149 (10th Cir. 1990); *Mekdeci v. Merrell National Laboratories*, 711 F.2d 1510 (11th Cir. 1983); *Barton v. Richardson-Merrell, Inc.*, Toxics L. Daily (BNA) (June 20, 1990), no. 85-C-28; *Rudell v. Merrell Dow Pharmaceuticals, Inc.*, no. 85-0115-CV-W-5 (W.D. Mo. June 8, 1988) (order); *Hill v. Richardson-Merrell, Inc.*, no. C83-74TB (W.D. Wash. June 7, 1988) (jury verdict); *Hagaman v. Merrell Dow Pharmaceuticals, Inc.*, no. 84-2202-S (D. Kan. June 6, 1988) (jury verdict); *Rosen v. Richardson-Merrell, Inc.*, no. 82-0513 (E.D. Pa. Feb. 26, 1987) (jury verdict); *Will v. Richardson-Merrell, Inc.*, 647 F. Supp. 544 (S.D. Ga. 1986); *Lanzilotti v. Merrell Dow Pharmaceuticals, Inc.*, no. 82-0183 (E.D. Pa. July 10, 1986) (mem. and order); *Bityk*

v. *Richardson-Merrell, Inc.*, no. C-302-225 (Cal. Super. Ct. July 1, 1987) (jury verdict); *Cordova* v. *Philips Roxane Labs, Inc.*, no. 432656, (Cal. Super. Ct. [Santa Clara Cty.] June 21, 1985) (jury verdict).

16. *Lynch* v. *Merrell-National Laboratories*, 830 F.2d 1190 (1st Cir. 1987); *Lee* v. *Richardson-Merrell, Inc.*, 772 F. Supp. (W.D. Tenn. 1991); *Whelan* v. *Merrell Dow Pharmaceuticals, Inc.*, no. 83-3108 (D.D.C. 1990); *Turpin* v. *Merrell Dow Pharmaceuticals, Inc.*, 736 F. Supp. 737 (E.D. Ky. 1990) *aff'd*, 959 F. 2d 1349 (6th Cir.), *cert. denied*, 113 S. Ct. 84 (1992); *Daubert* v. *Merrell Dow Pharmaceuticals, Inc.*, no. 84-2013-G (IEG) (S.D. Cal. Nov. 1, 1989) (mem. and order aff'd 951 112869 Ct. *cert. granted*); *Ambrosini* v. *Richardson-Merrell, Inc.*, no. 86-278 (D.D.C. June 30, 1989) (order); *Koller* v. *Richardson-Merrell, Inc.*, no. 80-1258 (D.D.C. May 30, 1989) (order); *De Luca* v. *Merrell Dow Pharmaceuticals, Inc.*, 131 F.R.D. 71 (D.C.N.J.) (mem. and order), *rev'd*, 911 F.2d 941 (3d Cir. 1990) *On remand*, 791 F. Supp. 1042 (D. N.J. 1992); *Hull* v. *Merrell Dow Pharmaceuticals, Inc.*, 700 F. Supp. 28 (S.D. Fla. 1988); *Cosgrove* v. *Merrell Dow Pharmaceuticals, Inc.*, no. 17451 (Idaho June 7, 1989), *aff'd as modified* (Mar. 29, 1990) (LEXIS); *Monahan* v. *Merrell National Laboratories*, no. 83-3108-WD (D. Mass. Dec. 18, 1987) (mem. and order); *Obiago* v. *Merrell-National Laboratories*, 560 So.2d 625 (1990); *Hagle* v. *Mount Clemens General Hospital*, no. 83-3300-NM (Mich. Cir. Ct. [Macomb Cty.] Nov. 28, 1989); *DePyper* v. *Merrell Dow Pharmaceuticals, Inc.*, no. 83-303-467 NM (Mich. Cir. Ct. [Wayne Cty.], Mar. 10, 1989) (opinion and order); *Thompson* v. *Merrell Dow Pharmaceuticals, Inc.*, 551 A.2d 177 (N.J. Super. 1988).

17. No. 83-3506 (D.D.C. May 20, 1987) (jury verdict).

18. Pollock, *Jury orders Merrell-Dow to pay couple $33.8 million in suit over nausea drug, Wall St. J.*, Oct. 7, 1991, B7.

19. See Bendectin, 18 *Prod. Safety & Liabil. Reporter* (BNA) 285 (March 23, 1991).

20. Board of Trustees of the American Medical Association, Impact of product liability on the development of new medical technologies 11, Report A-88, Resolution 6, A-87 (1988).

21. Quoted in C. Skrzycki, The risky business of birth control, U.S. News & World Rep., May 26, 1986, 42.

22. The details of this case come from the appeals court judges' opinion, *Houston Lighting and Power Company* v. *Klein Independent School District*, 739 S.W. 2d 508 (Tex. Ct. App.—Houston [14th Dist.] 1987).

23. *San Diego Gas & Electric Co.* v. *Daley*, 205 Cal. App.3d 1334, 253 Cal. Rptr. 144 (1988).

24. *Zappavigna* v. *State of New York*, no. 74085 (N.Y. Ct. Cl. Sept. 21, 1989), cited in N.Y. judge rejects "cancerphobia" damages against NYPA in line case, *Electric Utility Week*, October 23, 1989, 11.

25. Legal Beat, *Wall St. J.*, August 21, 1990, B4.

26. Something in the air, *Power Europe*, August 29, 1991.

27. Power line radiation fight heads to court, 23 *National J.* 2030 (1991).

28. Transmission/Distribution Health and Safety Report, January 1992, 9–10.

29. M. Granberry, Suit claims cancer link to power lines, *L.A. Times,* May 30, 1991, B1, col. 3.

30. Browning, G. Power-line radiation fight heads to court, high voltage debate, 23 *Natl. J.* 2030 (1991).

31. R. E. Roel, Low-level radiation becomes high-level concern, *Newsday,* March 25, 1990, 70.

32. Mangan, Deciphering the risks of ELFs, EMFs, and VDTs, *Best's Review,* September 1991, 92.

References

Bernstein, D. E. 1990. A contractual solution to the contraceptive crisis. 8 *Yale Law & Policy Rev.* 146.

Banks, R. S. 1992. *1991 EMF litigation. Transmission/Distribution Health and Safety Report* 9. January.

Brodeur, P. 1990. Calamity on Meadow Street. *New Yorker,* July 9, 38–72.

McCune, P. S. 1991. The power line health controversy: Legal problems and proposals for reform. 24 *U. Mich. J. L. Ref.* 429.

VDT News. 1987.

Weinberg, A. M. 1985. Science and its limits. 2(1) Iss. in Sci. & Tech. 59–72.

II

Just a Little Bit of Poison

All substances are poisons; there is none which is not a poison. The right dose differentiates a poison and a remedy.

Paracelsus

A phantom risk may be a *real* risk that has provoked disproportionate public concern. The authors in this section explore the risks from low-level exposure to substances that, at high levels, are certainly hazardous.

In the opening chapter, Ames and Gold discuss some common misconceptions about low-level environmental pollutants and cancer. They argue for a sense of perspective, noting that foods often contain natural pesticides and carcinogens at much higher levels than the traces of synthetic chemicals that have caused great public distress.

D'Agostino and Wilson discuss the asbestos issue. They note that the mineral occurs in different forms whose toxicity varies greatly. High-level exposure to asbestos (in the workplace, for example) is definitely hazardous; workers were surely injured through careless handling of the mineral in the past. But the authors argue that residential exposure, in buildings with intact insulation, presents no significant risk to occupants.

Another vexing issue is that of polychlorinated biphenyls (PCBs), which until the early 1970s were widely used in transformer fluids, plasticizers, and other applications. PCBs are now widely dispersed at low levels in the environment and can be detected in human body tissues. At high levels, these substances are clearly toxic to animals. But toxic effects have been much harder to demonstrate in people exposed to PCBs, and the risks from low-level exposure are very uncertain and possibly nonexistent.

In comparison to other organic solvents, trichloroethylene (TCE) is benign, and (as Jaeger and Weiss relate) was used until recently in dry cleaning and other industrial processes, where it entered the environment by evaporation. Obvious toxic effects in humans require high levels of exposure; long-term exposure of animals at somewhat lower levels produce various effects, including cancer. The public controversy about TCE, in contrast, pertains to cancer risk from exposure to TCE at very much lower levels. Despite one epidemiologic study that claimed adverse effects of TCE (Woburn, Massachusetts), present evidence (as Jaeger and Weiss argue) is insufficient to classify TCE as a human carcinogen.

The media have often presented dioxin as a uniquely potent carcinogen to humans; indeed, one member of this class of chemicals is the strongest animal carcinogen. Gough reviews the complex epidemiologic evidence regarding dioxin. Some workers, exposed to comparatively high levels of dioxin, developed a serious skin disease (chloracne), but no other major health effects have been documented in such people. Several epidemiologic studies have searched for a link between exposure to dioxin and cancer. Initial studies by two Swedish groups reported a pronounced increase in cancer risk associated with slight exposure to dioxins; later studies failed to confirm these results, and reported much smaller increases in risk, or none at all. Taken as a whole, Gough argues, the epidemiologic evidence makes no strong case that dioxin caused cancer in any exposed individuals.

This section concludes with a discussion by several authors of a uniquely vexing issue: risks from exposure to ionizing radiation. At high levels of exposure, ionizing radiation is truly hazardous; and some risks might reasonably be expected to persist even at low exposures. However, public reaction has often been out of proportion to the likely magnitude of such risks. Despite media reports of human illness, epidemiologic studies near Three Mile Island (reviewed by Tokuhata) failed to disclose significant health consequences of the accident to the nearby population apart from transient effects that might reasonably be interpreted as arising from psychological stresses from the accident. The uranium processing plant near Fernald, Ohio was the subject of extensive litigation; Cohen reviews the case, and argues that the projected health impact of the released uranium should be very low. Finally, the possible health effects of fallout from above-ground weapons testing has been the subject of decades-long controversy and extensive litigation, which Lapp reviews.

7

Environmental Pollution and Cancer: Some Misconceptions

Bruce N. Ames and Lois Swirsky Gold

The public has many misconceptions about the relationship between environmental pollution and human cancer. Underlying these misconceptions is an erroneous belief that nature is benign. Below we highlight eight of these misconceptions and describe the scientific information that undermines each one.

Misconception No. 1: Cancer Rates Are Soaring

Cancer death rates in the United States (after adjusting the rates for age and smoking) are steady or decreasing. According to an update from the National Cancer Institute (1988), "the age adjusted mortality rate for all cancers combined except lung cancer has been declining since 1950 for all individual age groups except 85 and above." (Overall, that represents a 13 percent decrease, 44,000 deaths below expected, and a 0.1 percent increase in the over-85 group.)

The decreases in cancer deaths during this period have been primarily from stomach cancer (by 75 percent, 37,000 deaths below expected), cervical cancer (by 73 percent, 11,000 deaths below expected), uterine cancer (by 60 percent, 9,000 deaths below expected), and rectal cancer (by 65 percent, 13,000 deaths below expected). The increases have been primarily from lung cancer (by 247 percent, 91,000 deaths above expected), which is due to smoking (as is 30 percent of all U.S. cancer deaths), and non-Hodgkin's lymphoma (by 100 percent, 8,000 deaths above expected). To interpret changes in mortality rates, one must consider changes in incidence rates (the number of people who are diagnosed with the cancer) and effects of treatment. The incidence rates have been increasing for some types of cancer. Sir Richard Doll and Richard Peto of Oxford University, two of the world's leading epidemiologists, in their definitive study on cancer trends point out that incidence rates should not be taken in isolation, because reported incidence rates for a disease might reflect increases in registration of cases and improvements in diagnosis (Doll and Peto 1981).

Even if particular types of cancer are increasing or decreasing, it is difficult to establish a causal relation between this fact and the many changing aspects of our lives. There is no persuasive evidence that life in the modern industrial world has in general contributed to cancer deaths.

Cancer is a degenerative disease of old age, although external factors can increase cancer rates (e.g., cigarette smoking in humans) or decrease them (e.g., eating more fruits and vegetables).

In the United States and other industrial countries life expectancy has been steadily increasing, while infant mortality is decreasing. Although the data are less adequate, there is no evidence that birth defects are increasing. Americans, on average, are healthier now than ever.

Misconception No. 2: Cancer Risks to Humans at Low Doses Can Be Assessed by Testing Chemicals at High Doses in Rodents

Animal cancer tests are conducted at near-toxic doses of the test chemical that cannot predict the cancer risk to humans at the much lower levels to which they are typically exposed. The prediction of cancer risk requires knowledge of the mechanisms of carcinogenesis, which is progressing rapidly.

Recent understanding of these mechanisms undermines many of the assumptions of current regulatory policy regarding rodent carcinogens and requires a reevaluation of the purpose of routine animal cancer tests. We summarize our current understanding of cancer mechanisms and their relation to animal cancer tests.

Mechanism and Causes of Cancer

It is generally agreed that several mutations (changes in the sequence of DNA bases) are necessary to convent a normal cell to a cancer cell capable of uncontrolled growth. When the cell divides, a DNA lesion (a damaged base in DNA) has a certain probability of giving rise to a mutation. Cell division increases mutation and cancer because DNA lesions are converted to mutations when the cell divides. There is little cancer in nondividing tissues. Thus the main cellular events leading to cancer appear to be DNA lesions and cell division. Mutagens are chemicals that cause lesions in DNA. Mutagens are often assumed to be only external agents (coming from outside the body). Most mutagens, however, are

DNA-damaging oxidants that are endogenous (produced inside the body) and are formed naturally during normal metabolic processes such as oxygen utilization, or by white cells during chronic inflammation. Thus, in a sense, normal oxidative metabolism or inflammation is equivalent to irradiating the body, since radiation is an oxidative mutagen. Studies in our laboratory have shown that normal metabolism causes chronic massive oxidative DNA damage: we estimate that the number of oxidative hits to DNA per cell per day is about 100,000 in rats and 10,000 in humans. The average young rat cell has a million oxidative DNA adducts, and this number increases with age. The number of oxidative lesions increases markedly during inflammation.

All mammals have numerous defenses to counter this damage, such as enzymes that repair damaged DNA, but this repair is imperfect. DNA damage in somatic cells accumulates with time because a considerable proportion of an animal's resources is devoted to reproduction at a cost to maintenance. Proteins can become oxidized as well. Some laboratories have shown that normal protein oxidation is extensive and that oxidized proteins accumulate with age, contributing to brain dysfunction. Thus, oxidative damage appears to be a major contributor to many of the degenerative diseases of aging, including cancer, because not all the DNA damage is repaired.

Agents that cause chronic cell division are indirectly mutagenic (and carcinogenic). Oxidants (e.g., from chronic inflammation) are dangerous because they effectively induce both cell division (the wound-healing response) and DNA lesions, thus producing a synergistic response. Agents that cause chronic cell division appear to be important in many of the known causes of human cancer: estrogen, for example, which causes cell proliferation in breast tissue, is a risk factor for breast cancer; hepatitis B and C viruses and alcohol, which induce chronic inflammation and subsequent cell division in the liver, are risk factors for liver cancer; high salt intake and *Helicobacter* bacterial infection, which induce chronic irritation of the stomach lining, are risk factors for stomach cancer; papilloma virus, which can cause chronic infection and chronic cell division of cells of the cervix, is a risk factor for cervical cancer; asbestos and tobacco smoke, which irritate the lungs, are risk factors for lung cancer. For the chemicals associated with occupational cancer, worker exposures usually have been at near-toxic doses that would be likely to increase chronic cell division.

We estimate that roughly three-quarters of human cancers, however, are preventable through a combination of good dietary and lifestyle practices. Even though one type of cancer may be prevented (lung cancer in smokers), risk increases sharply with age for all types of cancer. Of the preventable cancer, about one-third is due to diet—in particular, to eating too much fat and too few fruits and vegetables. Fruits and vegetables contain vitamin C and other antioxidants and nutrients that are essential parts of our defenses against oxidation and DNA damage. About another third of preventable cancer is due to habitual smoking, which chronically inflames the lungs, exposes tissues throughout the body to numerous mutagens and carcinogens, and decreases antioxidant defenses. About another third of preventable cancer, particularly in the third world, is due to chronic infections, many of which can be prevented by vaccination, antibiotic treatment, or the use of prophylactics during sexual intercourse. (Since cancer is due to multiple, overlapping causes, the fractions add up to more than 1.) About another quarter of potentially preventable cancer is due to hormones. The risk of breast cancer, for example, increases significantly for women who have not had children by their early thirties, and estrogen levels in breast tissue are higher in these women than in women with children. Hormone levels can be adjusted therapeutically. High occupational exposures may possibly cause a small percentage of cancers. Pollution appears to be an insignificant risk factor for cancer, with the exception of heavy air pollution, which might slightly increase the risk.

Animal Cancer Tests May Be Primarily Measuring the Effects of Chronic Cell Division

Animal cancer tests of chemicals are conducted chronically at doses near the maximum that the animals can tolerate—the maximum tolerated dose (MTD). Such high doses are used to increase the sensitivity of the experiment to detect a carcinogenic effect. Chronic dosing at the MTD often causes chronic cell death, which leads to chronic cell division in neighboring cells that replace the dead cells. High doses can interfere with cell–cell communication, which also stimulates cell division. Thus, chronic dosing of chemicals at the MTD can increase cancer incidence in animals.

Thus, many chemicals might be expected to be carcinogenic at chronic, near-toxic doses because they increase cell division. Indeed, about *half* of all chemicals tested chronically at the MTD are carcinogens (see below). About 40 percent of rodent carcinogens are not mutagens, which is consistent with our understanding of the importance of cell division in carcinogenesis.

Although toxicity at or near the MTD often induces cell division, below a certain dose no such effect is observed. Therefore, if animal cancer tests are primarily measuring the effects of cell division, then the response of the animals should fall off at lower doses, not linearly with dose, as is usually assumed. Thus, a tenfold reduction in dose in a rodent experiment would produce much more than a tenfold reduction in cancer risk. If a chemical or its metabolites are not directly mutagenic, there would be no risk at low doses, where there is no increase in cell division. This is another reason that high-dose animal experiments are very poor methods of estimating human cancer risk under low exposure conditions.

Misconception No. 3: Most Carcinogens and Other Toxins Are Synthetic

About 99.99 percent of all pesticides in the human diet are natural pesticides from plants (Ames et al. 1990). All plants produce toxins to protect themselves against fungi, insects, and animal predators such as humans. Tens of thousands of these natural pesticides have been discovered, and every species of plant contains its own set of different toxins, usually a few dozen. When plants are stressed or damaged (when attacked by pests), they greatly increase their output of natural pesticides, occasionally to levels that are acutely toxic to humans.

We estimate that a typical American eats about 1,500 mg per day of natural pesticides, which is 10,000 times more than the average daily consumption of synthetic pesticide residues. The concentration of natural pesticides is usually measured in parts per million (ppm) rather than parts per billion (ppb), which is the usual concentration of synthetic pesticide residues or of water pollutants. We also estimate that a person ingests annually about 5,000 to 10,000 different natural pesticides and their breakdown products.

Table 7.1 lists 49 natural pesticides (and breakdown products) that a person ingests from cabbage, and indicates which ones have been tested for carcinogenicity or clastogenicity (the ability to break chromosomes). Lima beans contain a different array of 23 natural toxins that occur in stressed plants in concentrations ranging from 0.2 to 33 parts per thousand fresh weight: none appears to have been tested for carcinogenicity or teratogenicity (the ability to cause birth defects).

Table 7.1
Forty-nine natural pesticides (and metabolites) in cabbage

Glucosinolates	2-propenyl glucosinolate (sinigrin)★
	3-methyl-thio-propyl glucosinolate
	3-methyl-sulfinyl-propyl glucosinolate
	3-butenyl glucosinolate
	2-hydroxy-3-butenyl glucosinolate
	4-methyl-thio-butyl glucosinolate
	4-methyl-sulfinyl-butyl glucosinolate
	4-methylsulfonyl-butyl glucosinolate
	benzyl glucosinolate
	2-phenyl -ethyl glucosinolate
	propyl glucosinolate
	butyl glucosinolate
Cyanides	1-cyano-2,3-epithiopropane
	1-cyano-3,4-epithiobutane
	1-cyano-3,4-epithiopentane
	threo-1-cyano-2-hydroxy-3,4-epithiobutane
	erythro-1-cyano-2-hydroxy-3,4-epithiobutane
	2-phenylpropionitrile
	allyl cyanide★
	1-cyano-2-hydroxy-3-butene
	1-cyano-3-methylsulfinylpropane
	1-cyano-4-methylsulfinylbutane
Indole glucosinolates and related indoles	3-indolyl-methyl glucosinolate (glucobrassicin)
	1-methoxy-3-indolylmethyl (neoglucobrassicin)
	indole-3-carbinol
	indole-3-acetonitrile
	3,3′-diindolylmethane
Terpenes	menthol
	neomenthol
	isomenthol
	carvone★

Table 7.1 (continued)

Phenols, isothiocyanates and goitrin	allyl isothiocyanate★
	3-methyl-thio-propyl isothiocyanate
	3-methyl-sulfinyl-propyl isothiocyanate
	3-butenyl isothiocyanate
	5-vinyloxazolidine-2-thione (goitrin)
	4-methylthiobutyl isothiocyanate
	4-methylsulfinylbutyl isothiocyanate
	4-methylsulfonylbutyl isothiocyanate
	4-pentenyl isothiocyanate
	benzyl isothiocyanate
	phenylethyl isothiocyanate
	2-methoxyphenol
	3-caffoylquinic acid (chlorogenic acid)★
	4-caffoylquinic acid★
	5-caffoylquinic acid (neochlorogenic acid)★
	4-*p*-coumaroylquinic acid
	5-*p*-coumaroylquinic acid
	5-feruloylquinic acid

★Discussed below; all others untested.

Clastogenicity: Chlorogenic acid and allyl isothiocyanate are positive. Chlorogenic acid and its metabolite caffeic acid are also mutagens, as is allyl isothiocyanate.

Carcinogenicity: Allyl isothiocyanate induced papillomas of the bladder in male rats and was classified by the National Toxicology Program (NTP) as carcinogenic. There was no evidence of carcinogenicity in mice; however, NTP indicated "the mice probably did not receive the MTD." Sinigrin (the glucosinolate, that is, thioglycoside of allyl isothiocyanate) is cocarcinogenic for the rat pancreas. Carvone is negative in mice. Indole acetonitrile has been shown to form a carcinogen, nitroso indole acetonitrile, in the presence of nitrite. Caffeic acid, a carcinogen and clastogen, is a metabolite of its esters 3-, 4-, and 5-caffoylquinic acid (chlorogenic and neochlorogenic acid).

Metabolites: Sinigrin gives rise to allyl isothiocyanate on eating raw cabbage (e.g., coleslaw); in cooked cabbage it also is metabolized to allyl cyanide, which is untested. Indole carbinol forms dimers and trimers on ingestion that mimic dioxin (TCDD).

Toxicology: The mitogenic effects of goitrin (which is goitrogenic) and various organic cyanides from cabbage suggest that they may be potential carcinogens. Aromatic cyanides related to those from cabbage have been shown to be mutagens and are metabolized to hydrogen cyanide and potentially mutagenic aldehydes.
Source: Ames et al. 1990a.

Surprisingly few of these thousands of plant toxins in our diet have been involved in animal cancer tests, but of those tested in at least one species of animal, about half (27/52) are carcinogenic (Ames et al. 1990a).[1]

The 27 natural pesticides that are rodent carcinogens occur naturally in the following foods (see Table 7.2) (those containing a single carcinogen at concentrations greater than 10,000 ppb are in italics): *anise, apple,* banana, *basil,* broccoli, *Brussels sprouts, cabbage,* cantaloupe, *caraway, carrot, cauliflower, celery, cherry,* cinnamon, cloves, cocoa, *coffee* (brewed), *comfrey tea, dill, eggplant, endive, fennel, grapefruit juice, grape, honey,* honeydew melon, *horseradish,* kale, *lettuce, mace, mango, mushroom, mustard* (brown), *nutmeg, orange juice, parsley, parsnip,* peach, *pear, pepper* (black), pineapple, *plum, potato,* radish, raspberry, *rosemary, sage, sesame seeds* (heated), strawberry, *tarragon, thyme,* and turnip.

Thus, almost every plant product in the supermarket probably contains natural carcinogens at levels that are commonly hundreds or thousands of times higher than those of synthetic pesticides. We need not be alarmed by the presence of low doses of synthetic toxins and a plethora of natural toxins in our food. As we discuss below, humans are well protected against low doses of toxins by many general defenses that do not distinguish between synthetic and natural toxins.

Dietary exposures to natural rodent carcinogens do not necessarily increase human cancer risk. Indeed, a diet rich in fruit and vegetables is associated with lower cancer rates, probably because of anticarcinogenic vitamins and antioxidants in these foods. Chronic exposures to naturally occurring rodent carcinogens in our diets, however, casts doubt on the significance of our far lower exposures to synthetic chemicals that are rodent carcinogens.

Teratogens and Clastogens Are Common

Many natural and synthetic chemicals are likely to be reproductive toxins at high doses. Rodent teratogenicity tests (which detect birth defects and other types of reproductive damage) show a high fraction of positive results, with one-third of the 2,800 chemicals tested in laboratory animals at high doses causing reproductive damage.

Tests of other kinds show that many chemicals damage cells at high exposure levels. Ishidate reviewed tests of 951 chemicals for clastogenic (chromosome breaking) properties, using cultured mammalian cells (Ishidate et al. 1988). Of these 951 chemicals, 72 were identified as natural plant pesticides. About half of the natural pesticides and about half of all chemicals tested—whether synthetic or natural—are clastogenic at the exposure levels employed, which were typically very high. These in vitro experiments do not necessarily simulate in vivo conditions, and a given level of exposure would probably produce less extensive chromosome damage in body tissues than in laboratory tissue cultures.

Cooking Food

Cooked food is a major dietary source of substances that cause cancer in rodents. The average person consumes about 2,000 mg per day of burned material, which contains many substances that are rodent carcinogens and many other substances that have not yet been tested. Roasted coffee, for example, contains about 1,000 chemicals. Only 26 have been tested, and of these 19 cause cancer in rodents. The 10 mg of known natural rodent carcinogens in a cup of coffee would be equivalent in amount ingested to a year's worth of synthetic pesticide residues (assuming half of the untested synthetic residue weight turns out to be carcinogenic in rodents). The other chemicals, about a thousand, remain to be tested.

Cooking causes many biochemical changes in food, including the formation of mutagens and carcinogens. When proteins are heated, mutagenic compounds known as heterocyclic amines are produced. Ten heterocyclic amines have been tested and shown to be carcinogens in rodents, and scientists are in the process of isolating and testing many others. Cooked food contains many other mutagens and rodent carcinogens.

It is interesting to compare the intake of carcinogens in the diet with that from air pollution. In a typical day a person consumes several hundred times more browned and burned material in the diet than is inhaled even from severe outdoor air pollution. Diesel exhaust contains three mutagenic nitropyrenes that have been shown to be rodent carcinogens, but a typical person consumes far more of these substances by eating grilled chicken than by breathing polluted air. Gas flames generate NO_2, which can form both carcinogenic nitropyrenes and nitrosamines in foods that are cooked in gas ovens. Such food may be a major source of dietary nitropyrenes and nitrosamines. All of these rodent carcinogens may not be relevant to human cancer because of the problems in dose extrapolation discussed above.

Residues of Synthetic Pesticides

In contrast with these natural chemicals in the diet, human exposures to residues from synthetic pesticides are minuscule. The Food and Drug

Table 7.2
Concentrations of some natural pesticides that are rodent carcinogens

Plant food	Rodent carcinogen	Concentration (ppm)
Parsley	5- and 8-methoxypsoralen	14
Parsnip, cooked	"	32
Celery	"	0.8
Celery, new cultivar	"	6.2
Celery, stressed	"	25
Mushroom, commercial	p-hydrazinobenzoate	11
Mushroom, commercial	glutamyl-p-hydrazinobenzoate	42
Cabbage	sinigrin★ (allyl isothiocyanate)	35–590
Collard greens	"	250–788
Cauliflower	"	12–66
Brussels sprouts	"	110–1,560
Mustard (brown)	"	16,000–72,000
Horseradish	"	4,500
Orange juice	limonene	31
Mango	"	40
Pepper, black	"	8,000
Basil	estragole	3,800
Fennel	"	3,000
Nutmeg	safrole	3,000
Mace	"	10,000

Food source	Compound	Concentration (ppb)
Pepper, black	"	100
Pineapple	ethyl acrylate	0.07
Sesame seeds (heated oil)	sesamol	75
Cocoa	α-methylbenzyl alcohol	1.3
Basil	benzyl acetate	82
Jasmine tea	"	230
Honey	"	15
Coffee (roasted beans)	catechol	100
Apple, carrot, celery, cherry, eggplant, endive, grapes, lettuce, pear, plum, potato	caffeic acid	50–200
Absinthe, anise, basil, caraway, dill, marjoram, rosemary, sage, savory, tarragon, thyme	"	>1,000
Coffee (roasted beans)	"	1,800
Apricot, cherry, peach, plum	chlorogenic acid★★ (caffeic acid)	50–500
Coffee (roasted beans)	"	21,600
Apple, apricot, broccoli, Brussels sprouts, cabbage, cherry, kale, peach, pear, plum	neochlorogenic acid★★ (caffeic acid)	50–500
Coffee (roasted beans)	"	11,600

1 ppm = 1,000 ppb.

★Sinigrin is a cocarcinogen and is metabolized to the rodent carcinogen allyl isothiocyanate. No adequate test has been done on sinigrin itself. The proportion converted to allyl isothiocyanate or to allyl cyanide depends on food preparation.

★★Chlorogenic and neochlorogenic acid are metabolized to the carcinogens caffeic acid and catechol (a metabolite of quinic acid); they have not been tested for carcinogenicity. The clastogenicity and mutagenicity of the above compounds are discussed in Table 7.1.

Administration assayed food for residues of the 200 synthetic compounds thought to be of greater importance, including most synthetic pesticides and a few industrial chemicals (Gunderson 1988). The FDA surveys indicated that an average person consumes about 0.09 mg of these residues per day. For comparison, we estimate that the intake of natural pesticides averages about 1,500 mg per person per day.

Misconception No. 4: Synthetic Toxins Pose Greater Carcinogenic Risks Than Natural Toxins

The possible carcinogenic hazards from synthetic pesticide residues are minimal compared with the background of possible hazards of natural pesticides. By far the greater part of the chemicals we eat are natural, and few of them have been tested systematically. Synthetic chemicals account for 350 (82 percent) of the 427 chemicals tested chronically at high doses in both rats and mice (Gold et al. 1992). Of the 77 *natural* chemicals tested, about *half* (37/77) are carcinogenic to rodents; a similar fraction is observed for synthetic chemicals (212/350).

The high proportion of carcinogens found in rodent studies is unlikely to be due solely to the way in which chemicals were selected for testing. Some synthetic or natural chemicals were selected because they had suspicious chemical structures; but most were chosen because of their widespread use, for instance, because they are high-volume chemicals, pesticides, drugs, dyes, or food additives. Moreover, the ability to predict carcinogenicity has been inadequate. Naturally occurring chemicals, the vast bulk of chemicals humans are exposed to, have never been tested systematically.

It is important to compare possible hazards and put them into a relative context so that priorities can be more reasonably set. In particular, the potencies of different carcinogens vary more than 10 million-fold in rodent tests, which must be considered in any comparison of human risks. A method of setting priorities among possible carcinogenic hazards has recently been developed. It is based on analyzing results of animal cancer tests using data from our carcinogenic potency database (Gold et al. 1984, 1990, 1992). For each chemical, we calculate from the test results a quantity, the TD_{50} (tumorigenic dose 50), which is the daily dose of the chemical (in milligrams of chemical per kilogram of body weight) that will give half of the animals tumors by the end of a life span.

Using the TD_{50}, we can construct an index to rank possible carcinogenic hazards. First, we estimate a typical daily lifetime human exposure to each chemical, expressed as milligrams of the chemical per kilogram of body weight. This exposure is then expressed as a percentage of the rodent TD_{50}, to yield a quantity we call HERP—human exposure dose/rodent potency dose. Both the human exposure and the rodent dose in this index are expressed as lifetime exposure at the indicated daily dose rates (see Table 7.3).

Since the exposures in Table 7.3 for natural pesticides are for typical portions while those for synthetic pesticides are for average daily intake, we examined whether the relative rankings of these two groups of chemicals would be changed if average consumption of each plant food was the basis for the HERP values of natural pesticides (Table 7.4). Generally, the average daily intake is within a factor of 5 of the typical portions reported in Table 7.3, except for some less common foods, e.g., mango and parsnip. Table 7.4 reports all exposures to natural pesticides (in boldface) and synthetic pesticides from Table 7.3 for which average consumption data are available. Strikingly, all HERP values that rank in the top third of Table 7.4 are for natural pesticides, even though few natural pesticides have been tested.

The HERP values do not estimate human risk directly, because it is not known how to extrapolate from high-dose animal studies to low doses in humans (see Misconception No. 2). Also, not all carcinogens work in the same way. The HERP comparisons and risk assessments can be refined as we learn more about mechanisms and species differences.

This analysis suggests that alcohol at moderate doses and chemical exposures in the workplace should be high on our priority list for epidemiologic studies on cancer. Conversely, possible cancer hazards from residues of synthetic chemicals in food or water pollution are probably trivial compared with those from naturally occurring chemicals or from cooked food.

We comment on a few specific issues and put them in a broader perspective.

Alar

To put the carcinogenic hazard of Alar in perspective, we estimate that the possible hazard from UDMH (a carcinogenic hydrazine formed by breakdown of Alar) in a 6-ounce glass of apple juice taken every day for life is less than one-tenth that from naturally occurring carcinogenic hydrazines ingested by eating a mushroom a day (Table 7.3), or from the aflatoxin in a daily peanut butter sandwich, or the caffeic acid in a pear, an apple, or a cup of coffee. The estimated hazard of UDMH in a daily apple is one-tenth that of a daily glass of apple juice. Other HERP comparisons are shown in Table 7.3.

Table 7.3

Ranking possible carcinogenic hazards from natural (in bold) and synthetic chemicals

Possible hazard: HERP (%)	Daily human exposure	Human dose of rodent carcinogen
140	EDB: workers' daily intake (high exposure)	EDB, 150 mg (before 1977)
17	Clofibrate (avg daily dose)	Clofibrate, 2 g
16	Phenobarbital, 1 sleeping pill	Phenobarbital, 60 mg
[14]	Isoniazid pill (prophylactic dose)	Isoniazid, 300 mg
6.2	Comfrey-pepsin tablets, 9 daily	**Comfrey root, 2.7 g**
[5.6]	Metronidazole (therapeutic dose)	Metronidazole, 2 g
4.7	**Wine (250 ml)**	**Ethyl alcohol, 30 ml**
4.0	Formaldehyde: workers' avg daily intake	Formaldehyde, 6.1 mg
2.8	**Beer (12 oz; 354 ml)**	**Ethyl alcohol, 18 ml**
1.4	Mobile home air (14 hour/day)	Formaldehyde, 2.2 mg
1.3	Comfrey-pepsin tablets, 9 daily	**Symphytine, 1.8 mg**
0.4	Conventional home air (14 hr/day)	Formaldehyde, 598 µg
[0.3]	Phenacetin pill (avg dose)	Phenacetin, 300 mg
0.3	**Lettuce, ⅛ head (125 g)**	**Caffeic acid, 66.3 mg**
0.2	**Natural root beer (12 oz; 354 ml)**	**Safrole, 6.6 mg (banned)**
0.1	**Apple, 1 whole (230 g)**	**Caffeic acid, 24.4 mg**
0.1	**1 Mushroom (15 g)**	**Mix of hydrazines, etc.**
0.1	**Basil (1 g of dried leaf)**	**Estragole, 3.8 mg**
0.07	**Mango, 1 whole (245 g; pitted)**	**d-Limonene, 9.8 mg**
0.07	**Pear, 1 whole (200 g)**	**Caffeic acid, 14.6 mg**
0.07	**Brown mustard (5 g)**	**Allyl isothiocyanate, 4.6 mg**
0.06	Diet cola (12 oz; 354 ml)	Saccharin, 95 mg
0.06	**Parsnip, ¼ (40 g)**	**8-Methoxypsoralen, 1.28 mg**
0.04	**Orange juice (6 oz; 177 ml)**	**d-Limonene, 5.49 mg**
0.04	**Coffee, 1 cup (from 4 g)**	**Caffeic acid, 7.2 mg**
0.03	**Plum, 1 whole (50 g)**	**Caffeic acid, 6.9 mg**
0.03	**Safrole: US avg from spices**	**Safrole, 1.2 mg**
0.03	**Peanut butter (32 g; 1 sandwich)**	**Aflatoxin, 64 ng**
0.03	**Comfrey herb tea (1.5 g)**	**Symphytine, 38 µg**
0.03	**Celery, 1 stalk (50 g)**	**Caffeic acid, 5.4 mg**
0.03	**Carrot, 1 whole (100 g)**	**Caffeic acid, 5.16 mg**
0.03	**Pepper, black: US avg (446 mg)**	**d-Limonene, 3.57 mg**
0.02	**Potato, 1 (225 g; peeled)**	**Caffeic acid, 3.56 mg**
0.008	Swimming pool, 1 hour (for child)	Chloroform, 250 µg
0.008	**Beer, before 1979 (12 oz; 354 ml)**	**Dimethylnitrosamine, 1 µg**
0.006	**Bacon, cooked (100 g)**	**Diethylnitrosamine, 0.1 µg**
0.006	Well water, 1 liter contaminated (worst in Silicon Valley, CA)	Trichloroethylene, 2.8 mg
0.005	**Coffee, 1 cup (from 4 g)**	**Furfural, 630 µg**
0.004	**Bacon, pan fried (100 g)**	**N-nitrosopyrrolidine, 1.7 µg**
0.003	**Nutmeg: US avg (27.4 mg)**	**d-Limonene, 466 µg**
0.003	**1 Mushroom (15 g)**	**Glutamyl p-hydrazinobenzoate, 630 µg**
0.003	Conventional home air (14 hr/day)	Benzene, 155 µg
0.003	**Sake (250 ml)**	**Urethane, 43 µg**
0.003	**Bacon, cooked (100 g)**	**Dimethylnitrosamine, 300 ng**
0.002	**White bread, 2 slices (45 g)**	**Furfural, 333 µg**
0.002	Apple juice (6 oz; 177 ml)	UDMH, 5.89 µg (from Alar, 1988)
0.002	**Coffee, 1 cup (from 4 g)**	**Hydroquinone, 100 µg**

Table 7.3 (continued)

Possible hazard: HERP (%)	Daily human exposure	Human dose of rodent carcinogen
0.002	**Coffee, 1 cup (from 4 g)**	**Catechol, 400 µg**
0.002	DDT: daily dietary avg	DDT, 13.8 µg (before 1972 ban)
0.001	**Celery, 1 stalk (50 g)**	**8-Methoxypsoralen, 30.5 µg**
0.001	Tap water, 1 liter	Chloroform, 83 µg (US avg)
0.001	**Heated sesame oil (15 g)**	**Sesamol, 1.13 mg**
0.0008	DDE: daily dietary avg	DDE, 6.91 µg (before 1972 ban)
0.0006	Well water, 1 liter contaminated (Woburn, MA)	Trichloroethylene, 267 µg
0.0005	**1 Mushroom (15 g)**	**p-Hydrazinobenzoate, 165 µg**
0.0005	**Hamburger, pan fried (3 oz; 85 g)**	**PhIP, 1.28 µg**
0.0005	**Jasmine tea, 1 cup (2 g)**	**Benzyl acetate, 460 µg**
0.0005	**Salmon, pan fried (3 oz; 85 g)**	**PhIP, 1.18 µg**
0.0004	EDB: daily dietary avg	EDB, 420 ng (from grain; before 1984 ban)
0.0004	**Beer (12 oz; 354 ml)**	**Furfural, 54.9 µg**
0.0003	Well water, 1 liter contaminated (Woburn, MA)	Tetrachloroethylene, 21 µg
0.0003	Carbaryl: daily dietary avg	Carbaryl, 2.6 µg (1990)
0.0002	Apple, 1 whole (230 g)	UDMH, 598 ng (from Alar, 1988)
0.0002	**Parsley, fresh (1 g)**	**8-Methoxypsoralen, 3.6 µg**
0.0002	Toxaphene: daily dietary avg	Toxaphene, 595 ng (1990)
0.00008	**Hamburger, pan fried (3 oz; 85 g)**	**MeIQx, 111 ng**
0.00008	DDE/DDT: daily dietary avg	DDE, 659 ng (1990)
0.00003	**Whole wheat toast, 2 slices (45 g)**	**Urethane, 540 ng**
0.00002	Dicofol: daily dietary avg	Dicofol, 544 ng (1990)
0.00002	**Cocoa (4 g)**	**α-Methylbenzyl alcohol, 5.2 µg**
0.00001	**Lager beer (12 oz; 354 ml)**	**Urethane, 159 ng**
0.000008	**Hamburger, pan fried (3 oz; 85 g)**	**IQ, 23.4 ng**
0.000001	Lindane: daily dietary avg	Lindane, 32 ng (1990)
0.0000004	PCNB: daily dietary avg	PCNB (Quintozene), 19.ng (1990)
0.0000001	**Hamburger, pan fried (3 oz; 85 g)**	**MeIQ, 1.28 ng**
0.0000001	Chlorobenzilate: daily dietary avg	Chlorobenzilate, 6.4 ng (1989)
<0.00000001	Chlorothalonil: daily dietary avg	Chlorothalonil, <6.4 ng (1990)
0.000000008	Folpet: daily dietary avg	Folpet, 12.8 ng (1990)
0.000000007	**Coffee, 1 cup (from 4 g)**	**MeIQ, 0.064 ng**
0.000000006	Captan: daily dietary avg	Captan, 11.5 ng (1990)

Note: *Daily human exposure:* Reasonable daily intakes are used to facilitate comparisons; details are reported in (12). The calculations assume a daily dose for a lifetime; where drugs are normally taken for only a short period we have bracketed the HERP. *Possible hazard:* The human dose of rodent carcinogen is divided by 70 kg to give a mg/kg of human exposure, and this dose is given as the percentage of the TD_{50} in the rodent (mg/kg) to calculate the Human Exposure/Rodent Potency index (HERP). TD_{50} values used in the HERP calculation are averages calculated by taking the harmonic mean of the TD_{50}'s of the positive tests in that species from the Carcinogenic Potency Database. Average TD_{50} values have been calculated separately for rats and mice, and the more sensitive species is used for calculating possible hazard.

Source: From Gold et al. 1992 (by permission of American Association for the Advancement of Science).

Table 7.4
Comparison of average exposures to natural (in bold) and synthetic pesticides

HERP (%)	Average daily human exposure	Human dose of rodent carcinogen
0.1	**Coffee (from 13.3 g) [3 cups]**	**Caffeic acid, 23.9 mg**
0.04	**Lettuce (14.9 g) [1/67th head]**	**Caffeic acid, 7.90 mg**
0.03	**Safrole in spices**	**Safrole, 1.2 mg**
0.03	**Orange juice (138 ml) [4/5th glass]**	**d-Limonene, 4.28 mg**
0.03	**Pepper, black (446 mg)**	**d-Limonene, 3.57 mg**
0.02	**Mushroom (2.55 g) [1/6th]**	**Mix of hydrazines, etc**
0.02	**Apple (32.0 g) [1/7th]**	**Caffeic acid, 3.40 mg**
0.01	**Celery, (21.6 g) [2/5th stalk]**	**Caffeic acid, 2.33 mg**
0.006	**Coffee (13.3 g) [3 cups]**	**Catechol, 1.33 mg**
0.004	**Potato (54.9 g; peeled) [1/4th]**	**Caffeic acid, 867 µg**
0.003	**Nutmeg (27.4 mg)**	**d-Limonene, 466 µg**
0.003	**Carrot (12.1 g) [1/10th]**	**Caffeic acid, 624 µg**
0.002	[DDT: daily dietary avg]	[DDT, 13.8 µg (before 1972 ban)]
0.002	[Apple juice (6 oz; 177 ml)]	[UDMH, 5.89 µg (from Alar, 1988)]
0.001	**Plum (1.86 g) [1/25th]**	**Caffeic acid, 257 µg**
0.001	**Pear (3.29 g) [9/100th]**	**Caffeic acid, 240 µg**
0.0009	**Brown mustard (68.4 mg)**	**Allyl isothiocyanate, 62.9 µg**
0.0008	[DDE: daily dietary avg]	[DDE, 6.91 µg (before 1972 ban)]

0.0006	Celery (21.6 g) [2/5th stalk]	8-Methoxypsoralen, 13.2 µg
0.0006	Mushroom (2.55 g) [1/6th]	Glutamyl-p-hydrazinobenzoate, 107 µg
0.0004	[EDB: daily dietary avg]	[EDB, 420 ng (before 1984 ban)]
0.0003	Carbaryl: daily dietary avg	Carbaryl, 2.6 µg (1990)
0.0002	Toxaphene: daily dietary avg	Toxaphene, 595 ng (1990)
0.0002	[Apple, 1 whole (230 g)]	[UDMH, 598 ng (from Alar, 1988)]
0.0001	Mango (522 mg) [1/500th]	d-Limonene, 20.9 µg
0.00009	Mushroom (2.55 g) [1/6th]	p-Hydrazinobenzoate, 28 µg
0.00008	DDE/DDT: daily dietary avg	DDE, 659 ng (1990)
0.00007	Parsnip (54.0 mg) [1/3300th]	8-Methoxypsoralen, 1.57 µg
0.00005	Parsley, fresh (324 mg)	8-Methoxypsoralen, 1.17 µg
0.00002	Dicofol: daily dietary avg	Dicofol, 544 ng (1990)
0.00001	Cocoa (3.34 g) [4/5th serving]	α-Methylbenzyl alcohol, 4.3 µg
0.000001	Lindane: daily dietary avg	Lindane, 32 ng (1990)
0.0000004	PCNB: daily dietary avg	PCNB (Quintozene), 19.2 ng (1990)
0.0000001	Chlorobenzilate: daily dietary avg	Chlorobenzilate, 6.4 ng (1989)
<0.00000001	Chlorothalonil: daily dietary avg	Chlorothalonil, <6.4 ng (1990)
0.000000008	Folpet: daily dietary avg	Folpet, 12.8 ng (1990)
0.000000006	Captan: daily dietary avg	Captan, 11.5 ng (1990)

Source: From Gold et al. 1992 (by permission of the American Association for the Advancement of Science).

In addition to possible traces of Alar, apple juice contains more than 100 natural chemicals, of which only 6 have been tested for carcinogenicity; 4 of these are carcinogenic in rodents at high doses.

Water Pollution

The possible hazards from carcinogens in contaminated well water in places like California's Santa Clara ("Silicon") Valley or Woburn, Massachusetts, should be compared with the possible hazards of ordinary tap water. Of the 35 wells that were shut down in the Santa Clara Valley because of a supposed cancer risk to humans (from traces of trichloroethylene), only 2 had water whose calculated possible hazard exceeded that of chloroform in ordinary chlorinated tap water. Well water is usually unchlorinated and hence lacks the chloroform that is present in concentrations of 83 ppb in average chlorinated tap water in the United States. The most polluted well water in the Santa Clara Valley had a relative possible hazard from trichloroethylene far below that for typical portions of common foods that contain natural rodent carcinogens.

In fact, animal studies provide no good reason to expect that either chloroform (from chlorination) or synthetic pollutants at current levels in tap water pose a significant cancer risk relative to the background, in the amounts that people consume (one or two liters a day). Epidemiological studies looking at the effect of water chlorination or pollution have difficulty adequately controlling for large risk factors such as diet and smoking. In terms of cancer risks from drinking water, natural arsenic (a known human carcinogen) appears to pose the highest population risk.

Moreover, the trace amounts of chemicals found in polluted wells are likely to be a negligible cause of birth defects, compared with known teratogens such as alcohol. The important known risk factors for birth defects and reproductive damage in humans are the mother's age, consumption of alcohol, poor diet, and exposure to the rubella virus.

Dioxin (TCDD) Compared with Broccoli and Alcohol

TCDD is one of the most feared industrial contaminants (see chapter 11), and is a potent carcinogen and teratogen in rodents. Typical human doses, however, are far below the lowest doses that have been shown to cause cancer and reproductive damage in rodents.

TCDD exerts many or all of its harmful effects in mammalian cells through binding to the Ah receptor. A wide variety of natural substances also bind to this receptor (tryptophan oxidation products), and, insofar as they have been examined, they have properties similar to those of TCDD.

Various food items contain substances that bind to the Ah receptor and have similar properties to TCDD. A cooked steak contains polycyclic hydrocarbons that bind to the Ah receptor, as do a variety of plant substances. Cabbage and broccoli, for example, contain indole carbinol (IC), whose breakdown products bind to the Ah receptor, induce enzymes and possibly cause cell division—just as TCDD does. IC is present in large amounts in broccoli (500 ppm), cabbage, cauliflower, and other members of the *Brassica* genus. At the pH of the stomach, IC forms chemical structures (known as dimers and trimers) that induce the same set of detoxifying enzymes as TCDD.

The relation between these chemicals and carcinogenesis is complex. IC, like TCDD, protects against carcinogenesis when given before aflatoxin or other carcinogens. However, when given after aflatoxin or other carcinogens, IC, like TCDD, stimulates carcinogenesis. Cabbage itself has been shown to stimulate carcinogenesis. IC derivatives appear to be more of a potential hazard than doses of TCDD being ingested by humans. However, it is not clear whether at the low doses of human exposure either IC or TCDD is hazardous. Many more of these natural "dioxin simulators" will probably be discovered in the future.

In comparison with alcohol, TCDD seems of minor interest as a teratogen or carcinogen. Alcohol is the most important known human chemical teratogen. In contrast, there is no persuasive evidence that TCDD is either carcinogenic or teratogenic in humans, although it is both in rodents at near-toxic doses. If one compares the potential of TCDD for causing birth defects with that of alcohol (after adjusting for their respective potency as determined in rodent tests), then daily consumption of TCDD at the EPA reference dose (the allowable dose) would be equivalent in teratogenic potential to a daily consumption of alcohol from 1/300,000 of a beer. That is equivalent to drinking a single beer (15 g ethyl alcohol) over a period of 8,000 years.

In humans, alcoholic beverages are carcinogenic as well as teratogenic. A comparison of the carcinogenic potential of TCDD with that of alcohol (adjusting for the potency in rodents) shows that ingesting the TCDD reference dose is equivalent to a person ingesting one beer every 294 years. The average per-capita consumption of alcohol in the United States is equivalent to more than one beer per person per day, and five drinks a day are a carcinogenic risk in humans. Thus the experimental evidence does not seem to justify the great concern over TCDD at levels near the reference dose.

Caution is necessary in drawing conclusions from the occurrence in the diet of natural chemicals that are rodent carcinogens. It is not argued here that these dietary exposures are necessarily of much relevance to human cancer. What is important in our analysis is that widespread exposures to naturally occurring rodent carcinogens may cast doubt on the relevance to human cancer of far lower levels of exposures to synthetic rodent carcinogens. What these results do call for is a reevaluation of the utility of animal cancer tests done at the MTD for providing information useful in protecting humans against low doses of rodent carcinogens when a high percentage of all chemicals appear to be rodent carcinogens.

Our results indicate that many ordinary foods would not pass the regulatory criteria used for synthetic chemicals. However, these results do not necessarily indicate that coffee consumption, for example, is a significant risk factor for human cancer even though it is thousands of times the HERP equivalent to the 1-in-1 million worse-case risk used by the EPA. Epidemiology, despite its difficulties, will have to tell us that. Adequate risk assessment from animal cancer tests requires more information about many aspects of toxicology such as effects on cell division, induction of defense and repair systems, and species differences.

With respect to natural pesticides in plant foods, strong epidemiological evidence indicates that low intake of fruits and vegetables doubles the risk of most types of cancer compared to high intake. This is likely to be due in good part to anticarcinogenic antioxidants and vitamins in fruits and vegetables. Since only 9 percent of adult Americans eat the recommended five servings of fruits and vegetables per day, we should be eating more of them, not less. Particular natural pesticides can be bred out of plants, and cooking methods modified, if further studies on mechanism or epidemiology indicate that it is important to do so.

Misconception No. 5: The Toxicology of Synthetic Chemicals Is Different from That of Natural Chemicals

It is often assumed that because plants are part of human evolutionary history, whereas industrial chemicals are not, animals have evolved mechanisms to cope with the toxicity of natural but not of synthetic chemicals. For example, Rachel Carson said, "For the first time in the history of the world, every human being is now subjected to contact with dangerous chemicals, from the moment of conception until death." This assumption is flawed for several reasons (Carson 1962).

A large number of natural chemicals might have toxic effects, yet humans have evolved general and specific defenses against them. General defenses offer protection against both natural and synthetic chemicals, and buffer humans well against toxins. They include the following:

1. The continuous shedding of cells that are exposed to toxins. The surface layers of the mouth, esophagus, stomach, intestine, colon, skin, and lungs are discarded every few days.
2. The ability of cells to respond to stress using a wide variety of general detoxifying enzymes, such as antioxidant enzymes or the glutathione transferases for detoxifying alkylating agents. Human cells that are exposed to small doses of an oxidant, such as radiation or hydrogen peroxide, respond by increasing antioxidant defenses and become more resistant to higher doses. These defenses can be stimulated both by synthetic and natural oxidants and are effective against both.
3. The active excretion of planar hydrophobic molecules (natural or synthetic) by liver and intestinal cells.
4. The ability of cells to repair damaged DNA. This mechanism is effective against damage to DNA by both synthetic and natural chemicals. Cells respond to damage by producing more repair.
5. The ability of animals to smell and taste bitter, acrid, astringent, and pungent chemicals, which warns them against a wide range of toxins. These stimuli are likely to be general defenses against particular types of toxicity. Mustard, pepper, garlic, and onions are pungent, acrid, or astringent, as are some synthetic chemicals, but humans often ignore the warnings.

Having general defenses, rather than specific defenses for each chemical, makes good evolutionary sense. Plant-eating animals presumably evolved such defenses to counter a changing array of plant toxins in an evolving world; an animal with only specific defenses would have difficulty obtaining new foods when favored plants became scarce.

Various natural toxins, some present during evolutionary history, cause cancer in vertebrates. Mold aflatoxins, for example, cause cancer in trout, rats, mice, monkeys, and humans. Eleven mold toxins have been reported to be carcinogenic, and 19 mold toxins have been shown to be clastogenic (break chromosomes). Many common elements (e.g., salts of lead, cadmium, beryllium, nickel, chromium, selenium, and arsenic) are carcinogenic or clastogenic at high doses.

Furthermore, epidemiologic studies in various countries show that some natural chemicals in food may be cancer risks to humans. The phorbol esters present in the *Euphorbiaceae,* some of which are used as folk remedies or herb teas, are potent inducers of cell division and a suspected cause of nasopharyngeal cancer in China and esophageal cancer in Curacao. Pyrrolidizine toxins are mutagens found in comfrey tea, various herbal medicines, and some foods; they cause liver cancer in rats, and may cause cirrhosis of the liver and other pathologies in humans.

The chewing of betel nuts with tobacco around the world has been correlated with oral cancer.

Plants have been evolving and refining their chemical weapons for at least 500 million years, and incur large fitness costs in producing them. Plants that lacked chemicals effective in deterring predators have been eliminated by natural selection.

Humans have not had time to evolve into a "toxic harmony" with all of the plants in their diet. Indeed, very few of the plants that humans eat would have been present in an African hunter-gatherer's diet. The human diet has changed drastically in the last few thousand years. Many plants have been introduced from one continent to another, including coffee, cocoa, tea, potatoes, tomatoes, corn, avocados, mangoes, olives, and kiwi fruit. Some vegetables, such as cabbage, broccoli, kale, cauliflower, and mustard, were used in ancient times primarily for medicinal purposes and were introduced as foods in Europe only in the Middle Ages. Natural selection works far too slowly for humans to have evolved specific resistance to the food toxins in newly introduced plants.

Humans have been poisoned by plant toxins in the milk of foraging animals. This was a common problem in previous centuries. Abraham Lincoln's mother died from drinking cow's milk that had been contaminated with toxins from the snakeroot plant. Since the plants foraged by cows vary from place to place and are usually inedible by humans, people cannot easily adapt to toxins in animal milk.

Some of these plant toxins are teratogenic in animals and humans. For example, when cows and goats forage on lupine, their offspring may show birth defects, such as "crooked calf" syndrome caused by a toxin (anagyrine) in the plant. This teratogen can be transferred to the animals' milk in sufficient quantities to produce birth defects in humans. In one rural California family, a baby boy, a litter of puppies, and goat kids all had a "crooked bone" birth defect. The pregnant woman and the pregnant dog had both consumed milk from the family goats that had consumed lupine, the main forage in winter.

Plants also have anticarcinogenic chemicals that play a major role in protecting humans against both synthetic and natural carcinogens (e.g., the antioxidants vitamin C, vitamin E, and beta carotene.

It has been argued that synergism between synthetic carcinogens could multiply hazards. However, this is also true of natural chemicals, which are by far the major source of chemicals in the diet.

This section began with a quotation from *Silent Spring,* one of whose targets was the synthetic pesticide DDT. DDT "bioconcentrates" in animal tissues because of its high solubility in fat. The same property is shared by fat-soluble natural pesticides, such as solanidine, which is found in the tissues of people who eat potatoes, which is known to cause reproductive damage in rodents. Many people view DDT as a particularly dangerous synthetic pesticide because of its bioconcentration and its years-long persistence in the environment. However, DDT is remarkably nontoxic to mammals, and has saved millions of human lives; it caused no demonstrable harm to people. As the first major synthetic insecticide, DDT replaced lead arsenate, which before the modern era was a major pesticide, and is carcinogenic and even more persistent in the environment. DDT was prudently phased out when its undesirable bioconcentration, persistence, and toxicity to some birds were recognized. Less persistent chemicals were developed to replace it.

Misconception No. 6: Storks Bring Babies and Pollution Causes Cancer and Birth Defects

The number of storks in Europe has been decreasing for decades. At the same time the European birth rate has been decreasing. We would be foolish to accept this correlation as evidence that storks bring babies.

Epidemiology tries to sort out the meaningful from the chance correlations and to determine those that may indicate cause and effect. However, it is hard to obtain persuasive cause-and-effect evidence by epidemiologic methods, because of the many methodologic difficulties that are discussed elsewhere in this volume (see chapter 1). Toxicology (the study of toxic properties of chemicals) can help us decide whether an observed correlation reflects a cause-and-effect relation or is merely accidental.

Epidemiology and toxicology provide no persuasive evidence that pollution is a significant cause of birth defects or cancer. Epidemiologic studies of the Love Canal toxic waste dump in Niagara Falls, New York, or of dioxin in Agent Orange (see chapter 11), or of air pollutants from refineries in Contra Costa County, California, or of contaminated well water in Silicon Valley, California or Woburn, Massachusetts (see chapter 10), or of the pesticide DDT, provide no persuasive evidence that such forms of pollution cause human cancer. In most of these cases, the people involved appear to have been exposed to levels of chemicals that were much too low (relative to the background of rodent carcinogens occurring naturally or produced from cooking food) to be credible sources of increased cancer. No systematic analysis of birth defects (using an index such as the HERP index discussed above for carcinogenesis) has been done so far on these chemicals.

Some chemicals increase cancer in the workplace, at high levels of exposure. In California, workers were allowed to breathe high levels of ethylene dibromide (EDB), a fumigant and leaded gasoline additive. It was testified in 1981 that the workers' exposure was greater than the dose that would produce cancer in half of the rats in a lifetime cancer test. California subsequently lowered the permissible exposure to this agent by more than a hundredfold.

Misconception No. 7: Trade-offs Are Not Necessary in Eliminating Pesticides

Plants need chemical defenses—natural or synthetic—to survive attack by pests. There is a trade-off between nature's pesticides and synthetic pesticides in providing such protection.

Cultivated plants commonly contain fewer natural toxins than their wild counterparts, as a result of domestication. For example, the wild potato, the progenitor of cultivated strains of potato, has a glycoalkaloid content about three times higher than that of cultivated strains and is more toxic. The leaves of the wild cabbage (the progenitor of cabbage, broccoli, and cauliflower) contain about twice as many glucosinolates as cultivated cabbage. The wild bean contains about three times as many cyanogenic glucosides as does the cultivated bean. Similar differences between cultivated and wild varieties have been reported in lettuce, lima bean, mango, and cassava.

Because of disproportionate concern about synthetic pesticide residues, some plant breeders are developing more insect-resistant plants that have more natural toxins. Two recent cases illustrate the potential hazards of this approach to pest control (Ames et al. 1990b).

As the first example, a major grower introduced a new variety of highly insect-resistant celery. This led to a flurry of complaints to the Centers for Disease Control that people who handled the celery developed rashes after subsequent exposure to sunlight. After some detective work, scientists found that the pest-resistant celery contained 6,200 ppb of carcinogenic (and mutagenic) psoralens, compared with 800 ppb in normal celery (see Table 7.2). It is not known whether other natural pesticides were increased in the insect-resistant celery as well. The celery is still on the market.

As a second example, a new potato, developed at a cost of millions of dollars, had to be withdrawn from the market because it was acutely toxic to humans when grown under particular soil conditions. This was a consequence of higher levels of the natural toxins solanine and chaconine, which block nerve transmission and are known rodent teratogens. These toxins were widely introduced into the world diet about 400 years ago, when potatoes were disseminated from the Andes. A typical 200 g potato contains 15 mg of toxins (75,000 ppb), which is less than a factor of ten below levels that are measurably toxic to humans. Neither solanine nor chaconine has been tested for carcinogenicity. In contrast, malathion, the main synthetic organophosphate pesticide residue in our diet (0.006 mg per day), has been tested and is not a carcinogen in rats or mice.

Certain crops have become popular in developing countries because they thrive without requiring costly synthetic pesticides. However, some of these naturally pest-resistant crops are highly toxic and require extensive processing to detoxify them.

For example, cassava root, a major food crop in Africa and South America is quite resistant to pests and disease. However it contains so much cyanide that extensive washing, grinding, fermenting, and heating are needed to make it edible. Ataxia (the inability to control body movements) from chronic cyanide poisoning is common in many cassava-eating areas in Africa.

A second example is the pest-resistant grain *Lathyrus sativus,* which is cultivated in parts of India for making some types of dahl. Its seeds contain a nerve poison (beta-N-oxalyl aminoalanine), that causes a crippling nervous system disorder, neurolathyrism.

To avoid synthetic pesticides, "organic" farmers can legally use natural pesticides from one plant species to protect plants of a different species. These include rotenone (which Indians used to poison fish) or pyrethrins from chrysanthemum plants. These naturally derived pesticides have not been as extensively tested for carcinogenicity (rotenone is negative, however), mutagenicity, or teratogenicity as synthetic pesticides. Their safety compared with synthetic pesticides should not be assumed prematurely.

Nonscientists often think of chemicals as only synthetic, and characterize synthetic chemicals as toxic, as if every natural chemical were not also toxic at some dose. Even a National Research Council report states: "Advances in classical plant breeding . . . offer some promise for nonchemical pest control in the future . . ." (1987, 9). The report was concerned with pesticide residues in tomatoes, but ignored the natural pesticides in tomatoes. Tomatine, one such pesticide, was introduced comparatively recently into the world diet from Peru 400 years ago. Neither tomatine nor a related natural product, tomatidine, has been tested in rodent cancer bioassays. A 100 g tomato contains 36 mg of tomatine (360,000 ppb), which is much closer to an acutely toxic level in humans than residues of synthetic pesticides.

Efforts to prevent hypothetical cancer risks of one in a million could be counterproductive if the risks of the alternatives are greater. For example, Alar was withdrawn from the market after the EPA proposed cancellation hearings on it and after the Natural Resources Defense Council went to the media to get the process accelerated. However, the potential problems from withdrawing Alar should be addressed. These include the possible increase in pesticide use, increase of molds in apple juice, and increases in price that might cause consumers to substitute less healthy foods. Apart from giving up smoking, eating more fruits and vegetables, and less fat, appears to be the best way to lower risks of cancer and heart disease.

Misconception No. 8: Technology Is Harmful to Public Health

Modern technologies almost always replace older, more hazardous technologies. Billions of pounds of TCE (one of the most important industrial solvents) and PERC (the main dry-cleaning solvent) are used in the United States every year because they are low in toxicity and are not flammable (see chapter 10). The replacement of flammable solvents by these and other chlorinated solvents was a major advance in fire safety, even at the minor cost of low-level (parts per billion) contamination in some water supplies.

Eliminating a carcinogen may have unwanted effects. For example, EDB was the main fumigant in the United States before it was banned in 1984. It was present in our foods in trivial amounts, about 0.4 ppb. The cancer risk from the average daily intake of EDB at such levels is about one-tenth that of the aflatoxin in the average peanut butter sandwich, which is itself a minimal possible hazard (see Table 7.3). The trade-offs in elimination of EDB fumigation should be addressed, such as greater insect infestation and greater contamination of grain by carcinogen-producing molds. The net results would be a reduction in public health. Fumigants intended to replace EDB appear to be less effective, and more hazardous and expensive.

Every living thing and every industry pollute to some extent. Scientists can now measure parts-per-billion levels of chemicals, and are developing methods to measure parts-per-trillion. This makes us more aware of toxicity chemicals, but does not mean that exposure to them is necessarily increasing or that the detected chemicals cause human disease. Minimizing pollution is clearly desirable for other reasons but is an issue separate from cancer prevention; of course, it is important to obtain the greatest reduction in pollution at the lowest economic cost.

Focusing on minor rather than major health risks is counterproductive. Excessive concern for pollution will not improve public health—and, in the confusion, may cause us to neglect important hazards, such as smoking, alcohol, unbalanced diets (with too much saturated fat and cholesterol, and too few fruits and vegetables), AIDS, radon in homes, and occupational exposures to chemicals at high levels.

The progress of technology and scientific research is likely to lead to a decrease in cancer death rates and incidence of birth defects, and an increase in the average human life span.

Acknowledgements

This work was supported by National Cancer Institute Outstanding Investigator grant CA39910, by National Institute of Environmental Health Sciences Center grant ES01896, and by U .S. Environmental Protection Agency grant no. DE-AC03-76SF00098. This chapter has been partially adapted from B. N. Ames, *What are the major carcinogens in the etiology of cancer: Six errors,* in V. T. DeVita, Jr., S. Hellman, and S. A. Rosenberg, eds., Important Advances in Oncology 237–247 (Philadelphia: J. B. Lippincott, 1989); from B. N. Ames and L. S. Gold, *Misconceptions regarding environmental pollution and cancer causation,* in M. Moore, ed., Health Risks and the Press: Perspectives on Media Coverage of Risk Assessment and Health 19-34 (Washington, DC: The Media Institute 1989); B. N. Ames and L. S. Gold, *Dietary carcinogens, environmental pollution, and cancer: Some misconceptions,* 7 Med. Oncol, & Tumor Pharmacother. 69–85 (1990); and L. S. Gold., T. H. Slone, B. R. Stern, N. B. Manley, and B. N. Ames, Rodent carcinogens: Setting priorities, 258 *Science* 261–265 (1992).

Notes

1. We have developed a data base (the carcinogenic potency data base) of chronic, long-term, high-dose animal cancer tests that have been published. A chemical is classified as a carcinogen in our analysis on the basis of the author's positive evaluation in at least one experiment. Clearly, rodent carcinogens are not all the same: some have been tested many times in several species while others have been examined at only one site in one species; some are positive in two species and they or their metabolites are mutagenic in animals; some are only positive at one site in one species and are not mutagenic.

References

Ames, B. N., M. Profet, and L. S. Gold. 1990a. Dietary pesticides (99.99% all natural). 87 *Proc. Nat. Acad. Sci.* 7777–7781.

Ames, B. N., M . Profet, and L. S. Gold. 1990b. Nature's chemicals and synthetic chemicals: Comparative toxicology. 87 *Proc. Nat. Acad. Sci.* 7782–7786.

Carson, R. 1962. *Silent spring.* Boston: Houghton Mifflin.

Doll, R., and R. Peto. 1981. *The causes of cancer.* Oxford: Oxford University Press.

Gold, L. S., T. H. Slone, B. R. Stern, N. B. Manley, and B. N. Ames. 1992. Rodent carcinogens: Setting priorities. 258 *Science* 261–265.

Gold, L. S., N. B. Manley, T. H. Slone, G. M. Backman, L. Rohrbach, and B. N. Ames. 1992. The fifth plot of the Carcinogenic Potency Database: Results of animal bioassays published in the general literature through 1988 and by the National Toxicology Program through 1989. 100 *Environ. Health Persp.*

Gold, L. S., C. B. Sawyer, R. Magaw, G. M. Backman, M. deVeciana, R. Levinson, N. K. Hooper, W. R. Havender, L. Bernstein, R. Peto, M. C. Pike, and B. N. Ames. 1984. A carcinogenic potency database of the standardized results of animal bioassays. 58 *Environ. Health Persp.* 9–319.

Gold, L. S., T. H. Slone, G. M. Backman, S. Eisenberg, M. DaCosta, M. Wong, N. B. Manley, L. Rohrbach, and B. N. Ames. 1990. Third chronological supplement to the Carcinogenic Potency Database: Standardized results of animal bioassays published through December 1986 and by the National Toxicology Program through June 1987. 84 *Environ. Health Persp.* 215–285.

Gunderson, E. L. 1988. FDR total diet study, April 1982–April 1984. Dietary intakes of pesticides, selected elements, and other chemicals. 71 *J. Assoc. Off. Anal. Chem.* 1200–1209.

Ishidate Jr., M., M. C. Harnois, and T. Sofuni. 1988. A comparative analysis of data on the clastogenicity of 951 chemical substances tested in mammalian cell cultures. 195 *Mutat. Res.* 151–213.

National Cancer Institute. 1988. 1987 Annual cancer statistics review including cancer trends 1950–1985. NIH pub. no. 88-2789. Washington, DC: National Institutes of Health.

National Research Council Board on Agriculture. 1987. Regulating pesticides in food. Washington, DC: National Academy of Sciences.

Biographical Sketch

Professor Bruce N. Ames is Director, N.I.E.H.S. Environmental Health Sciences Center, University of California, Berkeley, and was formerly on the board of directors of the National Cancer Institute (National Cancer Advisory Board). He received the most prestigious award for cancer research, the General Motors Cancer Research Foundation Prize (1983), and the highest award in environmental achievement, the Tyler Prize (1985). He has produced 250 scientific publications. Professor Ames has been elected to the Royal Swedish Academy of Sciences and the Japan Cancer Association. He is a member of the National Academy of Sciences.

Dr. Lois Swirsky Gold is a staff scientist at the Lawrence Berkeley Laboratory and is director of the Carcinogenic Potency Project. She is a member of the N.I.E.H.S. Environmental Health Sciences Center, University of California, Berkeley. She has served on the panel of expert reviewers that evaluates rodent carcinogenesis studies for the National Toxicology Program.

8

Asbestos: The Hazard, the Risk, and Public Policy

Ralph D'Agostino, Jr., and Richard Wilson

Introduction

According to the *Oxford English Dictionary,* the word *asbestos* originally meant "inextinguishable" or "unquenchable," and was applied by Diocorides to quicklime; Pliny used the word in a form then incorrect, but now more widely used, to mean "incombustible fiber." Although Pliny's extension would allow even man-made fibers, such as fiberglass, to be included in the definition of asbestos, this is now an unusual usage. In this article we further restrict our use of the word to a group of incombustible mineral fibers that are based upon silicon. Even so, there are several fiber types in this group, each coming from a different mineral. Each chemical has two mineral forms, one nonasbestiform, the other asbestiform (or fibrous) (Fig. 8.1).

Asbestos has been used for over a century as a fire retardant, because it can be easily woven into cloth. At one time, for example, every theater had an asbestos safety curtain, lowered at every performance, to separate the audience from the stage in the event of fire. Starting in World War II, the use of asbestos increased markedly. It was first used in quantity as a fire retardant on ships—much of the damage at Pearl Harbor was caused by fire. A little later builders and designers realized that asbestos was also a good thermal insulator. They found a way of installing asbestos by spraying. The use of asbestos expanded during World War II, and increased rapidly until the mid-1960s. In some cases the asbestos was sprayed wet, so that the occupational and environmental exposures would be expected to be lower than if sprayed dry.

As early as 1906, Auribault noted 50 deaths in the years 1890–1895 in an asbestos weaving mill in Calvados, France. A year later, Murray noted a death in the United Kingdom from acute fibrosis of the lungs. At the time, there was considerable question about the nature of the disease, which was then called "asbestos silicosis." Silicosis had been wide-

asbestiform   non-asbestiform

Figure 8.1

Source: *Report of The Royal Commission on Matters of Health and Safety Arising from the Use of Asbestos in Ontario*, Vol. 1 (Ontario Ministry of the Attorney General, 1984), pp. 78–79.

asbestiform   non-asbestiform

Figure 8.1 (continued)

spread in the mines for millennia. Pneumoconiosis, often referred to as black lung disease, had been identified among coal miners; the Bolton cotton spinners also had problems with cotton dust. It was not immediately recognized that the fibrous nature of the asbestos led to specific problems.

After 1910, with the development and widespread use of X-rays, more specific distinctions became possible. By 1927, X-rays revealed that two-thirds of all asbestos workers had abnormal lungs. Cooke coined the term "asbestosis" to describe the disease, which appeared after prolonged high exposure to asbestos in the workplace. Figure 8.2 is a graph showing the apparent threshold behavior at about 25 (product of fibers per milliliter of air and the number of years of exposure) integrated exposure (product of exposure and the duration of the exposure). In 1927 most scientists believed that asbestos behaved like a simple poison, and if the integrated exposure was kept below this threshold, there should be no problem. (However, if one forces a straight line through the points

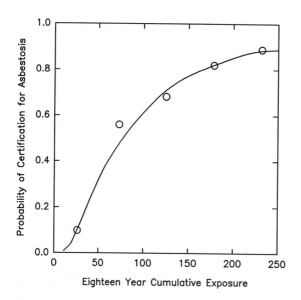

Figure 8.2
The cumulative probability of developing asbestosis, as evaluated at the end of 18 years of cumulative exposure
Measured in fibers/ml-years. [For example, 50 f/ml-years corresponds to breathing air with an average of approximately 3 fibers per milliliter for 18 years.] The line is a log-normal fit to the data.
Source: Adapted from Finkelstein 1982.

of Figure 8.1 and the origin, one might conclude that some risk is present at even low levels of exposure.)

In 1935, Lynch and Smith implicated asbestos in lung cancer, although their observation was complicated by the fact that almost all the victims in their study also smoked (Lynch and Smith 1935). Twelve percent of all asbestosis patients in their study developed lung cancer. The first good epidemiologic study seems to have been a seminal paper by Doll (1955). The first case of mesothelioma caused by asbestos was diagnosed in 1956 by Wagner (1985) in the pleura of a black adult male who had been a shower attendant in one of the Witwatersrand gold mines.

Many public health scientists had thought that the greatest asbestos exposures were in mines and weaving factories, and that they were comparatively small elsewhere. In mines and factories some effort was made to maintain exposures below the threshold for asbestosis, but there was comparatively little effort to reduce exposure from the use of asbestos. Thus, when Selikoff and collaborators in the late 1960s found that insulation workers had very high exposure to asbestos, it was a great surprise to many. In fact, the persons most at risk from exposure to asbestos include insulation workers and asbestos weavers, miners, and millers. More recently, concern has been expressed about widespread exposure to occupants of buildings.

The possibility that occupants of buildings might have adverse effects from asbestos therein has been called by some "the third wave of asbestos disease" (manufacturing workers and insulators being the first two waves). A whole issue of Proceedings of the New York Academy of Sciences has been devoted to this (NYAS 1991).

However, as will be discussed below, no firm evidence exists for any adverse effect with the possible exception of custodians and maintenance workers (Selikoff 1990b). Moreover, the measurements of asbestos concentrations, particularly the more recent ones, make this very unlikely (Upton 1991). It is the concern about this "third wave" that makes the asbestos risk a "phantom risk."

Now, 20 years after Selikoff's work, we may ask several questions:

1. Why did it take so long for the adverse health effects of asbestos to be noticed, and how can we present more of the many personal tragedies that resulted from excessive exposure?
2. Are our present actions to reduce asbestos exposure effective, or are we increasing exposure by improperly removing asbestos that is best left in place?
3. Is there an alternative to asbestos in each of its three major applications—fire

retardant, thermal insulator, and friction uses (brake linings)—that is as safe as the safest form of asbestos properly applied?

4. Is the U.S. plan to ban all future use of asbestos justified by scientific evidence?

Each of these questions has elicited heated disagreement, often including personal attacks on motives and integrity. But as the best-known authority on asbestos has stated: "Arguments should be evaluated on their merits and not by reference to the interest of those who make them" (Selikoff 1990a). As we shall see, direct data on the effects of the low exposures that now interest us are necessarily incomplete, and the available evidence is therefore often indirect.

Health Effects of Asbestos

Asbestos has a number of health effects, which are summarized below.

1. Benign conditions of the pleura, and in particular pleural placques. These may cause temporary problems but are not usually considered a danger; often they are present without causing symptoms of disease in the individual. They do, however, provide indication (though not definite proof) of exposure (Churg 1982, 1983; Hillerdal 1978).

2. Asbestosis, defined as fibrosis of the lung caused by asbestos dust. According to Doll and Peto (1982), the disease is indistinguishable from a rare "cryptogenic fibrosing alveolitis." Asbestosis is usually assumed, however, if there has been prior asbestos exposure; the probabilities certainly support that assumption.

Asbestosis seems to appear only after heavy accumulated exposure, and only if some threshold exposure level is exceeded. The medical literature has some confusion as to what is to be called asbestosis. Most authors use the term for interstitial fibrosis. Others distinguish pathological reactions in the respiratory bronchioles and alveolar ducts, and call them small airways disease. This distinction is useful, because a wide variety of other minerals, such as silica, cause small airways disease but do not cause (or cause less frequently) interstitial fibrosis (Churg 1983). (For an interesting history of the pathologist's role in this developing understanding, we recommend the article by Craighead (1987)).

3. Lung cancer (bronchial carcinoma). Exposure to asbestos correlates clearly with lung cancer. There is a long latency period of about 30 years after exposure. Figure 8.3 shows data from the study by Selikoff and Seidman. Figure 8.3a plots the relative risk—the ratio of the number of cancers in the exposed individuals to the number expected for unexposed individuals—versus the age of the subject. The relative risk shows a peak 30 years after the first exposure, then declines. Figure 8.3b plots the actual cancer rate in these individuals.

Figure 8.4 shows the principal asbestos diseases discussed above and their sites in the human body. Many cases of lung cancer arise in conjunction with asbestosis. The connection was strong enough for the chief inspector of factories in the United Kingdom to ask more than half a century ago: "Does silica or asbestos or the fibrosis of the lung they produce tend to inhibit cancer of the lung or to produce it? If the latter, do either of these two substances act as specific carcinogenic agents like tar, or is it that the disease they produce only prepares the soil for the occurrence of cancer?" . . . [A]mong 103 fatal cases in which asbestosis or asbestosis with tuberculosis were present, cancer of the lung was associated in 12 cases (11.6 percent) (Merewether 1938).

The connection between asbestosis and lung cancer bears directly on the relation between amount of exposure to the mineral and risk of lung cancer (the dose-response relation). There are no data that directly bear on this point, at least not at the low doses (under 0.01 fibers per milliliter of air) that are of public concern today, but several possibilities exist. If asbestosis develops first (and then sharply increases the risk of lung cancer), the dose-response relationships for lung cancer and asbestosis should be similar. Most scientists believe that exposures above some threshold are needed for asbestosis to develop. If lung cancer is directly connected to asbestosis, its risk should likewise be zero below some threshold of exposure. Conversely, if asbestos can cause lung cancer in the absence of asbestosis, an individual might incur some risk even at low levels of exposure. Some authors maintain that asbestosis is a necessary condition for lung cancer (e.g., Browne 1986), but this point cannot be directly confirmed because the risks, if any, are too small to measure at low levels of exposure.

The relation between asbestos dose and cancer risk is important; for a good general review see Zeise et al. (1987). A linear relationship between dose and cancer risk means that if the dose is halved, the risk is halved. Thus, some risk remains even at very low levels of exposure. In a nonlinear relation, the risk may fall off faster at low doses, perhaps exhibiting a threshold exposure below which the risk is zero. Thus, a linear dose-response relation will imply higher levels of risk at low doses than a threshold or other nonlinear model.

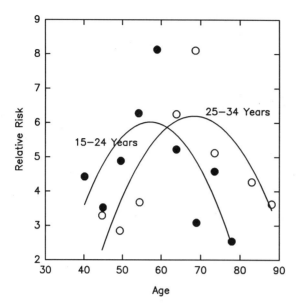

Figure 8.3a
Relative risk for lung cancer as a function of age
Note: The age of onset of exposure is shown in the graph. The lines are parabolic
fits to the data. The data show a latency of about 35 years between the onset of
exposure to asbestos and the greatest risk of developing lung cancer.
Source: Adapted from Nicholson et al. 1981.

Before 1980, most authorities believed that the relation between asbestos dose and cancer risk is nonlinear. Enterline (1981) discusses possible dose–response relationships for asbestos and cancer, and the use of
occupational data (with various assumptions) to predict risks at the much
lower exposure levels in environmental settings.

A related consideration is the latency (delay) between exposure and
development of a tumor. Enterline (1976) assumed that the cancer risk is
proportional to the exposure but that the latency increased at low exposure levels. Increases in latency of this sort were observed by Druckery
in animal tests with several chemicals, and by Davies (1985) for mesothelioma following peritoneal injection of asbestos in rats. Based on these
observations, Jones and Grendon (1975) suggested a formula in which
asbestos risk decreases faster than in a linear model at low doses. Mehir
et al. (1978) described the procedure the Consumer Products Safety
Commission (CPSC) used at that time to estimate cancer risk from asbestos, based on this method.

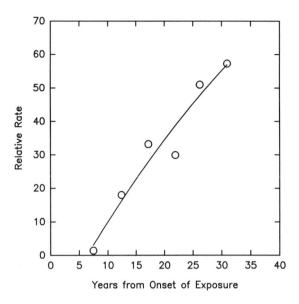

Figure 8.3b
The incidence of lung cancer as a function of time after onset of exposure to asbestos
Note: The rates are normalized to the first data point, to illustrate the rapid increase in incidence with age.
Source: Adapted from Nicholson et al. 1981.

The CPSC has, however, since changed its procedure (CPSC 1983). They assume that the dose-response relationship for asbestos remains linear at low doses. The new CPSC policy makes no allowance for the possibility that tumors may develop more slowly at low doses.

In 1978, when Mehir et al. published their report, one of us (Wilson) was urging other scientists in industry to calculate carcinogen risks by using a linear dose-response relationship. There were several reasons for taking this position. The linear relationship may be correct, as many academic scientists believe. It also seemed unwise for leaders of industry to insist rigidly on theoretical relationships between exposure and cancer risk that are not accepted by many academics. For example, Peto (1979), a highly renowned epidemiologist, supported the use of a linear dose-response relationship for asbestos for policy purposes.

It was also clear that scientists in the regulatory agencies were going to adopt a linear model, so as to be on the safe side. Indeed, in 1984 a committee of the National Academy of Sciences concluded that although a linear dose-response assumption "may not always be justified . . . it should lead to an appropriate upper bound for the committee's risk assessments for asbestos." The committee believed that "ruling out a linear dose term for exposure does not seem justified by the data now available."

Certainly, a linear dose-response model simplifies the estimation of risk. The dose used in all linear models can simply be the long-term average level of exposure. Other models may require special allowance for occasional exposures to high concentrations. Selikoff (1990b) and Brody (1990), for example, have expressed particular concern about intermittent high exposures of maintenance workers. This concern is automatically addressed if the average dose is used with a linear dose-response relationship. Nevertheless, no one can prove that a linear dose-response relationship is correct; sufficient data are (and will always remain) unobtainable at exposure levels where the risk of disease is exceedingly small.

Any discussion of dose-response relationships for asbestos and cancer is complicated by the fact that asbestos seems to exert its effect synergistically with cigarette smoke, that is, the cancer risk is more than that from asbestos exposure and smoking considered separately. The usual reference on this point is a study of insulation workers by Hammond et al. (1979). The first column of Table 8.1 lists the relative risks of asbestos exposure with and without smoking.

Based on their data, Hammond et al. suggested that the risks of asbestos and cigarette smoking combine in a multiplicative way. We describe the relative risk by the formula

Relative Risk = $(1 + a)(1 + c) = 1 + a + c + ac,$ (Equation 8.1)

Table 8.1
Risks of lung cancer caused by asbestos exposure and smoking

	Relative risk	Predicted by equation 8.1
Nonsmoker, non asbestos exposed	1.00	1
Smoker, non asbestos exposed	10.85	11
Nonsmoker, asbestos exposed	5.17	5
Smoker, asbestos exposed	53.24	55

Source: Hammond et al. 1979.

where *a* and *c* are proportional to asbestos exposure and cigarette smoking. For heavy exposure to asbestos *a* is equal to 4; for heavy smokers *c* equals 10.

In the above equation, the term *ac* expresses the synergistic effect between smoking and asbestos. Thus, compared with a nonsmoker with no asbestos exposure, a heavy smoker has an 11-fold higher risk for lung cancer, a nonsmoking asbestos worker has 5-fold higher risk, and a heavy smoker with heavy asbestos exposure has a 55-fold higher risk.

The results of this formula (Table 8.1, second column) agree extraordinarily well with the data (Table 8.1, first column); indeed, no other study has produced such a good fit to an equation like this that includes a multiplicative effect. By contrast, McDonald (1980) found something closer to an additive effect (Table 8.2), in which the relative risk is close to the sum of risks from smoking and asbestos considered separately.

4. Mesothelioma of the pleura or peritoneum. Mesothelioma is normally very rare except in individuals exposed to asbestos, and strongly associated with asbestos exposure. No evidence exists for a synergistic effect of smoking and asbestos on the risk of this disease.

Mesothelioma develops at least ten years after the exposure of an individual to asbestos; the risk increases very quickly with age, with no evidence that it subsequently declines. This suggests that the exposed tissues do not repair the damage caused by the exposure. Peto et al. (1982) accordingly suggested a model for mesothelioma risk, using Selikoff's data from insulation workers (Figure 8.5), that predicts a steady increase in relative risk in the years following exposure. Therefore, according to this model, mesothelioma poses the largest health risk for nonsmokers exposed to asbestos at young ages.

Table 8.2
Risks of lung cancer caused by asbestos exposure and smoking

| | Asbestos exposure | | |
	Little	Moderate	Heavy
Nonsmokers	1	2.0	6.9
Moderate smokers	6.3	7.5	12.8
Heavy smokers	11.8	13.3	25.0

Source: McDonald 1980.

5. Other cancers.   Figure 8.4 shows the locations of lesions known to be related to asbestos exposure. An increase of various other cancers has been found by Selikoff et al. (1979) among asbestos workers (see Table 8.3). Few of these cancers have been attributed reliably to asbestos, however; and any increases in risk, if real, for these cancers from asbestos exposure would be smaller than for lung cancer.

Probability of Causation

What is the probability that asbestos caused any particular case of mesothelioma, bronchial carcinoma, or pleural plaques? Mesothelioma is so rare that whenever it develops in an exposed individual, the cause is usually assumed to be asbestos. If the cancer appears less than ten years after exposure, however, this must be questioned. Several cases of mesothelioma in a small village in Turkey have been attributed to erionite, a locally obtained fiber used in building materials (Baris et al. 1988).

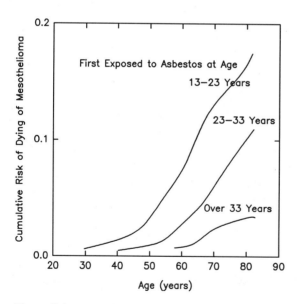

Figure 8.4
Cumulative risk of dying of mesothelioma in the absence of other causes among North American insulation workers first exposed to asbestos at different ages
Note: The increase in mortality occurs approximately 30–35 years after the onset of exposure. The latency for the disease is therefore at least 30–35 years.
Source: Adapted from Peto et al. 1982.

Table 8.3
Deaths among 17,800 asbestos insulation workers in the United States and Canada, January 1, 1967–December 31, 1986

Underlying cause of death	Expected*	Observed (BE)	Observed (DC)	Ratio Observed: Expected (BE)	Ratio Observed: Expected (DC)
Total deaths, all causes	3,454	4,951	4,951	1.43	1.43
Total cancer, all sites	761	2,295	2,127	3.01	2.79
Cancer of lung	269	1,168	1,008	4.35	3.75
Pleural mesothelioma	★★	173	89	—	—
Peritoneal mesothelioma	★★	285	92	—	—
	★★	0	55	—	—
Gastrointestinal cancer (esophagus, colon-rectum, stomach)	136	189	188	1.39	1.39
Cancer of larynx★★★	4.7	11	9	2.34	1.91
Cancer of pharynx, buccal★★★	10.1	21	16	2.06	1.59
Cancer of kidney★★★	8.1	19	18	2.36	2.23
All other cancer★★★	131.8	184	252	1.40	1.91
Non-infectious pulmonary diseases, total	145	507	465	3.50	3.21
Asbestosis	★★	427	201	—	—
All other causes	2,547	2,149	2,359	0.84	0.93

Notes:
*Expected deaths are based upon white male age-specific U.S. death rates of the U.S. National Cancer for Health Statistics, 1967–1976.
★★Rates are not available, but these have been rare causes of death in the general population.
(BE): Best evidence. Number of deaths categorized after review of best available information (autopsy, surgical, clinical).
(DC): Number of deaths as recorded from death certificates information only.
Source: Selikoff et al. 1979, 103 (Table 12). Updated in Selikoff and Seidman (1991).
★★★Deaths only until 1970.

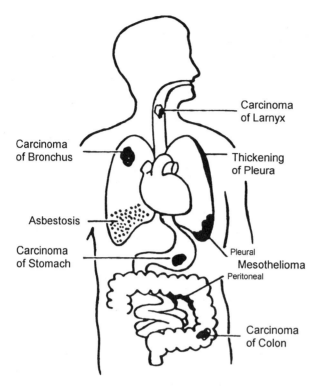

Figure 8.5
Principal asbestos-related diseases and conditions and their sites in the human body.
Source: Adapted from an illustration by Ferrell. (From Dupre et al. 1984).

Bronchial carcinoma is more difficult to attribute to asbestos because of the latter's strong synergistic effect with tobacco smoke in producing this disease. Bronchial carcinoma (and also fibrosis of the lung) in a non-smoker would normally be attributed to asbestos if there is any history of exposure to the mineral. With smokers the situation is much less clear. Certainly a nonsmoker exposed to asbestos is less at risk for bronchial carcinoma than a smoker not exposed to asbestos. Presumably, smoking is the main cause of lung diseases even if asbestos is also on the scene. On the other hand, the combined risks of smoking and heavy asbestos exposure far exceed those of smoking alone. The view of this matter by courts is suggested by the fact that the asbestos manufacturer Johns-Manville has been driven into bankruptcy while the tobacco company Philip Morris has not. Brodeur (1985) describes this attitude. The scientific evidence, however, suggests that the simplest and most direct apportionment is to rank smoking as five times as much to blame for lung cancers as asbestos, as shown by Tables 8.1 and 8.2.

Are All Fibers the Same?

Scientists are unsure precisely how asbestos causes disease, but many believe that its effect is physical, not chemical. If so, other fibers would entail similar risks, if they were of similar size and shape, and resided for similar times in the lung before decomposing or being expelled. Tests in animals and cells suggest that fiberglass fibers whose length and diameter are in a certain range may be as risky as asbestos (Hesterberg and Barrett 1984). No existing data contradict that view. But few people have been exposed to high levels of fiberglass in the past, so no good epidemiologic data exist. One recent epidemiologic report (Engholm et al. 1987) suggests that fiberglass is slightly worse than chrysotile asbestos in causing mesothelioma, but these results are not yet universally accepted by scientists.

Different types of asbestos have different health risks associated with them. Chrysotile asbestos, whose fibers are curly, seems to be less potent in producing mesothelioma than other types of asbestos such as crocidolite, whose fibers are straight and sharp. Peto made a summary of the data in various charts for (Table 8.4). The number of mesotheliomas in the chrysotile mine studied by McDonald is much less than the number among insulation workers exposed to crodilite. In a study of asbestos workers in Rochdale, Peto et al (1985) found few mesotheliomas, consistent with a small amount of crocidilite present. A critical analysis of the epidemiologic data by Langer and Nolan (1988) confirms the difference between chrysotile and other types of asbestos.

Some scientists do not believe that chrysotile asbestos causes mesothelioma in people. However, pure chrysotile asbestos does cause mesothelioma in rodents. But rodent tests also show dramatic differences in the effects of different kinds of asbestos. In one study, erionite particles (associated with the human mesothelioma in the Turkish village) induced 27 mesotheliomas in 28 laboratory rats; all the other asbestos varieties combined induced only 11 mesotheliomas in 668 rats (Wagner 1985). The reason for the different risks of different types of asbestos is not clear. One possibility is that chrysotile fibers are removed from the human lung more quickly than other asbestos fibers, and consequently result in lower exposure to lung tissues.

Table 8.4
Comparison of lung cancer and mesothelioma at different cohorts

Fibre	Lung and pleural cancer			Mesothelioma (B) O	Mesothelioma/Excess (B)/(A)
	O	E	(A) O-E		
Chrysotile and crocidolite (Enterline)	14	5.2	8.8	3	34%
	49	18.1	30.9	2	6%
Insulation (Selikoff)	533	105.6	427.4	175	41%
Crocidolite mine (Hobbs)	56	28.7	27.3	9	33%
Chrysotile and crocidolite(?) (Peto)	47	23.3	23.7	7	30%
Chrysotile mine (J.C. McDonald)	230	184.0	46.0	11	24%
Mixed (Newhouse)	180	46.8	131.2	96	43%
Amosite (Seidman)	116	19.1	96.9	16	17%

Source: Ontario, Royal Commission on Asbestos, Exhibit II-37, Tab 12, in RCA Transcript of Public Hearings, Evidence of Mr. Julian Peto, 29 July 1981, Volume no. 25(A), pp. 10, 61–63: Julian Peto, Assorted Transparencies. (Mimeographed.)

The size of the fiber seems to be important. Most scientists believe that fibers must be longer than 5 microns to be effective carcinogens, and must have a ratio of length to diameter of at least 5 to 1. Scientists generally agree that shorter fibers are less effective per fiber than longer ones, but more effective per unit of weight. The reason may be that macrophages (white blood cells that remove the particles from tissues) can envelop shorter fibers but not longer ones.

Lippmann (1988) reviewed the available data and concluded that fibers of different shapes and sizes cause different diseases, provided that their length is above a certain critical length (that varies with disease). This critical length is 2 microns for asbestosis, 5 microns for mesothelioma, and 10 microns for lung cancer. For asbestosis and lung cancer, where the fibers must be retained in the lungs, fibers with a diameter less than 0.15 micron pose no risk; for mesothelioma (which is caused by fibers that migrate from the surfaces of the lungs into deeper tissues) the hazard seems linked to fiber diameters greater than 0.1 micron.

These conclusions are plausible; however, the epidemiologic evidence is not firm enough to give them strong support, and they have not been universally accepted by scientists. But Lippmann's arguments support the general belief of scientists that low-level exposure to fibers longer than 5 microns leads to negligible risk of mesothelioma or lung cancer.

Risk at Low Doses

High exposures to asbestos are clearly hazardous. The public controversy today concerns risk at low doses. How large is that risk?

Dose-Response Model

There are no direct data on the risks of even long-term exposure to airborne asbestos at concentrations below one fiber per milliliter of air. Nor are there any direct data for exposures of people younger than the asbestos workers who were the subjects in the various studies.

Thus, a formula is needed for extrapolating from high-dose occupational exposures, for which data are available, to low-dose exposures for which no data exist. Scientists have proposed various formulas for this kind of extrapolation, which were summarized in a large table by Nicholson (1985). Most regulatory agencies use a linear dose-response model because it is most protective of public health.

Exposure Assessment

The next step is to estimate exposures. Defining an appropriate measure of exposure is extraordinarily difficult; as we discuss above, different forms of asbestos may present widely different risks that should be taken into account when estimating exposure. In the calculations that follow, we avoid these difficult questions, and use the calculations and procedures proposed by Nicholson.

Two methods are widely used to measure airborne concentrations: phase-contrast light microscopy, and transmission electron microscopy. The former is quick and cheap, but less sensitive. The latter provides more information, including the total concentration of fibers, their size, and their type. These data can sometimes tell us from where the fibers came.

Information about the fibers' origin may be important. In asbestos manufacturing plants of the past, it was safe to assume that airborne fibers were overwhelmingly asbestos. That assumption cannot be made in the typical environments of concern today. If the risk from an airborne fiber depends only on its size and shape, and the only question is whether a risk exists, then the fibers' origin is of no importance. But if the goal is to attribute responsibility for exposure, then investigators must attempt to distinguish asbestos from other kinds of fibers, and determine their source.

Typical exposure ranges are:

a. *Insulation workers:* average exposure 50–500 f/ml; maximum 2000 f/ml
b. *Textile workers:* average 30 f/ml; maximum 300 f/ml
c. *Asbestos miners and mill workers:* average 10 f/ml
d. *Asbestos cement workers:* average 6 f/ml up to 60 f/ml
e. *Office workers (1980):* average 0.003 f/ml up to 0.05 f/ml maximum
f. *School children (1980):* average 0.0005 f/ml; maximum 0.01 f/ml.

Table 8.5 is a summary prepared for Dupré et al. (1984). We emphasize that many of these data are from buildings with loose or friable (easily crumbled) asbestos and are for *oral* fibers only. Fibers longer than 5 microns (which presumably are the principal ones of health concern) account for only a small fraction of airborne fibers in the environment. More recent measurements (Gaeusler 1992, Upton et al. 1991) which use TEM only and restrict the count to *asbestos* fibers greater than 5μm, show primarily chrysotile asbestos fibers, and give smaller numbers, typically 0.0005 for office workers and 0.0001 for schools.

Dose vs. Exposure

Disease is caused by dosage, not exposure. The former depends on the concentration of the fibers in the lungs and how long they reside there; the latter refers to the concentration of fibers in the air a person breathes. An inhaled fiber might remain in the lungs long after exposure ends.

Some researchers have directly identified asbestos bodies and fibers in pulmonary tissues, and have even distinguished the different types of asbestos present. For example, Churg (1983) describes a woman who had a history of washing her husband's asbestos laden clothes. Her lung tissues contained amphiboles from commercial asbestos fibers at levels 30 times higher than normally present in lung tissues.

Such direct measurements are seldom feasible. Moreover, the absence of asbestos particles in a lung does not prove that no exposure occurred in the past. Some scientists have attempted to measure pleural plaques (small regions of damaged tissue) to indicate dose; but this approach is not generally accepted by scientists.

Thus, in almost all cases only the *exposure* of an individual can be measured. A person's *dose* must be estimated from the exposure multiplied by the total inhaled volume of contaminated air.

School Exposures

Much public concern today involves asbestos exposures in schools. This concern arises in part from the requirement of the Environmental Protection Agency (EPA) that every school assess the presence of any asbestos and make public the findings. This is usually done by "expert" assessors.

The EPA allows "expert" assessors to be in the business of removing asbestos, which is a conflict of interest. In our view, many assessors recommend removal of asbestos without properly relating their observations and measurements to hazards and risks. This has led to unnecessary fear and expense to the public.

The risks in question are in most cases exceedingly small. Estimating them requires several assumptions, each of which is open to debate. The entire procedure is called a DELPHI study, after the oracle at Delphi in ancient Greece. A preliminary attempt at such a study was made by D'Agostino and Wilson (1990).

Despite the uncertainties in its underlying assumptions, such a study yields reassuring conclusions. No one believed that Nicholson had *under*estimated the risk for a given exposure. Using Nicholson's tables, modified as explained in the following paragraphs, we estimate the risks shown in Table 8.6.

Table 8.5
Fiber exposures in buildings with asbestos (unless stated otherwise) [units of fiber/cubic centimeter, f/cc]

Author(s)	Type of building	Comment	Level
Nicholson et al. (1975)	(outdoors)	(83% less than)	0.0006
	(asbestos free)	(92% less than)	0.0006
	wet sprayed	(93% less than)	0.0006
	dry applied	(92% less than)	0.003
Sawyer and Spooner (1979)	Connecticut offices	mean	0.0024
	New York offices	lowest bldg. mean	0.000075
		highest bldg. mean	0.006
	disturbing custodial action		
	school	mean	0.019
	apt	mean	0.0089
Sebastian (1980)	outdoors	mean	0.00003
	asbestos free	mean	0.00006
	sprayed asbestos	median	0.00015
Pinchin (1982)	schools		0.00042★
Burdett and Jaffrey (1986)	miscellaneous	mean	0.00026★
Gazzi and Crockford (1987)	residence	mean	0.0003★
Rock (1987)	residence (both with and without asbestos)	mean	0.0001★
Crump (1990)	Minnesota University	mean	0.00003★
	Maryland, public bldgs.	mean	0.00009★
Corn (1991)	schools	mean	0.00024★
McCrone (1991)	schools	mean	0.0002
Lee (1992)	miscellaneous	mean	0.0001★

★Fiber length>5 μm ($= 5$ microns)
Note: Early mass measurements converted to f/cc from mass measurement by Dupré et al. (1984).

Table 8.6
Typical lifetime risk due to asbestos in a school

	Age Group	Lifetime risk (parts in a million)
Mesothelioma risk to females	10–15	4
	0–5	7
Interpolated age group	6–16	12
Adjusted for chrysotile only	6–16	2
Mesothelioma risk to males	10–15	3
	0–5	5
Interpolated age group	6–16	8
Adjusted for chrysotile only	6–16	1.6
Mesothelioma risk any asbestos	25–55	14
Adjusted for chrysotile only	25–55	3
Lung cancer risk (smoker)	25–55	20
Lung cancer risk (non-smoker)	25–55	<2

Source: Based upon Nicholson 1985, Table 6–3, and where noted, a modified average school-time exposure to chrysotile at 0.001 fibers/ml (fibers greater than 5 microns = 5 μm).

We consider a "typical" school that contains chrysotile asbestos in its fire retardant or thermal insulation. Our calculation uses Nicholson's methods as prepared for the EPA (1985), in particular his Table 6.3. We modify some of Nicholson's assumptions, but our results (Table 8.6) are in line with those of other authors (Hughes and Weill 1986).

Nicholson assumed that children were continuously exposed to asbestos in the school; we assume instead that children attend school 6 hours per day, 150 days per year. This is one-tenth of a full year. We assume that exposure lasts 10 years for a child (from ages 6 to 16), and 30 years for a teacher (ages 25 to 55). We use Nicholson's measurements of asbestos concentrations in buildings, which typically are 0.001 fiber/ml, with lower exposures if the asbestos was sprayed on wet and higher if sprayed on dry. In a survey of 71 schools (Crump 1990), the average concentration of airborne fibers longer than 5 microns was 0.00024 f/ml, one-fifth of Nicholson's figure.

Nicholson based his risk formula on data from exposures to forms of asbestos other than chrysotile. The risks of chrysotile asbestos are almost certainly lower than for other forms; and mesothelioma has never been definitely linked to chrysotile asbestos. Doll and Peto (1982) suggested that the risk of chrysotile asbestos is one-fifth that of other forms of the mineral; the actual risk may be far lower. We assume, as did Nicholson, that the risk is proportional to the exposure at low doses.

Finally, Nicholson did not distinguish between smokers and non-smokers. This lack of distinction is common in EPA documents, a fact that might be attributed to political pressure on EPA management by senators from tobacco-growing states. We allow for a doubling in Nicholson's estimate of the risk to adult males from asbestos due to smoking. We do not calculate the risk for children who smoke; such children face problems that are quite separate from any related to asbestos, that should be addressed separately.

The calculated risks from asbestos in a typical school (Table 8.6) are considerably lower than other risks that people commonly accept. For example, the *annual* risks of death for driving a car (200×10^{-6} per year) are 15 to 100 times higher than those from the asbestos exposure, and thousands of times higher if calculated over a lifetime of driving ($15,000 \times 10^{-6}$). Some people reject such comparisons because automobile driving is voluntary, whereas asbestos exposure in schools is not. However, a pedestrian's risk of being killed by a car is also much higher ($2,000 \times 10^{-6}$ per lifetime). The risk is also higher for a person who drinks chlorinated tap water in a typical U.S. city (200×10^{-6}, calculated by standard EPA methodology), although the numbers here are much more variable. The risks from the asbestos exposure are a factor of 10,000 below that of childhood death among blacks and minority groups (5×10^{-2})—which suggests where society can best spend money or direct its concern. From such calculations, many experts conclude that there is, in most cases, no significant risk from asbestos in buildings if it is in good condition.

Selikoff (1990a) accepts this conclusion for teachers and children, but suggests that school maintenance workers might suffer much higher risks. In a study of New York school custodians, Selikoff (1990b) found many radiological abnormalities and pleural plaques, and suggested that these may indicate asbestos exposure. He admitted that there were many problems in his study, and endeavored to correct for them. Most of the custodians had previous history of asbestos exposure, and most smoked cigarettes, which also scars lungs. Moreover "there was no relationship evident between mixing, fixing, and removing asbestos and the prevalence of asbestos abnormality," which makes his interpretation puzzling. As noted earlier (Churg 1982, 1983), pleural plaques may not be good indicators of asbestos exposure, and further work is necessary before such suggestions can be accepted.

The problem of asbestos risks to building custodians and maintenance workers is ultimately one of exposure. Monitoring asbestos exposure is unfortunately less easy than, for example, monitoring radiation exposure with a film-badge. Development of a simple portable asbestos monitor for workers would be helpful. Custodians of course must limit their exposure to asbestos, just as they must pay attention to other potential hazards, such as electrocution.

Long-Term Risk of Worldwide Asbestos Use

Asbestos is chemically stable and does not disintegrate, which makes it useful as an insulator and fire retardant. The same properties are related to one of its disadvantages—the problems it causes in the lungs.

Some people fear that continued mining of asbestos will lead to a progressive buildup of dangerous asbestos fibers in the environment, causing a steady rise in cancer. This has led to intense pressures for an absolute ban on asbestos, whether or not occupational or building exposures can be kept acceptably low. Similar concerns might apply as well to any stable toxic material, such as arsenic or lead.

Such speculation is impossible to prove or disprove. So far, however, no large increase in asbestos levels has been found in rural communities; any increases in cities are usually found at busy intersections where cars often brake. The incidence of mesothelioma among females has not increased; its increase among males is small and can be attributed entirely to occupational exposures. Finally, chrysotile asbestos is soluble in dilute acids, and environmental asbestos is often in the form of short fibers, which are less carcinogenic. Health concerns about low-level exposure to asbestos are therefore very speculative. Some monitoring of environmental asbestos might be appropriate, but drastic changes or a complete ban can be deferred without risk of disaster.

Substitutes

Risk assessors often walk where others fear to tread. What can be said about the risks of safety regulation itself, such as risks from banning asbestos? We address only a single dimension of that complex question, by considering the risk of an asbestos alternative, fiberglass. A whole issue of a journal was once addressed to risks of man-made fibers (Walton 1987).

Today fiberglass is much more carefully used than asbestos was in the early 1950s. Fiberglass is not sprayed on, nor is it held in place by gypsum, which is subject to deterioration. Glass fibers can easily be made large enough that adverse health effects would be very unlikely. We must make sure that such precautions are always taken.

These precautions seem obvious, but we know of no public health authority that monitors them. There are no regulations or standards for proper installation of fiberglass, and no studies to test our assumption that glass fibers are less likely to reach the environment than are asbestos fibers. Until such precautions are adopted, and adequate studies are conducted, the claim of more than one expert on the health effects of asbestos will remain correct: "There is no substitute for chrysotile asbestos that, if properly applied, is *known* to be as safe."

Acknowledgments

We acknowledge helpful discussions with many scientists, in particular with Drs. A. M. Langer, R. P. Nolan, and J. Peto.

References

Albelda, S. M., D. M. Epstein, W. B. Gefter, and W. T. Miller. 1982. Pleural thickening—its significance and relationship to asbestos dust exposure. 126 *Am. Rev. Respir. Dis.* 621–624.

Baris, Y. I., et al. 1978. An outbreak of pleural mesothelioma and chronic fibrosing pleurisy in the village of Karain/Ürgüp in Anatolia. 33 *Thorax* 181–192.

Breslow, L., et al. 1984. Report of a committee. *Asbestiform fibers: non occupational health risks*. Washington, DC: National Academy of Sciences.

Brodeur, P. 1985. *Outrageous misconduct: The asbestos industry on trial*. New York: Pantheon.

Brody, A. R. 1990. Asbestos, carcinogenicity, and public policy. 248 Science 795. Letter.

Browne, K. 1986. Is asbestos or asbestosis the cause of the increased risk of lung cancer in asbestos workers? 43 *Br. J. of Indus. Med.* 145–149. Editorial.

Burdett G. J. and S. A. M. T. Jaffrey. 1986. Airborne asbestos concentrations in public buildings. 30 *Ann. Occup. Hyg.* 185–190.

Churg, A. 1982. Asbestos fibers and pleural plaques in a general autopsy population. 109 *Am. J. Path.* 88–96.

Churg, A. 1983. Current issues in the pathologic and mineralogic diagnosis of asbestos-induced disease. 84(3) *Chest* 275–280.

Churg, A. 1988. Private communication.

Churg, A., and F. H. Y. Green, eds. 1987. *Pathology of occupational lung disease* 234–246. Tokyo: Igaku-Shoin Medical.

Consumer Products Safety Commission. 1983. Report of chronic hazards advisory panel on asbestos. Washington, DC: Consumer Products Safety Commission, Division of Health Sciences.

Craighead, J. E. 1987. Eyes for the epidemiologist: The pathologist's role in shaping our understanding of the asbestos-associated diseases. 89 *Am. J. Clin. Path.* 281–287.

Crump, K. S. 1990. Asbestos, carcinogenicity and public policy. 248 *Science* 799. Letter.

D'Agostino, Jr., R. B., and R. Wilson. 1990. An attempt at a DELPHI study on asbestos risks. Cambridge, MA: Harvard University. Privately circulated.

Davies, J. M. G. 1985. A review of recent experiments on the mechanisms of asbestos pathogenicity. In *Proceedings of Vth International Colloquium on dust measuring technique and strategy* 25. Asbestos International Association.

Doll, R. 1955. Mortality from lung cancer in asbestos workers. 12 *Br. J. Indus. med.* 81–86.

Doll, R., and R. Peto. 1982. Health and Safety Commission. *Effects on health of exposure to asbestos*. London: Her Majesty's Stationery Office.

Dupré, et al. 1984. *Report of the Royal Commissions on matters of health and safety arising from the use of asbestos in Ontario*. Toronto: Ontario Ministry of Public Services.

Engholm, G. Ö. 1987. Man-made fibers in the working environment. In W. H. Walton ed., 31(4b) *J. Br. Occup. Hygiene Soc.*

Enterline, P. E. 1976. Pitfalls in epidemiological research: an examination of the asbestos literture. 18(3) *J. Occup. Med.* 150–156.

Enterline, P. E. 1981. Extrapolation from occupational studies: a substitute for environmental epidemiology. 42 *Environ. Health Persp.* 39–44.

Environmental Protection Agency, Office of Toxic Substances. 1982. *Support document for final rule on friable asbestos containing material in school buildings: Health effects and magnitudes of exposure* 72. Washington, DC: EPA.

Finkelstein, M. M. 1982. Asbestos in long-term employers of an Ontario asbestos cement factory. 125 *Am. Rev. Resp. Dis.* 499.

Gaensler, E. A. 1992. Asbestos exposure in buildings. 13 *Clinics in Chest Med.* 5.1–5.12.

Gazzi, D. and G. W. Crockford. 1987. Indoor asbestos levels on a housing estate. 31 *Ann. Occup. Hyg.* 429–439.

Hammond, E. C., I. J. Selikoff, and H. Seidman. 1979. Asbestos exposure, cigarette smoking and death rates. 330 *Ann. N.Y. Acad. Sci.* 473–490.

Hesterberg, T. W., and J. C. Barrett. 1984. Dependence of asbestos-induced and mineral dust-induced transformation of mammalian cells in culture on fiber dimension. 44 *Cancer Res.* 2170–2180.

Hillerdal, G. 1978. Pleural plaques in a health survey; material frequency, development and exposure to asbestos. 559 *Scand. J. Resp. Dis.* 257–263.

Hughes, J. M., and H. Weill. 1986. Asbestos exposure—quantitative assessment of risk. 133 *Am. Rev. Resp. Dis.* 5–13.

Jones, H. B., and A. Grendon. 1975. Environmental factors in the origin of cancer and estimation of the possible hazard to man. 13 *J. Fd. Cosm. Toxicol.* 251–268.

Landrigan, P. J., and H. Kozimi, eds. 1991. Third wave of asbestos disease: Exposure to asbestos in place. 643 *Ann. N. Y. Acad. Sci.* 1–628.

Langer, A. M., and R. P. Nolan. 1988. Fiber type and mesothelioma risk. In *Symposium on health effects of exposure to asbestos in buildings.* Cambridge, MA: Harvard University Press.

Lee, R. J. 1992. Summary of measurements in 231 buildings quoted in Upton et al. (1991).

Lippmann, M. 1988. Review: Asbestos exposure indexes. 46 *Environ. Res.* 86–106.

Lynch, K. M. and W. A. Smith. 1935. Pulmonary asbestosis: Carcinoma of the lung in asbesto-silicosis. 24 *Am. J. Cancer* 56–64.

McDonald, J. C. 1980. Asbestos related disease: An epidemiological review. In J. C. Wagner, ed., 30 *Biological effects of mineral fibers* 587–601. Lyons, France: IARC Scientific Publications.

McCrone, W. C. 1987. Asbestos identification (2nd. Ed.) Chicago, IL: McCrone Res. Inst.

Mehir, R. M., S. P. Bayard, and J. Thomson. 1978. *CPSC regulation of nonoccupational exposure to asbestos in consumer products* 506. NBS special publication. Washington, DC: National Bureau of Standards.

National Institutes of Health. 1978a. *Asbestos, an information resource,* R. Levine, ed. Publication no. NIH 78-1681. Washington, DC: Dept. of Health, Education and Welfare.

National Institutes of Health. 1978b. *Asbestos and health: annotated bibliography.* Publication no. (NIH) 78-1842. Washington, DC: Dept. of Health, Education and Welfare.

New York Academy of Sciences. 1979. Health hazards of asbestos exposure. 330 *Ann. N.Y. Acad. Sci.*

Nicholson, W. J. 1985. *Airborne asbestos, health assessment update.* Environmental Health Laboratory report, Report EPA-600/8-84-003F. New York: Mt. Sinai Hospital.

Nicholson, W. J., A. N. Rohl, and I. Weisman. 1975. *Asbestos contamination of the air in public buildings.* Report EPA-450/3-76-004, Table 5 at 25, Table 6 at 26. Washington, DC: EPA.

Nicholson, W. J. et al. 1981. Cancer from occupational asbestos exposure: projections 1980–2000. In R. Peto and M. Schneiderman, eds. Banbury Report 9: Quantification of occupational cancer. Cold Spring Harbor, NY: Cold Spring Harbor Laboratory.

Peto, J. 1979. Dose response relationships for asbestos-related disease: Implications for hygiene standards: Part II, mortality. 330 *Ann. N.Y. Acad. Sci.* 195–203.

Peto, J., H. Seidman, and I. J. Selikoff. 1982. Mesothelioma mortality in asbestos workers: Implications for models of carcinogenesis and risk assessment. 45 *Br. J. Cancer* 124–135.

Pinchin, D. J. 1982. *Asbestos in Buildings,* Table I at 7.5, Table II at 7.8, Table III at 7.12. Royal Commission on Asbestos Study Series no. 8. Ottawa: Royal Commission on Asbestos.

Rock, A. M. 1987. Report in the first round of air sampling of asbestos in home study. Washington, DC: Consumer Product Safety Commission.

Sawyer, R. N., and C. M. Spooner. 1979. *Sprayed asbestos containing materials in buildings 1978,* Table 1-2-1 at 1-2-9. Report no. EPA-450/2-78-014. Washington, DC: EPA.

Sebastien, P., et al. 1980. Ministry of Health and Ministry for the Quality of Life Environment, *Measurement of asbestos air pollution inside buildings sprayed with asbestos* 14. Report no. EPA-560/13/80-026. Washington, DC: EPA. Translation of document prepared for the government of France.

Selikoff, I. J. 1990a. The third wave of asbestos disease; exposure to asbestos in place: public health control. *Asbestos Litig. Rep.,* February 18.

Selikoff, I. J. 1990b. *Radiological abnormalities and asbestos exposure among custodians of the NYC Board of Education.* Report to NYC Board of Education. New York.

Selikoff, I. J., E. C. Hammond, and H. Seidman. 1979. Mortality experience of insulation workers in the United States and Canada, 1943, 1976. 330 *Ann. N. Y. Acad. Sci.* 103.

Selikoff, I. J. and H. Seidman. 1991. Asbestos-associated deaths among insulation workers in the US and Canada 1967–1987. 643 *Ann. N. Y. Acad. Sci.* 1–14.

Upton, A. C., J. C. Barrett, M. R. Becklake, G. Burdett, E. Chatfield, J. M. G. Davies, G. Gamsu, A. Langer, R. J. Lee, M. Lippman, B. T. Mossman, R. Morse, W. J. Nicholson, J. Peto, J. Samet, and C. Wagner. 1991. Asbestos in public and commercial buildings—a literature review and synthesis of current knowledge. Cambridge, MA: Health Effects Institute.

Wagner, J. C. 1985. Mesothelioma and mineral fibers. 57 *Cancer* 1905–1911.

Walton, W. H., ed. 1987. Man-made fibers in the working environment. 31(4b) *J. Br. Occup. Hygiene Soc.*

Weill, H. 1983. Asbestos associated disease; Science, public policy and litigation. 84 *Chest* 601–608.

Zeise, L., E. A. C. Crouch, and R. Wilson. 1987. *Dose-response relationships for carcinogens: A review.* 73 *Environ. Health Persp.* 259–308.

Biographical Sketch

Ralph D'Agostino, Jr., currently a doctoral student in the Department of Statistics at Harvard University, is the staff statistician at the Eunice Kennedy Shriver Center for the study of Mental Retardation and consults for the Department of Anesthesia at Massachusetts General Hospital and the Channing Laboratory at Harvard Medical School. In 1990, he worked as a consultant with Professor Peter Kempthorne from the Sloan School at M.I.T. analyzing marketing techniques on new drugs. In 1989, he began research with Professor Richard Wilson, in the Harvard Department of Physics, studying the effects of low dosage of asbestos in the environment. This work is still in progress.

Richard Wilson is Mallinckrodt Professor of Physics at Harvard University. He is an adjunct member of the Center for Science and International Affairs of the Kennedy School of Government at Harvard and chairman of the Visiting Committee on Radiation Medicine at Massachusetts General Hospital. He has served on numerous scientific committees and as a consultant to government and private industry.

9

The Human Health Effects of
Polychlorinated Biphenyls

Renate D. Kimbrough

Polychlorinated biphenyls (PCBs) are 209 closely related chemical compounds—chlorinated biphenyls—that differ only in the number and location of chlorine atoms on the molecule. The stability and biological properties of these chemicals vary according to the number and position of the chlorine atoms on the molecule. As a group, PCBs are soluble in fat and, unlike many other chemicals, tend to accumulate in body tissues.

PCBs do not occur naturally in the environment. They were first produced commercially in the 1920s, and their use increased greatly in the 1950s. About 1.3 billion pounds of PCBs were produced and consumed in the United States between 1930 and 1975. They were used, for example, in capacitor, hydraulic, and transformer fluids, in carbonless copying paper, and as plasticizers in paint. In the United States, the Monsanto Chemical Company was the sole producer of commercial mixtures of PCBs.

As a result of these varied uses, PCBs have entered the environment and accumulated in the food chain. While their concentrations in urban areas are usually higher than in rural and remote areas, PCBs may be transported for long distances by air, and traces of PCBs are found even in remote areas (Kimbrough and Jensen 1989).

Once in the environment, the fate of a PCB molecule varies with its chemical composition. Isomers (chemical variants) with few chlorine atoms are metabolized and eliminated more easily by living organisms, and also are more easily broken down in the environment. Thus, the composition of a commercial mixture of PCBs changes after release into the environment. Some of the more toxic PCB isomers either were not present in commercial PCB mixtures manufactured in the United States or were present at very low concentrations. However, they may to some extent be preferentially concentrated in the environment; low levels of some these isomers have occasionally been found in human tissues. It is not clear whether they originated from commercial PCB mixtures or whether other sources exist.

In 1966, Jensen identified PCBs in wildlife. When better methods became available to detect them, scientists soon identified PCB residues in fish, birds, meat, and human tissues, usually at higher concentrations in fatty tissues. Today, a major source of human exposure to PCBs comes from eating some kinds of fish from polluted waters.

Scientists initially considered PCBs to be "safe" because single doses, even very large ones, did not promptly kill test animals. But these studies were designed to detect only acute toxic effects, and involved short-term observation of animals (usually for two weeks).

However, more sophisticated studies later uncovered toxic effects in test animals given daily doses of PCBs over much longer periods of time. Now, cumulative toxicity from low-level exposures to PCBs is the principal concern of scientists and the center of much legal and regulatory concern.

Much of the public concern about potential health effects of PCBs can be traced to the late 1960s and 1970s, with reports of illness in Japan in 1968 and in Taiwan in 1979 after people consumed rice oil contaminated with PCBs and other chemicals for a period of time. Initially, the illnesses were reported as having been caused by PCBs; investigators later found that the rice oil had also been contaminated with chlorinated dibenzofurans, polychlorinated quarterphenyls, chlorinated dibenzodioxins, and chlorinated napthalenes. The illness that these people suffered has been called *yusho* in Japan and *yu-cheng* in Taiwan (Lee and Chang 1985; Kuratsune 1989). These illnesses were not caused by PCBs but by other contaminants.

The mechanisms of PCB toxicity are complex. At very low doses, even cumulative exposures will not reach toxic levels in the body over a lifetime. The body eliminates PCBs in various ways, and the substances will reach an equilibrium concentration in the body even if there is daily intake. Some PCBs are eliminated or metabolized more easily than others; thus the mixture of PCBs in the body will change with time and may be quite different from that to which the organism was initially exposed.

Responding to health and environmental concerns about PCBs, government and industry have taken steps to reduce the use of these chemicals. Monsanto, the sole U.S. producer, voluntarily ceased production of many PCBs in 1971 and stopped marketing PCBs for open-ended use. Previously, it had marketed a range of PCBs, including more highly chlorinated biphenyl mixtures such as Aroclor 1248, 1254, and

1260; thereafter it produced only lower chlorinated biphenyls (Fed. Reg. 1982). In 1977, Monsanto stopped producing PCBs entirely.

The United States and other industrial nations have since taken further steps to limit the flow of PCBs into the environment. Although PCBs are no longer produced commercially in the United States (Fed. Reg. 1982), they remain present in many capacitors and transformers and in waste dumps, and their containment is still of concern. The removal of PCBs from the environment has proved difficult and expensive, and the effectiveness of various cleanup attempts is unclear, since no useful inventory of PCBs and their locations is available.

One complication in discussing the health risks of PCBs is that they are sometimes contaminated with another group of chemicals, polychlorinated dibenzofurans (PCDFs), some of which are far more toxic than PCBs. In the commercial mixtures produced by Monsanto, PCDFs were usually present in only trace amounts or not at all. However, they are formed when PCBs are heated to temperatures between 200 and 600°C (Morita et al. 1978). They may have caused some of the toxic effects attributed to PCBs in various animals and humans, and were definitely responsible for the incidents of *yusho* and *yu-cheng*.

Toxicity in Animals

Over the years, scientists have studied the toxicity of PCBs in various animals. Different animals apparently respond very differently to PCBs. The subhuman primates, guinea pigs, and mink, for example, appear to be more sensitive to PCBs than dogs, rats, mice, and rabbits. Also, the target organs (the organs that are principally affected by the chemicals) vary with species. For these reasons, it is unclear which species of animal is best for assessing the toxic effects of PCBs in humans.

I will briefly review the acute and chronic toxic effects of PCBs, and the organs that are primarily affected; more detailed reviews are available elsewhere (Kimbrough and Jensen 1989, Kimbrough 1987). In the rat and the mouse, and to some extent the rabbit, the primary target organ is the liver. For example, highly chlorinated mixtures of PCBs such as Aroclor 1260 produce liver tumors in rats and mice (for exposure levels, see Table 9.1A). By contrast, hormone-dependent tumors (such as tumors of the pituitary and the mammary glands) occur less frequently in rats fed PCBs than in controls without exposure to PCBs. However, lower chlorinated PCB mixtures do not produce the same increase in tumors in rodents at similar doses. PCBs can also produce skin lesions in rabbits and hairless mice.

PCBs produce other biological effects in addition to cancer. In chickens, PCBs cause fluid to accumulate in tissue underneath the skin, the sac around the heart, the chest cavity, and the abdominal cavity. In subhuman primates, PCBs do not particularly affect the liver but cause alterations in the lining of the stomach, and cause skin lesions of the type referred to in humans as chloracne. Some PCBs affect the reproduction in rats and mice and (at much lower doses) in subhuman primates (Table 9.1A).

PCBs and associated chemicals can affect the immune system. In animals, PCBs, particularly those containing appreciable amounts of PCDFs, suppress the immune system[1] (Vos and Luster 1989) at doses similar to those leading to reproductive effects. In humans, suppression of the immune system has been reported only in patients acutely poisoned by exposure at high levels to mixed PCDFs, PCBs, and chlorinated quarterphenyls. (It appears that in humans PCDFs were the culprit, not PCBs.) Reported immunological changes include depression of serum immunoglobulin, delayed-type hypersensitivity reactions, and enhanced in vitro proliferation of T-lymphocytes (Vos and Luster 1989).

It is difficult to judge the significance of such immunological changes to the health of the animal or of humans. Many laboratory tests of immune function, for example, yield abnormal responses for all sorts of reasons that have nothing to do with PCB exposure, which have no clear relation to clinical illness (Peter 1989).

The interpretation of the animal studies is also complicated by the fact that different PCB isomers have very different biological effects. Commercial PCBs consist of complex mixtures that have different effects on different organs, and require different doses to cause similar toxic effects in different animals. In one study (see Table 9.1A), investigators found that Aroclor 1260 required a dose 25 times higher than for Aroclor 1254 to produce the same reproductive effects in the same strain of rats. In another study, a German PCB mixture, Clophen A–30 (with a comparatively high concentration of lower chlorinated biphenyls), caused no increase in liver tumors in rats (Schaeffer et al. 1984, as reviewed in Institute for Evaluating Health Risks 1991). But a different mixture, Clophen A–60 (composed primarily of more highly chlorinated biphenyls), at the same dose, produced a pronounced increase in liver tumors in the rats.

The PCB mixtures with a great amount of chlorine are associated with the production of liver tumors in animals. In addition to Clophen A–60, Aroclor 1260 (a highly chlorinated biphenyl mixture produced in the United States) led to a statistically significant increase in liver tumors in rats. However, data are limited. Both mixtures were studied at only one dietary level (100 mg of PCBs per kg of body weight), and some commercial mixtures containing lower chlorinated biphenyls, such as Aroclor 1242 and Aroclor 1016, were not tested for carcinogenicity. In addition, scientists do not know which chemical component in the Aroclor 1260 and Clophen A-60 mixtures was responsible for the liver tumors in the rats.

Human Health Effects

PCBs are persistent and ubiquitous in the environment, and are found in the food chain and, at low concentrations, in the air. Thus it is often impossible to determine how, or in what amounts, a person has been exposed to PCBs. This is particularly true for the general population, whose members tend to have low body burdens of the chemicals. The general population has been, and will continue to be, exposed to trace amounts of PCBs, particularly in industrialized countries.

The accurate determination of exposure is a recurrent problem in assessing the health effects of PCBs and other environmental chemicals. Environmental sampling—measuring chemical concentrations in the soil or air—cannot accurately predict a person's actual exposure to and uptake of PCBs. Ten out of 12 recent investigations of sites contaminated with very high PCB concentrations in the soil (up to 13 percent PCB concentration by weight), or in material oozing into surface water (up to 0.002 percent), found no excess proportion of nearby residents with PCB levels in the blood serum above those found in the general population (greater than 20 parts per billion or ppb) (Stehr-Green et al. 1988). In other words, these "highly exposed" people did not have much higher body burdens of PCBs than other members of the general population. In the two studies that did report increases in serum levels of PCBs, the individuals had also been exposed to PCBs through their occupations or by eating PCB-contaminated fish.

In short, mere proximity to a PCB-contaminated site often does not lead to greater exposure. With persistent chemicals like PCBs, a person's exposure is best determined by measuring the levels of the chemical in the blood serum or body fat. These levels must be compared with those in the general population, to determine whether a person has had an increased exposure to PCBs.

Some people in the United States have been exposed to high levels of PCBs, particularly in the workplace. Workers who repair transformers or handle toxic waste may have high exposures (Kimbrough

1985). Because of their exposures, workers who produced PCBs, and PCB-filled transformers or capacitors, retain higher body burdens of PCBs than the general population. Nonoccupational sources of exposure include eating fish from contaminated waters. In the past, some farm families, and to a lesser extent the general population, were exposed to PCBs from some dairy products and meat.

PCBs are soluble in fat, and for this reason are primarily stored in fatty tissue. They are also present, to a lesser degree, in blood serum, other tissues, and human milk, in levels that are related roughly to the fat contents of these materials. The PCB concentration of human milk averages a few parts per million or less on a fat basis, that is, a few milligrams or less of PCBs per kilogram of fat in the milk (Kimbrough and Jensen 1989). Occasionally higher concentrations of PCBs are found in a person's tissues or blood despite the apparent lack of unusual exposure. Newborn babies may have measurable levels of PCBs, transferred from the mother through the placenta.

Scientists and public health officials have attempted to determine the health significance of body burdens of PCBs. One communitywide study in Triana, Alabama, examined 458 persons who had eaten a great deal of DDT-contaminated fish from a local river; among other things, the investigators measured levels of PCBs in the residents' blood serum (Kreiss et al. 1981). Most persons had serum PCB levels similar to those typically found in the general population; but in some the levels were higher. On the average, higher serum PCB levels were found in older residents and in males. The levels in these people tended to increase with higher alcohol consumption and with higher levels of serum cholesterol.

In the Triana study, Kreiss et al. attempted to relate serum PCB levels to the health of the residents. The Triana residents in general had a much higher prevalence of high blood pressure than expected from national rates, taking into account the distribution of sex, age, and race. Based on their initial analysis of the data, the investigators suggested that the increased serum PCB levels were associated with high blood pressure in these residents.

In another study, Lawton et al. (1985) examined workers who had been exposed to the commercial mixtures Aroclor 1016, 1242, and/or 1254. The serum PCB levels of these workers considerably exceeded those of the Triana residents, those reported in other community studies, or in the general population. Lawton et al. reported that increased PCB blood levels were positively associated with serum cholesterol, abnormal liver function, and hypertension (high blood pressure) in the subjects. However, when PCB whole-serum levels were adjusted to account for the amount of fat present in serum, these positive associations disappeared. It thus appears that the important variable was the fat content of serum rather than PCB levels: more fat will contain more PCBs and is also associated with more serum cholesterol and with altered liver function. Thus, in these two studies the increased body burdens of PCBs had not caused the increased serum cholesterol and hypertension. Rather, because these people had higher serum cholesterol, their whole-serum PCB levels were increased.

Other reported correlations between PCBs and health were spurious as well. Kreiss et al. (1981), for example, also reported a connection between PCB exposure and hypertension and abnormal liver function. But liver function and blood pressure are affected by many lifestyle factors, including consumption of alcohol; Mathews (1976) suggested that in developed countries, heavy drinking could account for 30 percent of all cases of hypertension. This makes it difficult to establish a correlation between these health conditions and a single variable such as PCB exposure.

Another problem is the variability in results of liver function tests. A recent study found that 2–3 percent of potential blood donors had sufficiently elevated liver function tests to require the blood banks to discard their blood (Saxena et al. 1989). Possible causes of this variability might include high intake of sucrose or alcohol, normal day to day variations in a person, obesity, ethnic origin, and measurement error if the serum contains a great deal of lipid.

Thus, before linking abnormal liver function with PCB exposure, an investigator must consider and rule out many other possible factors. That in turn requires the investigator to evaluate each subject in a study individually. An epidemiologic study that is based on simplistic interpretations of laboratory tests, without the clinical evaluation of individual subjects, cannot be analyzed completely enough to lead to useful conclusions for individuals.

Another problem is statistical. An investigator who performs many different tests on a group say of people living near a toxic waste site, and defines a "normal" result for each test as one that lies within two or three standard deviations of the mean for the entire population, will surely find some "abnormal" results. Such findings might arise from sampling errors, and are known in the jargon of statistics as "false positive" errors.

Indeed, using the statistical criteria commonly employed in science, a single test applied to a normal population will result in an "abnormal" finding 5 percent of the time; 10 tests will yield at least 1 "abnormal" finding 40 percent of the time; and 50 tests will yield at least 1 "abnormal" result 92 percent of the time (Galen and Gambino 1975). Thus an "abnormal" finding may or may not have clinical significance. If biologically plausible, it would warrant further investigation to determine whether it was a false positive result or a truly abnormal finding.

Diverse health problems have been reported in workers exposed to high concentrations of airborne PCBs, including upper respiratory irritation, skin irritation, and abnormal pulmonary function. When PCBs were first produced, some workers in plants manufacturing the chemicals developed a skin disease called chloracne that may have resulted from exposure to PCBs or other chemicals, such as PCDFs (Kimbrough 1987) that may have been present as contaminants.[2] Skin irritation and respiratory problems have been reported among workers exposed to other chemicals as well as PCBs, and it is not clear whether the PCBs were responsible for these complaints.

Other health problems that have sometimes been attributed to PCBs include fatigue, headaches, and nausea. Such problems, however, have many causes, and frequently occur in the general population for reasons that have nothing to do with PCB exposure. In one study of polybrominated biphenyls, a related class of chemicals, such complaints were more frequent among people with lower exposures who insisted on being examined than in more highly exposed people who had been invited into the studies (Landrigan et al. 1979). A cardinal axiom of toxicology is that real effects tend to increase with increasing dosage; thus more highly exposed individuals should exhibit more symptoms, even though individual members of the group may vary in their susceptibility (Cannon et al. 1978).

Reproductive Effects
PCBs have reproductive effects in animals (Table 9.1A), but no such effects have been conclusively demonstrated in humans. Taylor et al. (1989) surveyed female workers in a capacitor plant, and reported a small decrease (30 grams) in the average birth weights of their children, after accounting for other risk factors including cigarette smoking, alcohol consumption, and use of drugs by the mother; twinning; genetic factors; sex of the child; height of the mother; and illness of the mother during pregnancy. The workers had much higher exposure to PCBs than the general population and (as the investigators pointed out) the clinical significance of this small difference in the birth weight is unclear.

Rogan et al. (1986), in a follow-up study of 856 breast-fed infants, reported that higher exposure to PCBs in utero was associated with lower muscle tone and less well developed reflexes in the child. Again,

Table 9.1A
Animal tests using PCB mixtures

Aroclors tested	Daily dose mg/kg	Total dose mg/kg	Effect	Reference
Aroclors[1]	Single dose given in stomach	1,000– 10,000	Kills half of test animals	Kimbrough et al. 1978
Aroclor 1260[2]	about 25	4,650[5]	Some reproductive effects	Linder et al. 1974
Aroclor 1254[3]	about 1	186[5]	Some reproductive effects	Linder et al. 1974
Aroclor 1260[4]	about 5[6]	3,500	Cancer of the liver	Kimbrough et al. 1975

1. The lower chlorinated mixtures are generally more acutely toxic.
2. Highly chlorinated mixture.
3. Less chlorinated mixture.
4. Only mixtures with 60 percent chlorination caused cancer in the test animals.
5. Lower doses of PCBs produce reproductive effects in subhuman primates. However, some of these primates were exposed to other chemicals, making the interpretation of the results of this study uncertain.
6. This was the only dietary dose tested.

Table 9.1B
Human exposures to PCB mixtures[1]

Population	Daily dose mg/kg	Total or lifetime dose mg/kg	Reference
General population	0.00001 to 0.0003	less than 0.7[2]	World Health Organization 1988
Workers	Varied	195–260	Lawton et al. 1985

1. PCBs only; the accidental exposure leading to yusho-yucheng syndrome (from contaminated food) is excluded.
2. Mostly from dietary exposure.

the health significance of these findings is unclear. Their interpretation is further complicated by the fact that higher PCB levels were found in older women and women who regularly consumed alcohol—factors that might be related to the condition of the child. PCB levels were also higher in women bearing their first child (Rogan and Gladen 1982). Further follow-up of these children at ages three, four, and five showed that the deficits reported earlier were no longer apparent (Gladen and Rogan 1991).

Several investigators (Schwartz et al. 1983; Jacobson et al. 1984; Fein et al. 1984; Jacobson et al. 1983) reported changes in behavior or reduced gestation period in newborns associated with the mother's consumption of fish or exposure to PCBs. The investigators suggested that PCB exposure of the fetus during pregnancy may lead to behavioral abnormalities in the infant.

The significance of these findings is difficult to judge. The tests the investigators employed have not been widely used for predicting behavioral abnormalities of children. Obvious limitations of threshold studies included uncertainties in the exposure of the subjects to PCBs and lack of a clear relation between the extent of exposure and magnitude of the changes reported in the children. Other factors, such as exposure to heavy metals, the mother's lifestyle and well-being, and her genetic makeup may also have affected the results. This was also reviewed by Paneth (1991). In short, these observations warrant further study. Compared with other variables, we can conclude that PCB exposure has at most a minor or negligible influence on the birth weight, growth, and development of children.

Immunotoxicity

Immunotoxicity occurs when chemical agents or other factors adversely affect the immune system. No immunotoxic effects have been reported in people exposed only to elevated levels of PCBs. Such effects were reported in the victims of the rice-oil poisoning episodes in Japan and Taiwan, but contaminants other than PCBs were responsible.

Tests of the immune system might, for many reasons, yield abnormal results unrelated to chemical exposure. (Peter 1989). These include bacterial or viral infections during testing, drug treatment, some poorly understood diseases such as Sjögren's syndrome, systemic lupus erythematosus, motor neurone disease, recent surgery with general anesthesia, stress, aging, malnutrition, cancer, uremia, and extensive burns. Some immune-system tests yield a wide range of "normal" results in individuals with no clinical illness. Other tests are poorly reproducible even in the same individual.

An example of the difficulty of interpreting tests of the immune system is found in a study done by the Centers for Disease Control on individuals exposed to dioxin (specifically 2,3,7,8-tetrachlorodibenzo-p-dioxin). The study reported abnormal results of immune function tests in some individuals. But these initial findings could not be verified in a follow-up study. Moreover, none of the subjects showed clinical signs of disease from deficiencies of the immune system (Hoffman and Stehr-Green 1989). By themselves, many tests of the immune system are not useful for diagnosis of disease, and their interpretation requires the clinical evaluation of the subjects or patients in the study.

Cancer

Several investigators have studied cancer risk from PCBs by comparing tissue levels of PCBs in patients dying of cancer with those in patients dying from other causes. Some of these studies reported higher levels of PCBs in the adipose tissue of the cancer patients, suggesting higher cancer risk from PCBs. For instance, Unger and Olsen (1980) reported mean level of PCBs in adipose tissue of about 9 ppm (mg of PCBs per kg of tissue) in male and female cancer patients, 6 ppm in male noncancer patients and 4.5 ppm in female noncancer patients. While these differences were statistically significant, all of the PCB levels were within the range normally found in the general population at the time the study was done. Such small differences might have been caused by weight loss in the cancer patients, impairment of liver metabolism, or the effects of cancer treatment. In short, these differences—which were found in patients after their disease had developed—do not point to a cause-effect relationship between PCBs and cancer.

Numerous studies have attempted to measure the cancer incidence rates in groups of workers exposed to PCBs. Most of these studies compared the causes of death (as listed on death certificates) of the exposed workers with those of the general population, after taking into account any differences in sex and age at death in the groups being compared. Other studies used different comparison populations—such as other workers in the same factory who were not exposed to PCBs, or the population of the same geographic area.

One early, preliminary study (Bahn et al. 1976) reported 3 melano-carcinomas and 2 carcinomas of the pancreas among 92 workers who had been exposed to PCBs between 1949 and 1957, significantly more than expected. However, in this small group the calculated cancer rates are uncertain; the workers had also been exposed to other chemicals.

Other studies did not confirm these results. For example, Brown and Jones (1981) studied 2,567 present and former workers in two capacitor plants, of whom 163 had died. If the data from both work sites were combined, the workers had slightly more than the expected number of deaths from liver and rectal cancer, and cirrhosis of the liver; but these increases were not statistically significant. However, females at one of the work sites did exhibit a statistically significant elevation in incidence of cancer of the rectum. In a follow-up study, Brown (1987) found no additional cancers of the rectum among these workers, and the total number of cancers of the rectum was not nearly as elevated, compared with the controls, as previously reported. The follow-up study, however, observed two additional cancers of the liver and biliary tract, for a total of five such cases based on entries on death certificates.

A review of the medical records of these subjects, however, raised several questions. One autopsy report listed the cause of death as hepatic coma due to metastatic disease, with the primary site unknown (i.e., the cancer did not originate in the liver). Malignant tumors (cancers) commonly spread to the liver in advanced stages, and should not be counted as primary liver cancers in epidemiologic studies. In another case, the death certificate listed a primary cancer of the bile ducts as cause of death; the hospital pathology report, however, classified this tumor as an adenocarcinoma that probably originated in the bile ducts, and noted that the patient had a history of cancer of the uterus. This cancer might have originated in the uterus and spread to the bile ducts. It is also debatable whether a tumor originating in the bile ducts should be counted with tumors that originated from parenchymal liver cells. In a third case, the cancer may have originated in the gall bladder rather than the liver. Thus, a detailed examination of the workers' records does not make a strong case for a relation between PCB exposure and liver cancer. Moreover, in these workers the incidence of cancer did not seem to be related to dose, length of exposure, or time between exposure and development of the tumor—which further weakens the case that PCB exposure caused the tumors.

Bertazzi et al. (1981) surveyed 290 male and 1,020 female workers in an Italian capacitor plant. The investigators compared the number of cancer deaths among the workers with the expected rates, based on national mortality figures. Among the men, there were more cancer deaths than expected, particularly from neoplasms of the digestive system, the lining of the cavity that contains the digestive system, and the lymphatic and blood-forming tissues. Six men had died from cancers of the gas-trointestinal tract; the expected number was 1.5.[3] Of these, however, one was a liver cancer and another a cancer of the biliary tract, an entirely different disease. Three men had died from cancers of the lymphatic and blood-forming systems; only one such death was expected. The female workers had a higher overall death rate than expected from national mortality figures. Four had died from cancers of the hemopoietic system (including three cases of Hodgkin's disease), whereas only 1.5 such deaths were expected.

We can, however, draw no firm conclusions from this study. The total number of deaths was small, which makes any comparison of death rates very uncertain. Other problems include uncertainties about the workers' exposure to PCBs, and their exposure to other chemicals. The workers had a higher overall death rate than expected for the general population. By contrast, most epidemiologic studies on workers show lower death rates than for the general population, the "healthy worker effect." *Something* might have damaged the workers' health, unrelated to PCB exposure. Also, the cancers that were increased in this study were different from the cancers that were increased in other studies. This raises further questions about the role that PCBs played in all of this.

Cancer, like other chronic diseases, results from a complex series of events. And cancer risk is related to many factors, such as genetic predisposition, nutrition, lifestyle, and environment. These factors, and a host of other technical difficulties, greatly complicate the interpretation of mortality studies.

For example, consider the difficulties in the use of death certificates to study cancer mortality rates. Between 20 percent and 50 percent of death certificates disagree with autopsy reports in the cause of death (Cottreau et al. 1989). The cause of death (from death certificates) is coded for entry into computers by specialists in the classification of disease (nosologists), using the International Classification of Disease system (ICD), which for cancer is based on the site where the tumor originates. But nosologists are not physicians or pathologists, and may introduce errors of interpretation. For instance, a soft tissue sarcoma may be coded according to the organ site where it was found or as a malignant neoplasm of soft and connective tissue. A tumor may be misdiagnosed, particularly if rare, and misclassified (Brown et al. 1987). Such errors can have a major impact, particularly when the total number of tumors in the subjects of a study is small (Percy et al. 1981). To what extent the studies described above are affected by such problems is difficult to determine.

Sinks et al. (1990) reported a retrospective mortality study of workers at a capacitor plant. The investigators noted an excess mortality from malignant melanocarcinomas (two females, seven males) and brain cancer (five males, two females). For most of the brain cancer cases, the investigators could not confirm the diagnosis through medical records or pathology reports. Moreover, one brain cancer death occurred in an individual with less than six months' employment; in another, melanocarcinoma had been diagnosed before the employee had been hired (which suggests that the diseases were not connected with employment at the plant). In two of the other cases of melanocarcinoma, the date of diagnosis and the date of death coincided; in a third case these dates were only two months apart. Thus, in at least two of the cases, the primary cause of death does not appear to have been melanocarcinoma, and the number of reported cases does not represent true mortality rates. Furthermore, the workers' exposure to PCBs was not well defined, and no excess of these cancers was reported in any of the other studies. Further investigation is needed to elucidate these findings.

Conclusion

Relating a person's exposure to a chemical to health problems is difficult. Many diseases have unknown cause; scientists understand the health effects of few environmental chemicals; and exposure to a chemical may be associated with a disease without causing it. Thus, we need to assess cautiously all claims of an association between an environmental agent and a particular disease. Our final conclusion will depend on the overall weight of the evidence that has been accumulated and critically reviewed according to well-accepted criteria.

Hill's criteria are most often cited (they are summarized in chapter 1). By these criteria, the epidemiologic studies discussed above do not make a strong case that PCBs, at typical environmental levels, or even at high occupational exposures, cause cancer or other health problems.

Certainly, PCBs are toxic to animals, at relatively high levels of exposure; some PCB isomers and PCDFs and other substances commonly associated with PCBs are quite toxic. While not discussed in this chapter, ecological effects of these chemicals have also been reported in the literature. Outlawing the commercial uses of PCBs was a justified and prudent action.

By contrast, claims of association, based on epidemiologic studies, of chronic health effects such as cancer and trace exposure to environmental levels of PCBs are unjustified. One highly chlorinated mixture of PCBs does cause cancer in laboratory animals (Tables 9.1A and 9.1B)—but at levels that vastly exceed any to which the general population is exposed. People have overreacted to possible hazards from PCBs at typical environmental levels.

Notes

1. A suppressed immune system is less effective in fighting off infection or preventing the development of cancer (see chapter 16).

2. Chloracne has also been reported among workers exposed to some chlorinated dibenzo-p-dioxins (see chapter 11). The *yusho* and *yu-cheng* instances of human poisoning also resulted in chloracne which, in these cases, was caused by chlorinated dibenzofurans.

3. The reader might ask what is meant by "1.5 deaths." Death, like pregnancy, is an all-or-none phenomenon. For any group (e.g., the 290 Italian workers in this study) a statistician might apply national mortality rates and predict 1.5 deaths from a particular cancer. Because of chance (sampling effects) zero, one, or two (or even six) members of the group might succumb to the cancer, even though their risk might be the same as for the population at large. How to decide whether an unexpectedly high number of deaths in a group arises from sampling error or a real increase in risk is a crucial but sometimes difficult questions.—The Editors.

References

Bertazzi, P. A., C. Zocchetti, S, Guercilena, M. D. Foglia, A. Pesatori, and L. Ribaldi. 1981. Mortality study of male and female workers exposed to PCBs. Paper presented at the International Symposium on Prevention of Occupational Cancer, Helsinki.

Bahn, A. K., J. Rosenwaike, N. Herrmann, P. Grover, J. Stellman, and K. O'Leary. 1976. Melanoma after exposure to PCB. 295 *N. Engl. J. Med.* 450.

Brown, D. P., and M. Jones. 1981. Mortality and industrial hygiene study of workers exposed to polychlorinated biphenyls. 36 *Arch. Environ. Health* 120–129.

Brown, D. P. 1987. Mortality of workers exposed to polychlorinated biphenyls—an update. 42 *Arch. Environ. Health* 333–339.

Cannon, S. B., J. M. Veazey, R. S. Jackson, V. W. Burse, C. Hayes, W. E. Straub, P. J. Landrigan, and J. A. Liddle. 1978. Epidemic Kepone poisoning in chemical workers. 107 *Am. J. Epidem.* 529–537.

Cottreau, C., L. McIntyre, and B. E. Favara. 1989. Professional attitudes toward the autopsy. A survey of clinicians and pathologists. 92 *Am. J. Clin. Path.* 673–676.

Federal Register. 1982. Polychlorinated biphenyls (PCBs): Manufacturing, processing, distribution, in commerce and use prohibitions: Use in electrical equipment. 47:37342–37360.

Fein, G. G., J. L. Jacobson, S. W. Jacobson, P. M. Schwartz, and J. K. Dowler. 1984. Prenatal exposure to polychlorinated biphenyls: Effects on birth size and gestational age. 105 *J. Pediatr.* 315–320.

Fingerhut, M. A., W. E. Halperin, P. A. Honchar, A. B. Smith, D. H. Groth, and W. O. Russell. 1984. An evaluation of reports of dioxin exposure and soft tissue sarcoma pathology in U.S. chemical workers. 10 *Scand. J. Work Environ. Health* 299–303.

Galen, R. S., and S. R. Gambino. 1975. *Beyond normality: The predictive value and efficiency of medical diagnoses.* New York: John Wiley and Sons.

Gladen, B. C., and W. J. Rogan. 1991. Effects of perinatal polychlorinated biphenyls and dichlorodiphenyl dichloroethene on later development. 119 *J. Pediatr.* 58–63.

Hoffman, R. E., and P. A. Stehr-Green. 1989. Localized contamination with 2,3,7,8-tetrachlorodibenzo-p-dioxin: The Missouri episode. In R. D. Kimbrough and A. A. Jensen, eds., *Halogenated biphenyls, terphenyls, napthalenes, dibenzodioxins and related products.* 471–484. 2nd ed. Amsterdam: Elsevier Science.

Institute for Evaluating Health Risks. 1991. *Reassessment of liver findings in five PCB studies in rats.* Washington, DC: Institute for Evaluating Health Risks.

Jacobson, S. W., J. L. Jacobson, P. M. Schwartz and G. G. Fein. 1983. Intrauterine exposure of human newborns to PCBs: measures of exposures. In F. M. D'Itri and M. Kamrin, eds., *PCBs: Human and environmental hazards* 311–343. Boston: Butterworth.

Jacobson, J. L., S. W. Jacobson, P. M. Schwartz, G. G. Fein, and J. K. Dowler. 1984. Prenatal exposure to an environmental toxin: a test of the multiple effects model. 20 *Dev. Psychol.* 523–532.

Jensen, S. 1966. Report of a new chemical hazard, 32 *New Sci.* 612.

Kimbrough, R. D., R. A. Squire, R. E. Linder, J. D. Strandberg, R. J. Montali, and V. W. Burst. 1975. Induction of liver tumors in Sherman strain female rats by polychlorinated biphenyl Aroclor 1260. 55 *J. Natl. Cancer Inst.* 1453–1459.

Kimbrough, R. D. 1985. Laboratory and human studies on polychlorinated biphenyls (PCBs) and related compounds. 59 *Environ. Health Persp.* 99–106.

Kimbrough, R. D., J. Buckley, L. Fishbein, G. Flamm, L. Kasza, W. Marcus, S. Shibko, and R. Teske. 1978. Animal Toxicology. 24 *Environ. Health Persp.* 173–185.

Kimbrough, R. D., and A. A. Jensen, eds. 1989. Halogenated biphenyls, terphenyls, naphthalenes, dibenzodioxins and related products. 2nd ed. Amsterdam: Elsevier Biomedical Press.

Kimbrough, R. D. 1987. Human health effects of polychlorinated biphenyls (PCBs) and polybrominated biphenyls PBBs. 27 *Ann. Rev. Pharmacol. Toxicol.* 87–111.

Kreiss, K., M. Zack, R. D. Kimbrough, L. L. Needham, A. L. Smrek, and B. T. Jones. 1981. Association of blood pressure and polychlorinated biphenyl levels. 245 *J. Am. Med. Assn.* 2505–2509.

Kuratsune, M. 1989. Yusho with references to yu-cheng. In R. D. Kimbrough and A. A. Jensen, eds., *Halogenated biphenyls, terphenyls, napthalenes, dibenzodioxins and related products* 381–396. New York: Elsevier.

Landrigan, P. J., K. R. Wilcox Jr., J. Silva Jr., H. E. B. Humphrey, C. Kauffman, and C. W. Heath. 1979. Cohort study of Michigan residents exposed to polybrominated biphenyls: Epidemiologic and immunologic findings. 320 *Ann. N.Y. Acad. Sci.* 284–294.

Lawton, R. W., M. R. Ross, J. Feingold, and J. R. Brown Jr. 1985. Effects of PCB exposure on biochemical and hematological findings in capacitor workers. 60 *Environ. Health Persp.* 165–184.

Lee, T.-P., and K.-J. Chang. 1985. Health effects of polychlorinated biphenyls. In J. Dean, M. Luster, A. Munson and H. Amos, eds., *Immunopharmacology* 415–422. New York: Raven Press.

Linder, R. E., T. B. Gaines, and R. D. Kimbrough. 1974. The effect of polychlorinated biphenyls on rat reproduction. 12 *Food Cosmetic Toxicol.* 63–77.

Mathews, J. D. 1976. Alcohol use, hypertension, and coronary heart disease. 51(3) *Clin. Sci. Molec. Med.* suppl. 661–663.

Morita, M., J. Nakagawa, and C. Rappe. 1978. Polychlorinated dibenzofuran (PCDF) formation from PCB mixture by heat and Oxygen. 19 *Bull. Environ. Contam. Toxicol.* 665–670.

Paneth, N. 1991. Human reproduction after eating PCB contaminated fish. 5 *Health & Environ. Digest* 4–6.

Percy, C., E. Stanek, and L. Gloeckler. 1981. Accuracy of cancer death certificates and its effect on cancer mortality statistics. 71 *Am. J. Publ. Health* 242–250.

Peter, J. B. 1989. *The use and interpretation of tests in clinical immunology.* Omaha: Interstate Press.

Rogan, W., and B. Gladen. 1982. Duration of breast feeding and environmental contaminants in milk (abstract). 116 *Am. J. Epidem.* 565A.

Rogan, W. J., N. Carreras, B. C. Gladen, P. Hardy, J. D. McKinney, J. Thullen, J. Tingelstad, M. Tully. 1986. Polychlorinated biphenyls (PCBs) and dichlorodiphenyl dichloroethene (DDE) in human milk—effects of maternal factors and previous lactation. 76 *Am. J. Pub. Health* 172–177.

Saxena, S., I. A. Shulman, and J. Korula. 1989. A review of donor alanine aminotransferase testing. 113 *Arch. Path. Lab. Med.* 767–771.

Schaeffer, E., H. Greim, and W. Goessner. 1984. Pathology of chronic polychlorinated biphenyl (PCB) feeding in rats. 75 *Toxicol. Appl. Pharmacol.* 278–288.

Schwartz, P. M., S. W. Jacobson, G. G. Fein, J. L. Jacobson, and H. A. Price. 1983. Lake Michigan fish consumption as a source of polychlorinated biphenyls in human cord serum, maternal serum, and milk. 73 *Am. J. Pub. Health* 293–296.

Sinks, T., A. B. Smith, G. K. Steele, R. Rinsky, and K. Watkins. 1990. A retrospective cohort mortality study of workers at a capacitor plant, utilizing polychlorinated biphenyls. Paper presented at the 7th International Symposium of

Epidemiology in Occupational Health, Tokyo. Published in H. Sakurai, I. Okasaki, and K. Omae, eds., *Occupational epidemiology*. Amsterdam: Excerpta Medica.

Stehr-Green, P. A., V. W. Burse, and E. Welty. 1988. Human exposures to polychlorinated biphenyls at toxic waste sites: Investigations in the United States. 43 *Arch. Environ. Health* 420–424.

Taylor, P. R., J. M. Stelma, and C. E. Lawrence. 1989. The relation of polychlorinated biphenyls to birth weight and gestational age in the offspring of occupationally exposed mothers. 129 *Am. J. Epidemiol.* 395–406.

Unger, M., and J. Olsen. 1980. Organochlorine compounds in the adipose tissue of deceased people with and without cancer. 23 *Environ. Res.* 257–263.

Vos, J. G., and M. I. Luster. 1989. Immune alterations. In R. D. Kimbrough and A. A. Jensen, eds., *Halogenated biphenyls, terphenyls, naphthalenes, dibenzodioxins and related products* 295–322. 2nd ed. Amsterdam: Elsevier Science.

World Health Organization, Regional Office for Europe. 1988. *PCBs, PCDDs and PCDFs in breast milk: Assessment of health risks.* Environmental Health Series no. 29. Copenhagen: World Health Organization.

Biographical Sketch

Renate D. Kimbrough, M.D., is currently a senior medical associate with the Institute for Evaluating Health Risks, a non-profit organization. Prior to that, she was an adviser for medical toxicology and risk evaluation, Office of the Administrator, Environmental Protection Agency.

Dr. Kimbrough has worked in toxicology and environmental health since 1962, primarily at the U.S. Centers for Disease Control and Prevention until 1987. She was senior editor of and a contributor to *Halogenated Biphenyls, Terphenyls, Naphthalenes, Dibenzodioxins and Related Products*, published by Elsevier; senior author of *Clinical Effects of Environmental Chemicals, a Software Approach to Etiological Diagnosis*, published by Taylor and Francis.

Dr. Kimbrough was the 1987 recipient of the Clinton H. Thienes Award of the American Academy of Clinical Toxicology and the 1991 recipient of the Herbert E. Stockinger Award of the American Conference of Governmental and Industrial Hygienists. She is an honorary Fellow of the American Academy of Pediatrics.

10

Trichloroethylene: Toxicology and Epidemiology: A Critical Review of the Literature

Rudolph J. Jaeger and Arlene L. Weiss

Introduction

Pollution that drifts visibly into the atmosphere is easier to detect and regulate than that which seeps invisibly into the ground. One major contaminant of groundwater that has attracted much notice and controversy in scientific, regulatory, and legal circles is the chlorinated solvent trichloroethylene (TCE). What, if any, are its major health effects on humans at environmental exposure levels?

The answer offered is uncertain at best. Human experience with chronic low-level exposure to TCE in the absence of other confounding factors is sparse. Direct testing on humans would, of course, be unethical. Scientists have therefore estimated risks by extrapolating from acute overexposures, mostly in animal studies. But toxicology is unable to perform such extrapolations with precision, at least when toxicologists lack a mechanistic understanding of how the chemical acts in humans.

Background

TCE is a colorless, highly volatile, dense, nonaqueous liquid. At room temperature it smells sweet, not unlike chloroform. There are no known natural sources of TCE.

Most of the TCE produced in the United States is used for degreasing fabricated metal parts. The rest—between 5 percent and 20 percent—is either exported or used in such things as adhesives, paint strippers, industrial painting systems, and textile dyeing and finishing. At one time, TCE was commonly found in a variety of household drain cleaners and degreasing products. It is or once was present in various other consumer products, including typewriter correction fluids, paint removers and paint strippers, adhesives, drain cleaners, spot removers, cleaning fluids for rugs, and metal cleaners.

However, the production of TCE has been declining in recent years; it is being replaced by other solvents, largely because of regulation and concerns about pollution. TCE is no longer used as an inhalation anesthetic, as a fumigant mixture, or a solvent for removing caffeine from coffee (Office of Health and Environmental Assessment 1985).

Most of the TCE used in degreasing operations evaporates into the atmosphere, which likely accounts for the greater part of the TCE in the environment. Waste disposal sites may also release TCE to the air by evaporation. In the upper atmosphere TCE may undergo many chemical changes that can alter its atmospheric concentration (Altshuller 1980; Cox et al. 1976). TCE also contaminates groundwater by its deliberate or accidental release into the soil. Once in the ground, it sinks through the soil and forms a dense, nonaqueous-phase liquid (DNAPL) (Mackay and Cherry 1989). It is eventually removed from groundwater, mostly through attack by microbes, that is, biodegradation (Vogel and McCarty 1985).

Humans are exposed to TCE from environmental and occupational sources. Background levels of TCE in the outdoor air are typically 30 to 460 parts per trillion (ppt). Many groundwater and surface water sources that provide tap water for homes and businesses contain small amounts of TCE—1 or 2 parts per billion (ppb) or less. Industrialized areas generally have higher TCE levels than rural, agrarian areas. Some regions, where direct contamination has occurred, contain much higher concentrations of TCE.

The greatest human exposure to TCE probably occurs in the workplace, particularly in metal degreasing industries. TCE enters the body when workers inadvertently breath or ingest the chemical. Skin contact with TCE solutions is another potential means of exposure. This is probably not significant compared with inhalation and ingestion, but scientists disagree on this point. Industrial workers who handle highly concentrated solutions are warned, however, that skin contact may be an important means of exposure. There are currently no adequate means to measure directly or to calculate the importance of this pathway in human exposure to TCE.

From experience with workers exposed to high concentrations of TCE, physicians have learned that some personal factors increase the risk of adverse health effects from the chemical or its intermediates. These include consumption of alcohol, treatment with certain drugs, and exposure to substances that increase the body's production of certain enzymes. TCE may render a person intolerant to alcohol: a person who consumes alcohol after TCE exposure may develop "degreaser's flush" (facial and upper extremity skin vasodilation), a phenomenon produced by a chemical synergism (interaction) that results from increased levels of an intermediate in the breakdown of TCE and alcohol. This may also increase the risk of injury to the liver and kidney (Stewart et al. 1974; Reynolds and Molsen 1982). The drug disulfiram (Antabuse), used to treat alcohol abuse, increases the risk of injury from TCE by interfering with the detoxification of TCE metabolites in the body (Bartonicek and Teisinger 1962). This effect was first observed in humans; much of the rest of the data regarding such interactions is derived from high-dose animal studies whose relevance to low-dose human exposures is uncertain. Finally, people with cardiac abnormalities may be at greater risk from exposure to high concentrations of TCE because it sensitizes the heart to circulating adrenalin.

Health Effects

The health effects of TCE exposure have been comprehensively reviewed. The most important reviews are the toxicity profile document on TCE prepared by the Agency for Toxic Substances and Disease Registry (1987) and the health assessment document for TCE and its addendum prepared by the Environmental Protection Agency (Office of Health and Environmental Assessment 1985; EPA 1987). A brief summary of exposure dose and health effects in animals and man is given in Tables 10.1 and 10.2.

Table 10.1
Toxicologic effects of inhaled TCE

Exposure (ppm) in air	Effect	Reference
12,400 (rats) 8,450 (mice)	death to 50% of animals (4-hr. exposure)	Siegel et al. (1971) Kylin et al. (1962)
2,900	Lethal conc. to humans	NIOSH (1984)
81–110 ppm chronic exposure	Reports of headache and central nervous system effects in humans	Nomiyama & Nomiyama (1977)
27 ppm chronic exposure	Irritation to mucous membranes in humans	Nomiyama & Nomiyama (1977)

Table 10.2
Toxicologic effects of ingested TCE

Exposure (mg TCE/kg body weight) or ppm	Effect	Reference
7330 mg/kg one dose	Lethal to 50% of rabbits	NIOSH (1984)
7000 mg/kg (estimated) one dose	Lethal dose to humans	NIOSH (1984)
1000 mg/kg daily for 103 weeks	Cancer in mice	NTP (1982, 1986)

Certainly, very high exposures to TCE (2,900 ppm[1] and above) can be lethal (NIOSH 1984). TCE is an anesthetic, and when breathed at sufficiently high concentrations, it causes progressive loss of consciousness, depression of the central nervous system, and death from respiratory failure. Four-hour exposures of test animals kill half of the subjects at exposures of 12,400 ppm (for rats) and 8,450 ppm (mice) (Siegel et al. 1971; Kylin et al. 1962). In humans, anesthetic doses of TCE may produce cardiac arrhythmias (Dhuner 1951, 1957). However, studies on animals confirm that such effects occur at exposure levels above 1,000 ppm. They are enhanced if the subject exercises or increases ventilation, which increases the amount of TCE taken up by the body.

TCE is also toxic if ingested, but high doses are required to produce toxic effects. A single oral dose of 7,000 mg/kg[2] of TCE was reported to be lethal to humans (Sorgo 1976). A single oral dose of 7,330 mg/kg was lethal to 50 percent of a group of rabbits (NIOSH 1984). These are very high doses; in fact, the Consumer Products Safety Commission would consider TCE "not acutely toxic." No adverse effects were observed in rats exposed to TCE for eight weeks at levels below 3,160 mg/kg per day (National Cancer Institute 1976).

Toxicity to Other Target Organs or to the Immune System
Based on animal studies, the liver, the kidneys and the central nervous system are the most likely primary sites of action for TCE in man. Data linking TCE to toxic effects on other organs or to the immune system of humans are limited. Skin effects in workers, while common, are most likely due to a solvent action that requires excessive liquid exposure and

is not unique to TCE. The only reported effects of chronic TCE exposure at low levels in humans are anecdotal reports of irritation to mucous membranes and drowsiness. At slightly higher concentrations (81–110 ppm), headaches and mild effects on the central nervous system have been reported (Nomiyama and Nomiyama 1977). In one study in which human volunteers were exposed by inhalation to TCE at 110 ppm for two four-hour periods separated by an hour and a half without exposure, the subjects showed reduced performance on tests of perception, memory, reaction time, and dexterity (Salvini et al. 1971).

Only one study examined the effects of TCE on the central nervous systems of humans exposed for long periods to TCE (Grandjean et al. 1955). The subjects were workers who had been exposed occupationally to the chemical for periods averaging 3.75 years. Workers with higher exposure (85 ppm) to TCE reported problems such as vertigo, headache, and short-term memory loss more often than those with lower exposure (34 or 14 ppm). TCE at somewhat higher concentrations (greater than 200 ppm) produces effects on the central nervous system of rats similar to those of anesthetics, a purpose for which it had use in the past.

Likewise, limited information exists about the toxicity of TCE to the human blood and renal (kidney) systems. Most of the available data were collected after industrial accidents, in which workers were acutely overexposed to the chemical but at levels that could not be accurately determined. Such toxic effects have been well documented in experimental animals. Inhaled TCE affects the central nervous system, liver, kidneys, and blood system. In animals, inhalation of TCE leads to changes in the number or characteristics of blood cells. Studies with rats have demonstrated a slight, dose-related trend in the levels of a specific enzyme in the liver and bone marrow (Fujita et al. 1984). Rats exposed to 50, 200, or 800 ppm TCE for up to 90 days show a decrease in the hemoglobin concentration in their red blood cells (Nomiyama et al. 1986). Acute inhalation (150 ppm for 30 days) and longer exposures can lead to increases in the weight of the liver and kidney (Kimmerle and Eben 1973; Kjellstrand et al. 1983). Chronic oral (gavage) exposures to 500 or 1,000 mg/kg/day have led to enlargement of kidney tubular cells and kidney disease in various strains of rats and mice (National Cancer Institute 1976; National Toxicology Program 1982, 1986a). Mice given 240 mg/kg TCE orally for up to two weeks exhibited increased liver weights (Tucker et al. 1982); longer exposures also affected kidney function (Tucker et al. 1982; Stott et al. 1982).

The effects described above, however, required exposure and dosing at levels and in amounts of TCE far above those normally found in the environment (ppm range). There are no reliable reports linking TCE exposure at environmental levels with health effects such as dysfunction of the immune system in humans. One study, however, suggested an association between abnormalities in lymphocytes (a white blood cell that is part of the immune system) and suspected ingestion of water contaminated by several solvents, TCE among them, at concentrations of 270 ppb (Byers et al. 1988). No conclusions can be drawn from these data due to the multiple chemical exposures of the subjects.

Several animal studies have reported changes in the immune system in animals exposed to TCE. Mice exposed to drinking water containing TCE at concentrations ranging to 660 mg/kg/day for 6 months have exhibited depressed cell-mediated immune responsiveness, decreased humoral mediated immune response, and decreased bone marrow stem cell colonization (Sanders et al. 1982). An EPA study found that mice exposed to a complex mixture of contaminants in their drinking water had altered immune system function (Yang et al. 1989; Germolec et al. 1989). The total concentration of 25 contaminants was 756 ppm. However, these studies involve exposure of animals to mixtures of chemicals, and shed little light on the toxic effects TCE by itself. Two earlier reports involving in utero inhalation exposure of mice to such mixtures suggest that the effects on the immune system may, in fact, be due to benzene exposure (Keller and Synder 1986, 1988).

Developmental and Reproductive Toxicity

Several authors have reported higher risk for miscarriage in nurses exposed to certain anesthetics, including TCE (Corbett et al. 1973, 1974; Cote 1975). The data are inconclusive and the exposures were not well quantified.

So far, no epidemiologic data are available on possible associations between inhalation of TCE by pregnant women and altered development of their offspring. In animals, however, inhalation of TCE can be toxic to a fetus, often delaying development before birth. But, as several animal studies have shown, high levels of exposure are needed to produce such effects: doses that are sufficient to damage the health of the mother as well. TCE does not cause birth defects in animals.

Other animal studies should be mentioned, in particular the two-generation studies in mice and rats by the National Toxicology Program (1985, 1986b). When rats were fed diets containing 0.15, 0.30, or 0.60 percent TCE, the survival of their newborn pups decreased. In the mice given the highest doses of TCE (0.60 percent), the sperm showed reduced mobility. However, these rats showed no changes in fertility or reproductive performance, or in their reproductive organs, so the changes in sperm motility are probably not adverse.

In another study (Manson et al. 1984), female rats were given TCE orally before mating and through gestation; their newborn offspring had a higher death rate than controls. These effects were observed after high exposure to TCE and are more likely to result from toxicity to the mother than from any direct effect of TCE on reproduction or development of the offspring. No effect on mating performance or fertility was observed in the rats given 10, 100, or 1000 mg/kg/day TCE orally (gavage).

One epidemiologic study in particular (Lagakos et al. 1986) has often been cited as providing direct evidence of discernible risk from environmental exposure to TCE. This study examined residents of Woburn, Massachusetts, whose water came from wells contaminated by a variety of chemicals including TCE. The study reported a higher incidence of deaths among newborns and a higher incidence of anomalies (including anomalies of the eyes and ears, central nervous system anomalies, chromosomal abnormalities, and anomalies of the oral cleft) among children born in the town, taking into account other important risk factors, such as age and smoking habits of the parents.

However, this study can be criticized on several grounds. The investigators suggested that the increased health problems were caused by exposure to the contaminated well water. But the evidence satisfies few of Hill's criteria for causation (see chapter 1) and no strong case exists that the well water, much less the TCE that contaminated it, caused the reported problems. The study provided no useful measure of the actual exposures of the residents to the suspect chemicals, or even the amount of the suspected water they consumed. The investigators described one well (well G) as being used "intermittently" between 1967 and 1979, and another (well H) as used "intermittently" between 1974 and 1979, without explaining their use of the term "intermittent." Finally, the study did not consider other possible contaminants in the water, including natural radioactivity, polycyclic aromatic hydrocarbons, metal ions, and viruses. These omissions severely limit the usefulness of this study.

It appears that in the well water, the levels of TCE and other contaminants were similar to those found elsewhere in the United States. However, the mixture of chemicals in the water, and the actual levels of the residents' exposure to any of the contaminants, were not known.[3]

Interestingly, the Woburn study had been prompted by a different concern, raised by a cluster of childhood leukemia cases in the town. The investigators did report a positive statistical association between access to the water and incidence rates of childhood leukemia; but it appears that the association was too weak to account plausibly for the cluster. The investigators found no substances in the well water that are known to cause leukemia. No records exist of the incidence of leukemia in the area before 1964. However, the incidence of leukemia in the area continued to increase after the wells were closed. Most of this increase was in West Woburn, which was never supplied by wells G and H (Lagakos et al. 1986).

Carcinogenicity
Several studies have shown that inhalation of TCE can cause cancer in animals. The authors of one study (Maltoni et al. 1986) reported a statistically significant increase of testicular cell tumors and a slight increase of kidney tumors and carcinomas in male rats. Mice (two strains, both sexes) and rats were exposed to 100, 300, or 600 ppm 7 hours/day for 78 weeks and 104 weeks, respectively. Maltoni et al. also reported lung tumors and liver tumors in one strain of male mice and in female mice of a different strain. Other investigators (Fukuda et al. 1983) observed a significant increase in the incidence of lung carcinoma in another strain of mice exposed to 150 or 450 ppm TCE daily for 104 weeks. Yet another study found significant increases in the incidence of liver cancer in male and female mice chronically exposed to TCE, but no increase in cancer in rats exposed to the chemical (Bell et al. 1978).

Other studies report increased cancers in animals given oral doses of TCE. A study by the National Cancer Institute (1976) reported increased incidence of hepatocellular (liver cell) cancers in male mice given TCE orally for 78 weeks at two dose levels (time-weighted average doses of 1,169 and 2,339 mg/kg/day) and in females only in the high-dose group. No compound-related carcinogenic effects were seen in rats. The National Toxicology Program study (1982, 1986a) found excess cancer of the liver in mice of both sexes that had been given 1,000 mg/kg/day TCE orally for 103 weeks. However, the study reported an excess of kidney cancer in male rats at the high dose but no evidence of liver cell carcinoma in rats exposed chronically to TCE at 500 or 1,000 mg/kg/day for 103 weeks. These results, however, were inconclusive because of the high death rate of the rats, apparently a result of the high dosages of TCE.

In a later study (National Toxicology Program 1987) four strains of male rats were chronically treated with 500 or 1,000 mg/kg/day TCE. One strain showed an increase in kidney tumors in the low-dose group and another an increase in testicular tumors in the high-dose group. But this study also showed toxic effects of the chemical and high death rates of the animals, thereby rendering this study inadequate for assessing carcinogenicity. Still other investigators (Maltoni et al. 1986) observed a dose-related increase in one kind of leukemia (immunoblastic lymphosarcoma) in male rats that were given 50 or 250 mg/kg/day TCE orally for a year. The incidence of these tumors increased with increasing exposure to the chemical, which suggests that it was caused by the exposure. However, female rats in this study showed no such increase. It is important to emphasize that these studies employed quite high doses of TCE, far above those found in the environment.

Genotoxicity

The transformation of a normal cell into a cancer cell is associated with a mutation or damage to its genetic material. Thus, genotoxicity (capability of damaging the genetic material of cells) is linked with carcinogenicity, although genotoxic chemicals may not be carcinogenic. Genotoxic effects can be detected by examination of the chromosomes of cells taken from animals or humans, by searching for mutations in animals exposed to a chemical, or by other means.

Several studies have searched for genotoxic effects in humans occupationally exposed to TCE. Two studies of workers exposed to TCE reported an increase in hypodiploid cells (cells lacking the two full sets of chromosomes found in normal individuals) and greater response to the sister chromatid exchange test (which is designed to detect chromosomal abnormalities). However, one of these studies lacked matched controls (Konietzko et al. 1978), and the other provided inadequate information about exposure levels (Gu et al. 1981). Thus, one cannot conclude that TCE led to genetic damage in the exposed individuals.

Animal studies are more easily controlled. One test for genetic damage to mice (examination for dominant lethal mutations) found no effects of TCE (Slacik-Erben et al. 1980). Other studies using bacteria, fungi, mice, and cultured human cells found weak positive associations between mutation of genes and exposure to commercial preparations of TCE. However, these associations were observed only when the test cells were metabolically active. This suggests that the observed effects may not have been caused by TCE itself but by a chemical product that is formed when TCE is broken down and subsequently metabolized by cells.

An association was reported between abnormalities in mouse sperm and mice exposed by inhalation to 2,000 ppm TCE for 28 days (Land et al. 1979, 1981). These investigators did not determine whether these abnormalities were of any functional significance to the animals' reproductive ability.

In short, TCE may be weakly mutagenic in animals or humans. If so, it is a very weak mutagen that acts indirectly and requires changes in the chemical structure (by metabolic processes) for genotoxic effects to occur.

Epidemiologic Studies on Humans

No strong evidence exists for an increased cancer risk in humans from exposure to TCE. Four studies found no significant association between TCE inhalation and cancer (Axelson 1986; Tola et al. 1980; Malek et al. 1979; Shindell and Ulrich 1985). However, they were too limited to support any firm conclusions about cancer risk to humans associated with TCE exposure.

Dry cleaning processes formerly employed TCE, and dry cleaning employees were at one time exposed to this chemical and perhaps other solvents as well. In a proportionate mortality ratio study of dry-cleaning workers (Blair et al. 1979), the authors observed a significant increase in cancer at all sites, though not all of the increases were statistically significant. In this and other studies of dry-cleaning workers (Duh and Asal 1984; Katz and Jowett 1981), the workers had been exposed not only to TCE but also to tetrachloroethylene and carbon tetrachloride.

Other studies have been reported as well. One study found a slight excess of bladder cancer and lymphoma among workers exposed to TCE (Axelson 1986); another reported an association between naso- and oropharyngeal cancer and exposure to TCE and cutting oils (Barret et al. 1985). Still other studies found no association between TCE exposure and liver cancer (Paddle 1983) or malignant lymphoma (Hardell et al. 1981).

In our view, the available epidemiologic data are insufficient to confirm that TCE is a human carcinogen. They are also insufficient to confirm that it is not, though proving a negative is more difficult than proving a positive.

Metabolism of TCE in Animals and Humans

The biological activity of TCE is closely related to how the body metabolizes and excretes the chemical. Not surprisingly, this has been the subject of numerous studies.

One group of investigators (Mueller et al. 1982) administered TCE by injection to chimpanzees, baboons, and rhesus monkeys. The investigators found that metabolic products of TCE are excreted in the urine and feces. However, the TCE was broken down into metabolic products in considerably different proportions in these different species. In addition, the animals exhaled much of the TCE in unchanged form.

Others investigated the metabolism of TCE in mice and rats (Elcombe 1985; Elcombe et al. 1985; Green and Prout 1985; Prout et al. 1985; DeAngelo et al. 1989; Ikeda et al. 1980; Filser and Bolt 1979; Hathway 1980; Larson and Bull 1989; Herren-Freund et al. 1986, 1987), and humans (Monster et al. 1979; Nomiyama and Nomiyama 1979). Both rats and mice excrete most metabolites of TCE via the urine. Another group of investigators (Stott et al. 1982) found that mice metabolize more TCE than do rats at both low and high dose levels.

Some of the metabolic by-products of TCE are toxic, particularly to liver and kidney tissues. Miller and Guengerich (1983) studied the metabolism of TCE in tissue extracts from the metabolically active parts of rat, mice, and human livers. These investigators found toxic metabolic products of TCE, with higher levels in the mouse cells. It is known that metabolic activation by certain liver enzymes is necessary if TCE metabolites are to bind to DNA (Bergman 1983). Other work suggests, however, that carcinogenic effects of TCE metabolites are not directly due to their binding to DNA (Loew et al. 1983; Roe 1989; Kimbrough et al. 1985; Stott et al. 1982).

The fact that TCE is less carcinogenic in some animals than in others might be associated with the wide variation in the quantity and type of metabolites found in different animals. These differences occur in some strains of mice (Barnard and Weber 1979) and certain strains of rats (Banerjee and Van Duuren 1978). These findings support the theory that TCE may be more toxic to mice than to rats because of species-specific differences in metabolism and susceptibility to toxic metabolites. Much additional evidence reinforces this conclusion.

One metabolic product of TCE in particular, trichloroacetic acid—which is formed at different rates in mice, rats, and humans—may be responsible for the liver tumors observed in mice. However, this metabolite produces cancer in mice by a mechanism that is not thought to occur in humans. Rats appear to be susceptible, but less so than mice because of metabolic differences. This again suggests that both the metabolic chemistry and the ultimate carcinogenic effects of chemicals vary with species. If so, risk assessment based on extrapolation of data from one species to another is unjustified and probably inaccurate.

Assessment of Risk

Nearly 190 million people in the United States receive water that is uncontaminated or has extremely low levels of TCE. But approximately

42,000 persons are exposed to concentrations above 100 μg/liter. In view of the evidence discussed above, is this likely to pose a significant health risk?

It is easy to show that this exposure level corresponds to absorbed doses of TCE that are extremely low compared with those that acutely produce overt toxicity. A concentration of 100 μg/liter in water corresponds to a daily dose of 200 μg. Expressed another way, if all of the TCE in the water that a person drinks were absorbed by the body, we estimate that the total absorbed dose is roughly 0.003 mg of TCE per kilogram of body weight per day in a person who weighs about 150 pounds. This is far below the levels (tens to hundreds of mg per kilogram per day) that produce acute toxic effects in animals.

Nonetheless, the possibility remains that some chronic risk is present, even at low levels of exposure. It is important to estimate risks correctly, to define what levels of risk might be acceptable, and then set appropriate exposure limits.

A crucial first step toward setting human exposure limits is to estimate levels of TCE that are safe or that present minimum risk levels (MRLs). These MRLs, which some scientists also term risk reference doses, address effects other than cancer. For short term effects in humans, the best available data indicate that the no observed adverse effect level is 4 mg/kg/day for eye, nose, and throat irritation. Allowing for a factor of 10 variation in human sensitivity, one arrives at an MRL of 0.4 mg/kg/day. This is still two orders of magnitude higher than the exposure a person is likely to experience from drinking water, even water that has comparatively high concentrations of TCE.

These figures are based on the possibility of health effects other than cancer. However, the greatest public concern with TCE has been the risk of cancer. Any reliable estimate of cancer risk requires care in selecting reliable data and appropriate experimental subjects.

Several different methods might be used to estimate cancer risk from a carcinogen or to find acceptable levels of exposure for humans. These methods differ in their assumptions and yield greatly different results.

One method, which many scientists regard as the least conservative, sets the exposure levels below those found to increase the cancer rate noticeably in animals, with a large safety factor. Since animals differ greatly in their response to carcinogens, the investigator must take great care in choosing a suitable species for comparison.

A second method uses a mathematical approach—the linearized multistage model. This predicts an upper limit on the cancer risk for particular exposures. The model assumes that there is no threshold below which the cancer risk disappears entirely. It also assumes a linear relationship between risk and dose from low exposures. It further assumes that exposure occurs over a lifetime. The Environmental Protection Agency and other agencies take the view that this model is the most conservative.

Still other methods incorporate additional information, such as the time between exposure to a chemical and the development of a tumor in animals, or information on how animals metabolize the chemical. These methods usually yield risk estimates that are intermediate between those of the two other models.

These different models yield widely varying estimates of the safe dose of TCE from drinking contaminated water (National Cancer Institute 1976; National Toxicology Program 1982, 1987; EPA 1989). The first model, for example, yields an MRL of 10 mg/kg/day (lifetime exposure), using the result of the National Toxicology Program studies that TCE exposure of 1,000 mg/kg/day led to no detectable increase in tumors of any kind in rats, with an uncertainty factor of 100. (This uncertainty factor included a factor of 10 to account for possible variation in sensitivity to TCE among humans, and another factor of 10 to account for uncertainties in extrapolating data from rats to humans.) The second method (used by the EPA) yields an acceptable risk of 0.000086 mg/kg/day (based on 3 µg/1/day), about a million times lower than the first method. In other words, the risk calculations depend critically on the model one chooses; the wrong model could be grossly in error. Nevertheless, even the most conservative method yields maximum acceptable concentrations of TCE in drinking water that are still slightly above the highest concentration of TCE in wells G and H in Woburn, Massachusetts.

The EPA has labeled TCE a "Group B2" chemical, meaning that there is sufficient evidence that it causes cancer in animals (at high doses) but not in humans. The EPA has compared TCE with 58 other compounds, and ranks it among the bottom quarter of the group in its potency as a carcinogen (EPA 1987). Nevertheless, the agency operates on the assumption that all animal carcinogens lead to cancer risk in humans at all levels of exposure. On that basis, the EPA labels TCE a "probable" human carcinogen.[4]

Many scientists, including the EPA Science Advisory Board and the present authors, disagree with that classification. An increasing number of chemicals have been proven to cause cancer in some animals (usually at high exposure levels) but have never been proven to be carcinogenic in humans. TCE is one such chemical. Its proven toxic effects on humans are limited to the central nervous system and some reported cases of liver and kidney injury. Scientists have not been able clearly and unequivocally to attribute TCE exposure to human cancers; for reasons discussed above, the available epidemiologic studies are inconclusive. Many experts now believe that TCE poses no significant cancer risk to people at levels found in the environment. Moreover, the carcinogenicity of TCE in rodents may result from a mechanism of action that is specific to those species, and of no concern to humans. Thus, some scientists conclude that a quantitative risk assessment of TCE should look to specific cases and types of cancer (EPA 1987).

For reasons discussed above, rodents are probably *not* suitable animals for assessing the risk of TCE to humans. Current regulatory policy, however, often accepts extrapolation of scientific results between distantly related species, such as from rats and mice to humans. Because of the unsuitability of the available animals data, together with the lack of strong, consistent chronic health effects observed in humans, we do not believe that the present evidence is strong enough to classify TCE as a human carcinogen.

Notes

1. When TCE is administered in air (breathing), the concentration is expressed as parts of TCE vapor per million parts of air (ppm). On a volume basis, 1,000 ppm corresponds to 1 cubic centimeter of TCE vapor per liter of air.

2. When administered orally (in water or by stomach tube, that is, by gavage, the dose is expressed as milligrams of TCE per kilogram of body weight (mg/kg). The daily dose is given as mg/kg/day. These doses are contrasted with inhalation where exposure is measured as a concentration (e.g., ppm). The two units, ppm and mg/kg, are not directly comparable. Inhaled dose depends on the breathing rate and fractional uptake while oral dose is based on the amount administered.

3. Ames and Gold note (chapter 7), by one estimate, the cancer risk (from TCE contaminants) to these residents from drinking the well water are tiny but nevertheless comparable to those a typical American faces from drinking chlorinated municipal tap water (from chloroform, which develops in chlorinated water and is also a carcinogen).—The Editors.

4. The American Industrial Hygiene Association published in November 1992 (Appl. Occup. Environ. Hyg.) a notice of intended change for trichloroethylene. The TLV committee proposes that TCE be classified as Group A5, not suspected as a human carcinogen, because the substance has been demonstrated by well-controlled epidemiological studies not to be associated with any increased risk of cancer in exposed humans.

References

Agency for Toxic Substances and Disease Registry. 1987. Toxicological profile for trichloroethylene. Oak Ridge, TN: Oak Ridge National Laboratory. Draft.

Altshuller, A. P. 1980. Lifetimes of organic molecules in the troposphere and lower stratosphere. 10 *Adv. Environ. Sci. Technol.* 181–219.

Axelson, O. 1986. Epidemiological studies of workers with exposure to tri- and tetrachloroethylenes. 12 *Dev. Toxicol. Environ. Sci.* 223–230.

Banerjee, S., and B. L. Van Duuren. 1978. Covalent binding of the carcinogen trichloroethylene to hepatic microsomal proteins and to exogenous DNA in vitro. 38 *Cancer Research* 776–780.

Barnard, R. J., and J. S. Weber. 1979. Carbon monoxide: A hazard to fire fighters. 34 *Arch. Environ. Health* 255–257.

Barret, L., J. Faure, and V. Danel. 1985. Epidemiological study of cancer in a community of workers occupationally exposed to trichloroethylene and cutting oils. 23 *J. Toxicol. Clin. Toxicol.* 438.

Bartonicek, V., and J. Teisinger. 1962. Effect of tetraethyl thiuram disulphide (disulfiram) on metabolism of trichloroethylene in man. 19 *Br. J. Indus. Med.* 216–221.

Bell, Z. G., K. H. Olson, and T. J. Benya. 1987. Final report of audit findings of the Manufacturing Chemists Association: Administered trichloroethylene chronic inhalation study at Industrial Biotest Laboratories. Unpublished work cited in Environmental Protection Agency 1987.

Bergman, K. 1983. Interactions of trichloroethylene with DNA in vitro and with RNA and DNA of various mouse tissues in vivo. 54 *Arch. Toxicol.* 181–193.

Blair, A., P. Decoufle, and D. Grauman. 1979. Causes of death among laundry and dry cleaning workers. 69 *Am. J. Pub. Health* 508–511.

Byers, V. S., A. S. Levin, D. M. Oxonoff, and R. W. Bladwin. 1988. Association between clinical symptoms and lymphocyte abnormalities in a population with chronic domestic exposure to industrial solvent-contaminated domestic water supply and a high incidence of leukaemia. 27 *Cancer Immunol. Immunother.* 77–81.

Corbett, T. H., R. G. Cornell, J. L. Endres, and K. Leiding. 1974. Birth defects among children of nurse anesthetists. 41 *Anesthesiology* 341–344 (1974).

Corbett, T. H., G. Hamilton, M. Yoon, and J. Endres. 1973. Occupational exposure of operating room personnel to trichloroethylene. 20 *Can. Anesth. Soc. J.* 675–678.

Cote, C. J. 1975. Birth defects among infants of nurse anesthetists. 42 *Anesthesiology* 514–515.

Cox, R. A., R. C. Denwent, A. E. J. Eggleton, and J. E. Lovelock. 1976. Photochemical oxidation of halocarbons in the troposphere. 10 *Atmos. Environ.* 305–308.

DeAngelo, A. B., F. B. Daniel, R. E. Savage, P. Wernsing, and L. McMillan. 1989. Species and strain sensitivity to the induction of peroxisome proliferation by chloroacetic acids. 101 *Toxicol. Appl. & Pharm.* 285–298.

Dhuner, K. G. 1951. Cardiac irregularities due to trichloroethylene given during labor. 31 *Acta Obst. Ct. Gynec. Scand.* 478–482.

Dhuner, K. G. 1957. Cardiac irregularities in trichloroethylene poisoning. 1 *Acta Anaesth. Scand.* 121–135.

Duh, R.-W., and N. R. Asal. 1984. Morality among laundry and dry cleaning workers in Oklahoma. 74 *Am. J. Pub. Health* 1278–1280.

Elcombe, C. R. 1985. Species differences in carcinogenicity and peroxisome proliferation due to trichloroethylene: A biochemical human hazard assessment. 8 *Arch. Toxicol.* supp. 6–17.

Elcombe, C. R., M. S. Rose, and I. S. Pratt. 1985. Biochemical, histological, and ultrastructural changes in rat and mouse liver following the administration of trichloroethylene: Possible relevance to species differences in hepatocarcinogenicity. 79 *Toxicol. & Appl. Pharm.* 365–376.

Environmental Protection Agency. 1989. Trichloroethylene. Integrated Risk Information System (IRIS), CASRN 79-01-6.

Environmental Protection Agency. 1987. *Addendum to the health assessment document for trichloroethylene: Updated carcinogenicity assessment for trichloroethylene* 141. EPA/600/8-82/006FA. Washington, DC: Office of Health and Environmental Assessment/Office of Research and Development.

Federal Register. 1986. Guidelines for carcinogen risk assessment. 51:33992–34003.

Filser, J. G., and M. H. Bolt. 1979. Pharmacokinetics of halogenated ethylenes in rats. 42 *Arch. Toxicol.* 123–136.

Fujita, H., A. Koizumi, M. Yamamoto, M. Kumai, T. Sadamoto, and M. Ikeda. 1984. Inhibition of delta-aminolevulinate dehydratase in trichloroethylene-exposed rats, and the effects on heme regulation. 800 *Biochim. Biophys. Acta* 1–10.

Fukuda, K., K. Takemoto, and H. Tsuruta. 1983. Inhalation carcinogenicity of trichloroethylene in mice and rats. 21 *Indus. Health* 243–254.

Germolec, D. R., P. Blair, G. A. Boorman, M. F. Ackerman, R. S. H. Yang, G. J. Rosenthal, and M. I. Luster. 1989. Toxicology studies of a chemical mixture of 25 groundwater contaminants. II. Immunosuppression in B6C3F$_1$ mice. 13 *Fund. Appl. Toxicol.* 377–387.

Grandjean, E., R. Munchinger, V. Turrian, P. A. Haas, H.-K. Knoepfel, and H. Rosenmund. 1955. Investigations into the effects of exposure to trichloroethylene in mechanical engineering. 12 *Br. J. Indus. Med.* 131–142.

Green, T., and M. S. Prout. 1985. Species differences in response to trichloroethylene. II. Biotransformation in rats and mice. 79 *Toxicol. & Appl. Pharm.* 401–411.

Gu, Z. W., B. Sele, P. Jalbert, M. Vincent, F. Vincent, C. Marka, D. Chmara, and J. Faure. 1981. Induction of sister chromatid exchange by trichloroethylene and its metabolites. 3 *Toxicol. Eur. Res.* 63–67.

Hardell, L., M. Eriksson, P. Lenner, and E. Lundgren. 1981. Malignant lymphoma and exposure to chemicals, especially organic solvents, chlorophenols and phenoxy acids: A case-control study. 43 *Brit. J. Cancer* 169–176.

Hathway, D. E. 1980. Consideration of the evidence for mechanisms of 1,1,2-trichloroethylene metabolism, including new identification of its dichloroacetic acid and trichloroacetic acid metabolites in mice. 8 *Cancer Let.* 263–269.

Herren-Freund, S. L., M. A. Pereira, M. D. Khoury, and G. Olson. 1987. The carcinogenicity of trichloroethylene and its metabolites, trichloroacetic acid and dichloroacetic acid, in mouse liver. 90 *Toxicol. & Appl. Pharm.* 183–189.

Herren-Freund, S. L., M. A. Pereira, G. Olson, and A. B. DeAngelo. 1986. The carcinogenicity of trichloroethylene (TCE) and its metabolites, tricholoroacetic acid (TCA) and dichloroacetic acid (DCA), in mouse liver. 27 *Proc. Ann. Meet. Am. Assn. Cancer Res.* 91.

Ikeda, M., Y. Miyake, M. Ogata, and S. Ohmori. 1980. Metabolism of trichloroethylene. 29 *Biochem Pharmacol.* 2983–2992.

Katz, R. M., and D. Jowett. 1981. Female laundry and dry cleaning workers in Wisconsin: A mortality analysis. 71 *Am. J. Pub. Health* 305–307.

Keller, K. A., and C. A. Snyder. 1986. Mice exposed in utero to low concentrations of benzene exhibit enduring changes in their colony forming hematopoietic cells. 42 *Toxicology* 171–181.

Keller, K. A., and C. A. Snyder. 1988. Mice exposed in utero to 20 ppm benzene exhibit altered numbers of recognizable hematopoietic cells up to seven weeks after exposure. 10 *Fund. Appl. Toxicol.* 224–232.

Kimbrough, R. D., F. L. Mitchell, and V. N. Houk. 1985. Trichloroethylene: an update. 15 *J. Toxicol. & Environ. Health* 369–383.

Kimmerle, G., and A. Eben. 1973. Metabolism, Excretion and toxicology of trichloroethylene after inhalation. 1. Experimental exposure on rats. 30 *Arch. Toxikol.* 115–126.

Kjellstrand, P., B. Holmquist, P. Alm, M. Kanje, S. Romare, I. Jonsson, L. Mansson, and M. Bjerkemo. 1983. Trichloroethylene: further studies of the effects on body and organ weights and plasma butyrylcholinesterase activity in mice. 53 *Acta Pharmacol. Toxicol.* 375–384.

Konietzko, H., W. Haberlandt, H. Heilbronner, G. Reill, and H. Weichardt. 1978. Cytogenetische Untersuchungen an Trichloroathylen-Arbeitern. 40 *Arch. Toxicol.* 201–206.

Kylin, B., H. Reichard, I. Sumegi, and S. Yllner. 1962. Hepatotoxic effect of tri- and tetrachloroethylene on mice. 193 *Nature* 395.

Lagakos, S. W., B. J. Wessen, and M. Zelen. 1986. An analysis of contaminated well water and health effects in Woburn, Massachusetts. 81 *J. Am. Stat. Assn.* 583–596.

Land, P. C., E. L. Owen, and H. W. Linde. 1979. Mouse sperm morphology following exposure to anesthetics during early spermatogenesis. 51 *Anesthesiology* S259.

Land, P. C., E. L. Owen, and H. W. Linde. 1981. Morphologic changes in mouse spermatozoa after exposure to inhalational anesthetics during early spermatogenesis. 54 *Anesthesiology* 53–56.

Larson, J. L., and R. J. Bull. 1989. Effect of ethanol on the metabolism of trichloroethylene. 28 *J. Toxicol. Environ. Health* 395–406.

Loew, G. H., E. Kurkjian, and M. Regagliati. 1983. Metabolism and relative carcinogenic poetncy of chloroethylenes: A quantum chemical structure-activity study. 43 *Chem.-Biol. Inter.* 33–66.

Mackay, D. M., and J. A. Cherry. 1989. Groundwater contamination: Pump-and-treat remediation. 23 *Environ. Sci. & Tech.* 630–636.

Malek, B., B. Kremarova, and A. Rodova. 1979. An epidemiological study of hepatic tumor incidence in subjects working with trichloroethylene. II. Negative result of retrospective investigations in dry cleaners. 31 *Pracov. Lek.* 124–126.

Maltoni, C., G. Lefemine, and G. Cotti. 1986. 5 *Experimental research on trichloroethylene carcinogenesis*. Princeton: Scientific Publishing.

Manson, J. M., M. Murphy, N. Richdale, and M. K. Smith. 1984. Effect of oral exposure to trichloroethylene on female reproductive function. 32 *Toxicology* 229–242.

Miller, R. E., and F. P. Guengerich. 1983. Metabolism of trichloroethylene in isolated hepatocytes, microsomes and reconstituted enzyme systems containing Cytochrome P-450. 43 *Cancer Res.* 1145–1152.

Monster, A. C., G. Boersma, and W. C. Duba. 1979. Kinetics of trichloroethylene in repeated exposure of volunteers. 42 *Int. Arch. Occup. Environ. Health* 283–292.

Mueller, W. F., F. Coulston, and F. Korte. 1982. Comparative metabolism of [14C]-trichloroethylene in chimpanzees, baboons, and rhesus monkeys. 11 *Chemosphere* 215–218.

National Cancer Institute. 1976. *Carcinogenesis bioassay of trichloroethylene.* Case no. 79-01-6, NCI-CG-TR-2, NIH 76-802. Washington, DC: Dept. of Health, Education and Welfare.

National Institute for Occupational Safety and Health. 1984. KX4550000 Ethylene, trichloro-. *Registry of toxic effects of chemical substances* 906–907. Washington, DC: NIOSH.

National Toxicology Program. 1982. *Carcinogenesis bioassay of trichloroethylene in F344 rats and B6C3F1 mice.* Case no. 79-01-6, NTP 81-84, NIH 82-1799. Washington, DC: NTP.

National Toxicology Program. 1985. *Trichloroethylene: Reproduction and fertility assessment in CD-1 mice when administered in the feed.* NTP-86-068. Washington, DC: NTP.

National Toxicology Program. 1986a. *Toxicology and carcinogenesis studies of trichloroethylene in F344/N rats and B6C3F1 mice.* NTP-TR-243. Washington, DC: NTP.

National Toxicology Program. 1986b. *Trichloroethylene: Reproduction and fertility assessment in F344 rats when administered in the feed.* Final report. NTP-86-085. Washington, DC: NTP.

National Toxicology Program. 1987. *Carcinogenesis bioassay of trichloroethylene in four strains of rats.* NTP-TR-273. Washington, DC: NTP.

Nomiyama, H., and K. Nomiyama. 1979. Host and agent factors modifying metabolism of trichloroethylene. 17 *Indus. Health* 21–28.

Nomiyama, K., and H. Nomiyama. 1977. Dose-response relationship for trichloroethylene in Man. 39 *Int. Arch. Occup. Environ.* 237–248.

Nomiyama, K., H. Nomiyama, and H. Arai. 1986. Tetrachloroethylene and 1,1,1-trichloroethane are suitable substitutes for trichloroethylene as industrial solvent from the viewpoint of subchronic toxicity? 31 *Toxicol. Let.* (Amsterdam) 226.

Office of Health and Environmental Assessment. 1985. *Health assessment document for trichloroethylene.* EPA-6008-82/006F. Washington, D.C.: EPA.

Paddle, G. M. 1983. Incidence of liver cancer and trichloroethylene manufacture—Joint study by industry and a cancer registry. 286 *Br. Med. J.* 846.

Prout, M. S., W. M. Provan, and T. Green. 1985. Species differences in response to trichloroethylene. I. Pharmacokinetics in rats and mice. 79 *Toxicol. & Appl. Pharm.* 389–400.

Reynolds, E. S., and M. T. Moslen. 1982. Metabolic activation and hepatotoxicity of trichloroethylene. Biological reactive intermediates. In 2 *Proceedings of the second international symposium, chemical mechanisms and biological effects,* Pt. A, 693–701. New York: Plenum Press.

Roe, F. J. C. 1989. Animal tests for carcinogenesis: Relevance for man, 8 *J. Am. Col. Toxicol.* 1241–1246.

Salvini, M., S. Binaschi, and M. Riva. 1971. Evaluation of the psychophysiological functions in humans exposed to trichloroethylene. 28 *Br. J. Indus. Med.* 293–295.

Sanders, V. M., A. N. Tucker, K. L. White, Jr., B. M. Kauffmann, P. Hallett, R. A. Carchman, J. F. Borzelleca, and A. E. Munson. 1982. Humoral and cell-mediated immune status in mice exposed to trichloroethylene in the drinking water. 62 *Toxicol. & Appl. Pharm.* 358–368.

Shindell, S., and S. Ulrich. 1985. A cohort study of employees of a manufacturing plant using trichloroethylene. 27 *J. Occup. Med.* 577–579.

Siegel, J., R. A. Jones, R. A. Coon, and P. J. Lyon. 1971. Effects on experimental animals of acute, repeated and continuous inhalation exposures to dichloroacetylene mixtures. 18 *Toxicol. & Appl. Pharm.* 168–174.

Slacik-Erben, R., R. Roll, G. Franke, and H. Vehleke. 1980. Trichloroethylene vapors do not produce dominant lethal mutations in male mice. 45 *Arch. Toxicol.* 37–44.

Sorgo, G. 1976. Trichloroethylene, carbon tetrachloride, and gasoline intoxication as etiological factors in the development of arterio- and coronary sclerosis. 35 *Arch. Toxicol.* 295–318.

Stewart, R. D., C. L. Hake, J. E. Peterson. 1974. "Degreasers flush": dermal response to trichloroethylene and ethanol. 29 *Arch. Environ. Health* 1–5.

Stott, W. T., J. F. Quast, and P. G. Watanabe. 1982. The pharmacokinetics and macromolecular interactions of trichloroethylene in mice and rats. 62 *Toxicol. & Appl. Pharm.* 137–151.

Tola, S., R. Vilhunen, R. Jarvinen, and M. L. Korkala. 1980. A cohort study on workers exposed to trichloroethylene. 22 *J. Occup. Med.* 737–740.

Tucker, A. N., V. M. Sanders, D. W. Barnes, T. J. Bradshaw, J. White, L. E. Sain, J. F. Borzelleca, and A. E. Munson. 1982. Toxicology of trichloroethylene in the mouse. 62 *Toxicol. & Appl. Pharm.* 351–357.

Vogel, T. M., and P. L. McCarty. 1985. Biotransformation of tetrachloroethylene to trichloroethylene, dichloroethylene, vinyl chloride and carbon dioxide under methanogenic conditions. 49 *Appl. Environ. Microbiol.* 1080–1083.

Yang, R. S. H., T. J. Goehl, R. D. Brown, A. T. Chatham, D. W. Arneson, R. C. Buchanan, and R. K. Harris. 1989. Toxicology studies of a chemical mixture of 25 groundwater contaminants. I. Chemistry development. 13 *Fund. Appl. Toxicol.* 366–376.

Biographical Sketch

Dr. Rudolph J. Jaeger is president and principal scientist of Environmental Medicine, Inc., a consulting firm specializing in environmental risk assessment and industrial toxicology. He is a Diplomate of the American Board of Toxicology and an EPA accredited asbestos inspector. Dr. Jaeger serves on the Toxicology Information Program Committee, Board on Environmental Studies and Toxicology, National Academy of Sciences-National Research Council.

In 1971, Dr. Jaeger received his doctorate in biochemical toxicology from the Department of Environmental Medicine at the Johns Hopkins School of Hygiene and Public Health. He is a research professor on the faculty of the Institute of Environmental Medicine, New York University Medical Center and School of Medicine. Dr. Jaeger is currently visiting lecturer in industrial toxicology and environmental medicine at the Harvard University School of Public Health.

Arlene L. Weiss is president of Pharm Tox, Inc., a consulting firm specializing in epidemiology and toxicology. In addition to her other research activities, she is part-time staff scientist for Environmental Medicine, Inc. Ms. Weiss received her masters degree in environmental health sciences (epidemiology) from New York University in 1990. She is presently enrolled in the doctoral program of the Department of Environmental Medicine, New York University Medical School.

11

Dioxin: Perceptions, Estimates, and Measures

Michael Gough[1]

Dioxin exemplifies many toxic chemicals that are found in the environment.[2] Animal studies convincingly show that it is toxic, and there is no doubt that humans have been, and are, exposed to it. Yet, despite scores of investigations of possible associations between exposures to dioxin and various diseases, there is no convincing evidence that it has caused any human disease except chloracne, a serious skin disease, and *that* only in highly exposed persons.

But dioxin differs from all other chemicals found in the environment: it has become by far the most visible and the most controversial. It is the most potent carcinogen yet tested in animals. Because of its presence in Agent Orange,[3] it is intertwined with America's confusion and enduring public emotion about the Vietnam War. Many—perhaps hundreds—of legal actions around the country involve claims that dioxin has caused disease and death. The media routinely characterize dioxin as the "most toxic man-made chemical" and "most potent man-made carcinogen." Finally, the political stakes are higher for dioxin than for other toxic substances. Any change in popular perceptions of dioxin would be a sharp challenge to the idea that cleaning up tiny amounts of chemicals in the environment will significantly improve human health. After all, if some scientists and many others were mistaken about the worst of carcinogens, perhaps they are also mistaken about other chemicals, for which evidence of carcinogenicity and human exposure is far less certain.

Sources and Exposures

Exposures to many environmental chemicals can be controlled by banning or restricting a few production processes or by regulating a discrete number of releases. That is not the case with dioxin.

Dioxin has never been made commercially. First synthesized around the turn of the century, it remained a laboratory curiosity until 1957. It was then identified as a cause of chloracne in some chemical workers, and as an unavoidable by-product of the synthesis of the chemical 2,4,5-trichlorophenol (Gough 1986, chapter 2).

At one time, several industrial processes used large amounts of trichlorophenol. These included the manufacture of the bactericide hexachlorophene and, in much greater amounts, the manufacture of the herbicide 2,4,5-trichlorophenoxyacetic acid (2,4,5-T). In 1968, U.S. manufacturers made 7.9 million kg of 2,4,5-T, and it was also manufactured in other countries around the world. Some of the dioxin that was present in the trichlorophenol contaminated these products as well.

Health concerns have driven both products from the market in most of the world. Hexachlorophene largely disappeared from the world market following a tragedy in France in 1972, where large amounts of it, accidentally mixed into talcum powder, caused 36 infant deaths (Hay 1982). The herbicide 2,3,5-T at one time was widely used throughout the world, since it kills most broadleaf plants, including weeds, while leaving grasses such as wheat, rice, and maize, as well as evergreen trees, unharmed. Many countries restricted or banned its manufacture, and it is now produced only in New Zealand.

It appeared for a while that elimination of these products would reduce dioxin's importance as an environmental concern. It didn't. Dioxin is persistent in the environment, and may endure in some soils for hundreds of years (Yanders 1989). Many other sources of dioxin have been identified, including the burning of leaded gasoline, municipal solid wastes, and other combustible materials, and the bleaching of paper pulp. Airborne concentrations have been decreasing steadily as use of leaded gasoline declines, smoky incinerators are shut down, and dioxin-contaminated herbicides are banned (Czuczwa and Hites 1986).

Dioxin has entered the food chain as a contaminant in food (e.g., from farmers' use of the herbicide 2,4,5-T) and by deposition of combustion products from the air (Travis and Hattemer-Frey 1987). Every human is apparently exposed, and once inside the body, dioxin is taken up by and stored in body fat (called, more politely, "adipose tissue" or "lipid") from which it is only slowly eliminated. The question of how quickly or slowly dioxin is eliminated is an important one because estimates of exposure depend on it. If elimination is quick, then exposure years ago must have been higher to account for present levels. A few years ago Pirkle (1989) reported that the average half-life in 36 men who had sprayed Agent Orange in Vietnam was about seven years. (These men are called "Ranch Hands" because the spraying of Agent Orange was called "Operation Ranch Hand"). More recently, Air Force scientists who have examined data from 337 Ranch Hands (including the original 36) have revised their estimates upwards to about 20 years (Wolfe et al. 1992).

Among North Americans generally, the concentration of dioxin in body fat ranges from nondetectable levels to 20 parts per trillion (ppt). Even 70-year-old men who have spent their entire lives in the western deserts typically bear 6 ppt to 7 ppt of dioxin in their body fat (Houk 1989). Levels of dioxin in humans are now decreasing in parallel with declines in environmental levels. Concentrations decreased about two-fold in samples of adipose tissue collected from nonoccupationally exposed men between 1971 and 1982 (Kang et al. 1991; Gough 1991b).

Far higher levels are found in people who have been occupationally exposed to the chemical or who were exposed through an accident. In particular, detailed information is available for four groups of highly exposed people (see Table 11.1) who have been the subject of epidemiologic studies. The first group consists of Air Force personnel who served in Operation Ranch Hand and sprayed 90 percent of the Agent Orange used in Vietnam. The mean concentration of dioxin in the body fat of these people, some 20 years after exposure, is now 13 ppt, ranging up to 618 ppt in one individual (Epidemiology Research Division 1991). On the average, the dioxin concentration in Ranch Hands is about three times higher than the 4 ppt measured in other Vietnam veterans and in veterans who never served in Vietnam (CDC 1988).

Two other highly exposed groups are workers in chemical plants that formerly manufactured dioxin-contaminated chemicals in America and Germany. As can be seen on Table 11.1, dioxin levels in those workers are 100 to 1,000 times higher than those measured in nonoccupationally exposed people (Fingerhut et al. 1989; Sweeney et al. 1990; Beck et al. 1988). Furthermore, it is important to remember that because of the slow elimination of dioxin from body tissues, the concentration of dioxin in the bodies of Ranch Hands and the workers was far higher in the past.

The last highly exposed group consists of residents of Seveso, Italy, who were exposed to dioxin during and after a 1976 accident at the herbicide plant located there (Mocarelli et al. 1988). The concentrations of dioxin in those samples, all of which are from children, represent the concentrations soon after exposure because samples were obtained within a few days after the explosion. The mean dose to the Seveso children who developed chloracne (3,125,000 pg/kg)[4] is (pound for pound) about three times higher than would be sufficient to kill half of all guinea pigs so exposed (Gough 1991c).[5] Based on those limited data, people

Table 11.1
Concentrations of dioxin in highly exposed people

Exposed population	Number of people	Range of concentrations (ppt)	Mean concentrations (ppt)	Time between exposure and study
Ranch Hands[1]	886	0–618	13	18–28 yrs
unexposed comparisons	804	0–55	4	
U.S. workers[2]	5,172	2–3,400	233[3]	15–37 yrs[3]
exposed <1 year	2,583	46		
exposed >1 year	2,589	418[3]		
German workers[4]				
total	45	6–2,252	—	—
with chloracne	12	6–2,252	—	
Seveso children[5]				
highest level	1	56,000		few days
with chloracne	10	830–56,000	19,144	
without chloracne	9	1,770–10,400	5,240	

1. U. S. Air Force personnel who sprayed Agent Orange in Vietnam. Epidemiology Research Division 1991.
2. Fingerhut et al. 1991.
3. Mean concentration of dioxin and years since exposure based on concentrations reported for subsample of 253 workers in Fingerhut et al. 1991.
4. Beck et al. 1988.
5. L. L. Needham 1989.

seem to be less vulnerable to the acute toxic effects of dioxin than are the most sensitive animals.

As will be shown, studies of the highly exposed workers do not support the conclusion that dioxin has been a major cause of cancer in humans. In fact, those studies cast doubt on whether dioxin has caused human cancer at all.

Laboratory Toxicity

Dioxin became headline news in the United States in 1969 when the National Cancer Institute revealed that 2,4,5-T was the most potent man-made cause of birth defects (teratogen) ever tested in mice. Upon later study, scientists discovered that trace amounts of dioxin in the herbicide had caused the problems (Gough 1986, chapter 14).

Within a decade, other tests showed dioxin to be the most potent carcinogen ever tested in laboratory animals (Kociba et al. 1978; Kociba 1984). Furthermore, it affected almost every organ system in one experimental animal or another (Neal 1984; Poland and Kimbrough 1984).

Human Health Effects

There can be no question that dioxin has caused serious toxic effects in laboratory animals. The picture is much less clear for human health effects, but that is not for lack of studies. On the contrary, the volume of information about epidemiologic studies related to dioxin precludes making reference to every paper. In particular, the reader will notice that I do not discuss the possible effects of dioxin or Agent Orange on veterans of ground warfare in Vietnam. The reason is simple. There is no evidence (even) to suggest that many of those men were exposed to any significant amount of dioxin (Gough 1986; CDC 1988; Kang et al. 1991; Gough 1991b).

I will focus on research directly relating to dioxin, and consider studies on other chemicals only to the extent that they shed light on dioxin. I also will center my analysis on the specific tumors most frequently associated with dioxin: soft-tissue sarcomas. In addition, I will discuss two other types of tumors—non-Hodgkin's lymphomas and stomach cancers—that have been invoked in claims that dioxin has caused human cancers as well as overall increases in cancer rates. Finally, I will mention various studies that have raised concerns about other possible health effects. My conclusion is that there are no convincing data that dioxin has caused any long-term health effect in humans.

Soft-Tissue Sarcomas

About a decade ago, Swedish investigators published two papers that reported associations between exposures to phenoxy herbicides and soft-tissue sarcomas (Hardell and Sandstrom 1979; Eriksson et al. 1981). Hardell (1981) subsequently reviewed and expanded on the two papers.

These studies were case-control studies: the cases were men (living or dead) who had developed soft-tissue sarcomas; the controls were men of the same age who had lived or died in the same areas as the cases at similar times. Using information obtained from questionnaires mailed to the cases and controls (or next of kin in the case of the men who had died), which was sometimes supplemented by telephone interviews, the investigators classified men as "exposed" to phenoxy herbicides if they had reported at least one day's exposure at least five years before their cancer was diagnosed, or before their selection as a healthy control. (Case-control studies are frequently used in the study of cancer. Cancers such as soft-tissue sarcomas are rare and the case-control method is efficient in locating sufficient numbers of cases to study. Often—and this is clearly the case with some studies of dioxin and soft-tissue sarcomas—information about exposure is scanty and has to be obtained from the memories of the cases, the controls, and the next of kin.)

The Swedish investigators reported a sixfold to sevenfold increase in risk of soft-tissue sarcoma associated with exposure to dioxin-containing herbicides, such as 2,4,5-T (Figure 11.1). One of the studies also reported a fourfold increase in risk for the disease from use of phenoxy herbicides that do not contain dioxin, such as 2,4-D.

As the 1980s wore on, the Swedish investigators published additional studies, each of which chipped away at the high risks they had reported in their early papers. In 1988, after a number of other scientists' studies had not confirmed their findings, Hardell and Eriksson (1988) published a study of 55 patients with soft-tissue sarcomas in northern Sweden. This study confirmed the positive findings concerning phenoxy herbicides, but the associated risks were lower than earlier reported. When compared with the general population, as was done in the earlier studies, exposure to phenoxy herbicides was associated with an increased risk of about 3; when compared with other cancer patients, the increased risk was about 2. (People who have cancer may be more thorough in searching their memories about chemical exposures, and using cancer patients as comparisons is designed to reduce such "recall bias.")

Two years later, a 1990 paper from the Swedish investigators (Eriksson et al. 1990) reported only a nonstatistically significant association between dioxin exposure and soft-tissue sarcomas: "In this study,

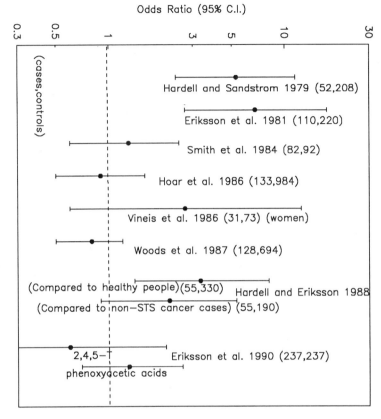

Figure 11.1
Case-control studies on soft tissue sarcoma associated with TCDD exposure.
The numbers in parentheses indicate the numbers of cases and controls in the studies.

exposure to 2,3,7,8-TCDD gave a nonsignificantly increased risk." Although the discrepancy between the earlier studies and the 1990 report might be explained by different levels of exposure, the same criteria for exposure were used in all studies. It is likely that the criticism by other scientists around the world (see, *e.g.,* Young and Reggiani 1988) of the techniques used in the earlier studies to decide on whether to classify a person as exposed or unexposed led to corrections in methods used for exposure classification in this latest study. Evidently, those corrections eliminated the apparent association.

It is interesting to note that the Swedish scientists also reported a threefold or sixfold increase in risk for soft-tissue sarcomas with exposure to chlorophenols in their early papers. In stark contrast, Hardell and

Eriksson (1988) found no association between exposures to chlorophenols and soft-tissue sarcomas. Then the association returned in Eriksson et al. (1990). Since these scientists used the same methods to study dioxin and chlorophenol exposures, the disappearance of both associations and reappearance of the chlorophenol association reinforces the suspicion that study results (for both chemicals) were influenced by some aspect of study design or execution.

The early, positive findings triggered many other studies of agricultural and forestry workers around the world. None confirmed the risks reported by the Swedish scientists. Five case-control studies, two from New Zealand (Smith et al. 1984; Smith and Pearce 1986), two from the United States (Hoar et al. 1986; Woods et al. 1987), and one from Italy (Vineis et al. 1986) reported no statistically significant association between exposures to phenoxy herbicides and soft-tissue sarcomas. Exposure criteria identical to those used by the Swedish scientists were used in the two New Zealand studies, and the exposures examined in the two U.S. studies were of longer duration than those in the Swedish studies. If there was an association between exposures to dioxin-containing phenoxy herbicides, it should have been seen in the other studies. It was not.

One could search through the studies that contradict the early Swedish results and find evidence that can be advanced to support an association between cancer and dioxin exposure. Italian scientists (Vineis et al. 1986) examined the health of women who had been employed as weeders in rice fields in Italy during the early 1950s, when phenoxy herbicides were widely used. They reported a nonstatistically significant increase in soft-tissue sarcomas (see Figure 1). However, when they focused on women who had been exposed between 1950 and 1955, who were still living at the time of the study, and who were less than 75 years old, the investigators reported an odds ratio of 15.5, indicating a large (nearly sixteenfold) and statistically significant increase in risk. But that group consisted of only four women, three of whom had developed soft-tissue sarcoma. Even the study's authors dismissed such a finding as having no importance.

Cohort studies involve the examination of the health status of groups of people (cohorts) who share common experiences or common exposures. Because cancers such as soft-tissue sarcomas are rare, cohort studies that involve such diseases must consider many people to detect an increased risk if it is present. Scientists have examined records from two large cohorts of agricultural workers and compared those with other workers, who presumably were unexposed or less-exposed to herbicides.

In the first of these studies, Riihimaki et al. (1982) examined death records of 1,926 Finnish workers who had sprayed 2,4-D or 2,4,5-T between 1955 and 1971. Among these workers there were no deaths from soft-tissue sarcoma. The investigators cautioned, however, that the workers' exposure was slight and the study had been undertaken too recently (between 1972 and 1980) for many dioxin-related cancers to have developed even if there was some effect. Yet the Swedish studies had very similar problems, and they had found an association. In the second study, Wiklund and Holm (1986) compared the cancer rates of more than 300,000 Swedish farmers and forestry workers with those of almost 2 million workers in other industries. The investigators found a slightly lower incidence of soft-tissue sarcoma among the farmers than among controls.

Despite the failure of other scientists to confirm the early Swedish results, and despite the fact that the latest Swedish results do not corroborate them, many people concluded from those studies that dioxin has caused human cancer. Two other results render that conclusion untenable. The only direct evidence we have about exposure of the men whom the Swedish scientists classified as "exposed" is inconsistent with those men ever having been exposed at all. The Swedish scientists had fat samples taken from some cancer patients who had been classified as exposed to dioxin and from others who had no record of dioxin exposure. There was no difference in the levels of dioxin; average levels of 2 ppt were detected in the "exposed" population and 3 ppt in the "unexposed" population (Nygren et al. 1986). This finding calls into question the entire classification scheme used in the Swedish studies. Not only was there no higher level in the "exposed" population, but the levels found in both groups of men were very low.

The other evidence arguing against the association between dioxin exposure and soft-tissue sarcomas reported by the early Swedish studies (or for any other cancer, for that matter) comes from an examination of the concentrations of dioxin in New Zealand herbicide sprayers (Smith et al. 1992). The scientists who examined the New Zealand sprayers selected 9 men who had sprayed 2,4,5-T for a range of 83 to 372 months, obtained blood samples from them, extracted lipid from the blood samples, and measured dioxin in the lipid. They found that dioxin concentrations increased roughly with months of spraying; concentrations ranged from 3 ppt to 131 ppt in the sprayers, with a mean of 53. None of the nine men had health problems, and earlier studies of New Zealand sprayers (Smith and Pearce 1986; Smith et al. 1984) had revealed no increased cancer risk. The mean of 53 ppt in a subset of a population that had no increased cancer rate can be compared with the 2 ppt measured in Swedish cancer patients who had been classified as "exposed." From that comparison, it seems clear that the Swedish workers were not occupationally exposed to sufficient dioxin to have any effect on the concentrations of it in their bodies.

The scientists who studied the New Zealanders estimated that one year's spraying, on average, resulted in a 3 ppt increase in dioxin in the men's bodies. They argued that the exposures reported in the early Swedish studies, which ranged from a day or more to, in a very few cases, more than a year, could not have resulted in substantial exposures:

Our finding that serum levels of TCDD increase only after several years of 2,4,5-T use suggests that exposure to TCDD was probably negligible in the Swedish studies . . . (Smith et al. 1992 p. 108)

As for the probable contribution of those exposures to cancer risk, they say:

. . . we can conclude that previous reports in other countries of increased cancer risks from brief exposures to phenoxyherbicides are probably not attributable to the TCDD that contaminates 2,3,5-T. (Smith et al. 1992 p. 108)

Inspection of the data in Table 11.1 shows that the factory workers who manufactured dioxin-containing chemicals have far higher concentrations of dioxin than do the Swedish "exposed" patients or the New Zealand sprayers. If there is any truth to the association between dioxin exposure and soft-tissue sarcomas, surely it would be evident from study of the German and American chemical plant workers.

Manz et al. (1991) reported no soft-tissue sarcomas in a study of 1,583 German chemical plant workers. Bond et al. (1989) compared death rates among Dow workers who had chloracne, a skin disease that is taken to indicate high exposure to dioxin, with the rates expected in the general population. There were two deaths from connective and other soft-tissue tumors—which can, for this discussion, be equated with soft-tissue sarcomas—among men who had had chloracne. Although those two deaths are a statistically significant excess, one of those tumors had been misclassified on the death certificate, and if it is removed from consideration, the excess is not statistically significant.

The most complete examination of a dioxin/soft-tissue sarcoma link is presented in a long-awaited study of U.S. chemical plant workers (Fingerhut et al. 1991). This study (sponsored by the National Institute for Occupational Safety and Health [NIOSH], and hence called the NIOSH study) examined the causes of death among 5,172 men who had worked in 12 U.S. plants that manufactured 2,4,5-TCP. As can be seen on Table

11.1, about half of the workers were exposed to dioxin-contaminated work spaces and dioxin-containing chemicals for more than a year; in fact, the median exposure of that group was about seven years. If the early Swedish results that associated exposures of only a few days or weeks with an increased risk of soft-tissue sarcomas were correct, a great number of deaths from that type of tumor might be expected in the NIOSH population. The NIOSH investigators reported that soft-tissue sarcomas were listed as the cause of death on four death certificates. Those four deaths were not statistically significantly different from the number of such deaths expected in the entire cohort of workers in the NIOSH study, but three of them occurred in the subpart of the cohort that had been classified as exposed to dioxin for at least a year and whose exposure had begun at least 20 years before data were collected for the study. Those three deaths were statistically significantly higher than the 0.3 deaths expected in that group.

In passing, it is of interest that two of the four tumors listed as soft-tissue sarcomas were not confirmed as such when expert pathologists examined them. To compare the number of these tumors with the number of "expected tumors" based on national data, one must assume that the classification errors occur with the same frequency for the chemical plant workers as for members of the general U.S. population. These four tumors occurred about a decade ago; they were extensively discussed at a 1984 meeting (Fingerhut et al. 1984). One other death from soft-tissue sarcoma was mentioned in Fingerhut (1991), but it did not meet the criteria for inclusion in the NIOSH study and was not considered in the reported analysis.

In addition to the two (or four, depending on how one counts) soft-tissue sarcomas listed on death certificates, the NIOSH investigators were aware of two other deaths attributed to those tumors by hospital records. (The classification of one of those two tumors as a soft-tissue sarcoma was confirmed by expert pathologists; the other's exact nature was not so verified.) And one more soft-tissue sarcoma was reported in a group of exposed workers who were excluded from the NIOSH study. The total of reported soft-tissue sarcoma deaths in the exposed U.S. workers is then 7; all but two (one a confirmed soft-tissue sarcoma; the other a misdiagnosed soft-tissue sarcoma) occurred in one of the 12 chemical plants in the study. That distribution, as well as the fact that the chemical plants manufactured many other chemicals in addition to 2,4, 5-T, suggests the possibility that some substance that did not contain dioxin and that was made in one plant, actually caused the bulk of the soft-tissue sarcomas. Indeed, the NIOSH scientists acknowledged that possibility: "Excess mortality from . . . soft–tissue sarcoma may result from exposure to TCDD, although we cannot exclude the possible contribution of factors such as smoking and occupational exposure to other chemicals" (Fingerhut, et al. 1991, p. 212).

Scientists at the Monsanto Company, which operates the plant where five of the seven soft–tissue sarcomas occurred, have concluded that another chemical, not dioxin, is associated with those tumors (Collins 1993). The chemical is para–aminobiphenyl, which has been known for years as a potent bladder carcinogen. That finding will fuel, not settle, the controversy about whether dioxin is associated with soft–tissue sarcomas, but it cannot fail to cast doubt on the dioxin/soft–tissue sarcoma link.

The initial reports from Sweden that dioxin was associated with soft–tissue sarcomas are supported only by some, but not all, of the studies done by the same Swedish scientists and, more recently, from the NIOSH study. Examination of the data shows that the Swedish method of classifying men as exposed to dioxin was faulty; "exposed" cancer patients did not have elevated levels of dioxin, and even if the classification scheme were correct, the men classified as exposed for a few days or weeks would not have had much exposure. It is unlikely that any more evidence can be brought to bear on the early Swedish results. The NIOSH findings, on the other hand, lend themselves to further analysis. Continued follow–up of that NIOSH population will reveal if any more soft–tissue sarcoma deaths occur, and if they occur more frequently in workers in plants contaminated with para–aminobiphenyl.

Even if no more support is produced for the dioxin/soft–tissue sarcoma link, it will be years before the reputed association drops from debate. The impossibility of proving the negative—in this case, that dioxin is not associated with soft–tissue sarcomas—means that an argument for the link can be kept alive with little or no additional support. The Swedish studies have been widely cited and will probably be cited for a long time to come. People who cite these studies in arguing for a link between dioxin and soft–tissue sarcomas will have to ignore the evidence that doesn't support the link, but that can be done.

Non-Hodgkin's Lymphoma and Stomach Cancer

The links between dioxin and non–Hodgkin's lymphoma, which also were originally reported by the Swedish scientists, have proved equally elusive. Hardell et al. (1981) reported a fivefold increase in risk of malignant lymphomas, including both Hodgkin's disease and non–Hodgkin's lymphoma, in herbicide–exposed workers.

In what appears to be a partial confirmation of this finding, National Cancer Institute (NCI) scientists found a twofold excess of non-Hodgkin's lymphoma in Kansas farmers exposed to herbicides. (This same study found no increase in soft-tissue sarcomas [see Figure 11.1] or in Hodgkin's disease [Hoar et al. 1986].) However, the NCI study stands in contrast with other, negative, studies. An earlier NCI study of farmers in Minnesota and Iowa had found no association between herbicide exposure and non-Hodgkin's lymphoma (Cantor and Blair 1986). Neither did studies of agricultural workers in New Zealand (Pearce et al. 1985, 1987), nor a study in western Washington, except in one group of men who had been potentially exposed for 15 years in the period 15 years before their cancers had been diagnosed (Woods et al. 1987). Wiklund and colleagues (1987, 1988) conducted cohort studies of non-Hodgkin's lymphoma among Swedish pesticide applicators and found no statistically significant increase in this disease.

Since the Hoar et al. (1986) study, which focused on the herbicide 2,4,-D, non-Hodgkin's lymphoma has become more closely associated with that chemical, which does not contain dioxin, than with 2,4,5-T, which does. With additional studies, that association may wax or wane, but currently it is supported by the original Swedish studies and by Hoar et al. (1986). Other results do not support it.

Thiess et al. (1982) reported three stomach cancers among workers exposed to dioxin in a German chemical plant, but neither of the large studies of American and German chemical plant workers discussed in the next section revealed any excess stomach cancers.

Except for the early Swedish studies, no evidence links dioxin to non-Hodgkin's lymphoma, although it remains an issue in discussion of the nondioxin-containing herbicide 2,4-D. There is no excess of that tumor or of stomach cancers in the two large studies of the German and American chemical plant workers (Manz et al. 1991; Fingerhut et al. 1991). Unless some new evidence develops for relationships between dioxin and these tumors, those associations will probably slip away.

Total Cancers

There is no prior reason to focus on any particular tumor in analyzing a possible connection between dioxin and human cancer, and a number of scientists have examined overall cancer rates. The problems in deciding whether a person was exposed are less in studies of chemical plant workers or the residents of Seveso than they are in studies of herbicide sprayers and other agricultural and forestry workers, but they remain nevertheless. A possible solution is to draw blood samples from each person in a study and determine the dioxin concentration. That is expensive, since analysis of each sample costs about $1,000, and the capacity of laboratories to analyze dioxin samples is limited; it would be years before samples from the thousands of occupationally exposed workers could be analyzed. Even if that were done, information about those who had already died, and who are the source of all the mortality data in the large U.S. and German studies, would be missing. Nevertheless, those two studies do have some information about exposure based on chemical analysis, and they will be discussed after a study that examined cancer mortality among Seveso residents and a study of workers in a chemical plant that lacks such information.

According to the Centers for Disease Control (CDC), 193 residents of Seveso developed chloracne, a skin disease associated with high exposures to dioxin (or other chlorinated hydrocarbons), after the accident. Bertazzi et al. (1989) reported that ten years after the chemical plant explosion, deaths from certain cancers were more frequent in the exposed Seveso population than in an unexposed, comparison population. But these results are difficult to interpret for several reasons (Centers for Disease Control 1989). None of the deaths in the exposed population had occurred among the 193 people who had developed chloracne, presumably those who had the highest exposure to dioxin. In fact, the overall mortality and overall cancer mortality were *lower* in the exposed population than in the comparison population. Given the long period required for chemically induced cancers to develop, there is little reason to expect the study to have observed any dioxin–related cancers in the ten-year period it addressed. A tumor registry has been established at Seveso, and more information from this population will become available in the years to come.

Scientists at the Dow Chemical Company compared the death rate of 2,192 Dow Chemical workers potentially exposed to dioxin with that of white American males (Ott et al. 1987). About half of the workers in question had been exposed in 1962 or earlier, more than 20 years before 1982, which was the cutoff date for collection of mortality data. That length of time is considered sufficient for the manifestation of cancers. Deaths from all causes in the workers was about 93 percent of the expected rate. Deaths from cancers were 102 percent of the expected rate, with 95 percent confidence limits of 81 to 127, which means there is no statistically significant difference in cancer death rate between the Dow workers and white men in general. Of particular interest in relation to dioxin, there was no excess of soft-tissue sarcomas, stomach cancer, or non-Hodgkin's lymphomas, all of which had been associated with dioxin exposure in other studies. The Dow study, however, did report a statistically significant excess of deaths from "other and unspecified malignant neoplasms." (Nine such deaths were observed, versus 3.7 expected in this population.) The increase was not associated with any particular work area or with higher potential exposures to dioxin.

Two years later, the Dow scientists (Bond et al. 1989) published a follow-up of the mortality study, which added mortality data for the years 1983 and 1984. The investigators reported no statistically significant increase in total cancers in the total worker population. When the investigators compared death rates among Dow workers who had chloracne and the rates expected in the general population, they found that the death rate from all causes was 79 percent of the expected rate, and the death rate from all cancers was 66 percent of the expected rate.

The Dow study used chloracne as a surrogate measure for high exposure in an attempt to reduce errors in exposure classification. That method has been replaced by direct measurements of dioxin concentrations in workers, subject to the constraints mentioned above.

Manz et al. (1991) examined the mortality experience of German workers who had been employed in a plant for which there was information about dioxin concentrations in some workers. They compared death rates of the dioxin-exposed workers with the rates in the West German population and the rates in workers employed by a gas supply company in West Germany. The second comparison is of a type commonly made in occupational studies in an effort to correct for the "healthy worker effect." [Workers, as a group, enjoy better health than the general population, which includes people too ill to work, so comparing workers with workers provides a comparison different from the general population.] The death rate of the dioxin-exposed workers was identical to that of the West German population but 1.34 times higher than that of the gas company workers. Similar results were obtained in comparisons of death rates from cancer: the dioxin-exposed workers had about the same death rates as the West German population but higher rates than the gas supply workers. When the investigators divided the exposed population into three groups based on estimated levels of exposure, the group with the highest exposure had a greater excess of cancer. Furthermore, exposed men who began work before 1954, when dioxin contamination was judged to have been higher, were at higher risk for cancer. These data lead to the conclusion that the cancer rate for the German chemical plant workers is higher than for the gas company workers and comparable with the West German population. Furthermore, the risk appears to go up with increasing exposures. The only specific cancers that were statistically significantly elevated in the chemical plant workers were lung cancer and cancers of the blood-forming systems, and those elevations were found only in comparison with the gas company workers. Manz et al. (1991) reported that the smoking rates among the dioxin-exposed workers and the gas company workers were comparable, but that comparison was based on a nonrepresentative sample.

This study can be criticized, as can all epidemiological studies, on several bases. A variety of methods were used to decide whether a person had been employed at the chemical plant; evidently neither company records nor union records were complete, because information from friends and families was used to supplement them. This introduces the possibility of recall bias, since people might more frequently remember a worker who got sick or died than one who moved, uneventfully, to another job. The source of information about death rates was not always death certificates, which introduces complications in interpretation, as was seen for the soft-tissue sarcomas in the NIOSH study. Workers who were employed for as little as three months at the chemical plant were included in the study, but all the gas workers included in the study had worked there for at least ten years. This complicates the study, because populations who work for short periods of time include people with poorer health than populations who work at the same job for long periods of time.

At the very least, the study of German chemical plant workers supports the contention that dioxin exposure increases overall cancer risk. In the months and years to come, that study will be examined and reexamined, and there may be additional follow-up of the population. The certainty to be attached to the study will go either up or down in that process. In any case, the study of Manz et al. does not appear to be as rigorous in design or execution as that of American chemical plant workers that I consider next.

NIOSH scientists who studied American chemical workers exposed to dioxin (Fingerhut et al. 1991) collected all their mortality information from death certificates, which could be supplemented from other sources, as in the case of soft-tissue sarcomas. The overall mortality in these workers was about the same as for U.S. men in general. However, there were statistically significant increases in all cancers, both in the whole group and in a "high-exposure" group of workers who had been exposed for more than a year at least 20 years before the study was done.

Subjects in this latter group presumably had enough time for any dioxin-related cancers to develop.

Some of the increase in cancers consisted of an excess of lung cancer among the workers. However, after the investigators corrected the data to account for smoking habits, the incidence of lung cancers in the workers was not significantly different from that of the controls. The excess in overall cancers persisted.

Despite the attempt to correct for smoking, exposures to other chemicals and to smoking may have influenced the results of the NIOSH study. For instance, smoking histories were obtained for men in two plants in the 1980s. The men who had already died and who were counted in the mortality data may have smoked much more, with the result that the effect of smoking may be underestimated. In addition, some workers had died from cancers known to be caused by other environmental exposures, such as mesothelioma (asbestos) and bladder cancer (para-aminobiphenyl). Those deaths are counted in the total even though they cannot reasonably be associated with dioxin exposure.

Thus, both Manz et al. (1991) and Fingerhut et al. (1991) reported higher than expected cancer mortality among dioxin-exposed workers. In both studies, lung cancer contributed to the excess, and neither study carefully examined the possible contribution of smoking to that excess, nor quantitatively estimated the possible contribution of other occupational exposures.

The clearest result is the failure of both studies to verify the very high risks reported by the Swedish investigators. In both studies, excess cancers were largely restricted to workers who had been highly exposed for long periods of time. That result weakens the claim that short-term, low-level exposures are associated with cancer.

Other Diseases
Essentially all the studies discussed above were mortality studies. To learn about the incidence of diseases, and about nonfatal diseases, it is necessary to study morbidity. The most thorough morbidity study is the United States Air Force study of the Ranch Hands (Epidemiology Research Division 1991a). Air Force physicians and scientists, and physicians and scientists under contract to the Air Force, make week-long physical and psychological examinations of the Ranch Hands and a comparison group at three- to five-year intervals. The study began in the early 1980s and is slated to end in 2003. The results from the 1988 examination, which were published in 1991, span over a foot of bookcase,

and indicate that the health of the Ranch Hands and the comparison group is comparable.

The report does highlight an association between higher dioxin levels and the frequency of diabetes and other lipid-related abnormalities in the Ranch Hands. I believe that the association is not causal. First, there is no statistical difference between the rates of diabetes in the Ranch Hands and the comparison group; and if dioxin did influence the frequency of diabetes, such differences would be expected because of the higher dioxin levels in Ranch Hands. Second, some of the comparison group have levels of dioxin as high as 55 ppt (see Table 11.1), and the frequency of diabetes increases at higher levels of dioxin in that group. If dioxin were the cause of diabetes, the disease should be much more frequent in the Ranch Hands where dioxin concentrations were higher than 55 ppt, but it is not (Gough 1991d). Finally, the U.S. chemical plant workers who have dioxin levels as high as 4,000 ppt more than 20 years after cessation of their exposure have no excess of deaths from heart disease or statistically significant deficits of deaths from circulatory system and digestive system diseases. An association of dioxin with lipid-related abnormalities would be expected to produce an increase in such deaths, not a decrease. I think that the apparent association between lipid abnormalities and diabetes and dioxin in the Ranch Hand study is explained by dioxin being a surrogate measure for some other factor that is associated with the diseases. I do not know what the factor is.

As the early, frightening reports of cancer rates among people classified as exposed to dioxin receive little or no support from later, more careful studies, it is possible that some people will claim other health effects from dioxin exposure. The Ranch Hand studies involve men with known levels of dioxin in their bodies—from which their exposure can be estimated—who received thorough health examinations. Those studies can be the source of much information to address other health concerns about dioxin exposure.

Comments on the Science

The evidence about human health effects of dioxin can be measured against Hill's criteria that are discussed in chapter 1. Clearly, the association of dioxin with chloracne meets most of those criteria. From the studies of chemical workers, dioxin may possibly increase the overall cancer rate in highly exposed people. But that conclusion must be tempered by the fact that part of the increase reported by the American and

German studies was from an unexpectedly high lung cancer mortality, yet neither study controlled carefully for smoking. The 12 plants considered by the U.S. study are located in different areas of the country, and a comparison of cancer rates in the individual plants against regional cancer rates rather than the nationwide average would provide additional information.

Furthermore, the workers in these studies were exposed to many occupational hazards in addition to dioxin. While it is tempting to ascribe any unexpected findings to dioxin, the data do not support that inference. To illustrate, consider that the NIOSH investigators reported *lower* mortality of dioxin-exposed workers for diseases of the circulatory and digestive systems, and alcoholism, and lower incidence of personality disorders. Surely no one would, without careful consideration, ascribe those beneficial effects to dioxin.

The American and German studies both reported increases in overall cancer and lung cancer, but the increase in soft-tissue sarcomas reported by the former study was not confirmed by the latter. Not one such tumor was reported in the German workers. Even in the American study, those tumors present analytical problems; they are difficult to diagnose, and no effort was made to assemble a comparison group of men and comb their records for evidence of soft-tissue sarcomas with the same diligence used in the study of the chemical plant workers.

Monsanto scientists interpret the data from their plants, where most of the soft-tissue sarcomas occurred, as showing that another chemical, para-aminobiphenyl, caused those tumors. That conclusion leads to a specific, testable theory. Because para-aminobiphenyl was identified as a potent cause of bladder cancer, it was not manufactured after 1955. The production of dioxin-containing trichlorophenol continued until 1969. If that chemical caused the soft-tissue sarcomas, those tumors should not be in excess in men who went to work in Monsanto plants after 1955. So far, that correlation holds up.

Whether or not further analysis support their general conclusions, the studies of U.S. and German chemical workers refute the Swedish reports of high risks from a few days exposure to dioxin. The studies that obtained information about dioxin exposure reported that cancers are increased only in highly exposed people, and even then it is questionable whether dioxin exposure is to be associated with increased cancer.

The early Swedish studies are the cornerstone of the contentions that environmental exposures to dioxin have caused cancer. As such, they have been reviewed by individual scientists and by government organizations. Two of the most critical reviews are those of Brian MacMahon (1988), for many years the chairman of the Department of Epidemiology at the Harvard School of Public Health, and of the Australia Vietnam Veterans Royal Commission. MacMahon flatly concluded that the findings of the Swedish investigators "were in error," and that "there is no reasonable basis" to conclude that Agent Orange caused "increased risk of STS [soft-tissue sarcomas] or NHL [nonHodgkin's lymphoma]." The Australian Commission concluded (quoted in O'Keefe 1988, p. 134):

[The] absence of replication, the absence of specific outcome . . . [the] admitted information bias, the presence of significant confounding factors, the unreliability of the exposure data and [other factors] . . . all indicate that the statistical associations asserted by Dr. Hardell are suspect. The Commission cannot, on the balance of probability, accept them as supporting an inference of causal connection between soft-tissue sarcoma, malignant lymphoma and exposure to phenoxy herbicides . . .

Various groups of scientists and physicians, including the American Medical Association (Council on Scientific Affairs 1984) and a committee of the British government (Department of the Environment 1989), have commented on dioxin and health effects. All have concluded that dioxin exposure has not caused elevated levels of cancer. The British committee also found no convincing evidence that exposures to dioxin have caused increased birth defects in human populations.

The authoritative International Agency for Research on Cancer (IARC) classifies evidence of carcinogenicity as "sufficient," "limited," or "inadequate." Its 1986 review of dioxin found "sufficient" evidence that dioxin causes cancer in laboratory animals. But it considered the evidence of *human* carcinogenicity "inadequate" (IARC 1987).

The U.S. Environmental Protection Agency classifies chemicals into one of five groups, depending upon the strength of evidence for human carcinogenicity (EPA 1986). It currently classifies dioxin as a "probable human carcinogen" based on very strong animal data; the ranking implicitly concedes that the evidence of human carcinogenicity is inadequate.

To date, dioxin's great toxicity in animals has not been translated into readily identifiable human effects. How can that be? There are at least three answers to that question:

1. We simply have not looked hard enough for human effects.
2. Humans are not as sensitive to dioxin as the test animals.
3. Humans have not been exposed to doses of dioxin comparable with those that caused toxicity in animals.

In my opinion, responses to these answers are as follows:

1. The epidemiology has been thorough and careful, and I do not think that additional studies will reveal new findings that will lead us to the conclusion that we've missed something.
2. It is very difficult to compare human and rodent sensitivities to dioxin, and differing sensitivities might explain part of the differences.
3. It is likely that humans have not been exposed to levels of dioxin comparable with those that have caused adverse effects in animals. Cancer, birth defects, and toxic effects on fetuses are seen in animals only at doses near or equal to those that cause overt toxic effects in adult animals. Some chemical workers have suffered a skin disease and a smaller number have suffered liver and neurological damage following dioxin exposure; cancer rates are barely elevated, if at all, in those populations. If there is a close relationship between dose levels that cause overt effects and cancer, it is no surprise that elevated cancer rates are not found in other, less-exposed populations.

Policy and Decisions

Dioxin remains, perhaps, paramount in the pantheon of chemicals that arouse public fear. There are several reasons for that. The simplest is that dioxin is clearly toxic to animals. But that can be said for many other chemicals that have aroused much less public concern. Politics and publicity have been far more important than science in creating dioxin's image.

The public's conviction that dioxin causes cancer in humans is nurtured by U.S. government policies directed at carcinogens. Several other countries estimate risks for carcinogens that do not cause mutations, such as dioxin, using models that assume that some critical dose must be exceeded before any cancer risk exists (Gough 1988). These nations and an expert committee of the World Health Organization (World Health Organization 1991) have established acceptable daily intake (ADI) levels at which dioxin exposure is considered acceptable (see Table 11.2).

American regulators, by contrast, use a model that extrapolates cancer risk from high levels of exposure to low levels, with no threshold. Because different federal agencies use slightly different risk assessment models, different government agencies predict different risks. The 1987 EPA risk number was a proposed revision (see Gough 1988) that was not adopted by the agency. Since no convincing data exist for cancer risk to humans, regulators base their extrapolations on animal data. Assuming that the maximum acceptable increase in cancer risk is 1 in 1 million (which is the de facto "acceptable" level for many risks considered by U.S. regulators), this leads to maximum acceptable exposure levels that

Table 11.2

Acceptable daily intake (ADI) levels and virtually safe doses (VSDs) for 2,3,7,8-tetrachlorodibenzo-p-dioxin (TCDD)

	NOAEL[1]	Safety factor	ADI or VSD[2,3]
ADIs			
Government			
Ontario	1,000	100	10
Netherlands	1,000	250	4
Denmark	1,000	200	5
Germany	1,000	100–1,000	1–10
Great Britain	1,000	100	10
WHO	1,000	100	10
VSDs			
EPA (1985)	—		0.006
CDC	—		0.028–1.200
FDA	—		0.057
EPA (1987)	—		0.100

1. NOAEL: "No observed adverse effect level" in laboratory animals in pg/kg/day.
2. The experimental basis for all calculations of ADI or VSD is Kociba et al. 1978.
3. ADI and VSD are in pg/kg/day.
Sources: All data from Gough 1988, except WHO, which is from WHO 1990, and Great Britain, which is from Department of the Environment 1989.

are as small as 1/1670 of those accepted in other countries, for instance, the ADI of 10 pg/kg/day in Great Britain compared with EPA's 0.006 pg/kg/day "virtually safe dose" that is equated with a risk of 1 in 1 million.

Moreover, the methods used by EPA lead to predictions of 83 to 333 excess cancers per million people with background levels of dioxin at 5 ppt to 20 ppt (which is typical of people with no history of dioxin exposure).[6] By this estimate, even background levels of dioxin—to which everyone in modern society is exposed—pose a cancer risk that exceeds the maximum cancer risk accepted by U.S. regulators. These estimates (which are greatly inflated, in my view) would justify drastic efforts at remediation if the possibility arose of even slight increases in dioxin exposures.

But current U.S. regulatory policy on dioxin specifically, and on carcinogens generally, is a product of history. In the mid-1970s, scientists believed that most carcinogens were also mutagens. According to this view, a single molecule might cause a mutation, and a single mutation (scientists postulated) might cause a cancer. As more chemicals were tested, however, the original postulate was found to be mistaken; there is no close correlation between mutagenicity and carcinogenicity. Only about half of the chemicals known to cause cancer in animals also cause mutations (Tennant et al. 1987).

Efforts to change U.S. regulatory policies on dioxin so far have met no success, but improved understanding of the biochemistry of dioxin has led the administrator of EPA to order his staff to reevaluate the method by which the risks of dioxin are estimated (Reilly 1991). The outcome of that effort, which is to be completed sometime in 1993, cannot be predicted (an effort to change EPA's estimate of the carcinogenicity of dioxin in 1987–1988 failed), but there is now far more biological information on which to base a new model. On the other hand, the idea that dioxin is very hazardous to humans is so ingrained in many people's minds that it may be impossible to revise the risk estimate downward.

Other government actions have maintained public concern about dioxin. In 1983, the federal government and the state of Missouri purchased the entire town of Times Beach, Missouri, because of dioxin contamination of the soil. No other substances, chemical or biological, has ever triggered such drastic action.

Litigation also maintains public concern about dioxin. The Agent Orange trial and settlement is the most famous. At its end, Judge Jack Weinstein declared that the evidence would be insufficient to convince any jury that Agent Orange had caused harm; and the settlement agreement stated that no causal connection had been demonstrated. But a settlement of $180 million will convince many people that "there must have been something there."

The psychological legacy of Vietnam has perhaps contributed most to our attitudes toward dioxin. Although the passage of time has dissipated some of the pain associated with the war, memories of Agent Orange remain a vestige of the nation's torment. Did the herbicide cause cancer and other diseases in some of the men and women who served there—or in the Vietnamese population that was so badly injured by the war? Animal tests and the current U.S. regulatory policies suggest that it may have. But studies of humans who have been far more heavily exposed to dioxin strongly indicate otherwise.

Many legislators and citizens are perhaps ashamed of our treatment of Vietnam veterans immediately after the war. That shame contributes, I think, to the idea that veterans should be compensated for some diseases, whether or not there is evidence that Agent Orange or dioxin caused any harm—or even in the absence of evidence of exposure (CDC 1988; Kang et al. 1991; Gough 1991d). Ironically, serious study of the mental and emotional anguish caused by war of any kind has been replaced by a vain search for a chemical culprit.

Risk assessment predicts the probability of adverse effects. But there are many uncertainties involved, and the process requires many questionable assumptions. There is no guarantee that predicted effects will actually occur or will occur in predicted numbers. Epidemiology can provide direct evidence for harm but will miss risks that fall below some statistical threshold of detectability (Gough 1987). Much of the controversy about possible health effects of dioxin concerns increases in risks for rare diseases that are at the very limit of the ability of epidemiology to detect reliably. Such debates are not likely to be resolved easily.

No experiment or study can prove the negative, the complete absence of risk. Moreover, the grounds of the debate can shift rapidly. If the link between soft-tissue sarcoma and dioxin is disproved, questions can be raised about dioxin and another cancer or another health effect, say, on the immune system. As each postulated connection dissolves, new ones can be proposed. Completing investigations of the postulated links takes far more time than demanding them. In the meantime, media attention and lawsuits can continue unabated.

The political stakes in the dioxin controversy remain very high. What if no harm had resulted to humans from "the most potent carcinogen" yet tested in animals? Would such a finding collapse a regulatory complex built around the extrapolation of risk from animal tests? Such a finding would be unwelcome to some environmental advocacy organizations, some regulators, some parts of the animal testing and risk assessment establishments, some citizens who are sincerely concerned about disease or property values, and some plaintiffs' lawyers.

Notes

1. The opinions expressed here are those of the author and not necessarily those of the Technology Assessment Board or the Office of Technology Assessment.

2. Hereafter, "dioxin" refers to the chemical 2,3,7,8-tetrachlorodibenzo-para-dioxin, which is also called 2,3,7,8-TCDD or TCDD. It is the most toxic of the 75 chlorinated dioxins and is closely related to 135 chlorinated furans, which are somewhat less toxic.

3. Agent Orange was a 50:50 mixture of two herbicides, 2,4,-D and 2,4,5-T, which was used during the Vietnam War. It always contained traces of dioxin, generally 1 or 2 ppm, but perhaps, at times, as high as 60 ppm.

4. pg/kg is picograms of dioxin per kilogram of body weight. A picogram is 10^{-12} gram.

5. See Gough 1986, 187.

6. Using Barry Commoner's estimate (see EPA 1988) that 10 ppt is associated with a daily dose of 1 pg/kg, 5 to 20 ppt would be associated with daily doses of 0.5 to 2 pg/kg. Using EPA's estimate that a dose of 0.006 pg/kg/day represents a 1 in 1 million risk, those doses translate to risks of 83 (0.5/0.006) and 333 (2/0.006) per million.

References

Beck, H., K. Eckart, W. Mathar, and R. Wittkowski. 1988. Levels of PCDDs and PCDFs in adipose tissue of occupationally exposed workers. 18 *Chemosphere* 507–516.

Bertazzi, P. A., C. Zocchetti, A. C. Pesatori, et al. 1989. Ten-year mortality study of the population involved in the Seveso incident in 1976. 129 *Am. J. Epidemiol.* 1187–1200.

Bond, G. G., T. E. Lipps, E. A. McLaren, and R. R. Cook. 1989. Update of mortality among chemical workers with potential exposure to the higher chlorinated dioxins. 31 *J. Occup. Med.* 121–123.

Cantor, K. P., and A. Blair. 1986. *Agricultural chemicals, drinking water, and public health: An epidemiologic overview.* Washington, DC: National Cancer Institute.

Centers for Disease Control. 1988. Veterans health study. Serum 2,3,7,8-tetrachlorodibenzo-p-dioxin levels in U.S. Army Vietnam-era veterans. 260 *J. Am. Med. Assn.* 1249–1254.

Centers for Disease Control. 1989. Comments on the paper: Ten-year mortality study of the population involved in the seveso incident in 1976, Pier Albert Bertazzi, et al. Attached to testimony of V. Houk before the Human Resources and Intergovernmental Relations Subcommittee of the Committee on Government Operations, U.S. House of Representatives. July 11.

Collins, J. J., M. E. Strauss, G. J. Levinskas, and P. R. Conner. (in press). The mortality experience of workers exposed to 2,3,7,8-tetrachlorodibenzo-p-dioxin in a trichlorophenol process accident. *Epidemiology* to be published in Jan or Mar 1993.

Council on Scientific Affairs, American Medical Association. 1984. *The health effects of "Agent Orange" and polychlorinated dioxin contaminants: An update, 1984.* Chicago, IL: AMA.

Czuczwa, J. M., and R. A. Hites. 1986. Airborne dioxins and dibenzofurans: Sources and fates. 20 *Environ. Sci. Tech.* 195–200.

Department of the Environment, Central Directorate of Environmental Protection. 1989. *Dioxins in the environment.* London: Her Majesty's Stationery Office.

Federal Register. 1986. Guidelines for carcinogen risk assessment. 51:33992–34006.

Environmental Protection Agency. 1987. A cancer risk-specific dose estimate for 2,3,7,8-TCDD. Washington, DC: EPA.

Environmental Protection Agency. 1988. Estimating exposures to 2,3,7,8-TCDD, EPA/600/6-88/005A. Washington, DC: EPA.

Epidemiology Research Division, Brooks Air Force Base. 1991a. Air Force health study, serum dioxin study. vol. 1, chs. 1–5, 18, 19. Brooks Air Force Base, Tex.: ERD.

Epidemiology Research Division, Brooks Air Force Base. 1991b. Air Force health study, serum dioxin study, vols. 1–9. Brooks Air Force Base, Tex.: ERD.

Eriksson, M., L. Hardell, and H. O. Adami. 1990. Exposure to dioxins as a risk factor for soft-tissue sarcoma: A population-based case-control study. 82 *J. Natl. Cancer Inst.* 486–490.

Eriksson, M., L. Hardell, N. O. Berg, et al. 1981. Soft-tissue sarcomas and exposure to chemical substances. A case-referent study. 38 *Br. J. Indus. Med.* 27–33.

Fingerhut, M. A., W. E. Halperin, D. A. Marlow, L. A. Piacitelli, P. A. Sweeney, A. L. Greife, K. Steenland, and A. J. Surada. 1991. Cancer mortality in workers exposed to 2,3,7,8-tetrachlorodibenzo-para-dioxin. 324 *New. Engl. J. Med.* 212–218.

Fingerhut, M. A., M. H. Sweeney, D. G. Patterson, et al. 1989. Levels of 2,3,7,8-tetrachlorodibenzo-p-dioxin in the serum of U.S. chemical workers exposed to dioxin contaminated products: Interim results. 19 *Chemosphere* 835–840.

Fingerhut, M. A., W. E. Halperin, P. A. Honchar, et al. 1984. Review of exposure and pathology data for seven cases reported as soft-tissue sarcoma among persons occupationally exposed to dioxin-contaminated herbicides. In W. W. Lowrance, ed., *Public health risks of the dioxins* 187–203. Los Altos, CA: William Kaufman.

Gough, M. 1986. *Dioxin, Agent Orange: The facts.* New York: Plenum Press.

Gough, M. 1987. Environmental epidemiology: Separating politics and science. 3 *Iss. Sci. & Tech.* 20–31.

Gough, M. 1988. Science policy choices and the estimation of cancer risk associated with exposure to TCDD. 8 *Risk Anal.* 337–342.

Gough, M. 1991a. Human exposures from dioxin in soil. 32 *J. Toxicol. & Environ. Health* 205–245.

Gough, M. 1991b. Agent Orange: Exposure and policy. 81 *Am. J. Pub. Health* 289–290.

Gough, M. 1991c. Human health effects: What the data indicate. 104 *Sci. Total Environ.* 129–158.

Gough, M. 1991d. Letter to Dr. Joel Michalek, U.S. Air Force School of Aerospace Medicine. March 25.

Hardell, L., and M. Eriksson. 1988. The association between soft-tissue sarcomas and exposure to phenoxyacetic acids. 62 *Cancer* 652–656 (1988).

Hardell, L., M. Eriksson, P. Lenner, et al. 1981. Malignant lymphoma and exposure to chemicals, especially organic solvents, chlorophenols and phenoxy acids: A case-control study. 43 *Scand. J. Work Environ. Health* 169–176.

Hardell, L. 1981. On the relation of soft-tissue sarcoma, malignant lymphoma, and colon cancer to phenoxy acids, chlorophenols and other agents. 7 *Scand. J. Work Environ. Health* 119–130.

Hardell, L., and A. Sandstrom. 1979. Case-control study: Soft-tissue sarcomas and exposure to phenoxyacetic acids or chlorophenols. 39 *Br. J. Cancer* 711–717.

Hay, A. 1982. *The chemical scythe: Lessons of 2,4,5-T and dioxin.* New York: Plenum Press.

Hoar, S. K., A. Blair, F. F. Holmes, et al. 1986. Agricultural herbicide use and risk of lymphoma and soft-tissue sarcoma. 256 *J. Am. Med. Assn.* 1141–1147.

Houk, V. 1989. Personal communication. November 7.

International Agency for Research on Cancer. 1979. *IARC monographs on the evaluation of carcinogenic risks to humans.* Supp. 7:350–354.

Kang, H. K., K. K. Watanabe, J. Breen, et al. 1991. Dioxins and dibenzofurans in adipose tissue of U.S. Vietnam veterans and controls. 81 *Am. J. Pub. Health* 344–349.

Kociba, R. J., D. G. Keyes, J. E. Beyer, et al. 1978. Results of a two-year chronic toxicity and oncogenicity study of 2,3,7,8-tetrachlorodibenzo-p-dioxin in rats. 46 *Toxicol. & Appl. Pharm.* 279–303.

Kociba, R. J. 1984. Summary and critique of rodent carcinogenicity studies of chlorinated dibenzo-p-dioxins. In W. W. Lowrance, ed., *Public health risks of the dioxins* 77–98. Los Altos, CA: William Kaufman.

MacMahon, B. 1988. Memorandum to Hon. Alan Cranston and Hon. Frank H. Murkowski. Cong. Rec. S12927–S12931 (September 29).

Manz, A., J. Berger, J. H. Dwyer, et al. 1991. Cancer mortality among workers in chemical plant contaminated with dioxin. 338 *The Lancet* 959–964.

Mocarelli, P., F. Pocchiari, and N. Nelson. 1988. Preliminary report: 2,3,7,8-tetrachlorodibenzo-p-dioxin exposure to humans—Seveso, Italy. 37 *Morbidity & Mortality Wkly. Rep.* 733–736.

Neal, R. A. 1984. Biological effects of 2,3,7,8-tetrachlorodibenzo-para-dioxin in experimental animals. In W. W. Lowrance, ed., *Public health risks of the dioxins* 15–29. Los Altos, CA: William Kaufman.

Needham, L. L. 1991a. Centers for Disease Control. Paper presented at the meeting "Human Exposures from Dioxin in Soil." Washington, DC, November 20. Summarized in Gough 1991a.

Nygren, M., C. Rappe, G. Lindstrom, et al. 1986. Identification of 2,3,7,8-TCDD-substituted polychlorinated dioxins and furans in environmental and human samples. In C. Rappe, G. Choudhary, and L. H. Keith, eds., *Chlorinated dioxins and dibenzofurans in perspective* 17–34. Chelsea, MI: Lewis Publishers.

O'Keefe, B. 1988. Soft-tissue sarcoma: Law, science and logic, an Australian perspective. In A. L. Young and G. M. Reggiani, eds., *Agent Orange and its associated dioxin: Assessment of a controversy.* Amsterdam: Elsevier.

Ott, M. G., R. A. Olson, R. R. Cook, et al. 1987. Cohort mortality study of chemical workers with potential exposure to the higher chlorinated dioxins. 29 *J Occup. Med.* 422–429.

Pearce, N. E., R. A. Sheppard, A. H. Smith, C. A. Teague. 1987. Non-Hodgkin's lymphoma and farming: An expanded case-control study. 39 *Int. J. Cancer* 155–161.

Pearce, N. E., A. H. Smith, J. K. Howard, et al. 1985. Non-Hodgkin's lymphoma and exposure to phenoxyherbicides, chlorophenols, fencing work, and meat works employment: A case-control study. 43 *Br. J. Indus. Med.* 75–83.

Pirkle, J. L., W. H. Wolfe, D. G. Patterson, L. L. Needham, J. E. Michalek, J. C. Miner, M. R. Peterson, D. L. Phillips. 1989. Estimates of the half-life of 2,3,7,8-tetrachlorodibenzo-p-dioxin in Vietnam Veterans of Ranch Hand. 27 *J. Toxicol. Environ. Health* 165–171.

Poland, A. and R. D. Kimbrough (eds). 1984. Banbury Report 18: *Biological mechanisms of dioxin action.* Cold Spring Harbor Laboratory: Cold Spring Harbor, NY.

Reilly, W. K. 1991. Memorandum: Dioxin: Followup to briefing on scientific developments. Washington, DC: EPA.

Riihimaki, V., S. Asp, and S. Hernberg. 1982. Mortality of 2,4-dichlorophenoxyacetic acid and 2,4,5-trichlorophenoxyacetic acid herbicide applicators in Finland. 8 *Scand. J. Work Environ. Health* 37–42.

Smith, A. H., and N. E. Pearce. 1986. Update on soft-tissue sarcoma and phenoxyherbicides in New Zealand. 15 *Chemosphere* 1795–1798.

Smith, A. H., D. G. Patterson, M. L. Warner, R. MacKenzie, and L. L. Needham. 1992. Serum 2,3,7,8-tetrachlorodibenzo-p-dioxin levels of New Zealand pesticide applicators and their implications for cancer hypothesis. 84 *J. Natl. Cancer Inst.* 104–108.

Smith, A. H., N. E. Pearce, D. O. Fisher, H. J. Giles, C. A. Teague, and J. K. Howard. 1984. Soft-tissue sarcoma and exposure to phenoxyherbicides and chlorophenols in New Zealand. 73 *J. Natl. Cancer Inst.* 1111–1117.

Sweeney, M. H., M. A. Fingerhut, D. G. Patterson, L. A. Piacitelli, J. A. Morris, A. L. Greife, R. W. Hornung, D. A. Marlow, W. E. Halperin, and L. L. Needham. 1990. Comparison of serum levels of 2,3,7,8-TCDD in TCP production workers and in an unexposed comparison group. 20 *Chemosphere* 993–1000.

Tennant, R. W., B. A. Anderson, W. Caspary, J. K. Haseman, B. H. Margolin, R. Minor, M. Resnick, M. D. Shelby, J. Spalding, S. Stasiewicz, E. Zeiger. 1987. Prediction of chemical carcinogenicity in rodents from in vitro genetic toxicity assays. 236 *Science* 933–941.

Thiess, A. M., R. Frentzel-Beyme, and R. Link. 1982. Mortality study of persons exposed to dioxin in a trichlorophenol-process accident that occurred in the BASF AG on Nov. 17, 1953. 3 *Am. J. Indus. Med.* 179–189.

Travis, C., and H. Hattemer-Frey. 1987. Human exposure to 2,3,7,8-TCDD. 16 *Chemosphere* 2331–2342.

Vineis, P., G. Ciccone, A. Cignetti, E. Colombo, P. Comba, A. Dunna, L. Maffi, R. Pisa, B. Terraani, E. Zanini, A. Cignetti, E. Columbo. 1986. Phenoxy herbicides and soft-tissue sarcomas in female rice weeders: A population-based case-referent study. 13 *Scand. J. Work Environ. Health* 9–17.

Wiklund, K., B. M. Lindefors, and L. E. Holm. 1988. Risk of malignant lymphoma in Swedish agricultural and forestry workers. 45 *Br. J. Indus. Med.* 19–25.

Wiklund, K., J. Dich, and L. E. Holm. 1987. Risk of malignant lymphoma in Swedish pesticide applicators. 56 *Br. J. Cancer* 505–508.

Wiklund, K., and L. E. Holm. 1986. Soft-tissue sarcoma risk in Swedish agricultural and forestry workers. 76 *J. Natl. Cancer Inst.* 229–234.

Wolfe, W., J. Michalek, J. Miner, J. Pirkle, S. Caudill, L. Needham, and D. Patterson, Jr. 1992. Dioxin half-life in veterans of Operation Ranch Hand. paper presented at "Dioxin 92," Tampere, Finland, August 24–27, 1992.

Woods, J. S., L. S. Heuser, B. G. Kulander, L. Polissar, R. K. Severson. 1987. Soft-tissue sarcoma and non-Hodgkin's lymphoma in relation to phenoxyherbicide and chlorinated phenol exposure in western Washington. 78 *J. Natl. Cancer Inst.* 899–910.

World Health Organization, Regional Office for Europe. 1991. *Summary report: Consultation on tolerable daily intake from food of PCDDs and PCDFs.* Bilthover, Netherlands: WHO.

Yanders, A. 1991a. Paper presented at the meeting "Human Exposures from Dioxin in Soil." Washington, DC, November 20. Summarized in Gough 1991a.

Young, A. L., and G. M. Reggiani, eds. 1988. *Agent Orange and its associated dioxin: Assessment of a controversy.* Amsterdam: Elsevier.

Biographical Sketch

Michael Gough, Ph.D., is currently Program Manager, Biological Applications of the Office of Technology Assessment (OTA). He received his Ph.D. in biology at Brown University. He joined the Center for Risk Management, Resources for the Future, in 1987 and was appointed Center Director in March 1990. From 1980 to 1985, he directed OTA's congressionally mandated oversight of Federal research into the possible effects of exposures to Agent Orange and to radiation from atomic bomb tests after World War II. He rejoined the Office of Technology Assessment later in 1990. His research interests include Federal carcinogen regulation policies, environmental policy, and scientific and policy issues related to Agent Orange and dioxin.

Dr. Gough served three years as chairman of the Department of Veterans Affairs Advisory Committee on health-related effects of herbicides, and currently chairs the Department of Health and Human Services' Ranch Hand Advisory Committee. He has published more than 20 papers in molecular and bacterial genetics and received Fulbright Lectureships to Peru and India.

12

The Three Mile Island Nuclear Accident and Public Health Consequences

George K. Tokuhata

On the morning of March 28, 1979, a series of "unlikely events" at the Three Mile Island (TMI) nuclear plant led to a loss-of-coolant accident that became the most serious accident yet to occur at a U.S. commercial nuclear power plant (Kemeny 1979). For several hours after the reactor first malfunctioned, its core overheated. Experts later estimated that up to 10 million curies of radioactivity escaped into the atmosphere in the following week (Nuclear Regulatory Commission 1980; Woodward 1979). The resulting exposure to humans was, however, very slight. According to one expert panel, the maximum[1] radiation dose to a person standing unprotected anywhere along the border of the plant site for the duration of the accident was 100 millirems (mrem)[2] (Ad Hoc Population Dose Assessment Group 1979), the approximate equivalent of one year of natural background radiation in the area. Gur et al. (1983) estimated that the average likely[3] radiation dose to persons living within five miles of the plant was 10 millirems. This is the approximate equivalent of one month's exposure to natural background radiation in the area and of one chest x-ray exposure.

At these low doses of radiation, no major physical health effects on the exposed population would be expected. One expert group, the Ad Hoc Population Dose Assessment Group, projected the health effects that were likely to occur among the 2.2 million people living within 50 miles of the plant over their remaining lifetimes. These effects include 1 excess cancer death[4] (in addition to some 450,000 cancer deaths that would normally occur among these people), 1 or 2 cases of nonfatal cancer, and 1 or 2 incidents of genetic damage that might be passed on to future generations (Ad Hoc Population Dose Assessment Group 1979). In short, the risk from the TMI radiation to the nearby residents is trivial compared with ordinary risks of everyday life.

Despite these reassuring assessments by academic, government, and industry experts, there was, and remains, much public anxiety. Some local residents reportedly developed a "radiation syndrome" including nausea, vomiting, diarrhea, and skin rashes, symptoms of the sort that might be associated with exposure to very high levels of radiation. Antinuclear activists and ordinary citizens questioned both the estimated radiation dose and the projected health risks.

The accident was accompanied by much confusion and uncertainty, particularly about the level of radiation released. For these reasons, and because this accident was the first of its kind, state and federal health authorities recommended that long-term epidemiologic studies be conducted on the population near the reactor (Committee of Federal Research in the Biological Effects of Ionizing Radiation 1979; Governor's Commission on TMI 1979; Tokuhata 1980).

Radiation Exposure

Certainly, exposure to high doses of ionizing radiation is harmful. Whether health is affected by exposures comparable with the level of natural background radiation is a matter of conjecture. Observations at high radiation intensities have implied that some health risks may be increased even at low levels of exposure, but such risks are difficult to measure. Radiation exposure may (a) damage genes and chromosomes (*mutagenic* effects); (b) adversely affect the growth and development of the embryo and fetus (*teratogenic* effects); and (c) increase the risk of developing cancer (*carcinogenic* effects) (Upton 1968, 1969).

The exposure to the residents living near TMI came almost entirely from xenon-133 (half-life 5.3 days), xenon-135 (half-life 9.1 hours), and traces of radioactive iodine (principally iodine-131, half-life 8.0 days), which escaped intermittently from the plant as gases[5] (Battist et al. 1979; Gerusky 1981) and followed prevailing winds. The resulting exposures to humans were short-lived because xenon dispersed rapidly and radioactive iodine was present only in barely detectable amounts. No releases of long-lived fission products, such as strontium-90, cesium-137, and plutonium-239, were detected.

Cancer, Genetic Damage, Teratology

One might predict, albeit uncertainly, the probable health effects in the population from the TMI exposure. One cannot study such effects directly since the exposure was comparable with that from natural background sources which would have similar effects.

Scientists estimate health effects from low-level radiation by extrapolating from observations at higher radiation doses and higher dose rates. This requires assumptions about dose–response relationships, that is, how rapidly the magnitude of an effect falls off with decreasing dose. These assumptions are inherently unverifiable, and the estimates of health effects are uncertain at best (National Research Council 1972; United Nations Scientific Committee on the Effects of Atomic Radiation 1977).

Most scientists assume that even low levels of radiation increase the risk of cancer. Animal studies done at intermediate-to-high dose levels show that the risk may depend on the type of cancer, the subject's age at time of irradiation, and the kind of radiation.

Several models can be used to estimate the cancer risk to the residents near TMI, and all show that the increase in risk is very small. In the *linear model,* a scientist will extrapolate linearly the data obtained at high doses, with no allowance for the ability of an organism to repair damage. This model was used by the Ad Hoc Population Dose Assessment Group (1979) to estimate the number of excess cancer deaths presented earlier. Many experts, however, believe that this method overestimates the risks of low-level radiation.

Other experts prefer a *linear-quadratic model,* which predicts risks 25 percent to 50 percent lower than with the linear model (Upton 1977; National Academy of Sciences 1980). It predicts less than one additional nonfatal cancer case among the 2.2 million people living within 50 miles of TMI.

Radiation may also cause genetic damage in human germ cells, leading to inherited disease or defect in future generations. Scientists have estimated that the incidence of genetic abnormalities in humans would be doubled by a dose of 20–200 rem (National Academy of Sciences 1972; United Nations Scientific Committee on the Effects of Atomic Radiation 1977). Extrapolating downward from this figure, one may predict that 1 descendant of the 2.2 million people living within 50 miles of TMI will be affected by genetic disorders resulting from the TMI accident.

The risks of damage to the human embryo and fetus are more difficult to estimate because there is little relevant data. Studies suggest that these risks are smaller than for carcinogenic and mutagenic effects at similar doses (National Academy of Sciences 1972; United Nations Scientific Committee on the Effects of Atomic Radiation 1977). No such effects are likely to be caused by the TMI accident in any individual in the exposed population.

Psychological Stress

The major health effects of the TMI accident were psychobehavioral. Many residents experienced psychological stress primarily because of fears associated with radiation. From this perspective, the accident cannot be considered a discrete, unique event; the prolonged recovery period created many new sources of stress and anxiety.

Stress may cause changes in body function that, if intense or chronic, may lower resistance to disease (Rahe et al. 1964). Stressful events may require more intense and prolonged coping efforts than others. The greater the strains on the coping mechanisms, the more likely that idiosyncratic or pathological physiological reactions may develop in the affected individual. In assessing these effects, we must consider both the individual's susceptibility to stress and society's network of support. Some people, because of their personality type and life history, are more vulnerable to certain diseases (Dunbar 1954).

Any stimulus that a person perceives as threatening a need will initiate a stress response. These stimuli need not be external to the individual: a person's imagination can lead to stress and prompt a physiological response that may threaten the individual.

Stress may cause disease by lowering or exaggerating the immune response (Stein et al. 1981), creating endocrine problems through either hypoactivity (too little activity) or hyperactivity (overactivity) and altering the balance of autonomic control (Lipton 1976). The result will be changes in the cardiovascular, respiratory, secretory, and visceral systems, which alter sleep patterns and affect brain function, which in turn may change eating, drinking, smoking, and other habits (Lisander 1979). It is unlikely, however, that psychological stress is a direct cause of any specific disease.

Pregnant women appear to be particularly susceptible to stress. Scientists have reported an association between anxiety or stress in a pregnant woman and health problems in her developing fetus or newborn child (Nuckolls 1972; Morishima 1978) and infant development (Barlow 1978). These effects are not fully understood, but several explanations are possible. Stress may affect the pregnant woman's behavior, such as smoking, drinking, or use of medication. It may cause her doctors to prescribe analgesic[6] or psychotropic drugs,[7] or to use special diagnostic procedures. Stress may affect the bonding of a mother to her child, or her child-rearing practices. Or it may act through more direct physiological mechanisms, such as by influencing the hypothalamic-adrenocortical mechanism[8] (Smith 1975).

Thus, the psychological stress resulting from the accident may have led to real health effects in the population. It became an important goal of health authorities to assess the possible extent of such problems.

Health Studies

Immediately following the 1979 accident, the Pennsylvania Department of Health developed a comprehensive research program to assess its potential health effects, including physical, psychological, and behavioral effects. As director of the Division of Epidemiology Research, I was responsible for developing and carrying out the overall research program, for securing the necessary financial support for the continuing program, and for handling public relations and media contacts.

Accurate information about emissions was at first unavailable; the public's anxiety, however, was immediately apparent. Many of the studies conceived during this critical time reflected the existing epidemiologic knowledge about the biological effects of ionizing radiation (National Academy of Sciences 1980) and psychosocial consequences of disaster (Melick et al. 1982). Some of the studies were conducted jointly with the University of Pittsburgh School of Public Health and the Pennsylvania State University College of Medicine, where I served as professor of epidemiology and biostatistics and behavioral science. The Health Department commissioned a scientific advisory panel to oversee the TMI Health Research Program.

TMI Area Census

One of the first projects was a special census of the nearly 36,000 people who resided within 5 miles of TMI (Goldhaber et al. 1983). Its chief purpose was to identify individuals who faced the highest risk of radiation exposure because of their close proximity to the plant.

The census obtained information about race, income, and other sociodemographic data for each subject. It also inquired into the subjects' smoking habits, medical history (including any cancer or thyroid diseases diagnosed prior to the TMI accident), pregnancy experiences, and radiation exposure from medical or occupational sources. Finally, it identified where each subject had been during the ten-day period when most of the radiation had been released from the plant. These data allowed the investigators to identify a cohort of individuals whose health and mortality could be tracked in long-term follow-up studies.

Evacuation during the Crisis

The governor did not order an evacuation of the general population in the vicinity of TMI. He did, however, issue an advisory urging the evacuation of pregnant women and small children in a 5-mile radius of the damaged plant; 64 percent of the residents did evacuate (Goldhaber and Lehman 1982). Compared with the general population, the evacuees tended to be younger and more highly educated, and to contain a greater proportion of females and white-collar workers. The people most likely to evacuate were those who lived closest to the damaged reactor, or who had one or more preschool children in the household. Doctors and other medical professionals were as likely to evacuate as other residents.

Radiation Dose Assessment

One of the most important, yet difficult, tasks was to determine the radiation exposure of individual residents (as opposed to the exposure of the population as a whole). This study was conducted by the Department of Radiation Health of the University of Pittsburgh, using additional data on census and evacuation provided by the Pennsylvania Department of Health (Gur et al. 1983).

For each individual residing within a five-mile radius, and for each pregnant woman residing within a ten-mile radius, the investigators estimated the maximum and likely doses to the whole body (gamma radiation[9]), the skin (gamma and beta[10] radiation combined), and thyroid tissues. The investigators based their estimates on detailed data about the evacuation, data from radiation dosimeters (such as the thermoluminescent dosimetry, or TLD), and other exposure readings. They also took into account meterological information, such as the direction and velocity of the prevailing wind during the accident.

When the investigators disregarded the evacuation of the residents, they could estimate the largest whole-body gamma dose to an individual (the maximum dose) within a 5-mile radius of the plant, but not on the plant site, to be 165 mrem; the average dose was 24 mrem. Taking the evacuation into account, the highest estimated exposure (the likely dose) was 80 mrem; the average dose was 10 mrem. The average dose to pregnant women within a 10-mile radius of the plant was estimated to be 10 mrem (without considering evacuation), and 4 mrem when evacuation was considered. These estimates made no allowances for shielding and probably exceed the true exposure (Gur et al. 1983). They are generally consistent with those provided by federal agencies (Ad Hoc Population Dose Assessment Group 1979). The total dose to the skin (from gamma and beta radiation) could have as much as 3 to 4 times larger than the whole-body gamma dose alone, if the protective effects of shelter and clothing were ignored (Battist et al. 1979). The dose from inhaled radioactive particles was probably no more than 3 percent to 7 percent of the total whole body dose.

Psychobehavioral Studies

A major concern following the TMI accident was its psychological and behavioral impact on the local population (Dohrenwend et al. 1979). How many people, and which ones, were affected psychologically? How did local residents cope with the crisis? What social and medical services were used? What kind of stress-related symptoms, mental and physical, did the residents report? How long did the psychological impact last?

To address these questions, investigators at the Department of Behavioral Science at the Milton S. Hershey Medical Center (Pennsylvania State University) and the Division of Epidemiology Research of the Pennsylvania Department of Health jointly conducted a series of psychobehavioral studies. The studies found that younger, more educated, married, and female residents were more likely to have been distressed, probably out of concern for their present and future children and their own future health (Dohrenwend et al. 1979).

Those residents who actively coped and those with poor psychological or physical health were highly distressed during the TMI crisis. The number of people who reported themselves as "extremely distressed" decreased shortly after the accident, but many of the people who lived closest to TMI remained distressed nine months after the accident. Some residents close to the reactor consumed more alcohol, tobacco, and sleeping pills and tranquilizers during the two weeks of the crisis than before the accident, but their use of these substances did not continue at the same level. They reported more psychosomatic symptoms, such as headache, chest pains, upset stomach, sleeplessness, loss of appetite, constipation, and difficulties in coordination and concentration. Eighteen months after the crisis, however, nearby and distant residents showed few differences in stress-related symptoms.

Bromet and Dunn (1982) reported a psychiatric study of three selected "high risk" groups: TMI employees, mothers with preschool children, and outpatients at mental health clinics. One year after the TMI accident, the psychological status of psychiatric outpatients residing near TMI did not differ significantly from that of their counterparts in a control group. The TMI workers experienced only slightly higher rates of clinical depression and anxiety. But mothers with preschool children who lived within five miles of TMI suffered more anxiety and depression than their counterparts who lived near a different nuclear plant where there had been no accident. Thus, clinically apparent mental health effects were found primarily within the two-months after the accident, but more subtle symptoms persisted as long as one year after the accident.

Pregnancy Outcome and Infancy
Both ionizing radiation and psychological stress can affect the outcome of pregnancy (Brent and Gorson 1972; Brent 1979; Morishima 1978; Gorsuch and Kay 1974). For this reason, the scientific advisory panel considered important an evaluation of the outcome of pregnancies through the neonatal period (the first 27 days after birth) and the health of infants of the residents in the TMI area.

Pregnancy Outcome. A carefully designed epidemiologic study of the outcome of pregnancies in the residents was initiated by the Pennsylvania Department of Health in August 1979. The study group included 3,946 infants delivered between March 28, 1979 (the day of the accident), and March 27, 1980, whose mothers resided within 10 miles of the reactor at the time of the accident. The control (comparison) group consisted of 4,046 infants delivered from March 28, 1980 (one year later), through March 28,1981, whose mothers resided in the same geographic area.

The study examined a range of problems. These included fetal deaths (stillbirths and spontaneous abortions that occurred 16 weeks or later in pregnancy), neonatal deaths (deaths of newborns less than 28 days after delivery), perinatal deaths (a combined measure of fetal and neonatal deaths), prematurity (duration of pregnancy less than 37 weeks), low birth weight (less than 2,500 grams), congenital anomalies (one or more developmental defects observed at birth), and low Apgar scores[11] (composite scores of less than 7 at 1-minute postpartum).

In addition, the investigators estimated the radiation exposures of each pregnant woman for ten days following the accident, using the methods already noted (Gur et al. 1983). They assessed the psychological stress to the mothers during and immediately following the accident, both directly, from the mothers' reports of anxiety or fear, and indirectly, from their use of extra medications (tranquilizers, sleeping pills, and antihypertensive drugs) and other behaviors used to cope with stress. Finally, the investigators collected data on other factors that can influence pregnancy outcome and fetal growth, such as sociodemographic and behavioral characteristics and medical histories of mothers, their health care providers, and the prenatal care the mothers received.

The investigators found no significant differences between the exposed and unexposed mothers on any of the measures of pregnancy outcome they examined. Neither radiation exposure nor psychological stress was significantly correlated with adverse pregnancy outcome, using the measures they employed.

The investigators did report some differences between the two groups, however. The women who had used "extra" medications (over and above their usual amounts) and were "extremely" stressed during and shortly after the accident had children whose Apgar scores (as measured one minute after delivery) or birth weights were significantly lower, on the average, than those of the control women. (The average Apgar scores measured five minutes after delivery were the same in both groups.) This finding on the Apgar scores might have minimal clinical significance. However, the association between low birth weights and stress, together with the use of extra medication by the mothers, may be significant and deserves further study. Low birth weight is known to be an important (and probably the most important) risk factor in child growth and development.

Congenital Hypothyroidism. Infants with congenital hypothyroidism are born with thyroid glands that produce insufficient thyroid hormone, a serious but treatable problem. It may result from exposure of the fetus to radioactive iodine, among other reasons.

The Pennsylvania Department of Health initiated a statewide screening program for congenital hypothyroidism in mid-1978, almost a year before the accident. In the one-year period after the accident, only one case of congenital hypothyroidism was identified among the 3,967 newborns whose mothers lived within a 10-mile radius of TMI. This is within the normally expected range.

However, in 1979, seven cases of congenital hypothyroidism were reported in nearby Lancaster County, most of whose residents lived more than ten miles from TMI and southeast (upwind) of the reactor. One possible explanation might have been exposure of their mothers to radioactive iodine released by the accident.

The interpretation of such an apparent cluster raises serious problems. Most are simply unusual groupings of cases that arise by chance, and have no particular epidemiologic significance or of a common cause, although that cannot always be excluded. But a cluster may reflect a real hazard, and each one needs to be investigated independently for evidence of a pattern in time or in space, or some other logical or biological reason that might indicate a common cause.[12]

Investigators from the Department of Health examined each case in the Lancaster County cluster of congenital hypothyroidism cases. The individual cases were diverse and had no apparent connection to the TMI accident. One of the seven cases had been reported before the accident. Another was a child born three months after the accident, who had other severe anomalies in the central nervous system as well. Because of the advanced stage of the mother's pregnancy at the time of the accident, and the presence of other anomalies unlikely to be related to radiation, this second case was probably not a result of the accident. A third case involved Amish twins, only one of whom was affected. Since both children had received the same radiation exposure from the accident but only one developed the disease, radiation exposure was unlikely to have been a factor. A fourth case was an Amish child whose condition had been inherited from the parents, that is, the disease was probably not a result of damage to the infant's thyroid from an external source but an inborn defect. A fifth child's hypothyroidism resulted from the displacement of the thyroid gland from its normal position in the fetus, and is unlikely to have resulted from radiation. The parents of the other two children would not allow diagnostic tests to study their condition.

Thus, investigators from the Department of Health concluded that the 1979 cluster of hypothyroidism cases in Lancaster County was not related to the TMI nuclear accident. The same conclusion was reached by an independent hypothyroidism investigative committee, organized by the State Health Department, that included experts in epidemiology, pediatric endocrinology, obstetrics, medical genetics, biostatistics, and radiation physics.

This conclusion is further supported by the absence of any other reported cases of congenital hypothyroidism during the nine months following the accident in the eight counties located downwind from TMI, taking into account the wind directions that in the first 48 hours after the accident. People living in these counties would be expected to have received the largest exposure to radioactive iodine released by the accident.

Moreover, the calculated exposure of residents near TMI to radioactive iodine was quite low. In their analysis, Health Department investigators estimated that the maximum dose of radioactive iodine to the thyroids of people residing in the vicinity of TMI following the accident was 7.5 mrad[13] (Gur et al. 1983). Doses at least 1,000 times higher would have been required to cause significant damage to the thyroid gland; even then, the body may repair much of the damage and still higher doses would probably be required to produce clinically apparent hypothyroidism.

These estimates are supported by studies on residents of the Marshall Islands who had been exposed to fresh radioactive fallout from atomic bomb testings, and atomic bomb victims in Japan. These data indicate that an exposure of 50,000 to 100,000 mrads would be necessary to damage the thyroid gland of a fetus irreversibly (Brent 1979; Morishima 1978). By comparison, the estimated maximum dose to the thyroid of any fetus carried by a woman near TMI was in the range of 75–200 mrad (depending on the assumptions). This exposure is far too small to be a plausible cause of congenital hypothyroidism.

Spontaneous Abortions. The fetus is particularly sensitive to ionizing radiation, showing biological effects following exposure to radiation at levels above 10 rem (National Academy of Sciences 1980; Brent 1979). However, exposures below 10 rem have not shown such effects, either because none exist or because they are too small to measure by current epidemiologic methods.

Some scientists have cited psychological stress as a risk factor for spontaneous abortions (Nuckolls 1972; Morishima 1978; Newton et al. 1979), although the relationship has not been quantified. Given the low levels of radiation exposure in the vicinity of TMI, any increase in spontaneous abortion would probably have resulted from psychological stress rather than from radiation.

To determine if there had been an increase in spontaneous abortions prior to 16 weeks' gestation (when the risk of miscarriage is highest), Goldhaber et al. (1983) conducted a study of women who lived near TMI. Three months after the accident, the investigators surveyed each female resident in a five-mile radius of the plant regarding their pregnancy status and other information. One year later, the investigators again contacted the women who had been pregnant, to ascertain the outcomes of their pregnancies.

The study found that the incidence of spontaneous abortion among the TMI area women was comparable with those reported in four studies used for comparison (Taylor 1964; French and Bierman 1962; Shapiro et al. 1971; Harlap et al. 1980). Of women who were between 4 and 16 weeks pregnant at the time of the accident, 15.1 percent experienced miscarriages. The incidence rose to 16.1 percent when later-term miscarriages and stillbirths were counted. Both figures were comparable with those in the studies used for comparison and, thus, were considered normal.

Fetal and Infant Mortalities. In-utero exposure to ionizing radiation
has been associated with fetal and infant mortalities (Kato 1970; Mac-
Mahon 1972). My group studied fetal and infant mortalities among residents in a ten-mile radius of the TMI plant (Tokuhata and Digon 1981).
Using vital statistics data compiled by the State Health Data Center, we
analyzed the numbers of fetal and infant deaths from 1970 through 1986,
covering both the pre-TMI and post-TMI periods, and compared them
with expected numbers. We examined the vital statistics data for particular time periods (a cross-sectional analysis) and searched for any variations in death rates with time (longitudinal analysis). In addition, we
searched for variations in the number of infant deaths in individual three-
month periods in years before and after the TMI accident.

This comprehensive analysis found no evidence for an effect of the
accident. The fetal, neonatal, and infant mortalities in the vicinity of the
TMI nuclear facility were neither significantly higher than expected nor
significantly different after the accident than before. When broken down
into three-month intervals, the infant mortality data immediately following the accident were not significantly different from what was expected. The data showed no pattern that might indicate an effect of the
accident on the fetus at any stage of the mother's pregnancy at the time
of the exposure.

Cancer Mortality and Incidence in Local Populations

Public concerns about health risks from the TMI accident were raised by
several developments. A local citizens' group conducted a survey of selected communities near TMI and claimed to have found an increased
risk of cancer among their residents. Moreover, antinuclear activists per-
sistently alleged that the local residents had suffered much higher radiation exposure than reported by government agencies. Further public
concern was raised by the Chernobyl nuclear accident in April 1986,
which resulted in much higher radiation exposure to workers and nearby
residents (including radiation deaths) than the TMI accident.

Much of the public concern about radiation exposure has centered
on radiation-induced cancer. Such cancers generally develop 10 to 20
years (or more) after exposure. Even leukemia, which has a relatively
short latency period, is not usually detected until four to five years after
radiation exposure.

In 1985, six years after the TMI accident, our group conducted an
epidemiologic study to search for a possible increase in cancer mortality
and/or morbidity in communities around TMI. Our task was also to

compare our findings with what is currently known about cancer caused by radiation (Tokuhata and Digon 1985).

This study examined cancer mortality in communities located within a 20-mile radius of TMI. In analyzing the data, we considered the mortality in all of the communities taken together, and in selected small communities downwind from the plant. We also compared the observed number of cancer deaths five years before and five years after the accident, with the cancer mortality for Pennsylvania as a whole. Cancer may be classified into eight major groups according to the part of the body in which it arises, each of which we separately considered.

The study found no evidence of excess cancer deaths in the five years after the TMI accident. On the contrary, residents in the area within 20 miles of the plant had *fewer* cancer deaths than expected during the 5-year period. The cancer death rates in the individual communities, in particular those downwind from TMI, showed no unexpected cancer patterns.

We also examined the pattern of newly diagnosed cancers between July 1982 and June 1984 (only time cancer incidence data were available in 1985) in four communities downwind from TMI, in comparison with national cancer rates (National Cancer Institute 1987). We found no indication of any excess of new cancer cases in the four communities. Some minor variations did exist between the observed and the expected numbers of new cases in these communities, which might have occurred by chance alone.

More important, we found no increase in the incidence of cancers that are known to be associated with radiation exposure. Leukemia, the cancer most likely to have been detected as early as four to five years after the accident, was diagnosed in only two area residents; four such cases would have been expected on the basis of national cancer rates.

Registry-Based Cohort Cancer Incidence and Mortality

Our group also analyzed the cancer incidence and mortality data from two cancer registries (Tokuhata and Digon 1985).

First, in 1985 we analyzed the data from the TMI Mother/Child Registry. Our analysis covered the period from July 1982 to December 1983, the only time period for which the necessary data on new cancer cases were available. The Mother/Child Registry included data from 3,582 women who were pregnant at the time of the accident and resided within 10 miles of TMI.

Four of the mothers in this registry were diagnosed of cancer during the period of our analysis—the expected number was 3.9, based on national statistics for women in the 10–44 year age group (National Cancer Institute 1987). Of the children in the registry (who had been exposed to the radiation from TMI in utero), two were diagnosed with cancer; one was expected on the basis of national cancer rates. Neither of these differences was statistically significant.

The Pennsylvania Department of Health continues to follow the women and children in this registry, because of the long time that is required for most radiation-induced malignancies to develop. At present there is no indication, however, of any increased cancer risk to these people.

A second analysis, conducted in 1988, examined the death records in the TMI General Population Registry, which included all people living in the vicinity of TMI. The data from the State Health Data Center and the National Death Index covered the six-year period from July 1979 to June 1985. In each case, the cause of death, the year, and the age of the person at time of death were verified against death certificates.

In this study, we used as a control the mortality experience of the Pennsylvania population (excluding Philadelphia). We also adjusted the death rates for the age and other demographic characteristics of the individual cases (Khan 1983; Cox 1972). During the six-year period we considered, we found no significant differences between the observed and expected death rates. This includes deaths from all causes combined, from ten leading causes considered separately, from all cancers considered together, and from the eight anatomical groups of cancers considered separately.

In these two registry-based studies, all of the subjects were known to have been in the vicinity of TMI during the accident. Such studies can provide better estimates of potential health risks from the accident than studies of local communities, which may include many subjects whose whereabouts during the accident were unknown.

Perhaps insufficient time has elapsed since the accident for some effects, such as cancer, to have been detected in our studies. Further studies are desirable, using other control populations and/or different methods of analysis.

Overview

The TMI nuclear accident was the most serious commercial nuclear accident in the United States, but it created a rare scientific opportunity. In response, the Pennsylvania Department of Health created the TMI

Health Research Program, which documented the radiation exposure of the population and searched for possible adverse health consequences of the accident. Few other studies have combined the extensive documentation of the exposure and the health of a human population exposed to low-level nuclear radiation. The TMI Health Research Program, which is an ongoing effort, contributes directly to science and public health.

Notes

1. The maximum radiation dose is the dose estimated without taking into account the evacuation of the residents.

2. A rem is a unit of dose equivalent. It is numerically equal to the absorbed dose of radiation, with adjustment to take into account the nature of the radiation, distribution of the absorbed energy in the body, and other modifying factors. The unit is often used to represent the whole-body exposure of an individual. 1 millirem (mrem) = 1/1000 rem.

3. The likely radiation dose is the dose estimated taking into account the evacuation of residents.

4. By contrast, Cohen notes (chapter 14) that a large coal-burning electricity generating plant in a metropolitan area results in an estimated 25–100 excess deaths *per year* from air pollution.

5. The half-life is the time required for half of a group of radioactive nuclei to decay.

6. Analgesics are painkilling drugs.

7. Psychotropic drugs are medications that act on the mind, such as sedatives and tranquilizers.

8. The hypothalamus (located in the brain) and the adrenal glands (located near the kidneys) are closely related physiologically. Together they regulate many bodily functions, such as temperature, carbohydrate-fat metabolism, sexual and emotional responses, sleep, and reaction to stress.

9. Gamma radiation consists of photons from decaying nuclei. In the present context, this radiation penetrates more deeply into the body than the other forms.

10. Beta radiation consists of high-energy electrons, which (in the present context) have less penetrating ability than the gamma radiation.

11. The Apgar score is a numerical expression (from 0 to 10) of the condition of a newborn infant, usually determined at one minute after birth. It represents the sum of points based on physicians' assessments of the *heart rate, respiratory effort, muscle tone, reflex irritability,* and *skin color.*

12. The interpretation of clusters was also significant in assessing the possible health effects of video display terminals (chapter 6)—The Editors.

13. The rad, a unit of absorbed dose in a medium, is expressed in terms of the total absorbed energy per kilogram of medium. The unit does not take into account the

different biological effectiveness of different forms of radiation, or the distribution of the absorbed energy. 1 mrad = 0.001 rad.

References

Ad Hock Population Dose Assessment Group. 1979. *Population dose and health impact of the Accident at the Three Mile Island nuclear station.* Washington, DC: U.S. Government Printing Office.

Barlow, S. M., A. F. Knight, and F. M. Sullivan. 1978. Delay of postnatal growth and development of offspring produced by maternal restraint stress during pregnancy in the rat. 18 *Teratology* 211–218.

Battist, L., F. Buchanan, F. Congel, C. Nelson, M. Nelson, H. Peterson, M. Rosenstein. 1979. *Population dose and health impact of the accident at Three Mile Island nuclear station. Preliminary estimates for the period March 28, 1979 through April 7, 1979.* Washington, DC: Nuclear Regulatory Commission.

Brent, R. L. 1979. Effects of Ionizing Radiation on Growth and Development. In M. A. Klingberg, ed., *Contributions to epidemiology and biostatistics* 1:147–183. Basel, Switzerland: S. Karger.

Brent, R. L., and R. O. Gorson. 1972. Radiation Exposure in Pregnancy. 2(5) *Cur. Prob. Radiol.* 1–48.

Bromet, E., and L. Dunn. 1982. *Mental health of Three Mile Island residents.* Pittsburgh: University of Pittsburgh. Psychiatric Epidemiology Program, Western Psychiatric Institute and Clinic.

Committee on Federal Research in the Biological Effects of Ionizing Radiation. 1979. *Follow-up studies on biological and health effects resulting from the Three Mile Island nuclear power plant accident of March 28, 1979.* NIH Pub. no. 79-2064. Washington, DC: Dept. of Health, Education and Welfare.

Cox, D. R. 1972. Regression models and life tables, 34 *J. Royal Stat. Soc.* B187–220.

Dohrenwend, B. P., B. S. Dohrenwend, S. V. Kash, and G. J. Warheit. 1979. Technical staff analysis report on behavioral effects. In *Report of the public health and safety task force to the President's Commission on the Accident at Three Mile Island.* Washington, DC: U.S. Government Printing Office.

Dunbar, H. 1954. *Psychosomatic diagnosis.* New York: Hoeber.

French, F. E., and J. M. Bierman. 1962. Probabilities of fetal mortality. 77 *Pub. Health Rep.* 835–847.

Gerusky, T. M. 1981. Three Mile Island: Assessment of radiation exposures and environmental contamination. 365 *Ann. N. Y. Acad. Sci.* 54–62.

Goldhaber, M. K., S. L. Staub and G. K. Tokuhata. 1983. Spontaneous abortions after the Three Mile Island nuclear accident: A life table analysis. 73 *Amer. J. Public Health* 752–759.

Goldhaber, M. K., and J. E. Lehman. 1982. Crisis evacuation during the Three Mile Island nuclear accident: The TMI population registry. Paper presented at the Annual Meeting of the American Public Health Association, Montreal, November 16.

Goldhaber, M. K., G. K. Tokuhata, and E. Digon. 1983. The Three Mile Island population registry. 98 *Pub. Health Rep.* 603–609.

Gorsuch, R. L., and M. K. Kay. 1974. Abnormalities in pregnancy as a function of anxiety and life stress. 36 *Psychosom. Med.* 352–362.

Governor's Commission on TMI. 1979. *Report on the [Pennsylvania] Governor's Commission on TMI.* Harrisburg: The Commission.

Gur, D., W. F. Good, and G. K. Tokuhata. 1983. Radiation Dose Assignment to Individuals Residing Near the Three Mile Island Nuclear Station. 57 *Proc. Pa. Acad. Sci.* 99–102.

Harlap, S., P. H. Shiono, and S. Ramcharan. 1980. A life table of spontaneous abortions and the effects of age, parity, and other variables. In E. B. Hook and I. Porter, eds., *Reproductive loss.* New York: Academy Press.

Houts, P. S., and M. K. Goldhaber. 1981. Psychological and social effects on the population surrounding Three Mile Island after the nuclear accident on March 28, 1979, in S. K. Majumdar, ed., *Energy, environment and the economy* 151–164. Pennsylvania Academy of Sciences.

Kato, I. I. 1970. *Mortality in children exposed to the atomic bombs while in utero 1945–1969.* Atomic Bomb Casualty Commission Technical Report 23. Hiroshima, Japan: Atomic Bomb Casualty Commission.

Kemeny, J. G. 1979. *Report of the President's Commission on the Accident at Three Mile Island.* Washington, DC: U.S. Government Printing Office.

Khan, H. A. 1983. *An Introduction to epidemiologic methods.* Oxford: Oxford University Press.

Lipton, M. 1976. Behavioral effects of hypothalamic polypeptide hormones in animals and man. In Sachar, ed., *Hormones, behavior and psychopathology.* New York: Raven Press.

Lisander, B. 1979. Somato-autonomic reactions and their higher control. In Brooks, Koizumi, and Sato, eds., *Integrative functions of the autonomic nervous system.* Amsterdam: Elsevier.

MacMahon, B. 1972. Radiation exposure in-utero and mortality. 95 *Am. J. Epidemiol.* 3.

Melick, M. E., J. N. Logue, and C. J. Frederick. 1982. Stress and disaster. In Goldberger and Breznitz, eds., *Handbook of stress: theoretical and clinical aspects.* New York: Free Press.

Morishima, H. O., H. Pedersen, and M. Finster. 1978. The influence of maternal psychological stress on the fetus. 131 *Obstet. & Gynecol.* 286–290.

National Academy of Sciences. 1980. *National Academy of Sciences advisory committee report on the biological effects of ionizing radiation.* Advisory Committee on the Biological Effects of Ionizing Radiation. Washington, DC: National Academy Press.

National Cancer Institute. 1987. *Annual cancer statistics review. SEER program: surveillance, epidemiology and end results, 1978–1981.* NIH pub. no. 88-2789. Washington, DC:

National Research Council, National Academy of Sciences. 1972 *National Academy of Sciences advisory committee report on the biological effects of ionizing radiation.* Washington, DC:

Newton, R. W., P. A. Webster, P. S. Binu, N. Maskrey, and A. B. Phillips. 1979. Psychosocial stress in pregnancy and its relation to the onset of premature labor. 2 *Br. Med. J.* 411–413.

Nuckolls, K. B., B. H. Kaplan, and J. Cassel. 1972. Psychological assets, life crisis and the prognosis of pregnancy. 95 *Am. J. Epidemiol.* 431–441.

Nuclear Regulatory Commission Special Inquiry Group. 1980. 1 *Three Mile Island, a report to the commissioners and to the public.* Washington, DC:

Rahe, R., et al. 1964. Social stress and illness onset. 8 *J. Psychosom. Res.* 35–44.

Shapiro, S., H. S. Levine, and M. Abramowicz. 1971. Factors associated with early and late fetal loss. 6 *Adv. Planned Parenthood* 45–63.

Smith, D. K. 1975. Modification of prenatal stress effect in rats by adrenalectomy, dexamethasone, and chlorpromazine. 15 *Physiol. & Behav.* 461–467.

Stein, M., S. Keller, and S. Schleifer. 1981. The hypothalamus and the immune response. In Weiner, Hofer, and Stunkard, eds., *Brain, behavior and bodily disease.* New York: Raven.

Taylor, W. F. 1964. On the methodology of measuring the probability of fetal death in a prospective study. 36 *Hum. Biol.* 86–103.

Tokuhata, G. K. 1980. Three Mile Island health research program. 54 *Proc. Pa. Acad. Sci.* 19–21.

Tokuhata, G. K., and E. Digon. 1981. Fetal and infant mortality and congenital hypothyroidism around TMI. Paper presented at the International Symposium on Health Impacts of Different Sources of Energy. Nashville, Tenn. June 22–26.

Tokuhata, G. K., and E. Digon. 1985. *Cancer mortality and morbidity (incidence) around TMI.* Harrisburg: Pennsylvania Dept. of Health.

United Nations Scientific Committee on the Effects of Atomic Radiation. 1977. *Report to the General Assembly, sources and effects of ionizing radiation.* New York: United Nations.

Upton, A. C. 1977. Radiobiological effects of low doses: Implications for radiological protection. 71 *Radiat. Res.* 51–74.

Upton, A. C. 1968. Effects of radiation on man. 18 *Ann. Rev. Nuc. Sci.* 495–528.

Upton, A. C. 1969. *Radiation injury: effects, principles, and perspectives.* Chicago: University of Chicago Press.

Woodward, K., Pickard, Lowe, and Garrick. 1979. *Assessment of offsite radiation doses from Three Mile Island unit 2 accident.* TDR-TMI-116, rev. O.

Biographical Sketch

Dr. George K. Tokuhata currently holds adjunct academic appointments at the University of Pittsburgh's Graduate School of Public Health as professor of epidemiology and biostatistics, and at the Pennsylvania State University's Hershey College of Medicine as professor of epidemiology and behavioral sciences.

He retired as Director of the Division of Epidemiology Research of the Pennsylvania Department of Health. Dr. Tokuhata holds a Ph.D. in behavioral sciences and a doctorate of public health in epidemiology and public health.

13

The Fallout Controversy

Ralph E. Lapp

Few issues have caused more fear and confusion than the question of the hazards of low-level radiation. There has been a remarkable failure to examine closely the evidence when discussing the issue and planning future studies. As a result, the public's radiation phobia has been needlessly reinforced, and public money is being used on studies that are bound to be inconclusive.

Yalow 1988, p. 11

In 1950 the Atomic Energy Commission (AEC) established a nuclear weapons test facility in Nevada, as a result of U.S. reaction to the Soviet breaking of our atomic monopoly in 1949. AEC officials knew that the Nevada tests would release radioactive debris into the atmosphere, and that some of it would return to earth in Utah and other states. The chances of such localized fallout would be greatest when powerful weapons were detonated close to the ground.

People who lived downwind of the test site reacted to the unsensed radiation with a fear that combined the dread of cancer and the mystery of radiation, symbolized by Hiroshima. This fear intensified when cases of childhood leukemia were reported in downwind communities—alleged by some people to be a result of the radioactive fallout. Many years later two dozen plaintiffs were picked for a bellwether trial in the U.S. District Court in Utah. Judge Bruce S. Jenkins, in *Allen* v. *United States*[1] addressed the issue of radiation causation of cancers linked to fallout. He applied a seven-point test that had been developed by Dr. David Gooden:[2]

1. Determine the level of the plaintiff's exposure to fallout radiation and find for the defendant if this level did not exceed applicable standards.
2. Determine the specific injury alleged and find for the defendant if this is not associated with fallout exposure.
3. Determine when the radiation exposure occurred and find for the defendant if the time from exposure to diagnosis of the malignancy was less than the latency period known to exist for radiation-induced cancers.

4. Require expert testimony on the number of radiation-induced cancers or leukemias that would be expected in a large population exposed to fallout in Utah.

5. Require expert testimony on the malignancies expected in such a population without this radiation exposure.

6. Find for the defendant if it is more likely than not that the probability that any plaintiff's malignancy was caused by radiation is less than that for a natural cause.

7. Find for the plaintiff if the probability for radiation-induced cancer is greater than that for natural causation, including exposure to other carcinogens.

The *Allen* trial began August 30, 1979, and lasted 13 weeks. It featured testimony by 98 witnesses and included submission of 1,692 exhibits. The court clearly faced some monumental problems. Cause and effect are easy to relate when a passenger's head is fractured on hitting a windshield in an automobile accident. They are much harder to relate for more subtle injury, such as radiation-induced cancer. In addition, the unfamiliar science of ionizing radiation challenged judicial comprehension. Experts disagreed on matters of fact (the exposure of the plaintiffs) and on basic scientific questions, such as the relationship between the exposure and the risk of cancer.

The court applied itself assiduously to mastering the technicalities of radiation exposure. Over 100 pages of the *Allen* decision are devoted to the rudiments of radiation physics. On May 10, 1984, Judge Jenkins handed down his decision: he ruled out the claims of 15 plaintiffs but awarded a total of $2.66 million to 9 plaintiffs. Five of the successful plaintiffs did not demonstrate probabilities of causation defined in Point 7 above. The court cited Prosser:[3] "If the risk is an appreciable one, and the possible consequences are serious, the question is not one of mathematical probability alone."

In *Allen* and several score of other cases, two experts, Dr. John W. Gofman and Dr. Karl Z. Morgan, appeared as expert witnesses for the plaintiffs. The high radiation risks they claimed and their unrestrained language were widely publicized by the media and helped to fuel public concern.[4]

The public then (and now) clearly viewed radiation as very hazardous, without distinguishing among the different risks that are associated with different levels of exposure. Some facts help to put the issue in a fairer perspective.

High doses of radiation can be immediately lethal, as tragically demonstrated at Hiroshima. Some of the survivors of the atom bomb showed an excess of cancer that was clearly linked to radiation exposure. But these exposures were far above those associated with fallout from weapons testing.

To better define the risk, we need some quantitative relationship between radiation dose and response, and some way to measure the dose that a person receives. To assess claims of radiation-induced cancer, we need to know the natural incidence of cancer and to estimate the probabilities of causation.

One of the first units of radiation exposure was the roentgen, named for Professor W. K. Roentgen (1845–1923), who discovered X-rays in 1895. Today scientists use the *rad* and the *rem* (roentgen-equivalent-man) to quantify radiation dose. The former describes the amount of absorbed energy in the body; the latter is equal to the rem with a further correction for factors, such as the distribution of dose and quality of radiation, that affect the biological effectiveness of the exposure. We use the rad in the discussion below.

Everybody is exposed to radiation from various natural and man-made sources. The greatest exposure to an average person comes from traces of uranium, thorium, and other radioactive elements in the earth, and their decay products (e.g., radon). Cosmic radiation from the sun and outer space is another natural source. Together, they result in an annual radiation dose of about 0.3 rad, or about 21 rads over the course of an average person's lifetime (National Council on Radiation Protection 1987). In addition, the average American receives 4 rads from medical X-rays. Far smaller contributions come from traces of radioactive materials in tobacco smoke and some consumer products. This exposure, of course, occurs gradually over the course of a person's lifetime.

The rate of exposure is another important variable. For example, in mice a single 300 rad dose produces leukemia. But exposure of mice to 300 rads at a rate of 6 rads per week produces no observable increase in leukemia (Bond 1989).

As another example, an exposure to humans of 400 or more rads, if given over a short period, will cause death in half of those so irradiated; the same exposure would probably not cause immediate death if it occurred over a period of many days but it may increase the risk for leukemia and other cancers later in life. Radiogenic (radiation-induced) cancers typically develop after a latency period of 20 years or more, although leukemia has a latency period of only about five years.

One source of data on health effects of radiation is the survivors of the atomic bombs at Hiroshima and Nagasaki. Beginning in 1950, a joint U.S.-Japanese program began to gather data on mortality among the Japanese bomb survivors, in what became the Radiation Effects Research Foundation (RERF). Researchers identified a study population of 75,991 persons who had received a collective dose of 1.2 million person-rads.

The average radiation dose was about 16 rads per person; more than 3,000 individuals had received more than 100 rads.

Statistical analysis of the death records of these people showed no excess mortality except for cancer, most significantly leukemia. From 1945 through 1985, investigators identified a total of 202 leukemia and 5,734 nonleukemic cancer deaths among the bomb survivors. To deduce the number of these deaths that could be attributed to the radiation exposure, the researchers compared the cancer mortality rates of the bomb survivors with those of people who were in Hiroshima and Nagasaki at the time of the bombing but sufficiently far from the bomb site to have received a negligible radiation dose. From this comparison, the investigators estimated that radiation accounted for 79 fatal leukemias (of the total of 202) and 254 other cancer deaths (of the total of 5,734) (Shimizu et al. 1989).

Another estimate of the cancer risk to the Japanese bomb survivors was presented in the fifth report of the Biological Effects of Ionizing Radiation Committee (BEIR) of the National Research Council (1989). These estimates were higher than those presented in its earlier report (BEIR 1980), a result of revised dose estimates, higher age-specific mortality and the choice of a new model for cancer risk.

Another source of human exposure is radium-based paint applied to watch dials early in the century (Rowland and Lucas 1984; Stebbings et al. 1984; Maitland et al. 1925). A long-term medical follow-up of workers who applied such paint by Stebbings and colleagues (1984) disclosed ten cases of leukemia, of which four were a form of leukemia (chronic lymphocytic leukemia) that is not associated with radiation exposure. This finding of ten leukemias is what would be expected for an unexposed population, indicating no detectable increase in leukemia risk.

However, radium workers do have a higher incidence of other kinds of cancer. Young women who worked in the radium industry during World War I used their lips to tip camel's hair brushes when applying luminous paint to dials, and in the process swallowed large amounts of radium. This passed into the bloodstream and found its way into the skeletal bone. During the 1920s some dial workers developed bone sarcomas or cancers of the jaw and skeleton. These tragic consequences jolted the scientific community into formulating a safety standard.

The question addressed by scientists was "How much radium can be allowed to reside in the human body without undue risk?" Dr. Robley Evans of the Massachusetts Institute of Technology developed techniques for measuring the radium body burdens in radium dial workers.

Based upon analysis of the number of radium workers who developed bone cancer, he proposed a maximum permissible body burden (MPBB) for radium. For Evans, a "safe" MPBB was the amount of retained radium that he would think safe if his wife or daughter were to have such a burden (Evans 1981).

The radium issue bears on the question of risks from long-term exposure to low-level radiation. Extensive long-term data on the dial workers disclose virtually no health effects in the workers, even those with body burdens of radium that greatly exceeded the MPBB. Some women accumulated bone doses of more than 1,000 rads without showing symptoms of radium poisoning. (In his paper Dr. Evans described one of his patients who had been a dial painter and died at age 93. The woman had an estimated skeletal dose of about 10,000 rads, yet a postmortem examination disclosed no symptom of radium poisoning.)

Additional evidence comes from cases in which people were deliberately irradiated for medical reasons. In Great Britain and Northern Ireland from 1935 until 1954, patients afflicted with ankylosing spondylitis, a crippling disease of the spine, were given X-ray therapy at 87 treatment centers. Systematic follow-up of 14,111 of these patients, who had received an average bone marrow dose of 330 rads, showed 31 leukemia deaths where only 6.5 would be expected (Smith and Doll 1982). Multiplying 14,111 by 330 yields 4.6 million person-rads or about 20,000 person-rads per excess leukemia mortality.

There are, however, great uncertainties in trying to extrapolate the data from the Japanese bomb survivors (and other people who sustained high levels of exposure) to people exposed to much lower levels of radiation. The BEIR estimates applied to a single, instantaneous flash of radiation from the atomic bomb, as opposed to a dose delivered over a period of years. Too few data were available from Japanese bomb survivors who received less than 50 rads exposure to calculate their cancer risk and the risks from low doses of radiation must be obtained by extrapolation.

Such extrapolation, however, requires the assumption of a dose-response function relating the cancer risk to the exposure. One approach (which most scientists regard as conservative) is the linear hypothesis which holds that the increase in risk is proportional to the dose.

With this assumption, we can predict that the exposure of a large number of people to radiation will result in 1 cancer death per 5,000 person-rads (National Council on Radiation Protection 1987). Thus, if a hypothetical group of 5,000 people receives a total exposure of 5,000 rads, we would expect 1 additional cancer death over the lifetimes of these people. Roughly 1,000 of these people will eventually die of cancer having unrelated causes. Assuming an average exposure of 0.3 rads per person each year, this would lead to 15,000 cancer deaths per year due to natural radiation background, or 3 percent of America's annual cancer death toll (National Council on Radiation Protection 1987).

These deaths, however, are statistical predictions only. There is no way to distinguish radiation-induced cancers from other neoplasms or measure their rates directly. Even if by some unimagined process we could divide the U.S. population into two groups—of people exposed and not exposed to natural background radiation—an impossibly large number of subjects would be required to enable an investigator to detect a 3 percent increase in the cancer rate. Dr. Charles E. Land, health statistician with the National Cancer Institute, provided this illustration (Land 1980):

For example, if the excess risk is proportional to dose and if a sample of 1,000 persons is necessary to determine the effect of a 100 rad exposure, a sample of 100,000 may be needed for a 10-rad exposure and about 10 million for 1 rad.

In their statistical analysis of the Japanese atomic bomb survivors, the investigators *could* separate people into "exposed" and "control" groups. These studies could not detect an increase in cancer risk in people who had received less than 50 rads exposure.

Thus, one can estimate the risk from low doses of radiation only on the basis of data from highly exposed individuals. Such estimates are necessarily based on untestable assumptions and cannot be directly verified by epidemiologic studies; they must be regarded more as opinion than fact. Our conservative assumption is that any dose of radiation causes *some* effect, although it may be too small to be detectable in a human population. Laymen often misinterpret this as implying that even a tiny dose causes a significant number of cancers. More precisely stated, near-zero doses may cause near-zero effects.

There may, in fact, be *no* excess cancers induced by low-level exposure. Some scientists argue that small doses of ionizing radiation may actually be beneficial by stimulating a positive response in an organism (Luckey 1980, 1989). This postulated effect, called radiation hormesis (the Greek *hormo* means "I excite") is similar to a hormesis effect that is known to occur in medical administration of chemicals and hormones. It is, however, difficult to prove by studies on human populations.

If one assumes a linear relationship between radiation dose and cancer risk, it is difficult to specify any dose as "safe," since any exposure, no matter how small, causes some theoretical increase in risk. However, workers in some industries necessarily face exposure to some radiation, and practical exposure standards are required. The U.S. Nuclear Regulatory Commission (NRC) has set a maximum exposure for a worker of 5 rads per year, with a lifetime dose of 235 rads. (The NRC standards do not specify a lifetime limit for occupational exposure; but the NRC limits correspond to a total of 235 rads for a working career that extends from age 18 to age 65.) For the general population the annual limit is 0.5 rad. These limits do not guarantee that exposure below these limits has no risk but, rather, that the calculated risk is negligible compared with other risks a person faces in everyday life or on the job.

It is useful to compare these figures with the exposures that many workers actually face on the job. The nuclear industry in the United States and elsewhere maintains extensive records of employees' exposure. In the 100 nuclear power plants operated by the American utility industry, the average lifetime exposure during the 1970s and 1980s of 600,000 workers was approximately 1 rad (Lapp 1989).

Workers in other industries also face some radiation exposure that is not subject to federal regulation. For example, airline crews are exposed to cosmic radiation, which is more intense at high altitudes. A pilot flying between New York and Minneapolis in the course of a year will accumulate 0.4 rad (Lapp 1989; Busick 1989). Over a 20-year career this pilot might receive a total dose of 8 rad from cosmic radiation.

Medical X-rays are another significant source of exposure. Each year over 4 million Americans receive a spinal/lumbar X-ray examination that delivers 0.4 rad. This is not a full-body exposure, to be sure, but it does involve irradiation of vital organs. These procedures are voluntarily undertaken,[5] and their possible risks are offset by the benefit of medical diagnosis; the same cannot be said for involuntary exposure to radiation from natural sources or fallout.

Some politicians have attempted to resolve these issues by fiat. Utah's Senator Orrin Hatch championed compensation for his constituents who lived downwind from the nuclear test site. He asked the National Institutes of Health (NIH) to prepare a set of tables listing the probability that a given radiation exposure had caused a specific cancer.

Senator Hatch had requested tables that covered exposures between 0.001 and 1,000 rads. However, NIH scientists balked at calculating cancer risk below 1 rad; they also identified some cancers (such as chronic lymphocytic leukemia) as nonradiogenic, that is, not caused by radiation. They eventually produced a 355-page document, the Radioepidemiological Tables, in 1985. The Tables provided a basis for calculating the probability that an observed cancer was caused by a radiation dose to the appropriate organ. These Tables do *not predict* the likelihood that an exposed person will develop a cancer but, rather the probability that a person who has already developed a malignancy had it arise as a result of radiation exposure.

It is instructive to consider how the Tables are meant to be used. If a person does not have any characteristic (such as smoking or heavy exposure to sunlight) that obviously increases cancer risk, the formula in the Table is

$$p = R_r/(R_n + R_r)$$

where p = probability that the cancer was caused by the
            radiation dose D (i.e., the probability of causation)
      R_r = risk of cancer due to
            a radiation dose D
      R_n = natural cancer risk.

The value of the term R_r depends on a person's age at the time of exposure and at the time of the cancer diagnosis, the type of cancer, and the person's sex. To illustrate the use of the Tables, we calculate the following probabilities for a man who had received a dose of 50 rads at age 30 and was diagnosed with cancer at age 50:

Cancer	Probability of Causation (%)
Liver	8.4
Stomach	2.8
Pancreas	1.9
Esophagus	0.8
Colon	0.8
Lung	0.6

Thus, if the person had been diagnosed with liver cancer, the table indicates an 8.4 percent probability that it was caused by the radiation; if the person had developed lung cancer, the probability is smaller (0.6 percent) but still non-zero. Needless to say, the radiation dose to this hypothetical individual was far greater radiation than any received by Utah residents from fallout from the weapons testing.

If one accepts the linear model (as have most courts), the major point of contention is shifted to the exposure that a plaintiff actually received. In court, different expert witnesses have presented juries with sharply different estimates of dose. In *Allen,* the plaintiffs' witness, Dr. J. W. Gofman, arrived at probabilities of causation that exceeded 50 percent for some downwind residents. These figures were based on very high estimates of dose, and a dose–response relationship that led to cancer risks a factor of 37 higher than those derived from the Japanese bomb victims. Dr. Gofman presented no direct evidence for his estimates of Utahans' exposure but relied upon data from an amateur epidemiologist, Dr. Carl Johnson. Dr. Gofman inferred an average organ dose of 25.6 rads for 24 cases, whereas estimates by government experts and other scientists averaged less than 1 rad (Schleien 1981; Beck and Krey 1983).

Even sharper disagreements between plaintiffs' and defendants' witnesses were apparent in *Johnston v. United States.*[6] Dr. K. Z. Morgan (witness for the plaintiffs) and Dr. C. J. Maletskos (for the defendants) presented the estimates shown below.

		Dose (rad)	
Case	Organ	Morgan	Maletskos
A.	Bone Marrow	37,712	0.06
B.	Colon	29,756	0.16
C.	Thyroid	412	3.2
D.	Lung	3,718	.49

Judge Patrick Kelly confronted an almost millionfold difference in estimates in Case A. He asked the Department of Justice and the plaintiffs to prepare a proposed findings of fact and conclusions of law. The Justice Department, in its 161-page document, analyzed other trials in which Dr. Morgan had appeared as expert witness, always for the plaintiffs, and critically analyzed the factual basis for his testimony. Regarding the two estimates of dose, the department concluded: "It [the court] cannot believe both and it cannot compromise such a vast difference. One expert must be right and one expert must be absolutely wrong." The judge recognized the validity of the estimates by the witnesses for the defense, and threw out Dr. Morgan's testimony.

Epidemiologic studies on the Utah residents have disclosed no increase in cancer risk that might be attributable to fallout. Health survey data in Utah do not indicate an association between childhood leukemia and residence downwind from the test site. However, the calculations are very uncertain because of the small numbers of cases involved. In the interior of southern Utah, for example, only 26 childhood leukemia deaths occurred from 1950 to 1978—an average of about 1 per year. This small number of cases imperils any conclusions about possible correlations between fallout exposure and childhood leukemia.

A number of scientists have estimated the collective exposure to residents in the fallout area during the eight years of atmospheric testing.

These assessments have been improved by using sophisticated instruments to measure the trace amounts of radioactive cesium remaining in the earth's surface from the fallout (Romney et al. 1983). They indicate a collective dose of 40,000 person-rads for Utahans living in the regions of measured fallout radioactivity. This corresponds to an average of 0.3 rads per person for an exposed population of 156,756 people. The most heavily exposed residents received an estimated radiation dose of 1 rad.

This low exposure should make one cautious when assessing claims of any radiation-induced cancer deaths in Utah. During the period 1950 to 1978, an average Utah resident received an estimated 8 rads from natural background radiation—which is 25 times higher than his or her average dose from the fallout. It would be futile to try to detect any excess in cancer deaths from such exposures.

The plaintiffs' witness Dr. Carl J. Johnson identified a group of Mormons living in Washington and other southwestern Utah counties who in 1981 recalled having "skin burns, eye burns, hair loss, change in hair coloration, nausea and diarrhea" at the time of the tests—characteristic symptoms of acute effects of high doses of radiation. Among these people, Johnson reported a 4,500 percent increase in leukemia and a 500 percent increase in all nonleukemic malignancies. Such symptoms are characteristic of far higher doses of radiation—100 rads or more—than measured for the population. Johnson's survey is questionable; perhaps he had selected individuals who had such problems regardless of radiation exposure.

Johnson's article "Cancer Incidence in an Area of Radioactive Fallout Downwind from the Nevada Test Site" (1984) raised a potentially serious public health issue. The National Cancer Institute (NCI) undertook an exhaustive epidemiologic study of the three southwestern Utah counties—Washington, Iron, and Kane—whose residents were most heavily exposed to test fallout (Machado et al. 1987). For Mormons living in these three counties, the study reported a relative cancer risk of 0.91 (slightly below that for all Mormons in the state) rather than the 1.61 as reported by Johnson.

The NCI investigators estimated the radiation dose to these residents as ranging from 0.01 to 2.7 rads, and indicated that this exposure was too small to produce a detectable increase in cancer. For example, in Washington County the collective fallout dose was 12,000 person-rads, which would be expected to have led to 2 excess cancer deaths in the NIH survey. But from the onset of testing to the time of the study, more than 500 cancer deaths had occurred in Washington County.

Apart from fallout, other sources of low-level radiation also led to controversy. Several uranium mills were located in southeastern Utah, including one near Monticello, a town of 2,000 close to the Idaho border. Over its operating life, the Monticello mill produced 903,000 tons of uranium tailings that were heaped up in piles at four sites. After the mill was closed in 1960, one to two feet of rock and soil was placed over the tailings and planted with vegetation to minimize erosion (U.S. Atomic Energy Commission 1963).

In 1980 seven plaintiffs filed a wrongful death action[7] in the U.S. District Court (Utah) alleging that the deaths were caused by radiation from the inactive Monticello Mill (Lapp 1979). One of the plaintiffs, a Monticello schoolteacher, recalled that as a boy he had played on the tailings pile and had drunk water from a small stream running through the mill site. Dr. K. Z. Morgan, the expert witness for the plaintiffs, presented estimates of radiation exposure to the plaintiffs that disagreed sharply with those of the defendants.

In this case the Department of Justice used scientific tests to establish the probable radiation dose to the plaintiffs. Scientists at the University of Utah removed small samples of brick from houses of the plaintiffs and measured their radioactivity. They showed that there was no difference between radiation exposures in the homes of the plaintiffs and other houses in the area.

The experts then estimated the schoolteacher's "playtime exposure" on the tailings piles by placing a human model on an uncovered tailings pile where the radiation was more intense than that atop the Monticello site. The model was equipped with numerous thermoluminescent dosimeters that recorded a maximum of 0.3 rad over an amount of time comparable with that spent by the plaintiff as a child playing on the tailings.

There remained the question of the internal dose from the plaintiff's ingestion of contaminated water or food. Here again scientific tests could provide objective estimates of exposure. Consultants used a whole-body counter, an elaborate instrument that measures the radiation emitted from the body by traces of any radioactive material it might contain. The tests disclosed no excess radioactivity in the teacher's body.

In the trial, radium experts such as Dr. Charles W. Mays of the University of Utah testified about the risk incurred by the Monticello teacher from his exposure to radium in the tailings. Dr. Mays deduced that radium taken in by the teacher produced no more than 0.005 rad dose to his bone marrow, far below the level needed to significantly increase the risk of cancer. On September 18, 1988, the Monticello lawsuits were voluntarily dismissed by the plaintiffs, in the face of overpowering evidence adduced by the defense.

Diverse other claims have been presented for health hazards from low-level radiation, in some cases by scientists. Dr. Thomas Najarian, a hematologist at Boston's Veterans Administration (VA) hospital, had a patient with hairy cell leukemia. The patient, a worker at the Portsmouth Naval Shipyard in Kittery, Maine, told Najarian that many other workers at the shipyard had died early of cancer. With the support of the *Boston Globe's* team of investigative reporters, Najarian surveyed 1,450 death certificates of persons believed to have worked at the shipyard. By contacting the next of kin who could be located, the team identified nuclear workers as having been "badged" (they had worn film badges at work).

Early in 1978 the *Boston Globe* ran a front-page story on a leukemia "epidemic" at the Portsmouth facility. Dr. Najarian reported (in an article in the British medical journal *The Lancet*) that in a group of workers in which only one leukemia death would be expected, he had found six (Najarian and Colton 1978). In response to the publicity surrounding the study, the U.S. Congress held a full-day hearing to investigate the report. Subsequently, the government authorized a study of all white males who had ever worked at the shipyard.

This year-long study surveyed 24,545 men, of whom 7,615 had received 2 rads of lifetime exposure at the naval facility (a figure obtained from the records of radiation exposure maintained by the U.S. Navy). These "exposed" workers had slightly fewer leukemia deaths than the workers at the shipyard who had received no exposure (Rinsky et al. 1981).

In another case, Dr. James E. Enstrom of UCLA's School of Public Health investigated the mortality of people living near the San Onofre nuclear power plant just north of San Diego, in response to claims of an excess of childhood leukemia deaths in the area. Enstrom's analysis showed no correlation of leukemia deaths in children in the area with radiation exposure from the plant (Enstrom 1983).

In addition to the tort litigation discussed above, many veterans have filed claims with the VA seeking compensation for cancers they believe were caused by radiation from the Nevada tests. Some of these veterans, in fact, may have received significant exposure. In some of the 199 tests that took place between January 1951 and July 1962, troops conducted postdetonation maneuvers near the test site to learn about the perils of nuclear warfare (Christoffel and Swartzman 1986).

In one of these tests, Operation Smoky, almost 4,000 soldiers participated. One participant, Army Sergeant Paul L. Cooper, recalled the test as a harrowing experience. As described in an AMVETS publication, he and 163 other soldiers witnessed the explosion (which had twice the power of that at Hiroshima) from a distance of 3,000 yards; then (to simulate maneuvers in actual combat) advanced to within 100 to 200 yards of ground zero. Nearly 20 years later, Sergeant Cooper presented at a VA hospital and was diagnosed as having leukemia.

Prompted by Cooper's congressman, the Defense Department tracked down radiation exposure records for servicemen who had participated in the tests. The Disabled American Veterans (DAV) urged the VA to compensate Cooper for his leukemia. The DAV viewed this case as a landmark, and it did succeed in getting Cooper a service-connected grant. However, the investigation by the Defense Department failed to establish a link between leukemia and veterans' exposure to the radiation from these tests.

By 1982 the VA had reviewed 1,982 cases alleging cancer linkage to radiation but had made only 20 awards, some to people who had received less than 1 rad. Pressure for granting more awards built up on Capitol Hill, and in 1983 Congress held hearings on the matter. Senator Dennis DeConcini from Arizona observed: ". . . of 3,224 veterans involved in a 1957 weapons test explosion there is an incidence of leukemia which is nearly three times higher than normal. Clearly, evidence such as this cannot be ignored." The senator was citing a report by the Centers for Disease Control on leukemia observed among the Operation Smoky veterans. The CDC investigators found 9 leukemia cases among the veterans; the expected incidence was 3.5 cases. However, the leukemia victims had received less radiation exposure from the Smoky test (0.9 rad on the average) than other Smoky veterans (1.1 rads) who had not developed the disease.

Congress then ordered the National Cancer Institute to develop the Radioepidemiological Tables and requested the congressional research arm, the Office of Technology Assessment, to investigate the issue. The highly publicized claims of excess leukemia among Smoky survivors led to an epidemiologic study by the Medical Follow-up Agency of the National Research Council. In this study, the mortality records of 46,186 participants in the bomb tests showed fewer cancer deaths than expected (Robinette et al. 1985). A study of 3,554 Smoky veterans showed "no evidence that the proportion of leukemia deaths in Smoky was significantly different from those in the other tests."

Meanwhile, a federal government task force called the Committee on Interagency Radiation Research and Policy Coordination (CIRRPC) reviewed the evidence and concluded that even in a group as large as all men exposed at the tests (222,000), there would be no chance of detecting a significant increase in radiation-related disease. This was confirmed by a sophisticated analysis prepared in 1985 by the Office of Technology Assessment.

With the issuance of the NIH Radioepidemiological Tables in 1985, the VA could evaluate the merit of some 6,000 radiation claims that had been filed. The problem remained to separate the few cases likely to have resulted from radiation exposure from the many other cancer cases that would develop among the veterans. By law the VA was to give the claimant the benefit of the doubt in making awards, so that the "more probable than not" criterion would not apply. But given the low radiation doses to the soldiers, even cases with a "probability of causation" of 10 percent would be infrequent. For criteria with which to identify valid claims, the VA had looked to CIRRPC for guidance. However, the draft CIRRPC report, "Use of Probability of Causation in the Adjudication of Claims by the Veterans Administration," was slow in moving through government circles.

Meanwhile, Congress debated bills to provide atomic test veterans with compensation for cancer claims. In the summer of 1988 it passed the Atomic Veterans Compensation Act and President Reagan signed it. Presumption of service connection (38 U.S.C. § 312) was amended to permit compensation for any veteran who could demonstrate service at a test site during the period of the weapons tests, and who later developed a 10 percent disability from any of 13 cancers, including thyroid, pharynx, breast, esophagus, stomach, small intestine, colon, pancreas, and bronchogenic carcinoma. The act allowed compensation for leukemias other than chronic lymphocytic leukemia and for certain liver cancers; it disallowed compensation for skin cancer, lung cancer, and certain liver cancers. Thus, Congress did not require a veteran to demonstrate radiation exposure to receive compensation for service-related injury. When I discussed this with Senate staffers, they agreed with my assessment of the comparatively high doses required for radiation exposure to account plausibly for a patient's cancer. They responded, "You're talking science; we're talking politics."

Ironically, the CIRRPC report appeared just as the radiation bill became law. The report noted that for exposures of 1 rad, the probability that a cancer diagnosed in a serviceman was caused by radiation was less than 1 percent. The report provided tables to allow the VA to screen cases for merit, and gave examples of how to use the screening data.

One example illustrates the use of the tables:

Example 2: A male claimant received a dose of 1.2 rad at age 25 and developed cancer of the stomach at age 50. The screening dose for stomach cancer is 10.8 rad for exposure at age 20 and 21.2 rad for exposure at age 30. The claimant's dose does not exceed 16 rad, the average of these values, and thus his claim is not given further consideration. In this case, the calculated PC [probability of causation] from the NIH Report is 0.46 percent. A dose of 126.3 rad is to yield a PC of 50 percent based only on the NIH Report. (U.S. Congress 1985)

A year after Congress passed the Atomic Veterans Compensation Act, some 220 veterans won their cases with the VA. Only the traditional slowness of the VA kept the number of awards so small. Whereas the judges had made their decisions based on science, the congressmen reacted politically in awarding claims, few of which could be justified by scientific arguments.

Overview

The issue of health effects from radioactive fallout—and other sources of low-level radiation—has been emotional and contentious. To some extent, this has been fueled by exaggerated claims by some scientists serving as expert witnesses for plaintiffs in lawsuits.

But even if exaggerated claims of radiation injury are refuted in court, and even if responsible scientists provide reasonable estimates of risks from low-level radiation, there remains the difficulty of informing the public. As Thoreau (1817–1862) put it: "It takes two to speak the truth—one to speak, and another to hear" (1849). The emotional nature of the issue and sensationalistic media coverage are barriers to accurate communication of radiation risk to the public. It is comforting to know that at least some courts have maintained a rational approach to radiation risk.

Notes

1. *Allen v. United States,* 588 F. Supp. 247 (D. Utah 1984), *rev'd,* 816 F.2d 1417 (10th Cir. 1987).

2. D. Gooden. 1989. Radiation injury and the law, *B.Y.U. Rev.* This is an excellent overview of the scientific and legal issues at stake in radiation litigation.

3. W. L. Prosser, *Handbook of the Law and Torts* (West, 1971).

4. See E. Klema, A. Shihab-Eldin, and R. Wilson. 1989. Some claims of unusually large effects of radiation (Harvard University) This is an excellent critique of var-

ious claims made by Dr. John Gofman and others. It is available from the office of Dr. Richard Wilson, Department of Physics, Harvard University, Cambridge, Mass. 02138.

5. Many x-rays, however, are taken as part of a required preemployment medical examination and their "voluntary" nature might be questioned.

6. *Johnston* v. *United States,* 597 F. Supp. 377 (D.C. Kan. 1984).

7. *Timothy* v. *United States,* 612 F. Supp. 160 (D. Utah C.D. 1985).

References

Baker, D. A. 1988. *Population dose commitments due to radioactive releases from nuclear power plant sites in 1984.* 6 NUREG/CR-2860. Washington, DC:

Beck, H. L., and P. W. Krey. 1983. Radiation exposures in Utah from Nevada nuclear tests. *220 Science* 18–24.

Bond, V. 1989. Justifications for the adoption of a "below regulatory concern" exposure level. 17 *Health Phys. Soc. Newsletter* 4.

Busick, D. D. 1989. Should airline crews be monitored for radiation exposure? Paper presented at Health Physics Society Annual Meeting.

Caldwell, G. G., C. W. Heath, and D. B. Kelley. 1980. Leukemia among participants in military maneuvers at a nuclear bomb test—a preliminary report. 244 *J. Am. Med. Assn.* 1575–1578.

Christoffel, T., and D. Swartzman. 1986. Nuclear weapons testing fallout—proving causation for exposure injury. 76 *Am. J. Pub. Health* 290–292.

Committee on Interagency Radiation Research and Policy Coordination. 1988. *Use of probability of causation by the veterans administration in the adjudication of claims of injury due to exposure to ionizing radiation.* Science Panel Report no. 6. Washington, DC:

Congressional record. 1983. May, S.5987. Daily ed.

Enstrom, J. E. 1983. Cancer mortality patterns around the San Onofre nuclear power plant, 1960–1978. 73 *Am. J. Public Health* 83–92.

Enstrom, J. E. 1980. *The nonassociation of fallout radiation with childhood leukemia in Utah.* Cold Spring Harbor, NY: Cold Spring Harbor Laboratory.

Evans, R. D. 1974. Radium in man. 27 *Health Phys.* 497–510.

Evans, R. D. 1981. Inception of standards for internal emitters, Radon and Radium. 41 *Health Phys.* 437–448.

Gofman, J. W. 1987. *Accident at Chernobyl—One year later: How to kill a half-million people, but "smell like a rose."* Committee for Nuclear Responsibility.

Hull, A. P. 1988. *Cancer clusters attract attention.* 16 *Health Phys. Soc. Newsletter* 4.

Johnson, E. S., E. Diamond, H. R. Fischman, and G. M. Matanoski. 1986. Occurrence of cancer in women in the meat industry. 43 *Br. J. Ind. Med.* 597–604.

Johnson, C. J. 1984. Cancer incidence in an area of radioactive fallout downwind from the Nevada test site. 251 *J. Am. Med. Assn.* 230–236.

Johnson, R. H. 1989. *The Maughan uranium mill tailings*. Schmeltzer, Aptaker & Sheppard.

Land, C. E. 1980. Estimating cancer risks from low doses of ionizing radiation. 209 *Science* 1197–1203.

Lapp, R. E. 1979. *Radiation controversy* 31. Greenwich, CT: Reddy Communications.

Lapp, R. E. 1989a. Cancer, courts and radiation. Paper presented at the International Conference on Criminal Justice and the Protection of the Environment, Hamburg, Germany.

Lapp, R. E. 1989b. *Radiation Exposure of Air Carrier Crewmembers*. Federal Aviation Administration, Advisory Circular AAM-624.

Lapp, R. E. 1989c. Radiation exposure and cancer mortality. Paper presented at the Annual Health Physics Conference, Edison Electric Institute. Clearwater, FL.

Luckey, T. D. 1980. *Hormesis with ionizing radiation*. Boca Raton, FL: CRC Press.

Luckey, T. D. 1989. Hormesis for health physicists. 17 *Health Phys. Soc. Newsletter* 9.

Machado, S. G., C. E. Land, and F. W. McKay. 1987. Cancer mortality and radioactive fallout in southwestern Utah. 125 *Am. J. Epidemiol.* 44–61.

Martland, H. S., P. Conlon and J. P. Knef. 1925. Some unrecognized dangers in the use and handling of radioactive substances. 85 *J. Am. Med. Assn.* 1769–1776.

Najarian, T., and T. Colton. 1978. Mortality from leukemia and cancer in shipyard nuclear workers. 1 *The Lancet* 1018–1020.

National Council on Radiation Protection. 1979. *Ionizing radiation exposure of the population of the United States*, Table 2.4. National Council on Radiation Protection Report no. 93.

National Council on Radiation Protection. 1987. *The use of thermoluminescence*. Paper presented at Proceedings of 23rd Meeting of National Council on Radiation Protection.

National Council on Radiation Protection. 1988. *Exposure of the population in the United States and Canada from natural background radiation*. National Council on Radiation Protection Report no. 94.

National Institutes of Health. 1985. *Report of the National Institute of Health Ad Hoc Working Group to Develop Radioepidemiological Tables*. NIH Publication no. 85-2748.

Prosser, W. L. 1971. "Handbook of the Law and Torts." St. Paul, MN: West.

Rinsky, R. A., et al. 1981. Cancer mortality at a naval shipyard. I *The Lancet* 231–235.

Rinsky, R. A., J. Melinus, and R. Hornung. 1981. *Epidemiologic study of civilian employees at the Portsmouth Naval Shipyard*. Washington, DC: NIOSH.

Robinette, C. D., S. Jablon and T. L. Preston. 1985. *Mortality of nuclear weapons test participants*. Medical Follow-Up Agency, National Research Council.

Romney, E. M., et al. 1983. ^{90}Sr and ^{137}Cs in soil and biota of fallout areas in southern Nevada and Utah. 45 *Health Phys.* 643–650.

Rowland, R. E., and H. F. Lucas. 1984. *Radium-dial painters*. In J. D. Boice and J. F. Fraumeni, Jr., eds., *Radiation carcinogenesis*. New York: Raven Press.

Shleien, B. 1981. External radiation exposure to the offsite population from nuclear tests at the Nevada test site between 1951 and 1970. 41 *Health Phys.* 243–254.

Shimizu, Y., et al. 1989a. *Cancer mortality in the years 1950–1985 based on recently revised doses (DS86)*. 9 *Mortality* Radiation Effects Research Foundation, Life Span Report no. 11, pt. 2.

Shimizu, Y., et al. 1989b. Studies of the mortality of A-bomb survivors 1950–1985. 1. Comparison of risk coefficents for site-specific cancer mortality based on the DS-86 and T65DR shielded kerma and organ doses. 118 *Radiation Research* 502–524.

Smith, P. G., and R. Doll. 1982. Mortality among patients with ankylosing spondylitis after a single treatment course with X-rays. 284 *Br. Med. J.* 449–460.

Stebbings, J. H., et al. 1984. Mortality from cancers of major sites in females radium dial workers. 5 *Am. J. Indus. Med.* 435.

Thoreau, H. D. 1849. *A week on the Concord and Merrimack rivers*.

U.S Atomic Energy Commission, Grand Junction Operations Office. 1963. A report of the Monticello mill tailing erosion control project.

U.S. Office of Technology Assessment. 1985. An evaluation of the feasibility of studying long-term health effects in atomic veterans. Staff memo, Special Projects Office.

U.S. Atomic Energy Commission, Grand Junction Operations Office. 1982. A nuclear cloud still hangs over the lives of hundreds of thousands of veterans' families. *Disabled Am. Vets. Mag.* at 12 (January).

Yalow, R. S. 1988. Unwarranted fear about the effects of radiation leads to bad science policy. 2 *The Scientist* 11–12 (June 13).

Biographical Sketch

Ralph E. Lapp was born in Buffalo, New York in 1917. He received his Ph.D. in Physics from the University of Chicago in 1946. From 1943–1946 he worked on the Manhattan Project, and was division director and later assistant director of the Metallurgical Laboratory, which later became the Argonne National Laboratory.

Dr. Lapp is well known for his work on radiation protection. He is the author or coauthor of numerous articles on biological effects of ionizing radiation, and 22 books including *Radiological Safety, Nuclear Radiation Physics, The*

Radiation Controversy, and *The New Priesthood.* He has been an independent consultant since 1949 in the areas of reactor accidents, radiation risk assessment, and radiological health.

Dr. Lapp has made many contributions on the issue of nuclear weaopns fallout, including coauthorship of the book *Radiation* (1957) urging the reduction of public exposure to fallout. He testified before Congress on this issue, and served as advisor to the Democratic Advisory Committee.

14

The Saga of Fernald

Bernard L. Cohen

The public has a strong impression that anything radioactive is extremely dangerous—*radiation can cause cancer* is the dominant thought. This view is oversimplified because many materials are only weakly radioactive and therefore present a negligible hazard. For example, hydrogen and carbon, two of the three most important elements for life, and potassium, a major constituent of our bodies and of the food we eat, are radioactive, and no one claims that they are dangerous; in fact we couldn't live without large quantities of them.

Similar considerations apply to uranium, which undergoes radioactive decay so slowly that about half of the uranium on the Earth when it was first formed 4.5 billion years ago has still not gone through the radioactive decay process. We are fortunate that it is not dangerous because it is a rather common element, more abundant in nature than antimony, iodine, arsenic, germanium, mercury, silver, cadmium, bismuth, and many other elements. It is about one-third as abundant as tin, and one-sixth as abundant as lead. Its average concentration in rock and soil is 2.7 and 2.1 parts per million (ppm), respectively, but some large rock formations contain as much as 3 percent uranium, and some individual rocks contain close to 50 percent. People ingest an average of 1.3 micrograms (a microgram is one-millionth of a gram) per day with their food, and their bones contain about 60 micrograms. Uranium has been used commercially for centuries, especially in making glass and ceramics—an Italian glass produced in A.D. 79 was found to be 1 percent uranium. With all of this, there is no evidence that any person has ever been harmed by the radioactivity of uranium.

In fact, in most situations the principal hazard from uranium stems from its chemical properties rather than from its radioactivity. All heavy metals are toxic, as are many other chemicals. Government regulations require that the concentration of uranium in airborne dust in a workplace be kept below 250 micrograms per cubic meter of air. The maximum allowable concentrations for some other substances are lead–200, copper fumes–100, ozone–200, mercury–100, nicotine–500, tetraethyl lead (formerly used in gasoline)–75, phosphorus (used on match tips)–100, cobalt–100, cadmium–20, platinum–2. Clearly, from these comparisons, uranium is not an exceptionally hazardous material.

Nevertheless, in the situation we will describe, some critics pictured it as such, taking advantage of the popular conception that anything radioactive is extremely hazardous. The words "radioactive" and "radiation" were used everywhere in a media crusade that will cost the American public a great deal of money.

Fernald

In 1951 the U.S. Atomic Energy Commission, which was then managing the nation's military nuclear program, started construction of a feed materials production center near the village of Fernald, Ohio, 20 miles northwest of downtown Cincinnati. We will refer to it as the Fernald plant. Production started in 1953. It was operated on a cost-plus basis by National Lead of Ohio, a subsidiary of National Lead Industries (headquartered in New York) until 1985, and since 1986 has been operated by Westinghouse Materials Company of Ohio, a subsidiary of Westinghouse Electric.

The mission of Fernald has been to carry out several chemical process and foundry operations on uranium. The most important of these were recovery of uranium from recycled materials; converting uranium oxide (UO_3) to uranium tetrafluoride (UF_4); converting uranium hexafluoride (UF_6) to UF_4; converting UF_4 to uranium metal in various forms suitable for further processing; machining and heat-treating uranium metal; recycling scraps; and analyzing and testing various products and materials. Each of these operations is housed in a separate large building. These and other service and administration buildings cover 136 acres of the 1,050-acre site.

Essentially all of the work at Fernald has been in support of national defense operations; none of it served the nuclear power industry or other commercial applications. Its largest single purpose is to produce feed materials for government reactors used in production of plutonium, and it is the only facility available for this purpose. Its finished uranium metal products are sent to the Rocky Flats (Colorado), Oak Ridge (Tennessee), Savannah River (South Carolina) and Hanford (Washington) plants. The first two of these plants fabricate nuclear bombs, and the last two produce the nation's plutonium.

U.S. military nuclear programs use vast quantities of uranium. Little unclassified information is available on the amounts used for various applications, but a typical commercial nuclear power plant contains 100 tons of uranium, one-third of which is replaced every year. To indicate the magnitude of the operations, the Fernald sampling plant that receives most incoming material has a capacity for crushing, grinding, and blending 10 tons of material per hour, and the plant for converting UF_6 to UF_4 can handle 18 tons per day. The level of activity at Fernald waxed and waned over the years. Employment reached a peak of nearly 3,000 in 1956, but it gradually declined as weapons stockpiles leveled off, reaching a low of 536 in 1979. There was a substantial revival in our military program, and hence in Fernald activities, in 1981, and employment in recent years has been about 1,500.

Fernald was always operated with emphasis on production. Environmental safety and health (ES&H) programs were designed to satisfy legal regulations existing at the time and generally succeeded in doing so, but there was no effort to make ES&H programs exemplary, as was the case at some other government-owned facilities.

Chemical and foundry operations by their nature release large quantities of airborne dust, particularly when handling molten metal at high temperatures. The UO_3 to UF_4 process uses temperatures up to 1,100°F, the UF_6 to UF_4 process requires up to 1,200°, and molten uranium metal is heated to 2,700°. The boiling of uranium-containing solutions releases large quantities of fine droplets. All of these sources were filtered before release from the plant, but filtering systems often failed or were overwhelmed. The principal impact of Fernald on the environment has been due to releases of airborne dust containing uranium.

The amount of uranium that the plant was allowed to release to the environment was governed by the Department of Energy (DOE) requirement that the total annual radiation dose to a hypothetical "maximally exposed individual" be less than 500 millirem (mrem) whole-body equivalent and less than 1,500 mrem to the "critical organ," in this case the lung. For purposes of developing the regulation, the maximally exposed individual was assumed to spend all of his or her time outdoors at the location beyond the plant boundary where exposure is the highest, and to derive all food and water from the most contaminated off-site sources. Table 14.1 summarizes the exposures to this hypothetical individual, as reported by Fernald.

Events Following 1984 Failure

From September 11 to December 7, 1984, the filtering system at Fernald failed, and the plant released an estimated 124 kg (273 lbs) of uranium as

Table 14.1
Calculated dose to a hypothetical "maximally exposed" individual from Fernald plant releases, 1980–1984

Year	Whole body (mrem/year)	Lung (mrem/year)
1980	10	4
1981	9	8
1982	12	12
1983	10	32
1984	66	100

Note: Over this period, the maximum permissible dose was 500 mrem. The increase in dose in 1984 was a result of the accidental release.
Source: International Technology Corp. 1989.

airborne dust. This led to extensive media publicity and stimulated investigations by the U.S. General Accounting Office responding to a request from Senator John Glenn, the U.S. Environmental Protection Agency, and the Ohio Department of Health.

Here we review the findings of these studies. An important element in the problem was that during the 1970s, DOE was considering shutting down the plant and therefore did not make improvements, causing some of the equipment to become obsolescent. The sudden increase in demand in 1981 put a severe strain on the plant and its management. In June, 1984, a task force from Oak Ridge National Laboratories that was charged with overseeing the ES&H program at Fernald complained that there was too much emphasis on production and recommended more emphasis on ES&H.

Following the large releases in late 1984, the Oak Ridge task force recommended that the ES&H program "be scrutinized carefully and changed accordingly." In response, DOE started a program estimated to cost $182 million for new process technologies and equipment, plus $200–$300 million for ES&H improvements to be completed by 1994.

In February 1985, the Environmental Protection Agency set much more stringent standards for allowable exposures to the public, reducing them from 500 mrem per year to 25 mrem per year for equivalent whole-body radiation, and from 1,500 mrem per year to 75 mrem per year to the lungs or other organs. This action was not taken in response to new information about the hazards of radiation; the former standards were still those recommended by the International Commission on Radiological Protection and were widely accepted around the world. The EPA action was, rather, a manifestation of the "ALARA" principle, which dictates that radiation doses should be kept as *low as reasonably achievable,* instituted by the U.S. Nuclear Regulatory Commission for regulation of the commercial nuclear industry. EPA decided that this principle should be extended to activities over which NRC has no jurisdiction, and that the lower allowable standards were reasonably achievable. In response, the Fernald plant installed additional exhaust stack emission monitors and took other actions to assure compliance.

The estimated doses to the hypothetical "maximally exposed" individual (Table 14.1) still complied with the new EPA regulation. The regulation referred to the doses to actual individuals, none of whom spend all of their time outdoors at the location of maximum dose. An individual who is indoors or away from the plant boundary will inhale a smaller amount of the airborne dust from the plant.

However, three investigations questioned the reliability of the data supplied by Fernald. An assessment by Oak Ridge Associated Universities (ORAU) published in August 1985, identified problems in the exhaust stack monitoring systems, including corrosion of the sample probes and inadequate flow measurement systems. It also questioned the location of the seven monitors for measurement of environmental dust, which were equally spaced around the plant's boundary, and suggested that data on wind velocities and directions be collected to determine optimum locations.

In July 1985, Fernald installed its first off-site monitors at local schools, and arranged for them to be operated by the Ohio State Air Pollution Control Agency. In response to the ORAU report, the deficient stack monitors were replaced and the plant began to collect data on winds. As an interim measure, the plant used wind data from a nearby airport to locate two additional on-site and two additional off-site monitors. As part of the capital improvement program, the plant is now installing high-efficiency particulate air filters that are expected to remove 99.97 percent of the dust remaining after the exhaust streams pass through the present bag-type dust filters. This should essentially eliminate the problem of uranium dust releases in the future.

Officials of the EPA and the state government also questioned the reliability of the plant's estimates before 1985 on the radiation dose to the public. EPA noted that calculated doses were quite sensitive to the distribution of size of the dust particles, and if the sizes were much smaller in earlier years, the doses would have been much higher. Fernald officials rejected this argument, contending that there was no evidence for such a change in the dust size distribution. The chief of the EPA Environmental

Studies Branch conceded that the EPA had no historical data to back up its assumption.

In addition to problems of air particulate emissions, there were problems of water contamination. DOE maintains strict guidelines for radioactivity[1] in water discharges from plants, that are stricter than the U.S. Public Health Service regulations for radioactivity in municipal drinking water supplies. Fernald always reported discharges within the DOE guidelines. As a further check, it routinely monitored water samples from a nearby stream, from the Great Miami River, from 8 surface water test stations, and from 13 on-site and 21 off-site wells.

In 1984, the plant reported that two of the on-site wells had levels of radioactive contamination that were as much as 90 percent of the DOE guidelines. Three off-site wells, including one used for drinking water, also had uranium contaminations that were below DOE guidelines but were a cause for concern. These contaminations were traced to a sewer problem, and several actions were taken to correct it. A new drinking water well was drilled to replace the contaminated one in February 1985. In addition, DOE contracted with the Ohio Department of Health to test local wells free of charge upon citizens' requests. A group of 134 wells was selected for routine monitoring.

An indication of how the performance of the Fernald plant was viewed by outside investigators was the payments under the award fee system. By its contract with the DOE, National Lead of Ohio (NLO) received compensation for all costs plus an award fee. Oak Ridge officials semiannually evaluated the performance of NLO, and determined what percentage of the contractually specified maximum fee should be awarded. The basis for determining this percentage was left to the judgment of the Oak Ridge officials, but environmental safety and health constituted an important element in it. Except for the period encompassing the accidental release in the fall of 1984, when no award was given, Fernald always received between 76 percent and 85 percent of the maximum award fee.

This was the situation as of the spring of 1985. At that point the accidental release of 1984 appeared to be a relatively minor incident. The reports by ORAU, the General Accounting Office, and Ohio state authorities gave little reason for excitement.

The Class Action Suit

In January 1985, a suit was filed in U.S. District Court for the Southern District of Ohio, Western Division, against NLO and its parent company, National Lead Industries. The suit named over 100 plaintiffs but claimed to represent all people residing within 10 miles of the Fernald plant.

To support their case, the attorneys for the plaintiffs used the Freedom of Information Act to obtain detailed plant records, which were provided to them piecemeal over a period of several years. The DOE, which owned the plant, recognized that its contract with NLO made the U.S. government responsible for any damages, and hence undertook the defense. To provide information for this purpose, it commissioned International Technology Corp. of Knoxville, Tennessee to study the radiation doses and cancer risk from Fernald emissions. The picture that emerged, described in the next section, was far worse than had been anticipated in early 1985.

Fernald became a hot political and media issue. As new information came out, media coverage escalated rapidly, reaching what seemed to be a peak in mid-1986, but with further increases for another three years. The plaintiffs' attorneys reportedly orchestrated the release of information so as to feed this process; if that is true, they did a masterful job.

Congressman Thomas Lukens of Cincinnati, chairman of the House Energy and Commerce Subcommittee on Transportation, Tourism, and Hazardous Materials, held hearings on the problem, and accused the DOE of "brazen criminal neglect" and of "waging a kind of chemical warfare" against the local community. He arranged for wide national and international publicity for his hearings and his remarks. Ohio senators John Glenn and Howard Metzenbaum became involved; Senator Glenn wrote an article for the *New York Times* headlined "Mini-Hiroshima near Cincinnati." During the 1988 political campaign, presidential candidate Michael Dukakis met with families from the Fernald area, and called the situation an example of the Reagan administration's laxity on environmental concerns. Ohio Governor Richard Celeste sent a well-publicized letter to President Reagan, asking that the Fernald plant be shut down immediately.

Most of the media coverage in the Cincinnati area and nationwide was reasonably factual, but often emotionally loaded. For example, in 1988 the *Cincinnati Journal News* ran a story about a worker who had been burned on the wrists by a small chemical explosion in 1956 and spent two days in the infirmary with standard treatment for burns. His health since that time has been normal, but now, 32 years later, his wife still worries about his getting cancer. This was a four-column story under a top-of-page headline.

A story in *U.S. News & World Report* stated, "They have counted

162 cancer cases among those living close to the plant," giving the unjustified impression that these cancers were caused by releases from the
plant. The story featured an insert headed "How a nuclear weapons plant
poisoned a community." Cancer develops in about one-third of all people
at some point during their lifetimes. Any survey of the 14,000 people
living within 5 miles of the plant would be bound to find many cases of
cancer, regardless of any effect of the releases themselves.

The media often referred to the released uranium as "radioactive
waste"; they constantly used the adjectives "dangerous" and "hazardous," with no attempt to put the risks into perspective. The principal
attorney for the plaintiffs, Stanley Chesley, was quoted extensively, frequently, and sympathetically, while quotations from the defendants' side
were few and generally had a legalistic and defensive tone.

Releases Announced by Westinghouse

Table 14.2 shows the annual uranium releases from the Fernald plant, as
announced by Westinghouse Materials Co. of Ohio (Boback et al. 1987).
The releases in 1984 exceeded 1000 kg, nearly 8 times higher than the
original estimates by the plant management; but even this was trivial in
comparison with releases during the 1950s. The originally announced

Table 14.2
Annual uranium releases from Fernald plant, 1951–1987

Year	kg released	Year	kg released	Year	kg released
1951	125	1963	6,375	1975	3,138
1952	543	1964	5,583	1976	3,539
1953	2,183	1965	7,494	1977	978
1954	15,486	1966	3,731	1978	261
1955	33,893	1967	3,726	1979	200
1956	15,519	1968	5,885	1980	317
1957	11,025	1969	4,708	1981	677
1958	9,055	1970	1,983	1982	395
1959	9,177	1971	1,092	1983	376
1960	9,153	1972	1,601	1984	1,014
1961	7,427	1973	1,739	1985	315
1962	6,942	1974	2,697	1986	130
				1987	302

Source: Boback et al. 1987.

release of 124 kg, which had attracted so much attention, led to the disclosure of releases that, by 1987, totaled 179,000 kg!

Moreover, the Fernald plant had released other radioactive products as well. Between 1962 and 1978 it had released 6500 kg of thorium, whose radioactivity is comparable with that of uranium. The releases also contained small quantities of radioactive fission products and transuranic elements, although by later estimates these added only about 15 percent to the radiation dose to the public. In addition it was found that in the early 1950s a St. Louis plant had processed pitchblende ore, a very rich source of uranium, to produce 5,000–10,000 tons of uranium, leaving a residue containing 1,600–3,200 curies of radium that was shipped to Fernald and stored in poorly sealed silos. Radium decays slowly to produce radon gas of an equal number of curies. For comparison, the typical levels of radon in homes that have caused so much concern are a few picocuries per liter of air.[2]

In addition to these releases as airborne dust, the plant discharged about 162,000 pounds of uranium into the water. Some occurred from leaking storage tanks. Another source was the settling tanks that the plant used to separate solid from liquid waste: after the solid material had settled to the bottom of the tanks, workers pumped the remaining liquid (which still contained some uranium waste) into the Miami River. In 1964 alone, the plant released 23,000 pounds of uranium in this manner.

In addition to these releases there remained 12.7 million pounds of uranium buried in pits, mostly with fewer precautions and safeguards than are now considered reasonable. There was some risk that this would eventually contaminate the groundwater in the region.

The International Technology Corporation Study

The International Technology Corp. (IT) estimated the health implications of these releases. Senator John Glenn had requested that the Centers for Disease Control (CDC) undertake an epidemiologic study of the situation. Instead, the CDC cooperated in planning the IT study recommending the formation of a peer review committee to oversee it. This committee was formed, and consisted of experts from the DOE Oak Ridge Office, EPA's Office of Radiation Programs, Oak Ridge National Laboratory, and two private firms, Chem-Nuclear Systems (Albuquerque, New Mexico) and Radiological Assessments Corporation (Neeses, South Carolina). The committee assisted in the selection of computer models and data used with the models, and it reviewed drafts of the report that the IT investigators produced.

The IT study relied on computer models for its analysis. These models, in widespread use for a variety of other applications, are well recognized in this field of study. They are, however, overly conservative, in that they assume that people spend all of their time outdoors. Our experimental studies have shown that being indoors typically reduces inhalation of dust of outdoor origin about four-fold (Cohen and Cohen 1980). Since people spend about 80 percent of their time indoors, the IT report exaggerates the effects about two and a half times. It appears also that the IT assumptions about dust particle size were too conservative, leading to inflated estimates of dose. For these reasons, the radiation doses and health effects discussed below are probably too large by a factor of 3 or more.

In performing their calculations, the IT experts gave extensive consideration to the chemical forms of the various releases; meteorological data on wind speeds and directions and on atmospheric stability, which determines the distribution of airborne dust versus altitude; the population distribution in the surrounding areas and its changes over time; the location of the emission sources; and the height above ground at which the material was released. All of these are important inputs for the calculations used to derive dose estimates.

The study estimated the dose to the "selected" person who was expected to have received the highest dose—the person who lived closest to the plant in the predominant downwind direction. The study also gave the sum of all doses to exposed individuals. It did not determine whether any person actually lived at this most highly exposed location for the full 34 years of plant operation. The selected individual was *not* the same for calculations of exposure to radon and uranium emissions.

The results of the calculations for the 34 years of plant operation are shown in Table 14.3 The "selected" individual received a total dose of 3,400 mrem from all sources of radiation other than radon over the 34-year period; 85 percent of this dose was due to uranium. This dose averages to 100 mrem per year—about 40 percent of what the average U.S. citizen receives from natural sources, and 20 percent of the extra radiation the average worker in the nuclear industry receives from job-related exposures.

Using the linear model for risk assessment (see chapter 13), one can project that the exposure to the "selected" individual will lead to a statistical loss of life expectancy of 6 days (U.S. National Academy of Sciences 1990). By comparison, the statistical losses of life expectancy due to some other risks are smoking (a pack per day)—2,000 days; being 15

Table 14.3
Summary of radiation dose and cancer risk from Fernald uranium emissions,
1951–1984

Due to all exposures except radon (mostly uranium):
—dose to "selected" individual: 3400 mrem
—sum of doses to exposed population: 53,000 person-rem
—risk of fatal cancer to "selected" individual: 0.00088
—cancer deaths expected in exposed population: 7.0

Due to radon and [mostly] radon progeny:
—exposure to selected individual: 1.05 WLM (working level months)
   (This is roughly equivalent to the exposure from radon at an activity of 0.16
   picoCurie per liter (pCi/L) in the home over this time period.)
—sum of exposures to public: 12,400 person-WLM
—risk of fatal lung cancer to selected individual: 0.00045
—cancer deaths expected in exposed population: 5.3

Note: WLM radon exposure is roughly equivalent to the exposure from radon at
an activity of 0.16 picocurie per liter in the home over this time period.
Source: International Technology Corp. 1989.

pounds overweight—500 days; motor vehicle accidents—200 days; fire
and burns—30 days; drowning—30 days. These losses are statistical projections (the length of any person's life depends on many factors) to provide a comparison of the risks of these various exposures.

The IT study also projected an excess of 7 deaths from 34 years of
exposure, an average of 0.2 deaths per year. For comparison, the air pollution from a typical large coal-burning electric power generating plant
results in an estimated 25–100 excess deaths per year (Wilson et al. 1980).
A large industrial plant that burns coal as part of its process would cause
one or more projected deaths per year from air pollution, at least five
times the toll from Fernald. Radioactive releases from coal-burning
plants (from natural sources in the coal) are similar to those from Fernald
(Cohen 1981).

The IT study separately estimated radiation exposure from radon.
By this estimate, the "selected individual" near the plant received a dose
from radon of 1.05 WLM (working level months). This is roughly
equivalent to the exposure a person would receive in a home with radon
activity of 0.16 pCi/1[3] over the same time period; the average American
home has roughly seven times higher radon levels. The people exposed
to radon from Fernald also were exposed to radon from natural sources
at levels that, during the same time period, were over 1000 times greater
than from the plant.

Studies Commissioned by Plaintiffs

The plaintiffs commissioned several studies, which claimed higher health risks than the IT study.

One of these studies, by Dr. Bernd Franke of the Institute for Energy and Environmental Research, Tacoma Park, Maryland, was roughly parallel to the IT study. Franke's report (which was submitted as evidence in the trial) was highly critical of the quantity and quality of data made available for his analysis. It emphasized the maximum doses that could have been received by a person during individual accidental releases. Such doses, according to the report, were as high as 410,000 mrem to the lung, which is equivalent to about 60,000 mrem whole-body radiation. This dose is 17 times higher than that estimated by the IT study for the total exposure to the maximally exposed individual over the entire 34-year period.

For several reasons, it is difficult to take Franke's report seriously. It gave only meager explanations of his methodology, not enough to check or understand it in detail. From his figures I deduced that Franke was assuming dust levels in the range of 100,000 micrograms per cubic meter, about 1,000 times the level that would set off an air pollution alert in a city; such a level would go unnoticed; and that people would be doing heavy exercise in it. It is questionable whether a person could avoid choking to death at such a dust level. Franke is not well known in the radiation health scientific community.[4]

The plaintiffs commissioned Carl Johnson and Alice Stewart, both well-known antinuclear activists, to evaluate Franke's report.[5] Both approved the report and suggested that it might have *under*estimated the health impacts (Johnson 1988; Stewart 1988). In addition, Dr. Arjun Makhjani, of Dr. Franke's institute, submitted a report that questioned the official estimates of the uranium releases, suggesting that the actual releases may have been nearly twice the official estimates.

The plaintiffs provided another report by L. Lehman and Associates of Burnsville, Minnesota, that dealt largely with groundwater problems (Lehman and Associates 1988). Its principal conclusions were that there should be additional sampling of sediments and surface water, and an additional well at one site to sample groundwater. The DOE agreed to these recommendations.

The plaintiffs also commissioned a study of the effects of the publicity about environmental problems from the Fernald plant on real estate values in the area (Gartside 1988). It found that selling prices for houses were not correlated with distance from the plant in 1983–1984, but in 1985–1986 the selling prices decreased with decreasing distance. For example, the average price for a home within one mile of the plant was $57,000 in 1983, $68,600 in 1984, $62,500 in 1985, and $59,100 in 1986. A similar but weaker pattern was found for houses one to two miles and two to four miles away. For houses four to six miles away from the plant, the selling prices increased steadily between 1983 and 1986. In contrast, the government contended that values of average properties in the vicinity of the plant increased from $63,500 in 1984 to $78,800 in 1988, and property sales were brisk, increasing at a rate of 15 percent per year in that four-year period (Real Estate Counseling Group of Connecticut 1987).

Court Proceedings

Legal issues are discussed elsewhere in this book, and only a few points will be discussed here. The defendants claimed that contractors are immune from liability, since they merely executed the government's directions. The plaintiffs' called this the "Nuremberg defense," referring to the trials of Nazi war criminals in which defendants claimed they were merely carrying out orders.

In support of their position, the defendants cited a long list of instances, included here in the Appendix, in which the contractor had requested money to make improvements. The DOE and its predecessor, the Atomic Energy Commission, had denied the requests and ordered the contractor to make no further requests. The defendants' strategy was based on the fact that it would be more difficult to obtain judgments against the government than against the contractor, and the government would have to pay judgments against the contractor anyhow. However, the plaintiffs publicized this tactic as admissions of guilt by the government, and the defendants' strategy backfired badly in the public relations arena.

There was heavy media coverage of the judge's statements in turning down a motion for dismissal. He said that the activities at the plant were "abnormally dangerous," that "they created a high degree of risk to neighbors," that "there was a likelihood that resulting harm from that risk would be great." He also said that the plant site was inappropriate from the beginning because the "defendants recognized when the plant was built that some hazardous materials would seep into property, springs, rivers, and wells owned or utilized by the neighboring public."

Together, both sides in this suit produced a tremendous amount of documentation. The trial records included 125 depositions, over 100,000 separate documents, and over 1 million sheets of paper.

The suit was eventually settled out of court. The agreement included payment of $73 million for the residents, plus up to $5 million for commercial and industrial claims; payments in the latter category were to be matched, dollar for dollar, by payments from the $73 million pool.

This settlement was to be for emotional stress and loss in value of real estate, but not for health effects. Thus, anyone who can prove that his or her physical health was injured by the emissions from the Fernald plant can still sue separately for those damages. However, past experience has shown that suits of this type have little chance of success because any health effects that might be caused by these very low levels of exposure are far more likely to be caused by other factors. Even if injuries were caused by radiation, a resident's exposure to radiation from the Fernald releases were far smaller than those from natural sources.

In the settlement, part of the $73 million fund would be used for medical monitoring; each of the 14,000 people living within 5 miles of the plant will have medical examinations at least once per year for the next 30–40 years. The nature of these examinations and their cost are yet to be decided.

The settlement also agreed that $3–5 million of the $73 million fund would be used for an epidemiologic study to determine whether there is an excess of cancer in the area that can be associated with Fernald releases. It was clearly understood that none of this settlement money would be used for cleanup, which remains a U.S. government responsibility, or as compensation for physical injuries. All the money was to be used for medical examinations, epidemiology, and compensation for emotional stress and loss of real estate values.

The court accepted the settlement in October 1989, and the $73 million was paid to the plaintiffs by DOE. In addition, DOE has spent $356 million on improvements since 1985, and EPA has declared Fernald a superfund site. Estimated costs of cleanup are $1.1 billion.

Discussion of the Settlement

National Lead of Ohio behaved irresponsibly in its management of the Fernald plant, and the problem was compounded by bad decisions by the DOE and the Atomic Energy Commission. National Lead failed to properly maintain the filtering systems designed to prevent large releases, and it apparently covered up a great deal of information about these releases. It most definitely was not a good neighbor, and deserved to be sued. However, neither National Lead of Ohio nor its parent company are the victims of the suit. U.S. taxpayers will have to foot the bill. How reasonable is this bill?

There can be no scientific justification for the medical surveillance or the epidemiologic study of the population around the plant. Radiation exposures to residents in the area were in all cases only a tiny fraction of the exposures they and everyone else receive from natural background sources. Even if effects are found by the epidemiologic surveillance, they could not plausibly be attributed to radiation from the Fernald releases.

The emotional stress and the loss of real estate value may be real. But these are indirect effects of the releases that were exacerbated by irresponsible media coverage. More responsible reporting would have put the risks in proper perspective by noting that the emissions from the plant were far less dangerous than emissions from each of the dozens of coal-burning plants in the area. Such playing on the public's irrational and greatly exaggerated fear of radiation is costing our nation dearly.

On the other hand, this is a relatively minor addition to the long list of existing samples. The $73 million cost is only a small fraction of the cost of not operating the Seabrook or Shoreham nuclear power plants. It is trivial compared with the billions of dollars that has been added to the cost of each nuclear power plant completed since the early 1980s. It is also trivial compared with the billions of dollars spent on super-supersafe management of radioactive waste. The price we pay for media-generated fear of radiation is very high indeed.

Notes

1. Government regulations often specify the maximum radioactivity, but not the particular radioactive isotope. This is a much easier quantity to measure.

2. One curie = 1 trillion picocuries.

3. Picocuries (pCi) of radiation per liter of air. 1 pCi/1 corresponds to about 2 radioactive decays per minute in each liter of air.

4. He became a member of Health Physics Society, the principal professional society of radiation health and radiation protection scientists, only in 1986.

5. Johnson was also prominent as an expert witness in litigation concerning health effects of nuclear fallout (chapter 13)—The Editors.

References

Berger, J. D. 1985. Environmental Program Review of the Feed Materials Production Center. DRAU internal report. Fernald, OH: unpublished.

Boback, M. W., T. A. Dugan, D. A. F. Fleming, R. B. Grant, and R. W. Keys. 1987. *History of FMPC discharges.* Cincinnati, OH: Westinghouse Materials Co. of Ohio Report FMPC-2082.

Cohen, A. F., and B. L. Cohen. 1980. Protection from being indoors against inhalation of suspended particulate matter of outdoor origin. 14 *Atmos. Environ.* 183–184.

Cohen, B. L. 1981. The role of radon in comparisons of effects of radioactivity releases from nuclear power, coal burning, and phosphate mining. 40 *Health Physics* 19–25.

Gartside, P. S. 1988. Independent analysis of patterns of real estate market prices around the Feed Materials Production Center, Fernald, Ohio. Submitted in evidence.

International Technology Corp. 1989. *Assessment of radiation dose and cancer risk for emissions from 1951 through 1984.* Knoxville, TN: International Technology Corp.

Johnson, C. 1988. Letter to L. M. Roselle, Attorney at Law, Waite, Schneider, Bayless and Chesley Co., L.P.A. Received March 16, 1988.

L. Lehman and Associates. 1988. Review of existing literature on Feed Materials Production Center.

Makhjani, A. 1988. Release estimates of radioactive and nonradioactive materials to the environment by the Feed Materials Production Center 1951–1985. Takoma Park, MD: Institute for Energy and Environmental Research.

Real Estate Counseling Group of Connecticut and Financial Consulting Group of Ohio. 1987. Report submitted in evidence.

Stewart, A. 1988. Report on Dr. Franke's preliminary assessment of radiation exposures and health risks associated with releases of radioactive materials from FMPC: 1951 to 1984.

U.S. National Academy of Sciences, National Research Council, Committee on Biological Effects of Ionizing Radiation (BEIR V). 1990. *Health effects of exposure to low levels of ionizing radiation.* Washington, DC: National Academy Press.

Wilson, R., S. D. Colome, J. D. Spengler and D. G. Wilson. 1980. *Health effects of fossil fuel burning.* Cambridge, MA: Ballinger.

Appendix

Cases in which the contractor, National Lead of Ohio, made requests for funds for avoiding environmental problems that were denied:

Concerning Water Pollution

1951: Atomic Energy Commission (AEC) officials tell the Ohio Department of Health it is possible to install a system to recover nearly all the 18 to 36 pounds of uranium being emptied into the Great Miami River daily, but that the $500,000 cost could not be justified.

1953: National Lead of Ohio (NLO) seeks money to upgrade the sewer system leading to Paddy's Run Creek so contaminated storm runoff can be reduced to "allowable limits." The Atomic Energy Commission refuses.

1962: NLO warns that further improvements in the storm sewer system are needed and says failure to do so could "contaminate the aquifer." The AEC agrees surface water runoff poses problems but rejects the improvements.

1978: NLO includes money in its 1981 budget request to improve the storm sewer system. DOE says it won't have the money for the project until 1983.

1984: NLO says it will shut down unless the government puts in writing that it won't "be held liable for the continued operation in violation of the existing [pollution control regulation] permit." On March 5, 1985, DOE orders operations continued.

Concerning Thorium, a Radioactive, Toxic and Corrosive Product Stored in Fernald

1979: Approximately 2,500 tons of thorium are delivered to the plant in corroding steel drums. They are placed in a steel-framed building, where they have remained. NLO wanted to process the thorium into less corrosive oxides which could be stored more easily. In 1980, DOE said no because it was too costly.

Concerning Leaking Radioactive Liquid Waste

1958: Plant management informs the AEC that one of the four six-year-old tanks containing liquid waste from Afrimet, a Belgian corporation, has "irreparable cracks in its concrete walls which allowed seepage of liquids from the tank." Government officials tell NLO to allow the seepage to continue "until the liquid level within the tank falls below the line of the lowest crack."

1963: AEC officials instruct NLO to bank soil around the tank as a bulwark against leakage. In 1964, NLO complies with the request.

Concerning Pits in Which Radioactive Waste is Buried

1952: Plant management opposes construction of any waste pits because it believes material buried there could contaminate the plant's water supply. The AEC ignores the warning and goes on to build five pits.

1962: Plant management warns that the Fernald operations may be contaminating the groundwater table and proposes draining the liquid wastes from pits. The idea is rejected.

1978: NLO again warns of problems with the waste pits and requests money to mine them and process the wastes into a safer form for long-term storage. The next year, DOE officials suggest that the contractor study the possibility of transporting the waste pit sludge to a processing facility. The say they don't have money for such work.

Concerning Emission of Radioactive Dust into the Air

1959: NLO warns that dust collection bags, which filter uranium particles from the air, rupture "on the order of once a month," releasing "relatively large amounts of uranium particulates into the atmosphere."

1970s and early 1980s: NLO repeatedly warns the government that the plant's equipment, including the dust collectors, is deteriorating and needs to be replaced.

1973: NLO suggests replacing the dust collectors with state-of-the-art filters. DOE fails to act on the request and instructs NLO not to put the requests in writing.

1984: In September and December, a dust collector malfunctions. The collector, which officials say has a life of 15 years, had not been replaced since 1963.

Biographical Sketch

Bernard Cohen is professor of physics at the University of Pittsburgh and adjunct professor of radiation health at the university's Graduate School of Public Health.

He is the author of six books, most recently *The Nuclear Energy Option* (Plenum Press, 1990), and over 250 scientific articles. He has won several awards, including the American Physical Society's Bonner Prize, and the Health Physics Society's Distinguished Scientific Achievement Award, and has served as a consultant to both the public and the private sectors.

Cohen has served as chairman of the American Physical Society's Division of Nuclear Physics and of the American Nuclear Society's Division of Environmental Sciences.

The Legal Context

Asbestos Property Litigation

Most asbestos property cases that at present are in litigation are part of the "second wave" of asbestos lawsuits. (The "first wave" consisted of claims by asbestos workers, such as workers in shipyards during World War II, for compensation for lung cancer and mesothelioma and other diseases contracted as a result of heavy asbestos exposure.) They hinge on the proposition that persons occupying buildings that contain asbestos insulation, tiles, or other materials are at risk of asbestos-induced disease. Over time, asbestos fibers will be released into building environments; there is some risk that they might cause disease, although (as D'Agostino and Wilson argue in chapter 8) such risks are very small.

Nevertheless, health concerns have led to an enormous amount of pending litigation on asbestos. An estimated 200 property cases are already pending in U.S. courts, including several major nationwide class actions. According to recent surveys, building-asbestos litigation has included a class action suit filed on behalf of all 34,000 U.S. school districts;[1] statewide class action suits on behalf of school districts in Alabama,[2] Michigan,[3] Ohio,[4] Pennsylvania,[5] Texas[6] and Wisconsin;[7] a statewide class action for all public buildings, excluding schools, in Pennsylvania;[8] statewide class action on behalf of all homeowners in California;[9] a class action on behalf of all hospitals in the United States and Canada;[10] two national class actions on behalf of all U.S. colleges and hospitals[11] and a class action on behalf of all owners of buildings leased to the federal government.[12]

The potential liability runs into the tens of billions of dollars. Virtually every owner of a building constructed before 1978 could have a claim for inspection and/or abatement costs.

In part, this litigation has been prompted by a federal law that requires elementary and secondary schools to inspect for asbestos and to develop appropriate response measures. In 1980 Congress declared that "the presence in school buildings of friable or easily damaged asbestos creates an unwarranted hazard to the health of children and school employees who are exposed to such materials."[13] Local governments and school boards have sought to shift the costs of asbestos monitoring and removal to asbestos manufacturers and others.

Most courts are allowing these cases to proceed to trial, finding sufficient allegation of injury in the property damage claims, regardless of the actual levels of underlying risk.[14] One court, for example, found that an appropriate claim had been stated for "contamination" of the building by virtue of release of the asbestos into the air.[15]

As of early 1992, almost three dozen such cases had been tried to a verdict. Their results have varied widely, although the current trend is in the defendants' favor. The verdicts for the plaintiffs, some of which were reversed on appeal or settled before the appeal could be heard, resulted in awards in the hundreds of thousands[16] and even millions of dollars.[17]

In some of these "second wave" cases, juries have awarded substantial punitive damages, amounting to $2 million in two different cases.[18] In 1990, a Minnesota jury ordered Keene Co., a building products manufacturer, to pay a total of $3.22 million, which included $2.4 million in punitive damages. The jury determined that asbestos-containing fireproofing in a district high school posed a potential health hazard to students, faculty, and staff.[19] More recently, a jury awarded the Kansas City Airport $8 million in actual damages and $6.25 million in punitive damages. The trial judge reversed the punitive award.[20]

Other cases have been settled out of court.[21] Three of the defendants in the nationwide school class action—Owens-Illinois, Proko Industries and LAQ—have settled; one other defendant, the National Gypsum Company, also settled with some of the plaintiffs in that case. Many individual suits have been settled as well.

PCBs

The range of litigation involving polychlorinated biphenyls (PCBs) is illustrated by the cases outlined below.

Mallory v. *Monsanto*[22] involved a claim by the estate of Paul Mallory, who had worked with transformers and capacitors filled with PCB-laden oils. Attorneys for the plaintiffs argued that Mallory's fatal colon cancer was caused or exacerbated by his exposure to PCBs.

Early in the proceedings, Monsanto moved for summary judgment. Its expert contended there was no proof of a causal link between the PCB exposure and Mallory's cancer. Mallory responded with the declaration of Dr. Selina Bendix, the president of an environmental and toxicological consulting firm and an expert witness for the plaintiff. Dr. Bendix declared that "job-related exposure to PCBs was a substantial factor in the development of [Mallory's] colon cancer," and buttressed her views with various statements regarding the physiological effects of PCBs. According to court records, Dr. Bendix has a Ph.D. in zoology with a specialty in physiocochemical biology.

Monsanto challenged Dr. Bendix's qualifications to express the opinion she had given on the cause of Mallory's disease. The trial judge acknowledged that Dr. Bendix's résumé "may suggest either some special knowledge or . . . experience in compiling data, or . . . experience as a journalist or essayist concerning certain tumor viruses; and upon carcinogenesis (in some unspecified aspect) [etc.]." But, concluded the court, "[a]s regards the basic issue of whether there is causal connection between exposure to PCBs . . . and colon cancer, none of the foregoing even suggests special knowledge. Nor does any of the foregoing, nor any of the witness' experience, training or education suggest qualifications as an expert *'on the subject to which her testimony relates'* [a requirement for qualification as an expert under California law]." The judge therefore granted summary judgment for Monsanto. An appellate court affirmed.

In *Scott* v. *Monsanto,* [23] plaintiffs alleged that Monsanto was liable for various physical injuries arising from their exposure to PCBs on the job. The trial judge ordered that eight plaintiffs be selected for a "bellwether trial." Over 60 witnesses appeared at the 2-week trial; the evidence centered on exposure and causality.

Dr. Daniel Teitelbaum, a witness for the plaintiffs, defined "PCB syndrome" as a cluster of disorders caused by exposure to PCBs. He identified the plaintiffs' claimed ailments—which included asthma, nerve damage, leukemia, toxic hepatitis, lung disease, chloracne, lung and skin cancer, and colon cancer—as caused by PCB exposure. He also cited the International Association for Research on Cancer, which categorized PCBs as "probable" human carcinogens.

Monsanto's experts argued that the plaintiffs had misrepresented the extent and nature of their exposure to PCBs, and that there is insufficient evidence to link PCBs to any human illness other than chloracne and liver disease. These experts found no evidence of chloracne among the plaintiffs, and attributed the plaintiffs' liver disease to alcohol consumption, and their other ailments to a variety of causes wholly unrelated to PCBs.

The jury returned a verdict for Monsanto on all the claims, the plaintiffs requested a new trial. The district judge granted the request to avert a "miscarriage of justice," expressing his view that the plaintiffs had been exposed to PCBs and that the exposure had adversely affected their health. Monsanto successfully appealed that ruling. "We would not expect disagreement between judge and jury upon the integrity of multiple witnesses to be a sound basis for a new trial," the appellate court declared.

In *Rubanick* v. *Witco Chem. Corp.*,[24] the heirs of Ronald Rubanick alleged that on-the-job exposure to PCBs had caused his colon cancer. Their evidence on causation came from Earl Balis, Ph.D., a biochemist involved in cancer research. The defendant, Witco Chemical Corporation, countered with three experts who testified that neither a majority nor even any substantial minority of mainstream scientists believe that PCBs are human carcinogens, or that there is a specific link between PCBs and colon cancer. They argued that Balis' conclusion should therefore be barred from the trial. The trial judge agreed: "Dr. Balis' opinions fail, having not been previously recognized by any recognized tribunal, having no substantial minority acceptance, and having no support in the scientific literature. . . ." The court later granted Witco summary judgment.

A divided panel of the New Jersey Superior Court reversed the decision. Expert testimony is admissible, the court declared, even if it is not generally accepted in the scientific community, "unless the opinion proffered would be either illogical, outlandish or totally speculative such that no reasonable jury could accept the opinion." Dr. Balis's testimony, the court concluded, should have been admitted. The New Jersey Supreme Court unanimously agreed.

This last case illustrates the difficulty the legal system has in handling questions of subtle environmental hazards. The court adopted a loose scrutiny test based on *Wells, Oxendine,* and other cases that had announced liberal standards for the admission of scientific evidence (see chapter 2). The court apparently believed that common sense, combined with minimal scientific evidence, is sufficient to create a jury question as to causation: "There are undeniable indications that persons do in fact suffer grave and lethal injury as a result of the wrongful or tortious exposure to toxic substances. *Those indications . . . conform to our common experience and informed intuition.*" (emphasis added.) The court added, "Our common sense, with some empirical support, tells us of the deleterious effects of PCBs." The court also relied on legal articles, prior cases, and regulatory statutes in support of the idea that PCBs are unusually dangerous. The problem, of course, is that common sense and legal precedent cannot accurately tell a court if PCBs are harmful at all, much less at the levels at which Rubanick was exposed.

In re Paoli Railyard PCB Litigation[25] is the probably most important—and certainly the most notorious—PCB case litigated thus far. The Paoli (Pennsylvania) yard has been a regional maintenance facility for various rail companies since the 1930s. For many years, railroads had stored, handled, and disposed of PCBs used as dielectric fluid in the transformers on railroad cars. The long-term presence and leakage of PCBs at the site caused of contamination at the yard and in the surrounding neighborhoods.

Twenty-four plaintiffs—local residents and employees—sued the various parties responsible for the yard's contamination. They alleged that PCBs had caused injuries including: hypertension, kidney cancer, asthma, myocardial infarctions, nephrectomy, cerebral ischemic attacks, pancreatic cancer, hepatitis, chronic cirrhosis of the liver, abnormal liver function, bruising, insomnia, irritability, anxiety, and depression, anemia, elevated triglycerides, immune system alterations, brain cancer, persistent skin rashes, joint irritation, stomach cancer, arthritis, gastrointestinal dysfunction, Parkinson's disease, benign prostatic hypertrophy, disorder of the spine, anorexia, wasting of quadriceps bilaterally, hepatomegaly, increased risk of future harm, emotional distress, and fear of increased risk.

The defendants assembled a panel of over a dozen medical doctors and scientists who filed a joint affidavit which stated: "We have reviewed the extensive literature on PCBs and have found that no reasonable medical or scientific basis exists for concluding that chronic exposure to PCBs causes cancer, hypertension, cardiovascular diseases, elevations in serum triglycerides or cholesterol levels, liver disease, joint irritation, pancytopenia [etc.]."

The plaintiffs countered with reports by their own experts. Among others, Dr. Deborah Barsotti claimed that PCBs were responsible for the plaintiffs' hypertension and asthma.[26] Dr. Arthur Zahalsky claimed that PCBs cause damage to the immune system and that tests (which had not yet been performed) would prove that PCBs had damaged the plaintiffs' immune systems, leaving them susceptible to a variety of ailments. Dr. Ian C. T. Nesbit, a self-described "professional environmental scientist," and Dr. Robert E. Simon criticized a study that showed that plaintiffs had suffered no higher exposure to PCBs than members of the general population. The plaintiffs also referred to reports of illness in people who had consumed rice oil that had been contaminated with PCBs and other substances (the yusho and yu-cheng diseases mentioned in chapter 9) as proof that PCBs are harmful to humans.

Trial judge R. F. Kelly ruled that (1) the plaintiffs had failed to prove they had more PCBs in their bodies than members of the general population; (2) the plaintiffs had not proved that they had suffered any legally cognizable injury; and (3) that even if (1) and (2) are incorrect, the expert opinions offered by the plaintiffs were inadmissible. As to the third point, Judge Kelly wrote the following:

[T]here is the question of whether the plaintiffs' experts are really experts. Many of them seem to have very little formal academic training in the areas in which they testify. . . . [T]here is [also] the lack of differential diagnoses. For example, an expert will claim that the plaintiff has asthma and that asthma is caused by PCBs to a reasonable medical or scientific certainty; but when asked how he knows that the asthma is not caused by one of the other causes of asthma that produce asthma even in people who are not exposed to PCBs, the expert has no intelligible response. I think that this is fatal to plaintiffs' claim.

On this basis, Judge Kelly dismissed the case.

The Third Circuit Court of Appeals overruled this decision in October 1990. The ruling discussed the problem of expert testimony at some length. It noted, for example, that Dr. Zahalsky has spent most of his time in recent years providing scientific consultation for litigation. It acknowledged that Zahalsky had completed "only one graduate-level course that included immunology," and that Zahalsky himself "conceded his lack of expertise in epidemiology, toxicology, and medicine, and admitted that because he is not a medical doctor, he is not qualified to examine patients, perform clinical tests, or render differential diagnoses." It noted that Zahalsky had offered diagnoses of immune system damage in a number of plaintiffs, even though he had not yet tested any of the plaintiffs for elevated PCB exposure.

The appellate court concluded that the trial judge "appears to have excluded much of Dr. Zahalsky's testimony regarding the effects of PCBs on human beings because he is not trained in differential diagnosis." But noting the "liberal" standard for qualifying experts embodied in the Federal Rules of Evidence, the appellate court found that Zahalsky's testimony should nonetheless have been admitted. The federal rules "embody a strong and undeniable preference for admitting any evidence having some potential for assisting the trier of fact and for dealing with the risk of error through the adversary process." The court also explicitly rejected "peer review" as the threshold requirement for admissibility.

Friedman v. *Myers* is another PCBs case from the same federal district as *Paoli*.[27] The plaintiffs claimed "pain and suffering, emotional distress, and fear of developing cancer" from exposure to water contaminated with PCBs. Once again, the defendants sought to exclude the plaintiffs' expert testimony. But the trial judge explicitly disavowed his colleague's ruling in *Paoli,* and ruled that the jury would make the call among the experts. The jury ultimately awarded one plaintiff $1,000, and another $15,000 in compensatory damages, with an extra $750,000 in punitive damages for one of the plaintiffs. The trial judge found the $750,000 excessive; he offered the plaintiff a choice between accepting $30,000 or holding a separate trial on the sole issue of punishment. The plaintiff chose the latter, and the case was settled for a confidential amount shortly thereafter.

TCE

Dougherty v. *Hooker Chemical Corp.,* [28] involved the claim of Wayne Dougherty, employed by Boeing Vertol Company as a helicopter transmission rebuilder. He worked in two buildings, each of which contained 200 gallons of heated trichloroethylene (TCE). After working for Boeing for several years, Dougherty died of cardiac arrest.

Dougherty's wife filed suit, blaming his death on exposure to TCE. The trial judge granted a directed verdict for the defense, on the ground that whatever the merits of the causation claim, the plaintiff could not possibly win because the defendants had given adequate warning. An appellate court reversed, holding that the adequacy of the warning was an issue for the jury to decide.

Peterman v. *Techalloy Co.*[29] was a class action alleging anxiety about health risks caused by the ingestion of water contaminated with TCE. The plaintiff alleged that the chemical had leaked from storage tanks on the defendant's property into well water in the village of Rhans, Pennsylvania. The trial judge granted summary judgment in favor of the defendants. Without some allegation of actual physical injury, or at least some physical manifestation of the effects of emotional distress, there could be no suit.

The best known TCE case is *Anderson* v. *W.R. Grace and Co.,* which involved claims brought by residents of Woburn, Massachusetts, against W.R. Grace and Company.[30] The plaintiffs alleged they had contracted leukemia and other illnesses from exposure to groundwater contaminated with TCE and other chemicals. They sought damages for actual injury, as well as for emotional distress and enhanced risk of future illness because of injury to their immune systems. The trial court dismissed part of the last claim, ruling that the plaintiffs had failed to establish to a "reasonable probability" that they would suffer future harm. After an initial jury finding on the question of responsibility for the pollution, the remaining claims were settled out of court for an undisclosed sum.[31]

The plaintiffs in *Higgins* v. *Aerojet-General Corp.*[32] claimed that drinking and bathing in water contaminated with TCE and other chemicals resulted in various physical and psychological injuries, including "immune dysfunction." This in turn caused gallstones, melanoma, headaches, fatigue, and miscellaneous other ailments. The defense established that all of these ailments are common to the general population, and presented experts who testified that none of these ailments is caused by exposure to TCE. The jury found for the defense.

In *Ayers* v. *Township of Jackson,*[33] residents of Jackson Township, New Jersey, alleged that TCE and other chemical contaminants from a township landfill had leached into the town aquifer. The plaintiffs sought damages for an unquantified enhanced risk of future disease, and requested funds for medical monitoring. The trial court denied both requests, concluding that the plaintiffs could not reasonably fear that they were at any serious risk of future disease because of the exposures in question.

The New Jersey Supreme Court upheld the rejection of the claim for enhanced risk, stating: "If such claims were to be litigated, juries would be asked to award damages for the enhanced risk of a disease that may never be contracted, without the benefit of expert testimony sufficient to establish the likelihood that the contingent event will ever occur." The court ruled, however, that the plaintiffs were entitled to damages for medical monitoring. Medical monitoring was justified whether or not future disease was likely because of the exposure; medical science may "necessarily and properly intervene where there is a significant but unquantified risk of serious disease."

The plaintiffs in *Stites* v. *Sundstrand Heat Transfer, Inc.*[34] claimed that TCE leaking from a manufacturing plant injured their immune systems, placed them at increased risk of cancer, and caused emotional distress from fear of cancer. On a motion for partial summary judgment, the defendants argued that TCE does not cause cancer, and that none of the plaintiffs were suffering from it. The trial court granted summary judgment on the risk-of-cancer claim, concluding that the plaintiffs had failed to provide evidence that there was a reasonable certainty that they would in fact develop cancer. But the court denied summary judgment on the fear-of-cancer claim. The plaintiffs had located experts who were prepared to testify that TCE is indeed a human carcinogen, so the plaintiffs could reasonably fear that those experts were right. The claim would therefore go to the jury.

Potter v. *Firestone Tire and Rubber Co.*[35] involved TCE that had been disposed of in the city-owned landfill but allegedly leached into the water supply. Here the plaintiffs recovered a total of $4 million including $200,000 each for their fear of cancer, and damages "for the general disruption of their lives after the contamination was discovered," for medical monitoring, and for emotional distress. The plaintiffs also recovered punitive damages. The court did reject, however, their claims for emotional distress caused by the increased risk of cancer in their children.

In *Clark* v. *United States*,[36] nearby residents brought suit against an air force base, alleging TCE contamination of their well water. They sought damages for property damage and emotional distress. The trial judge concluded there was "very little, very, very slight likelihood of any actual harm coming to any plaintiff as a result of consumption of this contaminated water . . . the risks are so slight as to not merit further worry or concern." He nevertheless awarded various damages, including $83,000 to nine plaintiffs for emotional distress.

In *Mateer* v. *U.S. Aluminum*,[37] the Mateer family of Columbia, Pennsylvania, alleged that TCE and other chemicals that had been dumped into a nearby quarry had contaminated their groundwater. They sought damages for emotional distress, fear of future disease, enhanced risk of future harm, and funds for medical surveillance. The trial judge granted summary judgment on the grounds that the plaintiffs had been unable to present any credible evidence of causation. The plaintiffs' experts' opinions were "not supported by the type of evidence reasonably relied upon by the scientific community to determine the health effects of exposure to toxic substances." There was no evidence the plaintiffs had suffered, or had a significant risk of suffering in the future, physical harm related to the contamination. The plaintiffs' expert witnesses had claimed that exposure might result in cellular damage and increased risk of future disease, but had failed to assess the dosage and duration of the exposure in question.

In one of the largest toxic tort settlements ever, in early 1991 Hughes Aircraft settled a class action suit against it for $84.5 million. The suit alleged that Hughes had contaminated part of Tucson, Arizona's, water supply with TCE, resulting in cancer and birth defects.[38]

Dioxin

The range of litigation involving dioxin is illustrated by the cases outlined below.

The *Agent Orange* litigation involved a defoliant herbicide that was used extensively in the Vietnam War.[39] Lawyers for a group of plaintiffs assembled a massive lawsuit against various chemical companies, alleging that the plaintiffs' exposure to dioxin in Agent Orange had caused miscarriages, cancer, birth defects, liver disorders, and other illnesses. Over 600 separate actions originally filed by more than 15,000 named individuals were consolidated into a single class action. Eventually the lead plaintiffs and lawyers in the suit would claim to represent 2.4 million Vietnam veterans, their wives, children born and unborn, soldiers from Australia and New Zealand, and a small number of civilian plaintiffs. The defendants consisted of 24 (later reduced to 7) corporations.

On the eve of trial, under intense pressure from trial Judge Jack Weinstein, the parties agreed to settle the action for $180 million, at that time the largest such settlement on record.[40] Thereafter, Weinstein sharply cut the legal fees sought by the plaintiffs' lawyers. He stated that there had been no convincing evidence of causation, and that he did not wish to encourage more litigation of this character. Since no plaintiff could possibly trace his individual injury to Agent Orange with any certainty, Weinstein ordered that "compassion—not scientific proof" be the basis for at least some of the awards.

Almost 400 individual claimants refused to take part in the class settlement. Their claims were adjudicated separately by Judge Weinstein.[41] In this separate proceeding, the plaintiffs cited studies in which dioxin was found to cause substantial harm in animals, to epidemiologic studies that allegedly showed Vietnam veterans were more susceptible than the general public to the same harms shown in animals, and to expect medical testimony that supposedly could show the causal link between the veterans' illnesses and exposure to Agent Orange.

Judge Weinstein nonetheless granted the defendants' motion for summary judgment. He found the animal and epidemiologic studies cited by the plaintiffs unpersuasive on the question of injury to humans. Weinstein ruled that the plaintiffs would have to procure an expert's affidavit for each plaintiff opining that "there is more than a 50 percent probability that their particular diseases were due to exposure to Agent Orange in Vietnam." The plaintiffs then submitted testimony by medical experts, the most prominent of whom was Dr. Samuel S. Epstein, author of *The Politics of Cancer* (1978). Epstein claimed that "a causal relationship exists between exposure to Agent Orange and a wide range of toxic multi-system and multi-organ effects," and that after reviewing the individual plaintiffs' medical conditions and history, he could say that "to a reasonable degree of medical certainty" the veterans' conditions were "much more likely than not caused by exposure to Agent Orange."

Judge Weinstein rejected this evidence, too. He analyzed the available epidemiologic studies and concluded there was no credible evidence that paternal exposure to Agent Orange causes birth defects, nor any difference in cancer rates between Vietnam veterans and the general population, nor any established relationship between herbicides and human illness. He dismissed the plaintiffs' studies as "irrelevant" and "flawed." The Judge quoted from Epstein's own book, which emphasized the manifold environmental causes of cancer, and pointed out that Epstein's testimony failed to consider the possibility that the plaintiffs' diseases were caused by those factors. The plaintiffs appealed, but an appellate court affirmed Weinstein's decision to dismiss their claims without trial.

The legal wrangling over Agent Orange was not quite finished, however. In December 1987, a Texas jury awarded a former U.S. Forest Service worker $1.5 million for a claim that exposure to Agent Orange in a weed control program had caused Hodgkin's disease. The verdict was upheld on appeal.[42]

In a recent case involving Agent Orange, 120 former plant workers, their families, neighbors, and business owners filed a $500 million damage suit against Diamond Shamrock Chemicals, whose plant in Newark, New Jersey had produced Agent Orange from 1966 through 1968. The plaintiffs claimed that the resulting dioxin contamination at the plant site and the neighborhood resulted in physical injuries and death.[43] The plaintiffs eventually settled for about $1 million, a result Diamond Shamrock's attorney considered a victory.[44] Diamond Shamrock had already won another case arising from exposure to dioxin produced at its Newark plant.[45]

The *Times Beach* litigation involved a small Missouri town of about 2,000 residents. In the mid-1970s, 2,000 gallons of a combination of oil and industrial wastes, contaminated by dioxin, were sprayed on unpaved roads near the town. In 1982, heavy rains caused flooding in the area, spreading the contamination. The Environmental Protection Agency ordered a complete evacuation of the town. The federal government eventually shut down the town and paid the residents some $33 million in compensation, some of which it later recovered from private defendants.[46]

Former town residents sued various companies connected with the dioxin, claiming that the exposure harmed their health and increased their risk of cancer. Four residents of nearby Lincoln County settled for $2.68 million in 1983;[47] 128 plaintiffs eventually settled in 1986 for $19 million.[48]

More than 1,500 other claims were still pending.[49] Another 180 claims were dismissed by a jury in June of 1988.[50] The plaintiffs relied mainly on the testimony of Dr. Bertram Carnow, who had testified in the Agent Orange case and in the *Sturgeon* litigation (discussed below). The ailments attributed to dioxin exposure included headaches, nausea, loss of sleep, vomiting, increased risk of cancer, precancerous conditions, and aggravation of preexisting heart conditions. After a seven-month trial, the jury returned a unanimous verdict that there was no medical evidence linking the plaintiffs' problems to dioxin exposure. A week before the case went to the jury, two of the chemical companies named in the suit had settled for $14.5 million.[51]

The *Sturgeon* case grew out of the January 10, 1979, derailment of a train just outside of Sturgeon, Missouri, which resulted in a spillage of 19,000 gallons of a wood preservative with trace contaminants of dioxin.[52] Part of the spill reached farmland owned by Frances E. Kemner, an 81-year-old matriarch, and her family. Members of the family were the lead plaintiffs in what became one of the longest civil cases in history. They were joined by local teachers, homemakers, construction workers, schoolchildren, farmers, and other residents of the half-mile area affected by the spill. All claimed that a broad range of ailments—including fatigue, headaches, joint pain, immune system suppression, and psychoneuroses—had been caused by dioxin. They sought $35.4 million in compensatory damages and $100 million in punitive damages.

The jury trial began in February 1984 and lasted over three and a half years. By the time jury deliberations began, 1 of the 67 original plaintiffs had died, 2 had dropped out of the suit, 4 of the jurors had been excused, and 1 of the defendants, Norfolk and Western Railway Company, had settled out of court. There was testimony from 182 witnesses, including toxicologists, neurologists, environmentalists, and family physicians; 6,000 exhibits; and more than 100,000 pages of trial transcripts.

On September 14, 1987, after three weeks of deliberation, the jurors reported to the judge that they could not make up their minds. The jury was sent back for further deliberation. Finally it returned a bizarre verdict for the plaintiffs. Two plaintiffs were awarded $14,000 and $500 in compensatory damages. The rest were awarded $1 each. But Monsanto was hit with a $16 million punitive award, which was eventually overturned by the Illinois Court of Appeals.[53] The state supreme court denied the plaintiffs appeal.

A separate lawsuit was brought by 47 railroad workers who claimed they were injured while cleaning up the spill.[54] In 1982 they won a jury verdict for $58 million against the railroad, which was later overturned on a technicality. The case was then settled for a reported $22 million.

The workers had previously settled for $7 million with Monsanto, the manufacturer of the chemical.

Other dioxin cases have produced similarly mixed results. A railroad brakeman suffering from porphyria won a $200,000 jury verdict against Monsanto; the Fifth Circuit Court of Appeals overturned, finding that the expert medical testimony had failed to connect dioxin to the illness.[55] In 1988 another federal jury rejected the claims of 95 Jacksonville, Arkansas residents who claimed illness and property damage from the dioxin-contaminated wastes from a nearby herbicide plant. The jury found there was insufficient exposure to cause any injury.[56] Before that verdict, however, one defendant in the case had settled for an undisclosed amount.[57] In the fall of 1990, a federal jury found no liability in a suit brought by six workers employed in the Jacksonville herbicide plant,[58] claiming a connection between dioxin exposure and nervous disorders. Once again, a defendant had settled with the plaintiffs before trial. In yet another dioxin case, six retired workers alleged that Monsanto had recklessly exposed them to dioxin on the job. After an 11-month trial, the jury found that the workers had been exposed to dioxin and that it had harmed their health, but that their claim for civil damages was barred by West Virginia's workers' compensation law.[59] More recently, the family of a deceased truck driver recovered $1.5 million after alleging that his death from cancer was caused by exposure to dioxin-laced oil sprayed at the freight lot where he worked.[60]

Three Mile Island

Within weeks of the Three Mile Island nuclear accident, prominent Philadelphia lawyer David Berger had filed a multimillion-dollar class action suit against the owner of the plant. The suit claimed economic losses, personal injury, and emotional distress. The trial judge refused to certify the last two of these claims, apparently because it was too early to judge whether injuries such as cancer and leukemia had been caused by the accident. But he dismissed them without prejudice, leaving open the possibility of certification at a later date.[61]

In 1983, four years after the accident, one large group of plaintiffs settled for a reported $14 million.[62] A trial on the claims of 2,000 other plaintiffs is set to commence in federal court, pending resolution of procedural issues. According to Ellen Scott, attorney for General Public Utilities, the owners of the Three Mile Island plant, dozens of other individual suits are still working their way through the courts.

The complaints in these suits allege that as a result of exposure to radiation released during and after the accident, the plaintiffs, all nearby residents, sustained injuries such as cancer, skin disease, chromosomal damage, and "other injuries and ailments presently undetected by current medical science."[63] The plaintiffs who remain healthy want to recover for their increased risk of becoming ill. Those with diseases allege that radioactive emissions from Three Mile Island were the cause.[64] The medical conditions allegedly resulting from exposure to the radiation from the accident include leukemia and other forms of cancer, hyperthyroidism, cleft lip and palate, hearing loss, respiratory disorders, elevated blood pressure, "traumatic neurosis," congenital heart defects, bronchitis and asthma, sterility, miscarriages, hypertension, diabetes, and hair loss.[65]

Fernald

As Cohen describes in chapter 14, the Fernald plant refined radioactive materials as part of a weapons program, and released tons of uranium into the surrounding area starting in the 1950s. In 1985, a class action was filed on behalf of 14,000 people living near Fernald.[66] The plaintiffs charged that radioactive emissions from the plant polluted their soil, air, and water, raised cancer rates in the community, and lowered property values. The claimants sought $300 million in damages for personal injury, emotional distress, and property damage. At the suggestion of the trial judge, S. Arthur Spiegel, the parties agreed to a "summary trial," a nonbinding jury trial meant to gauge potential jury reaction and encourage settlement. At the summary trial, the plaintiffs' attorney alleged that fear of cancer was prevalent among the class, as was a psychological disorder called "informed of radioactive exposure complex."[67] A lawyer for the Department of Energy responded that the plant posed no actual danger to the residents and had caused them no harm.[68]

The summary trial resulted in a $136 million verdict, including $55 million in punitive damages for reckless operation of the plant and "callous indifference" to the public's rights, with the rest for emotional distress and future medical monitoring.[69]

The Department of Energy then agreed to settle the case for $78 million. The government did not, however, acknowledge that the emissions had caused any actual harm.[70] The plaintiffs' lawyers announced they would use the bulk of the money to study the health of the plaintiffs. The memorandum of understanding signed by the Department of Energy and the plaintiffs explicitly noted that the settlement did not bar future "cancer claims, claims of genetic abnormality and other physical injury claims by members of the class," nor claims that might arise from "contamination, sufficient to cause a serious threat to public health and safety, which is not now known because relevant information was purposefully withheld from plaintiffs, with fraudulent intent and with wanton disregard for the public health and safety."

A new series of lawsuits soon emerged. In September 1991, the first phase of a trial began in U.S. District Court, brought on behalf of more than 6,000 workers and uncounted visitors at the Fernald plant. The suit alleges that the plaintiffs were exposed to radiation and other hazards without warning or adequate protection. The plaintiffs are asking for damages of $500 million.[71] Unless it is settled, the case is unlikely to be resolved for years.

Low-Level Nuclear Radiation

Silkwood v. *Kerr-McGee* involved Karen Silkwood, a laboratory analyst and union activist at the Cimarron plant of Kerr-McGee located near Crescent, Oklahoma.[72] The plant fabricated fuel pins containing plutonium for use as reactor fuel and Silkwood manipulated this highly toxic, radioactive material in sealed "glove boxes". On the afternoon of November 5, 1974, Silkwood began to work in two such glove boxes containing plutonium. When she withdrew her hands from one of the boxes, she monitored herself and found plutonium contamination. Further tests found contamination on Silkwood's left hand, right wrist, upper arm, neck, face, hair, and nostrils. Following regulations, the company immediately decontaminated her and placed her in a five-day program in which her feces and urine were collected for analysis. Government investigators tested the glove box, and found no leaks, and no significant airborne contamination in the laboratory.

Subsequent tests on November 6 and 7 showed that Silkwood was contaminated by plutonium, as was her apartment. Paradoxically, a urine sample that she brought to the plant also contained plutonium. Since plutonium is insoluble, it does not pass through the kidneys and cannot be secreted in urine. Silkwood's possessions were destroyed to prevent the contamination from spreading, and she was sent to Los Alamos Scientific Laboratory to undergo further tests. After work on November 13, Silkwood was killed in an automobile accident on her way to meet a *New York Times* reporter. A subsequent autopsy revealed that the amount of plutonium in Silkwood's body at the time of her death was between 25 percent and 50 percent of the permissible lifetime body burden allowed by the Atomic Energy Commission for plutonium workers.

After her death, the administrator of Silkwood's estate brought an action against Kerr-McGee to recover for injuries due to her contamination with plutonium. The plaintiffs claimed that the company, or Silkwood's coworkers, purposely contaminated her in retaliation for her union activities. The company claimed that she had either contaminated herself purposely or was the victim of an undetected industrial accident.

The trial judge instructed the jury that "if you find from a preponderance of the evidence that prior to her death . . . Karen Silkwood suffered any mental pain or anguish by reason of any physical injury [due to radiation] suffered, then plaintiff is entitled to recover. . . . [P]hysical injury can include a nonvisible or non-detectable injury, may include injury to bone, tissue, or cells."

The jury found for Silkwood, and awarded her $500,000 in actual damages for her injuries and $10 million in punitive damages. Kerr-McGee asked the trial judge to overturn the verdict, or at least the punitive award, but the judge refused. On further appeal, the U.S. Court of Appeals overturned the punitive award on the ground that such damages were preempted by federal law. The case proceeded to the Supreme Court, where only the issue of punitive damages was argued. The Court, making no substantive judgment on the rest of the verdict, restored the punitive damages award.

Allen v. *United States*[73] grew out of the above-ground atomic weapons testing program, in which the government detonated more than 100 atomic bombs in the atmosphere at the Nevada Test Site in central Nevada during the 1950s and early 1960s. Years later, when the possible dangers of radioactive fallout had been widely publicized, some residents of Nevada and nearby Utah concluded that cancer and leukemia in their communities could be attributed to the fallout from those tests. About 1,200 of them sued.

The federal district court in Utah selected 24 plaintiffs for a "bellwether" trial. The trial lasted 13 weeks and included 98 witnesses and 1,692 exhibits. The court dismissed the claims of 15 plaintiffs but found for the other 9, awarding a total of $2.66 million. The court explained its decision by noting that "[w]here the factual connections between radiation exposure and injury are as strong as the ones here, other largely hypothetical alternatives carry little force." The government appealed, and won a reversal based on governmental immunity; the appellate court did not reach the issue of causation. The plaintiffs have since attempted to persuade Congress to pay compensation, so far without success.

Johnston v. *United States*[74] involved an action by four plaintiffs for injuries allegedly caused by radiation exposure from luminous aircraft instrument parts. The plaintiffs used two expert witnesses, Drs. K. Z. Morgan and J. W. Gofman, who had previously appeared as experts for the plaintiffs in the Nevada fallout case and in *Silkwood*. The trial judge struck their testimony as unreliable and dismissed the case, noting that the two witnesses "represent the views of an extreme minority of scientists."

Notes

1. *In re Asbestos School Litigation*, 104 F.R.D. 422 (E.D. Pa. 1984), *aff'd in part, vacated in part*, 789 F.2d 996 (3d Cir.), *cert. denied*, 479 U.S. 852, 915 (1986) (class certification granted).

2. *Franklin Cty. School Bd.* v. *Lake Asbestos of Quebec, Ltd.*, 1986 WL 6906 (N.D. Ala. 1986) (dismissed).

3. *Board of Educ. of the School Dist. for the City of Detroit* v. *Celotex Corp.*, no. 84-429634 (Cir. Ct. Wayne Cty. 1988) (class certification granted).

4. *Cleveland Bd. of Educ.* v. *Armstrong World Indus., Inc.*, 476 N.E.2d 397 (C.P. Cuyahoga Cty. Ohio 1985) (class certification denied).

5. *School District of Lancaster* v. *Asarco*, no. 82-1414 (Cir. Ct. Phila. Pa.).

6. *Dayton Independent School Dist.* v. *United States Gypsum Co.*, no. B-81-277 (E.D. Tx. 1988); *Kirbyville Indep. School Dist.* v. *Gold Bond Bldg. Products Div. of Nat'l Gypsum Co.*, no. CA 9776 (D. Ct. Polk City) noted in L. Hoyle, Current Status of Asbestos-In-Building Litigation in the third annual asbestos in buildings seminar 245 (Law Journals Seminar Press, 1990).

7. *St. Robert's Congregation* v. *Owens-Corning Fiberglas Corp.*, no. 647656 (Cir. Milw. Cty.) cited in L. Hoyle, *supra* note 6.

8. *City of Erie* v. *Asarco*, no. 2544-A-1982 (Cir. Ct. Erie Cty. Pa.).

9. *Mullen* v. *Armstrong World Indust., Inc.*, no. 268517 (Cal. Super. Ct. 1985) (dismissed).

10. *Sisters of St. Mary* v. *Aaer Sprayed Insulation*, no. 85-CV-5952 (Wis. Cir. Ct. 1987), *aff'd*, 445 N.W.2d 723 (Wis. App., Dist. IV) (class certification denied).

11. *Clemson Univ.* v. *W. R. Grace & Co.*, no. 2: 86-2055-2 (D.S.C. 1988) (dismissed); *Central Wesleyan College* v. *W. R. Grace & Co.*, no. 2-87-1860-2 (D.S.C.) noted in L. Hoyle, *supra* note 6.

12. *Kalkus v. United States Gypsum*, no. 5388 (C.C.P. Phila. Cty.) noted in L. Hoyle, *supra* note 6.

13. L. Hoyle *supra* note 6.

14. See, e.g., *County of Johnson, Tenn.* v. *United States Gypsum Co.*, 580 F. Supp. 284 (E.D. Tenn. 1984); *Huntsville City Bd. of Educ.* v. *National Gypsum Co.*, no. CV83-325L (Cir. Ct. Madison County, Ala. Aug. 27, 1984); *Town of Hooksett* v. *W. R. Grace & Co.*, 615 F. Supp. 126 (D.N.H., 1984).

15. See, e.g., *School Dist. of Independence, Mo.* v. *United States Gypsum Co.*, 750 S.W.2d 442 (Mo. Ct. App., 1988); *City of Greenville* v. *W. R. Grace and Co.*, 827 F.2d 975 (4th Cir. 1987).

16. See, e.g., *Hebron Public School Dist. No. 13* v. *United States Gypsum Co.*, no. A1-86-184 (D.N.D. July 15, 1989), *aff'd*, 953 F.2d 398 (8th Cir. 1992); *St. Joseph's Hosp.* v. *United States Gypsum Co.*, no. CV186-047 (S.D. Ga. 1986), *rev'd on appeal; Kershaw County Bd. of Educ.* v. *United States Gypsum Co.*, 396 S.E.2d 369 S.C. (1990).

17. See, e.g., *City of Greenville* v. *W. R. Grace & Co.*, 640 F. Supp. 559 (D.S.C. 1986), *aff'd*, 827 F.2d 975 (4th Cir. 1987); *Mercer Univ.* v. *W. R. Grace & Co.*, no. 85-126-3-MAC (M.D. Ga. 1986), *rev'd*, 877 F.2d 35 (11th Cir.), *cert. denied*, 110 S. Ct. 408 (1989).

18. *Idem.*

19. *Independent School District 622* v. *Keene Co.*, no. C5-84-1701 (Minn. D. Ct. [Washington Cty.] Oct. 5, 1990), *cited in* Minnesota school district awarded $3.2M; punitive damages triple abatement costs, *Toxics L. Daily* (BNA), October 22, 1990.

20. *Kansas City Airport* v. *W. R. Grace & Co.*, no. CV 86-19615 (Cir. Ct. Jackson Cty. Mo., tried March 1991).

21. See Hoyle, *supra* note 6, at 256.

22. Dkt. No. 29843 (Super. Ct. Cal), *aff'd*, No. 3 Civil C000899 (Cal. App. 3d Dist. 1988).

23. 868 F.2d 786 (5th Cir. 1989).

24. 225 N.J. Super. 485 (1988), 542 A.2d 975, *rev'd*, 242 N.J. Super. 576 A.2d 4, 36 (1990), *modified and remanded*, 125 N.J. 421, 593 A.2d 733, (1991).

25. 706 F. Supp. 358 (E.D. Pa. 1988), *rev'd*, 916 F.2d 829 (3d Cir. 1990), *cert. denied*, 111 S. Ct. 1584 (1991).

26. *Idem.*

27. 706 F. Supp. 376 (mem. op.), 710 F. Supp. 118 (mem. op.) (E.D. Pa. 1989).

28. *Dougherty* v. *Hooker Chemical Corp.*, 540 F.2d 174 (1976).

29. 110 Mont. Co. L. R. 417 (1982).

30. *Anderson* v. *W.R. Grace & Co.*, 628 F. Supp. 1219 (D. Mass. 1986).

31. *N.Y. Times*, September 23, 1986, A16, col. 1.

32. 1 *Toxics L. Rep.* (BNA) 842, no. 287147 (Cal. Super. Ct. 1986).

33. *Ayers* v. *Township of Jackson*, 106 N.J. 557, 525 A.2d 287 (1987) *aff'g and rev'g*, 2020 N.J. Super. 106, 493 A.2d 1314 (1985) *modifying*, 189 N.J. Super. 561, 461 A.2d 184 (1983).

34. 660 F. Supp. 1516 (W.D. Mich. 1987).

35. 2 *Toxics L. Rep.* (BNA) 862 (Cal. Super. Ct. [Monterey Cty.] 1987).

36. 660 F. Supp. 1164 (W.D. Wash 1987), *aff'd*, 856 F.2d 1433 (9th Cir. 1988).

37. No. 88-2147 (E.D. Pa. 1989).

38. R. Valdez-Robinson, $50M payout in contamination suit, Gannett News Service, June 10, 1991.

39. The most complete account of the litigation is P. Schuck. 1986. *Agent Orange on trial: Mass toxic disasters in the courts.* Cambridge, MA: Belknap Press of Harvard University Press.

40. *In re Agent Orange Product Liability Litigation,* 597 F. Supp. 740 (E.D.N.Y. 1984).

41. *In re Agent Orange Product Liability Litigation,* 611 F. Supp. 1223, 1243–1248 (E.D.N.Y. 1985), *aff'd on other grounds,* 818 F.2d 187 (2d Cir. 1987), *cert. denied sub nom., Lombard v. Dow Chem.,* 487 U.S. 1234 (1988).

42. *Peteet v. Dow Chem. Co.,* 868 F.2d 1428 (5th Cir.), *cert. denied sub nom. Greenhill v. Dow Chem. Co.* 493 U.S. 935 (1989).

43. Plaintiffs call for strict liability against Diamond Shamrock in dioxin case, *Toxics L. Daily* (BNA), June 26, 1989.

44. Parties reach $1 million settlement in case over Diamond Shamrock plant, 6 *Toxics L. Rep.* (BNA) 1034 (1992).

45. *Vuocolo v. Diamond Shamrock Chem.,* 240 N.J. Super. 289, 573 A.2d 196, *review denied,* 122 N.J. 333, 585 A.3d 349 (1990).

46. See, e.g., *In re the Charter Co.,* Op. no. 84-289-BK-J-GP (U.S. Bankruptcy Ct. M.D. Fla. 1986), *cited in* 17 *Environ. Rep.* (BNA) 1025 (Oct. 31, 1986).

47. 17 *Environ. Rep.* (BNA) 1266 (Nov. 28, 1986).

48. Settlement is reached for 128 dioxin victims, *N.Y. Times,* November 20, 1986, A22.

49. *Idem.*

50. *Adams v. Syntex Agribusiness,* no. 832-05432A (Mo. Cir. Ct. June 7, 1988), *cited in* Verdict returned for chemical companies in case by former Times beach residents, 12 *Chem. Reg. Rep.* (BNA) 424 (June 17, 1988).

51. See 12 *Chem. Reg. Rep.* (BNA) 424 (June 17, 1988).

52. Background information is from Marathon trial on dioxin spill nears end in Illinois after 3.5 years, *N.Y. Times,* August 19, 1987, and Monsanto liable in '79 dioxin spill, *N.Y. Times,* October 23, 1987, § A, 12.

53. *Kemner v. Monsanto,* 217 Ill. App. 3d 108, 160 Ill. Dec. 192, 576 N.E.2d 1146, *appeal denied,* 142 Ill.2d 655, 164 Ill. Dec. 918, 584 N.E.2d 1301 (1991).

54. See Railroad settles claims arising from cleanup of chemical spill, reportedly for $15 million, 10 *Chem. Reg. Rep.* (BNA) 772 (September 19, 1986).

55. *Thompson v. Southern Pacific Transportation,* 809 F.2d 1167 (5th Cir.), *cert. denied,* 484 U.S. 819 (1987).

56. *O'Dell* v. *Hercules, Inc.*, nos. 88-1958, 88-2123 (8th cir. 1990).

57. See 12 *Chem. Reg. Rep.* (BNA) 1250 (November 18, 1988).

58. *Keister* v. *Dow Chem. Co.*, LR-C-87-236 (E.D. Ark. Oct. 4, 1990); Jury finds for Hercules Inc. and Vertac in suit alleging dioxin exposure in Arkansas, *Toxics L. Daily* (BNA) (October 18, 1990).

59. *Boggess* v. *Monsanto Co.*, no. 86-3081 (4th Cir. 1987), cited in 11 *Chem. Reg. Rep.* (BNA) 964 (September 11, 1987).

60. Jury awards $1.5 Million in death of man exposed to dioxin, U.P.I. B.C. Cycle (July 11, 1991).

61. J. Riley, Class inaction, *Natl. L. J.*, December 12, 1986, 22.

62. *Idem.*

63. See,e.g., Complaint at 11, *Nalda Ludwig et al.* v. *General Public Utilities*, no. 2536S (Ct. Com. Pleas Dauphin Cty., Pa. 1985).

64. *Idem.*

65. See idem. at 12-16; Complaint at 11-13, *Beck* v. *Metropolitan Edison Co.*, no. 2994S (Ct. Com. Pleas Dauphin Cty., Pa. 1985).

66. *In re Fernald Litigation*, no. C-1-85-0149 (S.D. Oh.).

67. Daily Report for Executives, October 5, 1989.

68. DOE to settle Fernald suit, *Fed. Cont. Rep.* (BNA), August 28, 1989, 406.

69. *Idem.*

70. M. L. Wald, Energy Dept. to pay $73 million to settle uranium case in Ohio, *N.Y. Times*, July 1, 1989, see 1, 1, col. 2.

71. B. L. Kaufman, Trial opens Tuesday in suit against Fernald, Gannett News Service, September 16, 1991.

72. *Silkwood* v. *Kerr-McGee*, 485 F. Supp. W.D. Okla. 566 (1979), *aff'd in part, rev'd in part*, 667 F.2d 908 (10th Cir.), *verdict restored*, 464 U.S. 238 (1984).

73. 588 F. Supp. 247 (D. Utah 1984), *rev'd on other grounds*, 816 F.2d 1414 (10th Cir. 1987), *cert. denied*, 484 U.S. 1004 (1988).

74. 597 F. Supp. 377 (D. Kan. 1984).

Reference

Epstein, S. S. 1978. *The politics of cancer.* San Francisco: Sierra Club Books.

III

Medical Controversy

. . . A theory is a good theory if it satisfies two requirements: It must accurately describe a large class of observations on the basis of a model that contains only a few arbitrary elements, and it must make definite predictions about the results of future observations.

Hawking 1988, p. 6

The final section considers legal issues that arise from questionable medical theories.

The first is the centuries-old theory of *trauma and cancer*. This theory was prompted by physicians' observations that some of their cancer patients had earlier suffered trauma; however, the theory was never supported by controlled studies. Claims of "traumatic cancer," however, have figured prominently in workmen's compensation cases and other litigation. Romsdahl (chapter 15) discusses the complex and rather murky connections between trauma in its various forms and cancer. Trauma, he relates, might increase the growth of an established tumor, or contribute to its spread. He concludes, however, that simple trauma is not a sufficient cause of cancer.

Quite a different medical controversy surrounds *chemicals and immunosuppression*. Luster, Rosenthal, and Germolec (chapter 16) describe the complex scientific evidence about the effects of chemicals on the immune system. Some powerful drugs, for example those used for cancer treatment or for preventing the body from rejecting a transplanted organ, suppress the immune system and increase the patient's susceptibility to infection or cancer. At high levels of exposure, some chemicals suppress the immune system or provoke allergic responses. Individuals vary widely in their susceptibility to such problems.

Several health problems have been reported from exposure to comparatively low levels of chemical exposure. For example, the sick building syndrome is a cluster of respiratory and other problems that workers in "airtight" buildings (energy-efficient buildings lacking outside ventilation) often report. The sick building sundrome is poorly understood, but is well established, and is associated with chemical vapors, tobacco residues, and other substances in the air.

A more controversial syndrome is "multiple chemical sensitivities" (MCS). Its victims suffer from a wide and loosely defined range of non-specific mental, emotional, and physical symptoms that some people believe are associated with exposures to chemicals at levels normally considered quite safe. The distress of MCS victims is certainly very real, but mainline physicians have been unable to identify just what the problem is, or treat it effectively. By contrast, clinical ecologists, a controversial medical group, have a simpler theory: that MCS arises from damage to a person's immune system by trace levels of environmental pollutants. Their methods, however, have been criticized on technical grounds by many immunologists, and the issue is still unresolved.

In chapter 17, Cornfield and Schlossman review and criticize immunologic tests conducted in one lawsuit in which plaintiffs claimed injury to the immune system by chemical exposure.

Reference

Hawking, S. W. 1988. *A Brief History of Time: From the Big Bang to Black Holes* 6. New York: Bantam.

15

Trauma and Cancer

Marvin M. Romsdahl

"Cancer" has long been recognized as one of mankind's most serious afflictions. Hippocrates is credited with introducing this term in the fourth century B.C. The idea that trauma might cause cancer also is very old. In 1676, a prominent English surgeon, Richard Wiseman, described two patients who developed cancer at the site of a previous contusion (Behan 1939). Physicians and laymen came to accept the idea that an injury could trigger a malignancy, a belief that has continued to present times.

Today, trauma and cancer, as separate entities, rank fourth and second, respectively, as causes of death in the United States. Consequently, each is an important health problem considering the burden to society, incurred in lost manpower, costs for health care and research, and psychological grief. As separate issues, trauma and cancer are of much greater concern than the somewhat ambiguous relationship between them. The importance of trauma as a cause of cancer has not ranked high as a scientific question. However, political, social, and legal factors now commonplace and firmly established in our society have led to extensive legal commentary and numerous scientific articles on this subject.

Cancer affects approximately one-third of our population at some point in their lifetime. The disease has attracted great interest in the scientific and medical communities, and in television and the mass media. Our failure to identify the cause of most commonly encountered cancers other than lung cancer has encouraged cancer victims to speculate about all conceivable factors. The increasingly litigious character of our society also makes "cause" an issue of paramount importance to the legal and medical professions.

I shall begin with certain definitions.

Trauma signifies any damage to the body. A clear definition has been important since 1913, when Gustav von Buengner linked tumor causation to a "single" trauma—an uncomplicated injury inflicted by a single mechanical force—as distinguished from "chronic irritation"—trauma associated with a series of repeated minor injuries (in Graef 1913). "Traumatic cancer" implies a malignant tumor caused by a single trauma, without extended infection or chronic irritation (Ewing 1935). Prolonged irritation, infection, and exposure to sunlight, chemicals, and abrasive elements could, by contrast, be considered forms of "chronic trauma" (Yamagiwa and Itchikawa 1917).

Cancer denotes all malignant tumors. A *tumor* (derived from the Latin *tumere*, "to swell") is perhaps best described as an abnormal proliferation of cells that serve no relevant function and may displace or disturb normal tissues. Whereas normal tissues have an orderly pattern of growth, atrophy, regeneration, and repair controlled by incompletely understood mechanisms, tumors are relatively autonomous. The term "tumor" can also be appropriately used to designate non-cancerous developments such as hemorrhages and edema—the excess accumulation of body fluids—in a region following trauma or inflammation. *Malignant* tumors usually grow more rapidly than *benign* tumors, infiltrate normal tissues, and metastasize.

Physicians customarily divide malignant tumors into two major groups. *Carcinomas* are derived from cells like those found on the surfaces of the skin, intestine, or lungs. *Sarcomas* arise from supporting structures, such as bone, cartilage, muscle, adipose tissue, and blood vessels. *Neoplasia* means literally "new growth." In practice it refers more specifically to autonomous new growth of tissue that fails to serve a useful purpose, which for most practical purposes means malignancy.

Traumatic determinism is a term introduced by Ewing[1] to describe the fact that tissues weakened or disordered by a tumor may be damaged by mechanical trauma that is insufficient to injure normal tissues. Susceptible organs include the testicle and the breast, and abdominal organs such as the spleen, liver, and kidneys. For example, skin tumors, particularly on the extremities, are more easily injured than normal skin. Bones afflicted by benign or malignant tumors, which might not be apparent to the patient or physician, are weakened and at high risk for fracture. Such fractures may be designated "traumatic fractures" although the injury would not have occurred if the bone were normal.

The Perceived Relationship of Trauma to Cancer

1900 to 1930

The enactment of compensation laws in Germany in the late Nineteenth Century, and similar laws in the United States some decades later, motivated the search for casual connections between on-the-job injury and disease. To qualify for compensation, a worker's disability had to have been caused by an accident "arising out of and in the course of employment." Cancer presented a difficult problem, in that the connection between the injury and disease was often remote in time and typically hard to establish.

At the turn of the century, most authorities accepted that trauma might be a cause of cancer, although with sufficient reservations to keep the question alive. William Coley, a highly reputable physician and cancer specialist in New York,[2] reported in 1898 that he considered the relationship between a history of trauma and sarcoma to be "fairly convincing" in 46 of his patients. In 1913 von Buengner studied the connection between single trauma and cancer in Germany by reviewing records from large clinics (cited in Graef 1913); he concluded that trauma had been the cause of 2 to 14 percent of the cancer cases. American experts at the time shared the view that a single trauma might be implicated as a cause of a person's cancer.

However, the kinds of evidence needed to implicate an antecedent trauma as a cause of a worker's cancer were unclear. Segond (1907) proposed several criteria by which to identify trauma-induced cancers:

1. There had to be proof that the body part in question had actually been injured.
2. The trauma must have been sufficiently important or severe.
3. There had to be reasonable evidence that the part had been intact prior to injury.
4. The site of injury had to coincide exactly with the site of the tumor.
5. A tumor had to appear at a date not too remote from that of the accident.
6. A diagnosis had to be established by clinical and X-ray evidence and to be supported (when possible) by microscopic evidence.

The Second International Conference on Cancer at Paris in 1910 agreed on similar postulates (Ewing 1940), undoubtably influenced by those of Segond. His postulates also influenced the views of physicians in the United States; they were moderately restated for medicolegal use by Mock and Ellis in 1926. The criteria were the following:

1. Reasonable proof of authenticity and adequacy of the trauma
2. Previous integrity of the wounded part
3. Origin of tumor at the exact point of injury
4. Reasonable time limit between the injury and the appearance of the tumor (three weeks to three years)
5. Positive diagnosis of presence and nature of the tumor
6. History of definite bridging signs.

Segond's fourth criterion was encompassed in the sixth requirement of Mock and Ellis (1926) of a history of "bridging signs." These are symptoms that remain evident from the time of injury until the time the tumor appears. An intervening period with no apparent symptoms would considerably weaken the inference of a causal relation between the trauma and cancer. Later postulates developed for legal purposes would incorporate more precise statements of the maximum time between the trauma and development of the tumor, and the requirement of a positive, or pathologic, diagnosis of the disease.

Also in 1926, Ewing expressed doubts that any widespread relationship existed between trauma and cancer. But he did accept the existence of traumatic cancer in some isolated cases. "There is no doubt that under certain circumstances a single trauma may produce a malignant tumor," he wrote.

1930 to 1950

Ewing's reservations about trauma as a cause of cancer were not shared by Coley and Higinbotham (1933). They reported that fully half of 360 cases of bone sarcoma presented histories of trauma. Additionally, 34 percent of 205 cases of breast carcinoma had histories of trauma. Segond's criteria, by then two decades old, were not applied by these authors.

Ewing continued to express concerns in his papers. He modified his opinions slightly, concluding (1940) that "single trauma" would not cause malignancy in "normal tissue," but might produce malignant growth in one predisposed or susceptible to neoplasia by heredity or other factors. He accepted that cancers would not have occurred without the trauma. The failure of investigators to produce cancer in experimental animals by a single trauma did not change his opinion; he believed the clinical evidence to be too substantial to dismiss on theoretical grounds.

In 1935 Ewing proposed five criteria by which to identify cancers of traumatic origin. They gained wide acceptance in the courts because of Ewing's stature as a pathologist and authority on cancer. Four of his postulates were almost duplicates of those proposed by Segond (1907) and Mock and Ellis (1926). The fifth, however, included a qualification concerning the "nature of the tumor." Ewing apparently believed that a tumor resulting from trauma had to involve reparative tissue, such as cartilage, bone, fat, or fibrous tissue. He argued (1926) that only a wound severe enough to require proliferation of reparative tissue should be considered a possible factor in cancer development.

In 1943 Warren[3] further modified the published criteria. He restricted the term "traumatic cancer" to that resulting from a single injury. Apparently echoing Ewing's views, Warren concluded that "the trauma must be sufficiently severe to disrupt continuation of tissue at the site and so initiate reparative proliferation of cells." Furthermore, the "tumor must be of a type which might reasonably develop as a result of the regeneration and repair of specific tissues that received the injury."

Stewart,[4] another learned pathologist of this period, dismissed traumatic cancer entirely. He believed that "attempts to rely on single trauma to explain cancer depend on the exercise of primitive forms of reasoning"; his much-quoted conclusion (1947) was that the "concept was propagated by a system of compensation medicine." Stewart may have been the person most responsible for raising real doubts about the relationship between trauma and cancer. In any event, the late 1940s were the turning point against the acceptance of trauma as a cause of cancer.

1950 to 1970

Between 1950 and 1970, some respected cancer authorities, including Ellenbogan (1954) and Rigdon (1962) continued to accept the trauma-cancer connection. Warren (1955) considered trauma to be a "very minor factor" in the etiology of malignant disease but still believed that the relationship did exist. As late as 1961, on the basis of an intense study of 445 patients, Byrd and colleagues concluded that acute or chronic trauma will often lead to formation of skin cancers. Skeptics of the trauma-cancer connection gained considerable support from scientists' complete failure to demonstrate the connection in animal tests.

In 1950 Pack,[5] a distinguished oncologist, declared that fewer than 1 court judgment in 50 in favor of traumatic-cancer claimants was justified. He pointed out how infrequently cancer is associated with traumas. Americans collectively experience approximately 10 million injuries per year that are sufficiently disabling to cause the loss of a day's work, thousands of fractured bones (with almost complete absence of subsequent sarcoma), war wounds, and thousands of surgical incisions every year. In Pack's abundant experience, he had observed only one instance of a sarcoma developing in a surgical incision.

In the 1950s, scientists began to consider a new theory for a possible link between trauma and cancer, based on an improved understanding of the mechanism of carcinogenesis. As one cancer specialist put it: "A single trauma might produce malignancy by destroying cells already diseased in some manner, but for one trauma to produce malignancy, there must have been a condition existing of cancer present or ready to develop." "Ready to develop" would soon come to be associated with cell mutations.

Mutations, which were defined in 1952 by Berenblum[6] as a sudden transformation or change of a gene, can be produced by many different chemical and physical factors, including ultraviolet light, heat, and X-rays. Reasoning along these lines, scientists have suggested that mutations in cells, associated with chronic tissue inflammation, may be the basis of a link between trauma and cancer (Warren 1955; Rigdon 1962). The continued proliferation of cells in the repair of chronic injury may increase the chance of mutation or otherwise stimulate their uncontrolled growth. Injury may, in other words, act as a cocarcinogen, which, according to Berenblum (1941), is a noncarcinogen that augments the carcinogenic potency of another agent. In 1961, Byrd examined the role of trauma as a possible cocarcinogen, and concluded that trauma "hastened" the appearance of malignant skin tumors. By 1958 most authorities agreed, however, that "there was no evidence that a single episode of trauma can produce cancer in any organ" (Flaxman 1958).

1970 to 1990

Case reports and a few epidemiologic studies connecting trauma and cancer continued to be published, however. One widely discussed connection has been meningioma developing at the site of a head injury. Harvey Cushing, an eminent neurosurgeon, had previously supported the theory that this cancer might have a traumatic origin (Cushing and Eisenhardt 1938). Some authors in the 1960s and 1970s identified meningioma patients whose accidents fulfilled the by-now familiar criteria developed by Segond, Mock and Ellis, and Ewing (Turner and Laird 1966; Walshe 1961; Whatmore and Hitchcock 1973).

In 1958 one authority still believed in "the existence of an etiological relationship between a local skull injury and the subsequent development of a meningioma in a significant proportion of instances of this tumor" (Flaxman 1958). A possible explanation for this phenomenon is the increased cell division induced as part of the reparative process, thus rendering cells more susceptible to genetic errors that, in turn, set the stage for development of cancer (Preston–Martin et al. 1990). Such a concept is consistent with the views of Warren and Berenblum previously alluded to. One might suggest that any agent or process stimulating cell proliferation contributes to the development of neoplasms, including cancer.

Other investigators have reported associations between protracted and severe infection or trauma and Hodgkin's disease (a malignancy of the lymphatic system) (Russell and Clark 1953; Bichel 1979). Previously, some authorities had dismissed such reports as mere coincidence (Chevallier and Bernard 1932), but new cases continue to be reported, and one cannot exclude the possibility that some real association may exist. One authority believes it is "reasonable to give the patient the benefit of the doubt," considering the scientific uncertainty on the issue (Bichel 1979). Hodgkin's disease is typically first detected in the lymph nodes and for a case to have been traumatically induced, it should at the very least be present in the lymph nodes that drain the traumatized region.

The absence of any major advance in the treatment of major tumors—carcinomas of the lung, breast, colon, and rectum—has made the prevention of these cancers all the more important, which calls for some understanding of their causes. Malignant melanoma, a highly lethal skin cancer, is unequivocally associated with exposure to the sun (Briggs 1984). Other authorities have expressed strong opinions both in favor (Briggs 1984) and against (McNeer 1961) the association of this disease with trauma. McGovern (1976) described a mole on the back of a woman that was constantly rubbed by a brassierre strap, which on biopsy revealed malignant melanoma. Other clinical reports have made similar observations. But these may be coincidences, and few authorities at present argue that trauma is causally linked with malignant melanoma. Nonetheless, it is prudent to remove moles that are subject to regular irritation or injury.

In 1988, Olsson and Ranstam reported a study, based on the Swedish national cancer registry, on the possible association between head trauma (brain concussions or skull fractures) and cancer. The investigators reported that men with breast cancer had experienced significantly more brain concussions and skull fractures than men suffering from lung cancer or lymphoma. (The first pair of associations, of breast cancer with brain concussions or skull fractures, is highly statistically significant; the second, with lymphoma, is at the edge of statistical significance). The investigators had previously reported a possible association between elevated levels of the hormone prolactin and breast cancer in males (Olsson et al. 1984). In this study, the time between the trauma and the diagnosis of breast cancer was 21 years (a sufficient time for any trauma-induced cancer to have developed). Another study, published a year earlier (Shy et al. 1983), reported that a history of skull trauma severe enough to require hospitalization was a significant risk factor for prolactinoma in women. These investigators proposed that the trauma had induced the prolactinoma by injuring a connection from the base of the brain to the pituitary gland.

These studies raise the possibility of a causal link between trauma

and breast cancer in men and women. Evidence concerning prolactino-
mas and prolactin might indicate a mechanism for a relationship. Even
if true, however, the number of patients with traumatically induced
breast cancer would be extremely small compared with the total number
of breast cancer victims. While a cause-and-effect relationship cannot be
definitely ruled out, the link is too weak to have any significant practical
implications.

One organ that is particularly subject to trauma is the testicle. Physicians' opinions vary on the possibility of a link between testicular
trauma and cancer; estimates range from 5 percent to 68 percent of the
fraction of patients with testicular cancer who had a prior history of testicular trauma (Swerdlow et al. 1988).

There is, however, an important difficulty in studying the possible
connection between trauma and testicular cancer. "Trauma" is impre-
cisely defined and difficult to verify, at least in its ordinary forms. Patients with testicular cancer might be more inclined to report previous
trauma to their testicles than healthy individuals (Field 1963). This creates a serious methodological problem known as recall bias. In their
study of 259 patients with testicular cancer, Swerdlow et al. (1988) found
no significant association between testis cancer and either temperature in
the patient's workplace or trauma to the testis. It thus appears that
trauma, at least in its commonplace occurrences, is not an important risk
factor for testicular cancer. Extreme forms of trauma or raised temperature, as occurring in cryptorchidism,[7] have not been excluded as possible
causes of malignancy.

Most authorities would agree that the once-firm belief of physicians
and laymen in traumatic cancer will continue to decline as more scientific
data accumulate. According to one authority, the problem of trauma and
cancer "would be relegated to limbo if it were not for lawyers constantly
keeping the question alive" (Auster 1961). Plaintiffs continue to win
compensation for such claims in some courts, however, which helps to
keep the issue alive. However, medical opinions are converging to dis-
count the role of single trauma as a cause of cancer, at the same time that
physicians are accepting the role of carcinogenic agents and ionizing irradiation as significant causes of cancer. Physicians recognize, however,
that some kinds of physical trauma are possible cocarcinogens in certain
types of skin cancer.

Chronic Irritation and Cancer

Chronic irritation is well known to be associated with some human cancers. For example, epidermoid carcinoma (a skin cancer) is associated

with chronically draining sinuses, which often accompanies chronic osteomyelitis (a condition that was prevalent before the introduction of
antibiotics)[8] (Bowers and Young 1960). Skin cancers are associated with
chronic scar tissue that sometimes develops after burns or irradiation
(Arons et al. 1965), or excessive exposure to the sun. Basal cell carcinomas are associated with exposure to ultraviolet rays (Ackerman and del
Regato 1962). Gallbladder cancer is strongly associated with the presence
of gallstones, which abrade the bladder wall (Henderson et al. 1991).

As Ames and Gold argue in a different context in chapter 7, rapidly
proliferating cells are at increased risk for mutations and thus are more
likely to become transformed into cancer cells. They suggest that the
tendency of many chemicals to produce cancer in experimental animals
at high doses may be a consequence of the chronic irritation they produce, rather than any direct carcinogen effect.

Chronic irritation is quite different from the sudden, uncomplicated
trauma that is the supposed cause of traumatic cancer. One obvious difference is that cell proliferation occurs over a much longer time period
than is required for the healing of a simple wound. It may be, however,
that even in the healing of simple wounds there is an increased chance of
the development of cancer, but the risk is too small to be detectable in
any human or animal studies.

Trauma and Cancer in Experimental Animals

Many studies have examined the effect of trauma on the growth or
spread of tumors in experimental animals. Many report that surgical or
other trauma accelerates the growth of tumors in test animals. Such findings are difficult to extrapolate to humans, but they raise questions about
whether trauma may in some way increase the spread of tumors in humans as well.

For example, cancer cells that are injected in the backs of rats will
grow into tumors in a predictable percent of animals. That percentage
more than doubles if the inoculation occurs immediately after an abdominal operation (Buinauskas et al. 1958; Slawikowski 1960). By contrast,
when the tumor cells are inoculated 48 or 96 hours after the operation,
tumors develop at about the normal rate. Thus, the factor (or factors)
that increase the tendency of surgically traumatized animals to develop
tumors are effective for only a short time after the operation. The limited
time of vulnerability in surgically traumatized animals has been independently confirmed in other studies (Pollock et al. 1984).

In my own studies, I have transplanted tumors into the legs of several strains of mice, which then develop secondary tumors in the lung.

The number and size of those lung tumors significantly increases in proportion to the magnitude of different surgical procedures performed on the tumor-bearing animal (Romsdahl 1964).

Nonsurgical trauma has similar effects. Liver damage induced in rats with carbon tetrachloride increases their incidence of liver tumors (Chan et al. 1958). Some forms of anesthesia may decrease the resistance of rats to tumor growth, but the results have been somewhat inconsistent (Schatten and Kramer 1958). Stress from hypothermia (body cooling) leads to increased growth of inoculated tumor cells in rats (Griffiths 1960). Cortisone acetate, a hormone secreted by the adrenal gland in response to stress, increases the metastatic spread of cancer cells inoculated into mice (Pomeroy 1954) and apparently reduces the resistance of hamsters to tumors induced by injected cancer cells (Toolan 1953). Various chemicals, including histamine, nitrogen mustard, boric acid, and dilute formalin increase tumor growth of cells inoculated on backs of animals (Gore et al. 1961; Woods et al. 1957). Acute starvation has also increased the growth of tumors in test animals (Griffiths and Hope 1954). These effects appear to be "systemic;"[9] that is, the chemicals need not come in direct contact with the tumor cells to produce their effects.

All this work clearly shows that many kinds of stress can increase the rate of growth or spread of a tumor in experimental animals. The mechanism of these effects appears to be complicated and indirect. Stress may lead to "decreased resistance," as described by Seyle.[10] Surgery may lead to general excitation of the sympathetic nervous system and the adrenal medullae,[11] and trigger an "alarm reaction"—an increased output of hormones by the adrenal cortex. Such increases have been observed in cancer patients (and other patients) after an operation and are a normal response to the stress of surgery. But we cannot assume that these reactions will lead to the kinds of accelerated tumor growth observed in the animal studies.

Investigations of body defenses against cancer have focused on the immune system, in particular the role of human natural killer cells. These cells are involved in the surveillance by the immune system of cancer cells (Herberman and Holden 1978); they have antitumor activity, and may be important in the control of neoplasma (Lotzova 1983). Pollock and associates observed that the stress from surgical amputation of a lower limb in mice impairs the ability of their natural killer cells to attack target cells (Pollock et al. 1987). Other experimental data indicate that natural killer cells fail to perform at peak efficiency for 12 days after a surgical operation (Pollock et al. 1987). Thus, at least in experimental animals, surgical trauma clearly interferes with one of the body's mechanisms for fighting tumors.

Other animal studies have shown that the development or growth of tumors may be associated with wounds. For example, chicken hatchings injected with the Rous sarcoma virus (RSV)[12] will develop a sarcoma only where the virus is injected or introduced into experimentally induced wounds (Dolberg et al. 1985; Bryan 1960). Sieweke and colleagues have shown (1990) that a chemical substance known as tumor growth factor-b (TGF-b) is present in wounds shortly after injury but not in noninjured control sites. This factor allows RSV tumors to become established at sites distant from a wound. A wound, or chemical substances associated with the healing process, might thus provide the environment necessary for the virus to generate tumors.

Several lines of experimental studies in animals have shown that prior injury to an organ makes it more susceptible to tumor(s) than noninjured areas when tumor cells are injected into the blood (Alexander and Altemier 1964; Agostino and Cliffton 1965; Fisher et al. 1967). Mice carrying transplanted tumors in the thigh, and subjected to an operation on a site remote from this area, will develop more and larger metastatic lesions in the lungs (Romsdahl 1964).

The relevance of these animal studies to human malignancies is unknown. They, do however, show that—at least in animals—trauma may be linked with the development and growth of cancer. I do not believe that these observations are sufficient to justify legal awards based on a claimed connection between stressful events and cancer. On the other hand, continuing experiments to neutralize potentially harmful effects of stress, including stress resulting from major surgery, remains a worthy scientific goal (Cole 1985).

Trauma and the Metastatic Spread of Cancer

Surgeons often worry that the trauma of an operation itself may somehow augment the growth of "dormant" tumor(s) caused by cells previously spread from the primary neoplasm. Many physicians and virtually all surgeons who deal with cancer patients, myself included, have observed seemingly "explosive" development of remote secondary tumors shortly after surgical removal of a primary epithelial cancer, such as carcinoma of the breast, or mesenchymal neoplasms, such as sarcomas.

These occurrences are infrequently reported, and are likely to be rare for several reasons. Tumors rarely occur in surgical incisions, where the trauma is most severe. Experiments have shown, however, that surgery can cause spread of cancer cells from the primary source (Romsdahl et al. 1965; Knox 1922, 1929). But tumor cells will in any event have had ample time prior to surgery to spread to distant sites. Any acceleration in the development of a tumor is likely to be a result of the stress accompanying the surgical removal of the primary tumor rather than a direct effect of surgical trauma to the tumor.

Clinicians often remove tumors so large that a skin graft is required. Occasionally in such patients, numerous metastases develop at the donor site for the graft, located far from the primary tumor (Mayo 1913; Jewell and Romsdahl 1965). Physicians believe that, in these cases, the cells responsible for the metastatic tumors are circulating in the blood at the time of the graft. The removal of the skin, and later repair processes, apparently provide a receptive environment for the development of new cancer growths.

Trauma and Aggravation of an Existing Tumor

Ewing believed that trauma may aggravate an existing tumor if it ruptures the capsule (the layer of connective tissue) that surrounds a tumor and allows it to expand into surrounding "normal" tissue, or if trauma introduces infection.

The reason for this can be understood by considering how a tumor grows and spreads in the body. Tumors grow by expanding (which pushes aside adjacent normal tissue) and by infiltrating into adjacent tissues. This growth is accompanied by the development of new lymphatic channels and blood vessels through which malignant cells can further spread throughout the body. Trauma may injure tumor tissue, blood vessels, and normal structural tissues within and about the tumor, and thereby evoke bleeding, edema, and other responses that increase the tendency for a tumor to grow and spread.

Schroeder (1966) proposed guidelines to help identify when trauma may have aggravated an existing tumor; similar guidelines were proposed earlier by Warren (1955). According to these guidelines, the tumor must have existed prior to injury and must have been perceptibly damaged by the injury. The subsequent growth of the tumor must also be visibly accelerated. These guidelines are reasonable and suitable for settling disputes on this subject.

The possibility that an operation might somehow aggravate a disease must be weighed against the real benefits of surgery, which often increases a patient's life expectancy or improves the quality of life. In fact, the vast majority of cancer "cures" result from surgery. Nevertheless, the evidence that "surgical trauma" may increase the spread of cancer in some patients cannot be ignored.

Emotional Trauma as a Cause of Cancer

Clinicians have noted that emotional trauma, including psychological depression, plays a role in onset and course of both infectious and neoplastic diseases. Emotions can have hormonal effects, which in turn may affect immunological stability (Bieliauskas 1983).

In 1987 Persky and colleagues reported a study of 2,020 men employed by Western Electric Co. in Chicago that suggested a link between depression and cancer mortality. The risk of cancer increased as much as twofold for depressed subjects, as indicated by an elevated score on the Minnesota Multiphasic Personality Inventory Depression (MMPI-D) scale. Depression remained a significant predictor of death from cancer even after statistical adjustment for other known cancer risk factors like smoking.

However, an editorial in the *New England Journal of Medicine* noted that later prospective studies found no connection between emotional distress and neoplastic disease (Angell 1985). For example, Zonderman and colleagues (1989) conducted a study that included almost 7,000 subjects from different regions of the United States, and used two different scales to measure depression. The study found no significant association between depression and risk of cancer death. It now seems likely that psychological trauma or depression, while capable of impairing immunological function in the same way as surgical stress, does not perceptibly increase cancer risk in humans.

Discussion and Conclusion

Interest in the possible connection between trauma and cancer developed not because of any scientific breakthroughs but because of great social changes associated with the industrial revolution. In 1884 Germany adopted the Accident Insurance Law, sponsored by Chancellor Otto von Bismarck.[13] The law provided worker's compensation insurance to most wage earners. In the 13 years following enactment of the law, more than 2,000 books and reports appeared in the German literature addressing the relationship of trauma to tumor development (Phelps 1910). Many authors suggested that a large fraction of cancers were a result of traumatic injury on the job. Lawyers and doctors began to debate the appropriate extent of employers' responsibilities.

However, physicians began to standardize trauma statistics in German clinics, and the number of cases of apparent trauma-induced cancer decreased sharply. The medical profession thus quickly developed a more rational approach to the question of trauma as a cause of cancer, but public perceptions did not change so readily.

The financial compensation of cancer victims appears to be the major factor in sustaining traumatic-cancer litigation to this day. The failure of the medical profession to identify the actual causes of most cancers has also contributed to the problem. The "cause" of cancer remains an enigma, despite continuing efforts by many scientists using extensive technical resources. But people often demand that the causes of untoward events be identified.

Physicians cannot yet identify with assurance the cause of most cancers, but we do have convincing knowledge about what does not cause them. Some of the most prominent and influential physicians of the past century have studied the supposed link between trauma and cancer. Their accumulated research and insight provides fairly clear, rational guidance. This understanding can be summarized as follows:

1. A single uncomplicated trauma is not a sufficient cause of cancer.
2. Trauma to an established tumor may accelerate and extend its localized growth.
3. Trauma may participate as a cocarcinogen, primarily in skin cancers.
4. Trauma resulting from certain environmental factors, or exposure to chemicals and ionizing radiation, is associated with development of cancer.
5. Trauma to an established tumor may help spread the disease to distant sites.
6. Trauma to an organ or region may increase the tendency of secondary tumors to form at that site.

As we learn more about the interrelationships between the central nervous system, pituitary and adrenal hormones, and the immune system, we may develop an interpretation of "trauma" that is much broader than the traditional one. This may lead to new insights on the relation of trauma and cancer.

Acknowledgment

The author gratefully acknowledges the Del and Dennis McCarthy Fund for Surgical Oncology Research and the RGK Foundation Fund for Sarcoma Research for their financial support, and Jean Farstad Fleming for editing and preparation of this chapter.

Notes

1. James Ewing (1866–1943), professor of oncology at Cornell University Medical College, New York City, and consulting pathologist, Memorial Hospital for Can-

cer and Allied Diseases, was a prominent authority on the origin, structure, and natural history of tumors.

2. William B. Coley (1862–1936), affiliated with Memorial Hospital for Cancer and Allied Diseases, New York City, was a prominent surgeon and authority on sarcomas of the bone and a pioneer in research on treatment of malignant tumors by bacterial products called Coley's mixed toxins.

3. Shields Warren (1898–), a distinguished American pathologist who was instructor in pathology (1925–1936) and professor of pathology (1948–1965) at Harvard Medical School. He conducted research on the effects of ionizing radiation on normal and neoplastic cells and was an authority on the pathology of tumors and diabetes.

4. Harold Leroy Stewart (1899–), a noted American pathologist, he worked in the Laboratory of Pathology, National Cancer Institute, National Institutes of Health. He conducted research and contributed numerous publications on experimental induction of esophageal, gastric, and intestinal carcinomas in mice, and on tumor progress and histogenesis.

5. George T. Pack (1898–1969), a distinguished oncologist and surgeon, was affiliated with the Memorial Center for Cancer and Allied Diseases, New York City. He was a proponent and practitioner of radical operations for cancer.

6. Isaac Berenblum (1903–), affiliated with the Weizman Institute of Science, Rehovot, Israel, is a research scientist and authority on mechanisms involved in causation of cancer. His investigations of effects of croton oil resin on skin suggested a multistage mechanism in the development of epidermal neoplasms, leading to the two-stage hypothesis of cocarcinogenic action.

7. Cryptorchidism is the failure of a testis to descend from the abdomen into the scrotum during development of the male fetus.

8. Osteomyelitis is inflammation of bone, most frequently due to the bacteria staphylococcus aureus and Group A and B streptococci. It was difficult to eradicate such bone infections, which often drained for long periods via sinus tracts through overlying skin.

9. "Systemic" is a term indicating an effect on the body as a whole, as well as of a diseased part.

10. Hans Seyle (1907–), was professor and director, Instit de Médecine et de Chirurgie Expérimentales, Université de Montréal. As a research scientist he was concerned with the general physiology and pathology of stress, defined as the sum of all nonspecific changes caused by function or damage, including biological phenomena necessary for the reestablishment of the normal resting state.

11. Adrenal medullae constitute the central zone of the adrenal gland, as opposed to the surrounding cortex. Stimulation of sympathetic nerves of the autonomic nervous system causes large quantities of epinephrine and norepinephrine to be released into the blood, to circulate to all areas of the body.

12. Francis Peyton Rous (1879–1970), an American physician and virologist, conducted research on cancer and viruses at the Rockefeller Institute in New York

City. He discovered the first ribonucleic acid (RNA) virus capable of transforming normal cells into sarcoma (RSV). With Charles Huggins he received the Nobel prize in medicine and physiology in 1966.

13. Otto Eduardo Leopold von Bismarck (1815–1898), called the Iron Chancellor, was a Prussian statesman and first chancellor of the German Empire. He put through many economic and social reforms, including workman's compulsory insurance and government ownership of industrial enterprises.

References

Ackerman, L. V., and J. A. del Regato, 1962. *Cancer: Diagnosis, treatment and prognosis.* 3rd ed. St. Louis: C.V. Mosby Co.

Agostino, D., and E. E. Cliffton. 1965. Trauma as a cause of localization of blood-borne metastases: Preventive effect of heparin and fibrinolysin. 161 *Ann. Surg.* 97–102.

Alexander, J. W., and W. A. Altemier. Susceptibility of injured tissues to hematogenous metastases: An experimental study. 159 *Ann. Surg.* 933–944.

Angell, M. 1985. Disease as a reflection of the psyche. 312. *N. Eng. J. Med.* 1570–1572.

Arons, M. S., J. B. Lynch, S. R. Lewis, and T. G. Blocker, Jr. 1965. Scar tissue carcinoma, Part I: A clinical study with special reference to burn scar carcinoma. 161 *Ann. Surg.* 170–188.

Auster, L. S. 1961. The role of trauma in oncogenesis: A juridicial consideration. 175 *J. Am. Med. Assn.* 946–950.

Behan, R. F. 1939. *Relation of trauma to new growths* 7. Baltimore, MD: Williams and Wilkins.

Berenblum, I. 1941. The mechanism of carcinogenesis: A study of the significance of cocarcinogenic action and related phenomena. 1 *Cancer Res.* 807–814.

Berenblum, I., and P. Shubik. 1949. An experimental study of the initiating stage of carcinogenesis, and a reexamination of the somatic cell mutation theory of cancer. 3 *Br. J. Cancer* 109–118.

Berenblum, I. 1952. *Man against cancer. The story of cancer research.* Baltimore: John Hopkins Press.

Bichel, J. 1979. Trauma and Hodgkin's disease. 205 *Acta Med. Scand.* 347–349.

Bieliauskas, L. A. 1983. Considerations of depression and stress in the etiology of cancer. 5 *Behav. Med. Update* 23–26.

Bowers, R. F., and J. M. Young. 1960. Carcinomas arising in scars, osteomyelitis, and fistulae. 80 *AMA Arch. Surg.* 564–570.

Briggs, J. C. 1984. The role of trauma in the etiology of malignant melanoma: A review article. 37 *Br. J. Plas. Surg.* 514–516.

Bryan, W. R. 1960. A reconsideration of the nature of the neoplastic reaction in the light of recent advances in cancer research. 24 *J. Natl. Cancer Inst.* 221–251.

Buinauskas, P., G. O. McDonald, and W. H. Cole. 1958. Role of operative stress on the resistance of the experimental animal to inoculated cancer cells. 148 *Ann. Surg.* 642–648.

Byrd, Jr., B. F., A. J. Munoz, and H. Ferguson. 1961. Cancer of skin following acute and chronic trauma. 54 *South. Med. J.* 1262–1266.

Chan, P., G. O. McDonald, and W. H. Cole. 1958. The role of hepatic damage on experimental "takes" of carcinoma. 22 *Proc. Instit. Med. Chicago* 72.

Chevallier, P., and J. Bernard. 1932. *La Maladie de Hodgkin.* Paris: Masson.

Cole, W. H., and L. Humphrey. 1985. Need for immunologic stimulators during immunosuppression produced by major cancer surgery. 202(1) *Ann. Surg.* 9–20.

Cole, W. H., G. E. McDonald, S. S. Roberts, and H. W. Southwick. 1961. *Dissemination of cancer: Prevention and therapy.* New York: Appleton-Century-Crofts.

Coley, W. B., and N. L. Higinbotham. 1933. Injury as a causative factor in the development of malignant tumors. 98 *Ann. Surg.* 991–1012.

Cushing, H. W., and L. Eisenhardt 1938. *Meningiomas, their classification, regional behavior, life history and surgical end results.* Springfield, IL: Charles C. Thomas.

Dolberg, D. S., R. Hollingsworth, M. Hertle, and M. J. Bissell. 1985. Wounding and its role in RSV-mediated tumor formation. 230 *Science* 676–678.

Ellenbogan, L. S. 1954. Traumatic cancer. 51 *J. Med. Soc. N.J.* (suppl.) 276–279.

Ewing, J. 1940. *Neoplastic diseases: A treatise on tumors.* 4th ed. Philadelphia, PA: W. B. Saunders.

Ewing, J. 1935. Modern attitude toward traumatic cancer. 19 *Arch. Path.* 690–728.

Ewing, J. 1926. Relation of trauma to malignant tumors. 40 *Am. J. Surg.* 30–36.

Field, T. E. 1963. The role of trauma in the etiology of testicular neoplasms. 109 *J. R. Army Med. Corps* 58–61.

Fisher, B., E. R. Fisher, and N. Feduska. 1967. Trauma and the localization of tumor cells. 20 *Cancer* 23–30.

Flaxman, H. 1958. Trauma and cancer. 2 *Med. Trial Tech. Qrt.* 223–247.

Gore, D. R., J. A. Anderson, and G. O. McDonald. 1961. The role of toxic doses of drugs on tumor "take" following inoculation of Walker 256 cells. 3 *Proc. A.A.C.R.* 205.

Graef, W. 1913. Trauma and tumor. 17 *Centralbl. Grenzgeb. Me. und. Chir.* 603.

Griffiths, J. D., and E. Hope. 1954. Effect of metabolic "stress" on development of tumor following inoculation of Walker carcinosarcoma cells. 77 *Proc. Soc. Exper. Biol. Med.* 480.

Griffiths, J. D. 1960. The role of hypothermia and hyperthermia in the takes of Walker 256 tumor cells in rats. 10 *Surg. Forum, Am. Coll. Surg.* 42.

Henderson, B. E., R. K. Moss, and M. C. Pike. 1991. Toward the primary prevention of cancer. 254 *Science* 1131–1138.

Herberman, R. B., and H. T. Holden. 1978. Natural cell-mediated immunity. 27 *Adv. Cancer Res.* 305–377.

Jewell, W. R., and M. M. Romsdahl. 1965. Recurrent malignant disease in operative wounds not due to surgical implantation from the resected tumor. 58(5) *Surgery* 806–809.

Knox, L. C. 1922. The relationship of massage to metastasis in malignant tumors. 75 *Ann. Surg.* 129–142.

Knox, L. C. 1929. *Trauma and tumors.* 7 *A.M.A. Arch. Pathol.* 284–309.

Lea, A. J. 1965. Malignant melanoma of the skin: The relationship to trauma. 37 *Ann. R. Coll. Surg. Eng.* 169.

Lotzova, E. 1983. Function of natural killer cells in various biological phenomena. 2 *Surv. Synth. Path. Res.* 41–46.

Mayo, W. J. 1913. Grafting and traumatic dissemination of carcinoma in the course of operations for malignant disease. 60 *J. Am. Med. Assn.* 512-513.

McGovern, V. J. 1976. *Malignant melanoma: Clinical and histological diagnosis.* New York: John Wiley and Sons.

McNeer, G. 1961. The clinical behavior and management of malignant melanoma. 176 *J. Am. Med. Assn.* 1–4.

Mock, H. E., and J. D. Ellis. 1926. Trauma and malignancy. 86 *J. Am. Med. Assn.* 257–261.

Olsson, H., and J. Ranstam. 1988. Head trauma and exposure to prolactin-elevating drugs as risk factors for male breast cancer. 80(9) *J. Natl. Cancer. Inst.* 679–683.

Olsson, H., P. Alm, U. Kristoffersson, and M. Landinolsson. 1984. Hypophyseal tumor and gynecomastia preceding bilateral breast cancer development in a man. 53 *Cancer* 1974–1977.

Pack, G. T. 1950. The relation of cancer to trauma. 3 Compensation Medicine 5–10.

Persky, V. W., J. Kempthorne-Rawson, and R. B. Shekelle. 1987. Personality and risk of cancer: 20-year follow-up of the Western Electric Study. 49 *Psychosom. Med.* 435–449.

Phelps, C. 1910. The relation of trauma to cancer formation. 51 *Ann. Surg.* 609–635.

Pollock, R. E., G. F. Babcock, M. M. Romsdahl, and K. Nishioka. 1984. Surgical stress mediated suppression of murine natural killer cell toxicity. 44 *Cancer Res.* 3888–3891.

Pollock, R. E., E. Lotzova, S. D. Stanford, and M. M. Romsdahl. 1987. Effect of surgical stress on murine natural killer cell cytotoxicity. 138(1) *J. Immun.* 171–178.

Pomeroy, T. C. 1954. Studies in mechanism of cortisone induced metastases of transplantable mouse tumors. 14 *Cancer Res.* 201–204.

Preston-Martin, S., M. C. Pike, R. K. Ross, P. A. Jones, and B. E. Henderson. 1990. Increased cell division as a cause of human cancer. 50 *Cancer Res.* 7415–7421.

Rigdon, R. H. 1962. Trauma and cancer: A relationship based upon cell mutation. 55 *South. Med. J.* 341–344.

Romsdahl, M. M., R. G. McGrath, E. Hoppe, and E. A. McGrew. 1965. Experimental model for the study of tumor cells in the blood 9(2) *Acta Cytol.* 141–145.

Romsdahl, M. M. 1964. Influence of surgical procedures on development of spontaneous lung metastasis. 4(8) *J. Surg. Res.* 363–370.

Russell, W. O., and R. L. Clark. 1953. Medicolegal considerations of trauma and other external influences in relationship to cancer. 6(4) *Vand. L. Rev.* 868–882.

Schatten, W. E., and W. M. Kramer. 1958. An experimental study of postoperative trauma metastases. II. Effects of anesthesia, operation, and cortisone administration on growth of pulmonary metastases. 11 *Cancer* 460–462.

Schroeder, Jr, O. C. 1966. Cancer aggravation by trauma of causal relationships. 40 *Postgrad. Med.* A-18.

Segond, M. P. 1907. Le cancer et les accidents du travail. 20 *Proc. Verb. Mem. Discuss. Assn. Fr. Chir.* 745–782.

Seyle, H. 1952. *The story of the adaptation syndrome.* Montreal, Canada: ACTA.

Shy, K. K., A. M. McTiernan, J. R. Daling, and N. S. Weiss. 1983. Oral contraceptives use and the occurrence of pituitary prolactinoma, 249 *J. Am. Med. Assn.* 2204–2207.

Sieweke, M. H., N. L. Thompson, M. B. Sporn, and M. J. Bissell. 1990. Mediation of wound-related Rous sarcoma virus tumorigenesis by TGF-Beta. 248 *Science* 1656–1660.

Slawikowski, G. J. 1960. Tumor development in adrenalectomized rats given inoculations of aged tumor cells after surgical stress. 20 *Cancer Res.* 316–320.

Stewart, F. W. 1947. Occupational and post-traumatic cancer. 23 *Bull. N.Y. Acad. Med.* 145–162.

Swerdlow, A. J., S. R. A. Huttly, and P. G. Smith. 1988. Is the incidence of testis cancer related to trauma or temperature? 61 *Br. J. Urol.* 518–521.

Toolan, H. W. 1953. Growth of human tumors in cortisone treated laboratory animals. 13 *Cancer Res.* 389–394.

Turner, O. A., and A. T. Laird. 1966. Meningioma with traumatic etiology. Report of a case. 24 *J. Neurosur.* 96–98.

Walshe, F. M. R. 1961. Head injuries as a factor in the etiology of intracranial meningioma. 2 *The Lancet* 993–996.

Warren, S. 1955. Criteria required to prove causation of occupational or traumatic tumors. *Univ. Chicago L. Rev.* 317–322.

Warren, S. 1943. Minimal criteria required to prove causation of traumatic or occupational neoplasms. 117 *Ann. Surg.* 585–595.

Whatmore, W. J., and E. R. Hitchcock. 1973. Meningioma following trauma. 60 *Br. J. Surg.* 496–498.

Woods, S., J. Yaroly, and E. D. Holyoke. 1957. The relationship between intravascular coagulation and the formation of pulmonanary metastases in mice injected intravenously with tumor suspension. 2 *Proc. A.A.C.R.* 260.

Yamagiwa, K., and K. Itchikawa. 1917. Experimental Studien Über Die Pathogenese der Epilhelialgeschwulste (II Mitteilung). 17 *Mitt. Med. Fakultät Kaiserl.* 19.

Zonderman, A. B., P. T. Costa, and R. R. McCrae. 1989. Depression as a risk for cancer morbidity and mortality in a nationally representative sample. 262 *J. Am. Med. Assn.* 1191–1195.

Biographical Sketch

Dr. Marvin M. Romsdahl is currently a professor of surgery at the University of Texas System Cancer Center (UTSCC) and a graduate faculty member of the Health Science Center at Houston, Graduate School of Biomedical Sciences. He received his MD. from the University of Illinois College of Medicine in 1956. In 1968, he completed his Ph.D. in biology and biochemistry at the University of Texas Graduate School of Biomedical Science.

Dr. Romsdahl has published many articles on cancer treatment, particularly in the area of soft tissue tumors and breast cancer. His published work is included in the books *Surgical Management of Breast Cancer: Insights into Current Practices and Treatment Options* (Meniscus, Ltd., 1990) and *Principles of Basic Surgical Practice* (Hanley and Belfus, Inc., 1987), and a joint work, published in *Primero Congreso Iberoamericano de Oncología por Excerpta Medica,* "Multidisciplinary Treatment of Breast Cancer."

16

Chemical Pollutants and "Multiple Chemical Sensitivities"

Michael I. Luster, Gary J. Rosenthal, and Dori R. Germolec

The immune system is a complex set of soluble proteins, cells, and bioactive chemicals that protects the body against foreign substances, such as infectious agents, and tumor cells that are created within the body. The major immune cells in the blood are white cells. They come in several types, including T- and B-lymphocytes, mononuclear phagocytes, natural killer cells, and polymorphonuclear leukocytes, which can be identified by the unique molecules on their surfaces (Table 16.1).

Medical scientists can evaluate the health of the immune system through a complex process of counting and testing the functions of immune cells. Such tests describe the functions of components of the immune system but may have only indirect bearing on a person's health or quality of life, in part because of the overlapping checks and balances inherent in the immune system. However, one would expect that the risk of developing disease would increase as immunosuppression increases.

The term "immunotoxicity" is used rather loosely to describe any adverse effect exerted on the immune system by environmental agents. Those agents, which we will term "xenobiotics," may include pharmaceutical drugs, pesticides, and many other artificial or natural chemical and biological materials found in agriculture and industry, or in food products. Their adverse effects have been variously labeled "immunodeficiency," "immunosuppression," "immune alteration," "immune dysfunction," "immune system impairment," or, most inappropriately, "chemical AIDS."

Immunologists distinguish several kinds of toxic effects of chemicals on the immune system (Table 16.2). The first is a change or suppression in immunological function, or altered development of blood cells, after exposure to chemicals (Luster et al. 1987; Dean et al. 1986). Such effects often, but not always, are associated with chemical exposure at levels not far below those needed to produce other signs of toxicity in the organ-

Table 16.1
Cells of the immune system

Cell Type	Function	Selected determinants
B-lymphocyte	Antibody production	CD19
T-lymphocyte	Cell-mediated immunity	CD3
T-helper	Amplify immune function	CD4
T-suppressor	Down-regulate immune response	CD8
T-cytotoxic	Destroy foreign cells	CD8
NK cells	Capable of destroying tumor cells	HNK-1
Monocytes	Regulate other functions, scavenging	CD14
Polymorphonuclear leukocytes	Scavenging, regulation	CD15

Note: NK = natural killer.

Table 16.2
General references for chemical-induced immunosuppression, allergy, auto-immunity, and MCS

Class of effect	References
Immunosuppression	Dean et al. 1986
	Luster et al. 1990
	Vos and Luster 1989
Allergy	Salvaggio 1990
	Goldstein et al. 1985
Autoimmunity	Bigazzi 1988
	Gleichmann et al. 1989
Multiple chemical sensitivities	Bascom 1989
	Ashford and Miller 1989

ism. Suppression of the immune system through one mechanism or another may lead to increased incidence or severity of infection or cancer. Severe suppression, such as that seen in AIDS patients, causes increased susceptibility to cancer and many infections, which may eventually kill the patient. However, this is an extreme example of immunodeficiency.

A second toxic effect involves an excessive reaction of the immune system—hypersensitivity—to environmental chemicals or therapeutic drugs. This may result in allergy or attacks by the immune system against the body's own tissues (autoimmunity). For example, the distress that a hay fever victim might experience after breathing pollen grains is a result of an excessive reaction of the immune system to a stimulus that, for other people, would be insignificant. Contact hypersensitivity induced by chemicals is demonstrated by skin testing methods (such as patch tests); respiratory allergy is demonstrated by lung challenge tests (Salvaggio 1990; Goldstein et al. 1985; Van Arsdel and Larson 1989).

These kinds of immune system problems are well established and accepted by the scientific community. In contrast, "multiple chemical sensitivities" (MCS)—also called "environmental illness," "chemical hypersensitivity syndrome," or "twentieth-century disease"—has no definition that is accepted by a consensus of the scientific community, and is not recognized by most scientists as an immune-mediated condition. MCS usually refers instead to a constellation of symptoms that some people believe are caused by exposure to low-molecular-weight organic chemicals at trace levels normally considered quite safe.

Immunosuppression and Autoimmunity

Since the late 1970s scientists have accumulated a large body of evidence demonstrating that certain chemicals can suppress the immune systems of experimental animals (Luster et al. 1987; Dean et al. 1986; Vos 1977; Koller 1980). The animals show decreased responsiveness to immunization and lowered resistance to infection or cancer. The chemicals include numerous industrial and environmental agents, many of which are listed in Table 16.3.

For example, extensive data from animal studies, and to a lesser extent clinical data, show that polyhalogenated aromatic hydrocarbons, including polychlorinated biphenyls (PCBs), can suppress the immune system (Vos and Luster 1989). (PCBs are discussed in chapter 9.) In laboratory animals, PCBs inhibit immune function and the ability to resist infection (Silkworth and Vecchi 1985). The immune system is compar-

Table 16.3
Examples of xenobiotics reported to inhibit immune function and decrease host resistance

Class	Example
Polyhalogenated aromatic hydrocarbons	dioxins, biphenyls
Metals	lead, cadmium, arsenic, mercury
Aromatic hydrocarbons (solvents)	benzene, toluene
Polycyclic aromatic hydrocarbons	benza(a)pyrene
Pesticides	trimethyl phosphorothioate, carbofuran, chlordane
Organotins	dibutyltin chloride
Aromatic amines	benzidine, acetyl-aminofluorene
Oxidant gases	nitrous oxide, ozone, sulfur dioxide
Particulates	asbestos, silica
Drugs	cyclosporine, methotrexate, azothioprine

Note: Most of these chemicals have been identified on the basis of animal studies involving exposure at higher levels than found in typical nonoccupational settings. Source: Adapted from Luster et al. 1990.

atively sensitive to these chemicals, and usually will show effects at doses below those needed to affect other organs or body systems.

Some scientists have speculated that chemical-mediated immuno-suppression may be related to the development of cancer (Urso and Gengozian 1980). For example, animals exposed to some polycyclic aromatic hydrocarbons exhibit immunosuppression; the same chemicals are often carcinogenic as well. Likewise, benzene is immunotoxic in humans and experimental animals (White and Gammon 1914). Benzene increases the susceptibility of mice to cancer (Rosenthal and Snyder 1987), and causes blood disorders and leukemia in humans (Luster et al. 1990). However, the connection between such effects on the immune system and cancer remains unproven.

Direct evidence regarding possible links between chemicals and human disease as a result of immune suppression is limited. Three lines of indirect evidence can be identified. The first comes from the use of powerful drugs for cancer treatment or to suppress the immune system of a patient after an organ transplant. For example, cyclophosphamide and mercaptopurine (two drugs used to treat cancer) have been linked to increased rates of infection and the development of other cancers in patients (Ehrke and Mihich 1985). Cyclosporine and azathioprine are immunosuppressive agents used to prevent the body from rejecting organ transplants; long-term treatment with these drugs is associated with high incidence of infections (Austin et al. 1989) and cancer (Penn 1985). These effects are well established and uncontroversial.

The second line of evidence includes the many studies that report immunologic changes in people associated with exposure to chemicals but do not document any clinically apparent health effects in the subjects. Most of these studies have involved occupational or inadvertent exposure to chemicals at levels below those at which acute toxic effects might be expected.

For example, Fiore and colleagues (1986) reported changes in the numbers of T-cells in the blood, but no adverse health effects, in women chronically exposed to groundwater contaminated with low levels of Aldicarb. Deo and colleagues (1987) reported immunologic effects in residents of Bhopal, India, who had been exposed to methyl isocyanate as a result of an accident in a pesticide plant in 1984. Bekesi et al. (1987) reported persistent changes in immune system function in Michigan residents who ingested polybrominated biphenyl (PBB) contaminated dairy products, though others (Silva et al. 1979) detected no abnormalities in a similarly exposed group of Michigan residents. Various immunological abnormalities have also been reported in individuals exposed to dioxin (TCDD), either occupationally or inadvertently via contaminated soil (Hoffman et al. 1986; Stehr-Green et al. 1989; Jennings et al. 1988; see also chapter 11). Other studies, by contrast, report normal immune function after apparently high-level exposure to immunotoxic chemicals such as heavy metals (Kimber et al. 1986) and TCDD (Reggiani 1978).

The third line of evidence includes scattered studies reporting both immune suppression and clinically apparent health effects in people following occupational or accidental exposure to chemicals (Dean et al. 1986; Luster et al. 1990). For example, Lee and Chang (1985) reported that Taiwanese residents who ingested PCBs and polychlorinated dibenzofurans in contaminated rice oil experienced immunological changes similar to those seen in laboratory animals exposed to such chemicals. These individuals, said to be suffering from *yu-cheng* disease, reportedly experienced immunosuppression together with increased rates of lung and sinus infections. Uber and McReynolds (1982) reported that humans occupationally exposed to airborne silica demonstrated decreased resistance to disease. Asbestos workers have reportedly suffered from altered immunity (reduced numbers of T-cells and natural killer cells) (Lew et al. 1986). Workers engaged in the manufacture of benzidine, a human bladder carcinogen, reportedly suffer depressed immune function (as judged by skin tests) and exhibit precancerous conditions and subsequent cancers (Gorodilova and Mandrik 1978).

Several controversial studies describe chemically induced immunosuppression followed by disease in humans. One study involved a cluster of individuals with Hodgkin's disease from a small town in Michigan. The authors ascribed the illness to "chronic immune stimulation and mitogenic substances" in the environment (Schwartz et al. 1978). In another controversial study, Byers and colleagues (1988) reported a high incidence of leukemia and recurrent infections in children exposed to high levels of industrial solvents. An increased number of their family members reportedly had altered ratios of certain immune cells and increased levels of autoantibodies, as well as increased infections and recurrent rashes.

None of the clinical studies cited above would be considered definitive for a variety of reasons. Many had an incomplete or inconsistent diagnosis of immunodeficiency. Most had been conducted retrospectively, that is, the investigators applied various batteries of tests to the subjects after their exposure. (This increases the chance of false positive results and creates other problems in interpretation of the data; see chapter 1). Other limitations include small numbers of subjects, the failure to establish the subjects' actual exposure to chemicals, and apparent contradiction by later studies.

It is much more difficult to demonstrate changes in the immune system of humans than of animals. Only noninvasive tests can be done, which in many cases are less sophisticated than invasive tests done in animals. Doses cannot be controlled and must be estimated after the fact, and effects from environmental exposures must be assessed in an extremely heterogeneous population. Even under normal conditions, the results of immune function tests in humans show considerable variation (over 30 percent) (Dorey and Zighelboim 1980), which makes it difficult to detect reliably any small changes associated with the exposure.

If exposure to environmental chemicals does affect the human immune system, the effects are likely to be subtle and difficult to identify. Physicians should perform multiple tests and base their diagnosis on a consistent pattern of results, rather than on the results of single tests. Of particular importance would be the search for patterns of changes similar to those observed in patients with primary or secondary immunodeficiency diseases. Such a holistic assessment is essential because the immune system has some redundancy, so that small effects disclosed in a few tests might have little or no consequence for health.

Such patterns can be detected reliably, with sufficient effort. Many tests measure the same immune functions, and their results can be compared to provide a more complete view of a patient's immune function. For example, changes in numbers of T-lymphocytes are often accompanied by changes in skin tests to recall antigens. Small changes in the numbers of a specific type of cell are not, by themselves, clinically significant. Indeed, such changes occur routinely with moderate exercise or other activities (Pedersen et al. 1990).

A World Health Organization monograph offers guidelines for evaluating the immune system in humans that should provide a basis for future work (IUIS/WHO Working Group 1988). However, these recommendations were principally intended to be allied to patients with primary immunodeficiency diseases (such as AIDS), who suffer from a high degree of immunosuppression. They may be of limited use for detecting possible immunosuppression induced by environmental pollutants. There is a need to develop and validate a battery of diagnostic immune tests, similar to those used in animal studies, to detect subtle changes in the immune systems of humans resulting from exposure to environmental chemicals. Such tests have been discussed in a document on immunotoxicology prepared by the National Academy of Sciences (National Research Council 1992). Most scientists today would agree that further clinical studies, using well-defined groups of subjects, will be required to determine whether low-level, chronic exposure to chemicals affects the immune system.

The scientific evidence on possible links between environmental chemicals and autoimmunity is of generally similar character. There are a number of excellent examples of drug-induced autoimmunity in animals and humans (such as from gold salts or hydrazine). But with the exception of autoimmunity induced by metals (Gleichmann et al. 1989), there is little reliable evidence that low-level environmental pollutants predispose either humans or test animals to autoimmune diseases (Bigazzi 1988). Apparent exceptions exist, such as reports that Spanish residents who ingested adulterated rapeseed oil exhibited "toxic oil syndrome" and a "graft vs. host" disease, possibly autoimmune in origin (Kammuller 1985), and idiopathic scleroderma observed in vinyl chloride workers.

Allergies and Hypersensitivity

Many industrial materials are known to cause skin or lung allergies in humans (Dean et al. 1986; Salvaggio 1990; Goldstein et al. 1985). Indeed, physicians believe that up to 15 percent of all asthma has an industrial or occupational origin; the rest is a response to foods, pollen, and animal products. Recently, a number of less obvious products, such as carbonless paper, have been shown to induce allergic responses. Table 16.4 lists some industrial materials that are known or presumed to cause allergic or hypersensitivity responses in humans.

Many different chemicals can produce hypersensitivity reactions, either from direct contact with the skin or by ingestion (Zeiss et al. 1983; Thomas et al. 1990; Nenne et al. 1980). Beryllium, a widely used industrial metal, is associated with hypersensitivity diseases (Reeves and Pruess 1985). Over 15 metals, including arsenic, chromium, and nickel, cause both allergies and cancer (Aaronson and Rosenberg 1985), al-

Table 16.4

Industrial materials known or presumed to cause allergic (or hypersensitivity) responses

Materials	Industry
Platinum salts, gold, mercury	metal refining
Cotton dust	textile
Formaldehyde	garment, laboratory
Grain and flour	farming, baking, mill
Ethylenediamine, phthalic anhydride, trimellitic anhydride diisocyanates (TDI, HDI)	chemical, plastic, rubber, resin
Wood dusts	wood mills
Vegetable gums (acacia, karaya), natural resins	printing
Organophosphate insecticides	farming
Pyrolysis products of polyvinyl chloride	farming
Beryllium	diverse industries, manufacturing, coal
B-lactam antibiotics, penicillin, sulfone, ampicillin	pharmaceutical

Source: Adapted from Luster et al. 1990.

though no physiological link between the two is evident. Among other problems, asbestos may cause autoimmune disorders. Such effects are of particular concern in the workplace, where individuals may be exposed to high concentrations of substances for extended periods of time.

"Sick Building" Syndrome

A syndrome has been described by some physicians that occurs in workers in "airtight" buildings, which lack natural ventilation and use recirculated air for heating and cooling. The ventilation systems save energy, but allow chemical vapors and residues from tobacco smoke to accumulate. People who work in such buildings often report inflammation of the mucous membranes and the respiratory system, eye irritation, and other symptoms. Such reports are scientifically supported by controlled studies that have demonstrated that individuals inhaling air from airtight buildings develop nasal irritation or blockage, dry throat, and headache (Berglund et al. 1984; Robertson et al. 1985). The World Health Organization (1983) calls this the "sick building" syndrome. It is apparently caused by vapors released from construction materials or office equipment, and/or tobacco smoke that may accumulate in inadequately ventilated buildings. In the absence of any clear means of alleviating the syndrome, the most effective remedy is to improve the ventilation in the building.

Multiple Chemical Sensitivities (MCS)

From the above discussion, it is clear that many chemicals can affect the immune system, and cause allergies or other health problems, sometimes at low levels of exposure. These problems, however, have well-defined clinical and pathological features, and usually occur under identifiable conditions.

In contrast, MCS has no characteristic features or unique symptoms. There are no distinguishing biological features or accepted tests of physiological function that correlate with the symptoms observed in MCS patients (American College of Physicians 1989). One medical group has defined MCS as causing "polysymptomatic, multisystem disorders" that often result in central nervous system disorders (Committee on Environmental Hypersensitivities 1985).

The concepts associated with MCS and the clinical ecology movement originated with a Chicago allergist, Dr. Theron Randolph, and his book *Human Ecology and Susceptibility to the Chemical Environment* (1962)

Randolph concluded that certain individuals suffer from acquired multiple food and chemical sensitivities induced by exposure to synthetic chemicals in the atmosphere and in foods. Many of his patients did not exhibit typical allergic reactions but suffered from an extremely wide range of mental, emotional, and physical disorders (Dickey 1976; Bell 1982).

Randolph invented the "environment control unit," which placed his patients in a fully controlled environment said to be completely free of chemicals. If the patient's symptoms disappeared, various materials (foods, chemicals, inhalants, etc.) were reintroduced until the offending material(s) was/were identified. Although Randolph's original diagnostic methods and therapies have been replaced with more extensive programs (Dickey 1976; Bell 1982), the term "clinical ecology" is still used by proponents of these concepts.

Reportedly, MCS can be caused by almost any organic chemical, with the most-cited examples being synthetic volatile organic chemicals (VOCs) with distinct odors. Such compounds are ubiquitous; they are found in the pharmaceutical, consumer product, farming, and chemical industries; they are used in pesticides, paints, and plastics, as well as in building and petroleum-based products. Airborne VOCs are created by combustion, including tobacco smoke and heating units, and vehicle exhaust, as well as by vapors released from synthetic materials in carpets and clothing. The many chemicals alleged to produce MCS have no common features in structure, chemical reactivity, or cellular toxicity, other than, in many but not all cases, a distinct odor.

Many individuals believe they suffer from MCS. They can be grouped according to the environment in which the exposure is said to have occurred (Ashford and Miller 1989). They include office workers and schoolchildren who occupy new, airtight buildings; industrial workers; residents of communities with allegedly contaminated air or drinking water; and individuals who believe they have had personal and unique chemical exposures. This latter group is the most homogeneous population: 70–80 percent of them are females 30–50 years of age (Johnson and Rea 1989), white middle to upper class; and professionals or farmers (Ashford and Miller 1989). Most MCS victims are women or individuals with a history of asthma (Ashford and Miller 1989), except for industrial workers, among whom most reported cases are men.

While many MCS victims are reportedly allergic to chemicals, they do not exhibit the traditional symptoms of allergies (Terr 1986). Other MCS victims exhibit neurological or emotional disorders that are reportedly connected in some way with real or presumed exposure to chemicals.

Some investigators have speculated that MCS may arise, in part, from toxic effects of chemicals on the nervous system (neurotoxicity) (Selner and Staudenmayer 1985). Many MCS victims have symptoms such as loss of memory, inability to concentrate, depression, anxiety, restlessness, confusion, and headaches (Shottenfield 1987; Cullen 1987) that may reflect toxic effects on the central nervous system, or many other possible causes. Certainly, at some level of exposure, many chemicals commonly found in the environment have neurotoxic effects in humans or experimental animals; more than 850 chemicals are thought to produce such effects (Anger and Johnson 1985). One professional group active in regulatory affairs, the American Conference of Governmental and Industrial Hygienists (ACGIH), recommends exposure limits for 588 chemicals, 167 of which are limited because of suspected effects on the nervous system (Anger 1984). It is important to note, however, that such toxic effects are generally associated with exposures far above those likely to be experienced by MCS victims, and the ACGIH guidelines are mostly of relevance to the workplace.

Without dismissing the real distress that MCS victims obviously experience, it should be noted that the link between their symptoms and chemical exposure may be indirect. Some authorities have suggested that MCS is linked with emotional disorders (Simon et al. 1990); for example, odors may produce a conditioned response in the patient, who may associate them with some traumatic experience in his or her life. Such very real problems can often be treated successfully by psychotherapy (Bolla-Wilson et al. 1988).

Reports of MCS are often difficult to evaluate because of the nonspecific nature of the symptoms. Many MCS symptoms—headache, depression, and so on—are common human afflictions whose causes are diverse and often hard to identify. Overstated articles in the lay press may have led to many reports of MCS by convincing people that their symptoms are a result of MCS; some physicians are more ready than others to make such a diagnosis.

In addition, many reports of MCS can be criticized on technical grounds. Most of the evidence for MCS comes from individual reports about patients rather than from controlled clinical or epidemiologic studies. Although some investigators have reported associations between MCS and alterations in the immune system, their methods have been highly criticized (American College of Physicians 1989); other studies provide evidence against a link between immune effects and MCS (Terr 1986). One group of medical practitioners, most of whom had formerly been traditional allergists or laryngologists, support Randolph's "clinical ecology" theories (Randolph 1962). But many of the diagnostic and therapeutic methods of the clinical ecologist are not accepted by the medical community at large.

Much of this ambiguity would be resolved if there were an objective, generally agreed-upon method of diagnosing MCS, as well as animal models that mimic similar responses. For example, skin tests or IgE antibodies are comparatively objective methods for identifying allergies in humans; but MCS victims commonly do not show positive responses for the chemicals suspected of causing their problems. Many of the tests that clinical ecologists use to identify MCS seem to be poorly controlled and subjective in their interpretation. An objective test for MCS would be useful for both treatment planning and resolving legal issues.

In response to this need, the American College of Physicians published "Position Paper: Clinical Ecology" (White 1989), which sets forth criteria and general guidelines for the clinical diagnosis of chemical hypersensitivity. This report recommends the performance of specific challenge testing with appropriate control subjects. In addition, it states that careful attention be paid to the method of patient selection, the method for allocating the order of the trials, appropriate statistical analysis, appropriate use of placebos and active extracts, and in-depth immune tests. These or more defined guidelines are needed to establish when (or if) impairment of the immune system plays a role in reported cases of MCS. In the absence of such guidelines, standard immunological tests by themselves are not likely to settle the issue of MCS.

Immunotoxicology and Litigation

Claims of "chemically induced immune dysregulation" have been appearing in the courts with increasing frequently (Table 16.5). Plaintiffs allege that immune changes caused by chemical exposure are responsible for numerous commonly occurring health complaints, including the common cold, allergies, and cancer. Clinical ecologists have been called upon to support these assertions in court. Though criticized by the scientific and medical communities, their testimony has figured in several successful claims. As Sugarman (1990) has observed, "The tort law system (including claims of immune system damage) ill serves the goal of individual justice in part because it assumes that lay juries can correctly decide complex scientific issues."

Table 16.5
Examples of court cases involving immunotoxicity claims

Anderson v. *W. R. Grace & Co.*, 1986
Elam v. *Alcolac Inc.*, 1988
Higgins v. *Aerojet-General Corp.*, 1986
In re "Agent Orange" Product Liability Litigation, 1985
In re Paoli Railroad Yard PCB Litigation, 1988
Moore v. *Polish Power Inc.*, 1986
Potter v. *Firestone Tire & Rubber Co.*, 1987
Schickele v. *Rhodes*, 1986
Sterling v. *Velsicol Chemical Corp.*, 1986
Stites v. *Sundstrand Heat Transfer, Inc.*, 1987
Viterbo v. *Dow Chemical Co.*, 1987

In *Elam* v. *Alcolac, Inc.* (1988), for example, residents of Sedalia, Missouri, claimed that exposure to chemicals (including toluene, methyl chloride, allyl alcohol and epichlorohydrin) from a nearby chemical plant caused numerous injuries to their health (see also chapter 17). The residents' major complaint was chemically induced immune dysfunction. They also reported eye problems, skin and lung irritation, tingling, loss of sensation and other signs of nerve damage, sexual dysfunction, cardiovascular problems, and liver toxicity. Clinical tests showed that, in several of the patients, some immune parameters fell outside a normal reference range. However, toxicologists and physicians who examined the plaintiffs on Alcolac's behalf found no functional abnormalities in the patients. A jury awarded damages of $49 million to the plaintiffs; a Missouri court of appeals affirmed the verdict though it remanded to the trial court for a recalculation of damages.

In addition to claims of actual physical damage to their immune systems, litigants have recovered damages through claims that "immunotoxicity" increased their future risk of developing illnesses and emotional distress. For example, in *Anderson* v. *W. R. Grace and Co.* (1986), 33 plaintiffs alleged that the defendant had contaminated the groundwater in areas of Woburn, Massachusetts, with numerous chemicals, including trichloroethylene and tetrachloroethylene. The plaintiffs argued that exposure to the chemicals via drinking water had caused physical injury, including impaired ability to fight disease and leukemia, as well as specific respiratory, digestive, ocular, and musculoskeletal injuries. In addition, the plaintiffs sought damages for emotional distress caused by the defendants, and for their alleged increased future risk of developing illnesses. The judge denied the defendant's motion to dismiss the claims by summary judgment, ruling that "certain elements of the plaintiff's emotional distress stem from the physical harm to their immune system allegedly caused by the defendant conduct and are compensable."

Finally, immunotoxicity has been cited in claims for increased medical surveillance of exposed individuals. For example, in *Potter* v. *Firestone Tire & Rubber Co.* (1987), employees claimed that their exposure to hazardous substances in the workplace might damage their immune systems and cause other injuries. The court accepted damage to the immune system as a compensable injury, and ruled that the plaintiffs should receive periodic medical monitoring because "they now live with an increased vulnerability to disease."

In several other cases, the testimony of expert witnesses has been excluded or attacked on the grounds that chemical-induced immune dysfunction is not an accepted scientific theory. In *Higgins* v. *Aerojet-General Corp.* (1986) and *Sterling* v. *Velsicol Chemical Corp.* (1988), plaintiffs claimed that exposure to contaminated water caused immunotoxicity. In both cases these claims were supported by tests showing that leukocyte counts fell outside a normal range. In both cases, a clinical ecologist testified that these tests demonstrated the presence of immune dysfunction that could lead to respiratory illnesses and increased risk of cancer. However, damages for "immune system impairment" were disallowed in both cases; both courts ruled that the theory of chemical-induced immune dysfunction has no widely accepted medical basis and lacks the foundation of traditional clinical support.

Some courts have not allowed traditional scientific evidence on immunotoxicity to be presented in MCS cases; others have admitted it so that litigants could counter MCS claims. In a case involving PCB contamination at a railroad yard (*In re Paoli Railroad Yard PCB Litigation* 1988), for example, the court excluded expert testimony on animal studies, citing a ruling by Judge Weinstein (*In re "Agent Orange"* 1987) that "animal studies are not helpful in this instance because they involve different biological species. They are of so little probative force and are so potentially misleading as to be inadmissible." The judge did, however, admit documents as evidence that were based on both animal studies and epidemiologic data, including a toxicology profile for selected PCBs prepared by the U.S. government.

Summary

Evidence exists that certain xenobiotics can influence the immune system by acting as "antigens" causing hypersensitivity or allergy, producing immunosuppression or, in rare cases, autoimmunity. While there are numerous reports of chemical-induced hypersensitivity in humans, immunosuppression is limited to experimental studies and certain inadvertently or occupationally exposed populations, with little evidence that these changes translate to clinical disease. Induction of autoimmune disease in humans is, so far, limited to certain drugs and heavy metals. Nonetheless, these examples, combined with current knowledge of disease pathogenesis, support the possibility that chemical-induced damage to the immune system may be associated with potential pathological conditions, some of which may be detectable only after a long latency. Likewise, exposure to immunotoxic xenobiotics may represent additional risk to individuals with already fragile immune systems (e.g., in malnutrition, infancy, old age). Animal immunotoxicology studies have been useful in establishing mechanisms of action, exploring the immunosuppressive capacity of suspect xenobiotics, and providing "warning signs" for potentially dangerous substances. In addition, these studies are providing a framework for risk assessment in which various mathematical models may be applied in an attempt to predict potential human health effects. Unfortunately, many animal studies have bypassed risk extrapolation experts and have been used directly in litigation involving human exposure. This is a gross misuse of animal toxicity data because it can be easily be taken out of context.

Environmental medicine presents many difficult issues. While "sick building" syndrome is becoming more defined, MCS is exceptional in the number of basic scientific and methodological problems that its proponents have not adequately addressed. Its alleged causes—which include many synthetic or natural chemicals found in the environment— are so broadly specified as to be considered unknown. Its symptoms consist of subjective complaints that point to many different organ systems. The mechanisms that lead to MCS are unknown; many conflicting theories have been proposed. Despite the obvious distress of many MCS victims, the medical and scientific communities have so far received little useful information to properly diagnose and treat individuals with these "environmental illnesses."

References

Aaronson, D. W., M. Rosenberg. 1985. Occupational immunologic lung disease. In R. Patterson, ed., *Allergic diseases: Diagnosis and management* 253. Philadelphia, PA: J. B. Lippincott.

Anderson v. W. R. Grace & Co., 628 F. Supp. 1219 (D. Mass.).

Anger, W. K. 1984. Neurobehavioral testing of chemicals: Impact on recommended standards. 6 *Neurobehav. Toxicol. Teratol.* 147–153.

Anger, W. K., and B. L. Johnson. 1985. Chemicals affecting behavior. In J. D. O'Donoghue, ed., *Neurotoxicity of industrial and commercial chemicals.* Cleveland, OH: CRC Press.

Ashford, N. A., and C. S. Miller. 1989. *Chemical sensitivity—A report to the New Jersey state department of health.* Newark, NJ: State Department of Health.

Austin, J. H., L. L. Schulman, and J. D. Mastrobattista. 1989. Pulmonary infection after cardiac transplantation: Clinical and radiologic correlation. 172 *Radiology* 259–265.

Bascom, R. 1989. *Chemical Hypersensitivity Syndrome Study.* Report prepared at the request of the State of Maryland Department of the Environment in response to 1988 Maryland Senate Joint Resolution 32. Baltimore, MD: Maryland State Department of the Environment.

Bekesi, J. G., J. P. Roboz, A. Fischbein, and P. Mason. 1987. Immunotoxicology: Environmental contamination by polybrominated biphenyls and immune dysfunction among residents of the state of Michigan. Cancer Detection and Prevention Supplement 1:29–37.

Bell, I. R. 1982. *Clinical ecology.* Bolinas, CA: Common Knowledge Press.

Bentwich, Z., P. C. L. Beverley, J. R. Kalden, L. Hammarstrom, P. H. Lambert, N. R. Rose, R. A. Thompson. 1988. Laboratory investigations in clinical immunology: Methods, pitfalls, and clinical indications. 49 *Clin. Immunol. Immunopathol.* 478–497.

Berglund, B., U. Berglund, I. Johansson, and T. Lindvail. 1984. Mobile laboratory for sensory air quality studies in non-industrial environments. In B. Berglund, T. Lindvail, and J. Sundell, eds., *Indoor air: Sensory and hyperreactivity reactions to sick buildings* 3:467–471. Stockholm: Swedish Council for Building Research, Stockholm.

Bigazzi, P. E. 1988. Autoimmunity induced by chemicals. 26(3–4) *J. Toxicol. & Clin. Toxicol.* 125–156.

Bolla-Wilson, K., R. J. Wilson, and M. L. Bleecker. 1988. Conditioning of physical symptoms after neurotoxic exposure. 30(9) *J. Occup. Med.* 684–686.

Byers, V. S., A. S. Levin, D. M. Ozonoff, and R. W. Baldwin. 1988. Association between clinical symptoms and lymphocyte abnormalities in a population with chronic domestic exposure to industrial solvent-contaminated domestic water supply and a high incidence of leukemia. 27 *Cancer Immunol. Immunother.* 77–81.

Committee on Environmental Hypersensitivities. 1985. *Report of the Ad Hoc Committee on Environmental Hypersensitivity Disorders.* Toronto, Ontario: Canadian Ministry of Health.

Cullen, M. R. 1987. The worker with multiple chemical hypersensitivities: An overview. 2 *State Art Rev. Occup. Med.* 655–661.

Deal, J. H., M. J. Murray, and E. C. Ward. 1986. Toxic responses of the immune system. In C. D. Klassen, M. O. Amdur, J. Doull, eds., *Casarett and Doull's toxicology* 245–285. 3rd ed. New York: MacMillan.

Deo, M. G., S. Gangal, A. N. Bhisey, R. Somasundaram, B. Balsara, B. Gulwani, B. S. Darbari, B. Sumati, and G. B. Maru. 1987. Immunological, mutagenic and genotoxic investigations in gas exposed population of Bhopal. 86 *Ind. J. Med. Res.* 63–76.

Dickey, L. D. 1976. *Clinical ecology.* Springfield, IL: Charles C. Thomas.

Dorey, F., and J. Zighelboim. 1980. Immunologic variability in a healthy population. 16 *Clin. Immunol. Immunopath.* 406–415.

Ehrke, M. J., and E. Mihich. 1985. Effects of anticancer agents on immune responses. 62 *Trends Pharmacol. Sci.* 412–417.

Elam v. *Alcolac, Inc.,* 3 *Toxics L. Rep.* 765, no. 38105 (W.D. Mo. Ct. App.).

Fiore, M. C., H. A. Anderson, R. Hong, et al. 1986. Chronic exposure to aldicarb contaminated groundwater and human immune function. 41 *Environ. Res.* 633–645.

Gleichmann, E., I. Kimber, and I. F. H. Purchase. 1989. Immunotoxicology: Suppressive and stimulatory effects of drugs and environmental chemicals on the immune system. 63 *Arch. Toxicol.* 257–273.

Goldstein, R. A., D. D. Sogn, and J. Ayers. 1985. Occupational and environmental lung disease: A perspective. In J. H. Dean, M. I. Luster, A. E. Munson, and H. Amons, eds., *Immunotoxicology and immunopharmacology* 489–496. New York: Raven Press.

Gorodilov, V. V., and E. V. Mandrik. 1978. The use of some immunological reactions for studying the immune response in persons presenting a high oncological risk. 8 *Sov. Med.* 50–53.

Higgins v. *Aerojet-General Corp.,* 1 *Toxics. L. Rep.* 842, no. 287147 (Cal. Super. Ct. [Sacramento Cty] 1986).

Hoffman, R. E., P. A. Stehr-Green, K. B. Webb, R. G. Evans, A. P. Knutsen, W. F. Schramm, J. L. Stoake, B. B. Gibson, and K. K. Steinberg. 1986. Health effects of long-term exposure to 2,3,7,8-tetrachlorodibenzo-p-dioxin. 255 *J. Am. Med. Assn.* 2031–2038.

Husman, K. 1980. Symptoms of car painters with long-term exposure to a mixture of organic solvents. 6 *Scand. J. Work Environ. Health* 19–32.

In re Paoli Railroad Yard PCB Litigation, 3 *Toxics L. Rep.* 843. no. 86-2229, slip. op. (E.D. Pa. Nov. 29, 1988).

In re "Agent Orange" Product Liability Litigation, 611 F. Supp. 1223, 1250–1255 (D.C.N.Y. 1985), *aff'd,* 818 F.2d 187 (2d Cir. 1987).

Jennings, A. M., G. Wild, J. D. Ward, and A. M. Ward. 1988. Immunological abnormalities 17 years after accidental exposure to 2,3,7,8-TCDD. 45 *Br. J. Indus. Med.* 701–704.

Johnson, A., and W. Rea. 1989. Review of 200 cases in the Environmental Control Unit. Paper presented at the Seventh International Symposium on Man and His Environment in Health and Disease, Dallas (February 25–26).

Kammuller, M. E., A. H. Penninks, J. M. deBakker, C. Thomas, N. Bloksma, and W. Seinen. 1985. An experimental approach to chemical induced systemic (auto)immune alterations: The Spanish toxic oil syndrome as an example. In *Mechanism of cell injury: Implications for human health* 175–189. Dahlem Workshop Life Sciences Research Report no. 37.

Kimber, I., M. D. Stonard, D. A. Gidlow, and Z. Niewola. 1986. Influence of chronic low-level exposure to lead on plasma immunoglobulin concentration and cellular immune function in man. 57 *Int. Arch. Occup. Enviorn. Health* 117–125.

Koller, L. D. 1980. Immunotoxicology of heavy metals. 2 *Int. J. Immunopharmacol.* 269–279.

Lee, T.-P., and K.-J. Chang. 1985. Health effects of polychlorinated biphenyls. In J. Dean, M. Luster, A. Munson, and H. Amos, eds., *Immunopharmacology* 415–422. Raven Press.

Levi, R. 1972. Effects of exogenous and immunologically released histamine on the isolated heart: a quantitative comparison. 182 *J. Pharm. & Exp. Ther.* 227–238.

Lew, R., P. Tsang, J. F. Holland, N. Warner, I. J. Selikoff, and J. G. Bekesi. 1986. High frequency of immune dysfunctions in asbestos workers and in patients with malignant mesothelioma. 6 *J. Clin. Immunol.* 225–233.

Luster, M. I., J. H. Blank, and J. H. Dean. 1987. Molecular and cellular basis of chemically induced immunotoxicology. 27 *Ann. Rev. Pharmacol. Toxicol.* 23–49.

Luster, M. I., A. E. Munson, P. T. Thomas, M. P. Holsapple, J. D. Fenters, K. L. White Jr., L. D. Lauer, D. R. Germolec, G. I. Rosenthal, and J. H. Dean. 1988. Methods evaluation: development of a testing battery to assess chemical-induced immunotoxicity: National Toxicology Program's guidelines for immunotoxicity evaluation in mice. 10 *Fund. Appl. Toxicol.* 2–19.

Luster, M. I., D. Weirda, and G. J. Rosenthal. 1990. Environmentally related disorders of the hematologic and immune systems. In *Medical clinics of North America* 74:425–440. Philadelphia: W. B. Saunders.

Maibach, H. 1983. Formaldehyde: Effects on animal and human skin. In J. Gibson, eds., *Formaldehyde toxicity* 166. New York: Hemisphere.

Menne, T., K. Kaaber, and J. C. Tjell. 1980. Treatment of nickel dermatitis. 10 *Ann. Clin. Lab. Sci.* 160–164.

National Research Council. 1992. Markers in immunotoxicology. Washington, DC: National Academy Press.

Nebert, D. W., H. J. Eisen, and O. Hankinson. 1984. The Ah receptor: Binding specificity only for foreign chemicals. 33 *Biochem. Pharmacol.* 917–924.

Norton, S. 1986. Toxic response of the central nervous system. In C. D. Klassen, M. O. Amdua, and J. Doull, eds., *Casarett and Doull's toxicology* 357–386. 3rd ed. New York: MacMillan.

Pedersen, B. K., N. Tvede, K. Klarlund, L. D. Christensen, F. R. Hansen, H. Galbo, A. Kharazmi, and J. Halkjaer-Kristensen. 1990. Indomethacin in vitro and in vivo abolishes post-exercise suppression of natural killer cell activity in peripheral blood. 11 *Int. J. Sports Med.* 127–131.

Penn, I. 1985. Neoplastic consequences of immunosuppression. In J. H. Dean, M. I. Luster, A. E. Munson, and H. Amos, eds., *Immunotoxicology and immunopharmacology* 79–90. New York: Raven Press.

Potter v. *Firestone Tire & Rubber Co.,* 2 *Toxics L. Rep.* 862, no. 81723, slip op. (Cal. Sup. Ct. Dec. 31, 1987).

Randolph, T. G. 1962. *Human ecology and susceptibility to the chemical environment.* Springfield, IL: Charles C. Thomas.

Rea, W. J. 1978. Environmentally triggered cardiac disease. 40 *Ann. Allergy* 243–251.

Reeves, A. L., and O. P. Pruess. 1985. The immunotoxicity of berylium. In J. Dean, A. Munson, M. Luster, and H. Amos, eds., *Immunotoxicology and immunopharmacology.* New York: Raven Press.

Reggiani, G. 1978. Medical problems raised by the TCDD contamination in Seveso, Italy. 40 *Arch. Toxicol.* 161–188.

Robertson, A. S., P. S. Burge, A. Hedge, J. Sims, F. S. Gill, M. Finnegan, C. A. C. Pickering, and G. Dalton. 1985. Comparison of health problems related to work and environmental measurements in two office buildings with different ventilation systems. 291 *Br. Med. J.* 373–376.

Rosenthal, G. J., and C. A. Snyder. 1987. Inhaled benzene reduces aspects of cell mediated tumor surveillance in mice. 88 *Toxicol. & Appl. Pharmacol.* 35–43.

Salvaggio, J. E. 1990. The impact of allergy and immunology on our expanding industrial environment. 85(4) *J. Allergy Clin. Immunol.* 689–699.

Schwartz, R. S., J. P. Callen, and J. Silva Jr. 1978. A cluster of Hodgkin's disease in a small community: Evidence for environmental factors. 108 *Amer. J. Epidemiol.* 19–26.

Selner, J. C., and H. Staudenmayer. 1985. The practical approach to the evaluation of suspected environmental exposures: Chemical intolerance. 55 *Ann. Allergy* 665–673.

Shim, C., and M. H. Williams. 1986. Effect of odors in asthma. 80 *Am. J. Med.* 18–22.

Shottenfield, R. S. 1987. Workers with multiple chemical sensitivities: A psychiatric approach to diagnosis and treatment. In M. Cullen, ed., *Occupational medicine.* Philadelphia, PA: State of the Art Reviews.

Silkworth, J., and A. Vecchi. 1985. Role of the Ah receptor in halogenated aromatic hydrocarbon immunotoxicity. In J. Dean, M. Luster, A. Munson and H. Amos, eds., *Immunotoxicology and immunopharmacology* 263–275. New York: Raven Press.

Silva, J., C. A. Kauffman, D. G. Simon, P. J. Landrigen, H. E. Humphrey, C. W. Heath, K. R. Wilcox, Jr., G. Van Amburg, R. A. Kaslow, A. Ringel, and K. Hoff. 1979. Lymphocyte function in humans exposed to polybrominated biphenyls. 26 *J. Reticuloendothelia. Soc.* 341.

Simon, G. E., W. J. Katon, and P. J. Sparks. 1990. Allergic to life: Psychological factors in environmental illness. 147(7) *Am. J. Psychiatry* 901–906.

Stankus, R. P., P. K. Menon, R. J. Rando, H. Glindermeyer, J. E. Salvaggio, and S. B. Lehrer. 1988. Cigarette smoke-sensitive asthma: Challenge studies. 82 *J. Allergy Clin. Immunol.* 331–338.

Stehr-Green, P. A., P. H. Naylor, and R. E. Hoffman. 1989. Diminished thymosinalpha-$_{alpha}$ levels in persons exposed to 2,3,7,8-tetrachlorodibenzo-p-dioxin. 28 *J. Toxicol. & Environ. Health* 285–295.

Sterling v. *Velsicol Chemical Corp.*, 647 F. Supp. 303, 422 (W.D. Tenn. 1986), *aff'd in part, rev'd in part,* 855 F.2d 1188 (6th Cir. 1988).

Struwe, G., and A. Wennberg. 1983. Psychiatric and neurological symptoms in workers occupationally exposed to organic solvents. 67 *Acta Psychiatr. Scand.* 68–80.

Sugarman, S. D. 1990. The need to reform personal injury law, leaving scientific disputes to scientists. 248 *Science* 823–827.

Terr, A. I. 1986. Environmental illness: A clinical review of 50 cases. 146 *Arch. Intern. Med.* 145–149.

Thomas, P. T., W. W. Busse, N. I. Kerkvliet, M. I. Luster, A. E. Munson, M. Murray, D. Roberts, M. Robinson, J. Silkworth, R. Sjoblad, and R. Smialowicz. 1990. Immunologic effects of pesticides. In S. R. Baker and C. F. Wilkinson, eds., *The effects of pesticides on human health* 261–295. Princeton: Princeton Scientific.

Uber, C. L., and R. A. McReynolds. 1982. Immunotoxicology of silica. 10 *CRC Crit. Rev. Toxicol.* 303–319.

Urso, P., and N. Gengozian. 1980. Depressed humoral immunity and increased tumor incidence in mice following in utero exposure to benzo (alpha) pyrene. 6 *J. Toxicol. & Environ. Health* 569–576.

VanArsdel, Jr., P. P., and E. B. Larson. 1989. Diagnostic tests for patients with suspected allergic disease. 110 *Ann. Int. Med.* 304–312.

Vos, J. G. 1977. Immune suppression as related to toxicology. 5 CRC Crit. Rev. Toxicol. 67–101.

Vos, J. G., M. I. Luster. 1989. Immune alterations. In R. D. Kimbrough and A. A. Jensen, eds., *Halogenated biphenyls, terphenyls, naphthalenes, dibenzoidioxins and related products* 278. Amsterdam: Elsevier.

White, L. J. 1989. *Clinical ecology.* 111(2) *Ann. Int. Med. 168–178.*

White, W. C., and P. M. Gammon. 1914. The influence of benzol inhalations on experimental pulmonary tuberculosis in rabbits. 29 *Trans. Assn. Am. Physicians* 332–337.

World Health Organization. 1983. *A sick building syndrome: a review*. European Report 78, presented at Indoor Air Pollutants: Exposure and Health Effects, meeting in Nördlingen, Germany.

Zeiss, C. R., P. Wolkonsky, R. Chacon, P. A. Tuntland, D. Levitz, J. J. Prunzansky, and R. Patterson. 1983. Syndromes in workers exposed to trimellitic anhydride. 98 *Ann. Intern. Med.* 8–12.

Biographical Sketch

Michael I. Luster is head of the Immunotoxicology Group at the National Institute of Environmental Health Sciences and adjunct professor in toxicology at Duke University Medical Center. He is a member of the American Association of Immunology, the Society of Toxicology, and the International Society of Immunopharmacology. Dr. Luster serves on the editorial board of *Environmental Health Perspectives, International Journal of Immunopharmacology, Food and Chemical Toxicology, Toxicology and Applied Pharmacology, and Environmental Research.*

Gary J. Rosenthal, Ph.D., received his doctorate at New York University Medical Center's Institute of Environmental Medicine in Sterling Forest, New York. He completed his postdoctoral training at the National Institute of Environmental Health Sciences, where he is currently on staff as a research toxicologist. Dr. Rosenthal is a diplomate of the American Board of Toxicology.

Dori R. Germolec is a biologist in the Immunotoxicology Group at the National Institute of Environmental Health Sciences and a doctoral candidate at North Carolina State University. Her research interests include the immunotoxicology of environmental chemicals and chemical mixtures, and the metabolism of xenobiotics by immune cells.

17

Immunologic Laboratory Tests:
A Critique of the Alcolac Decision[1]

Richard S. Cornfeld and Stuart F. Schlossman[2]

Introduction

Should courts and juries make decisions on scientific issues if there is no
scientific support for their decisions? It seems obvious that such decisions
would be incompatible with any notion of justice, yet the last few years
have seen courts and juries being asked to do just that. They have been
asked to find that individuals have suffered damage to their immune systems based upon evidence that would not withstand scrutiny in the scientific arena. In some cases this testimony has come from self-styled
"clinical ecologists," claiming that the supposed damage to the plaintiffs'
immune systems has rendered them susceptible to a seemingly endless
array of ailments in a variety of organ systems.[3] In others, the testimony
has come from expert witnesses using more traditional immunologic ter-
minology and diagnosing immunosuppression.

The decision in Elam v. Alcolac Inc., 765 S.W.2d 42 (Mo. Ct. App.
1988), is one example of the latter type of case. Reviewing a verdict in
favor of 31 plaintiffs for a total of $6.2 million in compensatory damages
and $43 million in punitive damages, the Missouri Court of Appeals
ruled, based upon a series of laboratory test results, that the plaintiffs had
suffered severe depression of their immune systems. Yet, as we show in
this chapter, the court did not cite any evidence of damage which any
competent immunologist would accept.

It is our thesis that courts should not consider claims of immune
system injury unless they are supported by evidence which would satisfy
competent immunologists. Using the *Alcolac* decision as a springboard,
we propose in this chapter a four-pronged evidentiary standard for the
consideration of immunologic claims. First, such claims must include, as
a sine qua non, a history of severe, unusual, and repeated infections.
Without such a history, no competent immunologist would even consider whether an individual has a suppressed immune system. Second,

even if an individual does have such a history, a diagnosis of immunological suppression must be based only upon laboratory tests that have
established diagnostic uses and not upon novel, experimental tests that
are for research purposes only. Third, in most instances, slight or trivial
deviations from a reference range have no diagnostic significance and
should not be used as evidence of immunosuppression. Fourth, even if a
laboratory result does deviate significantly from the reference range,
courts should not consider it to have diagnostic significance unless the
test is repeated and the result is substantially similar.

Admissibility of Scientific Evidence

The standard for admissibility of scientific evidence in complex product
liability and toxic tort litigation has received much recent attention.[4] In
cases such as *Sterling* v. *Velsicol Chemical Inc.,* 855 F.2d 1188 (6th Cir.
1988); *Viterbo v. Dow Chemical Co.,* 646 F. Supp. 1420 (E. D. Tex. 1986),
aff'd, 826 F.2d 420 (5th Cir. 1987); and *In re "Agent Orange" Product Liability Litigation,* 611 F. Supp. 1223 (D.C.N.Y. 1985), *aff'd,* 818 F.2d 187
(2d Cir. 1987), courts have used Federal Rules of Evidence 403 and 703
as authority to scrutinize expert testimony very carefully and to exclude
it if it lacks scientific foundation. As Judge Kelly stated in *In re Paoli
Railroad Yard PCB Litigation,* 706 F. Supp. 358, 368 (E.D. Pa. 1988):

> If Rule 703 is to be any limit on the ability of expert witnesses to give their
> opinions, a court must be permitted to examine the bases of the proffered opin-
> ions. Otherwise any case in which an expert was willing to use two sets of magic
> words would always survive motions for summary judgment and directed ver-
> dict. As long as the expert was willing to say "to a reasonable degree of scientific
> certainty" and "the basis of my opinion is X, on which experts in my field rea-
> sonably rely," every case requiring expert testimony would get to the jury. If a
> court is not permitted to examine the basis of an expert's opinion in order to rule
> on the admissibility of that opinion, then Rule 703 should read: "An expert may
> cite as the basis of his opinion anything he likes."

The precise nature of the scrutiny of expert testimony has varied
from case to case, but many courts have refused to receive expert testimony unless it has some minimum level of acceptance in the scientific
community. The district court in *Viterbo,* put the nature of the inquiry
this way: "If the underlying data is so lacking in probative force and
reliability that no reasonable expert could base an opinion on that data,
then an opinion that rests entirely on that data must be excluded" (646
F. Supp. at 1424).

Unfortunately, the court in *Elam* did not scrutinize the testimony of the plaintiffs' experts nearly so carefully. In that case, two expert witnesses, Arthur C. Zahalsky, Ph.D., and Bertram W. Carnow, M.D., testified that the plaintiffs had sustained severe damage to their immune systems from exposure to chemicals negligently emitted from the defendant's chemical plant. Drs. Carnow and Zahalsky characterized that damage with a number of terms, such as "chemically induced AIDS," "chemically induced immune disregulation" (CIID), "immunodeficiency," and "immune system dysfunction with suppression" (765 S.W.2d at 83, 100, 102, 213). The court approved the use of all these terms except for "chemically induced AIDS," which it held was "unnecessary and gratuitous" and unfairly prejudicial on the issue of punitive damages (765 S.W.2d at 214).

For that reason, as well as the trial court's erroneous ruling that the plaintiffs had made a submissible case on the issue of their alleged increased risk of cancer, the Missouri Court of Appeals remanded the case for a trial limited to damages. However, on the issue of the plaintiffs' alleged injuries, the court upheld the verdict. Without conducting any independent inquiry, the appeals court concluded that "the diagnoses of biological injury, disease and dysfunction Dr. Carnow entered for each of the 31 plaintiffs as attributable to exposure to the Alcolac toxins [was] derived by valid scientific principle, based on competent scientific proof, and rest[ed] on substantial evidence" (765 S.W.2d at 229).

With respect to each of the plaintiffs, the court set forth a summary of that evidence, which came entirely from two sets of laboratory tests performed on blood specimens. The first was a set of tests performed by Bioscience Laboratory in Chicago in August 1984 and consisted of a white blood count and differential, measurement of immunoglobulins, and mitogen stimulation testing. The second set of tests was performed by Midwest Organ Bank and Wheeler Laboratory in Kansas City in July 1985. It consisted of a peripheral blood measurement of white blood cells, lymphocytes, and various lymphocyte subsets.[5] Before describing the results which supposedly supported the conclusion that the plaintiffs' immune systems were deranged, it would be helpful to describe how immunologists typically go about evaluating a patient's immune system.

Typical Immunological Evaluation

The single most important aspect in evaluating an individual's immune system is the patient's history. In evaluating the history, the physician is attempting to determine whether the immune system has successfully been performing its function—to protect the individual against infectious diseases caused by organisms such as viruses, bacteria, fungi, parasites and protozoans, and against foreign substances or antigens.

Organization of Immune System

The importance of this history can be seen by describing the immune system and how it works (Table 17.1). There are actually two separate "immune systems" which provide this protection, the nonspecific immune system and the specific immune system. Some scientists do not consider the nonspecific system to be part of the immune system at all. This is because its components do not require any kind of recognition or sensitization to an infectious agent before being able to perform their function. The components of the non-specific system are very active at the first encounter with the agent. The specific immune system, on the other hand, requires prior stimulation with an infectious agent in order to become sensitized and perform its function. These branches, while distinct, often work together in fighting infections.

Non-Specific Immunity. The non-specific immune system is made up of several components: macrophages, polymorphonuclear leukocytes, complement, and natural killer cells. Macrophages (a word mean-

Table 17.1
Organization of the immune system

Nonspecific immunity	Specific immunity
A. Phagocytic cells:	A. T-Lymphocytes:
• Segmented neutrophils	[cell-mediated immunity]
• Eosinophils	• T helper
• Basophils	• T suppressor
• Monocytes	• T cytotoxic
• Tissue-based macrophages	
B. Complement system:	B. B-lymphocytes:
• Consists of at least 20 immunologically distinct plasma proteins	[humoral immunity]
	• Antibody producing
	• IgA
	• IgG
	• IgM
	• IgE
C. Natural killer cells:	
• Type of lymphocyte	

ing "large eaters") are white blood cells, or leukocytes, which engage in phagocytic activity, meaning that they engulf and destroy foreign materials. They are primarily located in bodily tissue, such as the skin or lung. In addition, a number of other types of white blood cells, called segmented neutrophils (or polymorphonuclear neutrophils or polys or PMHs), eosinophils, basophils, and monocytes are also engaged in the phagocytosis and digestion of infectious agents and foreign material. Except for tissue-based macrophages, these cells are generally found in the peripheral blood—i.e., the bloodstream. Complement is made up of many separate proteins. These proteins in association with antibody can lyse (or destroy) different infectious agents and help mediate an inflammatory reaction. The natural killer cells are, like macrophages, white blood cells—specifically, a subset of lymphocytes, which are another category of white blood cell. They were discovered only about 15 years ago, and their role in the immune system is not well understood. They appear to be responsible, in part, for natural resistance to some infectious agents and perhaps to some human cancers. (They are, at least, able to destroy malignant cells in the test tube.) They are the only type of lymphocyte that is not part of the specific immune system.

Specific Immunity. The specific immune system is again divided into two branches. The first, the humoral branch, exerts its effect by means of protein molecules called antibodies or immunoglobulins, which are produced by a subset of lymphocytes called B-cells or B-lymphocytes. There are five categories of immunoglobulins, three of which are principally involved in fighting infectious agents. These are IgG, IgM and IgA. A fourth, IgE, is involved in allergic reactions. The role of the fifth, IgD, is not known.

The other branch of the specific immune system is the cell-mediated branch. It gets its name because it requires the direct presence of the cell to exert its effect. The cells which make up this branch are yet another subset of lymphocytes called T-cells or T-lymphocytes. There are three principal types of T-cells: T-helper cells, which induce the B-cells to make antibodies; T-suppressor cells, which discourage the B-cells from making antibodies; and T-cytotoxic cells, which are sensitized to kill specific agents or to lyse (destroy) specific infected cells.

Typical Response to Infectious Agent

When a typical foreign agent, such as a virus, enters the body, it is taken inside a macrophage, which "digests" it by means of enzymes that break it down. This is known as the phagocytic function of the nonspecific immune system. In a relatively minor infection, this phagocytosis might end the process. In other cases, the macrophage directly transfers the broken-down or processed virus (or antigen) to its surface in the context of its major histocompatibility complex and then to T- and/or B-cells (depending on the particular virus involved).

The presentation of the antigen to the T-lymphocytes can result in the formation of a T-cytotoxic cell, sensitized to attack the particular kind of virus involved, but no other. At the same time, the B-cells receive chemical messages from the T-helper cells, encouraging production of antibodies, and from T-suppressors, discouraging such production. The result is the production of an appropriate amount of antibodies, again sensitized to the particular virus and no other. These antibodies attack the virus in a number of different ways, including attaching to the virus itself and preventing further infectivity.

With most infectious illnesses, the process of responding to the agent generally takes several days. During this time, the person may be sick. On the other hand, the immune system may fight the agent so well that the individual has little or no evidence of clinical disease. Furthermore, if the specific immune system becomes involved, on the next encounter with the same agent the sensitized B-cells and/or T-cells will immediately recognize the agent and successfully attack it before any clinical illness sets in. Unfortunately, many viruses, such as the influenza virus, can change their structure; this is why people get the flu year after year.

Aside from fighting infectious diseases, the immune system probably also has a role in protecting us against cancer. This area is highly controversial, and the method by which the immune system fights cancer is poorly understood. However, there is evidence that among individuals with severely—indeed, massively—impaired immune systems, forms of cancer occur in unusual numbers. For example, individuals with AIDS (acquired immune deficiency syndrome) tend to develop lymphoma or an unusual form of cancer called Kaposi's sarcoma. Transplant patients receiving immunosuppressive medications are likewise prone to develop leukemias or lymphomas. However, they do not develop other forms of cancer in unexpected numbers. Moreover, in the vast majority of cancer patients, there is no evidence of a preceding immune abnormality.

Studies have been done on cancer patients admitted to the Dana-Farber Cancer Institute to try to determine whether they have any defect in their immune systems. However, evidence of immune defects has been present only in patients who have previously been treated with potent agents such as chemotherapy or radiation therapy, agents which have the unfortunate side effect of suppressing the immune system. No pattern of immune defect has been found in cancer patients *before* being treated.

Furthermore, there is no immunologic test that has been found useful in predicting the development of cancer. One can only imagine the value such a test would have. Unfortunately, it does not exist. In short, the relationship between the immune system and cancer has yet to be fully delineated.

Effect of Immunologic Impairment

As is suggested by the role of the immune system in fighting infectious agents, individuals with impaired immune systems do develop frequent, unusual, severe, and even life-threatening infections. That is why a patient's history is the most important element of an immunologic diagnosis. Such infections are, in fact, the hallmark of a suppressed immune system.[6] As two prominent immunologists, Max Cooper and Alexander Lawton, have stated, " [i]mmunodeficiency syndromes, whether congenital, spontaneously acquired, or iatrogenic, are characterized by unusual susceptibility to infection. . . ."[7]

Immunosuppressed individuals develop major infections, repeat infections, and infections with organisms that do not affect healthy individuals. For example, they may develop recurrent bacterial pneumonia, recurrent abscesses, or recurrent fungal infections of the mouth. Such illnesses are uncommon in the general population but are frequently seen by infectious disease specialists treating AIDS patients or oncologists treating patients with immunosuppressive medication. No only do such patients develop these serious infections, but, because of the damage to their disease-fighting capability, they have difficulty fighting them off.

Immunosuppressed people do not, on the other hand, develop more frequent run-of-the-mill infections such as colds, flus, bronchitis, urinary tract infections and the like. Even individuals with AIDS get no more of these common infections than do healthy people. Nor do immunosuppressed patients develop the broad range of problems diagnosed by "clinical ecologists" as supposedly being due to environmental chemicals. Thus, if a patient has the kind of routine infections common to most people—even if he complains that he seems to develop one cold or sore throat after another—the astute physician will be able to conclude that there is nothing wrong in the immune system without needing any laboratory tests to reach that conclusion.

Laboratory Evaluation: Basic Tests

If the physician does perform laboratory tests, there are several that he might order, the most basic of which is a measurement of the white blood cell count and differential in the bloodstream. This is a measurement of the number of circulating white blood cells (i.e., the white blood cell count or WBC) with a breakdown of the different types, such as segmented neutrophils and lymphocytes (i.e., the differential).

The next test, in decreasing order of importance, is a quantitative measurement of the three important immunoglobulins, IgA, IgG and IgM. These results may indicate suppression of the immune system with an antibody deficiency, but only if the results are low—for example, total immunoglobulins of less than 400 mg/dl or IgG of less than 200 mg/dl.[8] As with the white blood count and differential, a result only a few points below the reference range has several possible causes—including normal individual variability—but does not indicate an immunodeficiency.

Measures of white blood count, differential, and measurement of serum proteins are derived from relatively common tests, which internists frequently perform and interpret. They were performed on the *Alcolac* plaintiffs. A specialist in immunology might perform more specialized tests, especially functional tests and quantitation of lymphocyte subsets such as B- and T-cells.

Functional Tests.   Functional tests measure the ability of lymphocytes to respond to a challenge. They are commonly done in two ways. The first, which was not done on the *Alcolac* plaintiffs, is a skin test which measures the delayed-type hypersensitivity response. This test is similar to the tuberculin tine skin test with which most people are familiar and involves pricking the skin with a number of different antigens. A healthy immune system will respond in a few days by causing the formation of one or more appropriately sized red lumps on the skin.

The other common way of measuring lymphocyte function is a test with a number of different names, including lymphocyte stimulation, lymphocyte blastogenesis, and mitogenic stimulation. In the *Alcolac* case, it was called mitogen challenge. This complicated test is performed by separating out the lymphocytes from a blood sample and challenging them with as many as three separate substances, called mitogens. Competent lymphocytes should respond to the challenge by synthesizing DNA. In addition, DNA synthesis is measured in lymphocytes which have been unchallenged, a so-called unstimulated response or background. After a number of days, a radioactive substance is added to each specimen and is incorporated into the DNA. The specimens are then put into a machine, similar to a Geiger counter, which measures radioactive counts. The more counts that are measured, the more DNA has been synthesized.

The absence of a response or a very low response might indicate immune suppression, but it must be found repeatedly to have any significance. And, again, results which fall below the laboratory's reference range are not diagnostic unless they are low, such as a stimulated result no more than three times the background (a so-called stimulation index of 3).[9] One reason is that many factors—age, stress, medications (including aspirin), difficulties in performing the test, just to name a few—can affect the results.[10] However, people with genuine immunosuppressions do not fall slightly below the reference range; they fall nearly to zero.

Lymphocyte Subsets.   Quantitation of the various lymphocyte subpopulations or subsets is done in tests that use substances called monoclonal antibodies. These antibodies were developed in the mid-1970s by Cesar Milstein and George Kohler, who won the Nobel Prize in medicine for their work.

Monoclonal antibodies are so called because they are derived from a single clone of a cell. They have the capability of attaching themselves, or binding, to molecules located on the surface of cells, generally called surface markers or surface antigens. Each cell has many such molecules on its surface, but different subsets of lymphocytes have certain distinct surface molecules, which can be used to differentiate them. For example, all human T-cells have a surface antigen called T3 or CD3 and will be bound by monoclonal antibodies directed against this antigen. They also have the T11 or CD2 antigen. T-helper cells have an antigen called T4 or CD4, and T-suppressors and cytotoxics have one called T8 or CD8. B-cells have an antigen called B-1 or CD20. Monoclonal antibodies therefore enable physicians to determine the number of total T-cells, T-helpers, T-suppressor/cytotoxics, B-cells, and other lymphocyte subsets in the bloodstream.

Various manufacturers have marketed monoclonal antibody reagents available for use by researchers, and they have given different names to their products. For example, the T-helper monoclonal antibody has been designated T4 by Coulter Immunological, OKT4 by Ortho Diagnostics, and Leu 3 by Becton-Dickinson. In 1984, a committee of the World Health Organization recommended that these names be supplanted by CD designations (for "cluster of differentiation").[11] Thus, the T-helper antibody was designated CD4. Initially, there were 15 CD designations, and additional CD designations have been added since that time. At the Fourth International Workshop and Conference on Human Luecocyte Differentiation Antigens held in Vienna in February [1989], the number of CD designations reached over 70.

The discovery of monoclonal antibodies has been one of the most exciting developments in the recent history of immunology. These remarkable molecules are enabling scientists to study differentiation and maturation of the lymphocyte and other cells in ways never before dreamed of. They are enabling scientists to determine the nature of different kinds of immunologic disorders and to follow the progress of patients with those disorders. They are enabling hematologists to study malignancies such as leukemia and lymphoma, with resulting new knowledge about the different forms these diseases may take. They have led to dramatically new and highly promising treatments for these diseases, such as the autologous bone-marrow transplant.[12]

However, the vast majority of these monoclonal antibodies are appropriate only for research, not diagnostic or therapeutic purposes. The U.S. Food and Drug Administration has approved only a few for diagnostic uses.[13] For example, of the 53 monoclonal antibodies currently being marketed by Coulter Immunology, only five—three which measure total T-cells, one which measures total B-cells, and one which measures a subset of B-cells—have been licensed for diagnostic use.[14]

There are several reasons why the bulk of the tests are not reliable for diagnostic purposes. For one, only a few of the monoclonal antibodies define distinct cell lines. For example, OKT-10 or CD38, one of the tests performed on the *Alcolac* plaintiffs, has been reported to measure B-cells at some stages of their development and maturation but not at others, plasma cells (B-cells in their terminal stage), thymocytes (cells in the thymus gland), immature T-cells, activated T-cells (T-cells which have been stimulated to respond to a foreign agent), monocytes, and some natural killer cells.[15] Thus, measurement of the number of cells reacting with such a monoclonal antibody does not indicate how many cells of any one type are present.

Furthermore, these tests tend to be difficult to perform accurately. In performing the tests, the monoclonal antibody is stained with fluorescent dye and then added to the cell sample so that it can bind to the appropriate surface antigens. The cells are then passed through a fluorescence-activated cell sorter. This machine counts the total number of cells that pass through the beam and the cells which are stained by the antibody.

A number of factors, however, make interpretation of a result difficult. First, there may be problems with the reagent which keep it from binding properly. In addition, problems in collection, preparation, or shipping the cell specimens are well known to cause errors.[16] It is sometimes difficult to set the cell sorter properly so that it can distinguish between stained and unstained cells—especially where, as with OKT-10, the antibody stains weakly. Furthermore, many factors other than the immunologic status of the patient can affect the results. These factors include the age and sex of the patient, the time of day at which the blood is drawn, recent drug intake, the presence of an infection in the patient (of which the patient may or may not be aware), and undoubtedly other factors which are currently unknown.[17]

Thus, even with those tests which are licensed by the FDA, a physician should not diagnose any immunologic condition unless the test is repeated and the results are similar.[18] In other words, if a patient has a low result on a CD3 test, indicating a possible reduction in the number of T-cells, the physician should not conclude that the patient actually has a deficiency in those cells unless he repeats the test and again finds such a reduction.

Furthermore, as with most of the other tests which we have discussed, no immunologic abnormality should be diagnosed unless the result is substantially outside the laboratory's reference range. In other words, a physician should not conclude a patient has a suppression of his immune system based upon an abnormally low result for the CD4 cells unless the result is so low it shows a virtual absence of helper cells.[19] Moreover, functional tests should be used to substantiate any phenotypic abnormality. Patients lacking CD4 cells will fail to respond to skin test antigens in vivo and their lymphocytes will not respond in vitro.

The Alcolac Decision

With these principles in mind, we can review the bases advanced by the plaintiffs' experts, and adopted by the court, for the diagnosis of immunosuppression in *Alcolac*. Of the 31 plaintiffs, there were diagnoses of immunological disorders in 29. These diagnoses were either "immune system dysfunction," "immune system dysfunction with suppression," or "immune dysfunction with depression." However, while those were the formal diagnoses, in his testimony Dr. Carnow was more colorful. He said one plaintiff's immune system was "zapped," another "completely zapped," and another in "total suppression" (765 S.W.2d at 116, 127, 130).

Were Plaintiffs Experiencing Infections?

What illnesses were these people with supposedly damaged immune systems experiencing? According to the court's opinion, none. The diagnoses were based entirely on the results of laboratory tests. Furthermore, in reviewing the clinical histories of the plaintiffs, the court did not describe any infections consistent with a total suppression, a severe suppression, or any suppression, of the plaintiffs' immune systems (765 S.W.2d at 100–162). The inquiry should therefore have stopped right there. Without any resulting infections, the finding of damaged immune systems—whether that damage be called "dysfunction," "suppression," "depression," "total suppression," or some of the more colorful phrases—makes no scientific sense.

Dr. Carnow apparently tried to explain away this problem with the amazing contention that deficiencies in T-cells do not lead to recurrent infection. According to the court, he claimed:

Recurrent infection is the consequence of B-cell abnormality, since the B system is that arm of the immune system which relates to infections. [Linda Sanders's] abnormality, as with most of the *Alcolac* plaintiffs, was to the T-cells—and they tend to relate "to very specific types of infections, like tuberculosis and things like that, and they relate more to cancer cells." (765 S.W.2d at 144)

This testimony is nothing more than scientific bamboozlement. Not only were all tests of Linda Sander's T-cells normal—and not only did she not have a "very specific type of infection like tuberculosis and things like that" (whatever that means)—but it is utter nonsense to suggest that an abnormality of T-cells does not lead to recurrent infections.[20] One only needs to think of AIDS patients to realize that. As a result of their loss of T-helper cells, AIDS patients suffer many repeated and severe infections. Moreover, abnormalities of T-cell populations are found in other severe immunodeficiencies as well. One example is agammaglobulinemia,[21] a type of immunodeficiency in which the bloodstream lacks immunoglobulins and repeated, severe infections result.

Were Tests Repeated?

Moreover, while there were two sets of laboratory tests on which the experts' conclusions were based, only three actual tests were repeated. Otherwise, an entirely different panel was performed each time. The repeated tests were measurements of white blood cells, lymphocytes, and T-lymphocytes, none of which showed consistent abnormalities. Of the seven plaintiffs said to have abnormalities of their white blood count in the first test, five had results within the reference range the second time.

Of the ten plaintiffs with lymphocyte "abnormalities" and of the four with T-lymphocyte "abnormalities," none had consistent results on the second test. Thus, whatever caused these "abnormalities," it was not a condition—such as an immunodeficiency—which persisted from the first test to the second.

Were Results Indicative of Immunologic Damage?
Furthermore, it is clear that even the results performed only once could not support a conclusion that any of the plaintiffs, with one possible exception,[22] had a damaged immune system. The appeals court did not always report the actual laboratory values, sometimes merely stating they were "abnormal," but of the values it reported, virtually none of them were so low as to cause legitimate concern—especially in the absence of a history of infections.

Immunoglobulins. For example, with respect to the immunoglobulins, which were tested as part of the first panel, there were three "abnormalities" on IgG—one simply called "abnormal" and two slightly elevated at 1510 (reference range 70–1500). Trivial elevations like these are insignificant, but elevation is clearly inconsistent with "suppression." There were nine results below the reference range (80–310) for IgM, the lowest being 61, not low enough to suspect an immunosuppression. The lowest white blood count was slightly depressed at 4100 (reference range 4500–11,000)—again, not enough to cause concern about an immune suppression.

Mitogen Stimulation Testing. On the mitogen stimulation testing, 14 of the 30 plaintiffs (not counting Mary Landon, who had cancer) had a least one result below the reference range. According to the appeals court's description of Dr. Carnow's testimony, he apparently placed great reliance on these results. It is remarkable, therefore, that he only repeated these tests on one plaintiff. These were the tests which were performed in 1983 on Gwendolyn Lawrence before most of the other plaintiffs were tested. Her results were below the reference range on each of the mitogen stimulation results, but not excessively so. For example, her PHA stimulation index (the ratio of her stimulated DNA production divided by the background rate) was 71. To cause any concern, the ratio would need to be in the vicinity of 3 or below.[23]

When Mrs. Lawrence's results were repeated, two—her CON A and PWM stimulation indices—were each significantly low at 2. These were the only results of any of the mitogen stimulation tests on any plaintiffs which were anywhere near low enough to raise the suspicion of an immunologic defect. Such results might have many causes other than damage to the immune system, but Dr. Carnow described her "entire immune system" as "irreparably suppressed" (765 S.W.2d at 130). Yet she had not had a single infection consistent with a suppressed immune system. At a minimum, if a physician were concerned, he should have repeated the tests. There is no basis, however, for concluding that these results were due to immune suppression.

Monoclonal Antibodies. The second panel, the one performed by the Wheeler/Midwest Laboratory, largely consisted of measurements of lymphocyte subsets by use of monoclonal antibodies. There were a total of eight or nine such tests. The court, and apparently Dr. Carnow as well, were confused about two tests called NKH1 and HNK1,[24] and it is unclear whether one or both were performed. In any event, the vast majority of the tests on this panel were developed at the Tumor Immunology Laboratory of the Dana-Farber Cancer Institute. These tests included B1 (CD20),[25] OKT-3 (CD3),[26] OKT-11 (CD2),[27] OKT-4 (CD4),[28] OKT-8 (CD8),[29] NKH-1 (CD56),[30] and OKT-10 (CD38).[31] In addition, researchers from this laboratory were the first to describe the T-4/T-8 or helper/suppressor ratio, on which Dr. Carnow relied.[32] The only other test performed on the plaintiffs with monoclonal antibodies was a test called by the court "natural killers." The court does not state what antibody was used for this test.

At the time these tests were conducted, none of the reagents used to perform the tests had been licensed for diagnostic uses by the Food and Drug Administration. Only one such reagent—B-I, a Coulter product—is licensed even today. In addition, Coulter markets licensed reagents corresponding to two of the other tests, T-3 (corresponding to the Ortho product, OKT-3) and T-11 (corresponding to the Ortho product, OKT-11).

Even if these unapproved tests are considered, however, there are no results which even suggest a suppression in any of the plaintiffs' immune systems. A summary of the tests appears in Table 17.2, which makes clear that there was no overall pattern to the results as one would expect if the plaintiffs had all been affected by a common chemical exposure. For example, with regard to NKH-1 (CD56), nine plaintiffs had results above the reference range and four below the reference range.

Moreover, some of the plaintiffs had results which were internally inconsistent. Lyle Turley had an elevated OKT-3 (CD3) and a depressed OKT-11 (CD2), even though those two tests are supposed to measure

Table 17.2
Results reported for lymphocyte subset testing on 30 *Alcolac* plaintiffs

Test	Above reference range	Below reference range	"Abnormal" without specification
B-1 (CD20)	2 plaintiffs	0 plaintiffs	1 plaintiff
OKT3 (CD3)	1	0	1
OKT11 (CD2)	0	4	0
OKT4 (CD4)	0	1	2
OKT8 (CD8)	3	0	0
OKT4/OKT8 Ratio	1	2	3
"Natural killers"	3	1	0
NKH1 (HNK1) (CD56)	9	3	0
OKT10 (CD38)	14	0	0

Source: Toxics L. Rep., Sept. 6, 1989.

the same thing—total T-cells. There were also inconsistencies in the two tests to quantitate natural killer cells, NKH-1 (CD56) and the test simply referred to as "natural killers." Although these tests presumably measured the same thing, only one plaintiff had a result out of the reference range on both. If the plaintiffs truly had natural killer abnormalities, as Dr. Carnow claimed, they should have had abnormalities on both tests.

There was similar confusion regarding OKT-10, the test which was reported to have 14 "abnormalities," the largest number found. With regard to Carl Berry, whose OKT-10 cells were more than twice the upper limit of the reference range and constituted nearly one-third of all his lymphocytes, Dr. Carnow said that these were "immature, unprogrammed lymphocytes, probably pre-leukemic cells." The court did not state the basis for Dr. Carnow's testimony, but we are aware of no literature in which OKT-10 cells have been found to be "pre-leukemic." Indeed, there is no monoclonal antibody yet developed which is capable of detecting "pre-leukemic cells" in the peripheral blood.

The testimony of Dr. Zahalsky about these tests was also fallacious. In summarizing Dr. Zahalsky's testimony, the court referred to "the natural killers of the T-4 population . . ." (765 S.W.2d at 85). Natural killers are not part of the T-4 population, a fact which was well known at the time of Dr. Zahalsky's testimony.[33] Dr. Zahalsky apparently also testified that the combination of elevated levels of HNK-1[34] and elevated levels of T-8 suppressor cells indicated a gross distortion in the ratio between the helper and suppressor cells, "an indication that the immune system balance was 'out of whack'" (765 S.W.2d at 85). However, the relationship between levels of HNK-1 and suppressor cells could indicate a distortion in the ratio between *helper* and suppressor cells only if HNK-1 were a test for helper cells. Yet, while HNK-1 may mark a few helper cells, it primarily marks other cells and is by no means a helper-cell antibody.

In short, the expert testimony in *Alcolac* was not only outside the mainstream of science, it was outside its widest perimeter. Court should require witnesses giving testimony like this to provide authoritative support for it in the scientific literature.[35] If, as in this case, there is no support for such testimony, they should exclude it. Because the jury is ill-equipped to evaluate the scientific validity of such testimony, the court must exercise its traditional power to exclude it as unreliable. We therefore propose a four-part evidentiary standard for the admission of the results of immunologic laboratory tests and expert testimony based thereon. We cannot, of course, foresee all the circumstances in which experts will purport to rely on such tests. This proposal is therefore designed to cover the *minimum* requirements for admissibility. There may be additional reasons to exclude laboratory results in individual cases.

A Proposed Evidentiary Standard

1. *Unless the plaintiff has a documented history of severe, prolonged, unusual and repeated infections, any results of immunologic laboratory tests are inadmissible.*

The only relevance of immunologic laboratory tests can be to assist the jury in determining whether an individual has an impaired immune system. As shown in this chapter, and as recognized by all competent clinical immunologists, suppressed immune systems are characterized by an unusual susceptibility to infections. Some individuals with suppressed immune systems may also develop other problems—such as autoimmune diseases—but without a history of susceptibility to infection, there can be no basis for diagnosing an immunodeficiency.

Thus, plaintiffs should be required, as a prerequisite to the introduction of laboratory results, to prove a history of the kinds of infections characteristic of damaged immune systems. This history must be documented in medical records of their treating physicians and would include such problems as repeated, prolonged bouts of pneumonia or meningitis, unusual fungal infections, abscesses, and the like. It would not include typical infections common in the general population, such as colds, influenza, strep throat, otitis media, urinary tract infections, and the like. Many parents complain that their children have frequent strep throat or other respiratory infections, but without a history of more unusual infections, these are not the result of an immunodeficiency.

2. *Only those laboratory tests which have been approved for diagnostic uses by the FDA should be admitted into evidence.*

Tests which have not been approved for diagnostic purposes do not yet have the necessary reliability to support a scientifically valid conclusion that an individual has a damaged immune system. In the *Alcolac* case, a handful of such tests were performed. Since that time, the number of novel, experimental, laboratory tests used in litigation has proliferated. For example, in the *Times Beach* trial in 1988, the plaintiffs' expert ordered no fewer than 18 monoclonal antibody tests on the plaintiffs.[36]

Perhaps in the future, data to support the use of these tests in diagnostic procedures will be developed, and if so we would then agree that juries should be able to consider them in appropriate cases. Clearly, immunological methodology is continually improving, and we would not propose an immutable list of tests which are forevermore inadmissible in evidence. The standard which we propose, in the interest of both scientific reliability and practicality, is one of FDA licensure. With regard to monoclonal antibodies, if the FDA has licensed a reagent for diagnostic purposes then juries should be permitted to consider the results of such tests. However, if the FDA does not yet consider such a test to be valid for diagnostic purposes—in other words, if the FDA believes that these tests are not sufficiently reliable for use by physicians in diagnosing immunologic abnormalities—then certainly juries should not be allowed to consider them for those purposes either.

3. *Only substantial deviations from a laboratory's reference range should be considered supportive of a suppressed immune system.*

It should be clear from the above discussion that, perhaps to a greater degree than in most tests, the range of immunologic laboratory results found in healthy individuals is great and that many causes other than immunosuppression—including random individual variability—can lead to "abnormalities."

Individuals with suppressed immune systems do not deviate from the norm by only a small degree. For example, results below a laboratory's reference range on mitogen stimulation tests do not support a diagnosis of immunodeficiency unless the stimulation index is in the range of 3.0 or less.[37] The total immunoglobulins in individuals with suppressed immune systems fall below 400 mg/dl.[38] Courts should require similar levels on these and other tests before allowing juries to consider whether plaintiffs have suppressed immune systems. Where to draw the line between significant and insignificant results is difficult. At a minimum, experts relying on such tests to prove immunologic damage should be required to provide literature support for their contention that results of that level are associated with clinical symptomatology.

4. *Courts should not admit results of immunologic laboratory tests into evidence unless those tests are repeated and the results are similar.*

As we have shown in this chapter, many immunologic tests are difficult to perform accurately.[39] Factors such as medications or temporary infections (of which the individual may not even be aware) may cause temporary alterations in some or all of these tests.[40] Therefore, physicians should not normally diagnose an immunodeficiency based on one set of laboratory tests alone. Neither should courts.

Courts should require that any tests with results diagnosed as "abnormal" be repeated and that the second set of results be similar before admitting the results into evidence. The second set of "abnormal" results should be from the same tests which had the "abnormalities" the first time. In other words, a depressed mitogen stimulation result on the second set does not support a conclusion that a depressed IgM on the first set was related to a damaged immune system. To be admissible into evidence, the IgM result should be depressed on each test.

Conclusion

Because a jury is ill-equipped to evaluate expert testimony that purports to be based on research on the frontier of science, the court must exercise control over the type of testimony a jury can consider. If courts refuse to allow into evidence testimony like that given in *Alcolac* and other cases, decisions based on such psuedoscientific untruths can be prevented.

Notes

1. Reprinted with permission from 4(14) *Toxics L. Rep.* 381–390 (September 6, 1989).

2. One of the authors of this article directs a research laboratory which has developed many of the laboratory tests which have been used to support both types of immunologic claims. The other author is an attorney who has handled the defense of immunologic claims.

3. In Sterling v. Velsicol Inc., 855 F.2d 1188 (6th Cir. 1988), the U.S. Court of Appeals for the Sixth Circuit ruled that expert testimony by clinical ecologists was

inadmissible under Fed. R. Evid. 702 because the principles upon which the testimony was based had not "gained wide acceptance. . . ." *Idem.* at 1208. Several earlier decisions by state courts were decided differently. In Menendez v. Continental Insurance Co., 515 So.2d 525 (La. App. 1987), the court reversed a worker's compensation ruling against the claimant on the ground that the trial court should have accepted the testimony of a clinical ecologist. The court ruled that, as the claimant's treating physician, the clinical ecologist was entitled to greater deference than the defendant's expert. In Kyles v. Workers' Compensation Appeals Board, 195 Cal. App.3d 614, 240 Cal. Rptr. 886 (Ct. App. 1987), and Grayson v. Gulf Oil Co., 292 S.C. 528, 357 S.E.2d 479 (Ct. App. 1987), the courts reversed benefit denials to claimants who alleged that PCBs had damaged their immune systems. The claims had been supported by the testimony of clinical ecologists. In Moore v. Polish Power Inc., 720 S.W.2d 183 (Tex. Ct. App. 1986), the court reversed a directed verdict for the defendant on the ground that the trial court had improperly excluded the testimony of a clinical ecologist. The issue was limited to whether the clinical ecologist had a sufficient basis for his testimony about formaldehyde content in a carpet. Neither the trial nor the appellate court was asked to rule on whether testimony based on clinical ecology was admissible.

4. See, e.g., Pagliaro & Benton, Courtroom Science: Toxic Tort Battleground, 3 *Toxics L. Rep.* 1336 (1989); Rothman & Maskin, Defending immunotoxicity claims, 3 *Toxics L. Rep.* 1219 (1989); Black, *A unified theory of scientific evidence,* 56 Fordham L. Rev. 595 (1988) [hereinafter Black]; *Rules for admissibility of scientific evidence,* 115 F.R.D. 79 (1987).

5. A third set was performed for the defendant by the University of Kansas laboratory, but the court refused to consider it—and did not report the results—because the laboratory had no reference ranges.

6. Chapel and Haeney, Essentials of clinical immunology 76 (2nd ed. 1988): "The major symptom of immunodeficiency is recurrent infection . . ."; Stiem, Immunodeficiency Disorders. In Immunologic disorders in infants and children 157, 163 (3rd ed. 1989): "The major manifestation of immunodeficiency is increased susceptibility to infection"; Waldmann, Immunodeficiency diseases: Primary and acquired, M. Santer, D. Talmadge, M. Frank, K. F. Austen, and H. N. Clamen, eds., in Immunologic Diseases 411, 415, (4th ed. 1988): ("Immunodeficiency syndromes are characterized by an unusual susceptibility to infection . . ."); Rose, Disorders of the immune system, N. Rose, F. Milgrom, and C. J. van Oss, eds., in Principles of immunology 277, 290 (2nd ed. 1979): "The common denominator of immunodeficiency disorders is heightened susceptibility to infection."

7. M. Cooper and A. Lawton, Immunodeficiency diseases, E. Braumwald, K. J. Isselbacher, R. G. Petersdorf, J. D. Wilson, J. B. Martin, and A. S. Fauci, eds., in Harrison's Principles of internal medicine 1385 (11th ed. 1987).

8. Stiem, supra note 6 at 167:

In older children and adults, a total immunoglobulin level above 600 mg/dl with normal screening antibody tests excludes antibody deficiency. By contrast, total immunoglobulins (IgG + IgM + IgA) under 400 mg/dl or an IgG-globulin level under 200 mg/dl usually indicates antibody immunodeficiency. Total immunoglobulin levels of 400 to 600 mg/dl and IgG levels of 200 to 400 mg/dl are non-diagnostic and must be correlated with functional antibody tests.

9. Rose and Friedman, Manual of Clinical Immunology 243 (2d ed. 1980); Oppenheim, Dougherty, Ehan, and Baker, Uses of lymphocyte transformation to assess clinical disorders, G. Vyas, D. P. Stites, and G. Brecher, eds., in Laboratory diagnosis of immunologic disorders 87, 99–100 (1975); Stiem, supra note 6 at 173, suggests the PHA stimulation index should be at least 10–100 and states that comparison with the laboratory's controls must be used.

10. Cooper and Lawton, supra note 7 at 1388; Stites, Clinical laboratory methods for detection of cellular immune function, D. Stites, J. Stobo, and J. Wells, eds., in Basic and clinical immunology 285, 294 (Table 18–5), 295 (6th ed. 1987); Mascart-Lemone, Delespesse, Servais, and Kunstler, Characterization of immunoregulatory T lymphocytes during aging by monoclonal antibodies, 48 *Clin. Exp. Immunol.* 148 (1982).

11. Bernard, Bernstein, Boumsell, Dausset, Evans, Hansen, Haynes, Kersey, Knapp, McMichael, Milstein, Reinherz, Ritts, and Schlossman, Nomenclature for clusters of differentiation (CD) of antigens defined on human leukocyte populations, 62 *Bull. World Health Org.* 809 (1984).

12. In this treatment, the patient's bone marrow is removed from his body and antibodies are made to the malignant cells in the marrow and used to destroy those cells. Then, while the bone marrow is being stored outside the body, the patient is treated with massive amounts of radiation therapy and chemotherapy that he could not normally tolerate because they would have destroyed his bone marrow. Finally, after this treatment, the patient is reconstituted with his own bone marrow, which has been rendered normal by the depletion of the malignant cells. *See, e.g.,* Nadler, Botnick, Finberg, Canellos, Takvorian, Bast, Hellman, and Schlossman, Anti-B1 Monoclonal antibody and complement treatment in autologous bone-marrow transplantation for relapsed B-cell non–Hodgkin's lymphoma, *The Lancet,* August 25, 1984, at 427; Ritz, Sallan, Bast, Lipton, Clavell, Feeney, Hercend, Nathan, and Schlossman, Autologous bone marrow transplantation in CALLA positive acute lymphoblastic leukemia after in vitro treatment with J5 monoclonal antibody and complement, *The Lancet,* July 10, 1982, at 60; Ritz and Schlossman, A review: Utilization of monoclonal antibodies in the treatment of leukemia and lymphoma, 59 *Blood* 1 (1982).

13. The use of monoclonal antibodies for diagnostic use is regulated by the Food and Drug Administration under the Medical Device Amendments of 1976, Pub. L. 94-295, 90 Stat. 539.

14. Coulter Immunology Catalog (1989). Of these antibodies, 26 have CD designations. The catalog states: FOR RESEARCH USE ONLY: "NOT FOR DIAGNOSTIC OR THERAPEUTIC USE. T1, T3, T11, B1 and B4 are for In Vitro Diagnostic Use." *Idem.* at 6. Becton Dickinson's catalog lists reagents for approximately 50 monoclonal antibodies, including over 20 with CD designations. Of these, only two, Anti-Leu-4 (CD3) and Anti-Leu-12 (CD 19), are approved for in vitro diagnostic use. The catalog states: "Unless otherwise specified, products listed herein are not for use in diagnostic or therapeutic procedures; they are for

research use only." Becton Dickinson, The Monoclonal Catalog 2 (1988). Ortho Diagnostics markets 19 monoclonal antibodies, only one of which (OKT-11 or CD2) is approved for diagnostic use. The current price list for these monoclonal antibodies clearly states, "These reagents are for research use only (except as noted) and are not for use in diagnostic procedures" (Ortho Diagnostic Systems, Inc., Price List Effective July 1989). Boehringer Mannheim Biochemicals' catalog lists over 90 monoclonal antibodies to human cells, including 8 with CD designations. Its catalog states: "All monoclonal antibodies are for research use only. Not for use in in vitro clinical diagnostic procedures." Boehringer Mannheim Biochemicals Catalog 67 (1989).

15. Ling, MacLennan, and Mason, B-cell and plasma cell antigens: new and previously defined clusters, A. McMichael, ed., in III Leucocyte Typing 303, 321–22 (1987): B-cells at some stages of development, plasma cells, activated T-cells; Preffer, Flow Cytometry, R. Colvin, A. Brian, and R. McClusky, eds., in Diagnostic Immunopathology 453, 463 (1988): activated T-cells, plasma cells, monocytes; Stiem, supra note 6 at 172: immature T-cells, activated T-cells.

16. Patrick, Schwartz, Harrison, and Keller, Collection and Preparation of Hematopoietic Cells for Cell Marker Analysis, 15 *Lab. Med.* 659, 659 (1984): "[O]ne must recognize that serious problems can occur and jeopardize the interpretation of data. Many of these potential errors happen during the collection, anticoagulation, handling and processing of the samples to be evaluated."

17. See, e.g., Brahmi, Thomas, Park, Park, and Dowdeswell, The effect of acute exercise on natural killer cell activity of trained and sedentary human subjects, 5 *J. Clin. Immunol.* 321, 321 (1985): association between exercise and the quantity of OKT-3, OKT-4, Leu-7 and Leu-11 cells, as well as natural killer activity; Hallgren, Jackola, and O'Leary, Unusual pattern of surface marker expression on peripheral lymphocytes from aged humans suggestive of a population of less differentiated cells, 131 *J. Immunol.* 191 (1983): association between age and the quantity of T-4, T-8 and T-10 cells; Matsumoto, Okubo, and Yokoyama, Distribution of marker-specific lymphocyte subsets in healthy human subjects, 16 *J. Clin. Lab. Immunol.* 143 (1985): association between age and the quantity of OKT-3 and OKT-10 cells and the OKT-4/8 ratio, association between gender and the quantity of OKT-4 and OKT-8 cells; Mescart-Lemone, Delespesse, Servais, and Kunstler, Characterization of immunoregulatory T lymphocytes during aging by monoclonal antibodies, 48 *Clin. Exp. Immunol.* 148 (1982): association between age and the quantity OKT-3 and OKT-4 in men but not women; Kus, Tse, Enarson, Grzybowski, and Chan-Yeung, Lymphocyte subpopulations in patients with allergic rhinitis, 39 *Allergy* 509 (1984): association between T-8 antibodies and allergic rhinitis; Phillips, Marshall, Brown, and Thompson, Effect of smoking on human natural killer cell activity, 56 *Cancer* 2789 (1985): although lymphocyte subsets were not measured, cigarette smoking was associated with depressed natural killer activity; Hong, Evaluation of immunity, 16 *Immunol. Invest.* 453, 479 (1987): "Increased numbers of CD8 + cells are common in viral infections."

18. Quoting Jack Dean, head of cell biology at the Chemical Industry Institute of Biology, a recent article in the authoritative journal *Science* stated: "Once an unusual pattern is discovered, it should be analyzed repeatedly. 'If there is an abnor-

mality, you need to reproduce it' to establish its validity." Marshall, Immune System Theories on Trial, 234 *Science* 1490, 1491 (1986).

19. Stiem, supra note 6 at 172, suggests that a CD4 less than $600/mm^3$ on an absolute count (rather than the percentage-of-lymphocytes basis used in *Alcolac*) suggests a T-cell deficiency and a result less than $200/mm^3$ indicates a profound deficiency.

20. Waldmann, supra note 6 at 416, states:

> Abnormalities of T cells and thus of cell-mediated immunity predispose to infection with a wide variety of agents, including viruses leading to disseminated viral infections, particularly herpes simplex, varicella zoster, and cytomegalovirus; fungi, leading to mucocutaneous candidiases; and parasitic organisms, including the protozoan Pneumocystis carinii.

21. Reinherz and Schlossman, The differentiation and function of human T lymphocytes: A review, 19 *Cell* 821, 825–26 (1980); Reinherz and Schlossman, Current concepts in immunology: Regulation of the immune response—inducer and suppressor T-lymphocyte subsets in human beings, 303 *N. Eng. J. Med.* 370, 372 (1980); see also Reinherz, Cooper, S. F. Schlossman, and F. S. Rosen, Abnormalities of T cell maturation and regulation in human beings with immunodeficiency disorders, 68 *J. Clin. Invest.* 699 (1981).

22. The only exception is Mary Landon, a 71-year-old cancer patient who had undergone chemotherapy, more than a sufficient reason to explain an immunosuppression.

23. See references cited in notes 9 supra; Stiem, supra note 6 at 173, states that the PHA stimulation index should be at least 10–100, a range within which this result falls, as do the results of all other plaintiffs, except Mrs. Lawrence's second result (see note 6).

24. NKH-1 and HNK-1 are different antibodies. NKH-1 (CD56) is a measurement of natural killer cells. Griffin, Hercend, Beveridge, and Schlossman, Characterization of an antigen expressed by human natural killer cells, 130 *J. Immunol.* 2947 (1983) (NKH-1 was called anti-N901). HNK-1, or Leu 7, is a measurement of some but not all natural killer cells as well as others that are not natural killer cells. Preffer, Flow Cytometry, in R. Colvin, A. Bhon, and R. McCusky, eds., Diagnostic Immunopathology 453, 462–63 (Table I) (1988). Indeed, HNK-1 fails to mark the most potent natural killers. Lanier, Le, Phillips, Warner,and Babcock, Subpopulations of human natural killer cells defined by expression of the leu-7 (HNK-11 and Leu-11 (NNK-15) antigens, 131 *J. Immunol.* 1789 (1983). Dr. Carnow, however, appears to have used NKH-1 and HNK-1 interchangeably. Since the court referred to the test, in most places, as NKH-1, we will assume that was the test that was done.

25. First described in Stashenko, Nadler, Hardy, and Schlossman, Characterization of a human B lymphocyte alloantigen, 125 *J. Immunol.* 1678 (1980).

26. First described in Kung, Goldstein, Reinherz, and Schlossman, Monoclonal antibodies defining distinctive human T cell surface antigens, 206 *Science* 347 (1979).

27. First described in Meuer, Hussey, Hodgdon, Hercend, Schlossman, and Reinherz, Surface structures involved in target recognition by human cytotoxic T lymphocytes, 218 *Science* 471 (1982).

28. First described in Reinherz, Kung, Goldstein, and Schlossman, Separation of functional subsets of human T cells by a monoclonal antibody, 76(8) *Proc. Natl. Acad. Sci.* 4061 (1979).

29. First described in Reinherz, Kung, Goldstein, and Schlossman, A monoclonal antibody reactive with the human cytotoxic/suppressor T cell subset previously defined by a heteroantiserum termed TH2, 124 *J. Imm.* 1301 (1980). The antibody was called T5.

30. First described in Griffin, et al., supra note 24.

31. First described in Reinherz, Hung, Goldstein, Levey, and Schlossman, Discrete stages of human intrathymic differentiation: Analysis of normal thymocytes and leukemic lymphoblasts of T-cell lineage, 77 *Proc. Natl. Acad. Sci.* 1588 (1980).

32. Reinherz, Morimoto, Penta, Schlossman, Regulation of B cell immunoglobulin secretion by functional subsets of T lymphocytes in man, 10 *Eur. J. Immunol.* 570 (1980).

33. Hercend, L. Reinherz, Meuer, Schlossman, and Ritz, Phenotypic and functional heterogeneity of human cloned natural killer cell lines, 301 *Nature* 158 (1983).

34. See note 24 supra, for a discussion of the apparent confusion in the case regarding tests referred to as HNK-1 and NKH-1.

35. See Black, supra note 4.

36. Tr. at Plaintiffs' Ex. 300, *Andre* v. *Syntex Agribusiness Inc.*, no. 832-05432 (Mo. Cir. Ct. [St. Louis] Jan. 6, 1988).

37. See note 9 supra.

38. See note 8 supra.

39. Stites, supra note 10 at 295; Patrick, et al., supra note 16.

40. Stites, supra note 10 at 294 (Table 18–5); Cooper and Lawton, supra note 7 at 1388; Brahmi et al., supra note 17; Kus et al., supra note 17; Hong, supra note 17.

Biographical Sketch

Richard S. Cornfeld is a partner in the St. Louis law firm of Coburn, Croft & Putzell, where he specializes in toxic tort and other complex personal injury litigation. He has defended such cases throughout the United States. In addition, he speaks and writes frequently on the defense of lawsuits involving sophisticated scientific issues. He has spoken before such groups as the National Association of Railroad Trial Counsel and the Chemical Manufacturers Association. His articles have appeared in the Toxics Law Reporter, Inside Litigation, and For the Defense. Mr. Cornfeld is a 1975 graduate of Northwestern University School of Law, where he was Notes and Comments Editor of the Law Review and a member of the Order of the Coif. He served as a law clerk for Judge John F. Grady of the United States District Court in Chicago.

Stuart F. Schlossman received his B.A. from Washington Square College, New York University, his M.D. from New York University College of Medicine, and his M.A. from Harvard University with honors. He is currently professor of medicine at the Harvard Medical School, as well as chief of the tumor immunology and immunotherapy division at the Dana-Farber Cancer Center of the Harvard Medical School. He is also senior physician in medicine at Brigham and Women's Hospital and associate physician at Beth Israel Hospital.

Dr. Schlossman is a fellow of the American Association for the Advancement of Science and a member of the National Academy of Sciences. Dr. Schlossman received the CIBA-GEIGY award in biomedical research, Harvey Society Lecture, the Solomon Berson Achievement Award in basic sciences, and the Robert Koch prize and medal. He has served on various editorial boards and currently serves on the boards of Cellular Immunology, Clinical Immunology and Immunopathology, Hybridoma, and Cancer Reviews. He has published over 500 articles in various journals.

The Legal Context

Traumatic Cancer

Legal interest in traumatic cancer can be traced back at least to 1884, with the advent of workers' compensation programs in Germany.[1] By 1901, German compensation boards had established medical criteria for deciding when cancer had been caused by trauma.[2] In the ensuing decades many hundreds (and probably thousands) of traumatic cancer cases were litigated in U.S. courts.[3] We describe a few cases for illustration.[4]

Canon Reliance Coal v. *Industrial Commission*,[5] a 1922 decision, is a typical example of an early traumatic cancer case. A worker was struck in the face by coal. His face remained swollen for two to three weeks; a carcinoma developed at the spot where he was struck. He filed a workmen's compensation claim that his employer contested. The worker submitted medical testimony that the blow had caused the cancer. The industrial commission found for the worker, and the state supreme court upheld the award, noting that the testimony "may be unreliable" and "by other experts disputed," but that the plaintiff's expert's testimony provided "'substantial and credible evidence' to support the findings."

Reasoning of this character was accepted in many courts from the 1920s until the 1950s and sometimes even later, particularly in claims for workers' compensation. Courts frequently accepted a suggestive sequence of events as sufficient proof that simple trauma had caused cancer. In a 1925 decision,[6] for example, the Supreme Court of Minnesota said the fact that the plaintiff suffered a blow and later developed cancer in that spot "is pretty strong evidence that injury was the proximate cause of the result, and would be quite convincing to the mind of a layman." The Virginia Supreme Court went even further in a 1927 ruling,[7] upholding the "significant" language of a workmen's compensation commission that said that "[w]hatever may be the medical theory as to connection between sarcoma or cancer and traumatism, it is nevertheless impossible . . . to separate the occurrence of the injury in this case from the condition of disability which has resulted."

Beginning in the 1940s, the growing medical consensus that physical trauma rarely if ever causes cancer forced a shift in courtroom tactics. Plaintiffs' attorneys in trauma cases began to allege that injuries aggravated preexisting cancers, rather than being sufficient causes for the disease. In a 1951 case that reflects the change in medical opinion, *Pittman* v. *Pillsbury Flour Mills*,[8] only one of six testifying physicians agreed that trauma had induced the plaintiff's cancer, but three stated that trauma had aggravated a preexisting tumor. The plaintiff won compensation for the aggravation alone.

Meanwhile, standards of proof in most states for causation were growing tighter. A breakthrough came in 1952 in *Dennison* v. *Wing*.[9] In that decision, a New York Appellate Division court held that accepted medical postulates must be applied as a minimum standard for proving causation. At about the same time as *Dennison,* the Minnesota Supreme Court ruled that traumatic cancer claims required medical testimony beyond "conjecture and speculation."[10] Other courts soon began announcing stricter criteria for determining traumatic-cancer causality in both tort and workers' compensation cases.[11]

Gradually, courts began to deny claims alleging trauma-induced cancer, and to overturn awards issued by workers' compensation tribunals. In a 1953 New York ruling, for example,[12] the plaintiff argued that a trauma to the back had aggravated a preexisting breast cancer. The compensation commission granted an award, but an Appellate Division court reversed. Another plaintiff attempted to prove that a bone fracture five to six inches from a preexisting tumor aggravated its growth.[13] The compensation commission granted an award, but the state supreme court reversed. In a 1980 decision,[14] the South Carolina Supreme Court rejected any possibility of traumatically induced cancer. As the justices noted, "People will have a tumor that's been sitting there for a long time [without realizing it, until a blow called their attention to it]. . . . The best analogy is [that] you really don't know how many times a day you hit your thumb until you have a sore thumb, and then it seems like you are hitting it every five minutes."

Judicial views on traumatic cancer have evolved, however, at different rates in different states. As late as 1970, an Ohio municipal court declared that a "sequence of events, if closely connected in time, is generally enough to present a factual question as to whether the cancer is the result of an injury."[15] Likewise, in a 1972 Louisiana ruling,[16] medical testimony was divided on the question of whether a trauma had aggravated a preexisting tumor. The attending physician in the case viewed the trauma as beneficial, because it brought attention to the cancer, thus allowing doctors to treat it at an earlier stage. The appellate court nevertheless upheld an award, noting that "one of the strongest, single factors supporting plaintiff's claim" was his healthiness prior to the trauma and his illness afterward.

In another Louisiana decision issued in 1981, an appellate court upheld a denial of compensation, stating that uniform medical testimony against a causal relationship overcame the "presumption" of causality that occurs where there is proof of an accident and a following disability, without any intervening cause.[17] Even then, medical testimony must establish a reasonable possibility of such a connection. These minimal criteria were overruled 4–3 by the state supreme court, which declared that "medical testimony must be weighed in the light of other credible evidence of a nonmedical character, such as a sequence of symptoms or events. . . ."

In a 1985 Kentucky case,[18] the plaintiff, a salesman in a department store, experienced sudden back pain. He was soon diagnosed with multiple myeloma, a form of cancer. Despite testimony by two physicians to the contrary, the commission concluded that the cancer was "aroused or brought into a disabling reality" by the sudden back pain. A circuit court affirmed the commission, but the Kentucky Court of Appeals reversed.

One of the most recent traumatic cancer decisions came in 1988.[19] John Mangasarian fractured his ribs in a car accident. Less than a year later he died of lung cancer. His wife claimed a connection between the accident and the cancer. The trial court allowed Dr. Rocco Marzilli, a specialist in gastroenterology and internal medicine, to testify that a causal link existed. The defendant's expert denied that any such link existed, but he admitted on cross examination that be believed the trauma may have aggravated the cancer and caused it to spread more quickly. The jury found for the plaintiff. The Rhode Island Supreme Court found no error in the admission of Dr. Marzilli's testimony, and upheld the jury verdict.

Clinical Ecology

Probably the most prominent case involving the methods and theories of clinical ecology was *Elam* v. *Alcolac, Inc.*[20] (The scientific evidence in that case is discussed in chapter 17 by Cornfeld and Schlossman.)

Alcolac, Inc., manufactured specialty chemicals for soaps and cosmetics. Plaintiffs alleged that pollution from that plant damaged the immune system of people living nearby. They blamed Alcolac's pollution for dozens of different afflictions, such as nerve damage and heart disease, brain damage and vomiting, kidney infections, headaches, and interrupted menstrual cycles. During the 4-month trial the jury heard from 165 witnesses.

The jury awarded $6.2 million in compensatory damages plus a $43 million punitive award. In a lengthy opinion, the appellate court affirmed the verdict but ruled that frequent references to "chemical AIDS" by the plaintiffs' experts were too inflammatory. It therefore ordered a new trial for recalculating damages.

Many cases have turned on allegations that exposure to environmental pollutants damaged plaintiffs' immune systems. A railroad employee who had been involved in cleaning up a chemical spill brought (an unsuccessful) suit, claiming he suffered "multiple illnesses and diseases which have been progressive."[21] Another unsuccessful claimant alleged that headaches, fatigue, heat intolerance, nausea, numbness, chest pains, and depression had been caused by exposure to a liquid solvent.[22] The Agent Orange litigation (see chapter 11) included allegations of impairment of the immune systems of plaintiffs. Another claimant maintained she had suffered chemical poisoning and damage to her immune system from formaldehyde vapors emanating from a carpet.[23] These suits were unsuccessful.

Other courts in Louisiana,[24] California,[25] and South Carolina[26] have addressed such claims (favorably) in workers' compensation cases. Some of these cases have resulted in substantial awards ($3.9 million[27] and $16.25 million,[28] for example) or settlements ($8 million and $19 million[29]).

As Cornfeld and Schlossman discuss in chapter 17, many such claims cannot be substantiated by standard immune function tests. Instead, the questionable theories and tests of clinical ecologists have been persuasive evidence for the plaintiffs' cases.

Notes

1. Stoll, Epithelioma from Single Trauma, *N.Y. St. J. Med.,* February 16, 1962.

2. *Ibid.* at 4.

3. That estimate is based on a conservative Lexis search.

4. Other illustrations appear in P. W. Huber, *Galileo's revenge: Junk science in the courtroom* (New York: Basic Books, 1991).

5. 72 Colo. 477, 211 P. 868 (1922).

6. *Austin* v. *Red Wing Sewer Pipe Co.*, 163 Minn. 397, 204 N.W. 323, 324 (1925).

7. *Winchester Milling Corp.* v. *Sencindiver*, 148 Va. 388, 138 S.E. 479, 480 (1927).

8. *Pittman* v. *Pillsbury Flour Mills*, 234 Minn. 517, 48 N.W.2d 735 (1951).

9. 279 A.D. 494, 110 N.Y.S.2d 811 (1952).

10. *Pittman* v. *Pillsbury Flour Mills*, 234 Minn. 517, 48 N.W.2d 735 (1951). A year later the Minneseota court reiterated its requirement in *Erickson* v. *Knutson*, 237 Minn. 187, 54 N.W.2d 118 (1952).

11. *Ricciardi* v. *Marcalus Manufacturing Co.*, 26 N.J. 445, 140 A.2d 215 (1958); *Stordahl* v. *Rush Implement*, 148 Mont. 13, 417 P.2d 95 (1966); *Cox* v. *Ulysses Cooperative Oil and Supply Co.*, 218 Kan. 428, 544 P.2d 363 (1975).

12. *Sikora* v. *Apex Beverage*, 282 A.D. 193, 122 N.Y.S.2d 64 (1953) *aff'd*, 306 N.Y. 917, 119 W.E.2d 601 (1954).

13. *Stordahl* v. *Rush Implement*, 148 Mont. 13, 417 P.2d 95 (1966).

14. *Glover* v. *Rhett Jackson Co.*, 274 S.C. 644, 267 S.E.2d 77 (1980).

15. *Hanna* v. *Aetna Insurance Co.*, 24 Ohio Misc. 27, 259 N.E.2d 177, 180 (1970).

16. *Reed* v. *Myllin Wood Co., Inc.*, 274 So.2d 845 (La. 1972).

17. *Hammond* v. *Fidelity & Casualty Co. of N.Y.*, 407 So.2d 13 (La. 1981), *rev'd*, 419 So.2d 829 (La. 1982).

18. *Wells* v. *Davidson*, 689 S.W.2d 610 (Ky. 1985).

19. *Mangasarian* v. *Gould*, 537 A.2d 403 (R.I. 1988).

20. 765 *S.W.2d* 42 (Mo. App. 1988), *cert. denied*, 493 U.S. 817 (1989).

21. *Freels* v. *U.S. R.R. Retirement Bd.*, 879 F.2d 335, 338 (8th Cir. 1989).

22. *Sparks* v. *Metalcraft, Inc.*, 408 N.W.2d 347 (Iowa 1987).

23. *Moore* v. *Polish Power, Inc.*, 720 S.W.2d 183 (Tex. Ct. App. 1986).

24. *Menendez* v. *Continental Insurance Company*, 515 So.2d 525 (La. App. 1987), *writ denied*, 517 So.2d 808 (La. 1987).

25. *Kyles* v. *Workers' Compensation Appeals Board*, 195 Cal. App. 3d 614, 240 Cal. Rptr. 886 (1987).

26. *Grayson* v. *Gulf Oil Co.*, 292 S.C. 528, 357 S.E.2d 479 (Ct. App. 1987).

27. *Potter* v. *Firestone Tire & Rubber Company*, 2 *Toxics L. Rep.* (BNA) 862 (1988).

28. *Kemner* v. *Monsanto*, 2 *Toxics L. Rep.* (BNA) 612 (1987).

29. See Marshall, Immune System Theories on Trial, 234 *Science* 1490 (1986).

IV

Conclusion:
Phantom Risk—A Problem at the Interface of Science and the Law

The reader is likely to come away with two strong impressions. The first is that much confusion, error, and ambiguity surrounds risk research, at least when searching for small risks. This is particularly true when the injuries are chronic diseases that appear long after the exposure to the toxic substance. The second is that this creates much controversy and expense in a legal system that sometimes raises more questions than it settles.

These problems are connected, of course. The legal controversy arises, in part, from the difficulty that science has in proving cause-and-effect relationships in individual cases. We are all surrounded by carcinogens, natural and synthetic. Many of us develop cancer sometime in our lives. Yet rarely can science identify the specific cause of any person's tumor. Some of us will bear children with grave defects—yet rarely can science identify the cause. We all get sick and die—yet the cause of most chronic diseases is unknown. Epidemiology can often only hint at the answers, and many caveats are needed when interpreting such evidence. The courtroom is not well suited to resolve such issues.

For at least two reasons, there can be no way to avoid all dubious litigation, at least in our legal system. It is, in part, the cost of a legal system that grants broad access to the courts, and which gives attorneys financial incentives to file speculative litigation.

It is also, in part, an unavoidable result of scientific error and honest differences of opinion. In the early stages of the controversy about spermicides and birth defects (chapter 4), the studies by Jick and colleagues, all respected scientists, *did* raise the spectre of a serious problem; it was only in the hindsight of later work that these concerns were recognized as unfounded. The exaggerated calculations of risk (from the viewpoint of conventional health physics) that Gofman and Morgan presented in numerous radiation exposure cases (chapter 13) may have reflected the sincere convictions of the witnesses. There is no way to prevent the scientific errors and differences of opinion that loomed so large in cases like these. But some people are injured, and should receive compensation.

How then can society reduce the costs of phantom risk litigation, without at the same time shutting off meritorious claims? Some observers have proposed "science courts" to resolve hazardous exposure issues by expert panels of scientists. The proposal has merit, but will founder on the objection that it is too elitist and undemocratic. Tort lawyers will probably fight such plans for strategic reasons as well, out of the justified fear that a jury of scientists would review the scientific evidence more critically than a lay jury. Lasagna and Shulman (chapter 5) report that plaintiffs in an early Bendectin case rejected a "blue ribbon" jury of educated laymen, and a "blue, blue ribbon" panel of knowledgeable scientists, perhaps for such reasons.

Other observers have called for a system of compensation for chronic diseases based on statistical calculations of "probability of causation." Such plans are attractive, for they explicitly consider the statistical nature of the evidence linking exposure and disease. They also directly address the usual legal requirement that the plaintiff must show that his or her injuries "more likely than not" were caused by the exposure. If both sides in a lawsuit can agree about the relation between exposure to a toxic agent and the probability of illness, the problem shifts to the more tractable one of exposure assessment.

Lapp (chapter 13) discusses one such plan, based on the Radioepidemiological Tables for estimating the probability that a plaintiff's cancer had been caused by exposure to radioactive fallout from above-ground weapons testing. These tables, prepared by the National Cancer Institute by order of Congress, undoubtably influenced the disposition of many claims for compensation for injury from low-level radiation. (Congress resolved the veterans' claims by political fiat, however, without using the Tables.)

Radioepidemiological Tables, or other similar analysis prepared by a prestigious organization outside of the context of litigation, can be a powerful statement of mainstream scientific understanding of an issue and have a strong influence in court. However, this approach is feasible only when a hazard has been unequivocally identified (e.g., cancer from exposure to ionizing radiation) and enough epidemiologic and animal data exist to allow scientists to make educated guesses about dose-response relationships, at least for comparatively high levels of exposure.

The problem—as the issues discussed in this book vividly illustrate—is that both sides often will *not* agree on the connection (if any) between exposure and risk of illness. What plaintiff's lawyer would accept a "probability of causation" table for cancer from weak magnetic fields (chapter 3), when there is no scientific consensus that a hazard exists at all? And who would prepare such a table? A "probability of causation" approach would not have been much use in the litigation resulting from trichloroethylene-contaminated well water in Woburn, Massachusetts, where the contamination was negligible (as viewed by mainstream toxicologists), but an epidemiologic study had been done that suggested that real health problems might have existed nevertheless.

The outcome of such cases is likely to depend on testimony of expert witnesses with radically different views of the supposed hazards involved. Even for ionizing radiation, whose hazards are surely well studied, one can pick and choose among the epidemiologic studies and find support for the claim that exposure to low-level radiation is far more hazardous than the consensus of scientific opinion would admit (see, for example, Morgan 1992 and the reply by Cameron 1992). The adversarial process naturally amplifies these differences, and often obscures the differences between well-established scientific fact, consensus scientific opinion, and idiosyncratic views of some scientists.

Probably the best that legal reformers can do is to suggest ways to help improve the quality of the scientific evidence that is presented in court. The goal is not to raise standards of proof to levels so high that no plaintiff could hope to win, but rather to ensure that the scientific testimony that is presented to juries is as reliable as possible. Expert testimony needs to be *verifiable*, and, where possible, *consistent with a consensus of scientific opinion*. It needs to address at least three issues: the existence of a hazard, the plaintiff's exposure, and the risks associated with that exposure. In legal terms, it needs to be more probative than prejudicial. We offer several recommendations.

1. Judges and Lawyers Should be More Careful in Appraising Scientific Evidence. The legal community as a whole, and judges in particular, need to become more sophisticated about the scientific basis of risk assessment. Judges should attend to the quality of scientific evidence more closely, and exclude marginal or unreliable evidence more often.

As the chapters in this book illustrate, science raises two core issues in evaluating risk research: the *relevance* of data to health and the *reliability* of scientific inferences. As our authors frequently point out, scientific data vary greatly in their relevance to human health. For example, many tests of the immune system are not useful for diagnosing human disease (chapters 9, 16, 17). High-dose animal studies have questionable relevance for predicting risks to humans from low-dose exposures (chapter 7). Much of the controversy about the biological effects of electromagnetic fields concerns the interpretation of in vitro or in vivo studies whose implications regarding human health are speculative and remote (chapters 3 and 6).

Scientists are best equipped to judge the relevance and reliability of scientific evidence, and to provide critical assessments of the data. This is not to say that only high priests of Science should be entitled to weigh scientific evidence about risk and disease. But if nonscientists are to consider such evidence, they must understand how very cautiously scientists themselves use it. Absent such an understanding, marginal evidence might be given more weight than it deserves; its "scientific" presentation will obscure the fact that it is, at best, only tangentially relevant to human health. The probative value of scientific evidence is a valid legal issue that courts need to address more carefully.

This does not mean that judges should become scientists too, or acquire expert knowledge of toxicology or other fields. The issues involved in risk assessment might be unfamiliar to laymen but are not difficult to understand. One mechanism for educating lawyers and judges is through the process of continuing professional education.

In judging the reliability of a scientific report, judges and lawyers often seem to misunderstand the nature of "peer review." Peer review is a minimum qualifying step for acceptance of a paper by a scientific journal; it is not (as some lawyers appear to believe) a certification of high quality by the scientific community. Nearly all of the 800 or so papers cited in this volume were peer reviewed, but many of them present questionable or incorrect claims. It is more appropriate to view peer review as a necessary, threshold step for qualifying any scientific paper. A more important criterion is that a paper be sufficiently complete to allow other competent scientists to judge the strength of its arguments and conclusions; many of the peer-reviewed articles cited in this volume fail to meet that standard.

2. Courts Should Maintain Traditional Standards of Proof. A plaintiff has traditionally been required to produce evidence establishing "more probably than not" that a given cause led to a given harm. These traditional standards have been eroded by other theories of recovery, which focus on such things as "exposure to risk" or "cancerphobia," by the progressive weakening of the *Frye* rule, and the slide toward a "let it all in" philosophy of scientific evidence.

Such developments, particularly in jury trials, in effect shift the burden of proof to defendants, requiring them to prove the absence of hazard, and thus the absence of any legitimate grounds for anxiety. But science can never demonstrate the absence of hazard, still less the absence of "reasonable" grounds for anxiety. Science can only place an upper limit on risk, and there will always remain confusion at the lower margins of risk. Judges must understand that when they reverse burdens of proof, either expressly or implicitly, they create an attractive environment for litigation in pursuit of phantom risk.

3. Reaffirm Traditional Standards for Qualifying Expert Witnesses and Testimony. Recently, as we have seen (chapter 2), some jurisdictions have begun to reaffirm traditional standards for the admission of expert testimony. This trend should be encouraged. In particular, the following should be required:

First, expert witnesses should testify within the scope of their expertise. This obvious requirement is often overlooked. A treating physician, for example, should be allowed to testify about injury or ill health of a patient and his or her treatment. But clinicians are not necessarily experts on the causes of injury or etiology of disease. For many years in traumatic cancer cases, for example, courts gave far too much weight to the opinions of treating physicians, and far too little to the experts in oncology (see part III).

Second, an expert witness's opinions should reflect the consensus of the scientific community as a whole (as contained, for example, in reports of broadly constituted consensus groups), and not just the views of members of a small subdiscipline. In extreme cases, the subdiscipline (e.g., clinical ecology) might be on the fringes of science. The best perspective on an issue is usually provided by a broadly constituted group, e.g., a committee of the National Academy of Sciences, rather than a committee of a small scientific society.

Third, courts should insist on peer review and independent evaluation of any scientific evidence that is presented. This is a necessary—though as discussed above, not a sufficient—minimum standard, a threshold test for the *Frye* rule itself. "Scientific findings" that have not been published in sufficient detail cannot be evaluated properly at all.

Fourth, scientific evidence must be palpably relevant to the causation questions before a court, and must be scrutinized firmly to ensure that it is more probative than prejudicial. Much scientific evidence can, and should be, excluded from the courtroom for lack of probative value. For example, Cornfeld and Schlossman (chapter 17) propose evidentiary standards for the admission of the results of immunologic laboratory tests and expert testimony based thereon. Standards of that character should be applied much more widely and frequently.

Fifth, an expert can identify an agent as the cause of an injury or illness only if he or she has studied and discounted alternate possible causes. To describe a sequence of events is not to prove a cause and an effect. Time and again, judges have been lenient about the *ergo* in *post hoc ergo propter hoc*. Phantom risk will continue to fuel a major litigation industry until judges finally crack down on this all-too-common fallacy.

4. Reduce Financial Incentives for Speculative Litigation. The financial stakes in phantom risk litigation remain highly asymmetric. It is much cheaper to bring a claim to court than to shoot it down. It generally agreed in the legal community, for example, that the potential economic value to a lawyer of a chemical pollution case depends on the number of claimants signed up. "The 'going rate' for settlements," reports E. Donald Elliott, "is $10,000 to $100,000 per plaintiff," of which the lawyers typically receive 30 percent (Elliott 1989). Judges must search for ways to readjust the economic equilibrium. The legal system is not so highly accurate that the prospect of losing discourages a lawyer from filing speculative claims.

5. Beware of "Hired Guns." As one of us has argued elsewhere (Huber 1991), the expert is in court to provide a bridge between the particular facts of a case and patterns of facts that can be observed and understood only through much wider study. An "expert witness" who engages in purely personal, idiosyncratic speculation is not fulfilling the proper role of expert at all.

Lawyers frequently complain about "hired guns" (usually referring to witnesses who testify for the opposing side). While the exact identification of a "hired gun" is problematic, the term implies that a witness is a partisan rather than objective expert.

One sign of a "hired gun" is an inordinate amount of time spent providing expert testimony, and too little time spent making original contributions to a technical field. A scientist who is actively doing science will probably have little time to spare in providing scientific exposition for lawyers and jurors. (At the going rate of $200–$400 per hour, many scientists make the time, however.)

Of course, many expert witnesses play a useful and honorable role in court. Many consulting engineers have made successful professional careers investigating bridge collapses and other disasters, and providing expert testimony in the resulting litigation. As environmental litigation increases, many opportunities will exist for consulting scientists to provide expert services and testimony relating to exposure assessment, toxicology, and other scientific issues. Earning one's livelihood providing expert testimony is not, by itself, cause for opprobrium.

At the minimum, such witnesses should reflect on the counsel once offered by Nobel physicist Richard Feynman. A scientist approached for advice on public matters must commit at the outset to come forward with his or her ultimate findings no matter whose position they may favor. Candor of this kind will not win much applause among lawyers. But it remains the very essence of serious, reputable science.

6. Encourage Judges to Use Their Own Expert Witnesses.

European judges routinely summon their own experts. American judges have similar powers, but few choose to exercise them (Lee 1988). Most trial lawyers vehemently oppose the use of court-appointed experts, perceiving (correctly, no doubt) that consensus cannot be good for a conflict-centered livelihood.

Lawyers might argue that there is no such thing as a neutral expert. But it is possible to find knowledgeable scientists of high principle, and a nonpartisan judge has a good prospect of finding a less partisan expert. Judges who have appointed experts, such as Federal District Judge Sherman Finesilver, have reported very positive results.

7. Professional Organizations Should Set Standards for Their Members.

Providing expert testimony is a rapidly growing, largely unregulated industry with no standard methodology and few clearly formulated standards, notwithstanding recent legislation in several states to deal with the issue (Bernstein 1990a, 1990b). Many expert witnesses are university faculty who are allowed (indeed, often encouraged) by their institutions to engage in outside consulting. The chief requirements for such work are scientific credentials that are acceptable to courts, and a skin that is thick enough to withstand the give-and-take of litigation.

The engineering profession has long employed various mechanisms for encouraging quality services by its members, that might serve as models for scientists in the testimonial business as well. One is registration. State boards, working with the engineering societies, certify candidates as Registered Professional Engineers if they have graduated from accredited engineering schools and pass a test. An engineer must be registered to provide testimony and other services, particularly in matters related to buildings and construction. Professional misconduct, false testimony, or other egregious acts might result in sanctions including loss of registration.

However, it is unclear how well registration actually works in raising the quality of engineering testimony. Few sanctions are ever applied, and few engineers other than civil engineers seek registration in any event.

Perhaps a more useful approach for scientists would be the articulation of standards by professional societies. Societies such as the National Academy of Forensic Engineers and the American Academy of Forensic Sciences have recently proposed or are now developing codes of behavior that, if followed, will help to improve the reliability of expert testimony.

Many of these codes directly or indirectly address the problems of eccentric or unreliable testimony and "hired guns." For example, the Recommended Practices of the National Academy of Forensic Engineers (adopted in 1988) include:

Recommendation 3. The expert should consider other practitioners' opinions relative to the principles associated with the matter at issue.

The accompanying commentary states that "experts who disagree with the opinion of other professionals should be prepared to explain to the trier of fact the differences which exist and why a particular opinion should prevail." A witness who cannot or will not describe for the benefit of the court the scientific consensus on an issue should not be considered an expert at all.

Recommendation 5. The expert should evaluate reasonable explanations of causes and effects.

The commentary states that ". . . experts should study and evaluate different explanations of causes and effects. Experts should not limit their inquiry for the purpose of proving the contentions advanced by those who have retained them."

These and other professional standards are voluntary, of course; *mandatory* standards would probably expose a society to the threat of antitrust suits. But they are useful guidelines nonetheless.

8. Rely More on Consensus Groups. In public and legal discussion it is important to present balanced, sensible, assessments of scientific evidence, recognizing that experts themselves frequently disagree about the interpretation of scientific findings. It is important to map out the broad areas of agreement about risks, and specify as clearly as possible the range of opinions that are held by competent scientists.

One effective mechanism for articulating such views is through expert consensus groups. Such groups are convened by government and nongovernment groups, and include diverse specialists with different viewpoints. Their reports indicate a consensus of informed scientific opinion, and sometimes include minority reports by dissenting members.

For example, the National Research Council (a part of the National Academy of Sciences) has a long and distinguished record of providing independent analysis and advice about scientific issues. Consensus groups of the National Institutes of Health serve a similar function for clinical medicine. Foster, in his bibliography to chapter 3, lists seven reports by consensus groups on health effects of electromagnetic fields. Their viewpoints vary (none makes any strong claims for cancer from magnetic fields, and they all recommend more research), but all are responsible discussions of the issue—much more so than many discussions of the issue presented by some witnesses in court or by the lay media. Any judge interested in giving real meaning to the *Frye* rule will place substantial weight on consensus reports of this kind.

Some judges clearly understand these issues. In July 1992, Judge Michael M. Mihm issued a judgment in a 7-year old lawsuit brought by James R. O'Conner against Commonwealth Edison Company (U.S. District Court, Central District of Illinois). O'Conner had worked briefly as a pipefitter in a nuclear power plant where he received slight exposure to ionizing radiation. He later developed cataracts, which he alleged were caused by the radiation. The plaintiff's witness was Dr. Karl Scheribel, an ophthalmologist who offered an unequivocal diagnosis of radiation-induced cataracts (despite the fact that O'Conner's father had also developed cataracts relatively early in life). The defendants' witnesses (who included some of the most eminent scientists in radiation health) argued that O'Conner's exposure was far below the level needed to produce cataracts.

The Judge issued a long and thoughtful judgment, in which he considered the plaintiff's exposure, evaluated the consensus scientific literature on radiation-induced cataracts and the scientific references cited by Dr. Scheribel, and reviewed the Federal Rules of Evidence. He wrote:

In science, a proposition is not true just because one claiming to be an "expert" is willing to make such a statement. In law, a statement is not admissible just because a self-proclaimed "expert" is willing to say it on the witness stand. Scientific truths must be verifiable or they are not *scientific* truths at all. Rules of both science and evidence require a scientist or an expert to have a verifiable scientific basis for his opinion. Such controls are important in both fields to minimize error due to "junk" science.

Judge Mihm excluded the testimony of Dr. Scheribel, granted the defendants' motion for summary judgment, and dismissed the case. One wonders whether the suit would have been filed at all had *Frye* retained its force.

This is a book about science and the law, but other questions leap from these pages as well. How much social benefit is there in toxic tort litigation? Lawyers often argue that litigation is an effective instrument for controlling behavior that creates risk. This is probably true when risks are obvious and the legal system performs quickly and predictably: the fear of a lawsuit encourages the shopkeeper to clean the ice from his doorstep.

With subtle hazards the situation is much less clear. Litigation of this kind (say) that developed in connection with the Fernald plant (see chapter 14) does not demonstrably reduce risk at all; it simply imposes costs. Tort law does not perform a useful or desirable social function when the link between exposure and injury is as remote and questionable as with the issues considered in this volume, nor is it an effective way of compensating real victims of the exposure.

Many of the ostensible social benefits of well-functioning tort litigation can be more efficiently obtained through other social mechanisms. Compensation for cancer, birth defects, or other health problems can be provided more fairly and reliably through health insurance or other contractual arrangements. Better health insurance might reduce to some degree the incentive to litigate. However, many of the litigants mentioned in this book did not allege any injury at all, only the possibility of injury at some time in the future. Better insurance is an important social goal but it will not solve the legal problems that we address here.

For all its imperfections, the regulatory process is far better suited than tort law for controlling subtle risks. Regulatory agencies seek to inhibit risk *ex ante,* just in case. Courts are only supposed to compensate people *ex post,* not for risk but for proven harm. Regulators can, at least theoretically, aim for a far higher level of protection than can possibly be achieved by tort law. For example, the Environmental Protection Agency attempts to regulate carcinogens to a level such that less than one excess death occurs in a million people over their lifetimes, which corresponds to less than three excess deaths per year in the entire country. Risks of this magnitude are far too small to be detectable by any conceivable scientific study, and thus far too small to lead to any tort litigation that meets conventional standards of legal proof.

The standards of proof employed by regulatory processes are quite different from those applied in court, which also works to increase safety. Before granting premarket approval to a new drug, for example, the Food and Drug Administration requires strong evidence that the drug will improve a patient's clinical outcome. Merely showing that the drug has some biochemical or physiological effect, without demonstrating clinical benefit, will not suffice. This standard of proof is very high. The FDA can likewise ban substances (e.g., saccharine) on the basis of animal studies and other laboratory evidence, even though its relevance to human injury might be questioned. This standard of evidence is far lower than the "more probable than not" standard that tort law imposes on a plaintiff before awarding damages.

The regulatory system is also far better than the courtroom at resolving contradictory scientific evidence. In the United States at least, the regulatory process is subject to extensive scientific review and public comment, which pushes it toward consensus solutions. Ultimately, the questions of how much safety a society should purchase for itself, to whose benefit and at whose cost, are political decisions that must be resolved through the political process. The goal is not to avoid all risk (which is impossible in any event) but to reduce risk to levels that society is willing to accept.

Another question that leaps from these pages is whether the scientific research itself might not be better managed. The issue of possible links between cancer and exposure to electromagnetic fields has been alive for over a decade, without resolution. Many biological effects of electromagnetic fields continue to be reported that cannot be independently confirmed by other scientists.

This dismal situation might be remedied in part by better management by funding agencies. Many of the bioeffects studies with electromagnetic fields were poorly conceived, undertaken as fishing expeditions, inadequately followed up, or done under inadequate quality control. Many have no clear relevance for risk assessment, and no clear value as basic science. The confusion that they created might have been avoided by more careful management of risk research, more careful selection of projects to be funded, more attention to quality control, and more willingness of agencies to fund follow-up and confirmatory studies. Risk research is not basic science, and it should be far more closely managed and subjected, where possible, to tighter quality control.

The controversies discussed in this book extract high costs, in several respects. First, there are the costs of the research itself. A good epidemiologic or animal screening study might cost a million dollars—about what it costs to treat a handful of cancer patients. However, on the scale of the national health budget, these costs are tiny.

At a different level are the opportunity costs. The capacity of the scientific research establishment is limited, and scientific efforts might be more productively directed toward other health issues. Some 70,000 chemicals are used in commerce, for example, and as of the mid-1980s only 2 percent had been extensively tested for human health effects; no health data existed for over 70 percent of the rest [National Research Council 1984]. No doubt some of these chemicals will be found to cause otherwise preventable illness, most likely from occupational exposures.

The issue has still other costs, that are high and not easily measured. By one estimate (Florig 1992) the very existence of the issue of possible health hazards from electromagnetic fields now costs the American public $1 billion a year, through increased costs to utilities, litigation, and *ad hoc* steps taken by many individuals and industries to reduce exposure. Considered as a health investment, that money is being very badly spent indeed. A billion dollars spent on prenatal and pediatric health care to inner city populations (for example) would produce important and easily demonstrable health benefits. The health *benefits* of electricity are incalculable but obviously very high.

Some of the issues discussed in these pages may never be conclusively settled. For example, scientists are running out of identifiable groups of people who have been heavily exposed to dioxin and can be studied feasibly, and it would be difficult to do a better job than some of the recent studies in any event. But the data remain sufficiently ambiguous that the issue of cancer risk from dioxin remains, at some level, unresolved. Society needs to find some way to live with uncertainties about subtle risks without being paralyzed by fear of litigation.

Finally, risks that are imposed on people involuntarily or unknowingly deserve special attention. But the evidence does not make a strong case that PCBs, dioxin, TCE, low-level electromagnetic fields, and the other things that caused so much public and legal controversy are very risky, or risky at all, at least at typical environmental exposure levels. Their risks (or non-risks) loom larger in the public's mind than the (very much larger) everyday risks that are under a person's voluntary control. A person who drives without seat belts, eats a rotten diet, smokes, or drinks too much has real risks to worry about, but can take effective steps to reduce them.

In the end, phantom risk is a problem of the law and not science. Future historians might look back on late-twentieth-century America and regard the abuses of toxic tort litigation as a bizarre aberration that reflects an essential failure of the law when the link between cause and effect is murky. Whatever the eventual solution to this problem may be, phantom risk remains a diversion that is too expensive for even our wealthy society.

References

Bernstein, D. E. 1990a. A contractual solution to the contraceptive crisis. *Yale Law & Policy Rev.* 146–162.

Bernstein, D. E. 1990b. Out of the Fryeing pan and into the fire: The expert witness problem in toxic tort litigation. 10 *Rev. of Litig.* 117–159.

Cameron, J. 1992. *Physics Today* 9. August. Letter to the editor.

Elliott, E. D. 1989. Toward incentive-based procedure: Three approaches for regulating scientific evidence. 69 *B. U. L. Rev.* 487.

Florig, H. K. 1992. Containing the costs of EMF litigation. 257 *Science* 468–490.

Huber, P. 1991. *Galileo's revenge: Junk science in the courtroom.* New York: Basic Books.

Lee, T. 1988. Court-appointed experts and judicial reluctance: A proposal to amend rule 706 of the Federal Rules of Evidence. 6 *Yale Law & Policy Rev.* 480.

Morgan, K. Z. 1992. *Physics Today* 9. August. Letter to the editor.

National Research Council. 1984. *Toxicity testing: Strategies to determine needs and priorities.* Washington, DC:

Specter, M. M. "Recommended practices for design professionals engaged as experts in the resolution of construction industry disputes." National Academy of Forensic Engineers (undated pamphlet).

Abbreviations and Acronyms

ACGIH	American Council of Government and Industrial Hygienists
AEC	Atomic Energy Commission
AHERA	Asbestos Hazard Emergency Response Act of 1986
ALARA	as low as reasonably achievable
AMVETS	American Veterans of World War II, Korea, and Vietnam
ANOVA	analysis of variance (a statistical test)
BEIR	(National Academy of Sciences) Committee on Biological Effects of Ionizing Radiation
CDC	(U.S.) Centers for Disease Control
CIID	chemically induced immune disregulation
CIRRPC	(U.S.) Committee on Interagency Research and Policy Coordination
cps	counts per second (of ionizing radiation)
CTS	carpal tunnel syndrome
DAV	Disabled American Veterans (a veteran's organization)
DES	diethylstilbestrol
DHEW	(U.S.) Department of Health, Education, and Welfare (now DHHS)
DHHS	(U.S.) Department of Health and Human Services
DNA	deoxyribonucleic acid
DNAPL	dense non-aqueous phase liquid
DOE	(U.S.) Department of Energy
EDB	ethylene dibromide
EFM	electronic fetal monitor
EMRCET	Electromagnetic Radiation Case Evaluation Team (a legal organization)
EPA	(U.S.) Environmental Protection Agency
EPRI	Electric Power Research Institute
ES&H	environmental safety and health

f/ml	fibers per milliliter
FDA	(U.S.) Food and Drug Administration
HERP	Human exposure dose/rodent potency dose
HKE	Henle-Koch-Evans (postulates)
HRG	Public Citizen's Health Research Group
Hz	Hertz (cycles per second)
IARC	International Agency for Research on Cancer
ICD	International Classification of Disease System
IEEE	Institute of Electrical and Electronics Engineers
IEHR	Institute for Evaluating Health Risks
IT	International Technology Corp.
IUD	intrauterine (contraceptive) devices
kV	kilovolt
MCS	multiple chemical sensitivities
mg	milligram
mG	milligauss
mg/kg	milligrams per kilogram
MPBB	maximum permissible body burden
mrem	millirem
MRL	minimum risk level
MTD	maximum tolerated dose
NAS	National Academy of Sciences
NCI	National Cancer Institute
NCRP	National Council on Radiation Protection and Measurements
NIEHS	National Institutes of Environmental Health Sciences
NIH	National Institutes of Health
NIOSH	(U.S.) National Institutes of Occupational Safety and Health
NK	natural killer cells
NLO	National Lead of Ohio
NOAEL	No Observed Adverse Effect Level
NRC	National Research Council; Nuclear Regulatory Commission
NRDC	Natural Resources Defense Council
NTIS	National Technical Information Service
NTP	National Toxicology Program
ODC	ornithine decarboxylase
OR	odds ratio
ORAU	Oak Ridge Associated Universities
OTA	(U.S.) Office of Technology Assessment

PCB	polychlorinated biphenyl
PCDD	perchlorinated dibenzodioxin
PCDF	polychlorinated dibenzofuran
PHS	(U.S.) Public Health Service
PID	pelvic inflammatory disease
PMH	polymorphonuclear neutrophil
PMN	polymorphonuclear leukocytes (a kind of white blood cell)
PMR	proportionate mortality (morbidity) ratio
ppb	parts per billion
ppm	parts per million
ppt	parts per trillion
RERF	Radiation Effects Research Foundation
RR	relative risk
SMR	standardized mortality (or morbidity) ratio
TCDD	2,3,7,8- tetrachlorodibenzo-para-dioxin (also called dioxin)
TCE	trichloroethylene
TCP	tetrachlorobiphenyl
TGF	tumor growth factor
TLD	thermoluminescent dosimeter
TMI	Three Mile Island (nuclear power plant)
UCLA	University of California at Los Angeles
VA	(U.S.) Veterans Administration
VDT	video display terminal
VDU	video display unit (same as VDT)
WBC	white blood cell count
WHO	World Health Organization

Index

Adair, Robert K., 19
Aflatoxin, 173
Afrimet, 335
Agent Orange, 13, 32, 40, 110, 175,
  249–272 (passim)
  litigation concerning, 345–347, 392,
  402, 428
AIDS, chemical, 17, 379
ALAR and cancer risk, 165–170
Allen v. United States, 299–300, 306,
  352
American Council of Government and
  Industrial Hygienists (ACGIH), 389
American Telephone and Telegraph
  Company (AT&T), 145
American Veterans of World War II,
  Korea, and Vietnam (AMVETS),
  311
Ames, Bruce N., 11, 12, 16
Anderson v. W. R. Grace and Co., 343–
  344, 391–392
Animal testing
  false positive and false negative
  results, 106
  relation of high-dose studies to
  human risk, 11, 106–107, 154–157,
  172
  and thalidomide, 106 (*see also* subjects
  of individual chapters)
Anxiety, claim in litigation, 33, 341,
  343
  and MCS, 389, 435 (*see also*
  Cancerphobia)
  and thalidomide, 279, 282, 293, 285–
  286

Aroclors (PCB mixtures), 212–215,
  219
Asbestos, 1, 8, 14, 29–32, 44, 62, 151,
  183–210
  asbestosis, 186, 188
  dose vs. exposure, 201
  dose-response, 189–192
  effects of fiber type, 197–199
  effects on immune system, 384
  exposure assessment, 200
  interaction with smoking, 192–193
  litigation, 27, 31, 337–338
  and lung cancer, 187, 188–193
  and mesothelioma, 193–194
  and pleural plaques, 188, 194, 201,
  205
  probability of causation, 194
  risks at low doses, 199
  in schools, 201–205
  and silicosis, 184, 200
  substitutes for, 206
  "third wave" of litigation, 187
Association, strength of, 5, 9, 71, 92–
  93
Atomic Energy Commission (AEC),
  299, 334–336
Atomic Veterans Compensation Act,
  312
Autoimmunity, 381, 385
Ayers v. Township of Jackson, 344

Bailar, John C., 3, 78
Balis, Earl, 340
Barsotti, Deborah, 341

Bendectin
  animal tests of, 105–107
  and birth defects, 1–6 (passim), 27,
    45, 101–116
  case reports, 101–102
  discontinuance of, 102, 108
  epidemiologic evidence, 103–105
  Food and Drug Administration and,
    107–110
  formulation of, 101
  litigation concerning, 35, 110–115,
    138–141
  normal rate of congenital defects, 102
  Public Citizen's Health Research
    Group and, 107–110
Bendix, Selina, 339
Berger, David, 349
Berman, Ezra, 126
Bhopal, 383
Birth defects, normal rate in
  population, 94, 102
Bladder cancer, 238
  and benzidine, 384
  and para-aminobiphenyl, 260, 267
  and TCE, 238
Blankets, electric, 64–65, 146
Brain tumors
  claim in litigation, 144, 341
  and electromagnetic fields, 51–66
    (passim), 72
  and spermicides, 88
  and workers in capacitor plant, 224
Brock v. Merrell Dow Pharmaceuticals,
  113, 114

Cameron, J., 18, 433
Cancer
  and ionizing radiation, 3, 281, 301
  mechanisms and causes, 154–156
  rates of, 153 (*see also* individual
    neoplasms)
Cancerphobia, 32, 143, 434
*Canon Reliance Coal v. Industrial
  Commission,* 424
Carcinogens
  from cooking food, 161
  natural and synthetic, 157–161

Carnow, Bertram W., 348, 403, 412–
  415 (passim)
Carpal tunnel syndrome
  litigation, 146
  and VDTs, 131–132
Carson, Rachel, 172
Carstensen, Edwin L., 18, 74
  as expert witness, 142
Case-control studies
  defined, 52–54
  susceptibility to bias, 53, 94
Cataracts, and radiation, 439
Causation
  assessing from epidemiologic studies,
    7–10 (*see also* Hill's criteria)
  and association, 3–4, 175–176
  legal vs. epidemiologic, 111–112
Celeste, Richard, 325
Centers for Disease Control (CDC)
  and Fernald, 327
  and immune system tests, 221
  study of dioxin and cancer, 262
  study of Operation Smoky veterans,
    311
  study of reproductive risks of VDTs,
    123
Chadkoff, Marvin, 142
Chernobyl, 290
Chloracne
  and dioxin exposure, 249, 250, 251,
    258, 262, 263, 266, 269
  and PCB exposure, 214, 218, 225,
    339
Chloroform, 170
Clark v. United States, 345
Classification
  bias introduced by exposure
    misclassification, 6
  of diseases, 223, 259
  of exposure, 255, 256, 259, 263
Clastogen, 157, 160–164 (passim)
Clinical ecology, 17, 387–390
  and litigation, 37, 427–428, 435
Clophens (PCB mixtures), 214
Clusters
  of congenital hypothyroidism and
    Three Mile Island, 287–289

of Hodgkin's disease in Michigan, 384
of leukemia near San Onofre nuclear
power plant, 310
of leukemia in Woburn, MA, 235–236
of miscarriages in VDT users, 19,
123–124, 132
problems in interpreting, 123–124,
287–288
Committee on Biological Effects of
Ionizing Radiation (BEIR), 302, 303
Committee on Interagency Radiation
Research and Policy Coordination
(CIRRPC), 312
Consistency, of epidemiologic
evidence, 4, 9, 67, 71, 91, 93, 130–
131
Consumer Products Safety
Commission (CPSC)
and asbestos, 190–191
and TCE, 232
Cooper, Paul L., 311
Cure, phantom, 20–22

Dalkon Shield, 1, 27, 30–31
Daubert v. Merrell Dow Pharmaceuticals,
141
Davis, Hugh J., 32
DDT, 175, 216
Death certificates
in epidemiologic studies, 221, 258–
259, 264, 292, 310
problems in interpreting, 51, 222–
223, 259, 264
DeConcini, Dennis, 311
Delgado, José M., 125
DELPHI study, 201
Dennison v. Wing, 426
Department of Energy (DOE), 321–
333 (passim), 334–335
litigation, 350–351
Dicyclomine, 101, 104–106, 110
Diethylstilbestrol (DES), 8
Dioxin (TCDD), 13–14, 32–40
(passim), 152, 163, 170–172, 221,
249–272, 383, 442
from accident at Seveso, Italy, 251
animal studies, 253

comments on the science, 266–269
diseases other than cancer and, 265–
266
dose-response relations, 269–270
environmental sources, 249–251
epidemiologic studies, 253–266
industrial exposures, 251–252
litigation, 34–35, 345–349
non-Hodgkin's lymphoma and, 260–
261
Ranch Hands and, 265–266
regulatory policy, 270–271
soft-tissue sarcomas and, 254–260
stomach cancer and, 260–261
total cancers and, 261–265
Vietnam and, 271–272
Disabled American Veterans (DAV),
311
DNA, 12, 154–156 (passim), 173, 239,
408–409
Doll, Richard, 3, 4, 20, 49, 53, 153–
154, 187, 188, 204
Done, Alan K., 139
Down's syndrome, 88, 90–91, 98
Doxylamine, 101, 104–106, 108, 110
Duesberg, P. H., 8
Dukakis, Michael, 325

Elam v. Alcolac, 401–418, 427–428
criticism of expert testimony in, 411–
416
Electromagnetic fields
assessing causation, 71–77
electric blankets and cancer, 64–65
in environment, 47–49
epidemiologic studies and cancer, 51–
75
evidence cited for link with cancer,
75–77
exposure assessment, 68–71
external and internal sources in the
body, 74
from Hill's criteria and, 71–74
individual's exposure to, 70
litigation concerning, 141–145
problems with bioeffects studies, 441
project HenHouse, 125–126

Electromagnetic fields (continued)
  resolution of the issue, 77–79
  teratological studies and, 126–127
  video display terminals, 124–125
  wiring configuration code, 68–71
Electromagnetic Radiation Case
  Evaluation Team (ERMCET), 144
Enstrom, James E., 310
Environmental Protection Agency, 14,
  32, 178, 201–204, 241–242, 268–270,
  322–324, 327, 332
  and dioxin, 268–270
Epidemiologic studies, problems in
  interpreting, 4–7, 52
Epstein, Samuel S., 11
  as expert witness, 346–347
Ethylene dibromide (EDB), 176, 178
Evans, Robley, 302–303
Ewing, J., 361–362
  views on traumatic cancer, 362
Expert witnesses
  with minority opinions, 17, 18, 37,
  38
  judicial scrutiny of, 402
  qualifying of, 37–41
  self-interest and, 37

Fallout, 3, 37, 289–313, 432
  criteria for deciding cancer claims,
  299–300
  epidemiologic studies and, 307
  exposures from, 308
  litigation, 299–300, 306–307, 309,
  352–353
  other sources of low-level exposure,
  309
  Radioepidemiological Tables and,
  304–306
Fatigue
  claims in litigation, 344, 348, 428
  and PCBs, 218,
Federal Rules of Evidence
  Frye rule, 38–40, 435, 440
  Rule 102, 41
  Rule 403, 40, 402
  Rule 702, 38–39
  Rule 703, 39–40, 113, 402

Feinstein, Alvan, 10, 52
Fernald Feed Materials Production
  Center, 319–333
  cancer risk from release, 329
  International Technology Corp.
  study, 327–330
  litigation and, 324–333, 350–351
  media coverage and, 325–326
  1984 release, 321–322
  releases announced by Westinghouse,
  326–327
  requests by National Lead of Ohio
  for improvements to avoid
  environmental problems, 334–336
  reviews of environmental safety and
  health programs, 321–324
  settlement of suit, 331–333
  studies commissioned by plaintiff,
  330–331
Fetal monitor, 30
Feynman, Richard, 437
Food and Drug Administration, 97
  and Bendectin, 107–109
  pesticide residues in foods, 161–164
Franke, Bernd, 330
Friedman v. Myers, 342–343
Frye rule, 38–40, 435, 440

Gallbladder cancer
  and gallstones, 367
  and TCE, 344
Genotoxicity, of TCE, 237
Glenn, John, 325
Gofman, John W., 300, 306, 353, 431
Gooden, David, 299–300

Hannon, Joseph M., 139
Hatch, Orrin, 305
Hayes, Arthur, 108–109
Headache
  claim in litigation, 344, 348, 428
  and MCS, 389
  and PCBs, 218
  and sick building syndrome, 387
  and TCE, 233
  and Three Mile Island accident, 285
HenHouse, project, 125–126

Henle-Koch-Evans postulates, 7–8
Higginbotham, Patrick, 39
Higgins v. Aerojet-General Corp., 344, 392
Hill's criteria for assessing causation, 8–10, 71–72, 92–93, 112, 224, 235, 266–267
Hiroshima, atomic bomb at, 3, 18, 299, 300–302, 311, 325
Houston Lighting and Power Company, litigation, 141–143
Human exposure dose/rodent potency dose (HERP), 165–169

Immune dysfunction, 379, 412
claims in litigation, 344, 391, 392, 411
guidelines for diagnosing, 390
Immune system
allergies and, 386–387
damage from environmental exposures to toxic substances, 384–385
difficulty of interpreting immune system tests, 221, 416–418
effect of impairment, 407
evaluation of in humans, 384–385, 403–404
hypersensitivity, 381, 386–387, 408
laboratory tests of, 408–411
response to infectious agent, 405–407
specific and nonspecific immunity, 404–405
Immunosuppression, 379–385, 409
claims of in litigation, 401, 402, 407–416 (passim)
Immunotoxicity, 379–390
claims in litigation, 390–392, 401
In re Agent Orange Product Liability Litigation, 345–347
In re Paoli Railyard PCB Litigation, 341, 343, 392, 402
International Agency for Research on Cancer (IARC), 268
Intrauterine device (IUD), 30–31

Jackson, Thomas P., 140
Jenkins, Bruce S., 299–300

Jick, Hershel, 88–90, 431
Johns-Manville Corp., 27, 196
Johnson, Carl J., 307, 308, 330

Kelly, Patrick, 307
Kelly, R. F., 342
Koch's postulates. *See* Henle-Koch-Evans postulates
Kuhn, Thomas S., 16–17

Lehman, L. and Assoc., 330
Leukemia
and benzene, 382
childhood leukemia and electromagnetic fields, 58–64
claims in litigation, 144, 339, 343, 349–350, 390, 391
and fallout, 299, 307, 308
and Hiroshima survivors, 302
and immunological disorders, 410
and immunosuppressive medications, 406
and industrial solvents, 384
and ionizing radiation, 3, 301
latency of developing, 290
in persons receiving X-ray therapy, at Portsmouth Naval Shipyard, 310
and radium watch dial painters, 302
near San Onofre nuclear power plant, 310
and TCE, 237
near TMI, 291
VA compensation of veterans of Operation Smoky, 311
in Woburn, MA, 235–236
in workers with electrical occupation, 51–57
Litogen, 28
Lung cancer and asbestos, 188–193
in chemical plant workers, 264–267 (passim)
claim in litigation, 427
and smoking, 4, 15, 49–50, 95, 153, 155, 156, 187–193
Lynch v. Merrell National Laboratories, 113–114, 140
Land, Charles E., 305

MacMahon, Brian, 103, 268
Makhjani, Arjun, 330
Maletskos, C. J., 307
Mallory v. Monsanto, 338
Mangasarian, John, 427
Martin, Alice, 73
Marzilli, Rocco, 427
Mateer v. U.S. Aluminum, 345
Mays, Charles W., 309
Media and risk, 32, 325
Mekdeci v. Merrell National Laboratories,
  138–139
Melanoma
  and abrasion by brassiere strap, 365
  claim in litigation, 344
  and electrical workers, 54
  and exposure to sunlight, 365
Merrell-Dow (Wm. S. Merrell)
  Bendectin litigation, 32, 35, 110–111,
  113–115, 138–141
Mesothelioma
  and asbestos, 8, 187, 190, 193–194,
  197, 199, 265
  claim in litigation, 337–338
  and other fibers, 197
Metzenbaum, Howard, 325
Mihm, Michael M., 439–440
Miscarriage
  and anesthetics, 234
  claim in Agent Orange litigation, 346
  claim in TMI litigation, 350
  and spermicides, 91, 97
  and TMI accident, 289
  and VDTs, 1, 2, 6, 19, 123–132
Mitogen stimulation test (of immune
  system), 403, 408
  role in litigation, 413–414
Montague, H. Dixon, 145
Morgan, Karl Z., 18, 37, 431, 433
  as expert witness, 300, 307–309, 352–
  353
Multiple chemical sensitivities (MCS),
  17, 380, 381, 387–390
  difficulty in evaluating, 389–390
  guidelines for diagnosing, 390
Multiple comparison problem, 6, 89,
  116, 130, 384

Nagasaki, atomic bomb at, 301
Najarian, Thomas, 310
National Academy of Forensic
  Engineers, recommended practices
  for expert witness, 438
National Cancer Institute, and
  Radioepidemiological Tables, 305–
  306
National Institute of Occupational
  Safety and Health (NIOSH)
  study on dioxin and cancer, 258, 259,
  264–265, 267
  study on VDTs and miscarriage, 130–
  131
Nausea
  claims in litigation, 308, 348, 428
  and PCBs, 218
  after TMI accident, 280
Nelson, Gaylord, 32
Nesbit, Ian C. T., 341
New York Power Lines Project, 60,
  73, 75, 143

O'Conner, James R., 439
Oak Ridge National Laboratories,
  study of Fernald plant, 322–323
Operation Smoky, 311
  and leukemia in veterans of, 311
Operation Ranch Hands, 251, 265–266
Ortho Pharmaceuticals, spermicide
  litigation and, 28, 137–138
*Oxendine v. Merrell Dow
  Pharmaceuticals,* 113, 115, 139, 340

Pack, George T., 363
Peer review of scientific papers, 22
  role in litigation, 40, 114, 342, 434
Pelvic inflammatory disease, and
  IUDs, 30–31
Pertussis vaccine, litigation
  concerning, 29
Pesticides
  natural vs. synthetic, 157–175
  (passim)
  tradeoffs, 176–178
Peterman v. Techalloy Co., 343
Peto, Julian, 193

Peto, Richard, 3, 11, 153
Phillips, Jerry L., 75–76
 as expert witness, 142
Pittman v. Pillsbury Flour Mills, 426
Pollution
 and cancer risk, 170, 178
 water, 170, 334
Polybrominated biphenyls, 383
Polychlorinated biphenyls (PCBs), 13,
 14, 32, 33, 211–224
 and cancer, 221–224
 effects on immune system, 220–221,
 381
 human health effects of, 215–218
 litigation, 338–343, 392, 402, 442
 as litogen, 34
 presence in the environment, 212–213
 reproductive effects, 218–220
 toxicity in animals, 213–215
 yusho/yu-cheng disease, 212–213,
 341–342, 383
Polychlorinated dibenzofurans
 (PCDFs), 212, 213, 218, 383
Portsmouth Naval Shipyard, 310
Post hoc, ergo prompter hoc
 deduction, 102
 fallacy, 436
Potter v. Firestone Tire and Rubber Co.,
 345, 392
Probability of causation
 for asbestos-related diseases, 194–197
 in determining liability, 116, 306–307,
 432
 of radiation-caused cancers, 306–307
Probative value of scientific evidence,
 434
 related to peer review, 40
 of high-dose animal studies, 113, 392
 of medical speculation, 140
Proportionate mortality studies,
 defined, 51–52
Prospective studies, 7
 advantages and disadvantages, 72, 89,
 94
Public Citizens' Health Research
 Group (HRG), 107, 108–109

Radiation Effects Research Foundation
 (RERF), 301–302
Radioepidemiological Tables, 304–305,
 311, 312, 432
Radiothor, 21
Radium
 Fernald and release of, 327
 maximum permissible body burden,
 303
 watch dial painters and, 302–303
Radon, 22, 179, 301, 327, 328
 exposure from Fernald plant, 328–329
Randolph, Theron, 387–388
Raytheon Corp., 145
Reagan, Ronald, 312, 325
Recall (reporting) bias, 5–6, 89, 90–91,
 95, 102, 104, 127, 128, 254, 264, 366
Retrospective studies
 advantages of, 94
 potential problems in interpretation,
 72, 95, 127, 384
*Richardson v. Merrell Dow
 Pharmaceuticals, Inc.,* 113, 114, 140
Risk assessment, National Research
 Council model of, 2–3
Rothman, Kenneth J., 53, 90–91, 103
Rozzell, Thomas C., 126
Rubanick v. Witco Chem. Corp., 340
Rubin, Carl B., 110, 139

Sandman, Peter M., 33
Sarcoma
 and chlorophenols, 255–256
 and dioxin, 254–260, 262, 267, 269,
 272
 misclassification of, 223
 and trauma, 15–16
Scheribel, Karl, 439–440
Schweiker, Richard, 107
Science, pathological, 17
Scientific evidence, judicial review of,
 116
Scott v. Monsanto, 339
Sedalia, MI, 391
Segond, M. P., 361–362
Shoob, Marvin, 138
Sick building syndrome, 387, 393

Signature disease, 8, 71
Significance of association, 5
 as issue in litigation, 115, 140
Silkwood v. Kerr-McGee, 351–353
Simon, Robert E., 341
Spermicides
 biological plausibility of link with
  birth defects, 89
 correction of study by investigators,
  98
 and Down's syndrome, 90
 establishing causation, 92–93
 Food and Drug Administration
  advisory committee and, 97
 litigation, 28–29, 137–138
 miscarriage and, 91
 prospective vs. retrospective studies,
  93–94
 recall bias in studies on, 90–91
Sterling v. Velsicol, 392
Stewart, Alice, 330
Stites v. Sundstrand Heat Transfer, Inc.,
 344
Stress
 and cancer, 368–369
 as cause of immune system changes,
  220, 409
 cellular response to, 173
 claims in litigation for psychological
  stress from Fernald plant, 331–332
 and pregnancy, 282, 289
 psychological, from TMI accident,
  282–287 (passim)
Strom, Robert C., 144
Sturgeon, MO, 348
Substation, electrical and health risks,
 21, 57, 58–59, 61, 71
 and litigation, 144
Supreme Court (U.S.), 41

Teitelbaum, Daniel, 339
Teratogens
 animal studies and human teratogens,
  92
 and Bendectin, 101–116
 difficulties in identifying human, 94
 and oral contraceptives, 87
 and spermicides, 87–98

and thalidomide, 101
and video display terminals, 123–132
 (passim) (see also Project HenHouse)
Thalidomide, 9, 101, 102, 106, 109,
 138
Three Mile Island (TMI) accident,
 279–294
 cancer rates and, 290–292
 congenital hypothyroidism cluster
  and, 287–289
 evacuation after accident, 284
 fetal and infant mortalities and, 290
 health studies on nearby population,
  283, 292
 litigation and, 349–350
 predicted health consequences, 280–
  281
 pregnancy outcomes and, 286–289
 psychobehavioral studies, 285–286
 psychological stress, 282–283
 radiation exposure from, 280, 284–
  285
 spontaneous abortions and, 289
 TMI area census after, 283
Thurber, James, 21, 47
Times Beach, MO, 271, 347, 417
Tort litigation
 fear and, 33
 financial incentives, 35–36
 media and, 32
 politics and, 32
Trauma
 aggravating an existing tumor, 370
 defined, 359–360
 emotional and cancer, 371
 and Hodgkin's disease, 364
 and metastatic spread of cancer, 369
Traumatic cancer
 animal studies, 367–369
 chronic irritation and, 366–367
 criteria for determining, 361
 Ewing's views on, 362–363
 head trauma and, 365
 testicular trauma and, 366
 traumatic determinism, 360
Triana, AL, 216
Trichloroethylene (TCE), 13, 229–242,
 442

and cancer, 236–237
carcinogenic ranking by
  Environmental Protection Agency,
  214
carcinogenic ranking by the American
  Industrial Hygiene Association, 242
developmental and reproductive
  toxicity, 234–236
in environment, 230
epidemiologic studies, 238
genotoxicity, 237–238
health effects in humans, 230–238
interaction with Antabuse, 231
and litigation, 37, 343–345
metabolism of, 238–239
relevance of rodent tests for assessing
  human cancer risk of, 242
risk assessment, 239–242
toxicity to organs, 232–234
Trichlorophenol, as source of dioxin,
  250, 267

Uranium
  maximum allowable concentration as
  dust, 319–320
  release by Fernald plant, 326–327

Validity of a study, 5, 10, 112, 116
  difficulties of juries in deciding, 416
  of case-control studies, 52–53 (*see also*
  Feinstein, Alvan)
Verifiability
  of effects of low-dose radiation, 281,
  304
  of expert testimony, 38, 402, 433, 439
  of trauma-cancer links, 366
Veterans Administration (VA), and
  fallout claims, 310–313
Video display terminal (VDT)
  carpal tunnel syndrome and, 131–132
  litigation and, 145–146
  miscarriages and, 123–132
  skin problems and, 132
Vietnam, War, 249, 271
  veterans' exposure to dioxin, 251
Viterbo v. Dow Chemical Co., 402

Wegener, Alfred, 16, 19
Weinstein, Jack, 40, 271, 346–347, 392
Wells v. Ortho Pharmaceutical, 137–138,
  340
Wertheimer, Nancy, 58–60
  as expert witness, 142
Wiseman, Richard, 15, 359
Woburn, MA, 175, 235–236, 241, 343–
  344, 391, 433
Wolf, Peter H., 139
Yusho/yu-cheng disease, 212–213,
  341–342, 383

Zahalsky, Arthur C., 341–343, 403,
  415